Human Diversity in Education

An Integrative Approach

Human Diversity in Education
An Integrative Approach

fourth edition

Kenneth Cushner
Averil McClelland
Kent State University

Philip Safford
Case Western Reserve University

Boston   Burr Ridge, IL   Dubuque, IA   Madison, WI   New York
San Francisco   St. Louis   Bangkok   Bogotá   Caracas   Kuala Lumpur
Lisbon   London   Madrid   Mexico City   Milan   Montreal   New Delhi
Santiago   Seoul   Singapore   Sydney   Taipei   Toronto

McGraw-Hill

A Division of The McGraw·Hill Companies

HUMAN DIVERSITY IN EDUCATION: AN INTEGRATIVE APPROACH,

Published by McGraw-Hill, a business unit of The McGraw-Hill Companies, Inc., 1221 Avenue of the Americas, New York, NY, 10020. Copyright © 2003, 2000, 1996, 1992 by The McGraw-Hill Companies, Inc. All rights reserved. No part of this publication may be reproduced or distributed in any form or by any means, or stored in a data base or retrieval system, without the prior written consent of The McGraw-Hill Companies, Inc., including, but not limited to, in any network or other electronic storage or transmission, or broadcast for distance learning.

Some ancillaries, including electronic and print components, may not be available to customers outside the United States.

This book is printed on acid-free paper.

1 2 3 4 5 6 7 8 9 0 FGR/FGR 0 9 8 7 6 5 4 3 2

ISBN 0–07–248669–4

Publisher: *Jane Karpacz*
Developmental editor II: *Cara Harvey*
Editorial coordinator: *Christina Lembo*
Media producer: *Lance Gerhart*
Project manager: *Karen Nelson*
Production supervisor: *Susanne Riedell*
Freelance design coordinator: *Gino Cieslik*
Supplement producer: *Nathan Perry*
Photo research coordinator: *Judy Kausal*
Photo research: *Mary Reeg*
Cover and interior design: *Kay Fulton*
Typeface: *10/12 Times Roman*
Compositor: *Electronic Publishing Services, Inc., TN*
Printer: *Quebecor World Fairfield, Inc.*

The credits section for this book begins on page 440 and is considered an extension of the copyright page.

Library of Congress Cataloging-in-Publication Data

Cushner, Kenneth
    Human diversity in education : an integrative approach / Kenneth Cushner, Averil McClelland, Philip Safford.—4th ed.
        p. cm.
    Includes bibliographical references and index.
    ISBN 0-07-248669-4 (softcover : alk. paper)
    1. Multicultural education—United States. 2. Individual differences in children—United States. 3. Sex differences in education—United States. I. McClelland, Averil. II. Safford, Philip L. III. Title.
    LC1099.3 .C87 2003
    370.117'0973—dc21   2002070262

www.mhhe.com

About the Authors

KENNETH CUSHNER is Associate Dean for Student Life and Intercultural Affairs, and Professor of Education in the College and Graduate School of Education at Kent State University, Kent, Ohio. A former East-West Center Scholar, he is a frequent contributor to the professional development of educators through writing, workshop presentations, and travel program development. Dr. Cushner is the author of several other books and articles in the field of intercultural education and training including *International Perspectives on Intercultural Education,* Lawrence Erlbaum Associates: 1998; *Intercultural Interactions: A Practical Guide* (1986, 2nd edition, 1996): *Improving Intercultural Interactions: Modules for Cross-Cultural Training Programs,* volume 2 (Sage Publications, 1997); and the workbook, *Human Diversity in Action: Developing Multicultural Competencies for the Classroom,* 2nd ed. (McGraw-Hill, 2003). He is past director of COST—The Consortium for Overseas Student Teaching, and is founding Fellow of the International Academy of Intercultural Research. In his spare time, Dr. Cushner enjoys photography, music, and travel.

AVERIL MCCLELLAND is currently an Associate Professor of Cultural Foundations of Education at Kent State University. She received her Ph.D. from Kent State University. Dr. McClelland has had extensive experience in curriculum design and program evaluation, as well as considerable experience with addressing issues of gender and education, and cultural diversity in education. She is a consultant to the international journal, *Gender and Education*, and she received the Distinguished Teaching award from Kent State University in 1996. Her special interests are the history and sociology of education, multicultural education, and the reconstruction of teacher education.

PHILIP SAFFORD is Emeritus Professor and former chair of Special Education at Kent State University. His Ph.D. was earned through the combined program in education and psychology at the University of Michigan, with specialization in special education and psychology. Previously he had been a teacher of emotionally disturbed children and also a coordinator and director of special education in residential treatment programs. Dr. Safford has authored four books, all concerning special education for infants, toddlers, and preschool age children with disabilities, as well as numerous journal articles. He has directed or co-directed a number of training, research, and demonstration projects supported by federal and state grants in special education.

Brief Contents

Contents

**2   CULTURE AND THE CULTURE-LEARNING
PROCESS**   31

3   CLASSROOMS AND SCHOOLS AS CULTURAL CROSSROADS   73

4   INTERCULTURAL DEVELOPMENT: CONSIDERING THE GROWTH OF SELF AND STUDENTS   105

9   DEVELOPING A COLLABORATIVE CLASSROOM: GENDER AND SEXUAL ORIENTATION   277

10 CREATING DEVELOPMENTALLY APPROPRIATE CLASSROOMS: THE IMPORTANCE OF AGE AND DEVELOPMENTAL STATUS 313

11 CREATING INCLUSIVE CLASSROOMS: THE ABILITY/DISABILITY CONTINUUM AND THE HEALTH DIMENSION 337

12 ASSESSING PROGRESS: THE IMPORTANCE OF SOCIAL CLASS AND SOCIAL STATUS   367

Preface

The rapidity of change and the monumental contexts in which it has occurred in relation to human diversity is indicative of what this book is really all about. It is difficult to believe that it has only been three years since the previous edition of *Human Diversity in Education: An Integrative Approach,* and so much has changed. Consider what has happened in just the last three years: the government has begun to access data collected in the 2000 census; scientists have mapped the human genetic code; experiments related to the cloning of organisms continue to develop; and on September 11, 2001, the United States was attacked by terrorists in the worst case of assault ever to occur on American soil, forever altering Americans' intercultural interactions as well as their need to better understand those who are different from themselves. The opportunities and challenges that people continue to face increasingly reflect the face of diversity. Educators in the United States as well as around the world continue to struggle with questions of how best to provide an education for all students that is responsive to the needs of different communities while maintaining a sense of unity. This struggle continues to be the basis behind this book.

This fourth edition of *Human Diversity in Education: An Integrative Approach* continues to address the preparation of teachers and human service providers for the wide diversity of students they are certain to encounter in their classrooms, schools, and communities. In addition, we continue to address the knowledge and skills that are necessary for teachers to have if they are to provide a foundation that will assist young people to be better informed and be proactive in an increasingly interdependent, global and multicultural society.

New to This Edition

The previous edition of this text continued to engender positive feedback from users, and because of this we have maintained much of the familiar format. Regular users, however, will notice some changes that accompany this fourth edition. The text continues to provide a broad treatment of the various forms of diversity common in today's schools, including nationality, ethnicity, race, religion, gender, class, language, sexual orientation, health, and handicapping condition. This text maintains its unique approach, which is research based with a cross-cultural and intercultural psychological emphasis. We continue to stress that it is especially at the level of the individual teacher in addition to the organizational structure of the school that significant change must occur with regard to how diversity is understood and accommodated. That is, little in terms of institutional or systemic change will occur until all individuals fully understand the role that culture plays in determining their thoughts and actions and how they can go about altering its powerful influence. Culture learning for both teacher and student, along with intercultural interaction, continues to be central to this book.

Special Features

 Case Study Approach. In this edition, the use of case studies and critical incidents has been expanded. Chapters begin with a lengthy case study that introduces major concepts and sets the context for what is to follow. A number of related critical incidents are then placed throughout the chapters.

 Web Links. Each chapter also identifies an expanded number of relevant web sites that students can access. An icon in the margin of the chapter identifies these web sites. Students can then go to the text's Online Learning Center at *www.mhhe.com/cushner4e* to link to these sites.

 Connections to Workbook Activities. Activities found in *Human Diversity in Action: Developing Multicultural Competencies for the Classroom,* 2nd ed. (by Kenneth Cushner, McGraw-Hill, 2003) are referenced in the text margins.

Organization

The general format of this edition remains similar to the previous one with a few modifications. Part 1 provides background to the broad social, cultural, and economic changes that confront society today (Chapter 1), paying particular emphasis to culture learning and intercultural interaction (Chapters 2 and 3). Chapter 4 is new in that it explores the concept of intercultural development and provides a model that teachers can use to gauge their own growth as well as that of their students. Historical aspects related to diversity, rather than being placed in a separate chapter, are interspersed throughout the text in relevant chapters. Part 2 of the book examines what teachers can do to make their classrooms and schools more responsive to diversity and to make them more effective learning communities, that is, to create classrooms that are collaborative, inclusive, developmentally appropriate, globally oriented, and religiously pluralistic. Each of the chapters in Part 2 centers on a major aspect of diversity: global understanding (Chapter 5), race and ethnicity (Chapter 6), language and learning style (Chapter 7), religious pluralism (Chapter 8), gender and sexual orientation (Chapter 9), age and development (Chapter 10), exceptionality and ability levels (Chapter 11), and social class and assessment (Chapter 12).

Student and Instructor Resources

Student Resources. The Online Learning Center, at *www.mhhe.com/cushner4e* houses a student study guide (with practice quizzes), web links, and additional resources for the student.

     Instructor Resources. The Instructor's Online Learning Center, also at *www.mhhe.com/cushner4e,* houses resources for the instructor. Through PageOut, instructors can create their own course web sites. Also available is an instructor's manual that includes activity ideas and test questions.

Acknowledgments

We would like to thank the following individuals for the feedback they provided during the development of this edition: Johnnie Thompson, Wichita State University; Howard Eliason, Miami Dade Community College; Carlos J. Vallejo, Arizona State University; Wilbert Nelson, Phoenix College; Funsho Akingbala, The University of Texas, Austin; Davie Tate, Jr., Clarion University of Pennsylvania; Joseph Nwoye, Illinois State University; Virginia Marion, Ursuline College; Godfrey Franklin, University of West Florida; Mary Nella Gonzales, California State University, Bakersfield; Pamela Soeder, Slippery Rock University; Fumie K. Hashimoto, Saint Martin's College; Scott McNabb, University of Iowa.

     We hope you continue to find benefit in this edition, and we certainly welcome feedback from you.

Kenneth Cushner
Averil McClelland
Philip Safford

part one

Foundations for Multicultural Teaching

Education in a Changing Society

*The illiterate of the twenty-first century will not
be those who cannot read and write, but those
who cannot learn, unlearn, and relearn.*

—Alvin Toffler

C h a p t e r   O u t l i n e

1.   What is the rationale for attention to diversity in education?

2.   What are some of the fundamental changes influencing American society and the world, including the aftermath of the September 11, 2001, attacks on America, and how might these changes impact you as an educator?

3.   What are some differences between schools designed for an industrial age and schools designed for an information or global age?

4.   Why is real change difficult?

case study   Tracy Harmon's Diversity Class

Activity 1: Mental Maps of Culture: An Ice Breaker

Tracy Harmon wants to be a teacher. She has wanted to be a teacher since she was seven and was constantly encouraging all the younger neighborhood children into playing "school," with herself as teacher, of course. She has heard all the arguments against it: it's a difficult and even sometimes a dangerous job; it's only moderately well paying; she could do more with her abilities. But she wants to be a teacher, and that's all there is to it.

Tracy is also a volleyball player. She has a full athletic scholarship to the university, and she hopes to coach volleyball in the high school where she has already been hired to teach mathematics in the fall. She has it all planned out: graduation in a few months, spend the summer using her new computer (an early graduation present!) to prepare for her first classes, and finally, finally, starting her new job in a suburban school system on the outer edge of a midwestern city that is just far enough away from her home to give her a needed sense of independence. Algebra . . . geometry . . . calculus . . . even general math! She can hardly wait!

Except . . . except, here she is, sitting in a required diversity course, wondering what in the world all this "diversity stuff" has to do with her future. It isn't as if the school district that has already hired her has much of a minority population; the high school principal said something about 20 percent, she thinks. And it isn't as if she has never spent any time with people who are different from herself. Her volleyball team has black players, a girl from Puerto Rico, a girl who is Jewish, even a girl who is a lesbian. They all get along fine; she knows all their parents and siblings; they will always be friends. And it certainly isn't as if she doesn't already know that some groups of people still suffer from discrimination—some of her community service credits have been spent working with kids in an urban poverty neighborhood, and she spent one whole summer helping build houses in rural Appalachia. She really liked those people, too, and wished she could have done more to help them.

Why, Tracy says to herself, I could probably teach this course!

And anyway, she thinks, I'm going to teach math! Math is math, isn't it? I might have to adjust my lessons for kids who learn in different ways, and some kids are just brighter than others, but after all, everyone needs to know math, don't they? And I know how to use all these new ways to teach math that show kids what math really means. Still, there was that time I spent tutoring in the city; some of those children didn't even speak English! And the kids I met in Kentucky made faces when I said I was going to be a math teacher—as if they hated it! And they said that I couldn't teach math because I was a girl! What's all that about? And now it looks as if I might have students with real disabilities in my classes; how do I handle that? I don't even really know anyone with a disability!

Tracy is finding that society is really changing—in lots of ways. If there is one thing she's learned in the past few years, it's that schools aren't like they used to be, even when she was in school. Her uncle teaches sixth grade in a nearby town, and in his class of twenty-five students, half live in families headed by a single parent (some of them, fathers); one-third are reading below grade level; and one-third are eligible for free lunches. His class, even in that small town, is far from being an all-white class; he has African American, East Indian, Vietnamese, and Central American children as well as white children. Half his students are Catholic, one belongs to the local Jehovah's Witness church, two are Muslim, one is Buddhist, and four are Jewish. One child had suffered injuries in an automobile accident and is in a wheelchair, and two children are still waiting (after six months) to be tested to determine their eligibility for the severe behavior disorders class, which is going to be eliminated next year anyway, because his school is going to implement full inclusion. Yes, for sure she will have children with disabilities in her classes.

Other changes are taking place as well. Her uncle now has several computers in his classroom and is experimenting with ways to integrate their use into his instruction, and Tracy herself is using the Internet and quite a few computer programs in preparing for her classes. In fact, she thinks, *I've already found a number of web sites that have really good ideas for teaching math!* But her uncle uses the computer in other ways as well. Since the September 11, 2001, attacks on the United States and the subsequent war on terrorism, her uncle has had to teach about things he really never knew much about—such as Islam, cross-cultural relations, and globalization. The computer has enabled his students to reach out to other young people around the world to discuss these issues, even some American students living in Saudi Arabia, while at the same time providing him with the information he needs that is not readily available in his textbooks. He and his students can also get up-to-the-minute access to world news. This access certainly makes the morning current events sessions more engaging.

And today is also the era of proficiency tests and teacher accountability—in fact, that is what the class is discussing today. "The good news," says the professor, "is that the proponents of accountability want all children to learn. The bad news is that we have never before really tried to educate all children to the same standard, and we are not altogether sure how to do that."

A classmate raises his hand. "What," he asks, "about kids who have really bad family problems, or kids whose parents aren't even there for them? What about kids with ADHD, or kids who just hate school? What about kids who are working thirty hours a week, or kids who just can't 'get it'? What about kids who don't speak English? What about kids who act out in violent ways?"

"Yes," says another classmate, "how are we supposed to teach everyone?"

"Perhaps," says the professor, "we'd be better off asking it another way: how are we to think about our practice of teaching so that everyone learns? The scene has shifted in schools today from an emphasis on teaching to an emphasis on learning. That's what accountability is about, and that's the reason for testing—to see what's been learned. And this change in focus makes it all the more important that we understand differences among students—all kinds of differences, visible and invisible, because those differences may influence a student's learning, and our job is to create a classroom in which everyone learns."

Tracy sighs. She really does want to be a teacher, but it seems to be a lot more complicated than she thought it would be.

The Reality of Social Change

As we get used to living in the twenty-first century, we all, along with Tracy, are witnessing two fundamental social changes that have widespread importance for the future of our country and our schools. The first is a rapid shift in the demographic makeup of our population, and the second is an equally profound shift in the nature of some of our basic institutions such as schools, health care institutions, and social service agencies.

Demographics in Transition

Demographics

Three factors are of primary importance in the shifting **demographics** of our population. First, immigration from non-European countries currently rivals the great immigrations from Europe that this country experienced at the turn of the twentieth century. There is an important difference, however. In the early part of the twentieth century, the majority—97 percent—of immigrants arrived from Europe. Except for language, it was relatively easy for these new immigrants to fit into the cultural landscape of the country; after all, many of these people looked similar to the majority of people around them. Today, 85 percent of the roughly eight hundred thousand immigrants who come to the United States come from Latin America and Asia.[1] Most look somewhat different from the mainstream, which immediately sets them apart. Indeed, many communities are becoming increasingly international as the phenomenon of globalization extends its reach.

Second, birthrates among nonwhite populations are considerably higher than they are among whites. Among European Americans, for instance, birthrates have dropped to 1.6 for every two people. This figure is well below the 2.1 replacement level. Birthrates for all other groups have remained the same. What this statistic means is that about the time that most current teacher education students were born (the early to mid 1980s), approximately one in four schoolchildren was a child of color (traditionally referred to as minority students). By the year 2020, it is likely that this figure will increase to one child in two, and many of these children will be poor. By mid-century, people of color will become the majority of Americans. In 1998, European Americans had become a numerical minority in 243 U.S. counties, with 42 of those counties making the transition since 1994.[2] And in 1994, in the twenty-five largest school districts in the United States, children of color comprised about 72 percent of the total school enrollment.[3] By 2056, the average U.S. resident, as defined by census statistics, will trace his or her descent to Africa, Asia, the Hispanic world, the Pacific Islands, or the Middle East—almost anywhere but white Europe.[4] Compounding this demographic phenomenon is the academic underachievement of many minority students. For example, the President's Initiative on Race reports the following percentages, or proportions, of the population age twenty-five to twenty-nine who have finished high school: whites, 93 percent; blacks, 87 percent; and Hispanics, 62 percent. The lower rate among Hispanics reflects lower average levels of education among immigrants, 38 percent of whom were foreign-born in 1997.[5]

Demographics for School Enrollment

Third, the total population of children in relation to adults in the United States is changing as the public grows older. The recent U.S. census reports that although the number of school-age children will increase from now until the year 2025, the number of American youth compared to citizens age sixty-five and older will continue to shrink.[6] An increasing concern is that there will not be enough workers to support the aging baby boom population, who will be a tremendous drain on the nation's social security system at a time when the system itself may be in jeopardy.

Institutions in Transition

Robert Biersted has defined **social institution** as "a formal, recognized, established, and stabilized way of pursuing some activity in society."[7] Another way to define a social institution is to think of it as a set of rules, or **norms,** that enable us to get through the day without having to figure out how to behave toward others, or whether to brush our teeth, or if in fact we should go to school or to work. In this society we have rules that govern the way we interact with family members; friends; people we see often, such as neighbors, teachers, or doctors; and even strangers who fill certain roles—the bus driver, the clerk in the store, the server in a restaurant. We know those rules because we have internalized them as children, and in a stable society, we can depend on the rules staying relatively the same over time.

All societies, even nonliterate ones, create social institutions that govern at least five areas of social need: economics (or ways of exchanging goods and services); politics (or ways of governing); religion (or ways of worshiping one or more deities); the family (or ways of ensuring the survival of children); and education (or ways of training the younger generation to take over).

Our society, and indeed most of the world, is witnessing profound changes in the nature of these basic institutions. Many scholars who study the past as a way to understand the future assert that these changes are so fundamental as to constitute a shift in the very nature of our civilization. Alvin Toffler, for example, claims that our institutions (what is normative in the society) are changing in specific and characteristic ways.[8] His writings were among the first in the popular literature to hint at the rise and the effect of globalization on us all. He writes:

Alvin Toffler

many of today's changes are not independent of one another. Nor are they random. For example, the crack-up of the nuclear family, the global energy crisis, the spread of cults and cable television, the rise of flextime and the new fringe-benefit packages, the emergence of separatist movements from Quebec to Corsica, may all seem like isolated events. Yet precisely the reverse is true. These and many other seemingly unrelated events or trends are interconnected. They are, in fact, parts of a much larger phenomenon: the death of industrialism and the rise of a new civilization.[9]

Prior to September 11, 2001, it was relatively easy to fall prey to exaggerated notions of the future. Today, Toffler's views are more than a little intriguing. Clearly, all our institutions are showing signs of transition, and the direction seems to be toward increased choice, increased diversity, and increased interdependency. Consider for a moment four of these five social institutions as they manifest themselves today (Education is discussed in its own section).

Economics and Politics

For much of our history, the American economy has been based on manufacturing done by companies whose production could be found within the borders of the country. The norm was that folks went to work for a particular company and stayed there throughout their working lives. Indeed, as recently as thirty years ago, people who changed jobs too many times were considered quite undependable. Today, our economy is firmly global in both scale and attitude; workers frequently change jobs (often because their companies are moving production to another country, but also often to enhance their own prospects); and it is more the norm *not* to work for the same company for thirty years. Indeed, the much-revered *American* corporation can hardly be said to exist any longer: the acquisition of raw material, manufacturing processes, and distribution of goods by such giants as Ford Motor Company, General Motors, or General Electric is done worldwide. In large measure because of advances in computer technology and high-speed travel, we find ourselves looking more and more often beyond our own borders for goods and services. Robert Reich, former secretary of labor, describes the situation in the following terms:

Consider some examples: Precision ice hockey equipment is designed in Sweden, financed in Canada, and assembled in Cleveland and Denmark for distribution in North America and Europe, respectively, out of alloys whose molecular structure was researched and patented in Delaware and fabricated in Japan. An advertising campaign is conceived in Britain; film footage for it is shot in Canada, dubbed in Britain, and edited in New York. A sports car is financed in Japan, designed in Italy, and assembled in Indiana, Mexico, and France, using advanced electronic components invented in New Jersey and fabricated in Japan. A microprocessor is designed in California and financed in America and West Germany, containing dynamic random-access memories fabricated in South Korea. A jet airplane is designed in the state of Washington and in Japan, and assembled in Seattle, with tail engines from Britain, special tail sections from China and Italy, and engines from Britain. A space satellite designed in California, manufactured in France, and financed by Australians is launched from a rocket made in the Soviet Union. Which of these is an American product? Which a foreign? How does one decide? Does it matter?[10]

North American Free Trade Agreements and World Trade Organization

Such economic realities have their counterparts in the political sphere as well. As we increasingly interact with people from other nations in matters of trade, we also increasingly interact with them politically, and political events occurring in other countries have a much more profound effect on our own political agenda than they used to. For example, the realization of the North American Free Trade Agreement and the

GATT (General Agreement on Tariffs and Trade) Treaty—as well as GATT's successor, The World Trade Organization—are political and economic responses to the facts of international trade. The end of the Cold War was a defining feature of international politics as the twentieth century drew to a close. Today, at the brink of the twenty-first century, the recurring ethnic and religious wars around the world and the September 11, 2001, attacks on American soil are expressions of new realities with which the United States must contend. Clearly, a day does not go by without some news of our entanglement with other countries that has political consequences for the United States. The norms have changed; we do economics and politics differently.

Marriage and Family Life

In the family too we are witnessing profound changes in structure and organization. Recent research on the changing demographics of our families graphically portrays the changing nature of family life. For instance, in 1942, 60 percent of families could be described as nuclear families consisting of two parents and their children. Furthermore, if you believe the images that until recently were often portrayed in basal readers, this nuclear family included a dog and a cat all living happily together in a white house surrounded by a neat picket fence. In these families, the father's role was to leave home every day to earn money to support the family, and the mother's role was to stay at home and raise the children. Those images were the norms. Today, less than 10 percent of American families match that ideal. The norms have changed.

Examples in Children's Readers of the "Traditional" American Family

   It is estimated today that about half of all marriages in the United States will be disrupted through divorce or separation. More than ten different configurations are represented by the families of children in today's classrooms—a most significant one being the single-parent family, often a mother and child or children living in poverty. Increasingly, this single parent is a teenage mother. Another increasing family configuration is one in which two adults of the same sex, committed to one another over time, are raising children who may be biologically related to one or the other adult, or who may have been adopted by them.

   There has also been a corresponding increase in intermarriage between individuals from different ethnic or religious groups. Nearly one-third of Latinos born in the United States, for instance, now intermarry, as do about 10 percent of African Americans. In some Asian American groups (Japanese Americans, for instance), more people marry outside the group than marry within the group[11]. And roughly 50 percent of American Jews marry outside their religion. Children of these mixed marriages will increasingly fill our schools.

   Consider also some of these facts: every thirty-two seconds a baby is born into poverty; every minute a baby is born to a teen mother, every two minutes a baby is born at a low birth weight; every three minutes a baby is born to a mother who received late or no prenatal care; every fifteen minutes a baby dies; and although the number has lessened a bit in the past few years, a teenager in the United States is more likely to give birth out of wedlock than in any other country in the world.[12]

   Another important family issue is poverty, and it is not limited to the children of children, nor even to children of single parents. In the United States, the number of children living in poverty has risen 43 percent since 1970, and more than 12 million American youngsters live below the poverty level. A quarter of all students are from poor or lower socioeconomic backgrounds, 20 percent live in single-parent homes, 14 percent are at risk of dropping out, 14 percent are children of teenage mothers, 40 percent will live with divorced parents before the age of eighteen, and 25 to 33 percent will be latchkey children with no one to greet them when they come home from school. Most disturbing is the fact that every nine seconds a child drops out of school, every ten seconds a child is reported abused or neglected, every two hours a child is killed by firearms, every four hours a child commits suicide, and every five hours a child dies from abuse or neglect.[13] Thus, a random sample of 100 children in the United States would reveal 12 born out of wedlock, 40 born to parents who will divorce, 15 born to parents who will separate in the next five years, 2 born to parents who will die in the next five years, and 41 who will reach age sixteen "normally." Clearly, the family pattern that was once considered the norm, that provided the image of the "right" and "proper" kind of family, that guided the policies of our other institutions, has changed.

Organized Religion

In times of transition such as we are experiencing, organized religion can serve as a stabilizing influence. Here too, however, the institutionalized churches of all faiths are undergoing change. Once largely a nation steeped in the Judeo-Christian heritage, the United States is now home to a growing number of faiths that are unfamiliar to many people. Buddhism, Islam, and other religions of the East and Middle East are growing as new immigrants bring their religious ideas with them; Islam is the fastest growing religion in the United States. Similarly, a wide variety of relatively small but active congregations built around scientific, philosophical, and psychological ideas are appearing to proliferate—the so-called New Age religious sects. At the same time, conservative branches of mainline Protestant, Catholic, Jewish, and Muslim religions serve as havens for people for whom social change seems too rapid and too chaotic, and fundamentalist denominations (usually Protestant) are the fastest growing religious organizations in the nation. Indeed, the tension between so-called liberal and conservative elements in the organized church may become one of the most profound social conflicts of contemporary life.

Schools as a Reflection of Social Change

Demographics

All the institutional changes discussed thus far are inevitably reflected in the institution of schooling—its purposes, policies, and practices. For example, the demographic statistics, cited in the previous section, that reflect the total population of the United States are first seen in our schools. It is projected that, by the year 2040, children of color will comprise more than half the children in classrooms, up from approximately one-third at the beginning of the twenty-first century.[14] Startling changes are already occurring in a number of places in the country. For example, more than a decade ago, students from so-called minority groups comprised more than 50 percent of the school populations in California, Arizona, New Mexico, Texas, and New York.[15] In these states, minority children may find themselves in the uncomfortable position of being the majority in a world whose rules are set by a more powerful minority, not unlike the former situation in South Africa. And recent census figures for California show that there is currently no majority cultural group in the state!

Language

Along with ethnic and racial diversity often comes linguistic diversity. Increasing numbers of children are entering school from minority language backgrounds and have little or no competence in the English language. It is estimated that there are between 2 million and 3.3 million limited English proficient (LEP) students in schools in the United States—73 percent of whom speak Spanish as their primary language,[16] making the United States the fifth largest Spanish-speaking country in the world! While 67 percent of these students can be found in the five states of California, Texas, New York, Florida, and Illinois, most school districts in the country have LEP students. Spanish is the most common second language spoken in America's classroom, but an increasing number of students are entering the schools speaking Arabic, Chinese, Russian, Hmong, Khmer, Lao, Thai, and Vietnamese. More than 50 percent of LEP students are in grades K–4, with 77 percent coming from poor backgrounds. A relatively high dropout rate characterizes this group of children—in spite of all our efforts at bilingual education. Since a person's language provides the symbols used to understand the world, children whose symbol systems differ from those of the dominant group are likely to see the world from a different perspective, to look for meaning in different ways, and to attribute different meanings to common objects and processes. Although these students may be perceived as a challenge to our educational system in the years ahead, one consequence of successfully accommodating this diversity is that all of us—students, teachers, and communities alike—must become more knowledgeable, more accepting, and better skilled at communicating with people from different backgrounds.

Ability

Life in classrooms is different in other ways as well. Before the enactment of the Education of All Handicapped Children Act of 1975 (Public Law 94-142), more than 1 million children with disabilities were excluded from public school because the community (or state) had not yet taken any responsibility for their welfare or education. In addition, many who were in school were given inappropriate labels and were segregated from their peers. With amendments enacted in 1990, 1992, and 1997, the law was renamed the Individuals with Disabilities Education Act and significant changes were made in the law that now affect not only children but all students through the age of twenty-one. As a result of Public Law 94-142 and its successors, students with a variety of disabilities now spend increasing amounts of time in traditional classrooms while still receiving the services they need. Indeed, some schools are becoming all-inclusion schools, and the preparation of special education teachers is also changing in a number of states, reflecting the changing role of those teachers in schools where students with disabilities spend most of their time in regular classrooms. The trend is toward more inclusion, which enables students with disabilities to be educated side-by-side with their nondisabled peers. While this arrangement benefits students with special needs, the benefits are not one-sided. Children do learn from each other, and students with disabilities also have *abilities* to share.

Gender

Over the last few decades there has emerged a new awareness in many classrooms of a difference among children that is so fundamental that it has been overlooked as a matter of inquiry throughout most of our history. That difference is gender. Because we have included both girls and boys, at least in elementary education, since the very beginning of the common school, and because our political and educational ideals assume that school is gender neutral, the effect of gender on children's education has not been analyzed until recently. In the last thirty years, however, considerable research has been done on differences in the social and educational lives of boys and girls in school. Shakeshaft writes:

> Two messages emerge repeatedly from the research on gender and schooling. First, what is good for males is not necessarily good for females. Second, if a choice must be made, the education establishment will base policy and instruction on that which is good for males.[17]

For the most part, girls have not been considered educationally different from boys. Yet the experiences of girls in school are in many ways quite different from the experiences of boys. Also, the educational outcomes of girls differ from those of boys. In short, girls who sit in the same classrooms as boys, read the same materials as boys, do the same homework as boys, and take the same examinations as boys, often are not treated in the same ways as boys and consequently may not achieve the same educational outcomes as boys do.

Students and Teachers: A Clash of Cultures?

There exists a considerable discrepancy between the makeup of the student population in most schools and that of the teaching force. Most of our nation's teachers continue to come from a rather homogeneous group; approximately 88 to 90 percent are European American and middle class. Indeed, the profile of the teacher education student that emerged from Zimpher's study in 1987 has not changed appreciably: "the typical teacher education student is a monolingual white female from a low-middle or middle-class suburban or rural home who wants to teach children who are just like herself."[18]

Women outnumber men by three-to-one in the teaching force, with nearly two-thirds of Pre K–6 teachers being women (male teachers in grades 7–12 do outnumber female teachers two-to-one). These figures contrast sharply with the student diversity that currently exists in schools and that is projected to increase in the years ahead. A considerable number of children are thus missing important role models who represent their background within the school setting—boys in the early years, and children of color in general. Majority students as well miss having role models who represent groups other than their own. Equally critical is the fact that teachers (like many other people) tend to be culture bound, to have little knowledge or experience with people from other cultures, which of course limits their ability to interact effectively with students who are different from themselves. Indeed, sixty-nine percent of white teacher education students report spending all or most of their free time with people of their own racial or ethnic background.[19] More disturbing, a substantial number of teacher education students do not believe that low-income and minority learners are capable of grasping high-level concepts in the subjects they are preparing to teach.[20] Finally, the traditional identification of teaching as women's work means that even multiculturally sophisticated teachers are usually powerless to make their school's culture more accommodating to female and underrepresented students because it is usually white males who are in key decision-making roles.

Rethinking Schools and Learning: The Effort to Reform Our Schools

In terms of traditional definitions of social order, it appears that most of our social institutions are not working very well in the beginning of this new millennium. Another way to state this observation is to say that the norms governed by our institutions have changed. In this context, the principle values of democratic equality, liberty, and community are once again called into question. What does equality mean when many culturally different people around the world are competing for the same jobs? What does liberty mean when language barriers prevent common understanding? What does community mean when allegiance to one's group prevents commonality with people in other groups?

Some scholars have argued that the changes we are experiencing require a shift from the ideals of a Jeffersonian political democracy (in which democratic principles are defined by individualism) to the ideals of a cultural democracy in which democratic principles are defined by cultural pluralism.[21] Such a shift involves a radical change in our beliefs about how we are to get along with one another, what kinds of information and skills we need to develop, and how we are to interpret our national ideals and goals. Among other changes, this cultural view of democracy requires a fundamental rethinking of our national goals and how we structure or organize schools in relation to those goals. Schooling is, after all, the institution charged not only with imparting necessary information and skills but also with ensuring that young people develop long-cherished democratic attitudes and values. While schooling alone cannot completely alter the larger society in which it exists,[22] schooling can influence as well as reflect its parent society. And since teachers can engender or stifle new ideas and new ways of doing things with their students, they are in a position to influence both the direction and pace of change in our society.

As Tracy is learning in her teacher education program, one of the most significant results of rethinking schools and teaching is the testing and accountability movement. Although there is considerable debate about both the means and ends of the movement, taken at face value it signals a major change not only in the way we think about schools but also in the way we think about teaching and learning. It is no longer acceptable to eliminate certain children from the ranks of the educable. Nor is it acceptable to think that it's all right if some children don't measure up to standards, or that you just can't "teach everyone." Indeed, the emphasis is now squarely on learning outcomes for *all* children.

Fortunately, there are teachers who have accepted this challenge and are learning to think about their practice in more inclusive ways. They work in classrooms in all regions of the country, sometimes alone and sometimes with colleagues who are also excited about new possibilities. They work with students of all backgrounds: white and nonwhite, wealthy and poor, boys and girls, rural and urban. They work with students of varied religions and of no particular religion, with students who have vastly different abilities, and with students who have different sexual orientations. They work in wealthy districts that spend a great deal of money on each student and in poor districts that have little in the way of resources. And most importantly, their classrooms reflect their belief that all children can succeed.

Schools in Transition

Twenty-first-century schools and classrooms, in which teachers must learn to see change as an opportunity rather than a problem and difference as a resource rather than a deficit, are fundamentally different from the traditional schools and classrooms that character-ized nineteenth- and twentieth-century America. Underlying these differences in past and future schools are fundamental differences in the larger society in which schools are found. During the nineteenth and twentieth centuries, most schools were designed to reflect the emerging industrial (factory) mode of organization. Toffler refers to this era as the "Second Wave Civilization" to distinguish it from its predecessor, the agrarian era, or "First Wave Civilization." Central to this industrial Second Wave Civilization, also often referred to as the "factory model," are the ideas of *standardization, synchronization, spe-cialization, centralization, and bigness.* Conversely, the organizational model that seems to be emerging as we enter the information and global age of the twenty-first century, which Toffler refers to as "Third Wave Civilization," differs sharply from its predecessor. Central to this model are the ideas of *individualization and choice* rather than standardi-zation, *decentralization* rather than centralization, *diversity* rather than specialization, and *smallness* rather than bigness.[23] The next two sections take a closer look at how the current progression from the industrial age to the information age is likely to influence the nature of twenty-first-century schooling and teaching. The text then examines where today's schools are in relation to this transition and the primary obstacles that must be dealt with as the change proceeds.

Characteristics of Classrooms for the Industrial (Factory) Age, or Second Wave

In industrial-age schools, administrators are viewed as bosses, teachers as workers, and students as raw material. The work of teachers is to lecture, ask questions, and give directions that will produce students who meet the vocational and citizenship needs of the society. Students, as befitting raw material, are largely passive.

Standardization

Standardization is important in Second Wave schools. Teachers and other school personnel are hired based on well-defined standards of certification. Standards of dress and behavior for both school personnel and students are enforced through well-publicized, standardized rules. Curriculum is based largely on standardized textbooks and on a districtwide standardized course of study that each teacher is expected to follow. Standards of performance for students and teachers are well-defined, and grades reflect a student's ability to learn standardized lessons as demonstrated through standardized paper-and-pencil tests. Competition for grades is encouraged, and work is normally done individually. "Keep your eyes on your own paper" and "Don't talk to your neighbors" are common statements made by teachers to reinforce ideals of individualism and competition. It is expected, and therefore accepted, that some students, being poorer raw material, will fail.

Children are initially grouped by age in standard grade levels without regard to individual development. Children who do not fit a particular grade level are either put down a grade level, kept back for a year, occasionally advanced a grade, or placed in remedial or special classes. In the past, the last option was likely to continue throughout the course of a child's schooling. Print is the instructional media of choice, while the use of art, music, drama, video, computers, and other alternative media is considered an extra if it is considered at all.

Synchronization

In Second Wave schools the synchronization of time is a major part of the school structure. The school year lasts a certain number of days. There is a time to come to school and a time to leave. Classes last for a certain number of minutes. Indeed, in some states, time allotments per subject per week are mandated by the state department of education. Special events like field trips and assemblies are carefully scheduled so as to offer the least interference with the standard school day.

Specialization

Specialization is also a central element of Second Wave schools. In elementary school, specialized subject areas are taught separately throughout the day. Above the elementary grades, knowledge is divided into disciplines and offered in specialized courses by different teachers separated from one another by physical distance, time, and often a hierarchy of value. Home economics, vocational education, music, and art, for example, are not valued as highly as mathematics, English, and science. Roles in Second Wave schools are also specialized. Administrators perform certain tasks, teachers perform other tasks. Teachers in secondary schools teach only certain subjects, whereas special teachers teach only special students. Other professional and nonprofessional staff (nurses, counselors, custodians) perform still other tasks.

Centralization

Similarly, Second Wave schools are highly centralized. Most rules and customs are decided by centralized district staff who usually work out of what is accurately called the *central office*. Curriculum decisions, budgets, purchasing, and school policies regarding attendance, discipline, acceptable teaching practices, and annual scheduling are effected from a centralized point. For students receiving special education, such responsibilities are administered separately, as a centralized system-within-a-system.

Large Scale

An inclination toward bigness is also characteristic of Second Wave schools, particularly at the secondary level. It's an old American belief that "bigger is better," and the belief applies to almost all aspects of schools except class size, where the norm is about twenty-five students per class. An elementary principal once said, sadly, "Every time my school population declines to its most educable level—about 300 students—the district talks about consolidating us with another school." Educators know from experience that the larger a school is, the more impersonal it becomes, the less chance there is for the school to become a community, and the more students will "fall through the cracks." Nevertheless, for financial reasons, consolidation of small schools is a major trend in the United States. Finally, most people seem attracted to the idea of bigness—and refer to a big football team, a big band, a big choir, or a big building.

Reich describes the school that expresses a desire to fit students for an industrial, mass-production society:

> Children [move] from grade to grade through a preplanned sequence of standard subjects, as if on factory conveyor belts. At each state, certain facts [are] poured into their heads. Children with the greatest capacity to absorb the facts, and with the most submissive demeanor, [are] placed on a rapid track through the sequence; those with the least capacity for fact retention and self-discipline, on the slowest. Most children [end] up on a conveyor belt of medium speed. Standardized tests [are] routinely administered at certain checkpoints in order to measure how many of the facts [have] stuck in the small heads, and product defects [are] taken off the line and returned for retooling. As in the mass-production system, discipline and order [are] emphasized above all else.[24]

Characteristics of Classrooms for the Information Age, or Third Wave

The model for Third Wave, or information-age, schools and classrooms is not the factory, it is the learning community. In learning communities, teachers, students, support staff, parents, administrators, and others who are involved in the school from time to time are viewed as members of a single community, whose common purpose, for everyone, is learning. Learning is defined not only as the acquisition of factual knowledge but also as the development of critical thinking skills and the ability to apply knowledge in varied situations (problem solving). Emphasis is placed not only on the acquisition of information and skills, but also on the *understanding* of their theoretical and research base. In such an atmosphere, *why* is often a more important question than *what*, and the *process* of learning—how material is structured and is presented in order to help students learn—is considered an important issue.

Individualization and Choice

Individualization and choice increasingly characterize Third Wave classrooms. Teachers and students often decide together, within a broad curricular framework, what to study and how to study it, what materials are required, what rules are needed, and how much time is given to various activities. Such collaboration enables teachers to share their individual knowledge and skills. Students and teachers are viewed as resources, each with unique contributions to the learning community.

Collaboration

As befits a community, tasks are often accomplished by people working together, using what they already know and figuring out what they need to know and how to get it. Since the primary goal of the community is learning, not sorting out those who have learned from those who have not, everyone's knowledge is put to use in the service of that goal. It is expected, and accepted, that everyone will learn and contribute to the learning of others. Cooperation is emphasized, and competition is reduced to an occasional activity. Mistakes are accepted and considered instructive, so the logical next step after failure is to try again. Some of these schools and classrooms have abandoned letter grades in favor of narrative progress reports or portfolio assessment. Where grades are given, they are sometimes given to groups rather than to individuals and, in any case, are used more as a measure of progress rather than a measure of the person.

In learning communities it is understood that children learn at different rates. Standardized grade levels are sometimes abandoned in favor of mixed age or ability groupings. Where grade levels are maintained, mixed age and ability groupings are often used for part of the day so that older or more advanced students can help those who are younger or less advanced. One way to accomplish this mixing is to block part of the day so that all students are simultaneously working on math or some other subject in different parts of the school. Another way is to organize learning in an individual classroom around small group projects, which allows students to collaborate in solving some problems. In this case, the acquisition of knowledge becomes a means to accomplishing the project. Still another community strategy is to study a particular object from an interdisciplinary point of view, utilizing knowledge from science, art, music, history, language arts, mathematics, and so forth to further understanding. For example, a unit on food production might integrate content from the sciences (plant growth), social studies (geography, economics, anthropology), language arts (writing from the perspective of a farmer), health (preservation of food), music (production of advertising jingles), and art (marketing and advertising). In most learning communities, all three strategies are present, sometimes sequentially and sometimes simultaneously.

Diversity

It is also understood in learning communities that everyone (students, teachers, support staff) has his or her own unique characteristics. Individuals learn, teach, and interact in any number of ways, depending on their innate characteristics and their cultural conditioning. Such social diversity is viewed as normal rather than deviant and as enriching rather than dividing the community. Consequently, in such schools and classrooms, social and physical differences are explicitly acknowledged and appreciated. This attitude has some important educational consequences.

First, a continuing effort is made to help all children understand and appreciate the characteristics of those who differ from themselves. Second, the tools of such understanding and appreciation—the skills of questioning, negotiating, and conflict resolution—are explicitly taught as a part of the ongoing routines of the day. And perhaps most importantly, teaching is seen as a process of adapting to different styles and needs.

Because learning communities are likely to "mix up" traditional divisions of age, time, and disciplines, both adults and children in the school are likely to find themselves working outside their normal age groups and knowledge specialties. Thus, everyone in the school, both adults and students, may serve as resources to one another. Students may find themselves working with many different adults and a wide variety of other students.

Decentralization

Because people in learning community schools and classrooms think of themselves as decision makers, the organization of these schools and classrooms is to a large measure decentralized. That is, the goals and objectives of learning are less dictated by external or centralized personnel and more directed by the participants themselves. Such decentralization is also applied to budgeting, attendance and dress policies, hiring of staff, and so forth. In many schools, this process is called *site-based management,* that is, the community's decision making is done on-site by those who will carry out, and be most affected by, these actions.

Small Scale

Finally, learning communities tend to be small enough to enable everyone to know everyone else reasonably well and to engage in the kind of face-to-face interaction that characterizes most communities. This issue of scale may be addressed in a variety of ways. In some schools, enrollment is deliberately kept low. In larger schools that have been formed for cost-saving purposes, students and teachers are often divided into schools-within-schools. For example, three or four teachers in an elementary school may teach 75 to 100 children, or five or six subject-area teachers may teach 150 high school students. This arrangement permits the greater flexibility and creativity that comes with smaller scale organization. The ultimate goal in all cases is to enable both children and adults to feel a sense of belonging to the community and a sense of responsibility for its welfare.

Where We Are Today

As we begin the transition to the twenty-first century and the information age, schools too are in transition. Few schools today can be described as being entirely Second Wave or entirely Third Wave in their organization and governance. Rather, most schools are somewhere between the two models. Furthermore, the Third Wave school is not entirely new. Some of its elements, such as cross-age grouping and the learning community atmosphere, have historical roots that go back to the one-room schoolhouse of the nineteenth century. What seems to separate the school as a learning community from the school as a factory are the characteristics associated with each model. And those characteristics in turn depend largely on the beliefs, attitudes, and values of the people who comprise the entity we call *school.*

The Difficulty of Change

Change is difficult, particularly when it deals with the fundamental beliefs, attitudes, and values around which we organize our lives. Attempts at such change often result in hostility or in an effort to preserve, at any cost, our familiar ways of doing things and thinking about the world around us. The universal nature of such resistance to change is illustrated in the following parable.

A Parable

Once upon a time there was a group of people who lived in the mountains in an isolated region. One day a stranger passed through their area and dropped some wheat grains in their field. The wheat grew. After a number of years, people noticed the new plant and decided to collect its seeds and chew them. Someone noticed that when a cart had accidentally ridden over some of the seeds, a harder outer covering separated from the seed and what was inside was sweeter. Someone else noticed that when it rained, the grains that had been run over expanded a little, and the hot sun cooked them. So, people started making wheat cereal and cracked wheat and other wheat dishes. Wheat became the staple of their diet.

Years passed. Because these people did not know anything about crop rotation, fertilizers, and cross-pollination, the wheat crop eventually began to fail.

About this time, another stranger happened by. He was carrying two sacks of barley. He saw the people starving and planted some of his grain. The barley grew well. He presented it to the people and showed them how to make bread and soup and many other dishes from barley. But they called him a heretic.

"You are trying to undermine our way of life and force us into accepting you as our king." They saw his trick. "You can't fool us. You are trying to weaken us and make us accept your ways. Our wheat will not let us starve. Your barley is evil."

He stayed in the area, but the people avoided him. Years passed. The wheat crop failed again and again. The children suffered from malnutrition. One day the stranger came to the market and said, "Wheat is a grain. My barley has a similar quality. It is also a grain. Why don't we just call the barley grain?"

Now since they were suffering so much, the people took the grain, except for a few who staunchly refused. They loudly proclaimed that they were the only remaining followers of the True

A Parable (continued)

Way, the Religion of Wheat. A few new people joined the Wheat Religion from time to time, but most began to eat barley. They called themselves The Grainers.

For generations, the Wheat Religion people brought up their children to remember the true food called wheat. A few of them hoarded some wheat grains to keep it safe and sacred. Others sent their children off in search of wheat, because they felt that if one person could happen by with barley, wheat might be known somewhere else too.

And so it went for decades, until the barley crop began to fail. The last few Wheat Religion people planted their wheat again. It grew beautifully, and because it grew so well, they grew bold and began to proclaim that their wheat was the only true food. Most people resisted and called them heretics. A few people said, "Why don't you just admit that wheat is a grain?"

The wheat growers agreed, thinking that they could get many more wheat followers if they called it grain. But by this time, some of the children of the Wheat Religion people began to return from their adventures with new seed, not just wheat, but rye and buckwheat and millet. Now people began to enjoy the taste of many different grains. They took turns planting them and trading the seed with each other. In this way, everyone came to have enough sustenance and lived happily ever after.[25]

This parable carries many metaphorical messages: it applauds diversity and recognizes that a society cannot function to its fullest when it ignores the ideas, contributions, efforts, and concerns of any of its people; it illustrates some of the consequences of unreasonable prejudice but also recognizes the powerful emotions that underlie a prejudiced attitude; it indicates the power of naming something in a way that is familiar and comfortable to those who are uncomfortable about accepting something new.

But perhaps most importantly, the parable recognizes the tendency people have to resist change. People are creatures of habit who find it difficult to change, whether at the individual level, the institutional level, or the societal level. People often work from one set of assumptions, one pattern of behavior. Because of the way in which people are socialized, these habits of thought and behavior are so much a part of them that they find it very difficult to think that things can be done in any other way. Some habits people develop are positive and constructive; others are negative and limiting. The story shows us that sometimes even a society's strengths can become weaknesses.

And yet new circumstances and opportunities arise in each generation that demand that new perspectives, attitudes, and solutions be sought. Such circumstances are evident today in the changing face of the American classroom, and much of the responsibility for change must lie with teachers and teacher educators.

Ideological Perspectives on Multicultural Education

Attention to social differences among students has a relatively long history in this society, beginning at least with the arguments for the common school (which was intended to give students of different social class backgrounds a "common" educational experience that would enable the society to continue to be governed by "we, the people"). During some periods of our history, the focus was also on assimilation to a "common culture," by which was meant a dominant, largely Anglo society. During other periods—notably in the early years of the twentieth century, when Black scholars began to develop curricular materials on the African American experience in America, and in the 1940s, when the Intergroup Education movement had as its main objective the reduction of prejudice and discrimination in the U.S. population—various attempts have been made to perceive difference as a strength rather than as a problem.[26]

The field now known as multicultural education emerged in the aftermath of the civil rights movement in the 1960s, first with the ethnic studies movement and later with a somewhat broader "multicultural" education effort. Within that effort (and outside it as well), there are a variety of perspectives on both the definition and the goals of multicultural education.

Multicultural Education

Some important questions emerge from what is in fact a healthy debate about our ability to provide educational opportunity and success for *all* children. Some of these questions have existed from the beginning; others have emerged as knowledge has increased and times have changed. Consider the following:

Is multicultural education for everyone, or for minority students alone?

Should multicultural education focus on the individual student, on the student as a member of a group, or on both?

If multicultural education takes as its focus the study of *group* identity and experience, which groups shall be included?

To what extent should multicultural education include the study of relationships of power along with the history and contributions of all people?

Is multicultural education academic or political or both?

Will multicultural education, as an ideological movement, divide us as a people or bring us closer together?

Are multicultural teaching practices good for everyone?

To what extent should multicultural education have as a goal the reconstruction of the whole society?

Is multicultural education centered on domestic (i.e., American) issues of diversity, or should it take as its central idea a more global understanding of difference?

All these questions are important ones, in part because they are inexorably related. Given the interdependent nature of the world in which we live, it is becoming less and less possible to think about purely American issues of difference. If the students being taught happen to belong mostly to one group or another, it is still the case that all of them, at some point in their lives, will need to learn how to understand and work with those who are different from themselves. If you think that local issues of inequality, poverty, and unequal access to education, housing, and jobs are central to Americans work concerns, consider that well over half the world's population is struggling with the same issues. Americans work to preserve and protect democratic institutions in this society while millions of people around the world try to understand what democracy really is.

Multicultural education, both as an organized field of study and practice and as an ideological perspective, has witnessed a continued broadening of its scope and interests over the years. Increasingly, the field and its ideologies are turning toward a more global sensibility. This change does not mean that local or national issues are no longer important; it means that what Americans have and continue to learn locally has important implications for global action. It also means that, inasmuch as we are not the only society struggling with issues of difference, there is much we can learn from others around the world.

This book is based in part on a notion of intercultural interactions and their cognitive, emotional, and developmental aspects. An intercultural interaction can be domestic, that is, between two (or more) Americans with different cultural backgrounds, or it can be international, between two (or more) people from different countries. The cultural identity of the parties involved in an interaction may come from a limited and mutually reinforcing set of experiences or from more complex and sometimes conflicting elements. The significant difference in an interaction may be race or class or religion or gender or language or sexual orientation; it may be physical or attitudinal in origin; it may be age-related or status-related or any combination.

Regardless of the *kind* of differences involved, all people tend to approach significant differences in similar, often negative, ways. That is, to understand the processes involved is a first step toward overcoming these differences; and *both* culture-specific knowledge and culture-general knowledge are prerequisites on the road to social justice.

Goals of This Book

This book is about change as well as about diversity. It is about teaching all children in a society that is growing more diverse each year. It is about changes in classrooms and in the act of teaching within those classrooms. It is about changes in schools and in the larger society in which these schools are embedded. It is equally about change within oneself, for change in the larger dimensions of society cannot occur without significant changes in one's own perception, attitudes, and skills. All these environments (self, classrooms, schools, and society) are connected, so that changes in any one of them produce disequilibrium and change in the others. Their connectedness and the mutual influence that each one exerts on the others is visually depicted in Figure 1.1.

As teachers in the twenty-first century, you will spend your careers in ever-changing schools, schools whose mission will be to help society make an orderly transition from a Second Wave civilization to a Third Wave civilization that is more inclusive. Your ability to feel comfortable and operate effectively within such a changing environment will require a unique set of cultural understandings and interpersonal skills that go beyond traditional pedagogy. These skills, perspectives, and attitudes that you as a teacher must adopt in order to coalesce diverse students into an effective learning community must also be transmitted to the students in your charge, who will live their lives in the same kind of highly interconnected and interdependent world. You are thus walking both sides of a double-edged sword, so to speak. The process that you undergo to become more effective working across cultures must ultimately become content that you teach to students. This feat will not be easy!

Figure 1.2 illustrates four basic goals of this book, which can be viewed as steps in understanding multicultural education and your role as an educator in an inclusive system. A word about each goal follows.

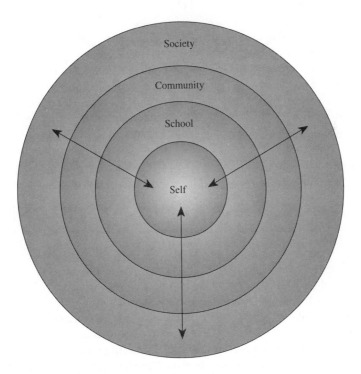

figure 1.1   Interconnected environments.

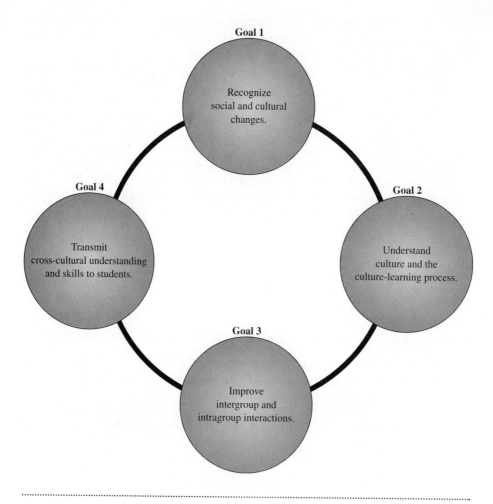

figure 1.2   Goals of this book.

Goal 1: To Recognize Social and Cultural Change

The first step in providing an education that is truly multicultural is to improve student understanding of the concept of pluralism in American society. Pluralism in this context must consider such sources of cultural identity as nationality, ethnicity, race, gender, socioeconomic status, religion, sexual orientation, geographic region, health, and ability/disability, and must look particularly at how each of these identities has had an impact on the individual as well as the group. This step requires that teachers understand the social changes that have historically and are currently taking place in our pluralistic society; these social changes provide the underlying rationale for multicultural education and are found in Chapter 1 as well as throughout the book.

Goal 2: To Understand Culture, Learning, and the Culture-Learning Process

After establishing the need for an education that is multicultural, it is necessary to understand just what is meant by that term. What does the term *culture* refer to, and how do people come to acquire different cultural identities? With what knowledge do children already come to school? Too often schools do not legitimize the experiences children bring with them to the school; instead schools label some children as failures because their backgrounds, including their language and culture, are not seen as adequate or legitimate. Teachers must thus expand their knowledge base of culture and the different groups found in the United States as well as abroad. This means that curriculum content must be expanded and pedagogy adapted to include the experiences of all students. Chapter 2 examines these issues and in the process provides models of the sources of cultural learning and of the culture-learning process. An important recognition here is that differences *within* groups are often as important as differences *between* groups. Individuals belong simultaneously to many different groups, and their behavior can be understood only in terms of their *simultaneous* affiliation with these many groups. These models illustrate how culture filters down to the individual learner who actively engages with it, accepting and absorbing certain elements and rejecting and modifying others.

Goal 3: To Improve Intergroup and Intragroup Interactions

Goal 2 is to examine how individuals come to acquire their particular cultural identity; goal 3 is to show how culturally different people interact with one another and how these interactions can be improved. We must work to improve intergroup as well as intragroup interactions. We must also learn how individuals develop sensitivity and improve their interactions with other cultures. Goal 3 demands attention to such issues as development of intercultural sensitivity, cross-cultural understanding and interaction, attribution and assessment across groups, and conflict management. Teachers in particular must broaden their instructional repertoire so that it reflects an understanding of the various groups that will be taught. To help teachers understand the interaction between culturally different individuals (whether from different groups or from the same group), Chapter 3 presents a model of intercultural interaction that applies culture learning to ourselves as well as our students and that develops a culture-general model of behavior. These models help us analyze the nature of intercultural interaction and they show how key concepts can be applied to various types of school situations. Chapter 4 offers some useful models of intercultural development and synthesizes them with a new and somewhat more sophisticated model of intercultural development that helps increase the number of concepts as well as the language with which we can profitably understand and discuss these issues.

Goal 4: To Transmit Intercultural Understanding and Skills to Students

The book's final goal is to help teachers transmit to students the same understandings and skills that are contained in (1) the model for explaining cultural differences, and (2) the model for improving intercultural interaction in order to prepare multicultural citizen-actors who are able and willing to participate in an interdependent world. That is, this book strives to empower action-oriented, reflective decision makers who are able and willing to be socially and politically active in the school, community, nation, and world. This book is concerned not only with developing the knowledge and skill of practicing teachers, but also with transferring this knowledge to the pupils in their charge. Thus, individuals become proactive teachers and reflective practitioners who can ultimately prepare reflective citizen-actors (their students) for an interdependent world. The content of these models is universal. It applies to all multicultural situations, not just those confronted by teachers in classrooms and schools. Teaching these understandings and skills to students can be accomplished both through teacher modeling and through explicit instruction, and both methods are illustrated in the remaining chapters of the book.

The Role of Stories, Cases, and Activities

Stories

This book contains many stories, because stories help us visualize and talk about new ideas and experiences. Some stories are about real people and events, while others, like the story of the wheat people, are folktales and parables. Stories contain the power to speak about complex human experiences; in this book, stories speak, about how people experience the fact of human diversity. Stories help us to see the universals within the experience. Everyone, no matter what his or her cultural or biological differences, goes through similar stages of experience when confronted with change. Stories, like no other literary device, help us cut through the morass of individual and cultural differences that separate us and allow us to focus on the universals of the experience as we come to grips with those changes.

Case Studies and Critical Incidents

Because it is difficult to imagine situations with which you have had little experience, this book develops a series of case studies and critical incidents describing multicultural teaching situations that you might encounter. These scenarios are actual or synthesized real-life situations that have been described by a number of researchers and practitioners. Think of them as scenes in a play about schools with a multicultural student population. Most cases have been generated from multiple sources, each of which is noted in the list of references.

Because the cases cover a variety of communities and classrooms with diverse kinds of people in them, multiple issues are embedded in most of the cases. Although each case is designed to illustrate one or more particular issues related to the topic at hand, the portraits of people, places, ideas, and activities are rich enough that they can also be used to discuss topics in other chapters. Taken together, these cases illustrate a number of complex classroom realities that defy simple right-and-wrong solutions. Rather, they present small dramas in which a number of interpretations are possible and in which a number of ideas can be used to develop plans of action and fallback positions.

Summary

This chapter provides an overview of some of the factors that are undergoing change in American society and that have an influence in the lives of children and teachers in schools. Such rapid social change has resulted in schools being caught in the transition from the Second Wave, an earlier factory model that offered a standardized curriculum for all, to the Third Wave, a more globally oriented dynamic model that attempts to address social change and prepare a citizenry that is more inclusive, integrative, and proactive. This book is designed to assist pre-service and in-service teachers to (1) recognize social and cultural change; (2) understand culture and the culture-learning process; (3) improve intergroup and intragroup interactions; and (4) transmit cross-cultural understandings and skills to students. The chapter also recognizes that change is difficult, yet is a force that we all must understand and accommodate—both as individuals as well as institutions.

 # Chapter Review

Go to the Online Learning Center at **www.mhhe.com/Cushner4e** to review important content from the chapter, practice with key terms, take a chapter quiz, and find the web links listed in this chapter.

Key Terms

Demographics   6   Norms   7   Social institution   7

Reflective Questions

1. Identify three changes that American society is undergoing, and discuss how those changes are reflected in schools.
2. Think back to your experiences in elementary and/or high school. What indication do you have that your school was reflective of a Second Wave, or an industrial-age, school? What indication do you have that your school was reflective of a Third Wave, or information-age, school?
3. In the case study, Tracy questions why she needs to be in a diversity course. What experiences have you had that might lead you to say that you are well prepared for diversity? In what areas do you not feel as well prepared?

References

1. C. Cortes, The Accelerating Change of American Diversity," *The School Administrator,* May 1999, pp. 12–14.

2. Ibid.

3. National Center for Educational Statistics, 1997.

4. William A. Henry III, "Beyond the Melting Pot," *Time,* 9 April 1990, p. 28.

5. The President's Initiative on Race, prepared by the Council of Economic Advisors, cited in the *Akron (Ohio) Beacon Journal,* 18 September 1998, p. A5.

6. "U.S. Census 2000," *Editorial Projects in Education,* 20, 4: 33, 2001.

7. Robert Bierstedt, *The Social Order* (New York: McGraw-Hill, 1974), pp. 329–332.

8. Alvin Toffler, *The Third Wave* (New York: William Morrow, 1980).

9. Ibid.

10. Robert Reich, *The Work of Nations* (New York: Vintage Books, 1992), p. 112.

11. Cortes, "Accelerating Change."

12. *America's Children Yearbook* (Children's Defense Fund, 1996).

13. Statistics on these kinds of categories vary depending on the methods (and often, the purposes) of those compiling them. These particular statistics can be found in the following publications: Center for Education Statistics, *Digest of Education Statistics* (Washington, DC: U.S. Government Printing Office, 1987); "Here They Come, Ready or Not," *Education Week,* 14 May 1986; H. L. Hodgkinson, *All One System: Demographics of Education—Kindergarten Through Graduate School* (Washington, DC: Institute of Educational Leadership, 1985); M. M. Kennedy, R. K. Jung, and M. E. Orland, *Poverty, Achievement, and the Distribution of Compensatory Education Services* (Washington, DC: U.S. Government Printing Office, 1986); and *America's Children Yearbook.*

14. National Center for Educational Statistics, 1997.

15. *From Minority to Majority: Education and the Future of the Southwest* (Boulder, CO: Western Interstate Compact of Higher Education, 1988).

16. L. Baca, "The Status and Future of Bilingual Education." (paper presented at the tenth annual conference of the National Association for Multicultural Education, 15 November 2000, Orlando, FL).

17. Carol Shakeshaft, "A Gender at Risk," *Phi Delta Kappan,* 67, 7 (March 1986): 500.

18. N. L. Zimpher, "The RATE Project: A Profile of Teacher Education Students," *Journal of Teacher Education,* 40, 6, (November–December 1989): 27–30.

19. Ibid.

20. Ibid.

21. Averil E. McClelland and Normand R. Bernier, "A Rejoinder to Steve Tozer's 'Toward a New Consensus Among Social Foundations Educators,'" *Educational Foundations,* 7, 4 (Fall 1993): 61.

22. George Counts, *Dare the Schools Build a New Social Order?* (Carbondale: Southern Illinois University Press, 1978 [1932]).

23. These ideas and categories are adapted from Toffler, *Third Wave.*

24. Reich, *Work of Nations,* pp. 59–60.

25. Told by J. E. Rash at the Mediterranean Youth Environment Conference, Cartagena, Spain, August 1985.

26. Carl A. Grant and Gloria Ladson-Billings, eds., *Dictionary of Multicultural Education* (Phoenix, AZ: Oryx Press, 1997).

Culture and the Culture-Learning Process

The first month or two in class I was always saying, "Look at me when I talk to you," and the (Navajo) kids simply wouldn't do it. They would always look at their hands, or the blackboard, or anywhere except looking me in the face. And finally, one of the other teachers told me it was a cultural thing. They should warn us about things like that. Odd things. It makes children seem evasive.

—Tony Hillerman, The Skinwalkers

Chapter Outline

focus   questions

1.   How is it that you became the cultural being that you are today?

2.   How have different individuals and institutions you have come into contact with influenced you?

3.   How has the media influenced your cultural identity? your religion? your community? What other forces operate to influence your cultural identity?

4.   What do you know about your own culture that you can use to better understand another culture, or that will enable you to talk intelligently about cultural differences with someone who is different from you?

The word *education* is derived from the Latin word *edu-care,* meaning "to lead forth." If we are to seriously engage in the education of students who will be proactive citizens in a multicultural and global society, then we must lead our students in such a manner that they understand where they have come from, are cognizant of current conditions that affect them and the world, and are able to take the necessary steps to adjust to change.

Clearly, *education* is a broader term than *schooling.* Indeed, one of the difficulties we all encounter in talking about education at all is that it is pervasive in human life. Not often emphasized, however, are the actual settings, apart from schools, in which education occurs and the precise nature of teaching and learning in those settings. Yet, it is in these settings—particularly in the home, the neighborhood, and our houses of worship—that we acquire the language, knowledge, attitudes, and values that let us engage in the dramatic conversation called culture. It is in these settings that we develop the cultural identities that we bring with us to school. And it is through these settings, including the school, that we must work to lead our students forward into the future.

Giroux and Simon speak directly to the importance of teachers understanding their own cultural identities and those of their students:

By ignoring the cultural and social forms that are authorized by youth and simultaneously empower and disempower them, educators risk complicity in silencing and negating their students. This is unwittingly accomplished by refusing to recognize the importance of those sites and social practices outside of the schools that actively shape student experiences and through which students often define and construct their sense of identity, politics, and culture.[1]

These ideas can be clarified through the use of a "thought experiment"— a community you can enter in your imagination, so as to consider the educational implications of living there. In this experiment, posit an imaginary medium-sized city of about three hundred thousand people—say it's close (about an hour) to one or more major metropolitan areas that have populations exceeding 1 million. Call this city Midland. Now, conditions in such a city will vary, depending on its ethnic and religious composition, its economic base, and its location (Is it in New England? the deep south? the Midwest? the mountain states of the west? the southwest? the northwest?). The size of Midland is also a factor to consider. If it were a city of several million, or a village of several hundred (or thousand) people, conditions might be different. In this thought experiment, Midland may assume a variety of characteristics: read on and see what you can surmise.

c a s e   s t u d y   Midland: A Thought Experiment

To begin with, the imaginary city of Midland is clearly a geographical community, in the sense that it is in some ways like a small city and in other ways like a large town. It has city limits, a mayor, and a city council. It has its own set of laws and is also under the jurisdiction of its county, its state, and the nation. Importantly, it also has a fairly good-sized river that runs through the very middle of the city, a fact that the residents acknowledge by using the terms north side *and* south side.

The city of Midland has a rather wealthy residential section, a number of middle-class neighborhoods, and a few neighborhoods that are rather poor. It has some manufacturing industry, a number of churches, two synagogues—one conservative and one reform—as well as a mosque and a Buddhist temple. It has numerous day care centers, a museum, a relatively large public library with several branch libraries, a television station, several radio stations, and a daily newspaper. There are three hospitals—one of them Catholic—and numerous "neighborhood" medical drop-in centers. It has department stores, discount stores, bars, neighborhood convenience stores, and several commercial and service businesses. It has a municipal park and a Class A professional baseball team with its own ballpark, a YM/YWCA, a welfare department, a children's services department, and a juvenile reformatory for boys. It has a community theater, several malls, and a downtown business district. It has an adequate number of lawyers, doctors, dentists, accountants, architects, and other professionals. Although the middle schools are all public, it has both public and private elementary and high schools. There are a few Catholic schools as well as one small Jewish day school. There is a well-established, well-endowed private school just outside the city limits. Midland has a university and a community college, both of which interact well with the community.

Within the geographical community that is Midland, there is also a set of educational communities—groups of people who are actively engaged in instruction and learning (formal and informal) as well as those organizations and settings in which deliberate and systematic teaching and learning occurs. It is in these educational communities that the dramatic conversations of culture take place—in particular ways in families, neighborhoods, businesses, religious settings, and voluntary associations. So the particular combination of settings in Midland sets the tone, so to speak, of the community itself and of the educational messages—both coherent and conflicting—available to its people.

Say, for the sake of the experiment, that Midland is in upstate New York and is a largely Protestant city (of all denominations, including three good-sized black churches). It also has a considerable number of Catholic families, enough to support several churches, as well as a few Catholic schools, 13 public elementary schools that feed into six middle schools, and four comprehensive high schools. There are relatively small groups of Jewish, Islamic and Buddhist families.

Say, further, that for the most part, Midland is a largely white, working- and middle-class city. The African Americans who live there have been there for at least fifty years, and they comprise about 12 percent of the population. Most migrated here from the deep south after World War II to work in the city's relatively small factories. Let's further suppose that these industries are suffering from severe competition, both domestic and foreign. Business is not good, and the residents of Midland are fearful that many jobs could be lost, thus creating a depressed economic situation for all income-producing businesses.

As in all communities, the cultural conversations of Midland have their roots in the economic, religious, social class, and family life of the town. The particular education received by an individual growing up in Midland depends, in large part, on the ethnic, religious, social class, and occupational character of the individual's family and the character of the housing and neighborhoods in which the individual lives, works, and plays. These factors—as well as others, such as the age of the individual, the individual's health, and the size and composition of the family of which the individual is a member—also have a great deal to do with the access the individual has to a broad or narrow range of educational resources and experiences available both within and outside the school.

Take a look, now, at four sixteen-year-old high school students who live in Midland. What cultural conversations do you think have meaning for them?

Michael Williams is an African American who has lived his entire life with his grandmother and grandfather (retired and at home), his mother (an assembly line worker at the light-bulb factory), his aunt (who works evenings cleaning at the museum), two brothers, and a sister in a house on the northeast side of the city. He doesn't know who or where his father is. His older brother works in a local factory and never went on to college after he graduated from high school. The family regularly attends the A.M.E. church. As a child, Michael played basketball at the community house near his home and continues to help out there with younger children. He attends the public North High School and is in the college prep academic program, where he earns excellent grades. He has a steady girlfriend; is a member of the high school golf team, which practices at the local golf course; is on the school newspaper staff, which is advised by an editor of the Midland newspaper; and works after school and weekends at the golf course.

Toni Catalano lives in a pleasant ranch house on a cul-de-sac on the south side of town. She is the youngest of a large, extended Italian Catholic family; her parents immigrated to the United States just before she was born. Although she attended Catholic parochial school through the eighth grade, she currently attends the public South High School, where she is majoring in business subjects and is planning to become a secretary—perhaps in one of the local banks. Her family has always been very involved in the local Italian community as well as in the church, and Toni gained a considerable amount of attention (not all of it positive) when she became the first alter girl at St. Mary's. Two of her aunts are nuns; one of them, Sister Rita, is a missionary in Central America. One of her uncles is a priest in a church in a neighboring suburb and disapproves heartily of her aunt's being in Central America. Nevertheless, her family keeps in close contact with Sister Rita, and Toni corresponds with her frequently—increasingly by e-mail. At home, the family speaks a fair amount of Italian, something that Toni finds rather embarrassing when her friends are around. In school, she earns reasonably good grades, is on the cheerleading squad, and is a scorekeeper for the wrestling team. She dates a number of boys, mostly athletes, and works on weekends at a department store in a local shopping mall.

Steven Wong lives in a large and comfortable house on The Hill, on the west side of town, with his parents and a younger sister. His father is a lawyer and his mother, an artist, is in charge of the adult volunteers (called docents) at the museum where Steve sometimes works as a guide for special exhibits. His family does not belong to any religious group. He attends a private high school for boys, where he struggles a bit for average grades, and is a member of the tennis and debate teams. As a child, Steve played Little League baseball, belonged to the Boy Scouts, and traveled extensively in the United States and China to visit family. He doesn't date much, and when he does it is usually with non-Asian girls who are children of his parents' friends. He takes karate lessons every week and participates in formal demonstrations of the martial arts. He is not certain that he wants to go to college, much to his parents' dismay.

Shameka Collins is living in one of only three African American families on her street, which is on the south side of town. Shameka lives with her parents, an African American mother who works as a bookkeeper for a local department store, and a European American father, who spends much of his time working out of state. She sees him only occasionally—perhaps once or twice a month. Shameka is the only biracial student in her school, although most other students are not aware that her father is white. She has an older brother who is stationed on a nuclear submarine presently on duty in the Persian Gulf. As a child, Shameka was a Girl Scout for a while, but dropped out. She has gone to Sunday school at the local Presbyterian church all her life. After school and on Saturdays, she works at the main branch of the public library downtown, saving most of the money she makes for college. She does not have either the time or the inclination to date much, but she does find time to go to all the exhibitions at the museum and to all the local community theater productions. Once she even had a small part in a play there. Since Shameka and her mother are generally alone, they spend as much time together as possible. Her mother has taught her to sew, and she makes almost all her own clothes. She worries about leaving home when she goes to college and is trying to decide whether to attend the local community college for two years before actually leaving home. Because she takes advanced placement courses in high school, she will be eligible for courses at the college in her senior year and will probably become a student there. She thinks perhaps she will become a doctor.

Each of these students, lifelong residents of Midland, participates in a particular pattern of educational life, out of which has emerged a cultural identity. The cultural knowledge, beliefs, attitudes, and values of these students, like those of most Americans, are multiple—none identifies with a single cultural group. Yet their cultural and educational patterns are different and sometimes surprising. How do you see their various cultural influences impacting their lives? What aspects of their upbringing do you think influences them most today? In what ways are they similar to one another? different? In what ways are they similar or different to you? Can you put yourself in Midland?

Exploring the Concept of Culture

One of the greatest difficulties people have when they begin to explore concepts related to culture and culture learning is that of agreeing on what it is they are talking about. This chapter looks closely at the concept of culture and the culture-learning process; that is, how we acquire a cultural identity. The chapter begins with some definitions of culture and with some of the analytical concepts devised by social scientists in their attempts to understand cultural differences among groups of people as well as individuals. This discussion sets the stage for subsequent analysis of cross-cultural interaction and intercultural development that occurs in the context of schools.

Activity and Reading 4: The Nature of Culture and Culture Learning

Defining Culture

Culture is studied by many different disciplines, including anthropology, sociology, education, psychology, business, and the military. If you were to peruse the literature of these various disciplines looking for the concept of culture, you would find literally hundreds of definitions. Some of these definitions are more useful than others in an examination of how culture influences the teaching-learning process. What all these definitions seem to have in common is the idea that culture refers to a human-made part of the environment as opposed to aspects that occur in nature. Culture determines, to a large extent, peoples' thoughts, ideas, patterns of interaction, and material adaptations to the world around them. This chapter explores this notion in greater detail as it looks at insights and practices from various disciplines.

Coon refers to culture as "the totality of socially transmitted behavior patterns, arts, beliefs, institutions, and all other products of human work and thought characteristic of a community or a population."[2] He likens culture to the act of cooking. When cooking, you begin with some basic ingredients, but then you add a few condiments, include a little bit more or less of certain items, adjust the cooking time, and so forth. The criteria by which cultures define themselves, and differentiate themselves from one another, vary a great deal. The basic ingredients determining a culture may be geography, ethnicity, language, religion, and history. The factors that divide cultures can consist of any combination of these elements plus the "condiments" of the local scene. In Bosnia, for instance, the split among Croats, Serbs, and Muslims is almost entirely religious. The situation is similar in India, where religion divides Muslim and Hindus; however, the Hindu majority is further split according to the caste to which one is born. In the United States and other modern nation-states, group loyalties based on cultural differences exist, but more or less as subsets of an overarching group loyalty called *nationalism* or *patriotism*. Ethnicity further divides these groups.

A culturally defined group can be as small as a group of Aborigines in the outback of Australia or as large as a nation-state. It can exist in a small, defined territory, or its members can share a territory with other culturally defined groups. It can be a closed system, or it can be open to new ideas introduced from other cultures. The only real requirement is that people who share the culture sense that they are different from those who do not belong to their group.

Culture in Everyday Use

Sociologists, who study culture in terms of various competing social groups within a society, have developed a number of concepts that are useful in discussions of cultural pluralism. Some of these terms are used interchangeably and often cause confusion. Five terms commonly used to describe social groups that share important cultural elements but that are smaller than a whole society are subculture, microculture, ethnic group, minority group, and people of color.

Subculture

Subculture refers to a social group with shared characteristics that distinguish it in some way from the larger cultural group or society in which it is embedded. Generally, a subculture is distinguished either by a unifying set of ideas and/or practices (such as the corporate culture or the drug culture) or by some demographic characteristic (such as the adolescent culture or the culture of poverty).[3]

Microculture

Microculture also refers to a social group that shares distinctive traits, values, and behaviors that set it apart from the parent macroculture of which it is a part. Although the terms *microculture* and *subculture* are often used interchangeably, *microculture* seems to imply a greater linkage with the parent culture. Microcultures often mediate—that is, interpret and transmit—the ideas, values, and institutions of the larger political community.[4] Thus, for example, the family, the workplace, or the classroom can each be thought of as a microculture embedded in the larger culture of the neighborhood, the business, or the school. These larger macrocultures are themselves embedded in larger professional, regional, or national cultures. Thus a particular entity, such as the school, may be simultaneously both a macroculture (the culture of the school as a model of society) and a microculture (the culture of the particular school).

Minority Group

Minority group refers to a social group that occupies a subordinate position in a society. Wagley and Harris define a minority group as one that experiences discrimination and subordination within a society, is separated by physical or cultural traits disapproved of by the dominant group, shares a sense of collective identity and common burdens, and is characterized by marriage within the group.[5] However, characterizing minority groups based on these criteria sometimes leads to confusion and inaccuracy. For example, women are often referred to as a minority group because they are thought to be oppressed, even though they constitute more than half the general population and do not, as a rule, marry within their group. Similarly, when students who are African American, Native American, or Hispanic constitute a majority of the population in a particular school, the school is often referred to as a "majority-minority school." The term *minority* can also be used in different ways in different countries. In the Netherlands, for instance, *minority* refers to immigrant groups that occupy a low socioeconomic status. Chinese, for instance, are considered minorities in the United States and Canada, but not in the Netherlands because they do not have low socioeconomic status.[6]

Ethnic Group

Ethnic group refers to groups who share a common heritage. When you are asked to complete the statement, "I am _____" using as many descriptors as possible to define yourself, those statements that reflect identification with some collective or reference group are often indicative of your ethnic identity. When you respond that you are Jewish or Polish or Italian, you are identifying with a group of people who share a common heritage, history, celebrations, and traditions, who enjoy similar foods and might speak a common language other than English. A sense of peoplehood, or the feeling that a person's own destiny is somehow linked with others who share this same knowledge, reflects identification with an ethnic group.

**Activity 10:
Who Am I?**

People of Color

People of Color refers to nonwhite minority group members, but reflects recent demographic realities of the United States. The phrase *people of color* refers to groups such as African Americans, Mexican Americans, Puerto Ricans, and Native Americans and is preferred over *ethnic minority* because these groups are, in many schools and communities, the majority rather than the minority.

As the United States and its schools grow increasingly complex with respect to cultural difference, many voices are beginning to criticize the use of collective terminology like *people of color.* These voices call for awareness and understanding of specific ethnic, racial, religious, and other groups. In this effort, it is recognized that the terms *Hispanic* or *Latino,* for example, are only umbrella terms for a number of Spanish-speaking ethnic groups, including Puerto Rican, Spanish, Salvadoran, and Mexican. Similarly, the term *Native American* is an umbrella term for an enormous variety of tribal identities (over 400 officially recognized by the Bureau of Indian Affairs), including the indigenous people of Alaska and Hawaii. Clearly, these groups can be as different from one another as they can be from the mainstream society.

Commonalities in Definitions of Culture

Many definitions of culture ask the question, What do all cultures have in common? Some try to answer this question by examining the functions or purposes of culture. Webb and Sherman, for example, describe culture in a functional way:

> Cultures solve the common problems of human beings, but they solve them in different ways. . . . Each provides its people with a means of communication (*language*). Each determines who wields power and under what circumstances power can be used (*status*). Each provides for the regulation of reproduction (*family*) and supplies a system of rules (*government*). These rules may be written (*laws*) or unwritten (*custom*), but they are always present. Cultures supply human beings with an explanation of their relationship to nature (*magic, myth, religion,* and *science*). They provide their people with some conception of time (*temporality*). They supply a system by which significant lessons of the culture (*history*) can be given a physical representation and stored and passed on to future generations. The representation usually comes in the form of dance, song, poetry, architecture, handicrafts, story, design, or painting (*art*). What makes cultures similar is the problems they solve, not the methods they devise to solve them.[7]

Culture can also be understood in terms of the assumptions or ideas inherent in the concept itself. Four of these assumptions seem particularly important.

Humans Construct Culture

Humans Construct Culture

Human beings are born with certain genetically determined predispositions, some of which underlie behavior while others direct physical features. Although these predispositions are not precise, they do help to determine the parameters under which humans develop. Humans have fewer biological instincts (e.g., breathing, swallowing) than any other species does, which means that we are born relatively helpless and remain so for a considerable amount of time, longer than any other organism in the animal kingdom. Unlike most members of the animal world, we are not biologically programmed so that we automatically know how to utilize our environment to find food and shelter. In short, we do not know how to survive without other people to care for us and to teach us. Therefore, humans must discover ways of effectively interacting both with their environment and with each other. They must learn how to *construct* the knowledge, including rules of living, that will enable them to survive. This knowledge, the manner in which it is presented (in the family, in the neighborhood, in literature, art, school lessons, etc.), and the meaning it has for us is called culture. Culture, then, is the one factor that determines the kinds of guidelines to which the individual is exposed.

The concept of culture usually refers to things (both physical and mental) that are made or constructed by human beings rather than to things that naturally occur in nature. When you look out over a body of water, for instance, neither the water itself, the undeveloped beachfront, nor the horizon is considered culture. These items are naturally occurring components of the environment. How we *think about* and what we *do* with the natural environment, however, is usually dependent on our culture. Thus, a beachfront such as Miami Beach has, in the United States, been viewed as a good place to build condominiums, piers, a boardwalk, and a marina. In another culture, this same beachfront might be regarded as a sacred space, with little human intervention allowed.

These physical artifacts of mainstream American culture are expressions of our underlying knowledge, attitudes, and values toward a part of the natural environment. Other expressions of our culture are our behavioral patterns, for example, our tendency to litter our oceans and beaches with various kinds of waste. Traditional Native American societies, on the other hand, have an entirely different view of the natural environment. Rather than seeing themselves as controllers of nature, many Native Americans (and others) believe strongly that human beings are an integral part of the natural world. And since in their view we live within rather than outside nature, they believe we should not interfere with it too much.

This example is interesting because it not only shows that different sociocultural groups perceive the world in very different terms but also that cultural beliefs and attitudes can and do change. Western peoples are now beginning to see the damage they have caused to the environment and to consider not only ways to clean it up but also ways of rethinking the very basis of the relation of human beings to nature.

Culture Is Shared

Culture is not only constructed; it is *socially constructed* by human beings in interaction with one another. Cultural ideas and understandings are shared by a group of people who recognize the knowledge, attitudes, and values of one another. Moreover, they agree on which cultural elements are better than others. That is, cultural elements are usually arranged in a hierarchy of value, which can also change over time. Mainstream American attitudes about children's place in the economy provide a good example. Before the middle of the nineteenth century, children in the United States were regarded as economic assets to their families and to the community. That is, they worked not only on the farm or in the shop but also often outside the family for money that went to help support the family. Zelizer makes a distinction between the "useful" and the "useless" child in talking about the change that occurred during the last half of the century:

> By 1900 middle-class reformers began indicting children's economic cooperation as unjustified parental exploitation, and child labor emerged for the first time as a major social problem in the United States. . . . By 1930, most children under fourteen were out of the labor market and into schools.[8]

This example illustrates the changing nature of cultural ideas. The notion that children do not belong in the labor market and that parents whose children bring income into the family may be exploiting them has become a highly valued idea in our society, but it is one that is relatively new. In contrast to early-nineteenth-century families, we believe that children should be in school when they are young. Moreover, when we encounter families that do send their children out to work, whether it be in the United States or elsewhere, we have a sense that they are doing something wrong. Thus, in contemporary mainstream U.S. culture, until our children are in mid-adolescence, we place a greater value on the "useless" (nonworking) child than we do on the "useful" one who works. Indeed, although many people find ways around it, we have in this country legal restrictions on the age at which children can be employed.

In nearly all instances, this shared cultural identification is transmitted from one generation to the next. One exception to this cultural transmission process, however, can be seen in the case of deaf persons whose primary language is a manual system, ASL (American Sign Language) in North America. Although most deaf persons have hearing parents, the Deaf normally form strong ties to their own community and tend to marry a deaf partner. Thus, cultural transmission in this instance is deferred until entry into the Deaf community occurs through instruction in schools for the deaf and through a network of social clubs, theater, political organizations, and publications. For some young people, their first enculturation into the Deaf community may come through enrollment at the world-famous Gallaudet University that provides schooling from preschool levels through college.

Culture of the Deaf

Culture Is Both Objective and Subjective

A third common feature of culture is that it is comprised of two components: objective elements and subjective elements.[9] The objective components of culture consist of the visible, tangible elements of a group, that is, the endless array of physical artifacts the people produce, the language they speak, the clothes they wear, the food they eat, and the unending stream of decorative and ritual objects they create. These elements are relatively easy to pick up or observe, and all people would describe them in a similar manner. It is the objective elements of culture that are most commonly thought of when cultural differences are considered. Subjective components of culture, on the other hand, are the invisible, intangible aspects of culture, including attitudes, values, norms of behavior, learning styles, and hierarchy of social roles—in short, the *meaning* that the more objective components of culture have for individuals and groups. In this respect, culture can be likened to an iceberg: only 10 percent of the whole is seen above the surface of the water. It is the 90 percent of the iceberg that is hidden beneath the surface of the water that most concerns the ship's captain who must navigate the water. Like an iceberg, the most meaningful (and potentially dangerous) part of culture is the invisible or subjective part that is continually operating at the unconscious level that shapes people's perceptions and people's responses to those perceptions. It is this aspect of culture that leads to most intercultural misunderstandings, and that requires the most emphasis in good multicultural or intercultural education.

Culture Is Nurtured

A final assumption about culture is the idea that it involves nurturing and growth, similar to the nurturing of plants. In the case of humans, however, the growing process involves teaching the young, both formally and informally. Thus, to **enculturate** a child is to help that child become a member of her or his social groups. In the United States enculturation may mean helping a child negotiate the different cultural perspectives found among the various social groups in which he or she participates.

Activity 5: Childhood Experiences

Culture is also related to growth through the fine arts (music, dance, literature, and the visual arts) as well as through social behavior. A "cultured" person is one who has been nurtured (helped to grow) by participation in such activities. However, observation tells us that it is people of comfortable circumstances who most frequently have the time, energy, and inclination to devote to such pursuits. Thus is born the notion of an elite (high-status) group.

High Culture

The idea that culture "belongs" to an elite group also carries with it the notion that this kind of "high culture" has more value than what we might call "folk" culture. In part, this idea has its roots in the late nineteenth century, when western anthropologists first developed their ideas from the study of so-called primitive peoples. Comparing these civilizations to their own more technological societies, they saw differences that were perceived not simply as differences but as deficits. Warren's 1873 textbook on physical geography introduced its readers to the "races of man" in the following manner:

> The Caucasian race is the truly cosmopolitan and historical race. The leading nations of the world, those who have reached the highest state of civilization and possess a history in the true sense of the word, belong to it. It has, therefore, not improperly been called the active race; while the others, embracing the uncivilized or half-civilized peoples, have been termed the passive races.[10]

Such quasi-evolutionary theories of culture have even been invoked to explain disabilities. Down's syndrome, for example, is named for John Haydon Langdon Down's ethnic classification, according to which individuals with "mongolian" features, whatever the "race" of their parents might be, represented regression to a more primitive state of evolutionary development. Tragically, before the discovery of its chromosomal basis in the 1950s, a newborn with Down's syndrome was often described as a "throwback," as were infants with a variety of congenital anomalies.

Western anthropologists' notion of cultural evolution was directed mainly at other (nonwestern) societies. At the top of the cultural hierarchy were the highly "civilized" peoples, mostly the Europeans who popularized the concept. At the bottom were the more primitive "savages" or "natives." Everyone else was placed in between and thought of as having the potential to climb up the cultural ladder. Inherent in this and other cultural models was the anthropologists' assumption that the natural progression of culture is upward. Indeed, the idea of a hierarchy of cultures existed well before anthropology was even accepted as a scientific discipline. In 1824, half a century before Warren wrote his textbook, Thomas Jefferson wrote:

> Let a philosophic observer commence a journey from the *savages* of the Rocky Mountains, eastwardly towards the seacoast. These he would observe in the earliest stages of association, living under no law but that of nature, subsisting and covering themselves with the flesh and skins of wild beasts. He would next find those on the frontiers in the *pastoral stage,* raising domestic animals to supply the defects of hunting. Then succeed our own *semi-barbarous* citizens, the pioneers of the advance of *civilization,* and so in his progress he would meet the gradual shades of *improving* man until he would reach his, as yet, most improved state in our seaport towns. This, in fact, is equivalent to a survey, in time, of the progress of man from the infancy of creation to the present day.[11]

Jefferson's categories foreshadow those of the early anthropologists. And in many ways our thinking has not moved very far beyond this framework. Books with such titles as *Affable Savages*[12] and commonly used terms such as *underdeveloped* and *developed nations,* or *Third World* versus *First World* perpetuate the idea of cultural movement toward something perceived as more ideal or better or more civilized. Moreover, the direction of this movement is generally toward a culture that looks a great deal like our own. While these ideas are largely discredited among modern anthropologists, they continue to exist in the minds of most Americans when contrasting U.S. society with other societies, particularly those that are less technological.

Traditionally, Americans have expected their schools to socialize all students into traditional European American, upper- and middle-class culture, generally referred to as "the best of western civilization." Although it is true that great art, beautiful music, and meaningful literature have been given to the world by western peoples, it is equally clear that western contributions do not represent all that is great and beautiful in the world.

Applying the Concept of Culture

When school programs are instituted to increase awareness and understanding of specific groups, they are called group-specific or **culture-specific approaches** and stress information about a particular group of people, usually identified by a single characteristic such as race, ethnicity, religion, or gender. Although these approaches have much to offer, several problems are associated with them. First, while they attend to differences *between* one group and another, these approaches still do not attend to important differences *within* groups. Consequently, they tend to give the impression that all people identified as belonging to a group (all Mexican Americans, all Jews, etc.) are alike, which is clearly not the case. Second, because these programs usually rely on students of certain *samples* of the larger group (e.g., *urban* African Americans, *white* middle-class girls, Navajo *who live on reservations*), they may promote stereotypes. Third, group-specific programs, because of their intentionally narrow focus, cannot attend to the wide array of differences that collectively control the teaching-learning process.

In contrast to the group-specific approach to understanding diversity is another, more inclusive approach that attempts to deal directly with the complex nature of cultural phenomena. Called a **culture-general approach,** it derives mainly from principles developed in the field of cross-cultural psychology and training. Cross-cultural psychologists are mostly interested in the effect of culture on the *individual* and on the interface or interaction between individuals of different groups. In addition to describing how culture affects an individual, these psychologists have also been developing a variety of training strategies to help individuals anticipate and deal effectively with problems that may arise in intercultural interaction.

**Cross-Cultural
Psychology**

Culture-Specific versus Culture-General Frameworks

It is important to understand the distinction between culture-specific and culture-general knowledge. A *culture-general* concept is one that is universal and applies to *all* cultural groups, as seen in the following example.

The way an individual "learns how to learn" depends on the socialization processes used by his or her culture. That is, learning style is related to socialization processes. This very general statement can be regarded as a cultural universal, or culture-general concept. It doesn't tell us anything about an individual's preferred learning style, but it does tell us that everyone has one and that it is formed by socialization experiences. Thus, knowing that socialization experiences vary from culture to culture, it follows that learning styles will also vary among cultures. Such a culture-general concept is valuable to teachers in that it warns them of the possibility that there will be many variations in learning style among their students; perhaps as many as there are cultural groups represented in their classroom. So informed, a teacher presiding over a multicultural classroom would be alert for signs of learning style differences and would attempt to develop alternative lesson plans or instructional approaches that match these differences.

A group-specific concept, on the other hand, is one that applies to a specific cultural group. For example, both Hawaiian and Native American children have historically acquired most of their knowledge, values, and attitudes about the world through direct participation in real-world events. Their teachers were usually other members of their family or ethnic group who were also participating in those events. Thus direct participation, or **in-context learning,** became their familiar and preferred learning style.

Contrast in-context leaning against the more formal schooling given to most urban and suburban middle-class children. These children are sent to a captive learning environment (schools) where specially trained teachers who are usually total strangers use books and other abstract learning tools to provide indirect participation, or **out-of-context learning,** about real-world events. In a classroom where both cultural groups are present, the teacher should anticipate learning style differences (culture-general knowledge), try to assess the culture-specific learning styles that are present, and then adapt instruction accordingly.

In short, teachers in multicultural classrooms need to have both culture-general and culture-specific knowledge. That is, they need to know that certain cultural universals (e.g., learning style differences, patterns of communication, value orientation) are at work in every multicultural classroom, and then they need to gather—through observation, inquiry, and study—the particulars of those variations so that they can plan and deliver instruction that is appropriate for *all* their students. To focus solely on culture-specific knowledge, which is always based on *samples* taken from some target culture, is to ignore not only individual differences within that group but also the cultural universals that cut across groups. Likewise, to focus solely on culture-general knowledge is to ignore the very real differences that separate groups and that provide a map for assessing and adapting instruction.

Themes from Cross-Cultural Psychology

Cross-cultural psychology also offers teachers the following set of themes or principles that can be used to study cross-cultural interactions in the classroom.[13]

Activity and Reading 6: Understanding Cultural Complexity

1. *People tend to communicate their cultural identity to others in the broadest possible terms.* For instance, on meeting someone for the first time, you may communicate many different things about yourself, for example, your age, nationality, ethnic group, religious affiliation, where you grew up, and the nature of your family. At other times you may describe your status at work or in the community, your health, your social class, or the way you have come to understand your gender. Each of these sources of cultural identity carries with it associated rules for behavior. We offer such information to new acquaintances because by doing so we give them cultural clues regarding what to expect from us and how to interact with us. People have multiple "cultures" influencing them at various times. Every one of us may thus be considered multicultural.

2. *Because we are all multicultural, our cultural identity is dynamic and always changing.* As our environmental circumstances and group associations change, we adapt our cultural identity and behavior accordingly. For example, in certain circumstances our gender-related knowledge and beliefs may be predominant; at another time our religious beliefs may stand out; and at still another, our ethnicity may be most important. Thus, our multicultural nature leads to behavior variations that are sometimes difficult to understand and appreciate.

3. *While culture is complex and variable, it is nevertheless patterned.* Culture helps individuals make sense of their world and thereby to develop routinized behavioral patterns to fit different environments. Common phrases such as the "culture of the organization," "the culture of the community," or the "culture of the society" refer to the fact that culture is not simply patterned for an individual but also for a setting, a community, or a society as a whole. When viewed from the outside, these patterns can appear quite complicated and difficult to understand. Yet each of us moves quite easily among the cultural patterns with which we are familiar. When confronted by someone whose behavior is *not* familiar, it is the responsibility of the outsider to listen, to observe, and to inquire closely enough so that the patterns of that person (or social group, or society) become evident and understandable. To do so decreases the possibility of misunderstanding and conflict and increases the possibility of new and useful understanding and appreciation.

4. *Interactions with other cultures can be viewed as a resource for understanding.* In this case, complexity can be an asset. The more knowledge and experience we have with other groups, the more sophisticated we can be in our interpretation of

events. The more complex our thinking is, then, the more lenses or insights we can bring to help understand a given situation. Culturally different encounters help prepare us to deal more effectively with the complexity that is increasingly a part of our lives. In short, the number of cultural variables we learn to accommodate will determine our ability to navigate within a fast-moving, ever-changing society.

5. *Behavior should be judged in relation to its context.* Observable behavior cannot be understood apart from the context in which it occurs. Seen outside its context, another's "different" behavior can, at best, seem meaningless and, at worst, be profoundly misinterpreted. Contextual inquiry allows us to be more accurate in our judgments of others. Consider this real-life example of an eleven-year-old boy who would become rowdy and disruptive in the classroom every day about 2:00 in the afternoon. Inevitably, the teacher sent the child to the office, where he was promptly sent home. Defined in terms of the middle-class cultural context of the school, this child was definitely a troubled child, and he was so labeled by nearly all the adults in the building. Eventually, however, an astute counselor recognized a pattern and did some inquiry. It turned out that the mother's boyfriend came home every day about 2:45, often quite drunk and abusive. In his rage, the boyfriend frequently abused the mother. The boy, quite accurately understanding the cultural pattern of the school, figured out that his misbehavior would result in his being sent home and that if he was sent home by 2:30, he would arrive before the boyfriend did and thus be able to protect his mother. Suddenly this so-called troubled boy's behavior makes sense, and he becomes something of a hero because he had found a way to protect his vulnerable mother. Without full knowledge of the context, behavior is often meaningless or badly misinterpreted. Culture thus provides the context from which to view others.

6. *Persons holding a multicultural perspective continually strive to find common ground between individuals.* In a sense, we must strive to be bifocal. That is, we must be able to see the similarities among people as well as their differences. While it is the differences that tend to stand out and separate people, it is precisely in our similarities where common ground, or a common meeting point, can be found. A multicultural perspective permits disagreement without anyone necessarily being accused of being wrong. If culture in all its complexity is understood as an individual's attempt to navigate the river of life, then cultural differences can be understood simply as pragmatic acts of navigation and judged accordingly. In this view, cultural differences become tolerable and the "we-they" or "us-them" debate is avoided. There are no winners and losers. We are all in this together. Either we all win—or we all lose.

The Culture-Learning Process

Individuals tend to identify themselves in a broad manner and in terms of many physical and social attributes. For example, a young man might identify himself as an attractive, athletic, Asian American who intends to be a doctor and live in upper-class society. Other people also identify individuals according to these attributes, and interactions among

Activity and Reading 11: The Culture-Learning Process

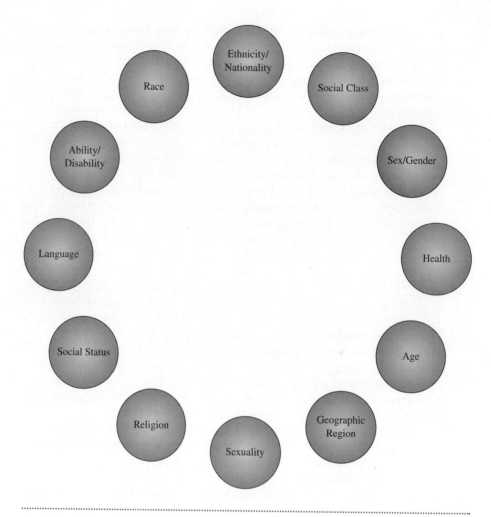

figure 2.1   Sources of cultural identity.

individuals are often shaped by such identifications. Figure 2.1 shows twelve sources of cultural identity that influence teaching and learning. Who learns what, and how and when it is learned, is briefly described here and is further illustrated and discussed in later chapters.

What Is Learned: The Sources of Cultural Knowledge

Race is a very amorphous term. Biologically speaking, it refers to the clustering of inherited physical characteristics that favor adaptation to a particular ecological area. However, race is culturally defined in the sense that different societies emphasize different sets of physical characteristics when referring to the same race. In fact, the term is so imprecise that it has even been used to refer to a wide variety of categories that are not physical, for instance, linguistic categories (the *English-speaking race*), religious categories (the *Jewish race*), national categories (the *Italian race*), and even to somewhat mythological categories (the *Teutonic race*).[14] Although race has often been defined as a biological category, it has been argued that race as a biological concept is of little use because there are no "pure" races.[15] As Yetman notes, "Many groups possess physically identifiable characteristics that do not become the basis for racial distinctions [and] . . . criteria selected to make racial distinctions in one society may be overlooked or considered insignificant or irrelevant by another. For instance, in much of Latin America skin color and the shape of the lips, important differentiating criteria in the United States, are much less important than are hair texture, eye color, and stature. A person defined as black in Georgia or Michigan might be considered white in Peru."[16] Recent research in mapping the genetic code of five people of different races demonstrates that the concept of race has no scientific basis.[17] Thus, race is an important social characteristic not because of its biology but because of its cultural meaning in any given social group or society. In the United States, race is judged largely on the basis of skin color, which some people consider very meaningful and use as a criterion for extending or withholding privileges of various kinds. Through subtle yet effective socializing influences, group members can be taught to accept as "social fact" a myriad of myths and stereotypes regarding skin color, stature, facial features, and so forth.

Racism results from the transformation of race prejudice and/or ethnocentrism through the exercise of power against a racial group defined as inferior by individuals or by institutions, with the intentional or unintentional support of an entire culture. Simply stated, racism is preference for or belief in the superiority of one's own racial group.[18]

Sex/Gender

Sex is culturally defined on the basis of a particular set of physical characteristics. In this case, however, the characteristics are related to male and female reproduction. Cultural meanings associated with gender are expressed in terms of socially valued behaviors (e.g., nurturing the young and providing food) that are assigned according to sex. Such culturally assigned behaviors eventually become so accepted that they are thought of as natural to that sex. Thus, gender is what it *means* to be male or female in a society, and gender roles are those sets of behaviors thought by a particular people to be "normal" and "good" when carried out by the assigned sex.

In all sociocultural groups, gender includes knowledge of a large set of rules and expectations governing what boys and girls should wear, how they should act and express themselves, and their "place" in the overall social structure. Beardsley notes that any social or psychological trait can be "genderized" in favor of one sex or the other.[19] Thus, in the dominant society of the United States, active traits such as aggressiveness are genderized in favor of males and against females, while more passive traits such as submissiveness are genderized in favor of females and against males.

Like cultural definitions of race, the specific set of traits assigned to males and females may vary by society. And within a society, these traits may vary by ethnicity, class, or religion. For instance, on a continuum of submissiveness to males (a norm in

U.S. society), many African American females might be located closer to the *less* submissive end of the scale, many Hispanic females might be located closer to the *more* submissive end, and many European American females would probably be located somewhere in between.

Health

Health is culturally defined according to a particular group's view of what physical, mental, and emotional states constitute a healthy person. The expert opinion of the medical profession usually guides a society's view of health. Although a medical model has dominated cultural definitions of health, most disabilities (mental retardation, deafness, blindness, etc.) are not judged in terms of this model's norms. Thus it is possible to be a healthy blind or retarded person. Nor would a person with cerebral palsy be considered sick.

In the United States and most of the industrialized world, the prevailing health system is almost totally biomedical. However, alternative systems such as acupuncture, holistic medicine, and faith healing are available, and the acceptance of alternative systems varies widely both within and between social groups. In other societies (e.g., China), what we deem alternative medicine may in fact be the dominant model, and our ideas of biomedicine may be operating at the fringes. The cultural meanings associated with health depend on which model, or which combination of models, an individual or family group accepts. For example, a four-year-old Russian child, who had recently immigrated with her family to the United States, suddenly suffered a high fever and flu symptoms. The child's nursery school teacher, who was European American and middle class, wanted the family to take the child to the doctor immediately for an antibiotic. The child's grandmother, on the other hand, who was the family expert on medical matters, prescribed a traditional treatment: the child should be put to bed, surrounded by lit candles and family members engaged in prayer. In this case, the grandmother was the final authority, and the child got better.

Ability/Disability

Like the term *health,* the terms *ability* and *disability* are culturally defined according to society's view about what it means to be physically, emotionally, and mentally "able." The categories of ability and disability refer to a wide variety of mental and physical characteristics: intelligence, emotional stability, impairment of sensory and neural systems, impairment of movement. The social significance of these characteristics may vary by setting as well. For example, the terms *learning disability* or *learning disabled* are primarily used with reference to schooling and are rarely used outside of school. Indeed, it may be that the current emphasis on learning disability in American schools is primarily a reflection of a technologically complex society's concern about literacy. In developing nations, specific learning disabilities among people who are otherwise unimpaired are of little concern. In fact, this "condition," as a category of exceptional individuals, is nonexistent in most of the world.

The cultural meaning of *ability* and *disability* is related to both the needs and the public perception of the ability or disability itself. For example, the culture of the Deaf "needs" a shared, rule-bound system of communication (sign language) as well as shared traditions and values among its members. However, the public acceptance of deaf individuals is far less positive than for those who are gifted. This lack of acceptance can be seen in the privileges accorded each group in schools. School experience might enhance the self-esteem of a gifted student while it threatens that of a student who is deaf. In the United States, the reaction to ability/disability hovers closely around a socially defined norm: we favor bright individuals but often exclude those who show evidence of extreme intelligence; we favor individuals who "overcome" their disabilities but often exclude those who, for one reason or another, cannot.

Social Class

Social class is culturally defined on the basis of those criteria on which a person or social group may be ranked in relation to others in a stratified (or layered) society. There is considerable debate about the criteria that determine social class. Some criteria identify class membership primarily in terms of wealth and its origin (inherited or newly earned). Other commonly used criteria include the amount of education, power, and influence.[20] Class structures vary widely among societies and social groups in terms of their rigidity and their importance to an individual's life chances.[21] In some societies, like Britain and India for example, the class structure is fairly rigid and determines to a large extent the opportunities each person will have. In these societies, a person is truly born into a particular social class and tends to remain there. In other societies, the structure is not so rigid, and although individuals may be born into a particular social class, it is expected that they may move up by virtue of their achievements. Societies also vary according to the value placed on leaving one's social class. In the United States, upward mobility is a value; in Britain it is not so valued. The consequences of these attitudes are not always salutary. In the United States, for example, if individuals do not succeed in moving up, the perception may be that something is wrong with them.

Social class differences are also tied to a person's social expectations and cultural tastes. For example, individuals who exhibit the child-rearing practices, speech, and general tastes of the upper classes in matters such as dress, food, and housing can affect their social image and thereby their chances for upward mobility.

Ethnicity/Nationality

Ethnicity is culturally defined according to the knowledge, beliefs, and behavior patterns shared by a group of people with the same history and the same language. Ethnicity carries a strong sense of "peoplehood," that is, of loyalty to a "community of memory."[22] It is also related to the ecological niche in which an ethnic group has found itself and to adaptations people make to those environmental conditions.

The category of *nationality* is culturally defined on the basis of shared citizenship, which may or may not include a shared ethnicity. In the contemporary world, the population of most nations includes citizens (and resident noncitizens) who vary in ethnicity. Although we are accustomed to this idea in the United States, we are sometimes unaware that it is also true in other nations. Thus, we tend to identify all people from Japan as Japanese, all people from France as French, and so forth. Similarly, when American citizens of varying ethnic identities go abroad, they tend to be identified as

"American." A tragic example of this misconception is the recent history of ethnic warfare in the former Yugoslavia. Americans in general are unaware of the role that ethnicity may play in dividing people. Most of the conflicts that occur across the planet are the result of long-held ethnic strife and do not cross national boundaries.

Religion/Spirituality

Religion and *spirituality* are culturally defined on the basis of a shared set of ideas about the relationship of the earth and the people on it to a deity or deities and a shared set of rules for living moral values that will enhance that relationship. A set of behaviors identified with worship is also commonly shared. Religious identity may include membership in a worldwide organized religion (e.g., Islam, Christianity, Judaism, Buddhism, Taoism) or in smaller (but also worldwide) sects belonging to each of the larger religions (e.g., Catholic or Protestant Christianity, or Conservative, Reformed, or Hasidic Judaism). Religious identity may also include a large variety of spiritualistic religions, sometimes called pagan or godless religions, that are often but not always associated with indigenous peoples in the Americas and other parts of the world. Like ethnicity, religious affiliation can engender intense loyalty, as recently witnessed through the actions of members of Osama bin Laden's Al Qaeda network in their attempts to live out their religious missions. Religion also engenders a sense of belonging or community and pride in a peoples' shared history. Because religious identity involves individuals' relationship with the earth and with forces perceived to be greater than themselves, the cultural meaning of religion is often expressed in terms of a rigid sense of righteousness and virtue that is linked to a belief in salvation or the possibility of an eternal life after death. It is thus often an extremely powerful determiner of behavior.

Geographic Location/Region

Geographic location is culturally defined by the characteristics (topographical features, natural resources) of the ecological environment in which a person lives. Geographic location may include the characteristics of a neighborhood or community (rural, suburban, urban) and/or the natural and climatic features of a region (mountainous, desert, plains, coastal, hot, cold, wet, dry). It has been argued that, in the United States, people's regional identity functions in the same way as their national heritage. Thus, southerners, westerners, and midwesterners are identified and often identify themselves as members of ethnic-like groups, with the same kinds of loyalties, sense of community, and language traits. This type of regional identity can also be found in some other countries of the world.

The cultural meanings of geographic location are expressed in terms of the knowledge a person has of how to survive in and use the resources of a particular area. This knowledge may include what foods are "good" (and how to grow and harvest them), how to protect oneself from the natural elements and common dangers of the locality, even how to spend leisure time. This kind of knowledge also applies to the type of community a person lives in. It is commonly acknowledged, for example, that "city people," "country people," and "suburban people" can be quite different from one another. The nature of that difference stems in part from their familiarity with and knowledge about how to live in a particular kind of community with particular resources and dangers.

Age

Age is culturally defined according to the length of time an individual has lived and the state of physical and mental development that individual has attained. Chronological age is measured in different ways by different social groups or societies. Some calculate it in calendar years, others by natural cycles such as phases of the moon, and still others by the marking of major natural or social events.

Mental and physical development is also measured differentially, in much the same way and under many of the same circumstances that health is determined. Most humans view such development as a matter of stages, but the nature and particular characteristics of each stage may differ widely. In most western societies, for example, age cohort groups are usually identified as infancy, childhood, adolescence, adulthood, and old age. "Normal" development markers include the acquisition of motor and language skills (infancy and childhood), the ability to understand and use abstract concepts (childhood and adolescence), and the ability to assume responsibility for oneself and others (adolescence and adulthood). In other societies, these cohort groups may differ. For example, in many nonwestern societies, the cohort group we define as adolescents may not exist at all, and the classifications of childhood and old age may be longer or shorter.

The cultural meaning of age is usually expressed in terms of the abilities and responsibilities attributed to it. Thus, in the United States, childhood is prolonged (hence the category of adolescence), and adult responsibilities are not expected until at least age eighteen, if not age twenty-one or beyond. In other societies (and indeed in the United States prior to the twentieth century), childhood is shorter, and adult responsibilities are assumed at younger ages.

Sexuality

Sexuality is culturally defined on the basis of particular patterns of sexual self-identification, behavior, and interpersonal relationships.[23] There is growing evidence that a person's sexual orientation is, in part, a function of that person's innate biological characteristics.[24] Culturally speaking, sexuality is tied to a number of factors, including sexual behavior, gender identity (both internal and external), affiliation, and role behavior. Like health, sexuality has a variety of orientations. Because sexuality is frequently linked to a person's deepest, most meaningful experiences (both religious and interpersonal), deviates from socially approved norms are often socially ostracized and sometimes physically abused or even killed, as in the case of the Matthew Shepard murder. In the United States, the prevailing view of sexuality is bimodal: only male and female are identified as possibilities. In other societies, additional possibilities are available. The Lakota Sioux, for example, approve four sexual orientations: biological males who possess largely masculine traits, biological males who possess largely feminine traits, biological females who possess largely feminine traits, and biological females who possess largely masculine traits. The female-identified male in Lakota society is called *berdache* and is accorded high honor because he possesses multiple traits and characteristics. *Berdache* tend to be teachers and artists, and if a *berdache* takes an interest in one's child or children, it is considered to be an advantage.

**Other
Approaches
to Sexuality**

Language

From a cultural standpoint, *language* is often defined as a system of shared vocal sounds and/or nonverbal behaviors that enables members of a particular group to communicate with one another. Language may be the most significant source of cultural learning because it is through language that most other cultural knowledge is acquired. Indeed, some researchers consider language and the category systems available in language to be *the* determiner of culture.[25]

Considerable research on the relation of brain function to language gives evidence that human beings are hardwired for language development at a particular stage in brain development.[26] That is, children who are in the company of other people appear to be programmed to learn whatever spoken language or sign system is used around them. Children even appear to invent their own language systems, complete with syntactical structures, if no other language is available.[27] It may also be that this program decreases in power (or disappears altogether) at a certain point, which helps to explain why it may be more difficult for older children and adults to acquire a new language. Language is meaningful in terms of both its verbal properties (what we name things, people, ideas) and in terms of its nonverbal properties (its norms regarding interpersonal distance, meaningful gestures, and so forth). Because language literally represents reality, the types and meanings of verbal and nonverbal behavior in any society or social group will reflect peoples' experience with their surroundings and the ways in which they interact with it. More than any other characteristic, language is a window into another person's life.

Social Status

Social status is culturally defined on the basis of the prestige, social esteem, and/or honor accorded an individual or group by other social groups or by society.[28] Social status cuts across the other categories, since every social group or society appears to construct hierarchies of honor, prestige, and value with which to "sort out" its members, often on the basis of such attributes as race, age, gender, ability, and so forth. In some cases, social status varies with social class; in many other cases, however, social class does not explain a person's status in a social group or society. Thus, persons may occupy a high place in the class system in terms of income and power but not be accorded prestige or honor. The children of a newly wealthy family who can well afford to send them to Harvard, for example, may have little prestige among the sons and daughters of inherited wealth. Similarly, there may be people accorded high status in the society who occupy relatively low-class positions. In U.S. society, many entertainers and sports figures fit this description. Social status is normally expressed through social roles. Thus, status assigned to a person's gender may determine the role that person plays in any situation; an individual's health status may determine the role he or she plays as a "sick" person; an individual's social class status may determine the role that person plays as a member of the upper, middle, or working class; and so forth.

While there is some overlap among these twelve attributes of culture, the important point to remember is that a particular society or social group culturally defines each of them. The cultural identity of all individuals (i.e., their knowledge, attitudes, values, and skills) is formed through their experience with these twelve attributes. Such experience is

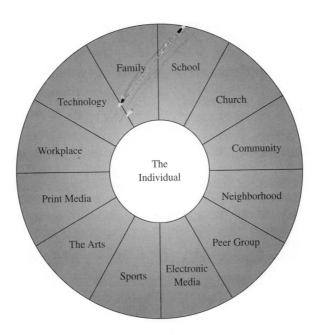

figure 2.2   Socializing agents that transmit culture.

gained through contact with socializing agents such as family, church, workplace, peer group, and the various forms of mass media. These socializing agents can be thought of as transmitters of cultural attributes. It is through these socializing agents (depicted in Figure 2.2) that individuals acquire the cultural knowledge that is defined by race, ethnicity, gender, language, and social class.

How Culture is Learned: The Socializing Agents

We acquire the specific knowledge, attitudes, skills, and values that form our cultural identity through a variety of socializing agents that mediate the sources of cultural identity and give them a particular "cultural spin." Thus, a person's understanding of race, gender, social class, disability, age, sexuality, and so forth depends in part on how that socializing agent is interpreted by those particular families, schools, neighborhoods, peer groups, workplaces, churches, and communities that the person affiliates with at a particular time. Each of these socializing agents has its own slightly different interpretation of a particular cultural attribute, which it passes on to its members.

Activity and Reading 12 How Culture Is Learned: The Socializing Agents

In contemporary social life, some socializing agents, such as families and peer groups, operate face-to-face, while others, such as the mass media, use technology to operate from a distance. Television, VCRs, the Internet, and the music industry, for example, exert significant influence on the self-perceived identity of many young people. Referred to by some researchers as the "third educator" (following family and school), television influences young peoples' acquisition of basic language and visual and aural skills. It also influences their ideas of "appropriate" dress, language, attitudes, and values.

Definitely College Material

Steven Wong is the child of a rather well-to-do professional family. Compared to many students in his community, he is well traveled, having had the opportunity to visit China as well as other countries throughout Asia in order to maintain family and cultural connections. He has also had exposure to many different opportunities as he was growing up. To his parents' dismay, Steven is not excited about attending college, sometimes saying he would rather study the martial arts as a professional and at other times saying he would like to leave the area, perhaps move out west, and "find" himself.

How might you explain Steven's apparent ambivalence toward college?

How would you explain the fact that at times he wishes to pursue the martial arts and at other times he is seemingly uncommitted to anything?

What factors in his school and community might contribute to his confusion?

If he were to come to you, a teacher, asking for guidance, how would you advise him?

Cortes suggests that the media functions much like the school curriculum and serves as a powerful teaching medium, especially with regard to multicultural understanding.[29] Like the school curriculum, he says, "the media curriculum is chaotic, inconsistent, multivocal, in many respects unplanned and uncoordinated, laden with conflicting messages, and offering myriad perspectives."[30] In addition, media often blurs information with entertainment, creating confusion in the minds of many people. For example, a survey of viewers of the television show *America's Most Wanted* revealed that 50 percent considered it to be a news program while 28 percent considered it entertainment.[31] These media lessons not only may affect young people's picture of themselves but also may affect the picture that adults have of them.

The media also teaches about older people, and again with conflicting messages. The visual image of the woman who has "fallen and can't get up" describes older people as weak, helpless, and slightly hysterical—and in need of a product that will alert some care-giving agency that she needs help. Conversely, commercials for vitamins for older adults often depict them as active people—hiking, swimming, traveling—no doubt as a result of taking the promoted vitamins. Because we live in a nation that is growing older, we can expect more commercials defining older people as active rather than passive.

Other technological tools, such as computers and microwave ovens, appear to exert significant influence on our notions of time. Teachers and other human service providers have noticed, for example, that over the last twenty years or so both children and adults exhibit a shorter attention span. People seem to have become accustomed to receiving information and accomplishing tasks in shorter periods of time and are unwilling or unable to persevere in tasks that take a long time.[32]

Other socializing agents of note include the performing and visual arts and, in the United States at least, sports. These widely available carriers of cultural messages help to shape people's attitudes, values, and behavior. The aesthetic value of design, language, music, dance, and theater as well as ideals of moral and ethical behavior are presented through the arts, and behavioral ideals such as fair play, personal achievement, and competition are taught through sport. It is also true that other qualities may be taught through these media; violence, for example, is an increasing part of movies, television, and sports. The contemporary nature of national sports teams as bottom-line businesses comes increasingly into competition with our cultural interest in providing a level playing field for all competitors.

Figure 2.2 provides a visual overview of how cultural knowledge is filtered by a variety of socializing agents to individuals through experience. Although sources of cultural knowledge (race, language, sexuality, etc.) are universal and appear in all cultures, the socializing agents (family, schools, media, etc.) that transmit them vary considerably from one culture to another. In most industrialized societies, for example, a wide variety of socializing agents bombard people daily, often with contradictory messages. In agriculturally oriented societies, on the other hand, a few primary socializing agents (e.g., family and gender group) may share the bulk of the culture-filtering process. As a result, individuals in different cultures develop very different worldviews.

When Culture is Learned: The Process of Socialization

One way to begin to understand how individuals acquire cultural knowledge, attitudes, values, and skills from the social groups with whom they have meaningful contact is to look closely at the concept of **socialization.** From the point of view of the outside observer (including such people as sociologists and anthropologists who use the term more than most people), *socialization* is "the imposition of social patterns of behavior."[33] These patterns may include the acquisition of a particular language, knowledge of social roles and role behavior, and particular understandings of all aspects of the physical and social environment and normative behaviors toward it. Berger and Berger note that "the socialized part of the self is commonly called identity."[34]

There is some consensus that the processes of socialization can occur at three stages of life: (1) primary socialization, which involves the socialization of infants and young children by families and other early caregivers; (2) secondary socialization, which in most contemporary societies involves the neighborhood, the religious affiliation, the peer group, and the school as well as television and other influences that surround and come into the home; and (3) adult socialization, which involves the socialization of adults into roles, settings, and situations for which they may have been unprepared by primary and secondary socialization (for example, taking a new job, marrying, moving to a new area, or becoming a parent).[35]

These stages of the socialization process are not entirely discrete but rather interact with one another in our lives. What we learn as children can be reinforced or modified, for good or ill, by what we learn as we grow up and have more experiences. In each of its three stages, the purpose of socialization is to teach the learner those habits of mind and action that will make him or her a loyal and functional member of a particular group. The use of the word *habits* in this context is important, for it points to another aspect of socialization, which is that the learner should internalize socially approved patterns of behavior so that he or she will voluntarily—and with little thought or effort—think and behave in an appropriate manner.

One important aspect of the internalization of particular knowledge, beliefs, attitudes, values, and behaviors is that the process by which they are acquired is, in a sense, a secret. Most people remember very little about their own socialization, the assumptions they make about the world, what has conditioned them, and the various cultural patterns that have become so ingrained in their makeup as to become nearly invisible.

Primary Socialization and Cultural Similarities

Most people share some aspects of primary socialization that are common to all or most of the people of their primary group. The primary group "Americans," for instance, would include at least those who have been born in the United States and speak English as a native language. Consider, for example, the rules they have learned about eating. When food is put before most Americans, they expect that it will be placed on a plate or in a bowl on a table at which they expect to sit on chairs. Once seated, the American automatically reaches for utensils called forks, knives, and spoons; cuts meat with the fork in the left hand and the knife in the right hand (except for left-handed folks); and then switches the fork to the right hand to carry the food to the mouth. In the same situation, a British person expects the plates, bowls, table, and chairs; cuts meat with the fork and knife in the same hands as an American; but then does *not* switch the fork to the right hand but continues to use it in the left hand. In the same situation, a Japanese person may expect the food to be placed on a low table, at which he or she will kneel, and the utensils used to carry food to the mouth will be two long, slender wooden or plastic implements that many westerners call chopsticks. In all cases, the people eating will not consciously think about these expectations and behaviors, they will simply expect and do them because they are "right," "appropriate," and "proper." Friedman's book *How My Parents Learned to Eat* is an interesting children's story that discusses Japanese and American eating customs. [36]

Within this general "American" set of rules for eating (as within any large nation-state), however, are many variations. How formally we set our tables, how many utensils we use, whether our plates are served for us or we serve ourselves (and how many different plates we use), what kinds of food we eat, what we commonly use as a beverage (water, milk, wine, soda or pop, coffee, tea), and whether we bring the beverage to the table in its original container or in a pitcher, all depend somewhat on the region in which we live, the ethnic, social class, and religious origins of our parents, our ages, and so forth. No matter what the particulars are of our personal and family rules for eating, however, we believe they are "normal" in part because we have internalized them.

Here is another example of both the secret nature of primary socialization and the degree to which knowledge acquired through primary socialization is internalized: the way people learn to speak. Do you remember how you learned to talk? If you have taken another language in school, perhaps it was difficult for you—but your *own* language, now that was easy! Or so it seems. It might, however, be very difficult for you to teach a non-English speaker to correctly pronounce the sentence "Can you tell me the time?" when that person might more easily say "Can you dell me the dime?" What might you tell this person about English that would correct his or her pronunciation? Go ahead. Try it. How would you teach someone to make the correct sounds?

If you have determined that a little puff of air passes out of the mouth when the *t* sound is made in such words as *tell* and *time* that is not passed in words beginning with the letter *d,* you are on the right track to discovering the secret. Correct speakers of English aspirate their stops; that is, some air passes out of the mouth when such letters as *t, p,* or *k* are spoken. This aspect of pronunciation is considered a secret because while most of us differentiate these sounds quite regularly and easily, you probably were not able to describe the difference to others. This practice has become so much a part of your behavior that you take it for granted; you must consciously think about it in order to describe it to others. This is not the end of the secret, however. If you think about it some more, you will realize that English speakers aspirate their stops only at the beginning and in the middle of words, not at the end. We do not aspirate the *t* in *hit, bit,* or *cat.*

That you have learned these rules is quite clear; you use them all the time. How these rules were learned, however, is considerably less clear. They were probably not taught in formal sessions with your parents or by reading appropriate language texts. Indeed, you may not have been able to talk about them at all because you did not have the language to use words such as *aspirate,* or *stops.* Rather, you probably learned these rules through trial and error while you learned to speak your native language. This particular language pattern is often hidden, as are its results. The same is true for other aspects of cultural learning; they, too, can be conceived as patterns that are hidden from our conscious thought and behavior.

Few people receive formal education in how to be an appropriate member of any particular cultural group. Rather, people are culturally socialized by observing others, by trial and error, and by continuous reinforcement. In other words, cultural knowledge such as the rules for speaking and eating are learned experientially, not cognitively. Consequently, it becomes difficult for many people to speak comfortably about the cross-cultural problems they might encounter. One of the difficulties people may face in their intercultural encounters, then, is that they may feel uncomfortable or unsure in a given situation *and may be unable to talk about the problem.* They may try to avoid situations in which they feel discomfort—certainly *not* one of the long-term goals of multicultural education. A reasonable goal is for people to become more knowledgeable and thus conversant about the issues at play in cross-cultural interaction.

Secondary Socialization

Perhaps the most important source of secondary socialization in most people's lives is the school. It is in school that individuals are often introduced to ideas and values that differ from those they acquired at home. In fact, one of the purposes of education is to "lead forth" or "liberate" individuals from the narrow confines of their primary socialization—in a sense, to expand their cultural identities. The difficulties of this process of alteration, however, should not be minimized, especially in situations where the cultural knowledge, beliefs, values, and skills required by the school may be in conflict with those of the home. Still, teachers often find themselves attempting to serve as "change agents" of their students' cultural identities.

The main goal of most school socialization in the United States has traditionally been to teach the rules of middle-class attitudes, values, and behavior. This cultural

critical incident

Who, Exactly, Am I?

Toni Catalano is a first-generation immigrant to the United States; her parents are recent immigrants. Toni's father works in a local factory and has learned to speak English rather well. Her mother, however, has never worked outside the home and, as a result, has not had as strong a reason to learn English. Thus, at Toni's home, more Italian is spoken than English, most meals reflect the family's Italian tradition, and most interactions are restricted to family or others from the Italian community. Toni feels as if she is under great pressure, caught between two worlds, torn between the expectations and demands of her own family and culture and those of her American classmates. She is embarrassed to have friends over to her house and has always been uncomfortable when her parents attend school functions as well as parent-teacher conferences.

What cultural factors can you identify that are immediately responsible for her conflicts?

If Toni came to you, her teacher, asking for advice, what would you focus your attention on?

If you were Toni, what would you want from your friends? from your teachers? from your parents?

socialization to the middle class is no less a secret than the varied cultural socialization of individual families. The school, like the family, does not make cultural socialization explicit; it is simply taken for granted as "normal." Thus, few people ever take a formal course in the variations of cultural knowledge that exist, and they almost never examine their own cultural patterns in contrast to others. Few ever learn why they behave the way they do, or why they think many of the things they think. Fewer still ever evaluate the assumptions they make. People thus generally lack the concepts and vocabulary with which to talk about these things. Yet cultural patterns that are a given, along with the assumptions, beliefs, and behavior associated with them, often do guide us along whether we are aware of it or not.

There is yet another aspect of socialization that must be analyzed: the power of early socialization when viewed from the inside. It is certainly true that as we grow up and meet people outside our childhood social groups, we learn that there are a variety of ways to interact with the physical and social environment. As children, however, we experience the imposition of patterns of socialization as absolute.[37]

There are two simple reasons for this absoluteness: (1) the power of adults in relation to young children, and (2) ignorance of any other possibilities. Berger and Berger describe the nature of this experience in the following way:

Psychologists differ in their view as to whether the child experiences the adults at this stage of life as being very much under his control (because they are generally so responsive to his needs) or whether he feels continually threatened by them (because he is so dependent upon them). However this may be, there can be no question that, objectively speaking, adults have overwhelming power in the situation. The child can, of course, resist them, but the probable outcome of any conflict is a victory on the part of the adults. It is they who control most of the rewards that he craves and most of the sanctions that he fears. Indeed, the simple fact that most children are eventually socialized affords simple proof of this proposition. At the same time, it is obvious that the small child is ignorant of any alternatives to the patterns that are being imposed upon him. The adults confront him with a world—for him, it is *the* world. It is only much later than he discovers that there are alternatives to this particular world, that his parents' world is relative in space and time, and that quite different patterns are possible.[38]

Some Results of Socialization

Ethnocentrism.   Because of the absoluteness with which the child experiences socialization, he or she begins, early on, to share the human tendency to view the world from his or her own perspective and to begin to believe that his or her way is certainly the *best* way. This perspective, called **ethnocentrism,** refers to the tendency people have to evaluate others according to their own standards and is an almost universal result of socialization. Think again about the example of eating behaviors: when confronted by someone from Bangladesh who eats with his or her fingers, most Americans will consider such behavior not as simply different but as *beneath* or *lesser* than their own. While a certain degree of ethnocentrism serves to bind people together, it can also become a serious obstacle when those who have internalized different ideas and behaviors begin to interact with one another.

Reading 13: Understanding Misunderstanding: Barriers to Dealing with Diversity

One major expression of ethnocentrism is a strong *resistance to change.* People resist change under the best of circumstances, as illustrated in the story of the Wheat Religion people in Chapter 1. If people believe that their way of doing things is best and if they have the power to choose to continue in familiar ways, why should they change? Consider the case of the United States and the adoption of metrics. At this time, *all* other countries of the world have adopted the metric system as their primary means of measurement. The United States is the only country to hold on to something they feel is very dear to them, and they hold on to it despite the difficulties it causes travelers, manufacturers, and others who must interact in a variety of ways with people from other nations. Failure to convert English measures to metric values by NASA scientists was the cause of the September 1999 loss of the Mars planet orbiter, a spacecraft that smashed into the planet Mars instead of reaching a safe orbit. This oversight resulted in the destruction of a $125 million spacecraft and jeopardized the entire Mars programs.

The Metric System

While these examples come from life outside of schools, other examples of ethnocentric behavior do not. There is, for example, the current insistence on the part of many educators and politicians that we need to strengthen a Eurocentric curriculum in our schools on the grounds that a curriculum based on "the best of western civilization" is the most valuable preparation any student could have. However, there is increasing interest among some educators to consider alternative perspectives. Consider this response to American educators in the mid-1700s about sending Native American children to American schools:

> But you who are wise must know that different Nations have different Conceptions of things and you will therefore not take it amiss if our Ideas of this kind of Education happen not to be the same as yours. We have had some Experiences of it. Several of our Young People were formally brought up at the Colleges of the Northern Provinces: they were instructed in all your Sciences, but when they came back to us they were bad Runners, ignorant of every means of living in the woods . . . neither fit for Hunters, Warriors, nor Councellors, they were totally good for nothing.

We are, however, not the less obliged by your kind Offer, though we decline accepting it. And to show our grateful Sense of it, if the Gentlemen of Virginia will send us a Dozen of their Sons, we will take Care of their Education, instruct them in all we know, and make Men of them.[39]

**Afrocentric
Curricula**

More recently, the growing debate over Afrocentric curriculum efforts is, for example, one that should be examined quite closely. Can a school experience that embraces an African perspective effectively reach African American children better than the standard Eurocentric curriculum? Is this curriculum worth embracing and evaluating? Similarly, there is increasing pressure for national, standardized, paper-and-pencil, computer-scored testing on the grounds that it is "objective" (a western idea) and, therefore, fair. The point here is that having the power to choose whether you will adapt to new ways of thinking about and doing things is an important factor in how you exercise your ethnocentric beliefs.

Perception and Categorization

Another result of socialization is that we learn to literally *perceive* the world and to *categorize* information about people and things in our environment in particular ways. Perception and categorization are both cognitive processes that are shaped by socialization.

People receive millions of bits of information every day through their senses. To think that people can respond to each and every individual piece of information is expecting too much; a person's physical and emotional systems would be overwhelmed. Because of the need to simplify things, people organize their world into categories; into each category they put items that share similar characteristics. People then generally respond to the category to which an individual item belongs.

Perception refers to the stimulation of the sense organs, that is, to what people immediately report seeing, hearing, feeling, tasting, and smelling. While no two people have exactly the same physiological structure and therefore no two people perceive stimuli identically, those with healthy nervous systems tend to perceive similar things in the environment in similar ways. Physicists, for example, tell us that the human eye can discern more than 8 million colors as distinguished by variations in wavelength. There is no practical reason, nor is it humanly possible, even to consider all these fine variations of shade and hue let alone to react to each individual color. Individuals, therefore, need some schema with which to group colors. The most familiar schema to you is probably the one based on the spectrum in which red, orange, yellow, green, blue, indigo, and violet are the major colors. When asked about the color of the sky, a westerner's response typically is "blue." A sapphire is blue, oceans depicted on a map are blue, and robin's eggs are blue. Grass, however, is green, as are the leaves of most trees and the inside of a kiwi fruit.

In traditional Japanese language, however, the term *aoi* refers to colors that span blue and green wavelengths. When asked the color of the sky, a Japanese individual's response would be "aoi." When asked the color of grass, the response would again be "aoi." How would you explain these responses? Certainly the entire Japanese population is not color-blind! Rather, whereas European Americans have learned to place these particular stimuli into different schemata, traditional Japanese have learned to place them in the same one.

What's Wrong with a Golf Scholarship?

Michael Williams, who comes from a working-class family and was raised by his grandparents and mother, is planning to go to college, although he does not have a particular major in mind. He is, however, pretty certain that he would like to continue with his golf and hopes to obtain a college scholarship through the sport. Many people in his community would have expected him to play basketball rather than golf.

To what would you attribute this?

To what would you attribute his love of golf?

What obstacles might Michael encounter as he pursues his goals?

If he came to you, his teacher, troubled because many people did not seem to support his wishes, what advice might you give him?

Clearly, sense perception alone is not sufficient. We also need to make sense out of the busy world around us, and to do so, we utilize schemata. Another term for such schemata is category, and **categorization** is the cognitive process through which human beings simplify their world by grouping similar stimuli. What kind of categories we use, how narrow or broad they are, and what meanings are attached to them are all shaped by culture and acquired through socialization. A good example of the relation between perception and categorization is the dog: how people perceive the animal and how they have learned to respond to the stimuli. While all people will see, or perceive, the dog in a similar way, they will certainly think about it differently. Most westerners think of dogs as pets, as companions, and in some cases, as important members of their families. A traditional Muslim, on the other hand, confronted by the same creature, would consider the dog filthy, a lowly animal, and something to be avoided at all costs—similar to the reaction a North American might have to a pig. People in some Asian or Pacific Island nations, on the other hand, might place a dog in the category of food. It is not uncommon to find dog meat as part of the human diet in many parts of the world.

The concept of a *prototype image* is a critical one in the analysis of categories. For most categories that humans create, there is one set of attributes or criteria that best characterizes the members of that category. In other words, there is a clear example of what the category encompasses. This example becomes a "summary" of the group and is the image most often thought of when the category is mentioned. If you were asked to think about a bird, for instance, you may conjure up an image of a creature about eight or nine inches long (beak to tail feathers), brown or perhaps reddish in color, that has feathers, flies, and nests in trees. You probably did not think of a turkey, penguin, ostrich, or even a chicken. For someone socialized in or near the jungles of South America, the prototypic image of a bird might be larger and more colorful, since those birds that we call exotic (e.g., parrots) are part of their everyday world. Yet robins, parrots, and penguins have all the critical attributes that characterize members of the bird family; they all have feathers, beaks, and hollow or lightweight bones, and they all lay eggs. Teachers must examine what their own prototype image of a student is and how they will respond to those who do not fit neatly into this image.

Activity 20:
Examining
Stereotypes
Held by Self
and Others

Stereotypes

Stereotypes.   Categories help people to simplify the world around them. That is, people put stimuli that have common characteristics into one category and then respond to the group. People do not, for instance, respond to each and every chair or table when they walk into a room but refer to them in their broader context of chairs, tables, or furniture.

People respond in a similar manner in their interactions with people. **Stereotypes** are examples of categories of people. Socially constructed categories designed to simplify the identification of individuals who are in some way "other" frequently become negative stereotypes associated with groups. Here we find that the processes of perception and categorization along with ethnocentrism combine to create a potentially harmful situation. Although any cultural group may teach its members to categorize other groups either positively or negatively, most stereotypes end up as negative labels placed on individuals simply because they are members of a particular group.

In the most general sense, the word *stereotype* refers to any sort of summary generalization (or prototypic image) that obscures the differences *within* a group.[40] Stereotypes obtain their power by providing categories that appear to encode a significant amount of information in a concise manner and that help us avoid having to pay serious attention to all the sensory data that is available. Negative stereotypes also enable us to keep our ethnocentric ideas intact by preventing us from seeing contradictory evidence before our very eyes. For example, it is much easier and quicker for us to think of all girls as stereotypically weak and/or passive than it is to notice that at least some of the girls in our classroom are stronger and more aggressive than the boys. Indeed, if we do notice such a thing, we tend to label those particular girls as "unfeminine," which helps us avoid the larger task of accurately differentiating one girl from another and also allows us to maintain a cultural value that teaches that boys are supposed to be strong and aggressive while girls are not. Stereotypic conceptions of others can be acquired through both early and later socialization and are powerful insofar as they promote group solidarity and ethnocentric beliefs.

Some Limits on Socialization

Although perception and categorization both depend in part on the cultural knowledge and meanings associated with the physical and social environment in which a child is socialized and although early socialization is a powerful factor in the development of identity, it is also true that the power of socialization has limits. Three of these limitations are particularly important to educators. First, socialization is limited to some extent by the nature of the child's physical organism. For example, while it is true that an infant or very young child can learn any language and any particular pattern of living, it is not true that any child can be taught beyond his or her biological limits. Socialization to color wavelength categories, for example, may be limited by color blindness

Am I Black or White?

Shameka Collins lives a life many people could not imagine. Being biracial in American society has presented for her both numerous opportunities and many challenges. Many doors were open to her, especially when she was young, but since her father began working away from home, she feels as though things have changed.

Shameka identifies herself as African American now, not because of what she thinks but because of what everybody else thinks. It's just become easier, she says. In seventh and eighth grades, soon after her father left, Shameka saw a counselor on a regular basis. She told her counselor that sometimes she doesn't feel like a black person because in many ways she was raised white. When she was younger, she would tell the counselor, she used to wish that she was just one race, because then she could say that's what she was and it was less confusing for people. But that wish created a dilemma for her. She felt that if she just said she was black, then she was denying her white side. And if she said she was white, she was denying the other side.

How might you help Shameka understand her internal conflicts?

If you were Shameka's classroom teacher, what might you do to make things easier in the classroom for her, or others like her?

Activity 25: Biracial Identity and the Classroom

to red and green. Similarly, socialization to musical sounds will not necessarily produce an operatic singer. However, sensory limits in one area may be, and often are, compensated for by increased attention to other senses, as in people with hearing limitations.

Second, because socialization is an unending process that is never completely finished, its powers of control are never absolute. Because a child is socialized according to one set of patterns (language, situational behavior, understanding of role, categorization) does not mean that he or she cannot learn new patterns. Indeed, the extension of socialization beyond childhood knowledge is one of the chief purposes of formal schooling.

Third, socialization is limited in its power because human beings are not simply passive recipients of socialization, they always act on that socialization in some way. Individuals resist or reject accepted norms, they reinterpret accepted norms, and they create new kinds of normative behavior. Thus, socialization can be seen not as an all-powerful force that totally molds the human creature but rather as a transactional process through which individuals are shaped but not totally determined. Your future students might become Nobel Prize winners, shuttle astronauts, or famous inventors.

Each of these limits on socialization is a resource on which educators can build. However, as Dewey noted repeatedly, the most effective learning takes place when it begins with what the child already knows and moves on from there.[41] Thus, it is important for teachers to understand not only the nature and purpose of cultural socialization in general but also the specifics of the cultural patterns to which they and their students have been socialized.

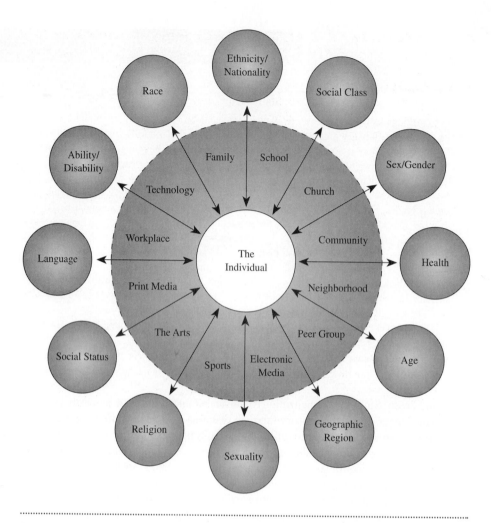

figure 2.3   The culture-learning process.

Understanding Cultural Differences

Variations in Cultural Environments: Returning to Midland

Figure 2.3 summarizes the discussion of the culture-learning process and points up its complexity in multicultural societies like the United States. Although the sources of cultural identity are the same for all societies, each society—indeed, each community—varies considerably in the number and character of its socializing agents. Thus, in a relatively simple society like the Maasai of Kenya, the sources of cultural identity shown in figure 2.3 will be transmitted through very few socializing agents, most notably the family and the members of other families in the community. Because these families have nearly every aspect of life in common, there is likely to be little conflict in the way the various attributes of culture (e.g., age, sexuality, social status, etc.) are transmitted to the individual in such a society. The same, by the way, can be said of small towns and villages in the United States, particularly in very poor areas such as Appalachia or widely separated regions such as the broad expanses of the Great Plains in Montana, where contact with the wider society may be limited, even in terms of radio and television.

In complex, multicultural societies like the United States and many other industrialized nations, however, most individuals interact daily with a vast array of socializing agents, each of which puts a slightly different spin on each of the cultural attributes. For example, your place of worship is likely to have a significantly different view of sexuality than your peer group or your favorite television program. Do you think, for instance, that in Midland, Toni Catalano finds a discrepancy between the teachings of her Catholic upbringing and the sexual ideas she views on television's sitcoms or soap operas? This daily interaction with a variety of socializing agents, each of which may have a unique interpretation of the cultural attributes, means that individuals are bombarded with a variety of conflicting cultural messages.

Furthermore, individuals are not simply passive recipients of incoming messages. Once a message is received, each individual interprets and acts (or not) on its content according to his or her own personality and prior experiences. This interactive aspect of culture learning is depicted in Figure 2.3 by the directional arrows that connect the individual to various socializing agents and through them to the universal cultural attributes. In short, culture learning is a two-way process in which individuals are both forming and being formed by incoming cultural messages. And in many ways, no two individuals construct their world in the same manner.

Perhaps another example would be helpful. Gollnick and Chinn describe two hypothetical women who live in New York City and who are both thirty years old, white, middle class, Italian American, and Catholic.[42] One woman identifies very strongly with her Italian American heritage and her church and not very strongly with her age group, her class status, her gender, or her urban life. The other woman defines herself as a feminist, enjoys her urban life, and is conscious of her age but does not pay very much attention to her ethnic background, her religion, or her social class. The significance of these patterns lies not in each woman's self-definition but in the attitudes, values, knowledge, and behavior that such definition entails. Thus, the first woman may well spend more time with family than with nonrelated friends, may be a member of a right-to-life group, might choose wine rather than Perrier, may be knowledgeable about and participate in Italian ethnic organizations, and is likely to understand, if not speak, Italian. The second woman may find her most intimate companions among women's groups, be pro-choice in her stand on abortion, choose to live in the city despite the possibility of living in a small town or the country, and—if she does not have children—hear her biological clock ticking. This example illustrates how individuals operating in relatively similar settings with relatively similar environmental demands and socializing agents can develop distinctly different cultures. Perhaps you can begin to imagine how different groups and individuals operating in different settings with differing environmental demands and using different sets of socializing agents can develop distinctly different cultures. Figure 2.3 can help you recognize the multitude of different factors that enter into the cultural identity equation.

In addition, consider that each of the three circles in Figure 2.3 can spin so that every cultural attribute can be filtered differently by each of the socializing agents, which results in a variety of personality types. For instance, a passive-reflective individual would interact with the many incoming cultural messages differently than a volatile, nonreflective person might. You can begin to see how complex culture learning can be; how variable individuals can be in the manner in which they receive, process, and output the various influences they encounter; and how these messages can be transformed into differing behavior and belief patterns. Although you might think that in reality an infinite number of cultural formations are possible, the three parts in Figure 2.3 can be used with a little practice as a diagnostic tool for analyzing any multicultural situation.

Activity 37:
Ethnic
Literacy Test:
A Cultural
Perspective
Differentiating
Stereotypes
from
Generalizations

Despite this enormous potential for variation among individuals and within groups, there are similarities, or generalizations, that can be made about groups of people, and these generalizations are referred to throughout this book. People have a tendency to use information that may or may not be reflective of all individuals within a given group. We must always be cautious when using culture-specific information to discuss whole groups because there will always be individuals who do not fit. Individual differences between two people who belong to the same group may be greater than between two people who belong to different groups. Generalizations differ from stereotypes about people, and this point must be kept in mind. **Generalizations** refer to the tendency of a majority of people in a cultural group to hold certain values and beliefs and to engage in certain patterns of behavior. Thus, this information can be supported by research and can be applied to a large percentage of a population or group. **Stereotypes,** on the other hand, refer to the application of a generalization to *every* person in that group. Thus, unsupported information blurs specific knowledge about other individuals. Such stereotypes would, for instance, say that Steven Wong *must* get very good grades because he is Chinese and male, and Shameka Collins *ought to* be more interested in a secretarial job because she is African American and female. Clearly, such stereotypes are in error, as life in Midland demonstrates.

Variations in Cultural Attributes, Socializing Agents, and Cultural Learners

Building a positive attitude toward differences requires a more sophisticated way of looking at diversity. Much of the educational research on individual differences related to culture rests on three assumptions. First, it is assumed that there is a standard or ideal against which difference can be seen, measured, or understood. In this society, people who are white, middle class, Protestant, English-speaking, healthy, physically and mentally typical, heterosexual, and male are said to make up the dominant cultural group. This "ideal" is, of course, a stereotype, much like the stereotypes of other cultural groups. It is important to note, however, that in the United States this particular stereotype refers to people who are socially privileged by virtue of birth characteristics over which they have little or no control.[43] They are also educationally privileged in that their preschool socialization tends to fit them for schooling, which is based on middle-class attitudes and values. One unfortunate consequence of belonging to this model group is that its members don't have to think of themselves as just one of many groups, each with its particular pattern of characteristics. Because they are the model group, they fit into perceived societal norms and thus do not have to think about their cultural patterns much at all (see the discussion of "white privilege" in Chapter 6). It also must be recognized that many of our institutions have been built with this stereotypical model group as their foundation—the very framework that is in conflict with an increasing number of Americans—and we must work to change this infrastructure.

The second assumption is that any deviation from this normative group is the very definition of difference. If a person speaks only Spanish rather than English or is Asian rather than European American; Jewish rather than Protestant; female rather than male; homosexual rather than heterosexual; working class rather than middle class; chronically ill or with a physical, emotional, or mental disability rather than healthy or typical, that person is likely to be perceived as different, and this difference is seen as a deficit to be overcome.

Finally, research on difference assumes that studies of large groups of children with certain characteristics will tell us a great deal about all children who possess some or most of these characteristics. This assumption has at least two serious problems, however. One is that while most research looks at only one characteristic at a time (e.g., gender or social class), no one ever belongs to just one group. Every individual, for example, simultaneously belongs to a gender, social class, and ethnic group. What these "single-characteristic" studies look for are central tendencies, ways in which each particular group of children are the same. It may be that this tendency to focus on one narrow point is problematic and may encourage stereotypes. In and of itself, such stereotypes are oversimplifications that tend to ignore the diversity of behavior differences that exist within a group.

While this single-characteristic research has taught us much, it does not enable us to focus on differences within groups, only on differences between groups. Furthermore, it compares groups according to only one characteristic. Thus, it does not help us understand how various characteristics (gender, social class, ethnicity, disability, etc.) combine with one another to form individual personalities and learning styles. For example, to be a deaf American who uses American Sign Language with other deaf people but uses English in interacting with hearing persons, as Humphries notes, is "to be bicultural and bilingual. This is just for starters. To be a deaf sign language user *and* African American, Hispanic, Asian/Pacific Islander, or American Indian in the United States is to be multicultural."[44]

The second serious problem is that such research is most often statistical and tends to be interpreted by practitioners (and the public) in more global terms than its results warrant. If, for example, 65 percent of a given group of girls are found to be less successful at math than a comparable group of boys, the tendency is to believe that *all* girls are less successful at math. Although this generalization is not warranted by the research, it tends to become "true" in the minds of many people and thus to influence their behavior toward girls. Similarly, educators' attitudes and practices regarding students with disabilities have too often been based on broad labels or classifications such as *mental retardation, learning disability,* and *behavior disorder,* all of which obscure wide individual differences.

This book tries to avoid this problem of group stereotyping by looking at the universal connections between culture and learning. These connections are universal in the sense that they seem to apply to all people no matter what their various group affiliations. Figure 2.1 illustrates the sources of cultural knowledge that, when mixed together, form the cultural identity of *all* groups and individuals. These attributes are, for the most part, societal designations that have little meaning for the individual except as experienced through various socializing agents such as the family, church, neighborhood, and peer group. In other words, individuals acquire a cultural identity within the larger society through their experiences with a variety of daily socializing agents.

What teachers must understand is that cultural-learning patterns vary considerably both between and within various cultural groups. Subsequent chapters describe in more detail some of the ways in which differences in cultural learning may lead to misunderstanding and conflict in schools and classrooms. This book also shows how these same differences can be used as a positive resource in learning-community classrooms. For now, play with the model in Figure 2.3. Ask yourself what the universal attributes mean to you in view of your own life experiences and which socializing agents have accounted for your understanding of them. Do the same for others who are close to you, that is, for family members and friends.

This book will ask these same questions about students, teachers, parents, and school administrators. With the help of the stories incorporated in this book for illustrative purposes and the cases presented for analysis, you will gradually become a sensitive and skillful teacher of *all* children, not just those whose cultural background matches your own. For as you have seen in Midland, while a person may *seem* to be quite different from you, by virtue of membership in a different race or class or religion, they may also share some important cultural aspects with you. And even when an individual *seems* to have many cultural aspects in common with you, they may in fact be quite different in some important ways.

Summary

All people, regardless of the culture in which they were raised, share certain common experiences. This chapter presented the dynamics of culture and the culture-learning process that all people, students as well as teachers, experience and bring with them to the school context. Of particular interest to educators are the primary and secondary socialization processes and the twelve sources of cultural knowledge that represent the diversity of knowledge and experiences to which people are exposed. Critical to educators concerned with improving people's skills in intercultural understanding and communication is the recognition that some of the results of the socialization process present barriers to cross-cultural interactions. Effective multicultural education understands and addresses such issues as critical process as well as content.

Chapter Review

Go to the Online Learning Center at **www.mhhe.com/Cushner4e** to review important content from the chapter, practice with key terms, take a chapter quiz, and find the web links listed in this chapter.

Key Terms

categorization 61	ethnic group 37	out-of-context learning 43
culture 36	ethnocentrism 59	people of color 38
culture-general approaches 43	generalizations 66	perception 60
	in-context learning 43	socialization 55
culture-specific approaches 42	microculture 37	stereotypes 66
	minority group 37	subculture 36
enculturate 41		

Reflective Questions

1. Look back at Webb and Sherman's definition of culture on page 38. Compare two different cultures or ethnic groups that you are familiar with in terms of the categories to which they refer. What categories are similar and which ones are different? How would you explain the differences and similarities?
2. Differentiate between objective culture and subjective culture. Can you provide two examples of each from the cultures or ethnic groups you identified in the first question?
3. Consider the twelve sources of knowledge described in the chaper. Complete an inventory on yourself. How might your inventory differ from one of your parents? Compare your inventory to that of a classmate. How are they similar? different? How would you explain some of the differences?
4. How does the way your parents or community socialized you to understand your social class differ from the way the popular media does? How about your understanding of your gender? How about your understanding of sexual relations?

References

1. Henry Giroux and Roger Simon, *Popular Culture: Schooling and Everyday Life* (Granby, MA: Bergin and Garvey, 1989), p. 3.

2. C. Coon, *Culture Wars and the Global Village: A Diplomat's Perspective* (Amherst, NY: Prometheus Books, 2000), p. 53.

3. Brian M. Bullivant, "Culture: Its Nature and Meaning for Educators," in *Multicultural Education: Issues and Perspectives* (Boston: Allyn and Bacon, 1989), p. 28.

4. James A. Banks, "Multicultural Education: Characteristics and Goals," in *Multicultural Education: Issues and Perspectives* (Boston: Allyn and Bacon, 1989), p. 7.

5. Cited by Christine L. Bennett in *Comprehensive Multicultural Education: Theory and Practice* (Boston: Allyn and Bacon, 1990), p. 42, from a discussion citing Wagley and Harris in J. R. Feagin, *Racial and Ethnic Relations* (Englewood Cliffs, NJ: Prentice-Hall, 1978), p. 11.

6. K. Cushner, "Intercultural Education from an International Perspective: An Introduction," in K. Cushner (Ed.), *International Perspectives on Intercultural Education* (Mahwah, NJ: Lawrence Erlbaum, 1998), pp. 1–14.

7. Rodman B. Webb and Robert R. Sherman, *Schooling and Society,* 2nd ed. (New York: Macmillan, 1989), pp. 49–50.

8. Vivian A. Zelizer, *Pricing the Priceless Child: The Changing Social Value of Children* (New York: Basic Books, 1985), pp. 61, 97.

9. Harry Triandis, *The Analysis of Subjective Culture* (New York: Wiley-Interscience, 1972).

10. D. M. Warren, *An Elementary Treatise on Physical Geography* (Philadelphia: Cowperthwait, 1873), p. 86.

11. Cited in Roy Harvey Pearce, *The Savages of America: A Study of the Indian and the Idea of Civilization* (Baltimore: Johns Hopkins University Press, 1965), p. 155.

12. Francis Huxley, *Affable Savages* (New York: Viking Press, 1957).

13. Paul Pedersen, *A Handbook for Developing Multicultural Awareness (*Alexandria, VA: American Association for Counseling and Development, 1988).

14. Norman R. Yetman, ed., *Majority and Minority: The Dynamics of Race and Ethnicity in American Life,* 5th ed. (Boston: Allyn and Bacon, 1991), p. 3.

15. Ibid.

16. Ibid. See Julian Pitt-Rivers, "Race, Color, and Class in Central America and the Andes," *Daedalus* 92, 2 (1967), for different interpretations of skin color, eye color, lip features, and so on.

17. "Ah, but the mystery," *Akron Beacon Journal,* 25 June 2000, p. A12.

18. J. Jones, *Racism and Prejudice*, 2nd ed. (New York: McGraw-Hill, 1996).

19. Elizabeth Beardsley, "Traits and Genderization," in *Feminism and Philosophy,* ed. Mary Vetterling-Braggin, F. A. Elliston, and Jane English (Totowa, NJ: Littlefield, 1977), pp. 117–123.

20. Gilbert and Kahl, for example, suggest that in the United States, individual or family income is the central variable from which other opportunities follow. For instance, income generally controls the neighborhood in which one lives. Neighborhood determines, to a great degree, the educational experience one has, in school and outside it. The education one has then influences one's profession or occupation, which determines the prestige that one obtains, and so forth (D. Gilbert and J. Kahl, *The American Class Structure: A New Synthesis* [Homewood, NJ: Dorsey, 1982]).

21. Max Weber, *The Theory of Social and Economic Organization* (New York: Free Press, 1957).

22. Robert N. Bellah, Richard Madsen, William M. Sullivan, Ann Swidler, and Stephen M. Tipton, *Habits of the Heart: Individualism and Commitment in American Life* (New York: Harper and Row, 1985), p. 152–155.

23. Gregory M. Herek, "On Heterosexual Masculinity: Some Physical Consequences of the Social Construction of Gender and Sexuality," *American Behavioral Scientist,* 29, 5 (May–June 1986): 570.

24. S. LeVay and D. H. Hamer, "Evidence for a Biological Influence in Male Homosexuality," *Scientific American* 270 (May 1994): 44–49.

25. See, for example, Edward Sapir, *Culture, Language, and Personality* (Berkeley: University of California Press, 1949); Benjamin Lee Whorf, "Science and Linguistics," in *Everyman His Own Way: Readings in Cultural Anthropology,* ed. Alan Dundes (Englewood Cliffs, NJ: Prentice Hall, 1968); and Lev Semenovich Vygotsky, *Thought and Language* (Cambridge, MA: MIT Press, 1962).

26. Noam Chomsky, *Cartesian Linguistics* (New York: Harper and Row, 1966).

27. Ibid.

28. Peter L. Berger and Brigitte Berger, *Sociology: A Biographical Approach* (New York: Basic Books, 1972), p. 127.

29. Carlos Cortes, *The Children Are Watching: How the Media Teach about Diversity* (New York: Teachers College Press, 2000).

30. Ibid., p. 19.

31. T. B. Rosenstiel, "Viewers Found to Confuse TV Entertainment with News," *Los Angeles Times*, 17 August 1989, p. A1.

32. Robert J. Cottrell, "America the Multicultural," *American Educator,* 14, 4 (winter 1990): 18–21.

33. Berger and Berger, *Sociology,* p. 51.

34. Ibid., p. 62n. Berger and Berger tentatively attribute the first use of the concept of identity in this sense to Erik Erikson.

35. Nicholas Abercrombie, Stephen Hill, and Bryan S. Turner, *The Penguin Dictionary of Sociology* (New York: Penguin Books, 1984), p. 201. See also Gail Sheehy, *New Passages: Mapping Your Life across Time* (New York: Ballentine Books, 1994).

36. Ina Friedman, *How My Parents Learned to Eat* (Boston: Houghton Mifflin, 1984).

37. Berger and Berger, *Sociology.*

38. Ibid., p. 51.

39. Response of the Indians of the Six Nations to a suggestion that they send boys to an American college in Pennsylvania, 1744.

40. Richard Brislin, *Understanding Culture's Influence on Behavior* (Fort Worth: Harcourt Brace Jovanovich, 1993).

41. John Dewey, *Democracy and Education* (New York: Free Press, 1966). Originally published in 1916.

42. Donna M. Gollnick and Philip C. Chinn, *Multicultural Education in a Pluralistic Society,* 3rd ed. (New York: Macmillan, 1990), p. 16.

43. For a fuller explanation of privileges that accrue to people who are associated with the dominant group, often without their being particularly aware of them, see Peggy McIntosh, "White Privilege," *Creation Spirituality,* January–February 1992, pp. 33–35, 53; and Gary R. Howard, "Whites in Multicultural Education: Rethinking Our Role," *Phi Delta Kappan,* 75, 1 (September 1993): 36–41.

44. Tom Humphries, "Deaf Culture and Cultures," in *Multicultural Issues in Deafness,* ed. K. M. Christensen and G. L. Delgado (White Plains, NY: Longman, 1993), pp. 3–16.

Classrooms and Schools as Cultural Crossroads

It is often hard to learn from people who are just like you. Too much is taken for granted. Homogeneity is fine in a bottle of milk, but in the classroom it diminishes the curiosity that ignites discovery.

—*Vivian Gyssin Paley*

C h a p t e r O u t l i n e

1.   How might the cultures of students and teachers be similar? be different? How might they be in support of one another? in conflict with one another?

2.   What cultural characteristics might be in common among people who appear to be different from one another?

3.   How might teachers become better prepared for the cross-cultural differences they are certain to encounter among students?

Schools, in particular, are cultural crossroads in a society where distinct but overlapping student, teacher, and school cultures intersect. This chapter examines what occurs when people from different cultures come together, as they increasingly do in our globally oriented pluralistic societies. It then takes an in-depth look at a culture-general model for understanding intercultural interactions. This book takes an intercultural perspective and draws from the work of cross-cultural psychologists who, more than any other group, have been developing practical strategies to help us understand and navigate the tricky waters of cross-cultural interaction. Finally, this chapter presents this model in action and provides opportunities for you to apply this model to the analysis of some common cross-cultural situations found in school settings.

case study   Robert's Induction Year Problem

Robert had just completed a degree in science education at a large southern university and was excited about the prospects of teaching in one of the area high schools. All through his teacher preparation he had been encouraged to pursue the sciences as an area of specialization. He had often heard about the shortage of science teachers and thought he might have an edge in terms of employment. Robert felt confident that he would obtain a position in a high school not too far from where he had grown up and gone to school. He had held this dream ever since his own high school years.

When Robert finally graduated, however, the employment situation was quite different. The teaching market in the immediate area was not as fruitful as he had been led to believe, so when school districts from the west coast came to recruit teachers at his university, Robert found himself seriously considering the possibility of relocating. After all, he did want to teach, and he felt well prepared for any classroom situation.

When offered a position at Alden High School near Los Angeles, Robert gladly accepted and eagerly made plans to move west. Alden High is an urban school of approximately 1,600 students in grades 9 through 12. Approximately 30 percent of the students are Latino, 30 percent are African American, 20 percent are European American, and 20 percent are Asian, Pacific Islanders, or Middle Eastern. A majority of students come from families at or below the poverty level. The school has a large vocational program in which more than half the juniors and seniors are enrolled. Approximately 20 percent of the faculty is a mix of Latino and African American; the rest are European American.

Alden has an aging faculty, with an average age of forty-two. Last year the principal, Mr. Henderson, was unable to hire any teachers of color. This year he was able to attract four new African American faculty members among the new teachers. Robert was one of three European Americans hired this year. He was excited about his first teaching situation and confident that he would be successful.

A few months after the start of the school year, Robert knew that he was confronting a reality far different from the one he had imagined. He felt unprepared for the student diversity that he faced each and every day, and he had no idea how to help students address what he felt were basic educational needs. He was unaccustomed to the variety of languages and dialects spoken by students, had little understanding of what went on in students' lives outside school, and struggled daily to present class lessons that motivated and involved students. And to top everything off, Robert found himself in the middle of significant racial strife.

It seems that in January of the previous year, Mr. Henderson had met with the African American teachers at their request. They had many concerns, ranging from insufficient minority representation on the teaching and coaching staffs to the way white teachers were interacting with many of the African American and Latino students. They felt that most white teachers did not appreciate the need for the proposed Martin Luther King recognition activities; they were disappointed at the lack of white response to a request for donations to the United Negro College Fund; and they felt a negative response to Black History Month activities and other efforts to make the curriculum more culturally sensitive.

As a result of this meeting, a Human Relations Committee was formed. This volunteer group planned and organized a two-day race relations institute. The results of the workshop were disastrous. Instead of improving race relations in the school, the situation became worse. A group of white teachers sent around a list of possible themes for the coming school year that were perceived as racist by the African American teachers. A group of concerned black teachers and parents sent letters to community leaders and higher level administrators voicing their concern. Once parents of the Latino students became aware of the situation, they started demanding equal attention to address the needs of their children. Not only the black students, but Latino and Asian students became increasingly alienated from school-related activities. Students formed a group they called "Students Against Racism" as a means to express their concerns and frustrations.

In March of last year, Mr. Henderson met with the equal opportunity officer in the district and with a racially mixed group of teachers. While concerns were aired, none of the problems were solved. A discussion was begun, but as Mr. Henderson puts it, "We have a long way to go. We definitely have some white teachers who are insensitive to the needs of others, as well as some African American teachers who perceive the white teachers as racist. I'm not quite sure how to begin addressing the students' needs, except to say that we will continue to bring the various parties together to address whatever needs arise. I only hope people will stay with me for the long haul."

Robert was quite uncomfortable attending faculty meetings, and the spin-off was affecting his classroom interactions. He was frustrated, unsure of what was really going on, and uncertain if he could remain in such an environment. He began to seriously question the preparation he had had and wondered how anyone could teach in such a stressful situation.

Schools and Classrooms: Where Cultures Intersect

Within the important limitations of economic circumstance, most people choose the neighborhoods they live in, the places they work and shop, and where they spend their leisure time. In schools, however, as nowhere else in American society, people of many different backgrounds are forced to come together in close quarters for significant periods of time. This section first examines the various cultures (student, teacher, and school) that come together in the context of the school. Second, it examines the role of the teacher as a cultural mediator who is responsible for developing a cooperative learning community within this potentially chaotic setting.

Student Culture

The students of "Generation Y"

Students make up by far the largest percentage of people in a school community. Roughly 33.5 million students were enrolled in public schools in the year 2000, with an additional 6 million attending private institutions.[1] And perhaps more than most social groups, students represent and exhibit the greatest diversity in American society. Not only do students reflect the cultural identities of their families (ethnicity, religion, social class, etc.), they also define themselves by creating their own particular in-school groups.

It is a cultural universal that all people categorize others into one of two major divisions: those with whom they identify and wish to spend their time (called *ingroups*) and those from whom they will keep a respectable distance (known as *outgroups*). Ingroup formation in school can be based on many different criteria, from the more potent cultural identities already discussed (e.g., ethnicity, race, gender) to the relatively fluid but no less important unifying features of academic groups (e.g., biology club, French club), special interest or skill groups (e.g., choir, football), or groups that are, from the point of view of most adults, less desirable but nonetheless purposeful, such as gangs. It should be relatively easy for you to construct many examples of the various student cultures that can be found in schools. Typically, individual students gain a certain school identity from participation in these groups. These microcultures within the school operate in ways similar to the macroculture outside it. Individuals learn appropriate rules of interaction, modes of communication, expression of values, and so forth. And as with larger groups such as nation-states, membership in these in-school microcultures (gangs, chess club, choir) often brings exclusion from other microcultures (other gangs, sports teams, band).

Teacher Culture

Teachers make up the other dominant social group within the school community, with approximately 2.9 million teaching in public schools and another four hundred thousand in private institutions.[2] But unlike the diversity found within the student population, teachers are a relatively homogeneous group. Indeed, a disturbing reality, given the increasing heterogeneity of students in public schools, is the relative cultural homogeneity of the teaching force. In the United States, about 90 percent of the teaching force are European American and two-thirds are female.[3] And even with recent efforts to recruit underrepresented groups into the teaching profession, it is projected that well into the twenty-first century the majority of new teachers will continue to be female and white. This statistic is not surprising. Teachers in the United States have always been mostly female and white, at least since the early part of the nineteenth century. However, this statistic raises interesting issues about the cultural and economic backgrounds of teachers in contrast to that of students.

The fact that a large proportion of our teachers are female is related to the power structure of schools. While it is true that teachers have a good deal of authority in their classrooms, it is not true that they have much authority in the schools. For example, teachers are only just beginning to have something to say about school policy or about the curriculum they are expected to teach. Reasons for this lack of authority may vary, but an important one has to do with the way in which large numbers of women entered the teaching profession in the 1830s and 1840s. Prior to that time, the person behind the schoolroom desk was a schoolmaster, a man. However, after about 1830, the growth of industry began providing more and more lucrative jobs for men, leaving teaching vacancies in the classroom. At the same time, the common school movement was evolving across America, opening up additional teaching positions. Conveniently, it was determined that women, who were "natural mothers" and therefore possessed the knowledge, skills, and talents needed to deal with young children, must also be "natural teachers." The elementary school was projected as an extension of the home and the teacher an extension of the mother. The fact that women would work for about one-third the wages paid to male teachers was also a significant factor in their employment in American schools.[4]

Women in Teaching

Given the history of their entry into the profession, female teachers have never had the status that male teachers once had. Unfortunately for all teachers, the low status of women teachers has become associated with teachers more generally. Administrators, who have greater authority, higher pay, and higher status, are mostly European American men. Thus, in our society, schools have become organized in such a way that leadership and policy are very often the exclusive province of white, male administrators.[5]

School Culture

Both schools and the teachers who inhabit them are, to a large extent, "culture bound," and the culture most are bound to is the dominant culture of European American, middle-class society, which is only one of the many culture groups in the United States. One purpose of public schooling has always been to transmit the cultural beliefs, values, and knowledge affiliated with the dominant group to those in the next generation. The danger, of course, is the ethnocentric tendency of most people, teachers included, to believe that their own cultural tradition represents the "best" way. Too often, the perception of both power and virtue combine to lessen the chance that white, middle-class teachers will make a real effort to understand the cultural differences that direct the lives of many of their students. At best, many of these teachers are predisposed to regard diversity as interesting; at worst, they are likely to regard it as a deficit. Teachers seldom come to their classes with the notion that diversity is an exciting and enriching phenomenon. Sara Lawrence Lightfoot, a professor of education at Harvard and someone who has committed her professional life to understanding and assisting with issues of diversity in schools, describes many good teachers as wishing that the diversity they see in September will somehow fade away as the class becomes a group.[6]

Teachers as Cultural Mediators

The cultural interplay between teachers, students, and their school produces a context within which significant culture learning can occur. In a sense, teachers must become *cultural mediators* in their classrooms and must walk both sides of a double-edged sword. On the one hand, teachers must become more knowledgeable about the role of culture in teaching and learning while becoming better able to address the educational needs of students and families from a variety of backgrounds. At the same time, teachers must turn this knowledge and skill into content that actively engages students in learning about and more effectively accommodating cultural differences. Students thus must learn how culture is formed and how to understand and handle the many intercultural interactions they are certain to encounter.

Throughout this process, it is imperative that teachers and students understand that a certain amount of adjustment and discomfort may occur. It is well to remember that when we as individuals are confronted by someone who looks, behaves, or thinks differently from ourselves, we suddenly become aware that our way of doing things may not be the only one. Such a confrontation often affects us at an emotional level— we may feel anxiety, uncertainty, and discomfort. Lacking a vocabulary to describe most cross-cultural differences and wishing to avoid discomfort, we may choose to avoid further interaction with those who are different from ourselves. Such avoidance behavior merely perpetuates the cycle of discomfort, mistrust, and ignorance and confounds our efforts to improve intergroup relations.

These same feelings often characterize teachers whose students are different from themselves and perhaps different as well from the value and behavior norms of the school. From the school's point of view, such students are often perceived as having deficits that need to be overcome through some type of remedial action. Sadly, such actions are often punitive to students, involving exclusionary practices such as tracking and negative labeling (e.g., at-risk students, learning disabled). Since most of us do not have a wide variety of experience with cultural patterns other than our own, deliberate instruction in culture, including acquiring a language in order to talk about its patterns, its substance, and its behavioral results, is one way to create a dialogue concerning differences. Such strategies help us to truly understand ourselves and others.

Reshaping Cultural Identity

It would be easy for teachers to give in to discouragement and try to find a school where the students were like themselves. The reality, however, is that such schools rarely exist in today's world. Teachers thus will have to adjust to the fact that they will find themselves in significantly diverse settings. Studies of cross-cultural experiences suggest an often predictable pattern of adjustment when one interacts with people one perceives as different from oneself. Early studies of international travelers led cross-cultural psychologists to identify a number of predictable phases people experience during their adjustment to an intercultural setting.[7] These early models, although brought into question in recent years, plot people's experiences on a graph, with emotional experiences along the vertical axis and time across the horizontal axis. The resulting image thus appears as a *U*. Hence, this description of the process of adjustment, or reshaping of identity, is often referred to as the *U-curve hypothesis* (see Figure 3.1).

Activity 14: Adjustment to Change

These early studies suggested that, at least initially, most people are intrigued and perhaps even enraptured by the prospect of an intercultural experience. They have some preconceived ideas of what the new culture will be like and how they might integrate into the new setting. In some cases, they do not initially perceive that the experience will be much different from experiences they have had in the past. Often they are excited at the idea of moving to a new place, of "starting a new life." In this stage, individuals enter what has been appropriately termed the *honeymoon phase,* where things are new and fresh; there are new people to meet, new ways of interacting, new foods to eat, new ideas to consider—nothing could be better!

After some time, however, when people begin to get a sense that what looks different really *is* different and that those differences are important, the constant demand to adjust to new stimuli and to function well in a new setting may become too difficult to accept. Most people react to the stress by entering a state of *hostility* and begin to move down the left side of the *U*. In this phase, people generally attempt to cope with three problems: (1) other people's behavior does not make sense to them; (2) their own

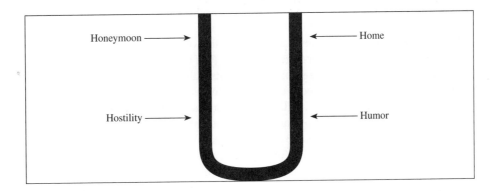

figure 3.1   U-curve hypothesis.

behavior does not produce the expected results; and, (3) there is so much that is new in the environment that they have no ready-made answers to the questions that may arise.

There are many examples of similar adjustment curves in the psychological literature (e.g., newlyweds, retirees). Beginning teachers and new students moving into the culture of a particular school, for instance, face a double challenge. Teachers must simultaneously adapt to the culture of the surrounding community and to that of the teaching profession, which, of course, has a culture of its own. In the school context, new teachers must integrate themselves into the norms and attitudes of both a well-established teaching staff and their students, who bring with them the norms of diverse communities. During the hostility phase, new teachers, like new arrivals in any new culture, may become so frustrated by their inability to make sense of their new world that they begin to react in an aggressive and perhaps hostile manner. At the same time, new students must also adjust not only to the school culture, which may be very different from their home and neighborhood cultures, but also to the behavioral and academic expectations of schooling and to the many possible student microcultures within the school. During the hostility phase, students may become so frustrated that they give up, act up, or drop out.

At this point the individual must make a critical choice: remain, and learn how to function effectively within the new setting; or allow the frustrations to build, and eventually retreat from the unpleasant situation. In this phase, those individuals most likely to succeed in their new setting begin to confront their new cultural environment. They learn to cope with embarrassment, disappointment, frustration, anxiety, and identity problems, while they begin to learn the subjective culture of the new environment.

Once this culture-learning stage begins, people typically begin to emerge from this reactive, hostile phase and enter the third phase, up the right side of the *U.* Often referred to as the *humor phase,* this phase is a positive step toward the reshaping of cultural identity. People who reach the humor phase begin to understand more of the new culture and can begin to laugh at some of their earlier misconceptions and mistakes.

Finally, people who succeed in altering their own cultural identities to include the new experiences climb the final leg of the *U* and enter the phase called *home.* In this phase, individuals are able to interpret the world and interact with others both from their own perspective and from the perspective of that which had been alien to them before. A major change occurs in an individual's ability to process information and to understand the world in ways similar to those who are different. The individual now shows indications of becoming more genuinely appreciative of differences, because the world now seems reasonable and acceptable from more than one point of view.

Most individuals require a significant amount of time before they can develop the in-depth understanding that is required for them to live and work effectively and comfortably with people from other cultural backgrounds. Some researchers suggest that this period may be as long as two years with the individual experiencing full immersion and speaking the local language. Bilingual learners whose primary language is not English often require two periods of adjustment. On one level, children may learn to speak English relatively quickly and within one or two years may appear to be quite fluent—on a surface, or objective, level. That is, non-English speakers may quickly be able to communicate effectively with other children on the playground and during their free time. Yet when these children are given standardized tests of educational achievement, they do not do as well—a secondary, deeper level of linguistic competence is at play.

That is, students may take between four and seven years to attain the level of linguistic competence in a second language that is typically required in schools. Clearly, if acquiring a cultural identity through primary socialization requires full immersion in a culture over a long period of time, it stands to reason that reshaping a cultural outlook as a result of secondary socialization will also take considerable time.

In Chapter 2, Figure 2.3 provided a visual overview of how the various sources of cultural identity are acquired by individuals through interaction with the many socializing agents they encounter. Although the sources of cultural identity (e.g., race, language, sexuality, etc.) are universal and appear in all societies, the socializing agents (e.g., family, school, media, etc.) that transmit them vary considerably from one society to another. In most industrialized societies, for example, a wide variety of socializing agents bombard people daily, often with contradictory messages. In agriculturally oriented societies, on the other hand, a few primary socializing agents (e.g., family and gender group) may share the bulk of the culture-transmission process. The result is that individuals with different cultural patterns develop very different worldviews.

Activity 3: Interpreting One's Own Intercultural Experience

Acculturation and Identity

Extended intercultural contact can have significant impact on individuals as well as groups. **Acculturation** refers to the changes that take place as a result of continuous first-hand contact between individuals of different cultures.[8] Such contact not only produces changes in people's attitudes, values, and behaviors, but may also significantly impact their cultural identity. The historical as well as present-day experiences of different groups may determine, to a great extent, the outcome. For instance, immigrants and refugees who enter a new culture with long-standing, distinctive cultural norms may have very different experiences from members of established ethnic minority groups.[9] Newcomers, for example, may have come from relatively homogeneous countries such as Japan, where cultural identity is rarely challenged, and may have had no experiences with the new host culture. Under such conditions, the pressures for cultural change are often intense, immediate, and enduring. For successive generations, the pressures may take on a different form as the groups evolve into established ethnic communities.

John Berry and his colleagues addressed two issues in an attempt to differentiate among acculturating groups.[10] Comparing the degree of mobility and the degree of choice (or voluntariness of contact), they identified four distinct groups that are of interest to educators: (1) those people with a high degree of mobility and who voluntarily made the contact are referred to as **immigrants** (relatively permanent) or **sojourners** (temporary visitors); (2) those with a high degree of mobility but little or no choice related to their contact are considered **refugees;** (3) those with a low degree of mobility but a high degree of voluntary contact with others are known as *ethnic groups* (see Chapter 2); and (4) those with a low degree of mobility and a low degree of voluntary contact reflect the native people, or **indigenous people,** of a nation. Members of each of these groups can have distinct needs and experiences within the school community.

Definition of Terms

People also differ in the degree to which they wish to remain culturally as they were or are willing to change. People's acculturation attitude can be determined by their responses to two distinct questions: "Is it of value to me to maintain my own cultural identity and characteristics?" and "Is it of value to me to maintain relationships with other groups?" Four distinct outcomes are possible in response to these questions. (1) In **integration,** people maintain relationships with other groups while at the same time they maintain their own cultural identity and characteristics. Integrated people keep their own unique cultural identity while working fairly well within a mainstream. They can, in a sense, walk in two worlds and are well on the way to being bicultural. American Jews are often cited as an example of an integrated group; there are often many well-established Jewish agencies, educational offerings, and community organizations that people can interact with while they maintain relatively positive interactions and involvement within the mainstream. (2) In **assimilation,** people maintain relationships with other groups but they do not consider those goups to be of value in maintaining their own cultural identity. An assimilation decision that is freely chosen is often refered to as the "melting pot." However, when assimilation is forced, a situation more akin to a pressure cooker might develop. Although American society has often been referred to as a melting pot, some people here contend that significant social and cultural barriers prevent many people from achieving assimilation and that many people simply do not wish to give up their heritage in favor of a mainstream. The pot, some would say, never melted. (3) In situations in which people value their own cultural identity but they do not value relationships with other groups, two possible outcomes exist. When the situation is by choice for both groups, it is referred to as **separation.** When such a scenario is forced on one group by another, more dominant group, the situation is called **segregation,** as was prominent in the American South in the first half of the nineteenth century or under apartheid in South Africa until 1994. (4) A unique situation occurs when people do not value their own identity nor do they value relationships with other groups. In such a scenario, **marginalization** may occur, and individuals may experience extreme cases of ethnocide or deculturation.

Members of each of these four groups can have distinct needs, experiences, and expectations of the school community. In fact, it is possible to observe each of the four acculturation attitudes within a given family unit. Imagine a family of four from a small village in Guatemala who recently immigrated to the United States. The father may lean toward integration for job prospects. He may work hard to learn English so he can fit in at work yet may still remain quite active with local Guatemalan/Latino community affairs. The mother, unable to enter the host society, may work hard to retain her Spanish language and her local social interactions. She then becomes a separatist. Hearing the Spanish language at home and eating Guatemalan food all the time may bother the teenage daughter. She may prefer assimilation, so she works hard to speak only English and to blend in through school activities. The brother, on the other hand, may not want to accept his Guatemalan heritage but may be rejected by his classmates. He may retreat and thus become marginalized.

A Model of Cross-Cultural Interaction

Cross-Cultural Communication

For years researchers from cross-cultural psychology have searched for methods that could be used to analyze, understand, and improve intercultural interactions. Cushner and Brislin developed a framework for understanding the dynamics of any cross-cultural encounter between individuals with different cultural patterns.[11] The approach is grounded in the recognition that people have similar reactions to their cross-cultural encounters regardless of the setting or the person they are interacting with, regardless of the role they adopt, and regardless of their own cultural background. Figure 3.2 illustrates three psychological stages through which individuals usually proceed when immersed in an intercultural encounter. Research suggests that these stages are universal, regardless of the particular shape or content of a cultural pattern. Consequently, these stages can be converted into an analytical model that anyone participating in an unfamiliar cross-cultural encounter can use as a tool for assessing or sizing up the situation. While most people assess informally, using whatever bits and pieces of relevant experience they may have, a general assessment model provides a more systematic and effective means.

Activity and Reading 15: A Culture-General Framework for Understanding Intercultural Interactions

Because this model is deliberately general, its usefulness lies in its adaptability to any cross-cultural encounter. It captures the *experience* of cultural differences from a variety of perspectives (emotional, informational, and developmental), and it offers frameworks within which specific problem situations can be addressed. However, it does not go beyond its diagnostic purpose. That is, the model does not offer prescriptive courses of action for dealing with difference. Such approaches are not only impossible, they are unethical given the complex realities of today's classroom. It is the individual student or teacher, empowered by culture-general knowledge, who must inquire into the causes and then propose solutions to the specific problems and issues that arise. The discussion that follows provides an in-depth examination of each stage in the culture-general framework, and the critical incidents provide an opportunity for you to apply this framework.

Stage 1: Understanding Emotional Responses in Intercultural Interaction

In any intercultural encounter, people's emotions are quickly aroused when they meet with unpredictable behavior on the part of others or when their own behavior does not bring about an expected response. The nature and strength of these emotional reactions quite often surprise the people involved, especially in the case of students who do not anticipate the differences between their own cultural patterns and those of the school. Strong emotions can also be experienced by teachers, like Robert in the case study, who find themselves in a school or classroom context that is significantly different from their prior experience. Recognizing and accommodating the strong emotional responses that

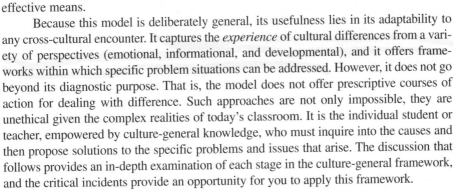

figure 3.2 Stages of intercultural encounters.

people are certain to have when they become involved in intercultural interactions is critical to successfully negotiating those interactions. Figure 3.3 identifies the emotional responses most commonly experienced by persons confronting an unfamiliar culture. A brief description of these responses follows.

Anxiety

As individuals encounter unexpected or unfamiliar behavior on the part of others, they are likely to become anxious about whether their own behavior is appropriate. Children and teachers in new schools, individuals in new jobs, and families in new communities will all experience some degree of anxiety as they attempt to modify their own behavior to fit new circumstances. Such feelings may be powerful, while their cause (cultural differences) may be unaltered. Feelings of anxiety may result in a strong desire to avoid the situation altogether, and individuals sometimes go to great lengths to do so, all the while rationalizing their avoidance behavior on other grounds.

Ambiguity

When interacting with those who are culturally different, people may often receive unclear messages; yet they must make decisions and somehow produce appropriate behavior. Most people, when faced with an ambiguous situation, try to resolve it by applying culturally familiar criteria. For example, it is quite common, when giving instruction to individuals who are just beginning to speak English, to ask them if they understand what has just been said. In an attempt not to seem ignorant or impolite, such individuals will often respond in the affirmative and act in ways consistent both with

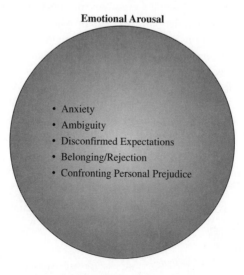

Emotional Arousal

- Anxiety
- Ambiguity
- Disconfirmed Expectations
- Belonging/Rejection
- Confronting Personal Prejudice

figure 3.3   Emotional responses in intercultural interaction.

their (perhaps incomplete or mistaken) understanding of the message and with familiar behavioral strategies. However, their later behavior may reflect only partial understanding of the message or an inappropriate response. Because the new intercultural situation may not fit familiar criteria, this strategy is often ineffective.

The uncertainty of ambiguous situations may be the most critical element in the development of anxiety and is one of the more important factors in cross-cultural misunderstanding. People who are effective at working across cultures are known to have a high tolerance for ambiguity. That is, in situations where they do not have full understanding of what is going on, they can tolerate a certain degree of discomfort, are skilled at asking appropriate questions, and are able to modify their behavior accordingly.

Disconfirmed Expectations

Individuals may become upset or uncomfortable not because of the specific circumstances they encounter but because the situation differs from what they expected. Despite the recognition that differences are all around, people have a tendency to expect others to think and behave in ways similar to themselves. Thus, when involved in intercultural interactions, most people are surprised and disconcerted when others do not respond in expected ways. For example, a child may consistently look at the floor when being spoken to by an adult rather than looking the adult in the eye. This reaction sets up a cycle in which unexpected behavior is attributed both negatively and inaccurately according to preconceived notions of what is right, or correct (this student isn't paying attention and is disrespectful). Further actions, such as the student being scolded for showing disrespect based on such negative or inaccurate attributions, also do not produce the intended result (the student continues to look at the floor). This situation is often very upsetting for all parties involved. For another example, teachers, especially new ones, want to succeed and do well in their classrooms. If the reality of the classroom does not meet the new teacher's expectation, discomfort may result.

Belonging/Rejection

People have the need to fill a social niche, to feel that they belong and are at home in the social milieu in which they find themselves. When they are immersed in an intercultural situation, this sense of belonging is difficult to achieve because they don't know the rules of behavior in the new situation. Instead, people may feel rejected as outsiders, and when this sense of rejection is strong enough, they may become alienated from the situation altogether. Students, for example, who feel alienated from the classroom or school are more likely to become discipline problems and have difficulty paying attention to classroom work. Similarly, teachers who work with youngsters very different from themselves may feel alienated from their students and their students' families and may respond with undue exercise of power or with burnout.

Confronting Personal Prejudices

Finally, a person involved in intercultural interactions may be forced to acknowledge that previously held beliefs about a certain group of people or certain kinds of behaviors may be inaccurate or without foundation. Such a revelation may result in embarrassment or shame. It may also require a basic change in attitudes and behavior toward others. For instance, it is not uncommon for young college students who grew up hearing from parents or other adults that certain groups of people were lazy or unintelligent to suddenly confront contradictory evidence when they encounter people from that group in their dormitories or classrooms. People confronting personal prejudices must decide to question their earlier beliefs and change their subsequent behavior, or maintain those beliefs even in light of their new information. Since change is difficult even in the best of circumstances, people often continue to harbor their prejudices even when faced with contradictory evidence. Making the cognitive shift can be very demanding, but it is essential. Teachers may have a difficult time working with others in this regard.

Stage 2: Understanding the Cultural Basis of Unfamiliar Behavior

In addition to accommodating their feelings, the parties in an intercultural encounter need to understand the particular cultural influences that have shaped one another's knowledge about the world. Individuals typically try to understand another person's behavior according to their own cultural knowledge base. Put another way, since most people do not have extensive experiences with people who think and act differently from themselves, they tend to interpret another's behavior in terms of their own cultural frames of reference. This tendency is the basis of ethnocentrism. In brief, people see what they expect to see, and with incomplete information or inaccurate knowledge, they may make inappropriate judgments about a given situation.

Consider the student who consistently looked at the floor when being spoken to by an adult. Some children from certain ethnic groups (e.g., Mexican American, African American) may be taught to demonstrate respect for elders or persons in authority by avoiding eye contact. Hence a child who is being spoken to by an adult would avoid gazing in that person's eyes. On the other hand, European American children (and the majority of teachers) were socialized to look a person of authority directly in the eye. Imagine the outcome of an interaction involving a Mexican American or African American child being addressed by a European American teacher. The child, as she or he may have been taught, looks away from the gaze of the teacher, thereby demonstrating respect. The teacher, expecting eye contact as a sign of respect, interprets the child's behavior as, "I am not listening to you" or "I do not respect you." This incorrect judgment may result in a reprimand, in response to which the child attempts to show respect by continuing to look away. Without understanding the cultural basis for this behavior, future interactions between this particular teacher and student may be in serious jeopardy.

The individual skilled in intercultural encounters learns to seek alternative explanations of unexpected behavior rather than to simply interpret such behavior according to his or her own cultural framework. The question "Why is this behavior occurring?" precedes the question "What is the matter with this child?"

As was discussed in Chapter 2, there are many aspects of cultural knowledge, each of which reaches the individual through a network of socializing agents. Regardless of the complexity of this socialization process, the resulting knowledge base functions to give us satisfactory explanations of our world and to tell us how best to interact with the people around us. Within this cultural knowledge base, however, the following kinds of knowledge are likely to differ across cultural patterns (see figure 3.4).

Communication and Language Use

Communication differences are probably the most obvious issues that must be recognized when crossing cultural boundaries. Language issues exist whether the languages involved are completely different (e.g., Japanese, Kiswahili, English, American Sign Language), are similar in root but not in evolution (e.g., French, Italian, Spanish), or are variations or dialects of the same language (e.g., French, French-Canadian; English, Ebonics). In any case, it is difficult to learn a second (or third) language. In addition, nonverbal communication customs such as facial expressions, gestures, and so forth also differ across cultural patterns, so that what a particular gesture means to one person may be very different from what it means to someone with another cultural pattern. The familiar head nod up and down that means "yes" to you may indicate "no" in Greece, for instance.

Values

The development of internalized values is one of the chief socialization goals in all societies. Values provide social cohesion among group members and are often codified into laws or rules for living; for example, the Ten Commandments for Christians and Jews or the Hippocratic Oath for doctors. The range of possible values with respect to any particular issue is usually wide, deeply held, and often difficult to change. For example, in the dominant culture of the United States, belief in progress is highly valued and

- Communication and Language
- Values
- Rituals
- Situational Behavior
- Roles
- Social Status
- Time and Space Orientation
- Relationship to the Group

figure 3.4   Analyzing unfamiliar behavior.

almost religious in character. A teacher holding that value may have a very difficult time interacting with parents who seem not to value their daughter's academic potential. The young woman's parents may believe that she should assume the traditional role of wife and mother after high school rather than seek a college education. The teacher, on the other hand, may believe that the young woman should "look to the future" in another way, "change with the times," and "make progress" for herself. These differences are not small.

Rituals and Superstitions

All social groups develop rituals that help members meet the demands of everyday life. Such rituals vary in significance from rubbing a rabbit's foot before a stressful event to the intricate format of an organized religious service. The difficulty, however, is that the rituals of one social group may be viewed as silly or superstitious by members of other social groups. Increasingly, children from a wide variety of religious and cultural backgrounds bring to school behaviors that are often misunderstood and labeled "superstition." Traditional Native American spirituality, for example, often includes rituals involving the personification of natural objects like trees, rocks, and animals. People who have been brought up with a scientific and technological mindset usually view such personification as superstition. Or consider the case of the preschool teacher in Chapter 2 who learned that one of her children was being treated for an illness through rituals involving lighted candles and prayer.

Situational Behavior

Knowing how to behave appropriately in a variety of settings and situations is important to all people. The rules for behavior at home, school, work, sporting events, and so forth are internalized at an early age. Such rules can be easily broken by an individual who has internalized a different set of rules for the same setting or situation. A child, for example, who has learned that learning is best accomplished by quiet and intense observation is likely to run afoul of a teacher who believes that learning is best accomplished by active participation with others in class.

Roles

Knowledge of appropriate role behavior, like that of situational behavior, may vary from role to role and group to group. How an individual behaves as a mother or father, for example, may be different from how that person behaves as a teacher. Similarly, the role of mother, father, or teacher may vary among sociocultural groups. Furthermore, role patterns change over time. For example, middle-class mothers now are increasingly also working mothers, which necessitates considerable alterations in the role of mother. Indeed, this change in middle-class motherhood brings it into closer correspondence with the pattern that has long been established by working-class mothers.

Social Status

All social groups make distinctions based on various markers of high and low status. Both social class and social status are the result of stratification systems whose role assignments may vary considerably from group to group. The role of the aunt in the African American community, for example, has a much higher status than it does in middle-class, European American society. Often the aunt of an African American child bears considerable responsibility for the well-being of that child. Middle-class, European American teachers who are unaware of this status and relationship may, when confronted by a proactive aunt, believe that the child's mother is somehow shirking her responsibilities.

Time and Space

Differences in conceptions of time and space may also vary among social groups. In addition to differences in the divisions of time (e.g., a week, a crop harvest), groups vary in the degree to which time is valued. It is common for many European Americans, for example, to value punctuality because it is seen as an expression of respect. Because time is so highly valued, such people pay much attention to its use—time is seen as money, something to be spent or saved, or in some circumstances, to be wasted. Measures of time and their value may be much more elastic in some less-industrialized societies where work is less synchronized. Similarly, the ease and comfort of a person's position in space *vis-à-vis* other people may vary. How close one person stands to another when speaking and the degree to which one person should stand face-to-face with another are both subject to cultural variation.

Relationship to the Group versus the Individual

All people sometimes act according to their individual interests and sometimes according to their group allegiances. The relative emphasis on group versus individual orientation varies from group to group and may affect significantly the choices a person makes. In the dominant culture of the United States, for instance, individualism is highly valued. Schools have traditionally reinforced this value through emphasis on "doing one's own work," the ability to "work independently," and the recognition of "individual responsibility." However, other social groups, such as the Japanese or some American ethnic groups, place much greater emphasis on group behavior, group solidarity, and group helpfulness and well-being. These social groups often consider it wrong to stand out, to be independent, to "rise above" the group. In a major study comparing national cultures on this dimension, the United States, Australia, and Great Britain stood out among the top nations on individualism. Guatemala, Ecuador, Panama, Indonesia, and Taiwan ranked among the highest on collectivism.[12]

Stage 3: Making Adjustments and Reshaping Cultural Identity

Finally, as a result of prolonged intercultural interaction, individuals may experience personal change. That is, people may alter their way of perceiving the world, processing those perceptions, and viewing themselves as well as others. Typically, for example, individuals who have had significant intercultural experiences become more complex thinkers. This accomplishment is, of course, one of the central goals of multicultural education, because it enables people to handle more culturally complex stimuli, to be more accurate in their interpretations of others' behavior, and thus to deal more effectively with the differences they encounter. As individuals continue to have intercultural experiences, they become less culture-bound and more understanding of how others perceive the world. Such individuals can now see from another's point of view; they are more complex thinkers and can handle a greater variety of diverse information. They are also less likely to make inaccurate judgments or attributions because they are more likely to inquire into puzzling beliefs and behavior, thereby improving their understanding. Think back to the gaze-avoidance behavior in the interaction between the European American teacher and the Mexican American or African American child. The interculturally knowledgeable teacher understands the meaning that underlies the child's gaze-avoidance and more accurately judges the child to be listening and demonstrating respect. Although even people who have considerable intercultural experience may have limited knowledge of the content of a particular cultural knowledge base, they do know that all people process information in similar ways, and they are willing to investigate the outcomes of such processes. Several important ways of processing information are listed in Figure 3.5, each of which can be investigated by the participants in intercultural exchanges.

Categorization

Since people cannot attend to all the information presented to them, they create categories for organizing and responding to similar bits of information. Cultural stereotypes, for example, are categories usually associated with particular groups of people. People involved in intercultural interactions often categorize one another quickly according to whatever category systems they have learned. Examples of this kind of categorization

- Categorization
- Differentiation
- Attribution
- Ingroup/Outgroup
- Learning Style

figure 3.5   Ways of processing information.

might be old/young, rich/poor, native/foreigner, and healthy/disabled. The context within which people categorize each other also influences the categorization process. Recall the example in Chapter 2 of the boy who was sent home from school before the end of each day. From one perspective, the boy was categorized as a troublemaker. Once the context of the situation was better understood, the boy was seen as a hero, doing whatever he could to help protect his mother. Of particular importance is the fact that category systems and their meanings not only differ from group to group but also are rarely neutral in value. Thus, "placing" another person in a particular category may also "place" that person in a more or less valued position (e.g., to be learning disabled is usually in a less valued position than not to be learning disabled).

Differentiation

Information related to highly meaningful categories becomes more refined or differentiated. As a result, new categories may be formed. Such refinement or differentiation is usually shared only among people who have had many experiences in common (e.g., doctors) and thus may be unknown even to those whose background, apart from occupation, is similar. A good example of this process is the way in which people in Asia might differentiate rice. Because it is an extremely important part of their diet and thus their way of life, rice can be referred to by many different terms and can have many different uses. For most European Americans, rice is not as important, and thus fewer references are made to it. A school-based example of differentiation might be found in the manner in which students in a particular high school differentiate their peers into groups such as brains, nerds, jocks, and so on. Although a similar type of differentiation may occur in most high schools, the particular categories and their meaning may differ considerably.

Ingroups and Outgroups

People the world over divide others into those with whom they are comfortable and can discuss their concerns (ingroups) and those who are kept at a distance (outgroups). Based on initial categorization and differentiation as well as on continuing interaction, individuals may identify one another as potential members of their own ingroup or as members of an outgroup. People entering new cultural situations must recognize that they will often be considered members of an outgroup, will not share certain ingroup behavior and communication, and thus will be kept from participating in certain ingroup activities. A really good, if somewhat mundane, example of this process is the situation experienced by a substitute teacher who is, by definition, an outsider in the culture of the classroom and school.

Learning Style

Sometimes called *cognitive style,* learning style refers to a person's preferred method of learning. Learning styles are partly the result of strengths and weaknesses in sensory perception (one's hearing may be more acute than one's vision, for example). However, cultural patterning may teach a child to attend to certain kinds of stimuli rather than others, as when children from collectivist societies learn better in cooperative groups. How (and what) an individual perceives, the categories into which that person places sensory stimuli, and whether that person prefers to learn through observation, listening, or action can all be based on cultural patterns. For example, some Native Hawaiian or Native American children, as they are growing up, learn from a variety of individuals, both adults and other children. Such children may also participate more in group learning; that is, they may learn and practice a skill with other children, not necessarily on their own. These children's preferred learning style (the way in which they have learned how to learn) may be more group oriented than the learning style of the majority of their European American counterparts, who have a tendency to learn how to learn in a more individualistic manner. Such children may not achieve as well in traditionally oriented classrooms as they might in cooperative learning situations.

Attribution

People not only perceive others according to familiar categories, they also make judgments about others based on the behavior they observe and its meaning in their own social milieu. They judge others, for example, as competent or incompetent, educated or naive, well-intentioned or ill-intentioned. Psychologists call these judgments attributions and tell us that within about seven seconds of meeting someone new, initial judgments are made. These initial "sizing-up" judgments, once made, are usually quite resistant to change. Human judgments, however, are fallible, and certain judgment errors occur repeatedly in human thought. One of these, called the *fundamental attribution error,* describes the tendency people have to judge others on different sets of criteria than they apply to themselves, particularly with respect to shortcomings. Thus, if I fail at a given task, I am more likely to look to the situation for an explanation: it was too hot, someone else was unfair to me, the task was too hard. If I observe someone else fail at a task, I am more likely to explain the failure in terms of the other person's traits: she is lazy, he is stupid, she is uncaring. This tendency is even more prevalent when individuals with different cultural patterns interact, because there is likely to be unfamiliar behavior in such situations. Given the speed with which people make judgments and the probable lack of intercultural understanding, attribution errors abound in intercultural situations. Couple this with the tendency people have to form categories (and thus, sometimes, negative stereotypes about people), and you can quite easily see how a very detrimental, complex situation can evolve.

Applying the Culture-General Model

**Activity 17:
Observing
Cultural
Differences**

At this point, you may appreciate the potential of the culture-general model but not know how it can be applied in your daily interactions. The main value of such a model is that it allows people to build a common, culture-related vocabulary that can be used to analyze intercultural interactions in a variety of contexts. That is, it provides a tool whereby people can more accurately judge the nature of the interactions they are reading about, witnessing, or participating in. The following discussion of Mexican Americans is paraphrased from Farris and Cooper's book *Elementary Social Studies: A Whole Language Approach.*[13] In the discussion, specific themes of the culture-general model are designated in italics, and following this discussion are a few cases for your analysis.

While tremendous diversity exists within the Mexican American culture, some generalities about the traditional Mexican American experience can be made. To begin with, there is strong identification with the family, the community, and the ethnic group at large (*belonging; relation to the group; ingroups and outgroups*). The individual achievement readily encouraged in many European American children is not stressed. Rather, achievement for the child means achievement for the family (*status; relation to the group; roles*). Parental involvement in the education of Mexican American children is important for the children's success. Because parents provide a positive support system, every attempt should be made to inform parents of their child's progress. Sending work home as well as accepting items from the home in school helps strengthen the necessary home-school relationship (*belonging; roles; values; learning styles*).

Mexican American culture typically encourages cooperation rather than the competition that is typical in European American culture. As a result, many Mexican American children may find the typical reward structure of schools confusing and frustrating. Teachers may find greater success when motivation is applied to a group activity rather than for personal gain such as a letter grade (*relation to the group; learning styles*).

Mexican Americans also tend to be sensitive to the emotional needs of others. Strong interpersonal relationships should be expected. As such, teachers should encourage children to help one another (*belonging; learning styles; relation to the group*). Mexican American children are also more likely to use both verbal and nonverbal means to elicit a teacher's attention. This may explain their reluctance to ask a teacher for help or to pose a question; their actual request may have been nonverbal (*communication and language use; attribution*).

The Mexican American humanistic orientation extends well beyond the nuclear family. Extended family actively includes *primos,* or cousins with the same last name but no blood relationship; *tocayos,* or namesakes, those with the same first name; *cuñados,* or brothers-in-law; *cuñadas,* or sisters-in-law; and the very important *padrinos,* or godparents, *ahijados,* or godchildren, and *compadres,* or natural parents to the godparents. All these individuals (and others) may play significant roles throughout the individual's life (*roles; ingroups and outgroups; relation to the group; belonging; categorization*).

In such an extended family, status and role relationships are rigidly defined. Younger children defer to older children, and females often defer to males. Respect for parents is expected, regardless of one's age. Sexual roles are well-defined, with females having responsibility for the condition of the home and the raising of children. Males, having higher status, are primarily the wage earners (*roles; class and status; categorization*). There is also a strong obligation to the family. Teachers should keep these roles and obligations in mind when hearing that students have responsibilities such as caring for younger children after school or working in the family business (*values; relation to the group; roles*).

Finally, among Mexican American families there exists a strong orientation and identification with Mexican Catholic ideology. This powerful force reinforces their value system, many of their daily actions, and their respect for parents, family, and tradition (*rituals and superstitions; values; belonging*).

Identifying Commonalities among Groups

In the brief Mexican American example, at least eleven cultural-general themes were evident; perhaps you have identified others. Used in this manner, the cultural-general model can help both students and teachers find commonalities among the cultural differences they encounter. For example, some aspects of the Mexican American experience are similar to those in other ethnic experiences, and some are different. Some may be similar to your own experience, while others will be different.

Viewed in the broadest terms possible, the goal of this model goes beyond simply negotiating cross-cultural interactions or adapting one's teaching in order to accommodate culturally diverse learning styles. Its search for commonalities among people of all cultures offers the possibility that all individuals in a pluralistic society will feel sufficiently similar that they can confront differences without going through the hostility stage shown in Figure 3.1. In short, awareness of similarities—kinship feelings, for example—can motivate people to learn about and appreciate differences. Thus, the model offers a way to go beyond tolerance, which often means "letting people alone," to begin to build a truly multicultural society.

Identifying Differences within a Group

The Mexican American discussion presented in this chapter has at least two dimensions in which the cultural-general model is useful: (1) in building a common vocabulary around differences; and (2) in using those concepts to analyze culture-specific information. The information about traditional Mexican American culture provided an example of using the model across ethnic/nationality boundaries—differences that are most commonly thought of as cultural differences—and of looking for commonalities among specific cultural ideas and practices. A third dimension of difference is also made more visible through the use of the culture-general model, and that is in identifying and analyzing differences within a specific cultural group. Such differences as, for example, social class, geographical location, sexual orientation, or religion are not always easy to "see" but may in fact be important differences in the way individuals perceive the world, interact with one another, and approach learning. Questions raised by a consideration of these kinds of differences can lead to inquiry about, for instance, whether *particular* Mexican American children are Catholic, whether *particular* Mexican American children have learned to operate in a cooperative manner, or whether *particular* Mexican American children identify strongly with their extended families. Research has shown, for example, that some of these cultural attributes may diminish in successive generations of Mexican American families. Indeed, to automatically assume that such characteristics will occur in all children and adults of Mexican American descent is unwisely to stereotype all individuals who "belong" to a particular ethnic group, and to run a grave risk of misinterpreting observable behavior.

Critical Incidents at Alden High

**Activity 16:
Critical
Incident
Review**

The next step is to apply the cultural-general model to the analysis of some school-based cross-cultural situations. Only by doing so is it possible to understand the degree to which culture influences teaching and learning in schools. This section examines the kinds of incidents that might occur in the fictitious Alden High School, described in this chapter's case study. You should realize, however, that the incidents reported here could easily occur in most schools in the United States

Go back to the case study and take a close look at Robert's induction year. Stop at this point and consider some of the culture-general themes that may be at play. It seems obvious that this situation is highly charged and emotional for many of the people

Andre's Role Problem

Andre is a twenty-three-year-old, first-year social studies teacher hired along with Robert. African American and from a middle-class background, Andre has always prided himself on knowing a lot about people at all socioeconomic levels and from many different ethnic groups. Andre began the year with the intent of relating especially well to the African American students. He intends to show them that he is really one of them and understands their needs.

While walking down the hall on his first day in school, Andre sees a group of black males standing near a wall of lockers. They are wearing typical casual clothes—jeans, T-shirts, and sneakers. Andre is dressed in slacks, shirt, tie, and sport coat. Andre greets the group with a hearty "What's happening, bro?" The students look at him and continue with their own conversation. Andre tries to strike up a conversation by asking about any good rap groups in the school, saying that he has done some "bad rappin'" himself. The boys eye him up and down, then slowly move on down the hall. Andre is puzzled. He'd thought that they would respond to his approach and would see him as a "brother."

The next day, Andre sees the same group again and begins to approach them. Seeing him coming, one of the group steps forward and quite sarcastically says, "Hey, bro! You be down in Room 104 (the teachers' lounge), not in my face!" Then the group walks away. Andre does not understand the group's obvious hostility and rejection.

Why do you think the students rejected Andre's attempts to be friendly?

involved. To begin with, Robert must reconcile the reality of this situation with his early expectations. Thus, Robert is clearly experiencing a case of *disconfirmed expectations*. Robert must begin to understand the real situation and adjust his behavior according to what is, rather than to what he expected.

He is also faced with a considerable amount of *ambiguity* in his new situation. While he is enthusiastic about the challenge of an urban teaching experience, he is quite unprepared for its specific dimensions. Such a situation promises to elicit a high degree of uncertainty or ambiguity. Robert is aware that certain actions are expected, but unsure of what those actions are or how to begin to learn them. At another level, Robert is certainly experiencing a high degree of *anxiety* as he strives to integrate into the faculty at Alden High. Such ambiguity and anxiety, while common, must eventually be negotiated if Robert is to be effective in his new setting. As Robert begins to build closer relationships with other teachers and gain a better understanding of his students, his emotions will come under control and he can begin to feel as if he *belongs* in this setting.

Robert's situation represents only one of many ambiguous situations that might arise in such a diverse setting as Alden High. Here are some other situations that could conceivably occur. Start by reading *Andre's Role Problem* above.

There are many possible explanations for Adre's situation. First, the group may feel that Andre's clothes are too different. They can't relate to this different-looking

Activity 34: The Triad Model for Developing Multicultural Understanding

Joao's Identity Problem

Joao is a teenager from Providence, Rhode Island, who has been sent to live for two years with his aunt and uncle who live near Alden High School. This is the first time that Joao has been away from his immediate family, who immigrated from Portugal when he was a child. His family is strongly united and feels a deep pride in their Portuguese heritage. Joao has heard that the school has a reputation as a place where students from different backgrounds get along well together, so he has not been worrying about being the only Portuguese in the student body. He has looked forward to attending his new school.

During Joao's first week in school, he discovered that several members of the faculty viewed him as belonging to a group of students who spoke Spanish. A few teachers greeted him in Spanish, and one suggested that he join a club for mainly Central American students. Joao was surprised and resentful that these teachers just assumed he was Hispanic. During his second week, a teacher gave him a notice to take home to his uncle; it was in Spanish. Joao startled the teacher by breaking into tears and loudly protesting, "Please try to remember; I'm Portuguese!"

How would you explain Joao's reaction?

adult (*outgroup; categorization*). Second, Andre's use of Black English may be incorrect to this particular time and place and thus may label him in their eyes as a "phony"— someone who can't be trusted (*communication; outgroup*). Third, it is possible that Andre came on too hard to these particular students and that he was seen as pushy and was rejected because of it (*role*).

Using the culture-general framework to analyze the situation suggests another possible explanation. The group may not accept Andre because they see him as an outsider regardless of his race or his language. Andre is still a teacher in the eyes of these students (*role; status*) and one that they do not yet know. Andre has been categorized by the students in a different way than he would categorize himself, that is, as an outgroup member rather than as the ingroup member he expected to be (*categorization*).

It is important to differentiate the particular criteria that others use to form categories and thus the meaning attributed to those groups. Although Andre may have been fairly close to their age and talked their talk, he is still seen as an adult teacher, an authority figure who may not be trusted, at least at the outset. As a teacher, he should not expect to be included as one of their group. Their response told him that he should be in Room 104, that he is a teacher and should act like one. New teachers are usually eager to be accepted by students. This need is normal, especially because teachers may not be far removed from the lives and concerns of high school students themselves. Given time, Andre can establish the rapport he wants, but he must do so in his role as a teacher. Now, read *Joao's Identity Problem* above.

Many different issues may be at play in Joao's situation. First, Joao might have felt some dislocation at being sent to live with his aunt and uncle in the first place. His

Rosita's Alienation Problem

Rosita Gomez arrived in the United States two months ago from El Salvador, an orphan being sponsored by a European American, middle-class family. Before her arrival, her American parents went to Alden High School and provided the administrators and faculty with information about her situation. To make her adjustment easier, a number of teachers organized a group of students to act as sponsors for Rosita. The students were to teach her about the school and community and help her with transition problems as well as to offer friendship.

During the last two months the appointed students have indeed helped Rosita in school and have been friendly to her. They have encouraged her to become involved in student council and to attend after-school extra-help sessions whenever needed. Rosita, though, is often left out of students' social activities such as parties, group movie dates, and volleyball games, and she thinks she is being treated as an outcast. She feels lonely and afraid and complains to her American parents and school counselor about her feelings. Her complaints confuse the Alden High students and teachers very much because they have tried hard to make Rosita feel at home. How might you explain this situation?

sense of unity with his family in Providence was very strong, and it is reasonable to suppose that he missed them very much (*belonging*). Second, in Providence Joao had been attending schools where many other students were native Portuguese. The idea of going to school with students from other ethnic and cultural groups—but not Portuguese—although initially interesting, might also have been somewhat frightening (*ingroups, and outgroups*). It is also possible that Joao's parents had kept him under such tight discipline that he never learned much self-discipline. Thus, his first experience of living away from home may have been so demanding that he was unable to control himself.

At another level, Joao was obviously upset about being identified as a member of a cultural group other than his own (*categorization; values*). Proud to be a native Portuguese and having shared this pride with other Portuguese students back in Providence, he couldn't adjust to being viewed as a Spanish speaker from Mexico or Central America. In addition, he was used to teachers who recognized the Portuguese language and culture, and he was perhaps shocked to find teachers who did not (*disconfirmed expectations*).

The teachers meant to be helpful to Joao, of course. They no doubt thought he came from one of the Spanish-speaking countries because they needed to quickly fit him into one of the ethnic and cultural categories already familiar to them. Because the Portuguese language is similar enough to Spanish that Joao could understand the teachers when they addressed him in Spanish, they found it convenient to categorize him with the other Spanish-speaking students. Now, read *Rosita's Alienation Problem* above.

It is possible that Rosita, having had a major transition in her life recently, is magnifying the situation. Perhaps the circumstances are such that she is experiencing what is

Rema's Communication Problem

Rema, a sixteen-year-old girl from Lebanon, came to the United States just one year ago. Although she still has some difficulties in speaking and writing English, her language skills are sufficient for her to be academically successful at Alden. Midway through the eleventh grade, Rema was achieving Bs and Cs in all her classes, including Andre's social studies class.

Actually, social studies is Rema's favorite subject, and Andre continually remarks to others on the breadth and depth of her reading. Rema reads voraciously and does not limit herself to that which is studied in class. She keeps up on international news and reads literature in two languages.

Andre is concerned, however, about Rema's test scores. When the class takes a multiple-choice, true-false, or fill-in-the-blank test, Rema's grades are usually among the highest. When the class is assigned an interpretive essay, however, Rema's grade is always much lower. Andre has said many times, "Rema just never really gets to the point; she tries to talk about everything at once." Despite repeated efforts to remedy this writing problem, Rema continues to write confusing analyses.

How might you explain this situation?

commonly referred to as culture shock. However, *culture shock* is a very generalized term that refers to an overall reaction to a complex series of events; the term isn't very useful when analyzing specific situations. There is something more specific going on here.

It is also possible that the students do not really like Rosita and are trying to have as little to do with her as possible. The appointed students may feel put upon by their teachers and are thus taking it out on Rosita. However, the students are having what appears to be extensive contact with Rosita in school. If they did not like her, they would probably forego school contact as well.

Viewed through the culture-general model, it is possible that Rosita's predicament can be understood in terms of ingroup behavior. In every culture there exist ingroups, people who are comfortable with one another, share similar values and casual language, and seek each other's company. Ingroups allow people to share their concerns, laugh and joke about problems as a way to reduce tensions, and generally just let their hair down. The students in this situation represent such an ingroup. Rosita has left her own ingroup behind in El Salvador and needs to reestablish herself as part of a new ingroup. The students, however, do not see Rosita as being part of their ingroup, at least not yet. She would not understand most of their jokes, does not share their intimate and extensive knowledge of other students and teachers, and could not enter into their conversation easily. The students thus do not invite Rosita to share in their social activities. Not belonging to an ingroup, Rosita feels like an outcast (*belonging*) and is missing the support system so needed during her difficult transition to a new culture. Now, read *Rema's Communication Problem* above.

Kaye's Communication Problem

 Issues of communication affect dialogue among teachers as well. Kaye Stoddard is in the middle of her first year as assistant principal at Alden High. Kaye is an energetic person who seeks out staff input concerning school policies and curriculum. She encourages staff participation through periodic surveys and group discussions at staff meetings. Lately, however, Kaye has been disturbed about the dearth of input she is receiving from Latino teachers. She is particularly interested in their ideas, since so many of the school's students are Latino. Although she has solicited feedback from everyone, most of her information comes from the European American teachers.

How might this situation be explained?

There are many ways to explain Rema's writing performance. It is possible that she lacks the basic writing skills and vocabulary necessary to write lengthy compositions of this kind. However, her overall academic performance indicates that she is competent in English vocabulary and writing. Her problems with written expression are probably not due to technical deficiencies.

It is also possible that Rema has misunderstood or misinterpreted the main elements of the work she is studying. But having read works of equal breadth and depth on her own, it is unlikely that Rema is unable to analyze and appreciate what she is reading.

Alternatively, Rema may not be able to think clearly under the pressure of tests. However, she doesn't seem to exhibit this problem in objective tests; she shows no particular "test anxiety." So Rema's problem seems to lie elsewhere.

Analyzed from the standpoint of cultural differences, however, it is possible that Middle Eastern and North American modes of learning, thinking, and communicating are very different. In many cultures, including Arab countries, communication is accomplished through associations. Everything that is associated with an idea is considered relevant when thinking about or communicating a concept. Such communication may seem highly indirect to a European American, who typically gets right to the point and reasons in a systematic, step-by-step fashion. In contrast, a Middle Easterner will often make many loops while communicating a particular point. In short, when viewed in terms of her native culture, Rema's highly associative compositions demonstrate both her knowledge of the subject and her overall intellectual ability. Once Rema and her teacher are aware of these culturally different writing styles, they can take some practical steps to improve the situation.

One simple explanation might be that the Latino teachers do not want to interact with Kaye because she is non-Hispanic. However, there is no justification for this explanation. The entire school population is mixed, thereby making it difficult for the Latino teachers to limit their interactions with non-Latinos. Also, Kaye does not feel that she is the target of hostility. Now, read *Kaye's Communication Problem* above.

It is also possible that the European American teachers dominate the Latino teachers, giving them little chance to express their opinions. Again, however, there is no indication that domination is the problem. Nor is there any indication that the Latino teachers are indifferent concerning the subjects Kaye includes in the surveys and meetings. Like other professionals, most teachers have strong opinions about their workplace.

A more probable explanation can be found in culturally different communication styles. Kaye has taken an impersonal approach to eliciting opinions, whereas the Latino teachers may favor a personalized approach. Latino culture strongly emphasizes the affective side of interpersonal relationships. Personalized contact is thus very important to many Latino teachers. Although Kaye is genuinely interested in the opinions of all her teachers, she has approached them impersonally through her written surveys and large-group staff meetings. The Latino teachers might respond more easily if approached individually or addressed personally at a meeting. At the same time, many Latinos feel strong affiliation with the group (*relationship to the group; individualism versus collectivism*), and the Latino teachers might respond even more enthusiastically if they were asked for their ideas and opinions together in a small group.

Each of these critical incidents has explored several of the many possible cultural issues always at work in diverse settings like Alden High School. They illustrate ways in which classrooms and schools function as cultural crossroads, as places where infinite variations of cultural knowledge, beliefs, values, and skills meet and are forced to interact. This chapter has presented a culture-general model that offers a language and concepts that provide a common framework for all such interactions, no matter what their variation. Perhaps you would like to analyze experiences you have had that might be understood in light of the culture-general model. See if you can think of some.

Activity 33:
Writing Your
Own Critical
Incidents

Part 2 of this book focuses on longer case studies in which teachers, students, administrators, parents, and others also experience various cross-cultural interactions in the context of evolving ideas of good practice in schools. Remember as you read on that there is never any "one best answer" to the issues that arise. Indeed, an understanding of the complexities of cultural diversity suggests that in many instances the idea of a single "best solution" is not only impossible but is also inimical to a culturally pluralistic environment. In short, teachers must learn to feel comfortable with, appreciate the possibilities of, and negotiate effectively in ambiguous situations.

Summary

In no other social setting in society does such a diverse gathering of people come together for a prolonged period of time than in the school. Thus, the potential for a wide range of intercultural interactions between students and teachers is great. This chapter introduces the eighteen-theme culture-general framework for understanding intercultural interactions between people, regardless of their cultural backgrounds, who they are interacting with, or the roles that they adopt. Such a framework provides an opportunity for people to better understand their emotional reactions to intercultural situations, the knowledge base that people bring with them as a result of being socialized within any given culture, and the manner in which people's cultural identity may be reformed. Such a framework also provides a vocabulary and categories with which people can discuss cross-cultural issues with others.

Chapter Review

Go to the Online Learning Center at **www.mhhe.com/Cushner4e** to review important content from the chapter, practice with key terms, take a chapter quiz, and find the web links listed in this chapter.

Key Terms

acculturation 81

assimilation 82

immigrants 81

indigenous people 81

integration 82

marginalization 82

refugees 81

segregation 82

separation 82

sojourners 81

Reflective Questions

1. Reflect on the eighteen culture-general themes introduced in this chapter. These themes are meant to identify issues that people are likely to encounter when interacting with people different from themselves. Using the following sentence as a starting point, fill in the blank with each of the eighteen themes and answer the questions accordingly.

    "Can you think of a time when _____ was evident in your life or in interactions with others? How might this have interfered with your ability to function effectively? When might it be an asset to you?"

2. Interview a student and/or family who has moved here from another country. What experiences can they recall about their cultural adjustment to a new land? What have you learned from them about their experience that would assist you as a teacher?

3. Reflect on the acculturation groups discussed in the chapter. What are some needs that would be similar and different among students who were immigrants, refugees, minority group members, members of an indigenous group, or short-term sojourners (such as year-abroad foreign exchange students)?

4. Locate a newspaper article that makes reference to cultural conflict in a school or community. How can you apply the eighteen-theme cultural-general framework to better understand the dynamics at play?

References

1. T. Snyder and C. Hoffman, "Digest of Educational Statistics: 2000," *Education Statistics Quarterly* 3, 1 (spring, 2001): 79–82.

2. Ibid.

3. Center for Educational Statistics, *Digest of Education Statistics* (Washington, DC: Government Printing Office, 1987).

4. Nancy Hoffman, *Women's True Profession: Voices from the History of Teaching* (New York: Feminist Press, 1981), p. xix.

5. Myra H. Strober and David Tyack, "Why Do Women Teach and Men Manage? A Report on Research on Schools," *Signs: Journal of Women in Culture and Society* 5, 3 (spring 1980): 494–503.

6. Sara Lawrence Lightfoot, in an interview with Bill Moyers as part of the *World of Ideas* series, American Broadcasting Corporation, 1989.

7. Gregory Trifonovitch, "Culture Learning–Culture Teaching," *Educational Perspectives* 16, 4 (1977): 18-22.

8. R. Redfield, R. Linton, and M. J. Herskovits, "Memorandum for the Study of Acculturation," *American Anthropologist* 38 (1936): 149–152.

9. C. Ward, S. Bochner, and A. Furnam, *The Psychology of Culture Shock* (East Sussex, England: Routledge, 2001).

10. John Berry, *Psychology of Acculturation: Understanding Individuals Moving between Cultures*. In *Applied Cross-Cultural Psychology,* ed. R. Brislin (Newbury Park, CA: Sage, 1990), pp. 232-253.

11. Kenneth Cushner and Richard Brislin, *Intercultural Interactions: A Practical Guide,* 2nd ed. (Thousand Oaks, CA: Sage, 1996).

12. G. Hofstede, "Dimension of National Cultures in Fifty Countries and Three Regions," In *Expiscations in cross-cultural psychology,* ed. J. Deregowski, S. Dzuirawiec, and R. C. Annis (Lisse, The Netherlands: Swets & Zeitlinger, 1983), pp. 335–355.

13. P. J. Farris and S. M. Cooper, *Elementary Social Studies: A Whole Language Approach* (Madison, WI: Brown & Benchmark, 1994).

Intercultural Development:
Considering the Growth of Self and Students

> One of the higher callings for young people in the
> coming century will be working to increase intercultural
> understanding. Such people will be the missionaries of
> the age, spreading light among groups . . . by giving
> them a modern vision of the new global community.
>
> —Carl Coon

Chapter Outline

1. Have you ever said to yourself something like, "I certainly wouldn't have thought that way a few years (or months) ago. I've changed and see things much differently than before"? As a teacher, you expect students to learn, to grow and to change as a result of certain experiences or encounters. What benchmarks might you use to determine if your students are becoming more sophisticated in their understanding and analysis of culture and intercultural effectiveness? What benchmarks might you use to determine if you were becoming more sophisticated in your understanding and analysis of culture and intercultural effectiveness?

2. What differences can you identify in people who are more ethnorelative in their orientation in comparison to those who exhibit more ethnocentric behaviors?

3. How might you design experiences that move students from an ethnocentric orientation to one that is more ethnorelative?

The following case study presents multiple perspectives and viewpoints on issues related to culture in a school and community. As you read the case study, try to identify the variety of points of view. The critical incidents at the end of the chapter refer you back to the case study as you explore the development of intercultural sensitivity.

case study   Dissent at Maplewood School

Sue Murray, fifth grade math and science team teacher: *It didn't begin with Mr. Jameson's letter to the editor in the local paper late in February, but that was when it did gain momentum and draw an increasing number of people into the issue. And now, just two months from the end of the school year, all kinds of people are angry and hurt, many are confused, teachers are getting anxious, and the students don't know what to think. Mr. Goodwin, the principal, seems to be doing all that he can to bring the various parties together, and as I understand it they are making considerable progress. Let's see if I can piece together all that has happened. I'll begin with the letter I just referred to. Then there are a few other letters to the editor that show the range of responses.*

Dear Daily Record Editor,

As a taxpayer and citizen of this fine city I resent what I see going on in the schools. As I know them, schools are meant to prepare young people for the future. If students are to go to college, then they should have the prerequisite courses they need to succeed. If they are to learn a trade, then the school is to provide them with the skills they will need to do their job. A student who is undecided on what the future will hold should be given an opportunity to try many different things. This is all well and good, and is as it should be. It is the way schools have operated since I went to them many years ago.

But since when have the schools become responsible for addressing all the demands of any group that comes along and claims they have been mistreated or ignored in society? I do not think the schools should be teaching multicultural education. What is it anyway? No one has shown me a book on multicultural education that students study from. It's not a part of the state proficiency test. We used to have good schools here that worked for everyone. Now they don't seem to be working at all. Why should teachers and students spend all their time holding debates, doing plays, having so-called cultural festivals and potluck dinners, and paying good money to invite some cultural dance group in to perform for kids? Let's get it straight, schools have a responsibility to prepare people for life, not to teach everyone about other groups' problems. With so many different people now living in America, there would be no more room in the school day if that were all teachers taught. Besides, aren't we all supposed to be Americans anyway? If people don't like the way things are, they should go back to where they've come from. After all, they came to America—they should do it the American way!

But perhaps it is not all the teachers' fault. Perhaps there is a lack of leadership in the schools—from the administrators to the board of education. And while I cannot stop paying my taxes, I can vote "NO" for the next school levy *and* vote to replace the current members of the board. I think many others would agree with me and follow my lead.

John Jameson, a disgruntled citizen
February 27

Editor, Daily Record,

I am writing in reference to Mr. Jameson's letter about issues in the schools. I agree. It's time we take a stand and stop pandering to every group that comes along. My husband has been out of work for almost one year now, and he can't seem to get a job because of such things as affirmative action. Yet I see many other people working in jobs that could go to real Americans. If people don't like it here they should just leave. I've traveled to other countries and each time I do I am reminded about how much better we have it here in America. I think the schools are part of the problem, and they'd better shape up soon.

Rebecca Reynolds
March 5

To the Editor of the Daily Record,

I wish to disagree with the letters written by Mr. Jameson and Ms. Reynolds who complained about the schools addressing multicultural education. As someone who works in the business community, I know how fast the world is changing—much faster than many people in this city seem to be—and our children must be prepared for these changes. School may be the only place where children can learn about other people—about other cultures, about how different people think and act, and about how to learn to get along with those who are different. Most parents are too busy or not experienced enough to tackle such a difficult task. We need the schools to do this for us. After all, it is in the school where children of different backgrounds come together for long periods of time. What better place is there for children to learn about diversity? I am in full support of our schools doing all they can to address diversity, and I hope others in this community come forward with their support as well.

Joyce Maples
March 8

Sue Murray: *As I already said, it wasn't the letters to the editor that started everything, but they do give you a sense of the variety of peoples' reactions. Ever since the start of the school year tensions have continued to mount. It seems as if no one is happy with the way things are, and I don't understand why. I was excited to begin teaching in the fifth grade team after teaching for five years in a fourth-grade self-contained classroom. But with all the developmental changes the children are going through and all the ethnic and racial tensions that have emerged, I don't know if I can take another year. We have parents who are angry that we are not addressing what they think are critical issues. We have had a number of parent meetings involving all the teachers as well as the principal where we attempted to discuss their concerns, but nothing seemed to help. And many parents and other local citizens have been showing up at school board meetings to voice their concerns.*

I think the problems began back in October at the school Halloween party. We have been concerned about violence in general and the increase in the number of slasher-type movies that influence many of the children's choice of costume. Rather than have children dress in whatever costume they might if they went out for trick-or-treating, we encouraged them to come dressed as some political or social figure. I was really surprised when two boys, Tom and Daniel, came dressed as Native Americans and three others, Keenan, James, and Troy, came dressed as sports mascots—one as a Cleveland Indian, one as a Washington Redskin, and one as an Atlanta Brave. What a social commentary they were making, and quite sophisticated, I might add, for a group of young middle school students. They had placards that challenged people's stereotypes: some demanded changing the team logos and some argued to maintain them out of tradition. Even the imbalance of power was evident in the three-to-two mix they presented. Many of the children were oblivious to the messages these students were trying to make, but not all. Some, in fact, were quite taken by their statement. Their presence even caused a stir among some of the parents who came to observe the annual Halloween march around the school. Mrs. Marks, the president of the PTO, took a photo of them for the school newspaper. The paper was printed just before Thanksgiving. I think it was this incident, in combination with some of the Thanksgiving plays and classroom activities, that really set things off. Some parents of the younger children in the school started complaining that putting on a traditional Thanksgiving play was perpetuating stereotypes. I kind of agree with some of them.

It was soon after we came back to school after the winter break that I really began to be bothered by all this attention to diversity. Some of the African American parents started complaining that not enough was being done to present their culture and that we shouldn't be doing things only during February for Black History Month. The PTO was asked to form a multicultural committee, and aside from Mrs. Marks, it seemed that there were mostly minority parents involved.

And then, what really got me was when Mr. Goodwin, the principal, called me in to his office. I think it was in early March. He said one of the African American parents complained that I wasn't a good teacher. The father said that his son wasn't learning from me and that I was treating some of the kids differently. I don't treat any of my students any differently. And I really think the parents would accuse me of playing favorites if I did start doing things differently for different groups. After all, we all want the kids to learn what's best for them. And we've been pretty good about being able to make that happen in this school—for everybody. I think the diversity is an asset for us. The more differences we have here, the better. More difference equals more creative ideas in the classroom, and I certainly wouldn't want all the kids to be the same around here. It's bad enough that most of the teachers are pretty much the same. If everyone were the same, it would be boring. The more cultures people can know about, the better off we'd all be. I have my master's degree with a specialty in math and I'm pretty good at science. I'm a good teacher. I can't help it if some of the kids don't catch on as quickly as the others. I work hard at what I do and I resent being accused of playing favorites or not treating certain kids right. Some of these parents should try to teach a room full of kids who are overloading on hormones. It's not easy work, you know.

I asked Mr. Goodwin to let me know which of the parents complained, but he wouldn't tell me. I told him that I'd rather meet personally with the parents to discuss the issue instead of them hiding behind the principal. He said he was arranging a parents' meeting soon and that would be the time for people to discuss their feelings. He said he was considering bringing in a facilitator to help keep the discussion in a positive light.

I wonder how my teaching team feels?

This book not only helps you develop an understanding of how individuals are socialized into their immediate social and individual identity groups (i.e., family, ethnic group), it also addresses your subsequent ability to accept and interact effectively with other people. This chapter looks at what it means to develop greater awareness and sensitivity to your own culture as well as the cultures of other people. It begins by presenting some general models of ethnic and racial identity and ends by looking closely at the developmental model of intercultural sensitivity as a means to become interculturally competent.

Developmental Models of Ethnic and Racial Identity

You have not always been the same physically, cognitively, emotionally, or experientially. What does it mean to develop; to change over time; to see and interact in the world from a new and different perspective? Developmental models propose a hierarchical scheme whereby an individual progresses from one level to the next, oftentimes as a result of direct experience and maturation. Numerous developmental or stage models have been proposed over the years that have relevance to educators: Erikson's concept of psychosocial identity formation,[1] Kohlberg's stages of moral development,[2] or Piaget's stages of cognitive development.[3] Models related to the study of culture and intercultural education have only recently emerged, the earliest can be traced to the various ethnic identity models proposed after the height of the civil rights movement.

Developmental Psychologists

Ethnic identity theory refers to "the process of defining for oneself the personal significance and social meaning of belonging to a particular ethnic group."[4] Often used interchangeably, but nevertheless qualitatively different, is the concept of **racial identity**. Race, as has already been stated, is sometimes socially defined on the basis of *physical* criteria (i.e., skin color, facial features), while an ethnic group is socially defined on the basis of *cultural* criteria (i.e., customs, shared history, shared language). You may identify as a member of an ethnic group but not think of yourself in racial terms. The opposite can also be true.

A variety of racial identity models have been proposed, most of them influenced by the black consciousness movement. Cross proposed a five-stage model that described a process of moving from low racial consciousness through a period of active examination of what it means to be black, and finally to internalize a positive black identity. These five stages are pre-encounter, encounter, immersion-emersion, immersion, and internalization.[5] Spring adapted this culture-specific model to other groups, including other dominated cultures, as well as to immigrant groups in general.[6] Following is a summary of Spring's adaptation

Pre-encounter

Individuals in the pre-encounter stage exhibit a certain amount of self-hatred, and they often buy into the negative stereotypes perpetuated by the mainstream society through television, radio, newspapers, and conversation. These negative stereotypes, then, are often internalized and become a part of the person's ethnic identity. Individuals at this level begin to see themselves as lazy, stupid, sloppy, thieving—whatever the prevailing stereotype happens to be. Once these feelings are internalized, young people at this level might speak of their entire group as lazy or stupid. A self-fulfilling prophecy takes over, and these individuals identify themselves as probable failures in school—and ultimately fail.

Young children are especially prone to the messages given by others. Immigrant children may face problems similar to those of other dominated groups as they become victims of negative stereotyping because of their speech patterns, different mannerisms, or dress. The Asian American stereotype of the "model" student, although seemingly positive, may also imply passivity and obedience. Asian adults, then, may suffer from being typecast as submissive and meek. And don't think that European Americans are exempt from having to confront negative stereotypes. A number of ethnic American groups (Polish Americans, German Americans, Jewish Americans, Italian Americans, etc.) have organized to combat the many negative images often perpetuated about them.

Encounter

In this stage, individuals confront an incident that forces them to question the negative stereotypes that have become part of their ethnic identity. Numerous incidents in recent years have caused many people to reevaluate their pre-encounter identity. Reactions to such highly publicized incidents as the Rodney King beating, the **racial profiling** by many law enforcement agencies, or incidents of racism in education have led many people to rethink their ethnic identity. At this stage, people begin to see self-hatred as a product of negative stereotypes and see themselves as part of a larger group experiencing similar social barriers. People begin to ask themselves, *"Why do I think this way about myself and my people?"*

Immersion-Emersion

In this in-between stage, people begin to rid themselves of their ethnic self-hatred, to rediscover their traditional culture, and to take on a new ethnic identity. People may adopt the symbols of their people, such as wearing the traditional clothing of their group, adopting new hairstyles that reflect their group, learning to make the traditional foods, and so forth. African Americans, for instance, may wear a dashiki, Italian Americans may purchase pasta machines, or Jewish Americans may don a kippa.

Immersion

This stage is represented by a complete immersion in a person's ethnic culture. Mexican Americans may join organizations focused on Chicano issues; Puerto Ricans may get involved in discussions about independence versus statehood; Native Americans may join active American Indian movements; people seek out the literature and music of their culture; and so forth. This stage represents a highly ethnocentric orientation, and people may adopt a "holier-than-thou" attitude. People may also adopt a somewhat militant stance, challenging existing social and institutional practices. Mexican American students in some public schools in Los Angeles, for instance, went on strike a few years ago, demanding that Chicano foods be served in cafeterias.

People's immersion in their ethnic culture changes their perspective on events. People may begin seeing the importance of their people's contributions to the greater society, such as the influence of Italian art and thought to Western art and literature, or West African contributions to the sciences and art. People begin to read various accounts of history from multiple perspectives, pointing out that most of what children learn in school has been told from the European point of view. The anger associated with this "I dare you, whitey" orientation provides people with the emotional energy to expel the final vestiges of domination in their minds.[7]

Internalization

At this stage, individuals come to terms with living within the culture of the United States (or other mainstream society) while maintaining a relationship with their ethnic culture. People become fully bicultural or multicultural and adopt a view of the mainstream culture that is both accepting and critical. They can identify with certain aspects of the dominant society (material abundance, perhaps) while rejecting other aspects (racism, for instance). African Americans may say, "Some whites are racist, but not all. Whether I like everything or not, I have grown up here and it is my home, too. Things can improve if we keep on working toward that goal." Anger becomes focused on certain aspects of society—combating discrimination in schools or racist impressions in textbooks, for instance.

Like Spring, Banks looked at the emerging stages of ethnic development of individuals within a particular group and proposed a similar six-stage model.[8] The first three stages—ethnic psychological captivity, ethnic encapsulation, and ethnic identity clarification—are similar to those of Cross.[9] The latter three stages speak more readily to a global society.

Banks's stage 4, called *biethnicity*, refers to individuals who have both a strong sense of their own ethnic identity as well as a healthy understanding and respect for others. Individuals at this stage participate equally as well and as comfortably in two different groups—their home ethnic group as well as that of at least one other, usually that of the mainstream. They have become bicultural. Think of the many American Jews who function effectively in numerous Jewish organizations while at the same time interacting in the greater society with relative ease. Similarly, many African Americans (or any other group for that matter) are able to move with ease and respect between their own community culture and that of the mainstream. This stage reflects people who are successfully integrating, not assimilating, as referred to in the discussion on acculturation in Chapter 3.

Stage 5 in Banks's model, *multiethnicity*, represents the idealized goal for citizenship identity within such ethnically pluralistic nations as the United States, Canada, or Australia. Individuals at this stage have an understanding and appreciation of many groups, are able to function somewhat effectively within a variety of ethnic or cultural communities, and maintain an allegiance to the nation state and its idealized values.

Finally, at stage 6, *globalism and global competency*, individuals reflect positive ethnic, national, and global identities while demonstrating the knowledge, attitudes, skills, and abilities required to function effectively in ethnic cultures from a variety of contexts. They have, as Banks states, "internalized the universalistic ethical values and principles of humankind and have the skills, competencies, and commitments needed to act on these levels."[10]

Cross suggests that internalized identity serves three main functions.[11] One, by providing a sense of psychological security, it protects people from the insults that may come from other groups. Two, it provides people with a sense of belonging to a larger cultural group. And three, it provides a foundation for dealing with people from other cultures.

So, how have our nation's schools addressed issues related to diversity and culture in education throughout time? The next two sections take a brief look at historical efforts as well as an analysis of more recent approaches to multicultural education. The subsequent section looks at recent conceptions of intercultural development and considers how these are fundamental to our efforts to deliver an education that addresses the goals of diversity.

Historical Perspectives on Multicultural Education

During the earlier years of massive immigration, from about 1870 to perhaps 1920, the "problem" of diversity in the schools was largely perceived as a problem of how to assimilate children of other nationalities. In short, it was thought to be the school's task to make immigrant children as much like white, middle-class, Anglo-Saxon Protestants as possible in as short a time as possible. Interestingly, a key strategy employed by public schools to accomplish this goal involved establishing the field of speech therapy (formally termed speech/language pathology). Immigrant children placed in New

York's "vestibule" or "steamer" classes were instructed in the proper use of English by speech teachers, who very soon, at parents' requests, were also assigned to work with children who had medically impaired articulation or fluency.

Anglo-Conformity and Assimilationist Ideology

Described as **Anglo-conformity** or the **assimilationist model,** the rationale for this strategy was typified by these words of Ellwood Cubberly, a prominent educator around the turn of the twentieth century.

> Everywhere these people settle in groups or settlements to set up their national manners, customs, and observances. Our task is to break up these groups or settlements, to assimilate and amalgamate these people as part of our American race and to implant in their children so far as can be done, the Anglo-Saxon conception of righteousness, law and order, and our popular government and to awaken in them a reverence for our democratic institutions and for those things in our national life which we as a people hold to be of abiding worth.[12]

The assimilationist strategy was applied to each new ethnic group as immigrants poured through Ellis Island and other ports of entry. Jews, Poles, Slavs, Asians, and Latin Americans all became the "raw material" from which the "new American" would be made. Between 1860 and 1920, 37 million immigrants became naturalized citizens. Their sheer numbers changed the ethnic makeup of America. By 1916, for example, only 28 percent of San Francisco's population claimed English as its first language.

Yet despite the high number of immigrants, the dominant American culture retained its English, Protestant identity. The nation's public schools, staffed largely by white, middle-class, Protestant women, did little or nothing to encourage the expression of ethnicity or address the special needs of an increasingly diverse student population. Indeed, in the eyes of the nativist population, the schools were supposed to prevent such expression. The idea of a melting pot was used to describe the process of helping immigrants shed their native languages, learn English, and assimilate into the dominant American culture.

The term *melting pot* actually came from the name of a play written in 1909 by Israel Zangwill. The goal of creating one homogeneous culture from the many that arrived on the shores of the United States is captured in the following speech from the play:

Israel Zangwill and *The Melting Pot*

> America is God's Crucible, the great Melting Pot where all the races of Europe are melting and reforming! Here you stand, good folk, think I, when I see them at Ellis Island, here you stand in your fifty groups with your fifty languages and histories, and your fifty hatreds and rivalries, but you won't be long like that, brothers, for these are the fires of God. A fig for your feuds and vendettas! Germans and Frenchmen, Irishmen and Englishmen, Jews and Russians—into the Crucible with you all! God is making the American . . . The real American has not yet arrived. He is only in the Crucible. I tell you—he will be the fusion of all races, the coming superman.[13]

James Banks suggests that assimilationists believe that a person's identification with an ethnic group should be short-lived and temporary because it presents an obstacle to an individual's long-term interests and needs.[14] Assimilationists believe that, for a society to advance, individuals must give up their ethnic identities, languages, and ideologies in favor of the norms and values of the larger, national society. The goal of the school, from an assimilationist perspective, should be to socialize individuals into the society at large so all can function in an "appropriate" manner—that is, in a manner that supports the goals of the nation as expressed through its leaders. Ethnic group identification, if it is to be developed, should be confined to small community organizations. In short, the goal for assimilationists is to make it possible for everyone to be "melted" into a homogeneous whole.

The assimilationist view, sometimes called a *monocultural* perspective, shares an image or model of American culture. In this view is a core American culture composed of common knowledge, habits, values, and attitudes. For people who think of American culture this way, these common characteristics might include the following: "real" Americans are mostly white, middle-class adults (or are trying to be); they are heterosexual, married, go to church (mostly Protestant but sometimes Catholic); they live in single-family houses (which they own, or are trying to); they work hard, eat well, stand on "their own two feet"; they expect their children to behave themselves; they wash themselves a good deal and generally try to smell "good"; they are patriotic and honor the flag; they are often charitable and, in return, expect that those receiving their charity will try to "shape up"; and they are not very interested in "highfalutin' " ideas found in books written by overly educated people, believing instead in "good, old-fashioned common sense."

Of course, this description is a composite picture and, to some respect, a generalization. Not all monoculturalists fit neatly into this view of "real" Americans. But most monoculturists share many of these characteristics, and divergence from any of these characteristics (for example, heterosexuality) almost automatically disqualifies a person even if that is the only way in which he or she differs. For people who see American culture in this narrow way, those who do not share these characteristics are clearly not real Americans, whether they happen to have been born in the United States or not. Moreover, their difference makes them dangerous to the maintenance of America as it is "supposed" to be. It is therefore a primary role of schooling to make the children of the culturally different into "American" children; that is, to teach these children those ways of thinking, behaving, and valuing that will help them fit harmoniously into the monoculturalists' culture. Children of monoculturalists, of course, do not need such help because they already match the model.

While exceptional individuals, people with disabilities, and people who are intellectually or otherwise gifted are considered real Americans, they too have been viewed in some sense as "others." Beginning in the 1870s, large urban school districts formed separate classes for "unrulies" and for "backward" or "dull" pupils. In actuality, most such classes were repositories for children who for one reason or another "didn't fit" the regular program. From these beginnings, special education emerged as a separate, smaller system within the public school.

Multiculturalism and the Pluralist Ideology

Cultural Pluralism

People who believed strongly in the idea of the melting pot have been both confused and angered by the fact that the contents of the pot never melted. Eventually, in opposition to the assimilationist ideology, came the call for **cultural pluralism** by a small group of philosophers and writers who argued that a political democracy must also be a cultural democracy.[15] To these pluralists, immigrant groups were entitled to maintain their ethnic cultures and institutions within the greater society. The analogy they used was that of a salad bowl and that in order to have a rich, nutritious salad (society) it was necessary to include a variety of cultures. In short, American society would be strengthened, not weakened, by the presence of different cultures.

Pluralists view one's social group as critical to the socialization process in modern society. The group provides the individual with identity and a sense of belonging or psychological support, particularly when faced with discrimination by the larger society. It is through one's group, usually the ethnic group, that one develops a primary language, values, and interpersonal relationships as well as a particular lifestyle. Pluralists believe identity groups (racial/ethnic, religious, and so forth) to be so important that the schools should actively promote their interests and recognize their importance in the life of the individual. Because pluralists assume a "difference" orientation rather than a "deficit" orientation, they stress the importance of a curriculum that addresses different learning styles and patterns of interaction and that fully recognizes students' cultural histories. The assumption is that the more congruent the school experience is with the other experiences of the child, the better the child's chance of success.

One set of programs that were responsive to cultural and other forms of diversity fell under the umbrella term *multicultural education.* Growing out of the civil rights movement of the 1960s, these programs tried to address the needs of racial, ethnic, and linguistic minorities. Specifically, Spanish-speaking Americans in the southwest, Puerto Ricans on the east coast, Asian Americans on the west coast, Native Americans on reservations and in urban settlements, and African Americans throughout the United States began to seek their fair share of what America had to offer and began to demand that the nation live up to the ideals it professed. The powerful buildup of unrest and frustration born of the discrepancy between American ideals and American practices sought an outlet. From the *Brown v. The Board of Education of Topeka* decision in 1954 through the Civil Rights Act of 1964 and to the Vietnam War, those groups marched out of the ghettos and into the courts.

Contemporary Multicultural Education Programs: They Are Not All the Same

Sleeter and Grant's Typology

In their analysis of multicultural education in the United States, Sleeter and Grant found five distinct categories of efforts described under the label *multicultural education* that are commonly found in schools.[16] While there is clearly some overlap among them, these five categories represent the variety of approaches that have been used by educational pluralists in their attempts to advance the cause of a positive approach to cultural diversity.

Teaching the Culturally Different

The main purpose of these approaches are to counter a cultural deficiency orientation and at the same time assist individuals to develop and maintain their own cultural identity. Such efforts attempt to help individuals develop competence in the culture of the dominant group while developing a positive self-identity. The focus of such efforts tends to be on aspects of the culture and language of specific target groups that a teacher can build on, such as culture (in the traditional sense), race, and ethnicity, and therefore the focus excludes attention to gender, exceptionality, and social class.

Kamehameha Early Education Program

Such education approaches are evident in situations where the majority group is rather homogeneous and of a different background than the teacher. Also characteristic of such approaches is an emphasis on the transmission of mainstream curriculum content. Examples of such education efforts include the extensive Kamehameha Early Education Program project in Hawaii, which aims to modify the school context so that it is more congruent with the culture of the child. Teacher training efforts that emphasize "all there is to know about teaching the _____ child" reflect such an orientation. Such efforts can transmit a considerable amount of culture-specific information; however, they may mask an assimilationist ideology.

Human Relations

The human relations category views multicultural education as a means by which students of different backgrounds learn to communicate more effectively with other people while learning to feel good about themselves. Such efforts provide practical ideas for how teachers can improve students' communication abilities and at the same time help students understand their culturally different peers.

While it is essential that individuals in a pluralistic nation learn to communicate more effectively with one another, such emphasis is only part of the solution. An education that effectively addresses diversity goes well beyond the limited scope of communication to include attention to such factors as curriculum expansion, curriculum inclusion, and empowerment.

Single-Group Studies

The single-group category addresses instruction that focuses on the experiences and cultures of one specific group. In response to the early demands by people seeking inclusion in the curriculum, specific courses that reflected the heritage, contributions, and perspectives of these "forgotten" groups were developed in many schools and universities across the nation. Such courses as African American History, Chicano Literature, and Native American Culture, typically monoethnic courses, were developed and taught, for the most part, by members of that particular group. Students who attended such courses were typically members of the target ethnic group. The primary goals of these courses were twofold: (1) to develop a content dimension, because exclusion from mainstream material typically resulted in a lack of information readily available about certain groups; and (2) to help individuals develop a more positive perception and self-image.

Although such efforts were needed, they may have had the tendency to perpetuate a rather ethnocentric orientation, albeit from a different group's perspective. Addressing diversity effectively today demands that _multiple_ perspectives be considered. The efforts of all who have contributed to the single-group studies can assist those working to expand the curriculum content for today's students.

Inclusive Multicultural Education

It soon became apparent that the adoption of single-group courses in and of themselves was not sufficient to enable many minority students to achieve in school at levels comparable to most of their majority counterparts, nor for them to advance along such a hierarchy. These early efforts seemed more akin to educational practices for minorities rather than practices for multicultural education.

A slow shift in direction began to occur that offered a new approach, a new way of looking at the question of what is appropriate multicultural education. Attention began to be paid to broader issues of school reform that focused on the total school environment. As more and more ethnic groups began to make similar demands, the pressure increased on schools and universities to develop and deliver courses that reflected the experiences of many different groups. As similarities in people's experience and perspective became evident, schools, colleges, and universities began to offer courses that attempted to link the experiences of ethnic groups from a variety of perspectives through the development of a conceptual core. Such course offerings as Ethnic Minority Music, Minority Literature, and The History of Minorities in America became popular.

Still other people became interested in educational reform that would consider the educational problems beyond those of ethnic minority groups. Such efforts attempted to address the needs of women, religious groups, individuals with handicaps, and those from particular regions of the country, such as white Appalachia. Teachers who employed such a multicultural approach in their teaching utilized material, concepts, and perspectives of many different individuals from diverse groups. English literature, for instance, was not limited to a study of the literature of the so-called dead white men, but included pieces written by women as well as by individuals from a variety of ethnic and cultural groups. In addition, the pieces selected for study were ones identified as relevant by members of that particular group.

These courses helped raise the consciousness of a number of people concerning the perspectives and contributions of various groups to a variety of disciplines and causes. Underlying this approach was a focus on such issues as the strength and value of diversity in a pluralistic nation, human rights as a basic tenet for all, the acceptability of alternative life choices, social justice and equal opportunity, and equitable distribution of power among members of all ethnic groups.

Education That Is Multicultural and Social Reconstructionist

The four approaches just identified did not seem to impact sufficiently on the experiences of many people to the degree that they were empowered to make a difference in their lives. A significant mismatch between the curriculum of the school and the daily experiences and cultural backgrounds of many people of color is assumed to exist, one that is nearly impossible for many to transcend. Essentially, the schools succeed at placing certain individuals at an advantage while successfully suppressing many others.

Sleeter and Grant speak of providing education that is multicultural and social reconstructionist.[17] This approach goes beyond multicultural education in its attempt to help students critically analyze their circumstances and the social stratification that keeps them from full participation in the society at large. The phrase "education that is multicultural" means that the entire education program should be designed to address the needs of diverse groups regardless of race, ethnicity, culture, religion, exceptionality, or gender. This approach also strives to provide students with the skills necessary to become socially active in creating the necessary changes. Such an effort is designed to enable individuals to shape their own destinies, hence the term **social reconstructionist**.

Sleeter and Grant cite four practices unique to education that is multicultural and social reconstructionist.[18] One, schools and classrooms that adopt such an approach are organized in such a way that democracy is put into action. That is, students are not told in a passive way what democracy should be like. Rather, children are given the opportunity to participate in constructing a system that exemplifies democracy in action. Students participate in such activities as determining the rules and consequences of classroom interaction, they may participate in determining portions of the curriculum, and they may be included in various aspects of program evaluation.

Two, students learn to analyze their life situation and to become aware of inequities found in society that impact their lives, such as the inequality of pay for equal work found between individuals from different groups or the assumption that an education automatically improves a person's life experience. Ogbu summarizes this issue through one individual's position:

> White people have always felt that they are superior to all other groups. And when the minority people begin to protest and challenge this superiority complex the white people begin to shout the slogan of "law and order." But the only solution to the problem, you say, is education. Education will do it. All right, now you take my wife. She has four years of college and yet she can't get a job. Now education is not the only answer. It is one of the answers but not all the answer.[19]

Attaining knowledge alone, however, is not sufficient. The third unique practice is that students learn social action skills so they are better prepared to put their knowledge and concerns into action in the political, economic, or social arenas. Only then can significant change occur with the potential to impact large numbers of people.

Finally, attempts are made to encourage groups to coalesce such that the efforts of smaller groups become concentrated and strengthened in their fight against discrimination and oppression. It is then that a large social movement can form. That is, when large numbers of people come together in their efforts to promote or resist change in society, formal organizations may be born. The feminist and civil rights movement of the past few decades resulted in the formation of many organizations that direct people's efforts and make significant change.

The Mitchell Typology

Over the years, a number of writers in addition to Sleeter and Grant have analyzed the wide variety of multicultural education programs and categorized them in ways that might help us understand their purposes and practices. Mitchell, for example, provides a slightly different typology. Writing clearly about the assumptions, expectations, and practices of various multicultural education programs, he argues that most if not all of such efforts fall into one of the following three models.[20]

Models of Cultural Understanding

The cultural understanding approach emphasizes improved communication among different ethnic and cultural groups. Proponents of these models assume that the United States is a culturally diverse nation-state where the presence of cultural diversity has helped to create a powerful society through the contributions of all Americans, no matter what their background. The schools, however, have not acted to promote this view of American society, with the result that prejudice and discrimination against particular racial and ethnic groups exist. To remedy this situation, schools and teachers should "positively endorse cultural diversity and foster an appreciation and respect for 'human differences' in order to reduce racial tension and estrangement of minority groups in the schools and in society."

In this approach, all social and ethnic groups are assumed to be relatively equal in worth, and ethnic identity is thought to be "a matter of individual choice or preference—the language of the shopping mall" or the banquet table. Proponents of this model advocate eliminating racial and sexual stereotypes; moving beyond simple awareness of cultural differences in food, dress, and so forth; and emphasizing the development of positive attitudes toward minority and disadvantaged groups. In other words, attitudes should change. Mitchell argues that these programs "take a benign stance towards racial inequality in schooling"; consequently, they focus most of their attention on the development of racial and ethnic harmony.

Expecting that schools will actively promote the cultural enhancement of all students, these programs place primary responsibility on the classroom teacher to provide information and enrichment activities designed to reduce prejudice. Mitchell indicates that these programs have not been very successful in changing attitudes; indeed, in some cases attitudes among white students toward African Americans and other minorities have deteriorated. In part, the lack of success of these programs has been attributed to problems with both content and methods.[21] In addition, these programs may, in fact, foster stereotyping by clustering individuals together on the basis of only one characteristic—race, ethnicity, religion, and so forth. Differences *within* these groups are rarely emphasized.

Models of Cultural Competence

Based on cultural competence models, it is not enough to appreciate other cultural groups. What is needed, according to Mitchell, is the ability to understand one's own cultural identity and, beyond that, to become "at home" in more than one cultural system. Advocates, says Mitchell, believe that traditional assimilationist approaches preserve Anglo dominance and that cross-cultural interaction will assist in the survival of minority language and culture as well as help decrease discrimination and prejudice. In the cultural competence model, minority students are encouraged not only to be proud of their own heritage but, in cases where their background is characterized by subjugation and prejudice, to become fluent in the dominant culture.

Critical of programs designed to remediate so-called cultural deficits, advocates of cultural competence programs argue for inclusive curricula in which knowledge and values rooted in minority cultures are examined. Mitchell asserts, however, that their twofold approach to cultural identity contains a fundamental contradiction. By affirming minority cultures, these programs challenge the dominant social norms that are promoted in the school. At the same time, by encouraging students to "build bridges" to the dominant culture, often by stressing language adaptation, these programs place students on the road to assimilation.

Models of Cultural Emancipation and Social Reconstruction

Models of cultural emancipation and social reconstruction share with other models the belief that cultural diversity in the United States is a positive force and that fostering positive self-concepts among minority students is a valuable enterprise. They differ from other models, however, in their focus on the attitudes of teachers and other school personnel and on the culture of the school, which, they claim, serves to suppress the development of ethnic and racial identity and thereby is partially responsible for underachievement and loss of job opportunities among minority students. It is thus incumbent on school personnel to act in ways that will redress past patterns of discrimination and increase educational and job opportunities for minority students.

Criticisms of this model, however, point out that it may be unduly optimistic to believe that improved school achievement based on an inclusive curriculum will translate into better job market opportunities for minority students. Prejudice and discrimination exist outside the school as well as in it, and the school has little power to alter pervasive attitudes in the larger community. In addition, the complexity of school culture itself has not been sufficiently addressed by emancipatory multiculturalists. They tend to ignore the complex social and political relations between the schools and the larger society in which they are embedded. Issues of policy formation, decision making, and trade-offs and the building of alliances for specific reformist initiatives have not been addressed by multicultural reformers. For these reformist educators, according to Mitchell, educational change hinges almost exclusively on the reorganization of the content of the school curriculum.

It might be of value for you to revisit the goals of this book that are presented in Chapter 1. How do each of the approaches to multicultural education that have been presented here meet those goals? What sort of model would *you* build in regard to an education that addresses diversity? Does the integrative model proposed in this book go beyond the approaches presented here? How can we begin to envision, and actualize, an approach that is not only inclusive but also assists people to develop the skills to collaborate effectively across groups? The discussion that follows addresses such concerns.

Intercultural Competence

Activity 2:
Inventory of
Cross-Cultural
Sensitivity
Just what does it mean to have an intercultural mind-set? What are the attitudes and behaviors of people who are comfortable and effective working across cultures? How would you recognize such an orientation in teachers and students? in yourself? How can we assist people to develop such an orientation?

Early studies in intercultural competence attempted to identify the specific behaviors that were evident in individuals who were effective at living and working across cultures. Such studies suggested that interculturally effective people have three qualities in common: (1) they are able to manage the psychological stress that accompanies most intercultural interactions; (2) they are able to communicate effectively across cultures—verbally as well as nonverbally; and (3) they are able to develop and maintain new and essential interpersonal relationships.[22] Other conceptualizations of intercultural effectiveness and sensitivity consider the interplay between the cognitive, affective, and behavioral domains.[23] People with an intercultural mind-set, for instance, move from an avoidance or a tolerance of difference to a respect and appreciation of difference. They move from an unconscious ethnocentrism to a more conscious awareness of their own and others' cultures. And instead of being conscious of what *not to do* to avoid racism, sexism and other prejudices, they understand what *to do* to create respectful, productive intercultural relationships. Interculturally effective people are thus proactive in nature and seek out diverse perspectives and contributions when making decisions and taking actions.

In learning to manage effectively across cultures, people should strive to develop a number of skills. They should respond to others in a nonjudgmental manner; attempt to propose more than one cultural interpretation for behavior (in other words, generate multiple attributions and check them out); learn to mediate conflicts and solve problems in culturally appropriate and effective ways; motivate others in the context of their cultural values; promote effective intercultural interaction through mutual adaptation to style differences; respect cultural differences through the analysis of strengths and limits of different perspectives, skills and knowledge; model culturally sensitive behaviors and attitudes; seek out new learning about cultural differences; and institutionalize an intercultural perspective in their personal and professional practice. Ultimately, intercultural competence refers to the maintenance of a vision that stresses the dignity of all cultures and the productivity of pluralism; to the development of a mind-set that recognizes ethnocentrism and seeks the value of difference; and to the adoption of a skill set that employs intercultural communication in effective and ethical ways.

Interculturally competent individuals are thus able to solve problems and take appropriate risks, shift their frame of reference as required, recognize and respond appropriately to cultural differences, listen empathically, perceive others accurately, maintain a nonjudgmental approach to communication, and gather appropriate information about another culture. In real life outside the classroom as well as within, such skills are critical when people engage in decision making, negotiation, or problem solving across cultures; when subordinates and authority figures from different backgrounds interact extensively; or when individuals or families make major transitions. The school and classroom provide an ideal context in which to practice and develop these skills.

Intercultural competence may be as much a tool for survival in today's world as is the development of literacy, mathematics, and technological skill. Educators today must strive to fully integrate an intercultural education and perspective while carrying on with the traditional educational needs of communities and nations. Yet these are not easy issues to adequately address. Intercultural education and training is a delicate and

**Intercultural
Competence**

difficult endeavor that must be approached with the greatest of sensitivity. Bennett points out that intercultural interactions among human populations have typically been accompanied by violence and aggression:

Intercultural sensitivity is not natural. It is not part of our primate past, nor has it characterized most of human history. Cross-cultural contact usually has been accompanied by bloodshed, oppression, or genocide. Education and training in intercultural communication is an approach to changing our "natural" behavior. With the concepts and skills developed in this field, we ask learners to transcend traditional ethnocentrism and to explore new relationships across cultural boundaries. This attempt at change must be approached with the greatest possible care.[24]

In addition to the intense reactions identified by Bennett, evidence for the unnaturalness of intercultural contact can be seen in people's everyday behaviors. Many people, including those who do not harbor intense prejudices, admit that interactions with culturally different others tend to be more anxiety provoking than are interactions with very similar people.[25] For a smaller number of people, this anxiety leads to a strong preference for interactions with similar others (a small ingroup) and an active avoidance of intercultural interactions. Such people, however, will not fare well in today's world, where intercultural interaction is increasingly commonplace.

Developing Intercultural Sensitivity

So how do people develop intercultural sensitivity? Of great concern is the relative lack of information most teachers and teacher educators have about intercultural development and sensitivity. Just what is meant by this concept? How do we know when we "have it"? What are the benchmarks that teachers should strive for with their students? If we are to aid peoples' intercultural development, where do we begin to understand how people move from an ethnocentric perspective to one that is more ethnorelative in orientation? These are all legitimate questions and issues to consider.

Researchers and practitioners in the fields of intercultural communication and training have something concrete to offer teachers and teacher educators when it comes to understanding how people develop intercultural competence. Bennett's developmental model of intercultural sensitivity (DMIS),[26] for instance, provides a framework for understanding individual development and awareness along a continuum from highly ethnocentric to highly ethnorelative, and this framework can help us better understand some of the dynamics that might occur in stages 5 and 6 in Banks's model of ethnic identity development. In explaining the DMIS, Bennett notes that an increase in cultural awareness is accompanied by improved cognitive sophistication. Specifically, as people's ability to understand difference increases, so does their ability to negotiate a variety of worldviews. As a six-stage model that describes the experience of cultural difference, the DMIS is linear to the extent that it allows us to address the question, "So, what do we do next?" Such a model provides a valuable tool to educators of both young people and adults as they struggle to achieve greater cross-cultural sensitivity.

The DMIS is based in grounded theory from the observations of thousands of subjects who appeared to develop in similar ways. Three stages lie on the ethnocentric side of the continuum, and three stages reflect increasingly ethnorelative perspectives and skills. The DMIS is a constructivist model, which helps us to better understand the complex phenomenon of culture and intercultural experience, and it explores the "experience or complexity, of difference." There is a strong affective dimension at most levels, especially in the early stages. As people move through the stages, their worldview becomes increasingly complex. On the ethnocentric side, an individual may be at denial, defense, or minimization. On the ethnorelative side, an individual may be at acceptance, adaptability, or integration.

Ethnocentric Stages of the DMIS

Denial

Denial, the inability to see cultural differences, is evident when individuals isolate or separate themselves in homogenous groups. Individuals at this stage ignore the reality of diversity and are often characterized by well-meant, but ignorant, stereotyping and superficial statements of tolerance. At this stage, an individual's construal of difference is minimal. Cultural difference is sometimes attributed to a deficiency in intelligence or personality. There is a tendency to dehumanize outsiders, viewing them as simple, undifferentiated aspects or objects of their environment, thus making them easy targets for discrimination, exploitation, or conquer.

At a societal level the denial stage can be exemplified by separatists, such as under apartheid in South Africa or segregation in the southern United States. Such people may have a very complex experience and many categories for dealing with their own reality, but they have limited, if any, experience and few categories for dealing with cultural difference. When experiencing difference, people in this stage tend to organize others in terms of already existing categories. They have a tendency to see others and the world as subversions of themselves and their own world. People in this stage emphasize familiar categories; they just don't see the differences.

If they are Americans in Paris, for instance, they have an "American" experience and say things like, "Paris is like the United States—cars, tall buildings, McDonald's." If thinking about immigrants, a person in denial sees major issues rather simplistically. Because they have the category of language differences (a general understanding), but not of assimilation or adjustment (a specific and more complex issue), they may support language development programs as a means to deal with the problem. While such efforts may be helpful on the surface, they tend to ignore other, more fundamental aspects of the groups' problems (such as racism and discrimination).

Bennett calls this stage the "stupid questions syndrome." People in denial tend to have a few, say perhaps four, ideas or pieces of stereotypic knowledge about a country or culture. Consider Africa. The stereotypic knowledge many European Americans have about Africa might include wild animals, poverty, black people, and jungle. Everything about Africa, then, is thought of in terms of these four ideas. When this individual meets an African, all these images come to the forefront. Such a person may think or ask, "So, when you leave your hut in the morning, aren't you afraid the wild animals from the jungle will attack you?"

Stop for a moment and think about the categories many people around the world might have of Americans. Do they tend to see Americans as overweight (lovers of fast food), lazy, and rich and as driving big cars? If so, this person from overseas, when meeting an American, might ask, "So, when you leave your big house in the morning, do you get in your big car and drive to McDonald's for your big breakfast?" They are bringing forth all their stereotypic information in their judgment of an American.

Outside of one's own context, things are rather fuzzy. People in denial see others as living in a different reality and, without having much knowledge of those people, may say such things as:

"Live and let live! That's what I say. Mixing just causes trouble."

"Business is business the world over."

"As long as they all speak English, there will be no problem."

"Technology doesn't care about culture."

"They were born here, so they should know how to do it the American way."

"With my experience, I can be successful in any culture without any special effort."

"I never experience culture shock."

Denial has profound consequences, and when people at this stage are brought together with others, unpleasant things can occur. Because these people have many categories for dealing with their own culture, but few, if any, for dealing with other cultures, they may have only one single category for foreigners—"people of culture." The title of a recent book on the Cambodian experience, *To Destroy You Is No Loss: The Odyssey of a Cambodian Family*, captures an extreme sentiment of someone in this stage.[27] An orientation such as this can lead to atrocities like the Holocaust, the recent wave of killings in Rwanda and Burundi, or the "ethnic cleansing" in the former Yugoslavia. People begin to believe that other people do not have feelings like they have, and they then treat those people as less than human.

Children in this stage are socialized that theirs is *the* view of the world, instead of learning that theirs is *one* view of the world. And while their thinking isn't necessarily evil, it is ignorant, and their behavior can become evil. Individuals at this stage are not capable of thinking about difference and must discover commonalties among people before they can move on. Moving individuals from this stage to the next involves helping them develop better skills of category discrimination and thus help them become more sophisticated in their thinking and more complex in their cognitive processing.

Defense

Defense is the next stage of the DMIS. Movement into this stage is driven by the inadequacies of the existing rudimentary categories. This stage is characterized by a recognition of cultural difference coupled with negative evaluations of most variations from one's familiar culture. The greater the cultural difference observed, the more negative the accompanying evaluation. Strong dualistic us-them thinking is common in this stage and is often accompanied by overt negative stereotyping. When forced into contact with others, individuals in this stage often become defensive. They tend to reflect a feeling that "we're all becoming the same" or "the world is becoming American after all." People at this stage generally separate themselves from others *because they don't have categories for dealing with difference.* Although they are beginning to develop a more differentiated view of others, they tend to have a "hardening of the categories" and a narrow focus on a small, typically elite sample of a society. Such people thus defend their way as the one best way.

Three areas of defense are typically found: denigration or derogation, superiority, and sometimes reversal. Denigration or derogation refers to belittling or actively discriminating against another person. Superiority assumes extreme ethnocentrism to the point where one looks down on another. Reversal refers to changing sides or evaluating one's own culture as inferior to another and identifying with the new one. In an intercultural context reversal is often referred to as "going native." Individuals in the defense stage who display reversal tendencies may avoid contact with fellow citizens and associate solely with host nationals. In the racial identity models discussed earlier in this chapter, such behavior might reflect the pre-encounter stage.

Defense protects an individual's own worldview of the possibilities of other realities. No longer hidden away, other (meaning different) people suddenly become a force to be reckoned with. Individuals at this stage tend to develop a polarized worldview. They put up a fence and raise their own flag, so to speak, and keep others at a distance. Such a scenario results in an us-them situation and may lead to the formation of militia groups or gangs. Both sides, the dominant group as well as the minority group, act to protect their own position. In reversal, nothing changes in one's worldview; one just changes sides and acquires the prejudices of the other group.

People in the defense stage may make statements such as the following:

"Genetically, they just don't have the capability to understand these things."

"The only way I can live around them is to spend most of my time at the expatriate (or country) club."

"We invented this stuff, and we're really the only ones who can make it work."

"This company was built on our values, so our opinions are the most important."

"These are American schools and they've worked really well for us. Others should just learn to do it our way."

"I am so embarrassed by my fellow citizens that I spend all my time with the locals." (This statement is an example of reversal.)

"Some people (like us) are the creators, and others (like them) are the consumers."

"Women are naturally passive so they wouldn't fit at this level."

"Asians are not assertive, hence they are poor leaders."

It's not uncommon for people to be in the defense stage, but they must be encouraged to move on. Because defense is a heavy affective state, people need to be supported in this stage. Developmental tasks require supporting people affectively while stressing the commonalities among people. People moving from this stage begin to say such things as "We're all in this together" and "We all came in different boats—but we're now in this one together." When considering how to move people from this stage, start with learning style and other inventories that demonstrate that all individuals and groups have differences. The eighteen-theme culture-general model also works well here.

Minimization

Movement from defense to minimization comes with the discovery of commonality. People begin to recognize and accept superficial cultural differences such as eating customs, money, and so forth, while they continue to hold the belief that all human beings are essentially the same. The emphasis at this stage is on the similarity of people and the commonality of basic values, with the tendency to define the basis of commonality in ethnocentric terms (i.e., "since everyone is essentially the same, they're really pretty much like me"). This perceived commonality could exist around physical universalism ("We are all the same—we all eat, sleep, breathe, bleed red, and die"; "We are all people of color after all") or around spiritual universalism ("Deep down we are all children of the same God, whether we know it or not").

Minimization is a very profound stage. There is evidence to suggest that most teachers are at this stage —and they are pleased to be here because they have transcended defense. It thus becomes difficult to move people from this stage, because they think they are doing okay. This stage, for instance, can become official institutional policy, which can be problematic as people tend to be "nice but color blind." Individuals at the minimization stage see people as basically the same, with little recognition of the differences that in fact do exist. People at this stage tend not to make reference to physical characteristics (race, for instance), believing that such characteristics are not important if they just treat all people the same. In minimization, people ignore the influence of culture and lived experience that may be quite different among people. They tend toward a belief that all people have the same needs—but in reality they don't.

In this stage exists an ethnocentric assumption that everyone should share one's own reality. People say and believe such things as, "If everyone knew of my religion, they'd all want to follow it." In schools, people might say, "They came to this country so they know we must have the best education system." At the corporate level, people may say, "We should introduce shopping malls everywhere because they work so well," or "We couldn't survive without computers." Internationally you might hear people say, "Australia is just like the United States, only twenty years behind." But you must keep in mind that everyone in the world does not aspire to be American.

At the minimization stage people may say such things as:

"The key to getting along in any culture is to just be yourself—authentic and honest."

"Customs differ, of course, but when you really get to know them they're pretty much like us."

"I have this intuitive sense of other people, no matter what their culture."

"Technology is bringing cultural uniformity to the underdeveloped world."

"No matter what their culture, people are pretty much motivated by the same things."

"If people are really honest with themselves, they'd recognize that some values are universal."

"It's a small world after all."

" I don't see any difference—race, gender or culture. We're all just people."

The developmental task to move people out of this stage is cultural self-awareness. Point out aspects of an individual's own culture and show how it might differ from another person's. However, resistance among people might develop around such things as strongly held values. Cultural awareness does not mean that people must like and accept everything; it is not a case of "anything goes." People can maintain a moral compass by contextualizing another's behavior and beliefs. Take nudity, for example. Is it appropriate to take off your clothes? Well, it matters—the context is critical. In certain circumstances it is appropriate to take off your clothes (as in the shower), but in other circumstance (out in public), perhaps not. The context legitimates the behavior. Culture thus becomes the context from which to explore another's values. When the context is set then individuals can decide if they will behave according to that context. Once cultural awareness is achieved, the person can move from minimization to acceptance.

Although minimization is the most advanced stage of the ethnocentric side of the DMIS continuum, people at this stage often negate the importance and value of cultural difference and tend to believe that "people are all alike," meaning that "everyone is just like me." Individuals at the minimization stage tend to see people as basically the same and make little recognition of the differences that are significant, that continue to divide people, and that underlie most intercultural interactions.

Bennett asserts that a paradigmatic shift in thinking must occur for an individual to move into the ethnorelative stages. Movement into the ethnorelative stages represents a significant change in one's view of difference, from something to be avoided to something to be sought out. Individuals in the ethnorelative stage search for ways to adapt to difference and begin to recognize that people live in culturally different contexts. The notion of context is not understood in ethnocentric stages.

Ethnorelative Stages of the DMIS

Acceptance

The first ethnorelative stage, acceptance of difference, represents an individual's ability to recognize and appreciate cultural difference in terms of both people's values and their behavior. Acceptance of cultural differences is seen as providing viable alternative solutions to the way people organize their existence and experience.

At this stage, the individual is beginning to demonstrate the ability to interpret phenomena within a cultural context and to analyze complex interactions in culture-contrast terms. Categories of difference are consciously elaborated. People at this stage say such things as, "They're not good or bad, just different." Later, the individual can

Activity 18: Learning about Others

see those beliefs, values, and other general patterns of assigning "goodness" and "bad-ness" to ways of being in the world that exist in all cultural contexts. People in this stage also begin to seek out cultural difference.

Acceptance, by the way, does not mean agreement. People may have respect and value for cultural differences, but do not necessarily agree with all they see. It is here that people begin to discriminate—they have "taste." People do have individual tastes and preferences, and not all cultures or cultural practices will be liked or valued by all people (the cultural belief that the role of all women should focus on home and family, for instance, is not universally accepted). The more sophisticated knowledge you pos-sess in a category, the more personal preference you can bring (as a wine connoisseur is able to do). This behavior is not ethnocentric as long as you assume that the other is equally complex and acceptable within a given context. While people find that they may not necessarily agree with all they see practiced within another culture, they can, at least, understand what they witness. Teachers at this stage, for instance, might under-stand that family or other collective influences may be greater for a Latino or Asian child than for an Anglo counterpart, and this understanding may temper their expecta-tion that students make their own independent choices on major life decisions. They may then seek out ways to work more closely with a student's family.

People in this stage may say things like:

"The more difference the better – more difference equals more creative ideas."

"You certainly wouldn't want to be around the same kind of people all the time—the ideas get stale, and besides, it's boring."

"I always try to study about a new culture before I go there or interact with the people."

"The more cultures you know about, the better comparisons you can make."

"Sometimes it's confusing, knowing that values are different in various cultures and wanting to be respectful, but still wanting to maintain my own core values."

"I know that my African American students and their families, and I, a European American man, have had very different life experiences, but we're working together as a learning community."

"Our new student is from Mexico. Where can I learn about Mexican culture so I can be more effective in the classroom?"

But acceptance alone is not sufficient to drive effectiveness with another culture. It is necessary to develop new skills in order to be more effective teachers or businesspeople.

Adaptation

Activity 36: Using the Interpersonal Grid to Expand Intercultural Understanding

In the next stage, adaptation, individuals begin to see cultural categories as more flexi-ble and become more competent in their ability to communicate across cultures. Indi-viduals are able to use empathy effectively, communicate cross-culturally, shift frames of reference and are better able to understand others and be understood across cultural boundaries.

Movement into this stage is driven by a need for action (better teaching, more profit) and cognitive empathy—the ability to change frames of reference. A significant amount of groundwork must be laid before a shift can occur and people are ready to learn new skills. The greater the cultural gap, the more difficult it will be to make the shift. The individual begins to experience reality in a more "other" way and can understand and feel about the world as the other would.

Two forms of adaptation exist: cultural adaptation and behavioral adaptation. Cultural adaptation refers to the ability to consciously shift perspective into alternative cultural worldview elements and to use multiple cultural frames of reference in evaluating phenomena. Behavioral adaptation refers to the internalization of more than one complete worldview. Behavior can shift completely into different frames without much conscious effort, and individuals can act in culturally appropriate ways. At this stage individuals say they are becoming bicultural or multicultural. Teachers at this stage, for instance, will be able to modify their responses to and expectations of students from lower versus middle socioeconomic groups as necessary when it comes to students' ability to participate in after-school extracurricular activities. Fellow students may understand that the needs of refugee students are quite distinct from those of international exchange students—even though they may both be from abroad—and will, in turn, respond differently to them.

But at this stage people are not simply acquiring skills. Nor are they simply regurgitating lists of dos and don'ts; this reaction creates emulation, not empathy. Knowledge and behavior here are linked by conscious intention. Category boundaries become more flexible and permeable, and intentional perspective taking and empathy occur.

In the adaptation stage, people may say such things as:

"To really help this student learn, I'm going to have to change my approach."

"I know they're really trying hard to adapt to my style, so it's only fair and right that I try to meet them halfway."

"I interact with my male and female colleagues somewhat differently to account for differences in the way respect is communicated."

"I can maintain my values and also behave in culturally appropriate ways."

"To solve this dispute, I need to change my behavior to account for the differences in status between me and my Arab customer."

"I interact with my Latino families from Central and South America differently to account for differences in the way respect and authority are communicated."

Integration

The final stage, integration, while rarely achieved, reflects those individuals who have multiple frames of reference and can identify and move freely within more than one cultural group. Integration refers to the internalization of bicultural or multicultural frames of reference. Individuals at this level are able to mediate between multiple groups. They tend to maintain a definition of self-identity that is marginal to any particular culture and to see themselves as "in process," characterized by acceptance of an identity that is not based in any one culture. People at this level are able to facilitate constructive contact between cultures and tend to become cultural mediators or cultural bridges. This level is a rare and difficult one for people to achieve, and it is difficult to measure.

People at this stage may say such things as:

"Sometimes I don't feel like I fit anywhere."

"Everywhere is home, if you know enough about how things work there."

"I feel most comfortable when I'm bridging differences between the cultures I know."

"Whatever the situation, I can usually look at it from a variety of cultural points of view."

Understanding that intercultural development is an evolutionary and not a revolutionary process should greatly influence the manner in which we educate both children and teacher education students. Intercultural competence is not achieved in one course or one experience. Rather, you recognize where one is on the developmental continuum, and you engage in systematic, oftentimes repetitious, and well-planned exposure to intercultural interactions that are designed to nudge one to increasingly complex levels. Moving too quickly along the continuum is akin to the scuba diver plunging immediately to a depth of 100 feet without taking the requisite time to equalize pressure and accommodate to the new environment—the shock can just be too great for the body to accept. Alternatively, gradual movement or immersion enables the diver to adjust to the changing circumstances and thus to function more effectively in the new environment. So too should it be with intercultural development. Understanding and integrating what we know about intercultural development and sensitivity into the education of young people and teachers will result in a more culturally effective and culturally competent citizenry.

Critical Incidents at Maplewood

The case study introduced at the beginning of the chapter ended with Sue Murray asking, "I wonder how my teaching team feels?" This chapter's Critical Incidents are perspectives from other teachers in Maplewood school. At the end of each, you will be asked to categorize the teacher's orientation according to the DMIS.

John Reading, Fifth Grade Social Studies and Language Arts Teacher

I'm in "seventh heaven," you could say. I came into the teaching field after spending two years as a Peace Corps volunteer teaching English in Kenya. It was the best two years of my life. I learned to speak Kiswahili fairly well and had a chance to teach in both a secondary school and a local teachers' college. I spent weekends working with younger children in the village in which I lived. We did general maintenance around the village, started all kinds of community action projects such as building a public shower, and organized a variety of community artists to showcase the local culture. That experience changed my life.

I grew up in a community not far from where I now teach. In many ways it was quite similar to this one—there were few minorities, although that has changed over time. I didn't have too many friends who were different from me—we were all pretty much the same. Not much diversity they'd say now, although that wasn't a term we used back then. We were all just "normal," I guess you'd say.

I became interested in the Peace Corps after many years of learning about different people in general. As a little kid I remember looking at *National Geographic* magazine at my uncle's house. He was a geologist and taught at a local community college. I was interested in the pictures—the different ways people dressed, or didn't dress. I was intrigued by the various ways people decorated themselves—from their jewelry to tattoos and body painting to body piercing. I guess even kids in this country today, when you think about how they pierce or tattoo their bodies, have much in common with some of the people I would read about then. But most kids probably wouldn't see the similarity.

In high school, I was active in the Exchange Student Club. I could never afford to be an exchange student myself, but I was always interested in other people. Then, I had one teacher, Mr. Philips, my eleventh grade English teacher, who had spent two years in Thailand as a Peace Corps volunteer. I was really intrigued by him and his experience. It was then that I began thinking about doing that myself. I applied during my student teaching semester and was accepted to the program in Kenya.

What an eye-opener that two-year experience was for me. I changed more in that time than I ever could have imagined. I became really attached to the people in my village. I'm now trying to arrange to have a more formal link between the village school and our school, but I haven't yet been able to raise enough money to do anything substantial.

I now want all my students to have similar experiences. But you know, it's hard to do. When I returned from Kenya most of my family and friends weren't very interested in hearing about my experiences—they wanted me to just fit right back into how I used to be and the way they were. But I couldn't. I had changed too much. Many of the things they were interested in seemed rather unimportant to me. This created some friction between my friends and me for a while. The Peace Corps tried to warn us about this problem when we returned. They said we would experience kind of a reverse culture shock, that coming back home would be difficult because we had changed so much and most others at home had not. Boy, were they right! I keep in closer contact with many of my old Peace Corps friends now than I do my older friends from home. Perhaps here in the school I can do something that can make a difference in the way young people view others. That's why I'm kind of glad all this discussion about diversity is happening now. I think it's a wake-up call that, if we're not prepared for it, will bring all kinds of trouble. There is a place for us as teachers to work with young people on these issues. Not only can I share some of my experiences, but perhaps I can create experiences for the students themselves that will help to introduce them to others in their world in a more personal and substantial way. I think it's critically important that people learn how to view the world from more than one perspective, and I hope to be able to develop this ability in my students. They have to begin to understand the plight of the world's indigenous peoples, understand the experiences of the African American and Native American in this country, and show greater concern for the environment. And teaching is a great vehicle from which to do this. I'm beginning to feel most comfortable when I'm helping people see the world around them from another perspective—kind of as a bridge builder. I can now look at most situations from at least two cultures' points of view. I think young people today need this mindset as well.

- Where on the continuum of the DMIS would you place John?
- What kinds of activities might John do with his current students that would build on his experiences in Kenya?

Fran Violet, Fifth Grade Language Arts Teacher

I'm really getting tired of all the commotion, although I won't come out and say it to too many people. I feel like an outsider at some of the teachers' meetings we've had. There seem to be two camps developing among the staff. There are those who are in favor of making changes to address the so-called needs of other groups, and others, like myself, who are rather quiet and in the background continuing to do a good job, or so we believe, just teaching kids. I've been teaching in the district for twenty-five years now and have seen all kinds of educational fads come and go. I'm pretty sure this attention to culture will just do the same. After all, we only have so much time in the day to teach all that we are supposed to teach. And there's such an emphasis today on competency tests, which don't even measure multicultural education. It's probably only a matter of time until all the hoopla dies down. It even angers me when I think that I've had to attend after-school workshops on multicultural education. They really didn't teach me anything I could use. They were more of a gripe session presented by some people who had a bunch of complaints to make. Then they handed us a list of multicultural books we should have the kids read. Come on. Give me a break. Do they really expect me to become motivated by that?

And the kids! I've seen quite a few changes since I began teaching here. That's what I think the problem is. It's not about culture. Yes, it's true that there are more minority children in the school now than there were a number of years ago. But the problem, as I see it, is about kids and their families. It doesn't matter what a child's cultural background is. I look at kids pretty much the same. Sure there are some differences, like some just pick things up quicker than others do. Some are better in certain subjects than others. Some are better in sports, or art, or music. But all in all, kids are basically the same. I want them all to succeed in school, and I do my best to teach them all. While people's cultures may differ, once you get down to it, kids are kids, and all people are pretty much the same. All people, after all, have the same basic needs. I have a general sense of other people; no matter what culture they are from, I can usually read them pretty well. If kids don't have a solid, stable family, then that's where there's going to be trouble. There has been such an increase in the number of children coming from broken families. Why, one year I had twenty out of twenty-eight kids who came from some sort of rearranged family. If you ask me, that's where the problem lies.

- Where on the continuum of the DMIS would you place Fran?
- What suggestions might you make to Fran to help her advance along the DMIS continuum?

critical incident

Steven Goodwin, Principal

Ever since I became principal of this school six years ago, I have been on a continuous learning curve. I had no preparation in college for issues of diversity. It wasn't even talked about when I first went to school twenty years ago. It's kind of been "trial by fire," you might say. As our community changed and as I became more involved in school administration, I suddenly had so many new things to which I had to adjust. I had training to be a school principal at a nearby university, but most of that training focused on leadership and management from a dominant-culture perspective. My professors were from, I guess you would say, the "old school," where everything was supposed to fit one particular orientation. But I quickly learned that things are different in the real world. Ever since our community demographics began to change and people began moving from the city to our suburb, the rules have never quite been the same. And I think I'm beginning to understand it quite well—although it still requires a lot of work on my part. And I'm not sure I always get it right.

Take this recent dispute, for instance. This community has always supported the local sports teams. Even our high school mascot is an Indian, and no one questioned it since it became part of our culture some sixty years ago. That is, until this year. And I'm beginning to understand the other side of the coin now. I guess the more time I spend with people from other groups and learn about their cultures, the more I begin to understand their point of view, their language, and their way of interacting. For so many years, all people have been forced to adapt to one mainstream point of view—like it or not! And I guess for the most part, at least for so many years, people tried pretty hard to adapt. Some might say they were forced to adapt. For many years we called it the "melting pot," all people were to become like the majority culture. For some it worked. As I understand it, and it makes sense to me, it was fairly easy for most European immigrants to fit into the mainstream culture in the early part of the 1900s. Most came from similar language backgrounds—at least they were all European—and shared relatively similar ways of life. Once they learned the English language, their physical features allowed them to pretty much fit right into the mainstream. And then their foods became part of the national diet, like Italian, Polish or German influences.

Many other immigrants, however, had quite different experiences. African Americans were forced or involuntary immigrants, never wanting to be here in the first place. And today, most immigrants come from countries whose languages, ethnicity, skin color, and general way of life are significantly different—not only from the mainstream, but from one another as well. This alone makes it very difficult for people to "just fit right in."

I guess I look at it this way. So many people have been struggling to adapt to our way of life for so long that it's only fair that we now try to make some changes. I guess for me that means that many people in the schools have been trying hard to adapt to my style that it's only fair that I try to meet them halfway. To solve some of the problems we face in our school and community, I'm going to have to change my approach. I'm beginning to understand that I can maintain my own culture's values, but at the same time I can learn to behave in ways that are appropriate for another culture. Now it's getting easier for me to say that about my behavior. But I recognize that for many others in the school community, including parents as well as some of the teachers, the situation is not so clear. Many of them are threatened and are not sure how to make the changes. I'm working real hard, in addition to all the other things I have to stay on top of, to encourage this school community to face these issues and address them in positive ways. I also recognize that I will have to continue to be a role model for others to demonstrate how this diversity can be accomplished. I constantly try to learn about other people and account for cultural differences in my interactions with them and to help our school community do the same.

- Where on the continuum of the DMIS would you place Steven?
- What are some things Steven might do to encourage development among his school community, especially among the more resistant teachers and families?

Summary

This chapter presents historical developments as they relate to the establishment of multicultural education in the United States. A survey of approaches to multicultural education currently in practice suggests that there are numerous ways in which people approach the topic. Fundamental to effective multicultural education is an understanding of the manner in which people develop their racial and/or ethnic identity and, in particular, intercultural development—how they develop their ability to understand and interact more effectively with people different from themselves. The Developmental Model of Intercultural Sensitivity (DMIS) was introduced as one means to understand how people can grow from being ethnocentric to becoming more ethnorelative in their orientation.

 # Chapter Review

Go to the Online Learning Center at **www.mhhe.com/Cushner4e** to review important content from the chapter, practice with key terms, take a chapter quiz, and find the web links listed in this chapter.

Key Terms

Anglo-conformity   113

Assimilationist model   113

Cultural pluralism   114

Ethnic identity   109

Racial identity   110

Racial profiling   110

Social reconstructionist   118

Reflective Questions

1. Return to the case study introduced at the beginning of the chapter. Where on the continuum of the DMIS would you place each of the individuals: Sue Murray, John Jameson, Rebecca Reynolds, Joyce Maples? Justify your decisions.
2. Draft a brief response to each of the three who wrote letters to the editor: John Jameson, Rebecca Reynolds, and Joyce Maples. As a teacher, what would you emphasize in your response?
3. Where on the DMIS would you place yourself? What criteria are you using to make your judgment?
4. Early in the chapter it is stated that while you may identify as a member of an ethnic group but not think of yourself in racial terms, the opposite can also be true. Can you provide examples from each perspective?
5. Differentiate race from ethnicity, and provide clear examples from each category. Then, provide one or two examples where there might be confusion between these terms.

References

1. E. H. Erikson, *Identity, Youth, and Crisis* (New York: Norton, 1968).

2. L. Kohlberg, *Stages in the Development of Moral Thought and Action* (New York: Holt, Rinehart and Winston, 1969).

3. J. Piaget, "The Theory of Stages in Cognitive Development," In *Measurement and Piaget,* ed. D. R. Green (New York: McGraw-Hill, 1971).

4. C. Grant, and G. Ladson-Billings, eds., *Dictionary of Multicultural Education* (Phoenix, AZ: Oryx, 1997), p. 106.

5. W. E. Cross Jr., *Shades of Black: Diversity in African-American Identity* (Philadelphia: Temple University Press, 1991).

6. J. Spring, *The Intersection of Cultures: Multicultural Education in the United States and the Global Economy* (New York: McGraw-Hill, 2000).

7. Ibid.

8. J. Banks, *Multiethnic Education: Theory and Practice,* 2nd ed. (Newton, MA: Allyn and Bacon, 1988).

9. Cross, *Shades of Black.*

10. Banks, *Multiethnic Education.*

11. Cross, *Shades of Black.*

12. Cited by Robert Trujillo in "Bilingual-Bicultural Education: A Necessary Strategy for American Public Education," in *A Relook at Tuscon '66 and Beyond,* report of a National Bilingual Bicultural Institute (Washington, DC: National Education Association, 1973), p. 21.

13. Israel Zangwill, *The Melting Pot* (New York: Macmillan, 1909), p. 37.

14. Banks, *Multiethnic Education.*

15. Ibid.

16. Christine Sleeter and Carl Grant, "An Analysis of Multicultural Education in the United States," *Harvard Educational Review* 57, 4 (November 1987): 421–444.

17. Christine Sleeter and Carl Grant, "Educational Equity, Education That Is Multicultural and Social Reconstructionist," *Journal of Educational Equity and Leadership* 6, 2 (1986): 105–118.

18. Ibid.

19. J. Ogbu, *The Next Generation: An Ethnography of Education in an Urban Neighborhood* (New York: Academic Press, 1974), p. 99.

20. Cameron Mitchell, *Multicultural Approaches to Racial Inequality in the United States* (Baton Rouge: Louisiana State University, 1989), typescript. This work is also the source of all subsequent quotations in the three sections that describe his models.

21. Ibid.

22. Cited in Richard Brislin and Tomoko Yoshida, *Intercultural Communication Training: An Instruction* (Thousand Oaks, CA: Sage, 1994).

23. M. J. Bennett, "Towards Ethnorelativism: A Developmental Model of Intercultural Sensitivity" in M. Paige, (Ed.), *Cross-Cultural Orientation*, ed. M. Paige (Lanham, MD: University Press of America, 1993), pp. 27–69).

24. Ibid., p. 21.

25. K. Cushner and R. Brislin, *Intercultural Interactions: A Practical Guide,* 2nd ed (Thousand Oaks, CA: Sage, 1996).

26. Bennett, "Towards Ethnorelativism."

27. J. Criddle, *To Destroy You Is No Loss: The Odyssey of a Cambodian Family* (Providence, UT: East/West Bridge Publishing House, 1996).

part two

Multicultural Teaching in Action

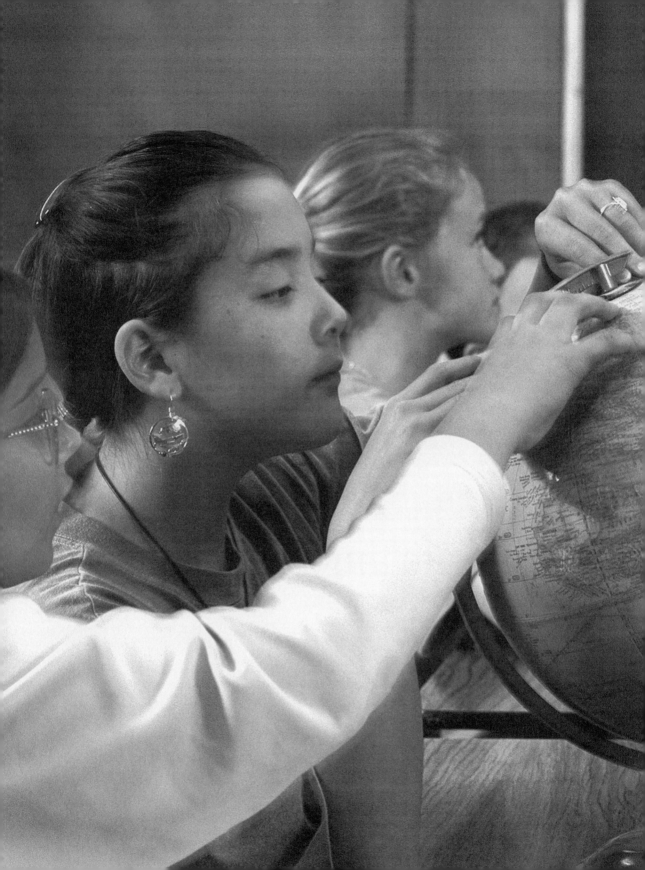

The Classroom as a Global Community:
Nationality and Region

> *We are living in a new age which itself is defined*
> *by the fact that challenges we face do not*
> *respect any conventional boundaries.*
> *They don't respect geographical boundaries*
> *and they don't respect old definitions*
>
> —*Richard F. Celeste*

C h a p t e r   O u t l i n e

focus questions

1. How have the attacks of September 11, 2001, altered what we do in schools?

2. What does it mean to be a globally connected society? What are some powerful concepts that underlie an international or global perspective?

3. What are some practical strategies that can be used to prepare students to better understand and interact with others around the world?

case study   A Global Classroom

It was 8:00 on a Tuesday morning in early February as Jerome Becker rushes into the front office with good news. Yesterday's mail had brought the package his class had been anxiously awaiting—a completed story from a school in southern India. Now he would be able to share its contents with the class. Jerome was eager to tell his principal, Mrs. Lewis, because she had seemed so certain that this project would fail and that the children would be let down. Well, this time it hadn't, and Jerome was delighted.

The school year had started with great difficulties. Within two weeks of the start of the school year the entire school, along with many other schools in the world, watched in horror as the World Trade Center and Pentagon were attacked by terrorists. Thousands of innocent lives were lost before everyone's eyes. For the first time, Americans watched helplessly as their world of predictability and security was transformed to a new degree of uncertainty and horror. The very strengths of the United States—the openness, trust, and freedoms that people had come to expect—suddenly became its greatest weaknesses and were replaced with fear, paranoia, and uncertainty. People responded to the tragedy with anger, resentment, fear, and mistrust.

Throughout the previous summer, children in the district had been in an increasing number of confrontations with one another in the malls, on playgrounds, even on recreation department ball fields. Vandalism and fighting, which had been relatively unheard of in this community of 60,000 in the suburbs of Grand Rapids, suddenly were appearing with far greater frequency. The troubles that people had read about in other major cities no longer seemed to pass by this peaceful area of Michigan; they had become an increasing part of the local picture. The problems didn't end with the summer; they came right into the classroom in full force with the new sixth grade class— name-calling, fighting, and threats of gangs. But tensions that at the start of the year seemed especially strong between the African American students and European American students suddenly had less significance. Now, a more common enemy was identified that seemed to bring most of the students together. And this development worried

Jerome even more. His students, like many other Americans, found it very difficult to differentiate between the many Arabs and Muslims who had lived in and around the state for years and had become trusted members of many communities and the Arab terrorists that were portrayed in the daily news as the perpetrators of the September 11 atrocity. Arabs and Muslims became the targets of much hatred, prejudice, and discrimination across the nation, and the hatred was finding its way into the classroom almost on a daily basis. Jerome saw that now was obviously an opportune time to address these critical issues in a very real manner, but he was unsure about how to do this in the most effective way. There were no textbooks available to guide a teacher through such a process, and he just was not certain where, and how, to begin.

After a couple of weeks, just after the U.S. bombing raid in Afghanistan began, Jerome decided that he just had to attempt something—it was time to alter the course of events in his classroom. He had taken some workshops in multicultural education, global education, and cooperative learning over the past few summers and was eager to try some of the strategies he had studied. He was also beginning to integrate various parts of his elementary curriculum; he saw several opportunities to link language arts, social studies, and the arts. He was even willing to try to integrate other areas of the curriculum while exploring how he might add a global perspective. After all, he had nothing to lose and everything to gain in his attempts to bring some peace to the class and to help his students live more peacefully with one another.

Because several of his students were first-generation children whose parents had recently immigrated to the United States, Jerome decided that an international perspective might provide them with concepts and activities that would cut across the various ethnicities and nationalities in his class. An international approach could also help his students better understand the circumstances faced by many of the Muslims and Arabs in the community. With this goal in mind, Jerome began with a unit on immigration that he hoped would develop empathy in his students for newcomers to this country. He also hoped this sense of empathy would be applied to the relatives and ancestors of students with long roots in America. An activity on immigration might also serve to bring the group together as they explored both the similarities and differences in their backgrounds. He asked his students to go home and interview family members about their own or their ancestors' experiences coming to this country, asking them to inquire specifically about the following topics:

**Activity 9
Family Tree:
Tracing One's
Roots and
Family History**

1. From what country did your ancestors come?
2. When did they leave their country of birth?
3. Why did they leave that place?
4. What was their experience when they first came to this country? Do people remember any hardships? Were any stereotypes and prejudice directed at them?
5. Where did they first arrive in this country?
6. How did they come to live in Michigan? When did they come here, and why?
7. Are there any traditions from the home country that are still practiced?
8. What makes our people unique in this country today?

A week later, Jerome had students come to the front of the room, share their stories, and locate their family's place of origin on the world map. He gave them each a

Table 5-1   Jerome Becker's Sixth Grade Class (Gender/Ethnicity/Origin)

Males	Ethnicity	Origin	Generation
Tony	Italian American	Italy	3rd
Karl	Danish American	Denmark	3rd
Guy	Scandinavian American	Sweden/Finland	hundreds of years
Bart	Irish American	Ireland	3rd
Mark	African American	West Africa	7th
Steve	Exact ethnicity unknown	Adopted at birth.	Adopted family is 3rd generation German
Ahmed	Jordanian	Jordan	1st
Peter	Hungarian American	Hungary	3rd
David	Native American and Polish	USA and Poland	mixed
Allen	European American	France, England, and Germany	6th
Kamal	African American	West Africa	7th or 8th
Tsuyoshi	Japanese	Hiroshima	short-term/new immigrant
Lenny	African American	West Africa	9th
Paul	Polish American	Poland	4th
Charles	Kenyan	Kenya	short-term/new immigrant

Females	Ethnicity	Origin	Generation
Jenny	Irish American	Ireland	4th
Mary	Irish American	Ireland	2nd
Hannah	Polish American	Poland	3rd
Gwendolyn	African American	West Africa	7th
Evgenia	Russian American	Russia	1st
Yoshiko	Japanese	Japan	short-term/new immigrant
Ronelle	Afrikaner and English	South Africa	short-term/new immigrant
Mariam	Lebanese American	Lebanon	1st
Susan	German American	Germany	3rd
Rebecca	European-American	Germany and Poland	3rd or 4th
Maria	Italian American	Italy	4th
Kathy	Danish American	Denmark	3rd
Monisha	Indian American	India	1st

piece of yarn, and as they located their country of origin, he asked them to attach it to the map at that country and extend the yarn to Grand Rapids. He was surprised by the results of this exercise. Table 5-1 shows the origins of his students.

A Sensitive Assignment

When Jerome asked his students to trace their ancestry and present their findings to the class, he was taken aback by Kamal's response. Jerome knew that Kamal's family was, perhaps more than many African American families in the school, emphasizing their African heritage with their children. Kamal stood up and, with a certain anger in his words, stated, "I'm African, and I don't know my exact heritage. You see, you white folks took my people from their lands, mixed us up with all the other Africans you stole, and now lump us all together. My father tells me that African American people come from more than fifteen different tribes in West Africa, and we don't even know which ones we belong to. That's why there's so much confusion in the world today. We've been stripped of our heritage."

- Jerome was not quite sure how to respond to Kamal. If you were Jerome, (1) what feelings might you be experiencing? (2) how would you initially respond to Kamal? (3) what advice would you offer to teachers who might do a similar exercise?

The discussion that followed the presentations was enlightening for both Jerome and his students. He was not surprised to see many of the students stand up and talk about their family history with a sense of pride. For many of them, this was the first time anyone had asked them about their ancestry. It seemed to Jerome that this was also the first time that the students had listened intently to one another's stories. There seemed to be a real sense of contribution for most of the students. They were especially interested in Guy's and Hannah's stories. Some of Guy's ancestors came to this country in the 1600s. He shared stories of people jumping ship off the New England coast and ending up in Vermont. Hannah shared stories of her grandparents' escape from Hitler's armies and how lucky most of her family had been to get out of the Holocaust alive. She did know, however, that two of her relatives had perished in the Holocaust.

What surprised Jerome, however, was the difficulty that some students had with the exercise, especially Steve and Ahmed. At first, Steve avoided participating in the exercise by offering the excuse that he had left his notes at home. The next day, when urged again to participate, Steve stood in front of the class and mumbled something like, "I'm adopted and I don't know anything about my parents." There was complete silence. An awkward moment or two followed, until Jerome quietly said, "My grandfather was adopted too, and he didn't know much about his background either. His adopted family helped him learn about their Polish background, and he grew up in that tradition. Perhaps there are some traditions that your adopted family follow that you can take for your own. What background is your adopted family?"

Steve began to relax when he replied, "Well, I guess they're all German. I mean, my grandparents speak a little German when they visit, and my parents make it a point to go to the Oktoberfest every year. My father really likes it when he has his German beer. They're even talking about visiting Germany in the next couple of years and plan on taking me and my sister. I guess I'm really German, but I'm not sure what it means to be German. I feel very much American, if you know what I mean."

Jerome asked how many others felt more "American" than affiliated with their ethnic ancestry. Almost all the students raised their hands. "Well," said Jerome, "it is good that we all feel American, because we are; but I want you to think about what being American means." He let the matter drop there for a time.

Ahmed's response to the exercise, however, was not as easy for Jerome to handle, but it was exactly what he knew had to occur. Jerome knew that Ahmed's family, and perhaps Mariam's as well, had been under a lot of stress since the attacks. Ahmed's father had kept him home from school the first few days after the attack and had asked Jerome to be especially sensitive to the actions and words of others. Jerome replied that he would and that he too was concerned. Ahmed stood up and, with a certain uneasiness and a few tears, stated, "I'm from Jordan, my father's a doctor, and he came here to study and practice medicine. Now everyone thinks I'm a terrorist and accuses me and my family of being responsible for the attacks in New York and Washington, and we had nothing to do with it. We too cried at our home the day of the attacks. We prayed at the mosque, both for peace and the safety of all of us in America. We're not the enemy. We love this country too, but no one seems to care what I think. Why do you all blame me?"

Jerome, taken aback by Ahmed's strong emotional outburst, wasn't quite sure what to say. At first Jerome remembered feeling a bit uncertain about, and perhaps threatened by, Ahmed's father's comments to him, but after taking a deep breath and pondering the situation for a moment, he could sense the anger and fear that must be felt by those everywhere who have been subjected to prejudice and stereotypes, especially during times of war and national conflict. A similar situation occurred in the United States just after Pearl Harbor was bombed by the Japanese. Except then, almost immediately, Japanese Americans were rounded up and placed in internment camps out of fear that they were the enemy. Although such extreme behavior was not happening this time and although the president of the United States along with many other civic leaders continuously urged understanding and compassion toward our Arab American and Muslim citizens, the apprehensions, tensions, and mistrust could still be felt. Jerome spoke with the class as they all reflected on the changes that had occurred over the past weeks. While most members of the class agreed that they weren't as angry with Arabs in general as they had been immediately after the attacks, Jerome knew there was still quite a lot of work to do to help his students understand and feel more comfortable with Ahmed and Mariam. Perhaps Ahmed's and Mariam's parents would be willing to come to class and share information about their heritage and culture; and both students said they would ask at home. Such presentations might help to build some bridges of understanding and trust, at least within the classroom and school community.

With that, Jerome returned to his desk, feeling that he was at least taking the first steps toward opening up some lines of communication between himself, his students, and their families.

In a larger group discussion of their ancestors, students were asked to identify generalizations in people's presentations and to pose hypotheses to explain what they observed. Peter noticed that most people seemed to come to the United States for better job opportunities, or for more money, as he put it, both in the past and today. A few people came for religious freedoms. Jeremy used this point as an opportunity to discuss religious freedom today for Muslims in America. Kathy noticed that everyone, except for one of David's relatives, came from somewhere else. When encouraged, she went on to suggest that almost everyone was an immigrant at least once in his or her past. Mark, an African American child in the class, reminded everyone that his ancestors didn't come here by choice and perhaps that explained many of the differences that exist between African Americans and other groups. Jerome took this opportunity to discuss with the class the differences between voluntary and involuntary immigration.

Jerome then began to probe into students' feelings about the immigrants they read about in today's news. Most were familiar enough with the Haitian refugees, the situation in Cuba, and the constant debate about Mexicans crossing the border into the United States. A few were aware of immigrant and refugee groups from Southeast Asia and the fact that many whites had left Zimbabwe and were now leaving South Africa. Jerome was hoping that a discussion about the plight of today's refugees and immigrant groups would enable students to identify with their situation and to compare it to that of their own ancestors. A few were able to make this leap, but most only nodded in half-hearted agreement. Jerome was content that perhaps he planted a few seeds for future discussion and activity, which he promised himself he would develop. He ended the discussion by asking the students to read the following parable:

A PARABLE

Once there were three men who had never seen oranges. They had heard many wonderful things about the fruit and wanted very much to have some. The first man set out with excitement. He traveled for many days and began to worry that he would get lost. The farther he went, the more he worried. Finally, he sat under a tree, deep in thought. "No silly fruit is this important," he decided. He got up and turned toward home.

The second man was a very bold fellow. He rushed off, dreaming about oranges as he traveled, and ended up at the same tree. Round orange fruits were all over the ground and in the branches. Thrilled with his success, he grabbed one of the fruits off the ground and bit into it. It was rotten and bitter. "Ugh! What a stupid fruit," he said, and returned home empty-handed.

The third man did research before he left home. He also asked questions of people he met as he traveled. Lo and behold, he found the same tree full of oranges. He examined many oranges and chose one that was not too hard, nor too soft. It was juicy and delicious. He took some seeds home, planted them, and eventually became a famous grower of fruit.

Jerome asked his students to think overnight about the possible meanings of the story. Tomorrow they would begin a writing assignment using this parable to link some of the issues that had been raised in their discussion.

Two months later, the classroom was alive with activity. Ahmed's and Mariam's parents had already been in to share part of their family traditions, as had the parents of three other children. The fact that the sixth grade social studies curriculum looks at world cultures made this project comparatively easy. It was also easy to integrate a number of books on various cultures into the language arts program. Jerome's focus was always on prejudice, discrimination, and how people might overcome the differences that existed between one another. The students had already read such books as "The Diary of Anne Frank" and had viewed and discussed a number of films. They were still to read a few more books by the winter holiday. Jerome had also started a Friday afternoon intercultural forum where students participated in a variety of activities designed to enhance their regular courses while expanding their horizons, always with an eye on how relations with Arab and Muslim students could be enhanced.

Activity and Reading 45: Creating Cross-Cultural Understanding through Internationally Cooperative Story Writing

One particular activity had excited the students so much that it expanded into the whole language arts program and involved all the students in the class. It was the end result of this activity that Jerome had been so excited to share with Mrs. Lewis, the principal. Jerome had read about a particular project, a partnership story project that was designed to integrate language arts, social studies, and cooperative learning.[1] Through small group activity, students in one country organize a story, decide on a topic or problem, identify the main characters as well as a setting, and write the first half of the story. This first half is then mailed to children in another country who are asked to complete the story and translate it into their own language. When completed, the classrooms have an internationally developed product translated in two languages. The book can also be coillustrated. In addition to collaborating on the story, classrooms can exchange a variety of artifacts, photos, letters, and so forth.

Jerome had written to a relative of Monisha's who worked in a school in Madurai, India. She was interested in the story-writing project and was willing to collaborate if Jerome's class would agree to begin the project. The class broke up into three groups, each writing the beginning of a story. Because they had been studying the environmental crisis in social studies, Jerome asked them to build their story line around this topic. Each group started a story. One was an adventure story involving a school of fish in a polluted lake. Another was a mystery involving a missing mineral. The third focused on abuses of the world's wildlife. Then they mailed all three unfinished stories to the Indian sixth grade class.

The students were very excited that morning when Jerome told them that the completed stories had been returned. It had been six weeks since the class mailed their story beginnings to India. Rather than just share the endings that had come back, Jerome decided to turn the activity into a real culture-learning experience by rereading his own students' unfinished stories and then asking them to imagine how they thought the Indian students would complete each story. After Jerome finished reading the first half of each story to his class, he showed them the beautifully written Tamil script and the pictures that the Indian class had used to complete the stories. Following is the first half of the third story written by Jerome's class.

PART ONE (UNITED STATES)

Once in a circus there was a tiger who would not perform because he was lonely. The circus owner sent his daughter, Maryetta, to the jungle to find a friend to perform with the lonely tiger. Maryetta's father gave her $1,000 to purchase a tiger. Her father told her to spend the money wisely.

The next day on a boat trip to the jungle, Maryetta met a trapper named Toby. Toby asked Maryetta why she was going to the jungle. Maryetta told him that she needed to purchase a tiger for her father's circus.

"What a coincidence," Toby remarked, all the while trying to figure out a way he might obtain Maryetta's money before the real trapper could reach her. "I am meeting a girl from a circus tomorrow."

"You are?" Maryetta asked, looking puzzled. "Do you know what circus she is from?"

"No," replied Toby, "but it must be yours. How many girls could there be going to the jungle tomorrow to buy a tiger?"

"I guess you're right. I'll meet you by the river at 10:00 tomorrow morning."

Toby wanted to get there before the real trapper did, so he said, "Why don't we meet at 9:00 and get an early start?"

They agreed to this and then went their own ways. The next day was a beautiful summer day, perfect for trapping tigers. Toby rented a boat and met Maryetta precisely at 9:00.

"I'll need to collect my fee of one hundred dollars each morning before we begin," Toby told Maryetta.

"I thought you told my father your fee was one hundred and fifty dollars per day," Maryetta said, wondering why he had lowered his fee.

"Oh, well, I guess I forgot what I said before. One hundred and fifty dollars it is then," said Toby.

"Alright, but I don't have a lot of money. Do you think we'll be trapping for a long time?"

"Probably only two or three days," Toby reassured. "Well, then, let's get going!" exclaimed Maryetta.

At first, the boat trip down the river was pleasant. About noon, however, the boat struck a huge rock which punctured its side. Maryetta and Toby spent the rest of the day repairing the boat. As a result, they had to spend the night on the river bank.

During the night, Maryetta thought she heard voices. When she peeked out of her tent she saw Toby talking to a wolf. She couldn't believe her eyes or ears! Although she had been raised around the circus and always knew that animals were special, she had never talked to one! She listened intently.

"Go make friends with the tiger and bring him back here," Toby told the wolf.

"When do you want me to bring back that stupid tiger?" asked the wolf.

"Five days from now will be good. Then I will have enough money to buy the secrets I want from the old wizard."

"Okay, I'll see you then," said the wolf, and he crept away.

Maryetta silently closed the flap of her tent and slumped to the ground. Something was very, very wrong. How was she going to get back to the circus safely with the tiger and not let Toby know that she knew he was a fake?

The next morning Toby told Maryetta the boat was fixed.

Toby then said, "I don't want to be rude, but where is my money?"

Maryetta answered, "I'll pay you later." She thought to herself, I have no intention of paying Toby. Toby said, "I want my money now!"

Maryetta said that because the boat accident was not her fault she should not have to pay for the first day. Toby replied, "Well, it's not my fault either, and besides, we had an agreement."

They argued for a while, and Toby finally agreed that Maryetta could pay him later. He told her he would begin to look for the tiger today.

They boarded the boat together to begin the search for the tiger. Along the way they spotted a beautiful tiger being chased by a wolf.

Maryetta said, "Toby, I know you sent the wolf after the tiger and you better make sure the wolf doesn't harm him or you won't be paid!" They anchored the boat and went ashore.

Toby and Maryetta began to chase after the tiger and the wolf. Suddenly, Maryetta tripped over a vine and broke her leg. Toby came along, grabbed Maryetta's money, and ran off with it!

At this point Jerome stopped reading. He asked how many students remembered this half of the story. All hands were raised. He then asked them to write down a few sentences about how they thought the story would end.

Of the twenty-six students in Jerome's class, eleven completed the story in a way that Maryetta's task is fulfilled. In these stories, Maryetta catches the tiger and takes it home, and it performs as desired in the circus. Three students resolved the story by creating a new character who saves Maryetta from her injury and from Toby. In six stories, the tiger frees Maryetta from her crisis, and in three of these stories, the tiger goes on to catch Toby. In two stories, Maryetta escapes, finds the wizard, and seeks revenge on Toby. In one case each the wolf helps Maryetta catch first the tiger and then Toby; Toby steals the money from Maryetta and does not catch the tiger; Maryetta is cured in a hospital and becomes friends with Toby; and Toby spontaneously recognizes and reconciles his evil ways.

Jerome could sense the excitement of the students as they waited to hear how their Indian colleagues had completed the story. He sat on the edge of his desk and continued with the second half.

PART TWO (INDIA)

The wolf who was chasing the tiger stopped after hearing Maryetta's cries and ran toward her. He finally reached her. He felt sad when he saw the flow of blood from her leg.

"Don't be afraid. I shall help you," said the wolf.

The wolf then ran into the forest and brought rare herbs and placed them on her leg. At once, Maryetta felt relief from the pain and felt pleasant again. Maryetta looked at the wolf with love and gratitude.

The wolf asked Maryetta, "How did you fall?"

She explained everything to him. The wolf felt bad when he heard of Toby's treacherous deeds. The wolf told Maryetta that he would get the money from Toby.

Maryetta saw the birds, trees, and other creatures around her. Suddenly she didn't feel lonely any more. She felt happy that she was a part of an endless creation of nature. She felt the encouragement and nourishment given by the surrounding birds and trees.

Toby went straight to the old wizard with the money he robbed from Maryetta. After getting the money from Toby, the wizard taught him the mantras (magic phrases) that he could use to conquer the animals and humans. Toby then quickly left, greedy to make more money.

Then Toby saw a tiger running towards him in a frenzy. He tried to conquer the tiger with the mantras he had learned from the wizard. But the tiger pushed him down and tried to attack him. At that time, the tiger heard the voice of a wolf and he ran away.

The wolf and Maryetta saw Toby struggling for his life. The wolf did not like to help the treacherous Toby. He thought that this was the right punishment for his terrible deeds. But Maryetta was deeply moved by Toby's suffering. She felt sad that she did not have the money to admit him to a hospital.

Maryetta pleaded with the wolf to help Toby. The wolf halfheartedly ran and brought rare herbs. Maryetta made a bandage with the herbs for Toby's wounds. She also gave him some juice from the herbs. He then recovered and could breathe easy again.

Toby slowly came to consciousness and appreciated the gentle qualities of Maryetta and apologized to her. He revealed that he had given the money to the old wizard. He felt sorry that he was spoiled by his own greed.

In the meantime, the wolf went to the tiger. He asked the tiger, "Why did you try to kill Toby?"

The tiger angrily replied, "It is but natural that we are angry towards men who prevent us from living independently in the forest and who try to hunt us. Toby is trying to destroy us totally by violence, tricks, and mantras. For him, money is bad."

The wolf said, "Toby not only cheats the animals, but also the humans. For this greedy fellow, money is everything."

Toby was truly sad. He felt ashamed of himself and asked to be pardoned. Then the wolf, the tiger, Toby, and Maryetta danced together in joy in a circle.

Then Maryetta told the tiger, "In my father's circus there is a male tiger suffering without a companion. If you can come with me, he would be very happy."

Maryetta looked at the female tiger with love and affection. The female was moved to tears. She began to wonder if that male tiger was the one that had been taken away from her long ago. She agreed to go with Maryetta.

All four returned to the circus. The male tiger was happy to see the female tiger that he had been separated from so very long ago. Soon they were able to identify one another. What a pleasure it is when separated ones come together again!

Maryetta was very happy. She had learned to talk with the animals. Her love toward them grew many times over. She looked after the tigers with special care.

One day, Maryetta fell asleep while playing with the tigers. She listened to the conversations of the tigers as she woke up. She pretended as if she was sleeping and continued to listen to them.

The female tiger said, "Maryetta is a wonderful girl. But she does not realize the fact that the forest is our heaven. Even this golden cage is still a cage."

Maryetta was deeply moved. The next day Maryetta's father called her and said, "Maryetta, I have grown old. I am retiring from the circus as of today. Hereafter, you should run the circus."

Maryetta said, "I shall free those wonderful animals from this sorrowful, tortuous caged life, and I will go and live in the forest."

And that she did.

Jerome followed this reading with a discussion. To begin the discussion he asked each student to respond, in writing, to the following questions.

1. In what ways is the ending different from what you expected?
2. What surprised you as you heard the end of the story?
3. What do you think you learned about Indian culture?
4. What might reading this story tell you about American culture?

The discussion that followed was lively. Most of the children thought that good would prevail over evil. What seemed to surprise them, however, was that the bad characters changed for the good. On further probing, some of the children questioned whether human nature could be modified so quickly, as if through sudden insight or experience, and wondered if it might be possible with terrorists. Many students were also struck by the use of herbs and mantras in the story as well as the apparent reverence for nature and living things.

While the children were discussing what they thought they had learned about Indian culture, Karl suggested that Indians seem to care about nature in general and animals in particular. He also asked about the possibility of humans really talking to animals. He remembered watching a television show about how researchers were trying

Maryetta saw the birds, trees and other creatures around her. She did not feel lonely. She felt happy she was part of an endless creation of nature. She felt the encouragement and nourishment given by the surrounding birds and trees.

Toby went straight to the old wizard with the money he robbed from Maryetta. After getting the money from Toby, the wizard taught him the mantras (magic phrases) to conquer the animals and humans. He then proceeded quickly, greedy to make money.

தன்னைச் சுற்றிலும் பறவைகள், மரங்கள், மற்றும் பிற உயிரினங்களை மரியட்டா பார்த்தாள். அவள் தனி-மையை எண்ணவில்லை. இயற்கையின் எல்லையற்ற படைப்பில் தான் ஒரு பகுதி என்பதை அவள் உணர்ந்து இன்புற்றாள். சுற்றியிருந்த பறவைகளும் மரங்களும் தந்த ஊக்கக்தையும் ஊட்டத்தையும் அவள் உணர்ந்தாள்.

டொபி நேரே, மரியட்டாவிடமிருந்து கொள்ளை-யடித்த பணத்துடன், சூனியக்கார கிழவியிடம் சென்றான். டொபியிடமிருந்து பணத்தை பெற்றுக் கொண்ட பிறகு, சூனியக்காரி மிருகங்களையும் மானிடர்களையும் வெல்லு-வதற்குரிய மந்திரங்களை அவனுக்கு உபதேசித்தாள். பிறகு பணம் சேர்க்கும் பேராசையுடன், அவன் வேகமாக வெளியே றினான்.

to communicate with dolphins, whales, and gorillas. Kathy seemed particularly moved by Maryetta's change of heart toward Toby and thought that Indians might care that other people are safe and peaceful. Kamal said he was learning about some of the ways African healers treated their patients and the fact that the Indians used herbs and mantras reminded him of this.

It was a bit more difficult, however, for the group to discuss what they might have learned about their own culture. With probing, Jerome was able to get something of a *discussion going. Some students thought that both countries were alike in many ways. Others were surprised that, while most of the American students would let the characters in the story die, the Indian children seemed to have compassion for them.*

The discussion of violence in the world in general as well as in American society, toward both people and animals, was the most lively. Finally, Maria pointed out that the way the story was completed showed that the Indian students believed that people's labels can change, whereas in the United States, she thought, a label might remain with a person for quite a long time. She was even bold enough to ask how many in the class still felt uncomfortable with Arabs and Muslims in the community. Jerome thought that Maria raised a good question, and he allowed it to develop into a whole class discussion about prejudice and racism in their classroom and in the community. At the end of the discussion, all of Jerome's students agreed with the Indian class that the two classrooms should continue a long-term friendship and an exchange of ideas, resources, and letters.

Rationale for the Classroom as a Global Community

It is the business of schools to prepare students for life in the larger societies that they are certain to encounter. In a democratic society this responsibility means preparing students not only to know about democracy, but also to be able to put it into practice. In a globally interdependent world this responsibility means preparing students for a future in which they will come into increasing contact with people different from themselves. It means a reality in which an increasing number of American firms have offices in overseas locations and, similarly, an increasing number of international firms have offices within the United States. It means political boundaries that are constantly shifting and rapidly changing, thus creating opportunities and challenges not imagined in recent decades. Moreover, it is not necessary to leave one's own community in order to come into regular contact with people from other nations or be significantly influenced by the actions of others from far away. As a result, educators are beginning to seek out concepts, skills, and strategies that will help students understand and function effectively in a globally interdependent world. A central focus of this effort is to develop an understanding of globalization and to attain an education that is international and intercultural in scope.

**Activity 35:
Future's
Window**

What is Globalization?

Globalization seems to be the defining concept at the beginning of the twenty-first century. Years before the millennial events began to unfold, nations around the world began preparing for the Y2K computer bug that threatened to wreak havoc on local and global systems that were increasingly interconnected. Today, we live in a world characterized by an interconnectedness in our economic, environmental, political, and social systems that brings about increasingly complex intercultural interactions, conflicts, and change. The world comes closer together through global terrorism, diseases such as AIDS,

Globalization

struggles for peace, drug trafficking, the threat of environmental decay, and the interdependence of our economic systems. The distinctions of what is local and what is global have blurred, and many people find it difficult to comprehend the new scenario in which we find ourselves. How can we begin to understand the phenomenon of globalization, and how does it impact teaching and learning?

Thomas Friedman and *The Lexus and the Olive Tree*

Friedman, in his book *The Lexus and the Olive Tree,* presents one of the clearest descriptions of globalization and its impact on society.[2] Friedman quite clearly points out how global changes in recent years have brought about a tremendous change in the way in which people across the planet live, work, and interact. It is critical that teachers understand this phenomenon and how it has changed the manner in which people interact, and consider how it might impact teaching and learning.

Characteristics of Globalization

Globalization replaced the Cold War in the late 1990s, and with it came many distinct changes in the way in which people around the world interact with one another and their immediate, as well as distant, environment. Friedman used the Lexus and the olive tree as symbols to differentiate the two extremes. He said, "the Lexus and the olive tree were actually pretty good symbols of this post–Cold War era: half the world seemed to be emerging from the Cold War intent on building a better Lexus, dedicated to modernizing, streamlining, and privatizing their economics in order to thrive in the system of globalization. And half of the world—sometimes half the same country, sometimes half the same person—was still caught up in the fight over who owns which olive tree."[3] Whereas the Lexus characterizes everything that is modern, faced-paced, and dynamic, the olive tree represents everything that keeps people rooted to a particular location, idea, or way of life.

Globalization is characterized by certain features that make it unique and quite different from the Cold War period, during which there were two superpowers, the United States and the Soviet Union. One overarching feature is integration; the world has become an increasingly interwoven place, and a person's opportunities are determined by whom that person is connected to. Another feature of globalization can be summarized in a single word—the Web. We have gone from a Cold War system built around division and walls with one of two superpowers in charge to a system built around integration and webs. During the Cold War we knew that at least two people were in control of events. In the globalization system we reach for the Internet, which is a symbol that we are all increasingly connected and nobody is quite in charge—unlike the Cold War.

Globalization is a dynamic, ongoing process. It is the inexorable integration of markets, nation-states, and technologies to a degree never witnessed before, with a powerful backlash from those brutalized or left behind by the new system. Globalization has its own dominant culture that tends to create a homogenizing set of circumstances. In previous eras this sort of cultural homogenization happened on a regional scale—The Romanization of Western Europe or the Islamification of Central Asia, North Africa, and the Middle East by Arabs. Today, globalization has tended to involve the spread, for better or for worse, of Americanization—from Big Macs to iMacs to Mickey Mouse. Whereas the Cold War was a world of friends and enemies, the globalization world tends to turn all friends and enemies into competitors.

The Cold War system of power was built around nation-states. Today, the globalization system is built around three balances that overlap and affect one another: (1) the traditional balance of power is now in the hands of one nation, the United States, which is the sole and dominant superpower and has tremendous influence over much of what happens in many nations around the world; (2) there exists a balance between nation-states and global markets, made up of millions of investors around the world; Friedman refers to them as the "electronic herd," who, with the click of a mouse, can influence financial markets around the world; and (3) there exists the sensitive balance between individuals and nation-states. Because globalization has brought down many of the dividing walls and because it simultaneously wired the world into networks, the individual suddenly has more power to influence both markets and nation-states than at any time in world history. As a result, in addition to superpowers and supermarkets, we now have super-empowered individuals, some of whom are quite angry and powerful. In the late 1990s, before the attack on the World Trade Center and the Pentagon, Osama bin Laden declared war on the United States. In response, the U. S. Air Force retaliated with a cruise missile attack on him, firing seventy-five cruise missiles that cost $1 million apiece—fired at one person. This action was an example of a superpower against a super-empowered individual, and he was not stopped.

An Educational Response

How can educators begin to respond to such changes in the social order, begin to understand the current state of affairs, and still empower their students with the knowledge and skills to be more effective with their international counterparts? The fact is that Americans (and others) are increasingly engaged with other people, thus demanding greater cross-cultural sensitivity, understanding, and a recognition of the shared values and challenges as well as differences among populations. We must begin asking ourselves such questions as: How do we learn about one another in ways that span boundaries and enlarge our understandings? How do we accomplish this learning in a way that respects the sacred while promoting the secular? How do we interact with others so as not to exploit but to grasp the essence of other peoples and their important contributions to a clearly global society?

The lack of barriers and walls that globalization brings presents its own set of new challenges. The concept of learning communities has been discussed in previous chapters, but those contexts were concerned mostly with integrating domestic diversity. This chapter discusses new learning communities as true global communities in which members are committed to thinking, growing, and inquiring with people who cross cultural as well as national boundaries. Americans are thus faced with new and significant challenges. For instance, how can we build the trust and intimacy that is essential to community with those who live in distant countries? Technology may be one tool that empowers us to reach further into the world, but we must be careful that we do not neglect the work that is needed to develop and maintain true interpersonal relationships and community. This issue is of grave concern, because we as Americans may tend to look to people in other countries as new customers or competitors and may interact with them at only a surface level. We may impose our own standards, for our own good, on other people and thereby neglect the impact our presence might have on them. We are then surprised when they resent our presence.

Education for a Global Perspective

A number of professional educational associations have addressed issues related to global and international education over the years. The National Council for the Social Studies defines a global perspective as the development of the knowledge, skills, and attitudes needed to live effectively in a world possessing limited natural resources and characterized by ethnic diversity, cultural pluralism, and increasing interdependence.[4] Teaching toward a **global perspective** emphasizes that:

1. The human experience is an increasingly global phenomenon in which people are constantly being influenced by transnational, cross-cultural, and multicultural interaction.
2. There is a wide variety of actors on the world stage, including states, multinational corporations, and numerous voluntary nongovernmental organizations, as well as individuals.
3. The fate of humankind cannot be separated from the state of the global environment.
4. There are linkages between present social, political, and ecological realities and alternative futures.
5. Citizen participation is critical at both local and international levels.

Education for a global perspective helps individuals better comprehend their own condition in the community and world and make more accurate and effective judgments about other people and about common issues. It emphasizes the study of nations, cultures, and civilizations, including our own pluralistic society, and focuses on understanding how these are interconnected, how they change, and what each individual's roles and responsibilities are in such a world. An education with a global perspective provides the individual with a realistic, balanced perspective on world issues and an awareness of how enlightened self-interest includes concerns about people elsewhere in the world. The catchphrase Think Globally, Act Locally has served the field of social studies education well. Making global concerns concrete, immediate, and meaningful to students is difficult yet critical.

Models of Intercultural Education

One way to better understand what underlies an international perspective is to consider how the cognitive demands placed on individuals have changed as societies have evolved.[5] Three levels of society can be distinguished, each having different subsequent cognitive requirements. At the first level, called the *local-traditional level,* people are able to attain their daily needs from within their rather small, closed society. Little interaction with outsiders is necessary to obtain these needs. When interaction with outsiders does occur, it is usually fraught with conflict, disagreement, apprehension, and fear. There is little need, or desire, to understand the perspective of others. Historically, these characteristics were associated with small hunting and gathering groups or large extended families or clans living in close proximity to one another. Few examples of such societies exist today, perhaps with the exception of some of the more traditional !Kung Bushmen of the Kalahari desert or Aboriginals of Australia.

At the second level, the *national-modern level,* individual and group needs have broadened to the point that they cannot be obtained within their immediate surroundings. Services, goods, and knowledge of outside groups may be desired and needed and may thus lead to barter, trade, and other means of negotiation. The need to communicate between groups increases, and money as a medium of exchange becomes very important. Such characteristics are associated with most modern societies from at least the latter part of the seventeenth century onward. The degree to which people and societies are interdependent at this level, however, is small. For the most part, nation-states remain relatively autonomous, while towns and cities maintain a local focus. Individuals may not have to go very far beyond their neighborhoods to trade, buy, or sell the things that are needed or desired.

The third level, the *global-postmodern level,* is one that many societies and nations of the world are entering today. At this level, people and nations are so inextricably bound together that they cannot satisfy their needs and wants without significant interaction and nearly instantaneous communication with outside groups. These characteristics are also associated with the daily lives of most individuals who live in societies at this level. People obtain their food not from their own or neighboring farms, but from a supermarket that carries foodstuffs from around the world. Their clothing comes, not from their own or their neighbors' fields, spinning wheels, looms, and needles but from stores that manufacture, buy, and sell on an international scale. People do not build their own or their neighbors' houses without materials from around the planet, nor do most people build their own machinery at all. An oil spill in the Bering Sea is likely to affect the lives of people in the Gulf of Mexico. Famine in India is likely to affect the lives of people in the United States. A large international company in the United States bought out by a large international company in Germany is likely to affect the jobs of people in Taiwan, Singapore, or China. When something happens in Tanzania or Venezuela or Saudi Arabia, people in Alaska, Sweden, Australia, and South Africa know about it within minutes or hours. When there is war, it affects everyone.

Indeed, it appears that mere survival of the planet today may be dependent on the smooth, interconnected functioning of many governments, economies, technologies, and communications systems and the people who make those institutions come alive. It is this third level that we refer to when we speak of a global society or a global economy. To the extent that these characteristics apply, people live in what has been referred to as a *global village* and are interconnected in many of the ways that were presented by Friedman and discussed in previous sections.

Most people would agree that in order to develop satisfactory relationships, to understand others' motivations and needs, and to interact effectively with those who are different, a certain degree of **empathy** (the ability to understand the world from another's perspective) must be achieved. The development of empathy is critical for a people to move from the local-traditional level to the national-modern level. Whereas empathy may be necessary for some (but not all) people at the national-modern level, it is indispensable for all people at the postmodern-global level.

Such a world has numerous players, each of whom may have distinct wants and needs, different perspectives, and different ways of thinking, interacting, and communicating. A healthy, well-functioning global society demands that individuals have the ability to think, perceive, communicate, and behave in new and different ways and with people from many different backgrounds. The goal of global or international education is to prepare individuals for these kinds of interactions.

Curriculum Transformation: The International Perspective

Most discussion of what is called global or international education refers to Hanvey's paper, "An Attainable Global Perspective."[6] In this work, Hanvey identifies five elements of a global perspective that educators can transform into teachable skills and perspectives that cut across academic disciplines and grade levels. Each of these elements is examined in the discussion that follows.

Perspective Consciousness

Perspective Consciousness refers to a person's awareness that he or she has a view of the world that is not universally shared, that this view is shaped by unconscious as well as conscious influences, and that others may have profoundly different views. This element differentiates opinion from perspective. Opinion refers to the surface layer of a person's innermost thoughts. It is the tip of the iceberg, so to speak, showing only a small portion of its totality. Underneath the surface lie the generally hidden, unexamined assumptions and judgments people make about life, about others, and about right and wrong. The assumption that human dominance over nature is both attainable and desirable is an example of a perspective that lies deep in many western minds. It was not until this traditionally unexamined assumption surfaced that many philosophical choices that previously escaped our attention were raised. As a result, debate involving our relationship with the environment ensued and stimulated considerable thought, activity, and discussion. Similarly, the feminist movement raised the consciousness of women and men regarding the role of women in society. In the process, deep layers of chauvinism inherent in much of our thinking about male and female roles were revealed. Likewise, concerned parents, addressing the unmet needs of their exceptional children, pointed out how the educational system (and society in general) discriminated against a large segment of society.

Children can develop perspective consciousness in a number of ways. Social studies curricula, for example, can help students examine their own culture's behavior from another point of view. Ethnocentrism suggests that most individuals will have a tendency to overemphasize their own culture's accomplishments and point of view. Children can be encouraged to question their own cultural perspectives and to consider how others might view them. When studying people in other parts of the world, for instance, students can be asked to explore why most people prefer to live in their native habitats despite sometimes difficult conditions. Why, children in your classrooms might ask, would anyone want to live in the Arctic, where people have to contend with extremes in temperature and have to hunt for their food? Or why would the Mundurucu people of

A Delayed Response

 A couple of days after Jerome's class received the completion of their partnership story, Jerome overheard Lenny and Paul giggling and talking about how silly it seemed that people in India would use rare herbs as medicines. The boys thought it even more unusual that Indians would consider using mantras to control people and animals, and the two began referring to Indians in derogatory ways.

- Why do you think Lenny and Paul would, after two days, begin to ridicule the people they had spent time studying about?
- How would you handle the immediate situation?
- What might you do to prevent this reaction from happening?

the Amazon River in South America want to live where the temperature was extremely hot year-round; where there are poisonous animals and annoying insects to contend with; and where the food staple, the poisonous manioc, has to be boiled and pounded over hot fires in the sweltering heat just to make it eatable? Likewise, children growing up in those regions of the world might ask the same of our young students: how can anyone live in an environment where the air is polluted, where the water is trapped in pipes and treated with chemicals, and where food is not freshly hunted and prepared but is packaged and loaded with preservatives so its shelf life can be extended? Point out to your students that our own behavior probably looks as strange to others as theirs might appear to us.

Children can also develop perspective consciousness by reading some of the numerous books that have been written either from another's perspective or from an insider's point of view. The children's book *The True Story of the Three Little Pigs as Told by A. Wolf,* for instance, is a good way to help children see that other points of view exist around most topics.[7]

State of the Planet Awareness

This awareness of prevailing world conditions and trends includes such aspects as population growth and migration; economic conditions; resources and the physical environment; political developments; advancements in science and technology, law, and health; and various forms of conflicts. Most people, even from highly mobile societies like the United States, spend the majority of their time in their local area. However, developments in communication technology have brought the world, if not into most people's homes, certainly within most people's reach. Extensive global media coverage via television news is making its impact felt at the diplomatic and war tables as well.

The liberal weekly *Die Zeit* of Hamburg, Germany, relates two incidents that capture the extent of the impact made by the aggressive CNN news broadcasting team:

In the summer of 1989, when the U.S. government was searching for a response to threats that hostages in Lebanon would be killed, a White House advisor was asked where President George Bush was spending the day. "He is in his office, watching CNN," the advisor said. "CNN is interviewing Middle East experts; maybe one of them will have an idea that the president can use." And when the Americans marched into Panama in December, 1989, Soviet leader Mikhail Gorbachev made use of the medium. CNN's Moscow correspondent was called to the Kremlin in the middle of the night. There, a press aide read a condemnation of the invasion for the camera. The official note to the U.S. ambassador was not delivered until hours later. The Kremlin's excuse was that it was counting on Washington getting the Kremlin's reaction immediately via CNN.[8]

Another illustration of the media's educational role can be seen in its coverage of the Gulf War in the winter of 1991. The U.S. military, knowing that Iraq was watching coverage of the war on CNN, actually planned their movements differently from those they were reporting to the American public so as to confuse the enemy. Thus, while the media makes state of the planet awareness a possibility as never before, it also makes the spread of misinformation easier and faster than ever before. Also, if we are not careful, we may find it very easy to believe that the real world consists only of televised images of the world according to CNN. Or recall the story line in the successful film *Wag the Dog,* which portrays a media-produced war created to divert public attention from unethical presidential behavior.

Another problem is that television and print news are selective. For example, an outbreak of the measles (as has happened in recent years in various parts of the United States) or a famine in Ethiopia is deemed newsworthy whereas the chronic hunger and disease that affects millions of Americans and others around the world is not. Also, not all parts of the world receive the same news. For example, a drastic rise in the rate of skin cancer in Australia during the late 1980s and early 1990s was thought to be tied to an increase in the size of the hole in the ozone layer. In recent years, the hole has spread from Antarctica to the southern parts of Australia. Consequently, major efforts were underway throughout the country to warn people against unprotected exposure to the sun. Parents went to all extremes to make certain their children's skin was covered while they played outside. Everyone wore hats. Even adolescents, who typically might go to any length to show off a suntan, were making efforts to protect themselves. Attempts were also being made to make high-SPF sunscreens prescriptive medications so people could deduct the cost from their income tax, thereby encouraging the use of sunscreens. For some reason, however, the American public was prevented from knowing about the extent of the hole and the severe impact it was having on life in Australia. This is an example of selective news coverage.

General public awareness of the state of the planet must become a priority. Children must be encouraged to reflect on national and world conditions and to ask questions that go beyond the obvious. For example, they should be aware that despite all of the United Nation's accomplishments, conditions for most of the world's people show serious deterioration.[9] For instance:

**Activity 30:
The Plight of
Women on a
Global Scale**

1.   The world's population has more than doubled in the last fifty years and is increasing by 250,000 people per day, over 90 million people every year! By the year 2050 there will be an extra 4 billion mouths to feed. This number is equal to what the total world population was in 1975.

2. Four hundred million people are unemployed in the "south" (the preferred term for those countries once referred to as undeveloped or third world). Forty million new jobs are needed each year just to maintain the present world condition. Under present north-south imbalances, there is not the remotest chance that these jobs will materialize.

3. Over one billion people live in poverty, 40 percent more people than in 1980. In 1960, the wealthiest one-fifth of the world's population were thirty times richer than the poorest one-fifth. By 1989, the wealthiest one-fifth of the world's population were sixty times richer than the poorest one-fifth. Viewed from the perspective of a single country, such conditions represent the classic condition for a massive and violent revolution.

4. Television, radio, and video has spread to the poor countries knowledge of the affluent lifestyles of the minority in the north and of some southern elites, permitting angry comparisons with the desperate poverty of the vast majority in the south.

5. The exhaustion of natural resources and lack of work opportunities are prompting massive migrations across frontiers in Africa and Asia. In the early 1970s there were 16,000 applicants for asylum within Western European countries. By 1991, there were 545,000 asylum seekers. By 1993, country after country was beginning to close its gates.

6. In 1951, when the United Nations High Commission on Refugees was founded, there were some 1.5 million legally classified refugees worldwide. In the mid-1990s, there were roughly 20 million refugees worldwide. A further 24 million people have been displaced within their own countries because of ecological, economic, and political causes.

7. World grain production per capita has shrunk by half since 1950. In Africa, grain production has dropped by 28 percent since 1967 because of the effects of drought, desertification, erosion, and population growth.

8. The rate of environmental deterioration continues unabated despite the best intentions of the activists and policy makers. The problems posed by global warming, ecosystem destruction, and ozone depletion demand urgent attention.

9. Between 1990 and 1994, the United Nations mounted as many peacekeeping missions as it has done in its entire history. On a global basis, only $1.90 is spent, per person per year, on the United Nations. This figures compares to $150 spent per person worldwide on weapons.

Within the United States, most people do not know that 43 million Americans are considered disabled or handicapped. Nor do people know that thirty-five thousand children around the world die each day because of hunger-related causes. How many people go hungry or are homeless in our own nation? How many children are born addicted to cocaine or suffering from AIDS-related complications? Students must be actively encouraged to expand their knowledge base, to review international news sources, and to inquire into the knowledge and perspective of international visitors. Such actions, incidentally, would help students develop the first dimension of global education, perspective consciousness.

Cross-Cultural Awareness

The cross-cultral dimension of global education includes an awareness of social and cultural diversity around the world and at least a beginning awareness of how one's own culture and society might be viewed from other vantage points. Hanvey suggests that this dimension may be the most difficult to attain, since people typically do not have the time or expertise needed to truly understand those who are different from themselves. We now know that understanding about others does not necessarily follow from simple contact. Lengthy and intimate contact under certain conditions is needed in order to "get into the heads" of those in another culture.

How can schooling best develop cross-cultural awareness in young people? To define what schools might reasonably hope to accomplish in this direction, it may be helpful to consider four levels of cross-cultural awareness posited by Hanvey.

The first level involves *awareness of superficial or extremely visible cultural traits,* the kind that often become the basis for stereotypes: skin color, dress, language patterns, ceremonies, and so on. Much of this information is obtained through textbooks, television, and tourism. At this level, the individual outside a given culture typically interprets observed actions of others as exotic, or worse, bizarre.

The second level involves *awareness of significant but more subtle cultural traits that contrast markedly with one's own.* Such information is gained as a result of culture conflict situations and is often interpreted as unbelievable. The reaction here, however, is more on an emotional level. Interactions are considered frustrating, irrational, and against "common sense."

The third level also includes an *awareness of significant and subtle cultural traits that contrast markedly with one's own.* However, this level is characterized by more intellectual emphasis and analysis. Others' behavior is then interpreted as believable because it can be understood.

The fourth level involves *awareness of how another culture feels from the perspective of an insider.* People attain this perspective through cultural immersion, that is, from living the culture. Information is perceived as believable not simply because it is understood at the cognitive level, but because of its familiarity at the subjective or affective level. This level might be likened to reaching the state called *home* on the U-curve introduced in Figure 3.1.

Effective culture learning is more of an affective and behavioral process than a cognitive process. A person truly learns about another culture by living it, not by being told about it. Development of intercultural competence may be, as Hanvey and others have noted, the most difficult, yet the most critical, of the five dimensions to achieve.[10]

However, strategies do exist that can assist people on their way to becoming interculturally competent. The culture-general framework used throughout this text can have a significant impact on cognition, affect, and behavior in cross-cultural settings. It is a cognitive tool that engages the emotions and may be just the tool for the school context.

The Importance of Systems Thinking

Knowledge of Global Dynamics or World Systems

Attaining this fourth dimension of a global perspective, knowledge of global dynamics or world systems, requires a modest understanding of how world ecosystems operate.

Educators can stress the interconnectedness of things by asking students to consider the impact one particular decision or action will have on another. The following examples illustrate interconnectedness.

In southeastern Australia, the fluctuation of various fish populations in area river basins was found to be caused by an increase in estrogen in the water. Following an extensive investigation it was determined that this hormone found its way into area waterways by being flushed out in toilet wastewater. Women using birth control pills eliminated higher-than-usual levels of estrogen in their urine. This increase of estrogen in the wastewater directly affected the behavior of fish downstream! This is a good example of an unanticipated, unintended outcome.

Now consider an example of the vulnerability of ecological systems to changes in distant parts of the world. The recent increase in mosquito populations across the United States can be directly tied to our tremendous appetite for inexpensive fast-food hamburgers. An increasing proportion of the meat in our diet comes from cattle raised on land that was once rain forest in Central and South America. These rain forests provided the winter nesting sites for many of the northern hemisphere's migrating bird populations. As an increasing percentage of the rain forest is destroyed, so too are the winter nesting sites for these birds, resulting in a greater than normal death rate for the species. The decline in bird population has resulted in fewer songbirds returning north and, consequently, an increase in the mosquito population that forms a major part of the birds' diet. This is a vivid example of the impact that individual choice, in this case eating habits, can have. Think Globally, Act Locally again becomes paramount.

When a new element is introduced into any system, it has unanticipated effects. Hanvey suggests that there are no *side effects,* only *surprise effects.* Thus, when we intervene in any system, we should be prepared for some surprising consequences. We confront numerous other examples of this principle in action almost every day. Depletion of the ozone layer, the greenhouse effect, the poisoning of groundwater, and the weakening of the eagle's egg as a result of DDT moving up the food chain are all examples of these surprise consequences, which we are now trying to correct. We must learn, as Hanvey suggests, to look for the "concealed wiring," the hidden functions of elements in a system.

Awareness of Human Choice

Hanvey's fifth dimension, awareness of human choices, represents the final critical step in developing a global perspective. The problems of choice that confront individuals, nations, and the human species as they increase their knowledge of the global system are addressed in this dimension. Until recently, people were generally unaware of the unanticipated outcomes and long-term consequences of their actions. This is no longer the case. A global consciousness or cognition is emerging. People now need to consider the implications of our expanded knowledge and communication base. Negligence, or even making an unwise choice out of ignorance, may set the stage for countless problems at some future time.

Fortunately, we know a great deal more than we used to, and choices do exist. Consider the use of chlorofluorocarbons (CFCs) and the growing problem of ozone depletion. We have two choices: we can continue to use CFCs because at the present time they make refrigeration and propellants possible, or we can stop using them because of their effect on the environment, while actively seeking a replacement product. The simple substitution of pump spray mechanisms for propellant sprays on a variety of products is a good example of a successful alternative. It is awareness of the problem, however, that often makes the difference in the success of alternatives.

Children can make remarkable strides toward realizing their power and ability to bring about change. In the 1970s, Israeli elementary schoolchildren went on a campaign to protect some of their nation's threatened wildflower populations. They raised the awareness of adults to such an extent that the adults stopped indiscriminately picking the flowers. Many of the threatened flowers have since been removed from the endangered species lists.

During the early 1980s, one of the authors of this text initiated a school exchange program between fifth and sixth grade children in northeast Ohio and schoolchildren in the Yucatan peninsula of Mexico and in Belize. Seventeen children went on the first trip from Ohio to Belize. One gesture of appreciation the Ohio children made to their host community was to present the village school with a world atlas signed by everyone at the visitors' school. The gift seemed to be the first book the Belize school actually owned. This discovery made such an impression on the students from Ohio that on their return home they decided to do something about the situation. All the fifth and sixth grade students in the school became involved in operating an after-school snack bar, collecting usable books from the community, and packaging them for shipment overseas. With the proceeds from their snack bar and their collection efforts, students were able to send more than 500 books to their peers in this small village in Belize. Needless to say, the children felt tremendous pride, realizing that they, personally, could have such an impact on individuals so far away. This lesson was one that no textbook could teach them and that they will never forget.

Characteristics of a Global Classroom

Most national systems of schooling typically address the needs of the nation they serve, paying particular attention to transmitting the "proper" attitudes and beliefs thought to be necessary to maintain the society. By its very nature, most schooling is an ethnocentric activity. However, long-term goals in most schools reflect some of the ideals of a global perspective. If you were to closely examine the philosophical goal statements of most schools, you would probably find statements such as: to appreciate people from other cultures; to develop sensitivity to the needs of people different from themselves; to increase knowledge about people around the world.

While the philosophical stage has been partially set, the methods for implementing such goal statements have created a problem. Schools in the United States, as well as most parts of the world, typically present curricular experiences from a predominantly cognitive Eurocentric point of view. In addition, until recently, curriculum development efforts have had little input or interaction from people of different backgrounds. Such assumptions and practices are presently being called into question.

In order to build true professional global communities in which teachers and students can begin to collaborate in real problem solving, we will need to help students learn firsthand about cultures of other countries; share what they are learning locally and globally with others; collaborate on common projects across national boundaries wherever possible; study and live in other countries with students from those countries; welcome global career opportunities; and develop capacities for success in a global village. But how can these goals be achieved?

In a classroom with a global perspective, global education is not merely an add-on to an already overcrowded curriculum. Relevant concepts and activities that develop a global perspective are woven throughout the curriculum. Most importantly, global classrooms seek to help students develop such critical cognitive skills and attitudes as empathy, interconnectedness, perspective taking, cross-cultural understanding, action orientation, and prejudice reduction. In such classrooms, students are active in building connections with others. They may have pen pals, or e-pals, with children in other parts of the world. In addition to communicating through writing with others and thus developing their language skills, students may be sharing audiotapes, videotapes, photographs, classroom materials, and other artifacts that reflect their own and each other's cultures. Children may read books about lives in other communities, which helps develop a global perspective while simultaneously achieving the goals and objectives of a language arts curriculum. Students may work on collaborative writing projects with peers in other countries, as Jerome's class was doing with students in India. In short, students go about developing their language arts and other skills with other people in mind.

Pedagogies: Old and New

All the pedagogical techniques discussed throughout this book also apply to the global classroom. Indeed, the use of developmentally appropriate practice, collaborative and cooperative groups, and student involvement in planning takes on a new and richer dimension when placed in the context of an international perspective. However, a global perspective can also be introduced in more traditionally oriented classrooms. What is important here is the notion of a broader perspective.

In addition, students in global classrooms may use technology in creative ways. Classroom computers can be connected to networks that enable children to communicate on a regular basis with others from around the world. Joint activities may develop whereby classes in two or more countries collaborate via computer to discuss some global issue. Classrooms or schools may also use fax technology or computer scanners to link classes, enabling them to transfer artwork, poetry, essays, and other student work to other schools. Similarly, an increasing number of schools are using video teleconferencing technology to motivate young people in social studies and foreign language education. Students can conduct conference calls with peers around the world while transmitting pictures of themselves, thus adding a highly personal dimension to the interaction. Rather than simulate a French café in a typical French language class, some schools have had video teleconferences in French cafés, thus allowing students to see and interact directly with overseas students in the real-life setting. Or young people from around the world can come together via technology to discuss a global current event.

Linking Students around the World

While it is helpful to have such technology in global classrooms, much can be done without it. Students can, for example, make excellent use of maps, local and national newspapers, encyclopedias and other books, taped television programs, and United Nations materials. Educators do not need more advanced technology than the mail service to introduce students to pen pals around the world. Or, when crises occur around the world, children's messages to others can have quite an impact. Rennebohm-Franz reports that the impact of a group of first grade children sending letters of emotional support to children in Kobe, Japan, following the earthquake in 1995 helped both her students and those in Japan feel connected to one another.[11] One child's drawing showed her family standing outside their house at night with the following message of hope and connectedness: "I hope you get your houses built. This is a picture of me and my family looking out at the night. Maybe you see the same stars and moon we do."[12] The class received a message back from the teacher, stating:

> We began receiving your heartwarming messages from around the world . . . We have posted the pictures, letters and messages in the classrooms and hallway bulletin boards of city schools that are serving as refugee centers. For those of us living among the aftermath of Kobe's quake, these messages have had an immeasurable heartwarming effect. They have given us an opportunity to realize that emotional support is just as important as material support and that we are all inhabitants of the same small planet.[13]

Roles: Old and New

In global classrooms the local members of the international community are considered to be an integral part of the school. As events unfold around the world, representatives from the various communities are invited into classrooms to share their experience and perspectives. These presentations may occur at regular specific times in certain classes (e.g., social studies, language arts) or during regular school assemblies devoted to world events. Such involvement serves to break down some of the personal barriers that tend to develop between people. Not only are students introduced to different perspectives, they are also introduced to various cultures and languages firsthand. Such activities add a personal element to the content under study that a textbook cannot. Thus, when a natural disaster occurs somewhere in the world or when a conflict breaks out, children can associate it with real people; it is no longer an abstract event unfolding in some far-off, abstract corner of the world. Finally, having adults from other parts of the world serve as teachers helps students understand that teaching and learning can occur in a variety of ways.

Place of Content Knowledge: Old and New

The Pacific Circle Consortium

Globally oriented classrooms, like collaborative classrooms, integrate subject matter from various academic disciplines. Often these integrated curricula are jointly developed by educators from many countries. This collaboration, of course, helps ensure the accuracy of the content being studied. For example, the Pacific Circle Consortium has, for well over a decade, been developing educational materials that integrate the perspectives and contributions of educators from the United States, Canada, Australia, New Zealand, and Japan as well as some Pacific Island nations. One of their products, The Ocean Project, uses the Pacific Ocean as a curriculum vehicle for students located in countries on the Pacific Rim. Two such projects have been developed. One provides fifth and sixth grade students in two different countries with an integrated look at the culture, environment, economics, and cultural interaction of the other group's region. At the beginning of the unit, each group of students studies local conditions (environment, culture, economics, etc.). Next, a simulated transoceanic voyage brings the students to the other country, where they study similar concepts in that location. Students in Honolulu, Hawaii, and Hiroshima, Japan, for instance, thus learn about one another's way of life and local environment. A similarly developed unit for upper secondary school students looks at the use of the world's oceans, treaties, international law, and so forth. A project on Antarctica has also been developed.

Assessment: Old and New

Assessment in global classrooms may generally be described as global itself. That is, because of the wide variety of activities and the emphasis on cross-disciplinary or interdisciplinary studies, global classrooms can easily use both traditional and alternative forms of assessment. One example is provided by Singer, who taught a class on the impact of industrialization on American society to students at Edward R. Murrow High School in Brooklyn, New York.[14] As part of their evaluation package, students were assigned to write or draw a political cartoon, poem, song, rap, poster, button, or flyer that illustrated the experience of one group with industrialization. The assignment counted as an "essay" on their final exam. Singer notes that, on the statewide regents exam that all students in New York must take, these Murrow students had at least as high a passing percentage as did students in more traditional classes.

If technology is used in global classrooms to stimulate curricular activities, it can also be used in evaluation. Everything from computer-generated tests in which students receive immediate feedback to the production of videos and computer games can be assessed for how they demonstrate what students know and can do. The central point to remember in the assessment of global classrooms, as well as of other kinds of classrooms described in this book, is that when a wide variety of activities enhances the curriculum, they can be evaluated in a wide variety of ways.

Case Analysis

How might all these suggestions look in action? Let's go back to Jerome Becker's sixth grade classroom and analyze what he was doing. Jerome's classroom activities reflect a number of strategies related to global or intercultural education.

1. Jerome has demonstrated that it is possible to combine global education with the development of traditional curriculum skills in such areas as language arts, social studies, and art.
2. He has not shied away from real but sensitive issues such as prejudice and interpersonal conflict that greatly affect the lives of his students. Rather, he has acknowledged these issues as real problems that are worth confronting and analyzing. And he has done this in a subtle, creative manner that will set the stage for subsequent activity once everyone has a common foundation.

3. By integrating traditional content areas, the day is not broken into short little time slots during which content and curricular experiences are segregated from one another. Rather, classroom activities are designed to be meaningful and relate to the lives and experiences of the students. Through the partnership story, for example, students have an opportunity to develop their language arts skills while they learn valuable social studies concepts about culture, specific countries, and interpersonal interaction. At the same time, students work in cooperative groups and develop linkages with others around the world.

4. He has actively sought to reduce prejudice, not by simply telling students that it is wrong but by enabling them to learn, firsthand, about similarities and differences among at least two groups of people.

These examples represent just the beginning of what is possible in a globally oriented classroom.

Perspectives on a Globally Oriented Curriculum

What Jerome has attempted to do in the first part of the school year is to integrate into his curriculum three types of knowledge that will help his students evaluate their interpersonal experiences both inside and outside school. First, he is integrating knowledge and understanding of prejudice formation and prejudice reduction. Second, he is tapping into the growing body of knowledge related to the development of an international perspective. Both of these points will be developed below. Third, he is applying cooperative learning strategies, thus providing students with necessary practice in developing the skills needed for collaborative living and working.

Teaching the Global Perspective

Development of a global perspective should be integrated throughout the school curriculum, not just in social studies. Although large-scale infusion is desirable,[15] an international perspective can be integrated into the curriculum by individual teachers through any of the following means: by offering international focus courses, by internationalizing instructional methods and materials, and by internationalizing the disciplines.[16]

International focus courses exist in such areas as anthropology, regional history, geography, global or world studies, foreign language study, art and music, world religions, ethnic group studies, and international business. Such courses seem most appropriate at the secondary level and quite readily emerge from the disciplines themselves.

Internationalizing instructional methods and materials might emphasize intercultural interaction in the classroom using the special experiences of immigrant and international students as resources. Teachers should employ culturally appropriate instructional and assessment strategies. Textbooks should be reviewed for balance. Partnership programs with other schools and countries such as those with the schools in India and Belize can also be developed.

Internationalizing the disciplines involves infusing key elements of a global perspective across the entire curriculum. There are numerous ways this infusion can be accomplished at all levels and in all content areas. For instance, in reading and language arts, students might study how non-American and non-British writers use the English language. World literature courses should strive to include numerous examples from a non-Western origin. And literature should be integrated with the social sciences as a way to introduce multiple perspectives on abstract concepts. Children's literature can be used to present concepts of interest in international education. Classic Dr. Seuss books, such as *The Lorax* and *The Butter Battle Book,* can be used in a study of the environment and the nuclear arms race, respectively. Students might also analyze the portrayal of minorities and internationals in basal textbooks.

Teaching the Global Perspective

In science education, teachers might help students observe and understand the natural world and study the problems created as a result of increased technology and innovation. Students should be encouraged to ask questions about drought in some parts of the world, about pollution, or about a growing hole in the ozone layer. Then, students should be encouraged to propose solutions to many of these problems, solutions that require knowledge and input from diverse peoples and cultures, all of whom "own" the problem. While technology may be universal, its application is quite specific. The study of what constitutes "appropriate" technology in a given situation demands sensitivity to such aspects as local environment, culture, history, and language. The topic of unplanned change can be introduced through the study of biology and evolution. Inequities of energy consumption across the planet can be explored. Finally, the global nature of such systems as the water cycle, the mineral cycle, and the energy cycle can be studied.

In foreign language education, cultural studies can be expanded beyond the mother country to include colonized people as well as immigrant and refugee populations. The role of translators in world diplomacy can be studied. Foreign languages can be taught through folk songs, and English as a second language can be introduced to foreign language teachers and students.

Mathematics education should stress the metric system. The United States is the only nation in the world not actively using metrics. Math concepts can be illustrated through problems that simultaneously teach about world trends and global issues. Traditional numeration systems from other cultures can be studied. The mathematics and possible computer application of Islamic art can be analyzed. Likewise, the impact of women on the development of mathematics can be introduced.

Finally, history and the social studies should look at various perspectives on similar issues. The American Revolution, for instance, certainly looked different through British eyes. Studying other nation's textbooks or discussing various events with international students can go far in helping students develop perspective consciousness. Issues of population growth, personal family migration, history, and cultural diffusion can become the focus of historical inquiry, as can the interaction between geography, culture, and the environment. Students should be encouraged to ask difficult questions and to explore possible reasons and solutions. Why, for instance, does one-fifth of the world's population (in the northern (developed) countries) use two-thirds of the world's natural resources, and what might be done to counterbalance this usage? What does it really mean to be an overpopulated nation when an individual in the north has the same

Studying the Global Environment

impact on the earth in terms of pollution and utilization of resources as twenty-four or twenty-five individuals in the south? And why should soybeans, for instance, be exported from Brazil to feed cattle in the Western nations, to the detriment of the small farmers in South America and the benefit of wealthy corporations in North America? These questions are difficult to explore, but are ultimately ones that have to be addressed if the people of the world are ever to live in true balance.

Ethical Issues

Clearly, there are a variety of ethical issues involved in developing a global classroom. Among them are the fair allocation of available resources (including computers and other technology), the need to consider families and communities when discussing global concerns, and perhaps most important, the need to balance advocacy with inquiry. While it is tempting for educators to become advocates when discussing the world's problems, the role of schooling remains one of inquiry. Assessing students on the degree to which they are able to use the tools of inquiry, on the breadth and depth of their research, on their analytical skills, and on their creativity in proposing solutions is more appropriate than assessing them on the degree to which they subscribe to a particular point of view.

Similarly, there are ethical considerations involved in the length of time given to new ideas such as global education. Its emphasis on attitude and behavior change may require educators to allocate large amounts of time in order to achieve even modest gains. Social psychologists have had a difficult time demonstrating that significant, long-lasting behavior change follows from short-term attitude change efforts. While it may be possible to demonstrate a change in attitude as a result of a short-term intervention (efforts at a summer camp program, for instance), there has been little evidence to demonstrate either that the attitude change persists or that it leads to a subsequent long-term change in behavior.

The converse may in fact be true, as seen in research concerning attitudes toward people with disabilities. An individual who has had little contact with persons with disabilities may initially react with discomfort and/or pity and be acutely aware of the disability. In one study, for example, teachers participating in an intensive five-week summer training institute on teaching young children with disabilities initially demonstrated a negative change in attitude, as measured by the Attitudes Toward Disabled Persons scale.[17] Positive attitudes, as defined by this scale, are those that regard a person with disabilities as essentially like everyone else, not as someone special. For many of the teachers in this study, this workshop was their first exposure to children with disabilities, and as a result, they had difficulty not being overly solicitous and eager to help. Later follow-up experiences with students with disabilities gradually led to more "normalized" attitudes.

Studies of classroom integration of children with handicaps generally have shown that mere exposure does not necessarily result in the formation of friendships. Teachers need to actively promote social interaction, model an accepting attitude toward all children, and design activities that enable children with handicaps and without handicaps to work together.[18] Too often insufficient time is provided for these activities, and consequently, initial assessments are disappointing. For example, in one study involving preschool children, initial observation revealed that typical children seldom selected peers with handicaps in play situations, but repeated observations several weeks later showed significantly more acceptance.[19]

Summary

This chapter takes as its starting point the reality that we live in an interconnected, interdependent, global society and that it is the responsibility of teachers and schools to prepare students to live productively in it.

Globalization has many meanings, but in this chapter it means actively introducing students to people and ideas from around the world; it means helping students learn to think in terms of whole systems (economic, political, social); and it means acquainting students with global issues that are certain to have an impact on their lives. Globalization should help students participate with other students from all over the planet in thinking through hard questions involving not only intercultural competence but also the ability to span all kinds of social as well as geographical boundaries.

When people encounter situations that induce or require them to behave in new and different ways for an extended period of time, there is a real possibility for long-term attitude and behavior change. If, for instance, school organizational structures can be modified so as to encourage or require intergroup interaction over an extended period of time, the likelihood that everyone may learn to regard themselves as tolerant, understanding, and able to get along with people increases. Government legislation that provides mandates for altering organizational structure on a national level is based on this idea. Official support and status for bilingualism in Canada or multilingualism in Switzerland are promising examples of this policy in action. Never believe, however, that mandates alone will do the job. What is required is persistent face-to-face activity and a good deal of trial and error!

 # Chapter Review

Go to the Online Learning Center at **www.mhhe.com/Cushner4e** to review important content from the chapter, practice with key terms, take a chapter quiz, and find the web links listed in this chapter.

Key Terms

Empathy 155	Globalization 152	Global perspective 154

Reflective Questions

The case study teacher, Jerome Becker, developed a number of activities and curricular redesigns that infused global awareness into his sixth grade curriculum. Still, he is bothered by several aspects of his work.

1. How can he continue to educate himself about new methods of global education while simultaneously keeping up with student needs and school requirements? Time is definitely a problem.
2. He knows that the United States is a widely diverse country with many unsolved problems regarding race and ethnicity. How can he justify moving to a global perspective when the problems at home remain so critical?
3. Although he has been relatively successful in incorporating a global perspective into social studies, language arts, and some of the arts, how can he do the same with such seemingly culture-neutral subjects as mathematics and science?

4. He has found that many students do not relate at all to the idea of ethnicity. Rather, they think of themselves as Americans and have neither knowledge of nor emotional ties to their own ethnic roots. How can he encourage these students to appreciate and value ethnic and racial diversity without seeming to denigrate the American way of life?

5. Not every teacher and administrator in his school appreciates the direction Jerome is taking toward a global perspective. How can he continue to broaden his students' perspectives in the face of criticism from his colleagues?

References

1. K. Cushner, "Creating Cross-Cultural Understanding through Internationally Cooperative Story Writing," *Social Education* 56, 1 (January 1992): 43–46.

2. Thomas Friedman, *The Lexus and the Olive Tree: Understanding Globalization* (New York: Anchor Books, 2000): 5.

3. Ibid.

4. National Council for the Social Studies, "Position Statement on Global Education" (Washington, DC: National Council for the Social Studies, 1982).

5. David Hoopes, *Intercultural Education. Phi Delta Kappa Fastback,* no. 144 (Bloomington, IN: Phi Delta Kappa Educational Foundation, 1980).

6. Robert Hanvey, "An Attainable Global Perspective" (New York: Center for Global Perspectives, 1978).

7. Jon Scieszka, *The True Story of the Three Little Pigs as Told by A. Wolf* (New York: Viking, 1989).

8. "CNN: Television for the Global Village," *World Press Review* 37, 12 (December 1990): 34.

9. E. Childers and B. Urquhart, *Renewing the United Nations System* (Geneva: United Nations, 1994).

10. Kenneth Cushner amd Gregory Trifonovitch, "Understanding Misunderstanding: Barriers to Dealing with Diversity," *Social Education* 53, 5 (1989): 318–322.

11. K. Rennebohm-Franz, "Toward a Critical Social Consciousness in Children: Multicultural Peace Education in a First Grade Classroom," *Theory into Practice* 35, 4 (autumn 1996): 265.

12. Ibid., p. 266.

13. Ibid.

14. Alan Singer, "The Impact of Industrialization on American Society: Alternative Assessments," *Social Education* 58, 3 (March 1994): 171–172.

15. A. DeKock and C. Paul, "One District's Commitment to Global Education," *Educational Leadership* 47, 1 (September 1989): 46–49; A. Crabbe, "The Future Problem-Solving Program," *Educational Leadership* 47, 1 (September 1989): 27–29.

16. K. Cushner, "Adding an International Dimension to the Curriculum," *The Social Studies* 81, 4 (July-August 1990): 166–170; Gail Hughes-Wiener, "An Overview of International Education in the Schools," *Education and Urban Society* 20, 2 (February 1988): 139–158.

17. J. Stahlman, P. Safford, S. Pisarchick, C. Miller, and D. Dyer, "Crossing the Boundaries of Early Childhood Special Education Personnel Preparation: Creating a Path for Retraining," *Teacher Education and Special Education* 12, 1 (January 1989): 5–12.

18. P. Safford, *Integrated Teaching in Early Childhood* (White Plains, NY: Longman, 1989).

19. K. Dunlop, Z. Stoneman, and M. Cantrell, "Social Interaction of Exceptional and Other Children in a Mainstreamed Preschool Classroom," *Exceptional Children* 47, 2 (October 1980): 132–141.

Creating Classrooms That Address Race and Ethnicity

All Americans are the victims of prejudice.

—*Shirley Chisolm*

Chapter Outline

1.   Do you believe that all people have prejudices? If so, in what ways do you display prejudice?

2.   Are there messages about certain groups of people that you grew up hearing and that you no longer support? How did you come to change your beliefs or point of view?

3.   How are factors of racism and prejudice evident in schools?

4.   What behaviors are effective when dealing with people who hold extreme prejudices? What responsibility should teachers assume to reduce prejudice in their students?

c a s e   s t u d y   The Chameleon[1]

The school board meetings were generally not as heated as they were that night in October when the issue of bilingual education was brought up for discussion. More than six hundred residents showed up for the meeting; so many that six police officers had been called into the auditorium as a precautionary measure. What had started a couple weeks earlier when a few students accused some teachers and administrators of prejudice and discrimination had now developed into a districtwide debate about the purpose and success of bilingual and multicultural education. The current state of affairs had certainly come a long way from the initial problem, which had been caused when a few Mexican American and Vietnamese students had not been chosen for the cheerleading squad. Some people were saying, in no uncertain terms, that students who were just learning to speak English could not be understood well enough to be on the cheerleading squad. Even one of the adults in the community was overheard to say, "If small groups of individuals had a difficult time understanding these particular students, how could a crowd of already screaming sports fans?" Over the past two weeks, majority students throughout the school began repeating these arguments. There had even been some fights between a group of Spanish-speaking boys and a group of African American football players.

Jane Myers, who had been teaching in this school for the past seven years, had never experienced such heated debate and outright antagonism before. And to top it off, the administration seemed to be dragging its feet and in no hurry to address the issue. True, they had been embroiled in the bilingual debate that was raging throughout the community, but dealing with student concerns at the moment seemed to be of the utmost importance.

Ms. Myers located the phone number of a presenter she had seen a year earlier and arranged a time for him to come to the school and meet with the junior and senior classes. She knew that something rather dramatic, but real, had to be done to get people talking with one another. John Gray could certainly facilitate that!

John Gray arrived on the planned day with plenty of time to have a cup of coffee, meet the principal, and arrange the auditorium for his needs. He had agreed to do the program, but only if persons in positions of authority would also attend; this group included Mr. Johnson, the principal; the two assistant principals; and even two of the school board members.

Ms. Myers welcomed the more than five hundred students once they settled into their seats in the auditorium. "This morning we have a speaker who will use a teaching approach known as psychodrama to help us explore issues related to prejudice and racism and the problems people of different groups can have when they live and work with those who are different from themselves. Mr. John Gray is a former personnel manager with a major Fortune 500 company and holds an MBA from Harvard University. Please join me in welcoming him to our school."

John Gray approached the stage as the students applauded. He was quite distinguished looking, really the picture of a rather successful, polite, white executive. He stood more than six feet tall and wore a gray business suit, white shirt, and a conservative red tie. His hair was straight and graying, and he had rather angular and prominent facial features.

He began in a pleasant manner, smiling and stating that he had not come with any kind of prepared speech. He would, instead, just share some ideas with the students and allow for some open discussion. But he did make some rather pointed comments. "I'll begin this morning by saying that if you are silent with me I will be making three assumptions about you and the silence. One, if you are silent, that tells me that you understand everything I am saying. Two, silence tells me that you agree with whatever it is I am saying. And three, silence tells me that you support what I am saying. Is this clear?" He paused.

"The only way I'll know anything different is if you break the silence. You see, silence, to me, is very critical. Silence suggests inaction, and the inaction then becomes a form of action." He waited again and took in the audience's silence. "So, you all just sent me the message that you understood what I just said, that you agreed with what I said, and you supported me by your silence."

There was some light laughter and apparent nervousness among the audience. A crucial contract had just been entered into with the group.

"Like any good teacher," Gray began, "I use three instructional approaches. You might think of these in terms of how you learn to do complex things, let's say learning to ride a bike. When I use the lecture method, I tell you about riding. Now while this approach may transfer a significant amount of useful information, it does not provide you the opportunity to practice the appropriate actions. Would you learn how to ride the bike? Probably not! The second approach I call the 'show-me' approach. I can demonstrate for you how to ride a bike. While this approach may enable you to see what is expected, once again, it probably will not result in you learning how to ride. There just is no opportunity to practice the skill. Now the third approach I call the 'involve-me' approach. Once you are involved, you really do begin to learn."

Gray went on to introduce the concept of prejudice and gave example after example of how people's preferences, or prejudices, can become problematic if they are extended and expected from all people. Whereas, he said, he had a prejudice toward apple pie, he did not think that all people should have only apple pie. At the same time, other people had no right to tell him what flavor pie to consume. But if Mr. Johnson, as the principal, went around and told all the students that they could eat only apple pie in school or they would be punished, then Mr. Johnson would be combining his prejudice with his power and discriminating against a certain group of people—cherry pie eaters, for instance. Then, Gray said, we get into a thing called 'pie-ism.' That, he explained, was when people and institutions, like schools, got into conflict, and then the silence had to be broken.

Gray posed a question to students. "How many of you think you are prejudiced?" Only a few hands went up. "Well, I for one think you are all prejudiced and that you are ignoring the reality in yourself. I think it's important that we all recognize that we have certain information about other people that we have been taught that may not be accurate, but yet we continue to support."

There was silence in the room.

"So, if I go by the silence, you are all agreeing with me. See, you are all prejudiced, you just weren't willing to admit it earlier."

Suddenly a hand went up from the middle of the auditorium. Gray called on the student, and he rose to speak.

"I don't think you can get away with calling me prejudiced," said the student. "I have many black and Hispanic friends, and I'm not alone. Many others in this school have friends from different backgrounds."

"Oh, I know where you are coming from," replied Gray. "You're just showing off in front of your friends to let them know how liberal you are. You can't fool most of us— we know your kind."

The student sat down quietly. Others in the room began to fidget in their seats. A female student then jumped up to defend the boy.

"How can you say that about him, you don't even know him? I think you're being prejudiced!" she challenged.

"You may be partially correct," replied Gray, "but I also know where you're coming from. Tell me," he asked, "are you Jewish?"

"No, I am not," she answered. "And why is that important?"

"Because I am a Christian, a good Christian, and I think if Jews want to believe in a God other than Jesus Christ, they should go back to Israel where they belong."

The students grew restless and agitated.

"How can you say such a thing? What does that have to do with anything?" another girl blurted out.

"What, may I ask, do you want to be when you grow up?" asked Gray.

"A politician," she replied.

"Oh, I don't think I'd spend my time doing that if I were you," he quickly responded. "Women can never really hold positions of authority and power because they are generally much more emotional than men. And there are many studies that prove that. In fact, a recent research study undertaken at the University of California at Berkeley—you know of it, I assume—stated that without a doubt women are more prone to tears and cry more when under pressure. Under pressure women just get too emotional, cry, and then fall apart. No one can be a successful leader when their emotions get in the way, and women have that problem all the time—just look at how you are acting with me.

Now you wouldn't want a leader to behave like this, would you? And I know that some of you in the audience will differ with me, but that's alright. That's your choice."

A few members of the audience laughed. Two students who were close to the back got up to walk out when Mr. Johnson approached them and quietly asked them to return to their seats.

"You know what really bothers me?" Gray continued without seeming to miss a beat, "is that affirmative action order. That order told me that I had to hire a certain number of minorities and women in my organization, and I resented that. I didn't like being forced into anything, especially having to hire people who could not do the job."

An African American male student jumped in. "What do you mean by people who couldn't do the job?"

"Well, you know," replied Gray. "Your people have trouble passing certain competency tests. Take teacher tests, for instance. Your people just can't pass those tests at the same rate that white teachers do. And you want to be teachers and teach my children? I think there's something terribly wrong with affirmative action. It's getting to the point where my children had to have a card saying they were minority or female before they could be considered for a job. That's just not right."

The students were silent.

"So I felt that I had to break the silence and fight back. I thought that if I could reach young people like yourselves in schools—because you are our future—I want to encourage you to speak out. Young man, may I ask you where you are from?"

"I'm from Africa. Nigeria to be exact. I was not born as an African American, although my family is working on getting our American citizenship."

"Well, let me suggest something to you. You're in a good school. When you learn to speak like a good American, then I can look to you as a good American who can understand what I'm trying to say. Why don't you solve the problems that you have in Africa before coming here and getting so upset with me? I see why your school is having such a debate about bilingual education. How many of you speak English as your first language, might I ask?"

The students—boy and girls, whites and blacks, Latinos and Asians—as well as teachers and administrators sat silently as more than half the hands went up.

"And what is this school doing to promote diversity?" Gray asked.

Mr. Johnson jumped in. "Mr. Gray, I did promise you academic freedom. But please try to keep your comments from being personal in nature. Students, if you have questions to ask of Mr. Gray, you can do that now. You don't have to wait for a question-and-answer period, but do ask one at a time."

"Well, I think that as a group you're showing disrespect for me," Gray continued, directing his comments toward Mr. Johnson. "Maybe I'm wasting my time with you. I really resent the way I've been treated. I don't know if you planted people in the audience to attack me, but I resent the laughter I've heard as well as some of the putdowns from those of you who may have a view that differs from mine. I've got better things to do than to stay here with you. No wonder you're having all these troubles about bilingual education in your school. I really resent the way I've been treated."

And with that, John Gray picked up his materials and walked off the stage. The students applauded as he left.

After Gray left the stage, Mr. Johnson approached the microphone. "I guess the lecture is over, and by the sounds of it, there are many people who have many things they'd like to say. I suggest we go back to our homeroom classes for a while and discuss what we have all just experienced. Then we can all come back together and meet here in the auditorium right after lunch."

There was much discussion among the students as they went back to their classes. When Jane's group reconvened in the classroom, it took her a few minutes to calm them down.

"Was he for real?" one of them asked.

"How could he be? Someone would kill him on the street if he went around talking like that to everyone!" another replied.

Jane jumped in. "How many of you know someone like John Gray?" she asked.

The room quieted down. About six hands went up.

"So," Jane continued, "It seems that some of you know someone pretty similar to Mr. Gray. Who might that person be?"

"My uncle Pete's a lot like him," a boy offered from the back of the room. "Whenever we're together at family gatherings he just rants and raves about 'those people' this and 'those people' that. He really seems to resent it when someone from another race appears to do well. He once moved out of a neighborhood that was becoming integrated. He gets so loud and forceful at times that we all just want to leave . . . but we can't . . . he's a close relative, you know. Boy, it really bothers me."

A girl from across the room picked up from there. "My sister has changed quite a lot since she got married a few years ago. I don't ever recall her being prejudiced at home. I'm not, and my parents don't seem to be. But ever since she married George she's become quite racist. I don't understand it. She has a college education, but her husband doesn't. She just seems to have adopted whatever he thinks. I've gotten into a few arguments with her, but not when her husband is around. I'm kind of afraid to speak up when he's in the room."

"What are you most afraid of, Sue?" asked Ms. Myers.

"Well," Sue continued, "He's quite loud when he gets upset. I've seen him insult people, and I'm just afraid I couldn't take his tirade. And besides, I don't want to upset my sister, so I just keep quiet. I don't know if that's the best thing to do."

"Let's think about strategies for dealing with such people a little later," Ms. Myers went on. "Does John Gray remind anyone else of someone they know?"

"Sometimes my father gets like him," Samantha added. "I've fought with him a few times when I've heard him say some rather negative things about people, especially about some of my friends at school. He gets quite upset with me when I challenge him, but it really bothers me that he can be so close-minded—and insult my friends at the same time!"

The discussion went on for quite some time, with student after student talking about someone they knew, about how they responded to such people, and how they might better respond in the future. The class, dismissed for lunch, was still talkative, as were many other students when they gathered in the lunchroom. One excited student ran into the cafeteria and reported that he had seen John Gray still in the building talking to the principal. Some of the students threatened to attack him if they saw him.

After lunch the students gathered back in the auditorium. As they settled into their chairs, Mr. Johnson walked onto the stage, took the microphone, and reported that there had been some very lively discussions in each of the homerooms. Mr. Johnson went on to report that he had been able to convince Mr. Gray not to leave because he thought it would be good to have Mr. Gray join them as they talked about their experiences and their various discussions.

There was quite a bit of talking and movement among the students when Gray returned to the stage. He took the microphone from Mr. Johnson and sat on a stool on the right side of the stage.

"I'm glad Mr. Johnson talked me into staying," Gray opened. "I understand you had quite lively discussions in your homerooms. That's good, because it is only after we begin talking about some of these issues that we will ever be able to solve them. In this case you were breaking the silence and I applaud you for that. I'd like to talk with you now about your reactions to me. I wonder if any of you have any questions for me now?"

There was nervous commotion throughout the room until one student stood up. "Are you for real? How would you deal with a person like yourself?" he asked.

"That's a very good question," replied Gray. "Let me tell you a few things about me, and then we can look at a few things about you. Would that be alright with you? And, by the way, what differences do you notice about me now?"

"Well, for one thing," a student replied, "You seem much more calm. You are not confronting us; you are sitting more relaxed, and you seem to be listening to what we are saying."

"How do you know I am listening?" asked Gray.

"Well, for one, you are responding to what I just said. You asked me a question and waited for my response."

"Yes, I will admit that sometimes I get to the point that I do not listen nor respond to the things you might say to me. But when I am doing that, I must tell you, I am not acting. I am not role-playing with you. What I am doing is what I call 'role-taking,' and let me define that. I did not memorize a script and come in here to play the role of a bigot. That's what happens in role-playing. But I was role-taking here with you this morning. I was sharing with you many messages that I heard when I was growing up—perhaps some of the messages you, too, have heard while you were growing up and perhaps still hear today. Maybe some of you shared that in your group discussions. Now while I may have heard those messages when I was younger, I do not support them today. But I do hear them in my head every now and then. I have to stop and remind myself that those are old messages, often prejudices, and I do not believe them anymore. They are like tapes that suddenly turn on in my mind when I'm in certain situations. But now that I am aware of them and now that I have more sophisticated knowledge and experience today, I know how to turn them off. So, in role-taking I was sharing messages that I grew up hearing and I was playing them all back for you. Do you recall what was said to you at the beginning of the session? You were told that you would participate in a psychodrama that would illustrate racism and prejudice in action. How many of you heard that? While you were told up front what was to happen, most of you were still personally drawn into the experience."

"I was also searching for your buttons with the hope that you would begin to feel what it might be like to be discriminated against for no other reason except being placed in a category based on some outward characteristic. That's in part what a prejudice is— it's making judgments about an individual based on some preconceived knowledge you may have about a group, even if that knowledge is incomplete or wrong. And, by the way, I apologize if I forgot 'your group.' Perhaps I neglected to talk about gays or the elderly or overweight people. All of us belong to a variety of groups that can be stereotyped and discriminated against. And that statement I made about research and women in leadership? That was not accurate. You have to be careful about how messages are presented. Sometimes they may sound quite authoritative, yet may not be truthful."

"What I'd like to do now is give you some feedback on how I saw you dealing with me so that when you are in a similar situation you can better evaluate what it is you would like to do. Is that alright?"

Many students signaled that that would be useful information.

"For one," Gray continued, "I heard quite a lot of laughter in the group. I remember in one group asking a man why he was laughing. He replied that he was laughing to prevent himself from coming up on stage and carrying me out the door—and that I better hope he kept on laughing. But consider the consequences of laughter in such a situation. Think of a young child, perhaps a brother or sister or niece or nephew. And think of when someone might laugh when they hear an ethnic joke or when they are watching a show on television like the Archie Bunker All In The Family *show. Is it possible that through the laughter we create stereotypes that may not have existed before? The child, seeing people laugh at ethnic jokes, may think, 'I like to see people laugh. Telling that joke makes people laugh.' Then he or she goes into the classroom and tells that ethnic joke and begins the whole process over again. So, it's important to think about the consequences of laughter and the role we play."*

"So, what can people do in a situation like this?" one student asked.

"I think it's important that we take a stand, tell others that we do not appreciate or support the telling of ethnic jokes, so others hear an alternative voice," said Gray. "You may not be the most popular person at the moment, but I can guarantee you that someone in the group will appreciate your sensitivity and your efforts."

"Now, related to this, let's talk about silence. Many of you were silent this morning. You may not have agreed with everything I was saying, and some of you may have actually agreed with some things you heard, but very few of you made your feelings known. Oh, you may have nudged someone sitting next to you and said something like, 'he can't be real.' But let me remind you that I am real. There are people all around you, people who, while they may not be as vocal as me, believe and act in such a manner in their neighborhoods and homes."

"But let's think about the consequences of silence. I think about Hitler. He got into power because people around him were silent and didn't challenge him. When you are silent, you are giving tacit approval of the messages you hear around you. So, my challenge to you is to break the silence. When you see an act that you know is wrong, or when you hear someone say something that you know is damaging, make yourself known. Even by simply standing up and stating something like, 'You know that statement you just made, I disagree with you and think it is wrong.' You will do wonders at drawing the

attention away from the bigot and will make those around you know that there is at least an alternative point of view. Your simple comments can go quite far at making change."

It was becoming obvious that the students had spent quite a bit of time talking about these difficult topics throughout the day. Gray sensed that it was time to bring the day to a close. The students had had quite an experience. Little did they know they were in for more.

"I know it's been a long day for us all, and I believe we've learned quite a lot. And if you think about it, you did most of the teaching here today. I think I spent less than an hour with you this morning, yet you have been engaged in this topic for most of the day."

"There is another part of myself that I have a need to share with you," he went on. "Sit back for a moment and think about me now. What images come to your mind? What judgments do you make about me now?" He paused a minute or two.

"Let me share something else with you. For over twenty years I have been using my physical appearance to illustrate the myth of race and the impact of color. Perhaps by sharing a little bit about myself I can make people stop to think about the judgments they make about others. You see, under the definition of race in this country, I would like you to know that I am black, or African American, my parents are black, both sets of my grandparents were black, I am married to a woman who is black, and I have five children of various shades."

There was silence and disbelief around the room. Students and teachers were looking back and forth at one another and at Gray. Then he showed some slides on the screen. One was of his family, showing the range of colors that were represented. Then there was one of his parents—obviously black, but light-skinned, with Gray, appearing white, among them.

"For many of you, your heads will be spinning right now. But I want you to know that what you see may not always be what you get. I am for real, and my experiences are real. Many of you may be confused because none of the visual cues about my ethnic identity are evident. Your judgments are now in question. I ask you to question all the judgments that people are so quick to make. And perhaps in your classes tomorrow you can further discuss issues related to color, race, and racism. I'd be interested in knowing what you do as a school and as individuals around these issues as the year progresses. Promise me you'll keep in touch."

And with that, John Gray left the school.

Lay versus Scientific Understanding of Race and Ethnicity

This chapter's case study vividly illustrates issues of racism and prejudice in action. It also provides a context in which to apply some of the eighteen culture-general themes introduced in Chapter 3. For instance, what attributions do you think the students were making about John Gray? What judgments were you making about John Gray as you read the case study? Did you ever imagine that he could be African American, given his physical description and the kinds of things he was saying? What attributions do you make about him now?

Pedagogies: Old and New

Teachers and school administrators who understand the deep-seated influence that race and ethnicity play in people's lives do not shy away from the topic. On the contrary, they understand the historical significance and current state of affairs that these sensitive and sometimes controversial issues assume in people's lives, and they believe they have an obligation to address these issues in their teaching. Such teachers understand the role that race takes, both in the lives of individuals and in society at large. Such teachers, especially those working primarily with children from the majority culture, understand that their students may be quite unaware of the impact that race can have on their own as well as others' lives. These teachers provide significant guidance, support, and structure to classroom and school environments that encourage new interactions and opportunities to discuss and learn about race and ethnicity.

Roles: Old and New

In classrooms that actively address issues related to race and ethnicity, teachers understand their role as active agents of change. They reach out to individuals as well as to community groups that represent various ethnic and racial groups' perspectives and experiences. Such an approach provides for authentic voices while building necessary bridges between the young people and the community. Not only are children exposed to authentic perspectives, they also interact with community representatives who are actively working to change the status quo. This exposure models for young people the desired outcomes of an effective multicultural curriculum: the skills and attitudes needed to become proactive agents of change. And these approaches get young people engaged in change efforts that impact their own school.

Place of Content Knowledge: Old and New

In recent years, race, like ethnicity, has been viewed less as a biological reality and more as a cultural construct, both of which are functions of the categorization process.[2] Americans categorize things in numerous ways, and the use of the term *race* is no exception. People may categorize themselves, or be categorized by others, according to such factors as language, religion, geography, history, ancestry, or physical traits. Think back to the range of socializing agents discussed in Chapter 2. When people assume that an ethnic group has a biological basis, they are referring to that group as a race. But there is increasing evidence that race has no biological basis. For instance, Hispanics or Latinos, referred to by some people as the Hispanic race, are quite a diverse group, with members tracing their heritage from Central and Latin America, the Caribbean, and Spain. Hispanics are an example of a linguistically based ethnic group (Spanish speaking), not a biologically based race.

Thus, not only is the term race used rather loosely, but it is also often used incorrectly. The concept of race is intended to reflect the shared genetic material, or **genotype,** within a group of people. Most people, however, scholars included, tend to use **phenotypic** traits, visible traits such as skin color, to classify people according to a given race. There are many problems with the phenotypic approach to race. For one, cultures vary in the importance given to a particular trait, and there is no agreement on which phenotypic characteristics should be emphasized. Skin color, the most apparent difference to early scientists, thus became the criterion most often used. Arbitrary cultural value was attached to skin color, and skin color then became the basis for discrimination.

It is not uncommon to still find textbooks that present the three great races as distinct from one another—white, black and yellow. This rather simplistic and inaccurate categorization scheme used race as a power mechanism by keeping white European colonizers separate from their Asian and African subjects. Attempts to make these groupings sound more scientific—by using such terms as *Caucasoid, Mongoloid,* and *Negroid*—cloud the reality that white people are really various shades of pink, beige or tan, black people are various shades of brown, and so-called yellow people are really various shades of tan or beige. Another problem with such a categorization occurs with such groups as Polynesians, Native Americans, and Australian Aborigines. No such clear-cut categorization of people based on skin color is sound.

Race as a cultural construct, however, is quite alive. But again, cultures vary in the manner in which race is construed. In the United States racial identity is acquired at birth as an ascribed status, not based on simple biology or ancestry. Consider the child of a racially mixed couple involving one African American and one European American parent. It is obvious that half the child's genetic material comes from each parent. However, American culture classifies the child as black, although it makes just as much sense to classify the child as white. In this case, heredity is being overlooked. And to confound the situation even more, racial categorization can vary from state to state. For instance, in some states, any person known to have any African American blood in his or her heritage will be classified as black. Such a situation is referred to as **hypodescent** (where *hypo* means "lower") because it automatically places the child in the minority group.[3]

A case from Louisiana vividly illustrates the role that the government can play in legalizing or inventing racial classification. Susie Guillory Phipps, a light-skinned woman with European facial features and straight black hair, discovered that she was black only when she was an adult. When she ordered a copy of her birth certificate, she found that her race was listed as "colored." She had, however, been brought up white and was twice married to white men. Phipps challenged a 1970 Louisiana law that classified as legally black anyone with at least one–thirty-second "Negro blood." The state insisted that her racial classification was correct even though the state's lawyer admitted that Phipps looked like a white person.[4] Do you think that John Gray may have had some of the same issues in his life?

The Susie Guillory Phipps Case

Assessment: Old and New

Assessment across cultural, racial, and ethnic boundaries has historically been a sensitive issue. The traditional cross-cultural research literature is filled with numerous studies that report the unfortunate but common practice of taking an assessment instrument developed and normed on one culture and using it with little or no modification in another cultural setting. Such use more often than not results in inaccurate judgments of people because:

(1) certain concepts that are important in one culture may be missed by some assessment instruments; (2) procedures developed in one country or culture may not be appropriate; or (3) it may be assumed that all people share in certain experiences that are not, in fact, universally practiced. Assessment that is sensitive to the role of race, ethnicity, and culture considers the sociocultural context of the learner and the learner's family as well as that of the examiner; it addresses such issues as biases, stereotypes, and prior experience as well as the selection of appropriate testing instruments or interview procedures. Awareness of such issues enhances the possibility of more relevant and culturally sensitive assessments. In addition, issues related to language and its complexities must also be considered when selecting and conducting assessments. The teacher who is sensitive to racial and ethnic concerns also struggles to understand that people display strengths and talents in many different ways. (See Chapter 12 for more information about assessments.)

Bias in Testing

Expanding the Discussion of Race and Ethnicity in Education

We Have Been Different from the Beginning

Activity 9: Family Tree: Tracing One's Roots and Family History

It is important to know a bit about our national history as well as how the educational establishment has responded to issues of race and ethnicity. Intolerance toward differences probably began in the Americas with the introduction of European culture in the 1490s. There is considerable evidence that the Native American populations that existed in the Americas before European settlement exhibited far greater tolerance toward diversity of thought and lifestyle than did the arriving Europeans. The Taino people, for instance, greeted Columbus with food, shelter, and open festivity when the Spaniards first arrived on their small Caribbean island in 1492. At first intrigued with the Taino people, Columbus thought them to be both decorous and praiseworthy. The Taino people's hospitality, however, was soon met with severe cruelty by the Spaniards. Within twenty years of Columbus's landing, the Taino were nearly extinct as a people. In fact, the Spainards' tendency toward intolerance of both religious and cultural diversity may have prevented them from becoming the dominant culture in North America. They spent so much energy repressing and fighting the native populations that the northern spread of Spanish culture was halted in the southwest.

The Taino People

The emergence of the English as the dominant force in the new lands may be partially attributed to their somewhat greater tolerance, which was perhaps born of their own need for religious freedom. However, even though the English government allowed and even encouraged immigrants from a variety of ethnic backgrounds to settle in America, it was the white, English-born Protestants who, by the time the United States became a nation in 1776, had emerged as the dominant group. This group, too, was fearful of "different" kinds of immigrants. In 1698, for example, South Carolina passed an act exempting Irish and Roman Catholics from new bounties (the granting of lands). In 1729, Pennsylvania placed a duty on all servants of Scotch-Irish descent. One official was concerned that if immigrants continued to come, they might make themselves proprietors of the province. Ironically, the very people who originally had come to the New World to escape religious persecution were among those who actively engaged in the persecution of others for their beliefs, values, and lifestyles.

The Civil War: Freedmen's Schools and the Issue of Race

Issues of race in public education became important only after the Civil War. In the pre–Civil War south it was against the law to educate black slave children, so no racial problem existed in southern schools. In the north, blacks who had bought or had been given their freedom achieved some education in the common schools, in African American church communities, and through abolitionist efforts. After the Civil War, the education of black children was still not perceived to be a "national problem" by most whites because, where African Americans were educated at all, they were educated in separate schools. Southern states, notably resistant to providing public education for blacks, were not above taxing them for white schools. In some places—Florida, Texas, and Kentucky, for example—black schools were built only after black citizens paid a second tax to build their own schools.

In 1865, Congress established the Freedmen's Bureau to help freed slaves with the transition to citizenship. In 1866, the law was amended to assist in the provision of black schools. Many of the teachers in these schools were northern white women, often daughters of abolitionist families. Indeed, the story of the women, both black and white, who taught in the "Freedmen's schools" is among the proudest in the history of teaching. By 1870, nearly seven thousand white and black "schoolmarms" were teaching 250,000 black students and were learning to cross the barriers of race and class that have characterized American history. The legacy of these teachers was enormous. Not only did they educate the children who later became the teachers in segregated schools, but they educated a generation of free black leaders who are too seldom talked about today.

The Freedmen's Bureau

Violence characterized the development of black schools after the Civil War. The burning of school buildings and the harassment of black teachers and students were commonplace. However, passage of the Fourteenth Amendment to the Constitution in 1868 made responsibility for civil rights a federal rather than a state function, and as a result, African Americans began to gain more access to public education. Fully aware that education was a way out of poverty, black parents saw that their children got to school, one way or another. When children were needed on the farm, they would alternate between school and work, as one Alabama boy describes:

> I took turns with my brother at the plow and in school; one day I plowed and he went to school, the next day he plowed and I went to school; what was learned on his school day he taught me at night and I did the same for him.[5]

Black children remained in segregated schools that were funded at minimal rates and often open for only part of the year. Indeed, despite efforts through the courts to equalize the rights of blacks in all spheres of public life, in the 1896 *Plessy v. Ferguson* decision, the Supreme Court held that segregation was not prohibited by the Constitution. *Plessy v. Ferguson*, which upheld the doctrine that "separate but equal" facilities for blacks and whites were constitutionally permissible, justified the separate (and usually inferior) education of African American children in both the north and south until 1954.

Plessy v. Fergusen

The situation was worse for African American children with disabilities because few received any schooling at all in the nineteenth century. The tiny number who did, mainly those with visual impairments, experienced double segregation. Among the thirty public and private residential schools for blind pupils established in the United States between 1832 and 1875 was the first school for "the colored blind" in North Carolina. By 1931 there were five such separate schools for black children and youth. Ten other black schools maintained separate (inferior) departments for blind students, most of which used secondhand materials such as badly worn Braille books that were virtually impossible to read. Moreover, "segregation not only kept black children in separate schools staffed by black teachers, but prevented those teachers from attending courses given at white southern colleges."[6] Black teachers' lower salaries made attendance at northern colleges prohibitive.

Legislative and Judicial Landmarks

Brown v. The Board of Education of Topeka

The start of events that led to desegregation in schools is usually marked by the 1954 Supreme Court decision in *Brown v. The Board of Education of Topeka.* This landmark decision stated that segregated schools were inherently unequal and that state laws that allowed separate schools for black and white students were unconstitutional. Passage of this law and others like it, however, did not guarantee equality of educational opportunity to all children. Frequently, court assistance was needed to ensure compliance with congressional mandates. A significant case in the development of multicultural and bilingual education was *Lau v. Nichols,* decided by a 1974 Supreme Court ruling. This decision declared that a San Francisco school district violated a non-English-speaking Chinese student's right to equal educational opportunity when it failed to provide needed English language instruction and other special programs. An important consequence of the *Lau* decision was the declaration that school districts across the country must provide students an education in languages that meet their needs.

Integration of Central High School in Little Rock, Arkansas

Perhaps the most controversial test of mandated efforts at desegregation, however, took place on September 4, 1957, when nine black teenagers attempted to enter Central High School in Little Rock, Arkansas, for the first time. The students were turned away by the National Guard, which was called out by Governor Orval Faubus "to preserve the peace and avert violence." While this event was not the final chapter in the story of the integration of Central High School, it was not the first chapter, either. It was, however, one that—shown widely on national television—riveted the nation. If any episode in the history of the civil rights movement in public education can be said to remain in the public mind, it is this one.

Contrary to what many people believe, the state of Arkansas and the city of Little Rock had made some strides in desegregating its public facilities prior to the integration of Central High School. As early as 1949, the School of Law at the University of Arkansas was integrated, and in 1951 the Little Rock Public Library Board approved the integration of its facilities. In 1956, the city's public buses were quietly desegregated with little fuss. However, as many other cities in the United States were discovering, integrating schools was a more difficult—and emotional—matter.

In May 1954, five days after the Supreme Court decision in *Brown v. Board of Education of Topeka,* the Little Rock School Board issued a policy statement offering to comply with the Brown decision "when the Court outlines the method to be followed and the time to be allowed." Two days later, the board voted unanimously to adopt the superintendent's plan of gradual integration beginning in September 1957 at the high school level and adding the lower grades over the next six years. But for those people who yearned for faster action, this plan was insufficient.

In January 1956, twenty-seven students attempted to register in all-white Little Rock schools and were turned down. One month later, the National Association for the Advancement of Colored People (NAACP) filed suit on behalf of thirty-three black children denied admittance to four white schools, and in August of that year, a federal judge dismissed the suit, ruling that the Little Rock School Board had acted in good faith in proposing its plan. The students would have to wait.

As the fall of 1957 approached, citizens opposed to integration began to organize. Specifically, a member of the Mother's League of Central High School attempted to block integration by asking for an injunction, which was granted in a local court on August 27 and then nullified in a federal court three days later. Central High School would be integrated in September.

But it was not that simple. On September 23, surrounded by an angry crowd of about a thousand people, the nine students again tried to enter the school—this time through a side door. When the crowd discovered that the students were inside, it became unruly, and police feared that they could not maintain control. The black students were taken out of the school, again through a side door. The next day, the mayor of Little Rock asked President Eisenhower for federal troops to maintain order; the president sent one thousand members of the 101st Airborne Division to Little Rock and federalized the Arkansas National Guard. On September 25, escorted by federal troops, the nine black students again entered Central High School.

During the 1957–58 school year, the "Little Rock Nine" (as the students came to be called) tried to maintain their composure and their studies in an atmosphere of student unrest and adult confrontations—in court and outside it. In December, one of the nine students, at the end of her patience with taunting by white students, dumped a bowl of chili on her tormentors in the cafeteria; she was suspended for six days and, after further altercations, ultimately for the rest of the year. She transferred to a high school in New York City.

In February 1958, the Little Rock School Board filed a request to delay integration until the concept, "all deliberate speed" was defined. In June, a federal judge granted the delay, writing that although black students had a constitutional right to attend white schools, the "time has not come for them to enjoy that right." The NAACP appealed that decision, and in August it was reversed by a federal court of appeals.

Over the summer of 1958, the school board asked for a stay of the appeals court ruling to enable them to appeal to the Supreme Court; the Supreme Court called a special session to discuss the Little Rock case; Governor Faubus asked the Arkansas legislature for a law enabling him to close public schools to avoid integration and lease the closed schools to private school corporations; the Supreme Court ruled that Little Rock must continue with its integration plan; the school board announced the opening of the city's high schools on September 15; Governor Faubus ordered Little Rock's three high schools closed. At the end of September, voters overwhelmingly opposed integration by a vote of 129,470 to 7,561. Public high schools in Little Rock were closed for the year.

In November 1958, five of the six members of the Little Rock School Board resigned in frustration, having been ordered to proceed with integration of the high schools even though it had no high schools to integrate. In December, a new school board was elected, evenly divided between pro and con factions. In May 1959, segregationist members of the school board attempt to fire forty-four teachers and administrators suspected of integrationist sympathies. Three moderates on the board walked out, refusing to participate. In June 1959, a federal court declared the state's school-closing law unconstitutional, and the new school board announced that it would reopen the schools in the fall of 1959.

Thirteen years later, in the fall of 1972, all grades in Little Rock public schools were finally integrated. Forty years later, in the fall of 1997, President Clinton—who was an eleven-year-old student in a nearby town when the first attempt to integrate Central High School occurred—held the door to the high school open for the returning members of the Class of 1957, including most of the Little Rock Nine.

The Civil Rights Movement and the Schools

Not long after the Little Rock Nine first attempted to enter Central High School, diversity in American society and in its schools again became the subject of major social turmoil. During the 1960s and 1970s, fueled by the general social ferment of the civil rights movement and the war in Vietnam, educational reform legislation was enacted in the areas of desegregation, multicultural and bilingual education, mainstreaming students with special needs into regular classrooms, and gender-sensitive education. These programs recognized the pluralistic nature of this society in a positive rather than a negative sense. Each one attempted to help some educationally disadvantaged group receive a better education within a pluralistic framework.

**Civil Rights
Legislation**

It is important to realize that these educational mandates were not achieved in isolation but as part of the larger human and civil rights struggles of the 1960s and 1970s. During this period, Congress passed a number of antidiscriminatory statutes: the Voting Rights Act (1963), dealing with voter registration; the Equal Pay Act (1963), which required that males and females occupying the same position be paid equally; the Civil Rights Act (1964), dealing with housing and job discrimination as well as with education; the Bilingual Education Act of 1968 (Title VII of the Elementary and Secondary Education Act), which established programs for children whose first language was not English; Title IX of the Education Amendments (1972), prohibiting sex discrimination against students and employees of educational institutions; and the Education of All Handicapped Children Act (1975), requiring schools to assume the responsibility for educating all children in the least restrictive environment possible. It was, in the words of one partisan observer, a period of "intensity of concern and commitment to do something about the problems in America stemming from the continued growth of its pluralistic character."[7]

In education the chief concerns were for access and equity: access to public education for excluded groups and a guarantee that such education would be equitable, that is, that it would be commensurate with the best that public education could offer. All these efforts rested on the belief that previously excluded groups had an inherent right to educational equity. Why was it important to emphasize the rights of racial and ethnic minorities, women, and persons with disabilities? Why was it important to enact legislation that protects their rights? Quite simply, these rights had not been recognized in the past, and large numbers of people had experienced discrimination and unequal opportunity in a society that rests on the principle that *all* citizens are equal under the law. The civil rights movement was a reaffirmation of beliefs that form the very basis of American society and an insistence that we live up to our ideals in education as well as in other aspects of social life.

What are some of the causes of ethnic or racial conflict in society? Why do these differences often lead to conflict and violence? What might educators do to prevent or help resolve situations rife with conflict? These are all legitimate questions to consider as you work to create more collaborative and inclusive classrooms and schools.

The causes of ethnic differences can be political, economic, religious, linguistic, cultural, or racial. Ethnic differences often lead to conflict or violence because of the sense of injustice that arises from differences in resource distribution, from economic or political competition, and from reaction to discrimination, prejudice, and other expressions of threatened or devalued identity.[8]

Curriculum Transformation: The Case of Prejudice

Discussions of categorization and stereotyping (see Chapter 3) inevitably lead into a discussion of issues surrounding prejudice and discrimination. It seems to be human nature to surround ourselves with others who provide social acceptance and help in times of need. As a result, people spend a considerable amount of time and energy learning the norms of the groups to which they wish to belong. One consequence of this tendency is that individuals begin to think that the familiar behaviors of their group are good and natural and that those of others are less good and less natural. Recall that *ethnocentrism* refers to the tendency people have to make judgments based on their own standards and to apply those standards to others. When people make nonreflective judgments about others that are harsh or discriminatory or that involve rejection, then the judgments are called *prejudicial*. The word **prejudice** implies a lack of much thought or care in making a judgment; prejudicial responses are quick, narrow in scope, and based on negative emotions rather than accurate information. Prejudice appears to be a cultural universal; that is, people around the world behave in similar ways toward certain other rejected groups.

Prejudice often seems to be an entirely negative phenomenon. It is easy to judge others' prejudices (and even our own) rather harshly. But we need to understand that if prejudice did not have a psychological function it would quickly disappear. Just as fear encourages people to prepare for danger and just as pain makes people aware of some problem, prejudice also serves an adaptive purpose. Researchers are seeking out the reasons for its existence. Katz, for example, suggests that prejudice serves at least four functions: adjustment function, ego-defensive function, value expressive function, and knowledge function.[9]

Prejudice and Prejudice Reduction

Adjustment Function

People need to adjust to the complex world in which they live, and if holding certain prejudicial attitudes aids that adjustment, they will be maintained. For instance, a teacher who believes that members of certain minority groups or people with disabilities are incapable of achieving at a high level then has an excuse for not finding alternative methods of reaching them. This attitude reduces the work-related responsibilities of the teacher, thus making life a bit easier. However, it obviously prevents these students from achieving their full potential.

Ego-Defensive Function

People may hold certain prejudicial attitudes because they protect self-concepts. If less successful students want to think of themselves as on equal terms with higher achieving students, they may be inclined to view the comparison group as cheaters. Holding this attitude protects the self-image of these individuals without any painful self-examination of the reasons for their own lack of success. The ego-defensive function also protects a positive view of one's ingroup. Rejection of others then becomes a way of legitimizing one's own viewpoint as well as a way of avoiding the possibility that others may have an equally legitimate point of view.

Value-Expressive Function

People use prejudicial attitudes to demonstrate their own self-image to others. If people believe they are custodians of the truth about the role of education, for instance, or that the god of their religion is the one true god, then other groups must be incorrect in their thinking. If one's group has attained success through the use of highly valued technology, then those who do not have this technology must be backward. The value-expressive function presents a certain image to the world whereas the ego-defensive function protects that image by blaming others when things go wrong.

Knowledge Function

Some prejudicial attitudes make the stereotypical knowledge of one's ingroup the basis of one's personal judgments and actions. Some groups, for instance, might consider certain outgroup members undesirable as peers or romantic partners. Holding these attitudes allows individuals to make quick (usually negative) decisions when faced with choices involving individuals from the outgroup.

There is often a close relationship between the knowledge and adjustment functions. The former has to do with the information that one's ingroup believes is important; the latter, with how people use that information in making decisions. Consider the example of friendships and romantic relationships with members of certain outgroups. There can be severe consequences for violations of the ingroup ideology. People can be expelled from their ingroup, shunned by their families, or excommunicated from their church for entering into relationships with the "wrong" partners.

critical incident

Nurturing a Gang?

Steve, Bart, and Allen had been spending quite a bit of time together, something not unusual for adolescent boys their age. Jane Myers, as well as many of the other teachers, was concerned that the boys seemed to be excessively close to one another while excluding most others. This behavior was especially apparent before and after school hours when the boys could be seen hanging around street corners close to the school. Other students had begun complaining that the boys were verbally abusive, were using derogatory names, and were occasionally even physically abusive. There was talk among some of the students that the boys might be involved in gang activity, which might explain their increase in fighting and verbal assaults on some of the ethnic minorities in the school. Ms. Myers, with the assistance of Principal Johnson, called the boys' parents in for a conference.

- How would you plan for this meeting with the boys' parents?
- What aspects of the boy's behavior would you focus on first? Next? Why?
- What strategies might you use to make the meeting as positive as possible?
- How would you use your knowledge of prejudice, the functions of prejudice, and prejudice reduction as a central part of your discussion?
- In your discussions with Principal Johnson and the teachers, what efforts at the school level might you integrate? Why did you choose these activities?

Prejudice Formation

The Components of Prejudice

Psychologists identify three components of prejudice: cognitive, affective, and behavioral. The *cognitive component* refers to the process of categorization previously discussed in Chapter 3. Narrowly constructed categories result in stereotypes. The *affective component* refers to the feelings that accompany a person's thoughts about members of a particular group. The affect attached to any statement can, of course, be positive or negative. The affective component is the one most often thought of as prejudice. The *behavioral component* is the discriminatory behavior that people who harbor prejudices are capable of directing toward others, especially when the same person possesses both prejudice and power. Power differentials are often evident between differing racial and ethnic individuals and groups.

Activity 20: Examining Stereotypes Held by Self and Others

How Children Learn Prejudice

Educators can work with each of these components in different ways. Chapter 3 pointed out that the categorization process is a cultural universal that helps people simplify the multitude of stimuli they confront each day. As educators, we must recognize this fact,

**Activity 21:
Stereotypes and
Their Impact
on Interaction
and Learning**

make a point of informing others about it, and work to broaden our students' (and our own) categories. One long-term goal of both multicultural and global education is for individuals to become broader, more complex thinkers. That is, people should develop the ability to perceive and evaluate situations from a number of perspectives, not just their native orientation. In addition to this cognitive dimension, the affective and behavioral components are also under the control of educators. Strategies and programs that have successfully reduced negative affect and behavior toward others will be discussed in the following sections.

Children are aware of differences in others from a very early age. It is in the early childhood and elementary school years that children's attitudes toward members of particular groups are being formed and crystallized. One critical role of schooling should be to provide positive experiences that cause children to rethink their beliefs about group differences.[10] On their own, children are unlikely to engage in reevaluation.

The literature on prejudice formation in children identifies four basic ways in which children may learn to be prejudiced: observation, group membership, the media, and religious fundamentalism.[11]

Observation

**Activity 22:
How to
Respond to
Stereotypes**

Children learn prejudice by observing the behavior of others, particularly respected elders. If those who surround a child hold biased beliefs about a particular group (the disabled, members of a certain religion, the physically unattractive, etc.), children may be inclined to follow suit. Although children learn much from the subtle messages given by others, some learn prejudice from more blatant efforts by parents and community.[12]

Group Membership

Children, like other individuals, want to feel that they belong to a group. If the group that the child identifies with excludes or devalues certain others, the child is likely to adopt that behavior and those attitudes. Thus, children may learn prejudice simply as a survival technique, as a way to fit into a group. Some children, for instance, are actively prepared from a very early age for adult roles in various religious cults or in secular organizations like the Ku Klux Klan.

The Media

The media presents another way in which children learn prejudice. While the media may not actively teach prejudice, it sometimes reinforces stereotypes or in some cases introduces stereotypes where they may not already exist. Cowboy and Indian films, for instance, have had a significant impact on children's views of Native Americans.[13] Both electronic and print media, through children's stories, often equate beauty with goodness and ugliness with evil. The symbolic association with evil of physical disabilities such as hunchbacks, peg legs, eye patches, and hooked arms may encourage a negative attitude toward disabilities.[14]

Religious Fundamentalism

The more orthodox or fundamental a person's religious beliefs are, the greater the prejudice toward other religious and cultural groups is likely to be. People's strict adherence to certain religious practices may actively encourage them to believe that all other doctrines, as well as the individuals who believe in them, are at best "wrong" and at worst dangerous.

Extreme Cases of Prejudice

Hate Groups

The *Dictionary of Multicultural Education* defines hate groups as any organized body that denigrates select groups of people based on their ethnicity, race, or sexual orientation or that advocates the use of violence against such groups or their members for purposes of scapegoating.[15] The term, as used in the United States, is generally applied to white supremacist groups such as the Ku Klux Klan, the White Aryan Resistance, and the Church of Jesus Christ Christians/Aryan Nations. While local chapters of hate groups tend to target racial or ethnic minorities in their immediate area, all of the groups are anti-black and anti-Semitic.

Hate Groups

It is difficult to obtain accurate figures on the number of hate groups or individual membership, but estimates range from between 250 to 400 groups, representing some 20,000 to 200,000 members. Some of these groups limit their activities to producing and distributing literature, actions that would be most typically observed in schools, while others are known to commit acts of violence, including vandalism, intimidation, assault, and murder.

But it should not be assumed that all hate groups are white. The Nation of Islam, a black Muslim separatist group, is regarded by some people as a hate group, with its main targets being whites and Jews. Their activities, however, as best as can be determined, have been restricted to verbal assaults and printed material.

White Privilege

People can in many ways unknowingly contribute to the existence of prejudice. A particular situation, referred to as *white privilege,* exists when white people, who may have been taught that racism is something that puts others at a disadvantage, are not taught to see the corresponding advantage that their color brings to them. Peggy McIntosh refers to white privilege as "an invisible package of unlearned assets that I can count on cashing in each day, but about which I was meant to remain oblivious. White privilege is like an invisible weightless knapsack of special provisions, maps, passports, codebooks, visas, clothes, tools, and blank checks."[16] White privilege, like its counterpart male privilege, remains largely unconscious for most perpetrators; people generally do not recognize their own oppressive behavior. Rather, individuals typically attribute success and status to personal traits rather than situational factors (recall the fundamental attribution error discussed in Chapter 3).

White Privilege

Activity 23: Privilege: The Invisible Knapsack

McIntosh identifies numerous instances where she (and whites in general) are at an advantage over people of color: she can arrange to be in the company of people of her own race most of the time; should she have to move, she can be pretty confident that she can find a home in an area she can afford and in which she would want to live; she can go shopping alone most of the time without being followed or harassed; her children will find examples of their race as the foundation of the school curriculum; she will not be asked to represent her entire race; and she can speak in public to a powerful male group without putting her entire race on trial.[17] In what ways can you see that you or others around you may have been privileged?

Racial Profiling

Although there is no single, universally accepted definition of racial profiling, it generally refers to the law enforcement practice of targeting someone for investigation while passing through some public space (public highways, airports, etc.) where the reason for the stop is a statistical profile of the detainee's race, ethnicity, or national origin (especially prevalent in times of national crises and war). In such instances, race may be used to determine which drivers to stop for minor traffic violations (sometimes referred to as "driving while black") and which motorists or pedestrians to search for contraband.

Racial profiling has increased in frequency in the United States in recent years. Despite the civil rights victories of thirty years ago, official racial prejudice is still reflected throughout law enforcement practices as well as the criminal justice system. Although some observers claim that racial profiling doesn't exist, there is an abundance of stories and statistics that document the practice.

Prejudice Reduction

**Activity 24:
Institutional
Discrimination**

In schools, perhaps more than in any other social setting, opportunities exist to have intimate and regular interactions with a wide diversity of people. It is thus critical that educators, at whatever levels they work, take the opportunity to become proactive in improving intergroup relations.

Critical to reducing prejudice and establishing an interculturally sensitive classroom is the teacher's understanding of, and ability to integrate, intercultural awareness and prejudice reduction activities into the curriculum. Intercultural education and training, however, is a delicate and difficult endeavor that must be approached with the greatest of sensitivity.

We are fortunate that the educational research literature supports our efforts to reduce prejudice. Indeed, there is some indication that we may even be able to decrease the likelihood that prejudiced attitudes will develop.[18] Educational strategies that have demonstrated the ability to reduce prejudice generally fall into four categories: (1) improving social contact and intergroup relations, (2) increasing cognitive sophistication, (3) improving self-esteem, and (4) increasing empathy and understanding of other groups.[19] These categories all have curricular implications, which are discussed in the following sections.

1. Improving Social Contact and Intergroup Relations

From a programmatic standpoint, the most promising of all change efforts stems from the work of researchers interested in intergroup interaction. Allport, in proposing the contact hypothesis, suggested that one way to reduce negative prejudice is to bring representatives of different groups into close contact with one another.[20] Sometimes this method proves helpful, but not always; occasionally, negative prejudice is reinforced or, in fact, formed where it did not previously exist. A different hypothesis suggests that it is the conditions under which groups come together that is critical. Certain characteristics of the contact situation are required to ensure positive outcomes. Considerable efforts under many different circumstances (bilingual classrooms, integrated housing and schools, summer camp programs) have led to recommendations concerning the best conditions under which social contact can be improved. These conditions relate to equal status, superordinate goals, encouragement, and personal familiarity.

Equal Status Contact

Amir, working in integrated school settings in Israel, found that if individuals coming together perceive that they have equal status, or equal access to any rewards available, conditions are set for improved relations.[21] In Switzerland, for instance, French, German, and Italian are all recognized as official languages of the country. Official documents are made available in all three languages. Speakers of diverse languages, therefore, are all appreciated, well informed, and encouraged to participate in the society at large.[22] (Note the current movement underway in many of our states to make English the official language, even though this country boasts the fifth largest Spanish-speaking population in the world!)

In the school context, equal access to rewards can be translated to equal access to knowledge, grades, or extracurricular offerings. In order for all students to have equal access to knowledge and grades, culturally appropriate curricula and instructional strategies need to be employed. Also at issue is the necessity to encourage all students to participate in extracurricular offerings, which may not occur in the "natural" course of events. Social class status has significant impact on the kinds of school experiences in which a child may participate. Children from lower socioeconomic groups tend to participate in fewer after-school activities than do their middle-class counterparts, and thus they do not reap the potential benefits of such participation. For example, the development of skills related to group and team thinking and acting that have been shown to be associated with managerial or other higher level employment are often learned through extracurricular activities rather than in formal classrooms. Recent legislation regarding equal rights for disabled persons is also intended to bring equal access to children with disabilities.

Superordinate Goals

Even when equal status is achieved, however, it alone is not sufficient. Individuals who come together and work toward achieving some superordinate goal or common task that could not be satisfied without the participation of all involved are more likely to learn to get along. This concept stems from the work of Sherif, who, although he was successfully able to create hostility and aggression between two groups of boys at summer camp, found it quite difficult to bring them back together again as one larger, cooperative group.[23] Finally, after much trial and error, he was able to bring both groups together after staging an incident in which a bus got stuck in the mud while on the way to a camp outing. In order for the bus to continue on its way, all the campers had to work together to push the bus back onto the road. This superordinate goal, which could not have been achieved without everyone's participation, enabled all the campers to work together.

In the school context, superordinate goals are readily available in the form of team sports, drama productions, and music performances as well as through cooperative learning activities that can be easily integrated in the classroom setting. When students with disabilities participate in the mainstream of school life (extracurricular as well as academic activities), such co-participation with nondisabled peers in pursuit of common goals is possible. Similarly, students who have opportunities to work with others across racial and ethnic boundaries in activities like sports, plays, and concerts tend to develop more positive attitudes toward one another. Educators who work in schools that are more homogenous will need to put more effort and imagination into planning activities that involve diverse groups. Such activities may teach students to "see" invisible differences, such as differences in learning style, differences in religious attitudes, or differences in knowledge and perceptions related to gender roles. Activities might also involve cooperative efforts with other communities and schools or efforts to encourage the implementation of international exchange students on a regular basis. Educators could encourage integrated activities between students with disabilities and without disabilities; across traditional age barriers; between high school and elementary school students; or between older people in the community and students of all ages.

Encouragement of Intergroup Interaction

In order to be effective, efforts to reduce prejudice must be seen as important at all levels of the school. Such efforts cannot be seen entirely as the whim or "cause" of a particular teacher or particular group. Teachers, school administrators, and as many other adults as possible must actively encourage and show support for such efforts. Do not interpret this caveat, however, to mean that an individual teacher cannot initiate such changes. Innumerable teachers acting independently or with a small group of colleagues have demonstrated that the initial efforts of a single individual can have broad effects, especially in curricular decisions. Although the school system controls much of a teacher's ability to make significant and permanent change partly in the way it controls available resources, it by no means controls everything. Indeed, many, if not most, school systems today are eager and willing to support a teacher who is trying something new in the way of curricular revision. Careful documentation of the revision process and its results are needed in order to institutionalize the changes that are effective and to refine the teacher's initial work.

Personal Familiarity

A high acquaintance potential must exist, encouraging close contact between individuals in a given situation. In other words, people must have the opportunity to get to know the "other" person in ways that render the stereotypic image clearly inappropriate. It is very difficult, for instance, for a student to believe that all people on welfare are lazy when that student knows firsthand that Susan and her mother are both working as much as they are allowed to within the welfare rules and that if Susan's mother took an available job that did not include health benefits, she would lose the health card she is using to treat Susan's chronic asthma.

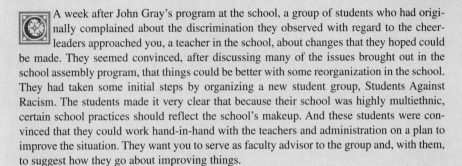

The New Student Activist Group

A week after John Gray's program at the school, a group of students who had originally complained about the discrimination they observed with regard to the cheer-
leaders approached you, a teacher in the school, about changes that they hoped could
be made. They seemed convinced, after discussing many of the issues brought out in the
school assembly program, that things could be better with some reorganization in the school.
They had taken some initial steps by organizing a new student group, Students Against
Racism. The students made it very clear that because their school was highly multiethnic,
certain school practices should reflect the school's makeup. And these students were convinced that they could work hand-in-hand with the teachers and administration on a plan to
improve the situation. They want you to serve as faculty advisor to the group and, with them,
to suggest how they go about improving things.

- How would you use your knowledge of prejudice, the functions of prejudice, and
  prejudice reduction as a central part of your discussion?
- In your discussions with Principal Johnson and the teachers, what efforts at the school
  level might you integrate? Why did you choose these activities?

Time for informal activity, perhaps even structured into the day or on weekends,
must occur. Students can be placed in different heterogeneous groups for a variety of
purposes, and they can be encouraged (or required) to participate in mixed team sports
or any other scheme that will enable them to get to know others on a personal basis.

Some Cautions in Applying the Contact Hypothesis

While application of the contact hypothesis generally proves beneficial, applying it in
the real world of school settings has always been problematic for a variety of factors.
Many schools are relatively monocultural and thus provide little opportunity for intergroup contact to occur. In such situations it might be best to stress the diversity that is
evident within a group, such as socioeconomic differences or gender differences.

But even when cultural, ethnic, racial, and socioeconomic diversity is evident in
the school, other factors often mediate against regular, meaningful intergroup interaction.
Problematic issues of applying the contact hypothesis in schools may center on the
criterion of equal status contact. Although equal status contact provides much of the
foundational structure that underlies many group activities in the classroom, including
cooperative learning strategies, it may be difficult to bring about in the somewhat artificial setting of the school primarily because groups do not have equal status outside the
school. Students do not leave their social status at home when they come to school.
Social contact efforts, therefore, may lead to increased stereotyping among groups. Some
schools continue to experience patterns of racial and ethnic segregation, often as a result
of segregated housing patterns, which reduces the possibility of intergroup contact. And

in many instances, integrated schools may end up resegregating themselves through the practice of ability or achievement tracking. Tracking, or segregation by group, may relegate a disproportionate number of low-income students and students of color to lower-tracked classes in which they receive inferior education, thus perpetuating the problem. Tracking can occur for a variety of reasons and in many different contexts. Grouping students by academic ability has long been, and continues to be, practiced in many schools, and it may result in the unintended segregation of students by ethnicity or race. In some schools, students may segregate themselves into like-groups in classrooms as a result of participation in extracurricular activities, on the playground, or in the lunchroom. Schools, too, may be segregated simply by the neighborhoods that they serve.

Another problem with the equal status concept is that it may not generalize beyond the immediate context in which an intervention occurs. That is, while intergroup relations may appear to improve among individuals who come into contact in the school setting, such attitude change may not transfer to other contexts. Equal status between two groups may not generalize to other outgroups or when status is not equal, as in a community context.

2. Increasing Cognitive Sophistication

Strategies designed to increase cognitive sophistication have been shown to have a positive impact on prejudice reduction. A considerable amount of research points to the fact that individuals who think in narrow terms are more likely to have a high degree of prejudice. Strategies that are designed to help individuals avoid stereotypes and overgeneralizations and become aware of the biases in their thinking and behavior do help them become less prejudiced. This research means we must focus our teaching efforts on improving students' critical thinking skills. Thinking in a critical manner is antithetical to prejudicial thinking. Rather than reacting quickly because of an emotional response, students must search for and examine the reasons or motivations behind their thoughts and actions. People who think critically tend to question, analyze, and suspend judgment until all available information is collected and examined.

Activity 38: Determining Bias in Textbooks

D'Angelo identified ten essential criteria in the development of critical thought:[24] intellectual curiosity; being objective and relying on evidence in making one's argument; being open-minded such that there is a willingness to consider a wide range of possibilities; flexibility in one's thinking; intellectual skepticism, or evaluating considerable evidence before accepting a hypothesis; intellectual honesty, or a willingness to accept evidence even if it conflicts with a previously held belief; being systematic, or trying to be consistent in one's line of reasoning; being persistent; being decisive when enough supporting evidence is available; and being attentive, or having respect for other points of view and responding, in an appropriate manner, to what others are saying.

Teachers should work hard to create the kind of classroom environment that encourages critical thought. In such classrooms, students feel respected and have a certain degree of trust, because students cannot function at higher levels of cognitive activity when their anxiety level is high. Feelings of safety and trust are thus a corollary of student risk taking. Recall the role that the culture-general themes of anxiety, belonging, and status play in people's sense of emotional stability.

The classroom should reflect, as Lipman states, a "community of inquiry,"[25] or as described in Chapter 7, "a learning community." Such an environment is characterized by questions of all kinds—those for which there are "right" answers and those that have more than one right answer. Indeed, some educators feel that in order to prepare students for the real world outside school, teachers' questions must force students to consider all sides of the problem, some of which may, in fact, be conflicting.

A balance should be maintained between teacher talk and student talk. Students must believe that their ideas are important and that what they have to say is critical. It is through discussion with others and through the sharing of ideas and problems that critical thinking develops. Within the context of a safe, open classroom discussion, all students should be allowed to participate and to feel that their participation was successful.

Students should be taught to think about their thinking and should be able to justify their reasoning with evidence. An emphasis should be on *metacognition,* or becoming aware of how one has come to a decision. Students who are aware of how they arrive at defensible positions are on their way to becoming independent, self-regulated learners.

To think critically means to think broadly, to take all sides of a problem into account, and to weigh the resulting evidence. In short, to think critically is to avoid simplistic approaches. Too often, students are encouraged to "learn what is in the book," which frequently means to avoid "thinking" altogether. Teachers who create an environment in which risk taking is encouraged, in which cooperation in problem solving is stressed, and in which mistakes are not perceived as sins or personal faults are more likely to engender achievement in students. In such classrooms, an emphasis on thinking skills is not seen as an addition to an already overcrowded school day. It does not require a special course or time of day. Rather, critical thinking is a goal that permeates each and every lesson and all teacher-student contact.

3. Improving Self-Confidence and Self-Acceptance

Pettigrew established a clear inverse relationship between the degree of prejudice a person harbors and the individual's sense of self-worth.[26] That is, the more confident a person is in his or her own sense of identity and competence, the lower is that person's degree of prejudice, and vice versa. While the relationship is not necessarily cause and effect, there are strong indications that self-acceptance is critical to mental, physical, and emotional health. Classroom activities designed to increase self-confidence also tend to bring about a decrease in levels of prejudice. Children can develop confidence in themselves when they are in educational environments where they feel secure and accepted, where their participation is valued, and where they know the boundaries or limits.[27] Creating such environments should be of prime concern to educators.

4. Increasing Empathy for and Understanding of Others

Although prejudice reduction is enhanced through social contact, cognitive sophistication, and the increase of self-esteem, long-term gains require educational activity that actively engages the emotions. Activities designed to help students see the world from another's perspective are useful to achieve this purpose. Classroom simulations are an

Activity 27: What Does It Feel Like to Be Excluded?

excellent tool for helping children become sensitive to others who act or look different. Shaver and Curtis, for example, offer a simulation to help children understand what it is like for those with speech difficulties.[28] They suggest students put something in their mouths (such as a small clean rubber ball or dental cotton—something large enough that it won't be swallowed) and then make a telephone call to a store and ask for information. Students can then discuss how it feels to be unable to communicate effectively.

The classic cross-cultural simulation Bafa Bafa, or the children's version Rafa Rafa, provides an excellent way for students to gain an understanding of what it is like to move into another cultural group.[29] In this experience, individuals learn "proper" behavior associated with the creation of two distinct cultural groups. After some time, members of each group have the opportunity to interact with one another. They very quickly experience feelings of anxiety, rejection, apprehension, and confusion—those feelings often referred to collectively as culture shock. Most individuals who have made a significant move from one country or culture to another encounter such feelings. This simulation allows students (and teachers or parents) to explore the feelings and experiences of immigrant, migrant, or refugee students; international exchange students; students in newly desegregated schools; newly mainstreamed children with disabilities; or just about anybody cast in the role of "new kid on the block."

Students may also write stories or act out plays and dramatizations of situations that characterize acts of prejudice and discrimination. In this manner, students "step into the shoes" of another, thereby gaining an insider's perspective of what it is like to be discriminated against.

Summary

Prejudice and racism have both been rampant in many forms throughout American society. This chapter provides an overview of issues related to prejudice and racism, beginning with a historical perspective and then tracing some of the major developments in efforts designed to address its occurrence in society. The chapter then explores the concept of prejudice, prejudice formation, and prejudice reduction, emphasizing that various actions taken by teachers, schools, and communities can go a long way toward reducing, and in some instances preventing, its occurrence.

 # Chapter Review

Go to the Online Learning Center at **www.mhhe.com/Cushner4e** to review important content from the chapter, practice with key terms, take a chapter quiz, and find the web links listed in this chapter.

Key Terms

Genotype   182   Phenotype   183   Prejudice   189
Hypodescent   183

Reflective Questions

1. What are some ways in which Jane and the other teachers could continue to educate themselves about new methods related to prejudice reduction while simultaneously keeping up with student needs and school requirements, especially when time is such a problem?
2. Not every teacher and administrator in the school appreciates the direction Jane and some others are taking toward antiracist education. How might Jane continue to broaden her students' perspectives in the face of criticism from her colleagues?
3. What experiences have you had in educational institutions that were effective at developing positive intergroup relations? What aspects of the contact hypothesis were evident?

References

1. This case study is based on the video program *Chameleon* by John Gray and Associates; and on a section from the book *A Country of Strangers: Blacks and Whites in America* by David K. Shipler, (New York: Vintage Books, 1997).

2. C. P. Kottack and K. A. Kozaitis, *On Being Different: Diversity and Multiculturalism in the North American Mainstream* (Boston: McGraw-Hill, 1999).

3. Ibid.

4. N. Yetman, *Majority and Minority: The Dynamics of Race and Ethnicity in American Life,* 5th ed. (Boston: Allyn and Bacon, 1991).

5. Quoted in Meyer Weinberg, *A Chance to Learn: A History of Race and Education in the United States* (New York: Cambridge University Press, 1977), p. 46.

6. F. Koestler, *The Unseen Minority: A Social History of Blindness in the United States* (New York: David McKay, 1967).

7. William A. Hunter, ed., *Multicultural Education through Competency-Based Teacher Education* (Washington, DC: American Association of Colleges of Teacher Education, 1975), p. 17.

8. S. Ryan, *Ethnic Conflict and International Relations* (Brookfield, MA: Dartmouth, 1990).

9. D. Katz, "The Functional Approach to the Study of Attitudes," *Public Opinion Quarterly* 24 (1960): 164–204.

10. P. A. Katz, "Developmental Foundations of Gender and Racial Attitudes," in *The Child's Construction of Social Inequality,* ed. R. H. Leahy (New York: Academic Press, 1983), pp. 41–78.

11. Deborah A. Byrnes, "Children and Prejudice," *Social Education* 52, 4 (April–May 1988): 267–271.

12. R. M. Dennis, "Socialization and Racism: The White Experience," in *Impacts of Racism on White Americans,* ed. B. P. Bowser and R. G. Hunt (Beverly Hills: Sage, 1981).

13. Deborah A. Byrnes, "Teacher, They Called Me a . . . ! *Prejudice and Discrimination in the Classroom* (New York: Anti-Defamation League of B'Nai Brith, 1987). See also Carlos Cortes, *The Children Are Watching: How the Media Teach about Diversity* (New York: Teachers College Press, 2000).

14. D. Bicklin and L. Bailey, eds., *Rudely Stamp'd: Imaginal Disability and Prejudice* (Washington, DC: University Press of America, 1981).

15. C. Grant and G. Ladson-Billings, *Dictionary of Multicultural Education* (Phoenix, AZ: Oryx Press, 1997), p. 129.

16. P. McIntosh, "White Privilege: Unpacking the Invisible Knapsack," *Creation Spirituality* (January/February 1992): 33–35, 53.

17. Ibid.

18. G. Pate, "What Does Research Tell Us about the Reduction of Prejudice?" (paper presented at the 1987 Anti-Defamation League Conference titled American Citizenship in the Twenty-First Century: Education for a Pluralistic, Democratic America; Washington, DC).

19. Byrnes, "Children and Prejudice."

20. Gordon Allport, *The Nature of Prejudice* (New York: Doubleday, 1958).

21. Yehuda Amir, "Contact Hypothesis in Ethnic Relations," *Psychological Bulletin* 71, 5 (May 1969): 319–343.

22. Ibid.

23. M. Sherif, "Superordinate Goals in the Reducation of Intergroup Tension," *American Journal of Sociology* 63, 4 (1958): 349–356.

24. Edward D'Angelo, *The Teaching of Critical Thinking* (Amsterdam: B. R. Gruner, 1971).

25. Matthew Lipman, *Philosophy in the Classroom* (Philadelphia: Temple University Press, 1980).

26. T. F. Pettigrew, "The Mental Health Impact," in *Impacts of Racism on White Americans,* ed. B. P. Bowser and R. G. Hunt (Beverly Hills: Sage, 1981), pp. 97–118.

27. S. C. Samuels, *Enhancing Self-Concept in Early Childhood* (New York: Human Sciences Press, 1977).

28. J. P. Shaver and C. K. Curtis, *Handicapism and Equal Opportunity: Teaching about the Disabled in Social Studies* (Reston, VA: Council for Exceptional Children, 1981).

29. R. Gary Shirts, *BAFA BAFA: A Cross-Cultural Simulation* (Del Mar, CA: SIMILE II, 1977).

Developing Learning Communities:

Language and Learning Style

> *When we study human language, we are approaching what some might call the "'human essence," the distinctive qualities of mind that are, so far as we know, unique to man and that are inseparable from any critical phase of human existence, personal or social.*
>
> —*Noam Chomsky*

Chapter Outline

1. Do you remember learning to talk? If not, why not?

2. Think of occasions when you were speaking to someone and they seemed not to understand what you meant. What do you think the reason was?

3. What is the difference between an accent and a dialect?

4. Have you ever been speaking to someone who was standing too close to you for your comfort? Why do you think you felt uncomfortable?

5. How do you learn best? If faced with the need to learn something new, what would you do (e.g., read about it, talk to someone about it, have someone show you)?

6. What do you think about bilingual education? Is it necessary for some children? Does it hamper English language learners?

c a s e   s t u d y   **Language and Learning Style
in a Learning-Community Classroom**

It is 4:00 on a Friday afternoon in mid-September, and Martina Chandler stands by the windows in her third-floor classroom watching the sun glinting off San Francisco Bay. Typical of many high school classrooms, this one is a large rectangle, with a blackboard on one end, windows along one side, and a variety of furniture and equipment for student use. Unlike many high school classrooms, however, the space in this room is organized for active work rather than for passive listening. Most of the furniture is adaptable to many uses: low, three-shelf bookcases on wheels can be moved around to create a variety of spaces; individual desks have been replaced by several round tables with moveable chairs that can accommodate four or five students at a time; individual carrels made of large boxes that fold up when not in use can be set up on small individual tables or on one long table so that students can work or study alone; learning center areas for various purposes can be created and re-created from a number of bright plastic "orange crates," also on wheels. Also in the room is a large, cushioned porch rocker inherited from Martina's grandmother. Even Ms. Chandler's desk is lightweight and movable when required by the classroom activities.

In addition, the walls are covered with maps, posters, and pictures from around the world. One striking poster has the Greek, Hebrew, Cyrillic, Spanish, Japanese, Arabic, French, and English alphabets side by side in bright colors. Another has a variety of drawings of students engaged in different styles of learning—reading, talking to one another, writing, building, singing, and dancing. Still another displays a language tree that shows the roots of the world's major languages.

Now that the last student of the day has left, Chandler is thinking about the progress her students have made in the first two weeks of school. Although she has five classes, she is particularly interested in her tenth-grade English class, which has shown strong interest in setting class goals for the year and in deciding how they are going to achieve them. These students have caught the spirit of the learning-community classroom earlier than her other classes and seem to be enjoying themselves a great deal.

Unlike some teachers in her school, Ms. Chandler has chosen to teach heterogeneous classes. The twenty-four students in this particular class come from backgrounds that vary by family income, ethnic heritage and/or country of origin, religion, native language, past school achievement, and race. She views this variation as potentially enriching for herself and her students. It is very important to her that the class becomes a community of learners in which the sociocultural and linguistic backgrounds of all her students are known, appreciated, and used.

Prior to the beginning of school, Ms. Chandler began assembling her usual set of student files by looking up their official records in the school office. She recorded their full names, their birthdays, their parents' occupations, and any information available concerning their English-language abilities as well as their abilities in languages other than English and their ninth grade achievement scores. From this information, she knew that this class was more linguistically diverse than others she had taught. Also, for the first time, she was going to have a deaf student and her interpreter in class. She was fairly certain that differences in the cultural and language backgrounds of these students would mean differences in their learning styles and personal interests. To aid her planning, she made up a variety of charts that let her see the demographic composition of the class at a glance. (See Tables 7.1 and 7.2.)

The First Week: Exploring Names and Languages

Since beginning school two weeks ago, Chandler has devoted much of her classroom time to activities designed to help her students get to know one another and to begin forming a classroom community. At the end of the first class, she asked her students to talk with their parents about the origins of their first and middle names and what nationality their names represented. She also asked them to find out if their names had a special meaning in another language. "Tomorrow," she announced, "we will begin interviewing one another for the Class Bulletin Board."

When her students came to class the next day, Ms. Chandler used a technique she had read about to form the students into pairs.[1] She had the students line up around the room according to their birthdays and then asked each student to be a partner to the student who had a birthday closest to him or her. When partnerships were established, she handed out the following list of questions for students to use in interviewing one another:

t a b l e 7.1   **Tenth Grade English Class: Gender/Ethnicity/Religion**

	Ethnicity	Religion
Males		
Tomas	Mexican American	Catholic
Ricardo	Mexican American	Catholic
Tran	Vietnamese	Buddhist
Peter	Japanese American	Methodist
Yoshi	Japanese American	Shinto
Ritchie	African American	Conservative Baptist
Dontae	African American	Nonaffiliated
Jacques	Haitian American	Catholic
Joe	Bohemian American	Nonaffiliated
Steve	Hungarian American	Catholic
Abdul	Kuwaiti American	Muslim
Females		
Grace	Mexican American	Catholic
Rosita	Mexican American	Catholic
Maria	Puerto Rican American	Presbyterian
Juanita	Mexican American	Catholic
Wei-Ping	Chinese	Methodist
Komiko	Japanese American	Shinto
Elaine	Japanese American	Baptist
Houa	African (Niger)	Muslim
Anna	German American	Catholic
Natasha	Russian American	Jewish
Kate	Scottish American	Presbyterian
Hannah	Scotch-Irish American	Assembly of God
Tammy	Scotch-Irish American	Nonaffiliated

1. What is your name? What do you like or dislike about your name?
2. What do you know about how you got your name? Were you named after someone else? Who named you?
3. Are there members of your family who have the same name?
4. Do you have any friends who have the same name as you do?
5. Are there any famous people who have the same name as yours?
6. Are you at all like any of these people who have the same name as yours?
7. Does your name have any other meaning?
8. Was your name originally in another language? Was it spelled differently in that language? Does it have a special meaning in that language?
9. What does your family call you? Do you have a nickname?
10. What do you like to be called?[2]

table 7.2   **Tenth Grade English Class: Social Class (Based on Parents' Occupation)**

Name	Father's Occupation	Mother's Occupation
Poor (25 percent)		
Jacques	Migrant laborer	Migrant laborer
Hannah	Not available	Waitress
Joe	Merchant seaman	Waitress
Dontae	Not available	Not available
Tammy	Not available	Cleaning lady
Juanita	Farmhand	Wife and mother
Working Class (29.2 percent)		
Tran	Truck farmer	Truck farmer
Tomas	Not available	Office worker
Maria	Restaurant cook	Waitress
Komiko	Merchant seaman	Data entry worker
Grace	Not available	Secretary
Rosita	Salesman	Teacher's aide
Steve	Longshoreman	Not available
Middle Class (33.4 percent)		
Ritchie	Minister	Nurse
Wei-Ping	Architect	Wife and mother
Yoshi	Computer specialist	Teacher
Peter	Banker	Social worker
Natasha	Teacher	Professor
Elaine	Store manager	Store clerk
Anna	Teacher	Teacher
Kate	Doctor	Nurse
Ricardo	TV videographer	Day care director
Upper-Middle Class (8.4 percent)		
Houa	Diplomat	Wife and mother
Abdul	Oil company executive	Wife and mother

The class spent about fifteen minutes interviewing one another. Then Chandler asked them each to introduce their partner to the class by telling what they had learned. While each student was talking, she listened carefully and took notes. At the end of each introduction, Martina took a snapshot of each student and repeated the student's name. Class ended before they finished, and Chandler told them they would complete the introductions the next day.

On Wednesday, after the introductions and picture taking were completed, the students were asked to hand in the notes on their question sheets. Then the class spent the rest of the period discussing the number of different languages, accents, and dialects represented in the class. One exercise that all the students liked was to pronounce aloud the following words:

greasy	*here*	*car*	*bath*	*dog*
get	*aunt*	*because*	*idea*	*park*
house	*fit*	*Mary*	*were*	*right*
fire	*sorry*	*log*	*child*	

The students were surprised to discover that, although everyone spoke at least some English, all of them also spoke dialects of some kind, some of which were regional and some of which were social in their origin. Anna and Mrs. Thomas (the deaf student and her interpreter) also participated by signing each of the words and talking about how the signs developed and how they might be used in sentences.

The students also considered English words that have been borrowed from other languages. Divided into groups of four and using one of the several dictionaries and other reference books in the room, students first tried to guess and then looked up the derivation of the following words:

algebra	*Arabic*
gingham	*Malay*
chocolate	*Nahuatl (Native American)*
khaki	*Hindi*
linen	*Old English*
safari	*Arabic (through Swahili)*
home	*Old English*
klutz	*Yiddish*
prairie	*French*
zombie	*Congo*
seersucker	*Persian*
skunk	*Algonquian (Native American)*
satin	*Chinese*
shampoo	*Hindi*
kimono	*Japanese*
piano	*Italian*
tycoon	*Japanese*
boondocks	*Tagalog (Philippines)*
smithereens	*Irish*
gorilla	*West Africa (through Greek)*[3]

Ms. Chandler was pleased that the students had become so interested in the subject of "word borrowing" that they were determined to develop a Borrowing Dictionary to leave with Martina for her other classes. By Friday of the first week, the pictures of all the students had been developed, and the class spent the period designing and putting together the Class Bulletin Board. Right in the middle of the pictures, they put a printed sheet that read:

A FABLE

In a house there was a cat, always ready to run after a mouse, but with no luck at all.

One day, in the usual chase the mouse found its way into a little hole and the cat was left with no alternative than to wait hopefully outside.

A few moments later the mouse heard a dog barking and automatically came to the conclusion that if there was a dog in the house, the cat would have to go. So he came out only to fall into the cat's grasp.

"But where is the dog?" asked the trembling mouse.

"There isn't any dog—it was only me imitating a barking dog," explained the happy cat, and after a pause added, "My dear fellow, if you don't speak at least two languages, you can't get anywhere nowadays."[4]

Over the weekend, Chandler looked at the notes she had made from the students' official files, the notes she had taken in class as the students were introducing one another, and at the question sheets that the students had filled out. From these three sources, she developed a chart on the linguistic variability of the class. (See Table 7.3.)

The Second Week: Exploring Learning Styles and Family Stories

The second week, Ms. Chandler began class by asking students if they knew how they learned best. "They tell me that we're going to get a computer for our classroom soon, and we'll all have to learn how to use it. How many of you are already familiar with computers?" About a third of the class raised their hands. "OK," she said, "what would be the very first thing the rest of you would do in order to go about learning how to use the computer?"

Students answered in different ways. Some said they would get a book on computers or on a particular program and start that way. Others said they would get someone who was familiar with computers to tell them about it first. Still others said there was no way they could learn without sitting down in front of one and actually doing it. Steve and Joe said they would first try to take the computer apart.

Using this short discussion as an introduction, Chandler divided the class into four groups, asking each group to look at and discuss the materials on learning style she had placed on their particular table. At one table were materials on field dependence and field independence (two types of cognition that are at the heart of learning style).[5] At the next table were materials on the need for structure in the learning environment,[6] while at a third table were materials on perceptual modalities (i.e., visual, auditory, and kinesthetic approaches to learning).[7] On the last table were materials on a broader based approach to learning styles called the Learning Style Inventory.[8] After

t a b l e   7 . 3   **Tenth Grade English Class: Linguistic Background/Language Proficiency**

Name	Native Language/Dialect	Comments
Tran	Vietnamese	Recent immigrant; limited English but able to make himself understood if necessary; also speaks French; needs help with many words; clever use of gestures to get meaning across; no record of reading or writing scores.
Anna	ASL	Speaks English as a second language; speaks standard English reasonably well; prefers to sign; reading and writing scores good.
Peter	English	Second-generation Japanese American; has some Japanese but uses it only with his grandparents; reading and writing scores fairly high.
Tomas	Spanish/Mexican	Speaks English with a slight Spanish accent; reading scores moderate; writing scores fairly low.
Wei-Ping	Chinese/Mandarin	Speaks standard English well but very formally; does not use vernacular English; reading and writing scores high.
Grace	English	Monolingual in English; speaks standard English reasonably well but uses a good deal of slang; reading scores moderate; writing scores moderately low.
Joe	English	Monolingual in vernacular English; does not appear at all comfortable speaking in front of the class; reading and writing scores moderately low.
Rosita	Spanish	Bilingual in Spanish and standard English; has a pronounced Mexican/Spanish accent; reading and writing scores moderate.
Ritchie	English	Bidialectal in Black English and standard English; seems to be able to switch back and forth easily, depending on whom he's talking to and what he's talking about; reading and writing scores moderately high.
Natasha	Russian	Bilingual in Russian and standard English; speaks well in front of people; reading and writing scores high.
Steve	English	Monolingual in standard English; uses vernacular English mostly; lives with his father and grandmother, who are bilingual in Hungarian and English; reading scores moderate; writing scores moderately low.
Yoshi	English	Bilingual in English and Japanese; is second-generation Japanese and lives near his grandparents, with whom he speaks Japanese regularly; reading and writing scores moderate.
Maria	Spanish/Puerto Rican	Came to United States at age five; fluent English speaker but still speaks some Spanish at home; reading scores moderately high; writing scores moderately low.
Kate	English	Monolingual in standard English; speaks easily and fluently in front of class; reading and writing scores high.

table 7.3 Tenth Grade English Class: Linguistic Background/Language Proficiency (cont.)

Name	Native Language/Dialect	Comments
Dontae	English	Monodialectal in Black English; recently moved here from South Los Angeles; has a lot of energy and speaks easily and quickly in his own dialect; reading and writing scores in standard English low.
Ricardo	Spanish	Bilingual in Spanish and vernacular English; speaks standard English with effort; reading and writing scores moderately low.
Hannah	English	Monolingual in vernacular English.
Komiko	English	Monolingual in standard English; third-generation Japanese American; parents do not speak Japanese and she has no one to learn it from; reading and writing scores moderate.
Abdul	Arabic/French	Trilingual in Arabic, French, and standard English; speaks standard English formally; reading and writing scores high.
Juanita	Spanish/Mexican	Bilingual in Spanish and English.
Tammy	English/Appalachian	Monolingual in vernacular rural English; has a strong West Virginia "twang" accent; reading scores moderately high; writing scores low.
Jacques	French	Recent immigrant; speaks vernacular French, some vernacular Black English, some standard English; reading and writing scores moderately low.
Elaine	English	Third-generation Japanese American; monolingual in standard English; uses considerable slang; reading scores moderate; writing scores moderately high.
Houa	Tribal/French	Trilingual in her ethnic-group language, French, and standard English; speaks somewhat less formally than other nonnative-born students; reading and writing scores moderately high.

each group had had a chance to discuss the materials and after a spokesperson at each table summarized their materials for the rest of the class, Martina handed out a questionnaire she had designed to help students assess their own patterns of learning. She also pointed out additional books, articles, and materials in the classroom to which students could go for further information.

"I don't want you to think of this as some kind of intelligence test, or that you are 'stuck' with the main learning style you appear to have. All of us use many different approaches to learning all the time, and we are all quite able to learn new ones. The point of thinking about learning style is, first, that it is one more piece of the puzzle that is you and, second, that it will help explain to you why this class may be a bit different from others you have had. It's important to me that everyone in this room learns as much as possible. To do that, we'll always have a variety of ways of approaching knowledge and skills. I'll always encourage you to try out new approaches as well as to use ways that are familiar and comfortable for you. OK?"

The students looked a bit skeptical, but they more or less willingly answered the questionnaire. The real discussion occurred when they compared their answers with others at their tables. It was still going on when the class was over.

For the rest of the week, Ms. Chandler and her students worked on family stories, building on some of the comments that had come out of the introductions exercise on the second day of class. Steve, for example, said that his grandmother always called him "Stefan," which is his name in Hungarian; Komiko commented that the only thing Japanese in her house were her family's names! Martina then introduced the notion of family stories as discussed by Stone.[9]

Stone interviewed over a hundred people from various backgrounds, regions of the country, and ages in order to see if there was a pattern to the influence that family stories had on the beliefs, values, and behavior of individuals. She concluded that family stories give us a sense of our past, of the norms and values held by the family, and perhaps most important, of the future that we might be able to expect by virtue of belonging to this particular family. She tells, for example, of one Irish family in which, because of too much drinking and a curiously morose temperament, many of the males committed suicide before the age of fifty—a kind of "tragic O'Connor curse." A young African American, Stone writes, speaks proudly of his Creek Indian ancestors who burned all their corn as they were dispatched on the Trail of Tears so that their white oppressors couldn't benefit from their hard work—a story that describes a tradition of self-assertion and bravery in his family.

"Now, what I want you to do," Ms. Chandler said to her students, "is think about the stories of your family members that you've heard ever since you were little. Many of these stories may be about how your families came to the United States, or about how someone conquered terrible odds to achieve something, or about how your family regards love, courtship, and marriage. Some stories may be very short and some may be quite complex, but all of them usually teach you something about yourself as a member of your first 'culture.' Eventually, we're going to write these stories and share them with the rest of the class. Then, we're going to look at some common characteristics of your stories and some common characteristics of narratives in general. Tomorrow, friends of mine are coming in to tell some of their family stories, and then we'll start on our own."

Now it was Friday afternoon. The students had heard stories about family members escaping from Nazi Germany during the Holocaust, about a family in which one ancestor coined the word "robot," and about a family in which several generations of women had "fallen in love at first sight" and married because of it. Next week the students will begin their own stories and will help each other by offering critiques and suggestions.

"Maybe," she thought, "we'll have the computer by then and can actually publish them!"

Case Analysis

The following list shows a number of strategies that Martina Chandler used both to create a learning-community classroom and to take advantage of various language backgrounds and learning styles so as to help her students explore and become more proficient in the English language.

1. She organized her classroom so that it could be altered by herself and the students to fit a variety of activities.

2. In the first two weeks of school she helped students get to know one another through the introductions activity, the Class Bulletin Board, the learning-style discussions, and the family stories. Each of these activities is designed to increase understanding of differences and commonalities among members of the class.

3. She got to know students through the use of student files and her own charts.

4. She introduced other adults into the class as storytellers. She will continue to include family and community members as well as other school staff in her classroom.

5. She began the process of democratic experience by encouraging the students to develop their idea for a Borrowing Dictionary as a collaborative project.

6. She used a variety of teaching methods, including questioning, describing, collaborative learning, and the development of "voice," all of which coincide with her initial emphasis on names, individual language backgrounds, and family stories.

7. She used culturally based word exercises and learning-style activities to put her students' similarities and differences at the center of the educational enterprise rather than at the margins. Given the linguistic diversity in this class, she is setting up situations in which such diversity can become a resource rather than a hindrance in the exploration and practice of standard English.

8. Finally, she did all of these things in the context of expanding students' awareness of language and, especially, improving their ability to use standard English. In just two weeks Martina has provided a number of opportunities for oral and written expression that she can use to diagnose her students' language proficiency and then plan both the content and pedagogy for the class. The content of the English class—principally reading, writing, and speaking—is not only central to, but also enhanced by, the approaches and methods she employs.

Martina Chandler's impressive accomplishments during the first two weeks of school are just the tip of the iceberg of what she needs to know in order to accomplish the goals that she and her students set. In addition to the personal knowledge of one another that she and her students now share, Martina also needs three kinds of general language-related knowledge. First, she needs to understand the central role of the family in the acquisition and use of language. Second, she needs to understand how language functions as a communication tool and how it is possible to have different variations of that tool. Third, she needs to understand the relationships between language tools and parental culture and how this relationship influences learning style. Each of these dimensions of language is explored in this chapter, but first it is necessary to look closely at what it means to develop a learning community.

Characteristics of a Learning Community

Education for democratic citizenship implies active participation in the life of the school and classroom community. What many school people are struggling with is the shift from *adding* these ideas to traditional classrooms to focusing on them as the *basis* for educational practice. In schools and classrooms where students and adults have succeeded in altering their focus, the look, feel, and sounds of classroom life are easily discernible.

Learning Communities

First, learning-community schools and classrooms are organized for activity. Student work covers the walls of halls and classrooms. There may be an absence of "posted rules carefully outlining what one can or cannot do."[10] Arrangements of classroom furniture and equipment vary according to the work being done in them: easy chairs or sofas for reading and conversation, darkrooms for photography, tables for assembling books and newspapers, tables and counters for scientific work, computer corners, and open spaces for gathering people together. There is a sense of "purposeful clutter in these schools and classrooms. They are places to do things in, not places to sit and watch."[11]

Second, everyone present in the school participates in this activity-oriented environment. Young children are eager to show off the books they have written; older students are engaged in activities that range from interviewing older community members to completing a scientific inventory of nearby plants and animals. Parents and teachers are often found working together to develop and implement instructional goals.[12] Principals, teachers, parents, and students often work collaboratively on joint projects such as publishing a newspaper or refurbishing the library. Because of all this ongoing activity, such schools and classrooms are rarely quiet, at least in the traditional sense of a school where adults talk and children listen. "Children are doing things, not just watching someone else. These are schools where learning is not a spectator sport."[13]

Third, in learning-community schools and classrooms, there is a sense that everyone belongs to the community: students, teachers, parents, administrators, support staff, volunteers, and other members of the broader community outside the school. Relationships among all people are collaborative, and each individual perceives all others as both teachers and learners. In a learning community, each individual is valued: cultural and linguistic identity is affirmed by using what each person brings to school as starting points and building blocks.[14]

Rationale for Learning-Community Classrooms

Building communities of learners centers on the traditional goal of preparing students to be citizens in a democracy. While not a new idea, citizenship education has sometimes been obscured by an overemphasis on the preparation of students for the workplace. At its core are two tenets: (1) the need to negotiate differences through sharing a common curriculum, and (2) the need for students to learn citizenship by *practicing* democracy. With respect to the need for a common curriculum, Dewey and his daughter argued in 1915 against the separation of students into academic and vocational tracks:

It is fatal for a democracy to permit the formation of fixed classes. Differences of wealth, the existence of large masses of unskilled laborers, contempt for work with the hands, inability to secure the training that enables one to forge ahead in life, all operate to produce classes, and to widen the gulf between them. Statesmen and legislation can do something to combat these evil forces. Wise philanthropy can do something. But the only fundamental agency for good is the public school system. . . .

There must not be one system for the children of parents who have more leisure and another for the children of parents who are wage earners. The physical separation forced by such a scheme . . . brings about a division of mental and moral habits, ideals and outlook. . . . A division of the public school system into one part that pursues traditional academic methods, and another that deals with those who are to go into manual labor means a plan of social predestination totally foreign to the spirit of democracy.

The democracy which proclaims equality of opportunity as its ideal requires an education in which learning and social application, ideas and practice, work and recognition of the meaning of what is done, are united from the beginning and for all.[15]

With respect to the need to practice democracy in order to learn democracy, Wood describes the requirements of the democratic life in the following terms:

Educating for Democracy

Fundamentally, democracy requires citizens who participate broadly in informed public decision-making with an eye toward the common good. Citizens must thus be literate, able not only to master the rudiments of reading, writing, and computing, but able to use these tools as ways of understanding the world and making their voices heard in it. We must also know how to find and evaluate information, how to sift through the items that bombard us daily, to sort the useful from the superfluous, and the clearly propagandistic from the approximate truths.

Members of the republic must also have an ongoing sense of community, an obligation to the common good. Citizens should see themselves as members of a community that makes their individuality possible, and they should value and nurture that community. Democracy also requires that we each have courage, that we believe our actions are important and valued, and that we have not only a right, but also an obligation to participate publicly. The democratic citizen is, in sum, the individual who has the intellectual skills and conviction necessary to participate publicly in making the many choices that confront us, in ways that will promote the common good.[16]

One way to provide a common curriculum in which all students practice the required skills of democratic participation is to create communities of learners in which all those involved—students, teachers, parents, administrators, counselors, nurses, and volunteers—actively participate in decisions regarding the educational process.

Pedagogies: Old and New

Much has been written lately about new ways of teaching that are presumed to benefit a wider variety of students. Included in these new ways of teaching are labels such as *interactive learning, engaged learning, feminist pedagogy, inquiry learning, emancipatory curriculum, critical pedagogy, discovery learning, whole language,* and *collaborative learning.* While there are indeed some "new" aspects contained in these ideas in general they can all be grouped into the much more traditional category of *good teaching.* Moreover, most of them have been around for a long, long time.

Dialogue, for example, or what is sometimes known as interactive teaching and learning, is Plato's dialectic in contemporary dress. Discovery learning, or the use of

critical incident

The Art Awards Ceremony

Ritchie, one of the African American students in Martina Chandler's class, had a strong interest in art that he typically pursued on his own by visiting museums, reading books, sketching, and painting. Much of his work reflected his African American heritage. At mid-year, Ritchie's family moved across the bay where he was enrolled in a predominantly white high school. He took an art class and was encouraged by his teacher to develop his talent. Ritchie entered several paintings in the school art show, received praise and attention for his work, and went on to enter the all-city show, where he also did well. The longtime principal of his school, a middle-aged Caucasian man named Mr. Tarbell, was present at the awards ceremony and was delighted that one of his students received rave reviews and an award. Congratulating Ritchie, he said, "Good work, Ritchie. We are proud to have such a talented black student representing our school. You have an uncanny ability to paint." Mr. Tarbell was surprised when Ritchie simply walked away from him with no comment.

- What happened in this incident?
- If Ritchie was to telephone Ms. Chandler and complain about Mr. Tarbell, how could she best help him understand the situation?

teaching techniques that present students with questions and/or materials that impel students to active investigation, was the centerpiece of Abelard's teaching in the twelfth century.[17] Critical pedagogy, inquiry learning, feminist pedagogy, and collaborative learning all hearken back at least to John Amos Comenius in the seventeenth century. He believed that understanding was more important than rote learning, that demonstration was more effective than listening to experts, that education should follow the natural development of the student, that students should teach and learn from one another, and that both text material and learning activities should incorporate the student's own experience as a starting point.

What is relatively new in learning-community classrooms is not that such varied methods of instruction should exist, but that they should exist more or less simultaneously and be exercised by both children and adults. Their emphasis depends on the age of the student, the nature of the subject matter, and the kind of learning activities used. Thus, in a learning-community classroom there is plenty of room for *all* the old methods of dialogue: telling, demonstrating, modeling, and problem posing. In addition, several relatively new ideas about teaching are often incorporated into learning communities. One is that teaching strategies should attend to the development of "voice" among students. That is, teaching should encourage the expression of distinctive beliefs and experiences based on both biological and sociocultural differences. In addition, because learning-community classrooms include parents and other community members as part of the classroom community, family or adult literacy may also be a pedagogical goal.

Roles: *Old and New*

As with pedagogy, traditional roles of adults and children in learning-community class-rooms are not so much changed as they are expanded. Thus, the role of teacher as teller is expanded to teacher as guide, as coach, and sometimes as cheerleader! The role of teacher is also expanded to include other adults—parents, administrators, and community members who provide various types of specialized assistance to the regular classroom teacher. Similarly, the role of teacher is also extended to students, who serve as teachers and critics to one another. The role of learner, like that of teacher, is also expanded in learning-community classrooms. Because everyone (teachers, students, administrators, parents, and community members) has unique experiences and specialized knowledge to share, it follows that everyone (adults included) will be a learner as well as a teacher.

Place of Content Knowledge: *Old and New*

In a learning-community classroom, the place and function of content knowledge also varies, although it is certainly no less important than in traditional classrooms. Thus, mathematics, language, history, science, and the arts serve in dual capacities. Sometimes such knowledge is learned as an end in itself, which is the more traditional approach to content. At other times, content knowledge serves as a means to another end, such as solving a problem or constructing a new way of looking at the world, which is the newer approach to content learning. More often than not in learning-community classrooms, subject matter knowledge is acquired in the service of other goals. Thus, if students need to produce a newspaper, they must know how to use language in intelligible ways. If students are going to measure the amount of rainfall during a storm, they must know about fractions and forms of measurement. Conversely, in traditional classrooms, it is likely that such subjects as language and mathematics are taught as ends in themselves, with applications of that knowledge coming later (or maybe not at all). In learning-community classrooms, the project or activity often comes first, and the acquisition of knowledge and skills needed to accomplish the activity become necessary tools in the service of that activity. In this way, students come to appreciate the relevance of subject matter knowledge.

Assessment: *Old and New*

In traditional classrooms, assessment or evaluation of student achievement is largely accomplished through the practice of paper-and-pencil testing. Moreover, the results of such assessment are often used to separate (track) students into homogeneous groups, presumably for their own benefit. Standardized commercial tests indicate to administrators and the community how "well" or "poorly" an individual student or teacher or class or school is doing in relation to other students, teachers, classes, and schools.

In learning-community classrooms, such traditional paper-and-pencil forms of assessment are also used, although for somewhat different purposes. For example, unit tests are used mostly for instructional feedback to individual students rather than for the purpose of grouping students or to provide interim or final grades. In addition, other forms of assessment including peer evaluation, portfolios, group tests, and self-evaluation are used. Teachers combine these various measures when judging what grades a student has earned.

At this point, you might be wondering how the ideas of a learning-community classroom are related to the issues of individual biological, psychological, and socio-cultural differences discussed in the first four chapters of this book. As an example, look at the ways in which one important source of cultural identity—language—might play out in a particular learning-community classroom.

Perspectives on Language Acquisition

It is often said that language is what makes us human. Certainly, language is the primary means for socializing us into our families and our social groups and, through them, to acquiring our cultural identity.

**Activity 26:
Interviewing
Nonnative
English
Speakers
about Their
Experiences in
This Country**

Language and the Family

Berger and Berger refer to language as the first institution encountered by the individual. This conclusion may surprise you if you think of the family as being the first institution, the one that introduces us to language. Infants, however, can't know what a family is until they have acquired some form of language.[18] Language *objectifies, interprets,* and *justifies* reality for the child, thus structuring the child's environment (pp. 68–69). It puts labels on roles (mommy, police officer, teacher, priest) and permits the child to extend those roles into the wider community. It also brings the meanings and values of the wider community onto the small stage of the immediate family. Consider the case of the father in the act of punishing the child:

> As he punishes, he talks. What is he talking about? Some of the talking may just be a way of giving vent to his own annoyance or anger. But, in most cases, much of the talking is a running commentary on the offending act and the punishment it so richly deserves. The talking *interprets* and *justifies* the punishment. Inevitably, it does this in a way that goes beyond the father's own immediate reactions. The punishment is put in the vast context of manners and morals; in the extreme case, even the divinity may be invoked as a penal authority. . . . The punishing father now represents this system (pp. 69–70).

Institutional Aspects of Language in the Family

Language has several characteristics in common with other social institutions (pp. 70–75). First, language is external. It is experienced as "out there," in contrast to the individual's private thoughts or feelings (which, incidentally, are also structured by language and its meanings). Further, when an individual hears language spoken by another person, that person is speaking according to a particular language *system* that was created neither by the speaker nor the listener. It is external to them both.

Second, language has objectivity; that is, everyone who shares it agrees to accept the norms and conventions of its particular symbol system. Berger and Berger note that "the objectivity of one's first language is particularly powerful" (p. 72). They write:

Jean Piaget, the Swiss psychologist, tells the story somewhere of a small child who was asked whether the sun could be called anything except "sun." "No," replied the child. How did he know this, the child was asked. The question puzzled him for a moment. Then he pointed to the sun and said, "Well, look at it" (p. 72).

Third, language has the power of moral authority to direct us. As children learn to speak their native language, they are usually excused small lapses in pronunciation and usage. As they grow up, however, inappropriate use of language may very well expose them to ridicule, shame, and guilt. Consider the child who speaks a language or dialect different from that of the school; the working-class college student who is expected to engage in polite conversation at a formal reception, and the adult who tries to speak in the rapidly changing vernacular of her teenage children. Not only are these individuals often misunderstood, they are also often the objects of considerable disdain.

Finally, language is historical. It was there before we were born and will continue after we are gone. Its meanings were accumulated over a long period of time by a myriad of individuals now lost forever. Furthermore, language is a living, changing tool, with new words and meanings constantly being added, some for a few days, others for much longer. Some regard language as a "broad stream flowing through time" (p. 75). Berger and Berger write:

An Austrian writer, Karl Kraus, has called language the house in which the human spirit lives. Language provides the lifelong context of our experience of others, of self, of the world. Even when we imagine worlds beyond this one, we are constrained to put our intimations or hopes in terms of language. Language is *the* social institution above all others. It provides the most powerful hold that society has over us (p. 75).

Given the power of language to shape us in many ways, it is well to keep in mind that it is not only our "own" language—formal or informal—that has such power. As Gonzalez notes,

There is no such thing linguistically speaking as a good language or a bad language, a superior language or an inferior language. Each language is appropriate for its time, place, and circumstances. All languages are complete in this respect.[19]

Perspectives on Language Variation

A number of Martina Chandler's classroom activities are designed to show how language varies from one cultural group to another, as well as between individuals within the same group. Likewise, teachers and students sometimes speak different historical languages, but more often, they speak the same language in different ways. Moreover, teachers and students use both verbal and nonverbal means to communicate significant messages to one another.

Verbal Communication

Through an extensive process of evolution, humans have developed the ability to produce, receive, store, and manipulate a variety of symbolic sounds. Human beings, more than any other creature, depend on the production of sound in the form of verbal language as their primary means of communication.

Within any given language, however, vocabulary, pronunciation, syntax (grammatical structure), and semantics (the meaning of words) may differ widely. When Martina's students took turns saying words like *greasy, fire, log,* and *aunt,* they were clearly able to hear differences in pronunciation. Furthermore, the form in which language is conveyed may also differ, as, for example, in sign language where syntax is composed of a combination of specific movements of the fingers, hand, and arm as well as facial expressions. Most people are fascinated to watch this kind of speech, made public in recent years by signers who accompany performances on television or talks by public officials. Martina's students were also very interested in Anna's and Mrs. Thomas's use of sign in class. As Martina's students interviewed one another and then introduced their partners to the rest of the class, they were able to hear other variations in language, such as accents and dialects, as well.

Accents

An **accent** differs from the standard language only in the way words are pronounced, and it often results from pronunciation habits shared by people from a geographical region. Thus, people with a typical New England accent may pronounce the words *car, far,* and *bar* as if they were spelled *caaa, faaa,* and *baaa.* Similarly, people who have learned to speak English in Appalachia, the South, or the West may have significant differences in the way they pronounce the same words. People whose first language is not English may have difficulty pronouncing certain English words. Japanese speakers, for example, often have trouble with the letter *l,* and Russian speakers may have difficulty with the letters *w* and *v* as they are used in English words. Note that such speakers may be speaking quite proper standard English, but with accents.[20] In Martina's classroom, Hannah and Tammy, who had both moved to California from West Virginia, had the softness and somewhat slurred accent of the West Virginia hills. Yoshi, who speaks both English and Japanese, can imitate his grandparents' Japanese accent as they speak English. Rosita speaks English with a pronounced Spanish accent.

Dialects

Accents and Dialects

A **dialect** is a variation of some standard language form that includes differences in pronunciation, word usage, and syntax. Such differences may be based on ethnicity, religion, geographical region, social class, or age. Dialects differ not only in their origin but also in the specifics of their expression. Regional differences, for example, usually involve variations in the pronunciation of vowels (recall the example of people from New England). Similarly, Tammy and Hannah, as well as having Appalachian accents, speak a dialect of English sometimes referred to as **Mountain English.** Social dialects, on the other hand, are most often distinguished from one another by variations in the pronunciation of consonants, particularly the *th* sound and the sound of the consonants *r* and *l*. Dontae, the young man from Los Angeles, exhibited this language pattern. Regional and social dialects and accents may vary together or be a combination from a number of sociocultural origins, depending on the life experiences of the speaker.[21] Although there are a variety of dialects spoken in the United States, the three most widely known are **Black English** (or Ebonics), **rural English,** and **standard English.**

Ebonics (also called Black English or African American Language) is a dialect spoken primarily but not exclusively by urban African Americans.[22] Although it is often associated with those who live in low-income communities,[23] it is also spoken by African Americans from a variety of social classes and serves, in part, as an expression of cultural identity.[24] The influence of social class on Ebonics is seen mainly in the ability of Black English speakers to switch back and forth between Ebonics and standard English. Dontae, who speaks Ebonics fluently, has difficulty switching to standard English and is not certain that he wants to do it. One explanation for the origin of Ebonics is that it is derived from Gullah, a Creole dialect developed by Africans brought to the United States as slaves, which puts English words into a syntax similar to many African languages. Another explanation sees it as a version of a regional English dialect spoken by early English settlers on the East Coast. Gullah is still spoken by some residents of the Sea Islands off the Carolina coast, and while many of the distinctive features of Black English are similar to Gullah, Black English is also similar to other dialects spoken by European whites in some rural areas of the United States and England.[25]

Not too long ago, a nationwide debate was sparked when the Oakland, California, school board decided to incorporate Ebonics into its plans to improve student achievement. Although this event is discussed in more depth later in the chapter, here it is enough to say that much of the controversy was because the press misrepresented the district's intent. The public was led to believe that students would be taught Ebonics instead of, or in addition to, standard English. The policy, however, never stated that Ebonics would be taught to students, only that their learning would be enhanced when teachers and others recognize and understand Ebonics. In reality, only teachers would be taught Ebonics, enabling them to better understand and communicate with their students.

Rural English, sometimes called mountain English, is a dialect spoken primarily in Appalachia and is derived from the language of early English settlers in the area. People from Appalachia are often ridiculed for their speech, but some linguists say that mountain English is the "purest" English spoken in the United States and the closest to the English spoken in Shakespeare's time. It has been preserved, in part, because of the isolation of mountain people, in the same way that Gullah has been preserved off the coast of the Carolinas.

Finally, middle-class European Americans may be surprised to learn that so-called standard English is also a dialect of the English language. Although the term *standard English* is usually taken to mean that version of the English language most acceptable or most "correct," there are, in fact, many varieties of standard English. Gollnick and Chinn, for example, note that "Standard English may vary from community to community: 'standard' is what is normative in that community."[26] Moreover, standard English as it is spoken in countries such as Australia, India, Nigeria, and England differs significantly from standard English as it is spoken in the United States.[27] Standard

English, as the term is used in U.S. schools, usually refers to that dialect spoken by educated middle and upper classes and to the formal written and oral English that dominates print and broadcast media.

Bidialectalism

Code-switching

Bidialectalism refers to the ability to speak two (and sometimes more) dialects and to switch back and forth easily. Examples of people engaging in bidialectalism are the country boy who has become an executive in a large city and switches dialects when he goes back to his hometown, or the African American woman who has become a professor and speaks standard English but switches to Ebonics when speaking informally to African American colleagues, students, or friends. The ability to "code-switch" is often encouraged in schools as a way of enabling youngsters to both broaden their language horizons and receive the perceived economic and social benefits of speaking standard English. Although research does not support the belief that it is necessary to speak standard English in order to read or write it, it is often the case that prejudice against those who speak nonstandard dialects may lead to economic and social discrimination.[28] In Martina's class, Ritchie is able to switch back and forth between Ebonics and standard English easily and does so often.

Sign Language

Sign Language

A form of nonverbal language is the language of signs spoken by the deaf. Several varieties of signed communication exist, notably **American Sign Language** (ASL), which is the only sign system recognized as a language; signed English, which translates oral or written English into signs; and finger spelling (sometimes called the manual alphabet), which literally spells out English words letter by letter. Anna acquired ASL in infancy in the same way that her hearing classmates learned oral language. Like other languages, ASL has its own syntax and rhythms. Anna learned to think in it and translates other sign languages and lip reading into it.[29] Closely associated with the culture of the deaf, ASL is the subject of often-heated debate in educational circles. Some educators believe that all deaf or hearing-impaired children should learn to speak orally, while others believe that signed communication is not only sufficient but also should be universally acknowledged as a complete and legitimate form of communication. In fact, many individuals—both hearing and hearing-impaired—are bilingual in ASL and English. Such is the case with Anna, who has learned to speak oral English but much prefers to use sign.

Like other languages, English and its dialects usually have two sets of norms, one for formal situations and writing and one for informal situations. Thus, people usually speak informally, using different vocabulary and grammar, to their friends and family but more formally to strangers or in formal situations. Formal English is also generally used when writing, except perhaps in letters to friends or family or in personal journals.

Nonverbal Communication

Nonverbal Communication

Although sign language is often thought of as nonverbal communication, it is also a form of verbal expression. Nonverbal communication, used by both hearing and hearing-impaired individuals, refers to body movements, facial expressions, and a variety of word replacement strategies. It has been estimated that nonverbal communication accounts for 50 to 90 percent of the messages we send and receive.[30] Leubitz has identified four functions of nonverbal communication: (1) it can convey messages; (2) it can augment verbal communication; (3) it can contradict verbal communication; and (4) it can replace verbal communication.[31] For purposes of analysis, three aspects of nonverbal behavior are usually studied: **proxemics, kinesics,** and **paralanguage.** It is well to remember, however, that they are seldom used or experienced individually; rather, they combine in various ways with one another and with verbal language to produce the innumerable nuances we take for granted in ordinary communication.

Proxemics

Proxemics, often called "social space," refers to the normal physical distance between speakers when they are communicating with one another and is normally acquired as part of a person's culture. For European Americans, particularly those of northern European ethnic heritage, a comfortable distance between speakers is about twenty-one inches.[32] Standing closer than that may be interpreted as hostile or in-your-face behavior, while standing farther away is likely to be interpreted as disinterested or standoffish behavior. In contrast, southern Europeans, Arabs, and Latin Americans normally stand much closer, while African Americans stand farther apart.[33] Social space and other forms of nonverbal communication, because they are so closely linked to cultural norms, are not issues we ordinarily think about; rather, they are so much a part of us that they become unconscious behaviors.

Kinesics

Kinesics is the study of body movements, often called body language, and includes gestures, posture, facial expressions, and eye contact. Like social space, body language is often involuntary, which accounts for the ability of nonverbal communication to contradict or replace verbal communication. That is, we often say with our bodies something opposite to that which we say with words, or we communicate attitudes and feelings without the use of words at all. Body language is also closely tied to culture. Indeed, cultural variations in the meaning of particular facial expressions or gestures or in the presence or absence of eye contact often account for serious misinterpretations among people from different cultural backgrounds. Consider, for example, the case of eye contact. African American speakers tend to look more directly at their conversational partner while speaking than while listening, which is the direct opposite of most European Americans. Thus, in conversation, a black listener is likely to look at the white speaker less than the white speaker expects. Likewise, while a black speaker is speaking, both parties in the conversation are likely to be looking at one another more than either expects. Imagine the range of misinterpretations or misattributions that are possible.

Paralanguage

Among the most interesting and least recognized forms of nonverbal communication is paralanguage, which is concerned with vocalizations that are not words. Two categories of paralanguage are distinguished. *Vocalizations* include (1) sounds such as crying, coughing, laughing, and sighing; (2) the intensity and pitch with which words are expressed; and (3) vocal segregates, which are sounds that act as word replacements such as "shhh" and "uh-huh." *Vocal qualifiers* lend meaning to words by means of rhythm, tempo, resonance, and control of articulation. Gollnick and Chinn note that "Vocal cues can enable listeners to distinguish between male and female speakers, African American and white speakers, and older and younger speakers, and to distinguish educational level and area of residence within a certain dialect region. A person's social class and status can often be determined based on the vocal characteristics of the individual."[34] Indeed, the almost magical ability of Henry Higgins to identify a speaker's geographical and social origins in the musical *My Fair Lady* is attributable in no small measure to his knowledge of paralanguage.

Differences in verbal and nonverbal language can lead to harmful misinterpretations in both student-to-student and teacher-to-student communication. When teachers and students belong to the same cultural groups, accurate interpretation is likely to proceed without too much difficulty. When teachers and students come from different cultural groups, however, misinterpretation is likely to be an ongoing problem unless both are aware of these differences and make an effort to accommodate them.

Culture, Language, and Learning Style

A third important area of language concerns its relationships to culture and learning styles. Language provides the names for ideas, people, and things that enable us to make sense of the world around us, and it does so at such an early age that it helps to structure the very ways in which we think. Thus, the language that students and teachers bring with them to school inevitably affects the mental processes by which they perceive, think, solve problems, learn, and approach learning. Language is also both a product and a shaper of culture. The two are inextricably intertwined.

Originally conducted in the 1950s by psychologists interested in perception and other forms of cognition, **learning style** research has in the past decades become increasingly available to educators interested in the variation they see in patterns of learning. Definitions of *learning style* vary, but the National Task Force on Learning Style and Brain Behavior has adopted the following tentative definition:

> Learning style is that consistent pattern of behavior and performance by which an individual approaches education experiences. It is the composite of characteristic cognitive, affective and psychological behaviors that serve as relatively stable indicators of how a learner perceives, interacts with, and responds to the learning environment. It is formed in the deep structure of neural organization and personality [that] molds and is molded by human development and the cultural experiences of home, school, and society.[35]

Components of Learning Style

Perhaps the most widely used dimension of learning style was also the first to be investigated. Studying variations in perception, Witkin and his colleagues discovered that most individuals could be grouped according to whether they were **field dependent** or

field independent.[36] An individual who is field independent easily perceives discrete parts, is good at abstract analytical thought, tends to be individualistic and less dependent on others, has less well-developed social skills, prefers working alone and self-organizes information to be learned, and tends to be intrinsically motivated and unresponsive to social reinforcement. In contrast, an individual who is field dependent (now more often referred to as field sensitive) perceives globally or holistically, does less well at analytical problem solving, tends to be sensitive to the social environment with well-developed social skills, prefers an observational approach to learning and will accept information to be learned as it is presented, and tends to be extrinsically motivated and responsive to the social environment.[37]

Learning Styles

A second dimension of learning style has to do with an individual's *preferred* sensory mode for learning. Although, barring physical disability, all six senses (sight, sound, smell, touch, taste, and movement) are normally open to learning stimuli, some individuals tend to learn most easily and efficiently through one of the sensory modes. There is also some evidence that preferred modes change as a factor of age. Barsch, for example, found that younger children make efficient use of taste, smell, and touch, while older children come to rely on movement, hearing, and vision.[38]

Activity and Reading 40: Learning Styles

Other variations in learning style include differences in response to the immediate environment, emotionality, social preferences, and cognitive-psychological orientation.[39] Responses to environmental influences include an individual's preference for quiet or noise, bright or soft illumination, or warm or cool temperatures. Emotionality includes such factors as motivation, persistence at tasks, and sense of responsibility as well as a person's response to the structure of a given context. Social preferences refer to the degree to which the presence of others facilitates learning. Included in this category is the degree to which an individual prefers to work alone, in pairs, in cooperative groups, or with adults. Finally, the psychological dimension refers to the tendencies individuals have to be global or analytic learners, right-brain or left-brain dominant, reflective or impulsive.

Multiple Intelligences

Related to the idea of learning style is the idea of multiple intelligences, extensively researched and promoted by Howard Gardner and his many colleagues and followers.[40] Based on considerable research on the brain and on aspects of cognition, Gardner's concept suggests that human beings have not only preferred learning styles but also different ways of expressing intellectual ability. Initially, Gardner conceptualized seven different kinds of intelligence: visual/spatial, verbal/linguistic, logical/mathematical, bodily/kinesthetic, musical/rhythmic, interpersonal, and intrapersonal. Individuals who have strengths in any (or several) of these kinds of intelligence tend to have preferred modes of *thinking*. For example, people who are strong in verbal/linguistic intelligence tend to think in words and love reading, writing, playing word games, and so on, while those who are strong in visual/spatial intelligence tend to think in images and pictures and love designing, drawing, and doodling.[41]

Multiple Intelligences

The importance of multiple intelligences and learning styles in school lies in the ability of teachers to identify preferred modes of learning and to adapt instruction so that all students get to practice learning in multiple ways. Notice that no one recommends that

c r i t i c a l   i n c i d e n t

The Chemistry Lab

Ricardo, a sixteen-year-old Mexican student in Martina's class, had been in the United States for one year and can speak and understand English well enough to function in school. He has done well in his studies, carrying a 2.5 grade point average with his highest grades in literature and history courses. He struggled through the first semester of chemistry, however, with D's and F's on most tests, which were based on class lectures. His lab reports salvaged his grade because they were always of the highest quality—a fact that his teacher, Mr. Thompson, attributed mainly to the influence and help of Ricardo's lab partner, Dave, the best student in the class.

When everyone was assigned a new lab partner for the second semester, Ricardo was paired with Tim, who was failing the course. Ricardo's lab reports, however, continued to be excellent, and Tim's also improved significantly. Mr. Thompson was puzzled by Ricardo's performance.

- How might Ricardo's performance in chemistry class be explained?

students learn only in their preferred style but rather that they have opportunities to develop learning *strategies* that can maximize their natural strengths and minimize their weaknesses.

Origins of Learning Style

Although the exact origins of a person's particular learning style are still a matter of conjecture, it is clear that learning patterns develop from a combination of biological, psychological, and sociocultural (including linguistic) factors. Also, much research indicates that child-rearing practices and other forms of socialization are heavily implicated in the development of learning style. Since language is the medium through which much socialization occurs in the family, it is not unreasonable to surmise that the relation of language to patterns of learning is considerable. In addition, because language is closely linked to culture, learning-style differences may be more readily understood if we look at the connections between language, culture, and learning style.

The Relation of Language and Learning Style to Culture

Geography, history, and cultural experience all influence the way a person acquires language, which language that person learns, and what meanings are attributed to words. The family is normally the first mediator of the culture to a growing child. Nevertheless, language and cultural knowledge are inextricably bound together.

Of primary importance, of course, in the development of language is the acquisition of vocabulary—what are the "right" words for ideas, people, actions, and things. But words themselves are arbitrary. Indeed, the very concept of "word" may differ among

From a Fishing Village to a School in Town

Natasha, one of the tenth grade students in Martina Chandler's class, was part of a special program to encourage young people to become teachers. One of the opportunities Natasha had was to assist in a district elementary school two days a week. She was asked by the classroom teacher to observe a new student, Jimmie, who had recently moved to San Francisco from a small fishing village outside Anchorage, where he had spent most of his young life among his father's people, the Tlingits. Before coming to San Francisco, Jimmie often accompanied his father, provided for his family by fishing for salmon and hunting for the winter food supply.

Jimmie's mother taught him at home, and he pursued his studies on his own with her guidance. When he came to San Francisco he tested at grade level and was placed with other nine-year-olds in the fourth grade. In social studies, the class was broken into small groups, each having a different topic for group inquiry and presentation. Natasha noticed that Jimmie usually sat quietly at the edge of the group and did not share or discuss with others in the group, even after several meetings, although he did seem to have his report outlined and completed. Natasha approached the classroom teacher concerned that Jimmie was not doing his fair share of the work.

- Why do you think Jimmie was not doing his work?
- How might Ms. Chandler help Natasha better understand why Jimmie is not doing his work?

language groups. The Japanese word *ikimasu,* for example, may have any of the following English meanings: I (you, he, she, we, they) am (is, are) going.[42] A Japanese listener will decide which of these meanings is correct by the context of the conversation.

An even more complex concept of "word" can be found in the Yana Indian language in northern California. The word *yabanaumawildjigummaha'nigi* has the following subparts:

ya	=	several people move
banauma	=	everybody
wil	=	across
dji	=	to the West
gumma	=	indeed
ha'	=	let us
nigi	=	we

In English, we might say, "Let us each move to the West," but as Tiedt and Tiedt note, "Even with the parts of the long word defined, we still do not understand [the Yana word] because we arrange our thoughts differently and do not repeat words as the Yanas did."[43]

Even in the same language, the same words may have different meanings. Consider the word *tip*. Tip can mean to push something over or off an edge. It can also refer to payment for some service over and above the stated price. A tip can also refer to a good idea or suggestion that one person might give another, or it can mean a slender point at the end of something. In some parts of the world, a tip refers to a garbage dump. Such common English words as *love, bread, chicken, turkey, bat,* and *top* all have many meanings. Linguists have estimated that the fifty most often used words in the English language can produce over fourteen thousand different meanings.[44]

Language also plays a critical role in the maintenance of subgroups within a larger cultural/language group. Recall that ingroup membership is granted to those with whom the group feels comfortable and with whom the group has perceived similarities. One function of language is to distinguish those who should be considered potential members of the ingroup from those who should not. In this way, language helps people develop a sense of social unity. Thus, a variation from a language standard that contributes to a group's sense of identity is nearly as important as the parent language itself.

Language reflects the thought processes of a culture. English writing and thinking, for instance, is relatively linear in comparison to many other languages.[45] That is, the speaker or writer tries to get right to the point by eliminating reference to issues and topics that seem irrelevant to the message. The task for such a speaker is to communicate the message quickly and efficiently. Speakers who do not keep to the topic can be quite frustrating to English listeners, as is witnessed by the English colloquialism "He just keeps beating around the bush!" On the other hand, speakers of Semitic languages (Arabic and Hebrew) use various kinds of parallels in their thinking. References to past events, for example, are quite common and expected. Another important function of verbal communication among Semitic speakers, as well as many others, is the building of personal relationships through language use.

No pattern of communication is right or wrong; all have evolved to express and satisfy particular cultural patterns and needs. Some, however, may stress the development of interpersonal relationships more than others. If those interpersonal relationships are not expressed in the message (for example, when an American is speaking with an Arab), the person receiving the message may interpret it in a way that the speaker does not intend. Consider the American discussing plans to meet later in the week. While the American is interested in establishing the exact time, place, and purpose of the meeting, the Arab intersperses the conversation with questions about the health of family members, the last time the two parties met, and other significant events in the lives of the two conversants. Both speakers are using language for cultural purposes in cultural ways: the American to get something done, and the Arab to indicate a committed relationship. It would not be surprising, in this instance, if misunderstanding occurred!

Learning style is also developed, in part, as an expression of culture, since what we attend to and how we attend to it are culturally shaped adaptations to the physical and social environment. Christine Bennett, for example, cites a story told by an Anglo-American speech student who had two experiences that illustrate this point, one with a Hopi Indian and the other with Trukee islanders.

> "Look at those clouds!" I exclaimed one afternoon. "We'll probably have rain later today."
> "What clouds?" my Hopi companion asked.

The Students Balk

Mrs. Allen teaches an elective class in English as a Standard Dialect that meets just down the hall from Ms. Chandler's classes. Her students (most of them African Americans, with some Hispanics) have been identified by English teachers or guidance counselors as speaking an excessive amount of nonstandard English. The students and their parents have chosen to take advantage of this special class. A few students from Ms. Chandler's tenth grade English class take this class as well.

Mrs. Allen's classroom is supplied with library carrels and tape recorders along with the usual individual desks arranged in slightly cramped quarters at one end of the room. Mrs. Allen went to a great deal of effort to collect copies of written materials from a variety of sources and to make audiotapes for oral work. Each student took a placement test at the beginning of the year and received a binder full of individualized lessons geared to her or his particular needs.

On the days when the class stays together, working from a common textbook, the students concentrate and participate. Other days when they work individually, the students complain, they do not do much work, and some constantly visit others around the room. The only way Mrs. Allen can get individual work done is to act in a very authoritarian manner, which she is not comfortable doing.

- If she were to approach Martina Chandler for advice, how do you think she would explain the situation, and what advice might she offer?

"Right there!" I responded in amazement, pointing to obvious puffs of white and gray.
"All I see is the sky."
"You mean you really don't see those clouds?"
"There's nothing there but sky."

Several months later, this same student was in the opposite situation with a group of Trukee fishermen.

I thought we were lost. There had been no sign of land for hours. My companions tried to reassure me that we weren't lost at all. They read the wave patterns like I'd use a map. All I could see were waves. Even when they pointed to specific signs, I couldn't see anything. Here we were looking at the same body of water. It felt strange to know that I simply could not perceive what they actually saw.[46]

Research has indicated that particular patterns of learning (or learning style) can be associated with particular cultural groups. For example, many African Americans and many females tend to be field sensitive, while many Japanese and Japanese Americans tend to be field independent. It is important to note, however, that *there may be more difference within these groups than between them.* As Figure 2.2 points out, a large number of factors can contribute to an individual's own particular pattern of culture, and this also holds true for the development of an individual's language and learning style.

critical   incident ....

Conversation at Lunch

Ranjani and Sathie are two female students from India who are in another of Martina's classes. They often eat lunch together in the cafeteria, usually by themselves. They are both very pleased to have found another person from their country with whom they can share their concerns. They often have quite animated discussions, in English, giving each other help and advice.

Steve, a Hungarian American student usually sits nearby. One day when Ms. Chandler happens to walk by, Steve asks her, seemingly out of frustration, "Why do those two students from India argue so much?" Ranjani and Sathie look at him in astonishment and do not know what to say. Martina, too, is a bit taken back by his comment.

- How would you best explain the situation?

Communication Style

Central to the issue of how we communicate is another set of culturally learned characteristics associated with both language and learning style called **communication style.** Grossman has written extensively on the subject, and the categories and analysis that follow are based on his work.[47]

Formal versus Informal Communication

All languages have sets of norms for both formal and informal communication. However, some cultural groups (and some languages) are much more rigid than others in this differentiation. "Strict codes of communication may be designed to show respect for others, to avoid open demonstrations of conflict and disagreement, or to avoid causing individuals to 'lose face'" (p. 173). Many Asian students, for example, are shocked to discover how informally American students talk to teachers.

Emotional versus Subdued Communication

Some cultural groups are more concerned with the sensibilities of other people, whereas other cultural groups are concerned with protecting the individual's right to express her or his intense feelings. In the United States, such a distinction can be seen in the African American pattern of emotionally intense speech versus the general pattern of subdued, less emotional speech more common among European Americans.

Direct versus Indirect Communication

Cultural groups vary in terms of their emphasis on frankness and direct communication. Asian and Pacific Islanders, for example, are more likely than Americans to communicate in indirect ways, and Americans are often surprised at the even more direct speech patterns of Russians. One variation of the direct-indirect distinction is the use of poetic or analogous communication. "Educators who prefer direct expression may also mistakenly think that some African American and Hispanic American students who use a more poetic speech pattern are 'beating around the bush,' that they cannot think straight, or that they have communication problems" (p. 174).

Objective versus Subjective Communication

While no culture places an emphasis on total and complete honesty, cultural groups differ on the emphasis placed on accuracy and "truth." To some groups, the need to save face or the importance of maintaining interpersonal relationships may be more important than honesty. Nguyen, for instance, writes that

> Falsehood carries no moral structure for a Cambodian, Laotian, or Vietnamese. The essential question is not whether a statement is true or false, but what the intention of the statement is. Does it facilitate interpersonal harmony? Does it indicate a wish to change the subject? Hence, one must learn the "heart" of the speaker through his/her words.[48]

Responses to Guilt and Accusations

Cultural groups also differ in the ways their members respond to accusations of wrongdoing and to guilt. For example, European Americans will usually respond vigorously to accusations of which they are innocent, but will show guilt by lowering their eyes and appearing embarrassed. African Americans, on the other hand, tend to lower their eyes as a sign of respect rather than guilt and may feel no particular need to defend themselves against false accusation. It is easy to see that, unaware of these differences, European Americans and African Americans are likely to interpret such signs inaccurately.

A number of other issues fall under the general rubric of communication style, such as cultural and language differences in the way people handle conflict, how and when they avoid blame, what they consider appropriate topics of general conversation, and whether and how they indicate affection. What is clear from this discussion is that teachers must be aware of some of these distinctions in language, learning, and communication styles if they want to interact effectively with their students.

Perspectives on Bilingual Education

Perhaps no other issue pertaining to diversity in American public schools has been as emotional and divisive over time as the debates over **bilingual education.**

Social and Legal History

Contrary to popular belief, bilingual education is not a creation of the 1960s, although the civil rights movement gave it renewed emphasis. Indeed, Ohio was the first state to pass a bilingual education law in 1839—allowing German-English instruction if parents requested it. Similar laws were enacted in Louisiana for French and English in 1847 and in the New Mexico territory for Spanish and English in 1850. By the turn of

History of Bilingual Education

the twentieth century, many local districts and nearly a dozen states were providing bilingual education in languages including Norwegian, Italian, Polish, Czech, and Cherokee.[49] At that time, at least six hundred thousand children in primary schools (public and parochial) received part or all of their instruction in German—about 4 percent of all American elementary students.[50]

Nativist fears stemming from World War I changed the political winds, however, and by the mid-1920s bilingual education provisions were replaced by English-only laws in a majority of states. The ferment surrounding civil rights in the 1960s brought renewed interest in bilingual education. In the twelve-year period from 1963 to 1975, private and governmental studies and hearings and a series of lawsuits regarding rights to native language instruction, placement of children with disabilities, and desegregation produced many mandates for the schooling of minority students. Concurrently, new educational strategies and curricula, especially in bilingual and bicultural education, appeared in districts across the nation. The Bilingual Education Act was passed in 1968 as Title VII of the Elementary and Secondary Education Act. President Lyndon Johnson clarified the intent of this law in the following words:

> This bill authorizes a new effort to prevent dropouts; new programs for handicapped children; new planning help for rural schools. It also contains a special provision establishing bilingual education programs for children whose first language is not English. Thousands of children of Latin descent, young Indians, and others will get a better start—a better chance—in school.[51]

In 1970, the Office of Civil Rights Guidelines tried to make special training for non-English-speaking students a requirement for public schools that receive federal aid. The office stated:

> Where inability to speak and understand the English language excludes national origin–minority group children from effective participation in the education program offered by a school district, the district must take affirmative steps to rectify the language deficiency in order to open its instructional program to these students.[52]

A significant case in the development of multicultural and bilingual education was *Lau* v. *Nichols,* decided by a 1974 Supreme Court ruling. This decision declared that a San Francisco school district violated a non-English-speaking Chinese student's right to equal educational opportunity when it failed to provide needed English language instruction and other special programs. An important consequence of the *Lau* decision was the declaration that school districts across the country must provide students an education in languages that meet their needs.

Bilingual Education Legislation and Court Cases

Although *Lau* v. *Nichols,* filed on behalf of eighteen hundred Chinese American pupils, did not involve special education directly, the ruling underscored the responsibility of schools to address language differences in making decisions about placing students as well as in teaching them. Two previous judicial decisions in class action suits brought by parents had directly addressed the issue of overrepresentation of minority children in special education. In 1970, in *Diana* v. *State Board of Education,* parents charged that the number of Hispanic students placed in special classes for children with mental retardation in California was approximately twice what would be expected based on the proportion of Hispanic children enrolled in that state. In *Larry P.* v. *Riles,* similar overrepresentation of black children was found in the San Francisco Unified School District. In both cases, disproportions were attributed to invalid use of IQ tests for bilingual or bidialectical children as the basis for placement decisions; *Diana* revealed that Spanish-speaking children were administered tests in English, while African American pupils in *Larry P.* v. *Riles* were found to score within the normal range when retested.

In 1981, a pedagogically sound plan for limited English proficient students was set by the fifth Circuit Court in Texas in *Castenade* v. *Pickard.* The plan required a sufficient qualified staff to implement the plan, including hiring of new staff and training of current staff, as well as the establishment of a system to evaluate the programs. It is important to note that a formal "bilingual education" program was not required; however, it did require that "appropriate action to overcome language barriers" be taken through well-implemented programs.

Responses to Bilingual Education Programs

Responses to Bilingual Education Programs

In terms of schooling mandates, educators and the public have responded (and still respond) to multicultural efforts in various ways. Opponents of special programs fall into several categories. First are the people who believe that the American educational system in its traditional form has always provided for the upward mobility of all people who were "willing to work." Another group of opponents believe that the nation-state will be destroyed if the schools do not continue offering a monocultural and monolinguistic education. Some people in the latter group moralize that pluralistic approaches to education, especially bilingualism, can "handicap a child—perhaps permanently— by offering him a crutch that won't hold up in the work-a-day world in which he must live in later life."[53] Other opponents worry that "ethnics" would be mandated for available teaching positions. Still others warn that ethnic (and racial) identity movements serve to weaken the cultural glue that holds the nation together, thereby aggravating tensions rather than diminishing differences among groups.

Proponents, composed primarily of educators and speaking in a somewhat softer voice, assert that pluralism in education should not be viewed as a remedial effort nor a form of reparation but rather as the long overdue affirmation of a social reality. Pluralism, in their view, is not an ethnic or racial property but a national characteristic, long ignored in education. In the year 2000, for example, delegates to the National Education Association Representative Assembly, who meet to decide policy for the organization, passed a Resolution on Educational Programs for limited English proficiency students that said, in part,

> The National Education Association believes that limited English proficiency (LEP) students must have available to them programs that address their unique needs and that provide equal opportunity to all students, regardless of their primary language.[54]

The Bilingual Education Backlash

The Oakland Ebonics Controversy

Since the 1990s, a growing backlash against teaching students in any other language but English seems to rival the backlash after World War I. Two significant responses surfaced in California. The first one was the largely symbolic decision (since partially amended) of the Oakland schools to recognize the use of Ebonics among some of its students and to attempt to use that fact as a tool to improve student performance. At no time did the Oakland Board of Education plan to teach students *in* Ebonics. Rather, the policy was part of a larger effort to "stop blaming children and start demanding more accountability from teachers and administrators in a district where the average grade among African American students is a D+."[55] The approach was to "train teachers to recognize and respect Ebonics as the everyday language of many African American students and, instead of declaring them wrong when they use it, helping them translate to standard English."[56] In other words, teachers would *begin* with the students' own language (or, in this case, dialect) in order to take them more effectively toward the understanding and use of the standard English of the typical American workplace.

So sensitive are some Americans to the bilingual education issue, however, that something of a firestorm erupted when the Oakland board announced its plans. What most critics missed was that such an approach was only part of a *process* of teaching standard English, not its aim.

Bilingual Education Backlash

A second major response had more far-reaching consequences, in California, in Arizona, and in the rest of the country as well. In 1998, voters in California passed Proposition 227, which required California public schools to teach limited English proficient (LEP) students in special classes that were taught almost entirely in English. It also shortened the time that most LEP students would stay in special classes, normally not longer than one year. Arizona's Proposition 303 followed in 1999, and similar measures are under consideration in Massachusetts, Oregon, Colorado, and Rhode Island.[57]

Research conducted by University of California researchers two years after Proposition 227 offers several insights into the early impact of the revised approach to language instruction. First, the percent of English learners in special classes dropped by 29 percent to 12 percent statewide. Second, in part due to confusion regarding the responsibilities of districts in informing parents of their rights to seek waivers from the English immersion program, only 67 percent of districts formally so notified parents. Third, teachers' initiatives in their own classrooms seemed to depend "on what they had done prior to 227, and on their own skills, experience, and beliefs about students' learning. However, it was rare to encounter a teacher who contended that his or her instruction and class organization had not been affected."[58] Moreover, research conducted by members of the same University of California research team at Stanford suggests that oral proficiency in English may take three to five years, while proficiency in academic English may take four to seven years.[59]

Given the debate among proponents and opponents of bilingual education, it is perhaps worthwhile to inquire why people become so upset about bilingual education. Two major factors seem to be at work here. The first is whether children will suffer if they participate in bilingual instruction. Advocates for Proposition 227 argued that although bilingual education began with good intentions in the 1970s, it has failed in actual practice and that Latino immigrant children are its principal victims, as evidenced by their high failure and dropout rates. The assumption here is that bilingual education results in students *not* learning to speak, read, and write English and thus being injured for life both economically and socially. A subtext of this argument—a fear of overwhelming numbers of *unassimilated* students entering the adult American world—is reminiscent of arguments for assimilationist practices at the beginning of the twentieth century. A second, related issue deals with the effects of a bilingual education. The assumption of many parents and teachers is that children cannot achieve as much in a bilingual context. Children, it is thought, cannot cope with the demands of schooling in two languages.

Other Bilingual Education Issues

Bilingual education is further complicated by the difficulty of defining just who is and who is not bilingual. While someone may be able to speak in two languages, use of one of those languages may be restricted to a particular setting. People may use their native language, for example, only at home or among other speakers of that language, whereas they use their second language at school or at work. No definitive cutoff points can be identified that distinguish a monolingual from a bilingual.[60] The 1984 Bilingual Education Act defines LEP individuals as those not born in the United States, those whose native language is not English, those from environments in which English is not the dominant language, and those from the various Native American groups where languages other than English are commonly used.[61] An estimated 3.5 and 5.5 million LEP students are enrolled in schools today, less than two-thirds of whom receive the support they need to succeed in school.[62] This lack of support is unfortunate, because children's psychological security and their sense of belonging as well as their general school adjustment is better when they are able to communicate effectively in the language of the school.

Types of Bilingual Education Programs

Bilingual education for language minority students has three goals: (1) students should attain high levels of proficiency in the English language; (2) students should achieve academically in all the content areas in school; and (3) students should experience positive personal growth. To achieve these goals, schools in the United States have adopted one of four general models of bilingual education: submersion, English as a second language, transitional bilingual education, and structured immersion. The distinctions among these models are somewhat blurred, but they can be differentiated according to their primary emphases and methods.

Submersion Programs

In **submersion programs,** language minority children are placed in the regular classroom with native speakers of English. This approach can accurately be described as a "sink-or-swim" approach. Some unexamined myths commonly exist about the effectiveness of the submersion experience. It is quite common to hear statements such as, "My parents or grandparents came to this country without speaking a word of English. They received their education only in English, and they didn't suffer." People who make such statements are probably ignorant of the feelings their ancestors actually experienced. Language use plays a critical role in identity, both for the group and the individual. Most people have a strong need to use their first language as a means of self and group preservation, particularly for first- and second-generation members. The Supreme Court in *Lau v. Nichols* ruled that submersion programs were unlawful.

English as a Second Language

In most instances, **English as a second language** (ESL) programs have replaced the typical submersion approach. In ESL instruction, the student's background and cultural experiences become the focal point for learning English. Children in ESL programs are kept in the regular classroom for most of the day, as in the submersion experience, but are pulled out at various times for English instruction. This approach to English language learning has become so popular that even a cursory investigation on the Internet produces a large variety of resources and instructional activities for students and teachers.

Transitional Bilingual Education

In **transitional bilingual education,** efforts are made to phase out the student's native language while developing the student's facility in English as quickly as possible. The thinking behind such an effort is that unless children's skill in English develops rapidly, they will soon fall behind their English-speaking counterparts in the regular classroom. In such programs, instruction in the child's first language is gradually withdrawn as facility in English grows.

Structured Immersion Programs

In **structured immersion programs** (which is the general direction mandated by Proposition 227), students are taught by teachers who are fluent in the native language of the child. While students are allowed to speak in their first language, the teacher usually responds in English. In this way, students receive instruction in subject matter that is comparable to their English-speaking peers while simultaneously learning to speak English, at least for a short time.

The distinction between submersion and immersion programs is important. Baker provides a good analogy in differentiating the two programs by comparing language learning to learning how to swim.[63] *Submersion* embodies the idea of a nonswimmer being thrown into the deep end of a pool. In submersion programs, students are forbidden to use their home language. The entire school program is presented in the majority language. It is assumed that second-language learners will be surrounded by expert users of the majority language who will assist students in their language development. In reality, however, the second-language learner is likely to have considerable difficulty keeping up with the ideas and interaction of fluent speakers.

In *immersion* programs, the student gradually moves from the shallow to the deep end of the pool. Pupils are allowed to splash about using their first language while slowly being taught the skills necessary to acquire the second language. The swimmer who moves slowly into deeper water eventually learns all the swimming strokes and is able to swim unaided. Similarly, the language student can listen, speak, read, and write in either language as needed. In immersion programs, students are homogeneous in their ability to use the new language; they are all nonswimmers. Slowly, as ability and confidence grows, children naturally switch to the second language. Successful immersion programs enable children to dive into either language pool equally well.

Ethical Issues: Local and Global

Teaching linguistically diverse students also entails ethical and moral issues. Martina Chandler, for example, is aware that students who speak another language, or who speak dialects of standard English, are likely to be stigmatized by other students as well as by school policies, particularly in schools without well-developed programs for English language learners.

Most U.S. schools, and a majority of the general public, are committed to the proposition that all students learn and perform effectively in standard English, which is the language of choice by the dominant social group. Therefore, debates about bilingual education and English as a second language revolve as much around issues of cultural domination and subordination as they do around what is best for individual students. In short, the debate about bilingual education is part of a larger debate about who controls the school curriculum and for what purposes.

Another ethical issue is the degree to which assessment of student progress is measured by culture-biased tests that favor students who are already fluent in standard English. It is likely, for example, that a student may be quite knowledgeable about a subject matter but cannot express his or her knowledge in the manner required by certain kinds of tests. Similarly, most traditional assessment instruments tend to favor students who are field independent rather than global learners, who are visual learners rather than auditory or kinesthetic learners, and who prefer to work alone rather than in cooperative groups. In recent years, alternative forms of performance-based assessment have been designed that enable teachers to accurately assess progress for those students who do better with other styles of learning. However, such assessments are relatively slow in being incorporated into statewide, government-mandated tests. In the meantime, teachers like Martina Chandler must find ways to demonstrate that their students are, in fact, learning effectively according to current, proficiency-based assessment strategies.

A third ethical issue is a global one and concerns the degree to which language provides the keys to understanding other peoples in an increasingly interdependent world. Globalization, worldwide television (especially cable news networks such as CNN), and the Internet have tended to make English a worldwide standard language. Indeed, more than sixty countries now use English in an official capacity.[64] In part because of this international acceptance of English, many languages are disappearing. Indeed, one author asserts that

> During the past century, due to a variety of factors, more than 1,000 of the world's languages have disappeared, and it is possible to foresee a time, perhaps 100 years from now, when about half of today's 6,000 languages will either be dead or dying. . . . This startling rate of linguistic extinction is possible because 96 percent of the world's languages are now spoken only by 4 percent of the world's population.[65]

This important ethical question is similar to ethical questions about preserving the biodiversity of the planet: "Is the maintenance of cultural and linguistic diversity as important as the preservation of pandas"[66] and other endangered life forms? Without diverse languages, diverse cultures become assimilated. And diverse cultures on the planet contribute to a healthy cultural "ecosystem," just as diverse species contribute to a healthy biological ecosystem. Clearly, some balance needs to be made between protecting "small" languages and encouraging international exchange.

The consequence of ignoring the languages of other peoples raises a final (and related) ethical issue, one newly and dramatically important to most Americans. Although English is spoken around the world, Americans generally take a dim view of learning other languages for any reason. Mila Saskova-Pierce, a foreign-language professor at the University of Nebraska at Lincoln, for example, believes that in our rush to assimilate immigrants, Americans have "failed to exploit an 'unbelievably potent' gift: the children of immigrants." These children, she says,

> could help America erase the ignorance it too often has of other cultures. It's just like little gems covered by sand. If you dig them up and shine them up a little bit, they have great value. . . . They have learned the kitchen-level language at home. If we took that gift that was given to them by the family and give them the ivory-tower instruction like we do to all the kids in English . . . we would raise a generation of true bilingual Americans.[67]

The American attitude of not encouraging the acquisition of other languages by native English speakers tends to hinder both our knowledge and our understanding of peoples around the world. Suddenly, with the destruction of the World Trade Center on September 11, 2001, it became evident that the United States was caught off-guard. Saskova-Pierce notes that.

> Five months before terrorists hit American soil, the New York Times reported that the country faced a critical shortage in language experts to help unravel other nations' secrets. Since the attacks . . . the CIA and FBI have descended on universities such as Harvard and Georgetown in search of students schooled in the language and culture of Afghanistan. Meanwhile, thousands of educated Afghans in America have spent their time washing dishes or driving taxicabs. The country could have drawn on their expertise . . . For Americans to understand Afghanistan, they must learn the language and thus unlock the code to the culture. The outrage over the terror attacks makes that more difficult, however. If you hate the language, you can't really learn it. . .
>
> The Pashtun language helped ignite the Renaissance in Europe, transmitting great medical, mathematical and cultural advances to thaw intellectually frozen medieval monarchies. But the irony of America's approach to language is evident: The well-to-do pay good money to place their children in bilingual schools in Washington, D.C., as a prerequisite to international business and political careers. Meanwhile bilingual education in California is under attack by those who would compel immigrants to abandon their language for English.[68]

Whether Americans will sufficiently realize the importance of knowing more than one language is an open question at this point. If the current data on efforts toward English-only instruction in the United States is correct, the picture does not look particularly encouraging. But it is perhaps a hopeful sign that upcoming generations of teachers are being increasingly exposed to the importance of diversity, and they may, in fact, lead this country in the direction of a broader emphasis on bilingualism.

Summary

Classrooms that are learning communities seem to be at the heart of effective teaching and learning in the twenty-first century. Of particular importance in this regard is attentiveness to the language or languages of students and teachers and to the ways in which all individuals naturally approach teaching and learning. Clearly, language structures the very thoughts and ideas we have as human beings. Not only do we have particular vocabularies that have meaning for us, but we also structure our sentences and pronounce our words in particular ways that we have learned as part of our primary socialization as young children and that therefore seem comfortable and "right" to us.

In classrooms where children of diverse backgrounds attempt to learn a proscribed curriculum, teachers must pay attention to the students' linguistic backgrounds so that they can be certain that all children are effectively understanding and participating in all learning activities. Teachers who are working with children whose first language is not English must remember that each child's language is an integral part of that child's personhood, and must make every attempt to regard that personhood with respect. Both the proponents and opponents of bilingual education want children to learn; both disagree—sometimes profoundly—on the best means (and the best language) to achieve that goal. Because of the history of the bilingual education debate and because of the increasing interconnectedness of today's world, teachers must be clear in their own minds about the relative merits of bilingual education.

Chapter Review

Go to the Online Learning Center at **www.mhhe.com/Cushner4e** to review important content from the chapter, practice with key terms, take a chapter quiz, and find the web links listed in this chapter.

Key Terms

Accent 222

American Sign Language 224

Bidialectalism 224

Bilingual education 233

Black English 223

Communication style 232

Dialect 222

English as a second
language 238

Field dependent 226

Field independent 227

Kinesics 225

Learning style 226

Mountain English 222

Paralanguage 225

Proxemics 225

Rural English 223

Standard English 223

Structured immersion
programs 238

Submersion programs 237

Transitional bilingual
education 238

Reflective Questions

Clearly, establishing a learning-community classroom like Martina Chandler's tenth grade English class is fraught with both difficulties and possibilities. Put yourself in Martina's place, at this early point in the school year, and answer the questions Martina is asked herself.

1. How am I going to create a democratic, interactive learning community when my students come from such different backgrounds?
2. How am I going to discourage standard English speakers from stigmatizing those students like Tran and Dontae whose language differences are often rejected in American schools?
3. How am I going to provide ways in which Anna, with Mrs. Thomas's help, can participate fully in the life of the classroom?
4. How am I going to create a classroom environment in which students can teach each other effectively?
5. How am I going to organize instruction so that students with different learning styles can have equal access to the material at hand?
6. If the school wants to put Jacques and Tran in an immersion program, should I argue against it?
7. How many of my students' parents are able and willing to come into the classroom to assist in teaching? How many other community members can I interest in these students?
8. Can my nonstandard-English-speaking students learn to write in standard English without also learning to speak standard English?

References

1. Frank Siccone, *Celebrating Diversity: Building Self-Esteem in Today's Multicultural Classrooms* (Boston: Allyn and Bacon, 1995), pp. 14–16.

2. Adapted from "Name Interview Work Sheet," ibid., p. 16.

3. Taken from Jim Carnes, "An Uncommon Language," *Teaching Tolerance* (spring 1994): 56–62; and from Pamela L. Tiedt and Iris M. Tiedt, *Multicultural Teaching: A Handbook of Activities, Information, and Resources,* 4th ed. (Boston: Allyn and Bacon, 1995), p. 162.

4. Found in Tiedt and Tiedt, Multicultural Teaching, 4th ed., p. 168; reprinted from BBC *Modern English* 2, 10 (December 1976): 34.

5. H. A. Witkin, C. Moore, and F. J. McDonald, "Cognitive Style and the Teaching/Learning Process" (American Educational Research Association Cassette Series 3F, 1974); A. Casteneda and T. Gray, "Bicognitive Processes in Multicultural Education," *Educational Leadership* 32 (December 1974): 203–207.

6. D. E. Hunt, "Learning Style and Student Needs: An Introduction to Conceptual Level," in *Student Learning Styles: Diagnosing and Prescribing Programs* (Reston, VA: National Association of Secondary School Principals, 1979).

7. H. Reinert, "One Picture Is Worth a Thousand Words? Not Necessarily!" *Modern Language Journal* 60 (April 1976):161–169.

8. R. Dunn and K. Dunn, *Teaching Secondary Students through Their Individual Learning Styles: Practical Approaches for Grades 7–12* (Boston: Allyn and Bacon, 1993).

9. Elizabeth Stone, *Black Sheep and Kissing Cousins: How Our Family Stories Shape Us* (New York: Viking Penguin, 1989).

10. George H. Wood, *Schools That Work: America's Most Innovative Public Education Programs* (New York: Penguin Books, 1992), p. xviii.

11. Ibid., pp. xiii–xiv.

12. Sudia Paloma McCaleb, *Building Communities of Learners: A Collaboration among Teachers, Students, Families, and Community* (New York: St. Martin's Press, 1994).

13. Wood, *Schools That Work*, p. xv.

14. Adapted from McCaleb, *Building Communities,* p. xii.

15. John Dewey and Evelyn Dewey, *Schools of Tomorrow* (1915); cited in R. Freeman Butts, *Public Education in the United States: From Revolution to Reform* (New York: Holt, Rinehart and Winston, 1978), pp. 222–223.

16. Wood, *Schools That Work,* p. xvii.

17. See Harry Broudy, "Historic Exemplars of Teaching Method," in *Research on Teaching,* ed. Nat Gage (Chicago: Rand McNally, 1963), pp. 1–43.

18. Peter L. Berger and Brigitte Berger, *Sociology: A Biographical Approach* (New York: Basic Books, 1972). Page numbers of subsequent citations are noted in the text.

19. G. Gonzalez, "Language, Culture, and Exceptional Children," *Exceptional Children* 40, 8 (1974): 565.

20. Donna M. Gollnick and Philip C. Chinn, *Multicultural Education in a Pluralistic Society,* 3rd ed. (New York: Macmillan, 1990), p. 213.

21. Ibid., pp. 214–215.

22. Tiedt and Tiedt, *Multicultural Teaching,* 4th ed., p. 163.

23. Gollnick and Chinn, *Multicultural Education,* p. 217.

24. Tiedt and Tiedt, *Multicultural Teaching,* 4th ed. p. 163.

25. Ibid., p. 164.

26. Gollnick and Chinn, *Multicultural Education,* pp. 216–217.

27. Tiedt and Tiedt, *Multicultural Teaching,* 4th Ed. p. 158.

28. Herbert Grossman, *Teaching in a Diverse Society* (Boston: Allyn and Bacon, 1995), pp. 164–166.

29. Gollnick and Chinn, *Multicultural Education,* p. 212.

30. Dean Barnlund, *Interpersonal Communication: Survey and Studies* (Boston: Houghton Mifflin, 1968), pp. 536–537.

31. L. Leubitz, *Nonverbal Communication: A Guide for Teachers* (Skokie, IL: National Textbook, 1973), cited in Gollnick and Chinn, *Multicultural Education,* pp. 218–219.

32. Gollnick and Chinn, *Multicultural Education,* p. 219.

33. Ibid., p. 219.

34. Ibid., pp. 221–222.

35. J. W. Keefe and M. Languis (untitled article), *Learning Stages Network Newsletter* 4, 2 (summer 1983): 1, cited in Christine L. Bennett, *Comprehensive Multicultural Education: Theory and Practice,* 3rd ed. (Boston: Allyn and Bacon, 1995), p. 164.

36. Herman A. Witkin, *Psychological Differentiation* (New York: Wiley, 1962).

37. Adapted from Bennett, *Comprehensive Multicultural Education,* p. 168.

38. R. H. Barsch, "The Processing Mode Hierarchy as a Potential Deterrent to Cognitive Efficiency," in *Cognitive Studies,* 2, *Deficits in Cognition,* ed. J. Hellmuth (New York: Bruner/Mazel, 1971).

39. Rita Dunn, Jeffrey Beaudry, and Angela Klavas, "Survey of Research on Learning Styles," *Educational Leadership* 46, 6, (March 1989): 50–58.

40. Howard Gardner, *Frames of Mind: The Theory of Multiple Intelligences* (New York: Basic Books, 1983); *The Unschooled Mind: How Children Think and How Schools Should Teach* (New York: Basic Books, 1991); and *Intelligence Reframed: Multiple Intelligences for the Twenty-first Century* (New York: Basic Books, 1999).

41. "Multiple Intelligence Learning Styles," at Chemistry and Environment Science web page of the University of Lake Superior State University. Available at http://dalton.lssu.edu/unsem/mistyles.htm.

42. Tiedt and Tiedt, *Multicultural Teaching,* 4th ed., p. 175.

43. Ibid., p. 176.

44. Larry Samover, Richard Porter, and Meni Jain, *Understanding Intercultural Communication* (Belmont, CA: Wadsworth, 1981).

45. Robert Kaplan, "Cultural Thought Patterns in Inter-Cultural Education," *Language Learning* 16, 1 and 2 (1966): 15.

46. Christine Bennett, "Teaching Students As They Would Be Taught: The Importance of Cultural Perspectives," in *Culture, Style, and the Educative Process,* ed. Barbara J. Robinson Shade (Springfield, IL: Charles Thomas, 1989), pp. 76–77.

47. Herbert Grossman, *Teaching in a Diverse Society,* pp. 172–184.

48. L. D. Nguyen, "Indochinese Cross-Cultural Adjustment and Communication," in *Identifying, Instructing, and Rehabilitating Southeast Asian Students with Special Needs and Counseling Their Parents,* ed. M. Dao and H. Grossman (ERIC ED 273-068, 1986), pp. 6, 7.

49. "History of Bilingual Education." *Rethinking Schools* 12, 3 (spring 1998). Availlable at http://www.rethinkingschools.org/Archives/12_03/langhst.htm.

50. Ibid.

51. Cited in Pamela L. Tiedt and Iris M. Tiedt, *Multicultural Teaching: A Handbook of Activities, Information, and Resources,* 3rd ed. (Boston: Allyn & Bacon, 1990), p. 9.

52. Ibid.

53. Editorial, "Two Language Teaching," *Albuquerque (NM) Tribune,* 19 May 1975, p. 54.

54. "Educational Programs for Limited English Proficiency Students," Resolution of the National Education Association (2000–2001). Available at http://www.nea.org/resolutions/00/00b-22.html .

55. Elliot Diringer and Lori Olszewski, "Critics May Not Understand Oakland's Ebonics Plan: Goal Is to Teach Black Kids Standard English," *San Francisco Chronicle,* 21 December 1996, p. A17.

56. Ibid.

57. Lisa Anderson, "Bilingual Debate Reaches Boil Point," *Chicago Tribune,* 29 May 2001.

58. Kenji Hakuta, Yuko Goto Butler, and Daria Witt, "How Long Does It Take English Learners to Attain Proficiency?" University of California Linguistic Minority Research Institute, Stanford University, January 2000.

59. Patricia Gándara, Julie Maxwell-Jolly, Eugene Garcia, Jolynn Asato, Kris Gutiérrez, Tom Stritikus, and Julia Curry, "The Initial Impact of Proposition 227 on the Instruction of English Learners," University of California Linguistic Minority Research Institute Education Policy Center, University of California at Davis, April 2000.

60. Colin Baker, *Key Issues in Bilingualism and Bilingual Education* (Clevedon, UK: Multilingual Matters, 1988).

61. H. Hernandez, *Multicultural Education: A Teacher's Guide to Content and Process* (Columbus, OH: Charles E. Merrill, 1989).

62. Data from the 2000 census has not been completely tabulated. Continually updated information on the numbers of children who speak a language other than English can be found on the web site of the National Association for Bilingual Education at http://www.nabe.org/faq.asp.

63. Baker, *Key Issues.*

64. Huang Changzhu, "Linguistic Diversity a Concern in Global Village," *China Daily,* 12 November 2000. Available at http://www.chinadaily.com.cn/cndydb/2000/12/d4-1lang.c11.html.

65. Ibid.

66. Ibid.

67. Mila Saskova-Pierce, quoted in Joe Dejka, "Language Key to Unlocking Foreign Culture," *Omaha World Herald,* 19 November 2001. Available at http://www.nabe.org/press_detail.asp?ID=27.

68. Ibid.

Religious Pluralism in Secular Classrooms

Without knowledge, the people perish.

—Book of Proverbs

Chapter Outline

1. Do you remember a time when you attended a religious service with someone of a different denomination or faith? What was it like? Did it feel odd or strange? Why?

2. Do you know anyone who attended or did *you* attend, a parochial school? How did it differ from a secular public school?

3. How and in what ways do you think religious knowledge should be a part of public schooling?

4. Do you believe that public funds should be used in support of parochial schools?

5. Why do you think the framers of the Constitution prohibited the establishment of a state religion and also guaranteed the free exercise of religious beliefs?

c a s e   s t u d y   **Religion in a Secular Classroom**

Melissa Morgan had been teaching fifth grade in a small town in her home state of Georgia for four years and she loved it. She had been married for two years, lived only five blocks from the school, and walked to work most mornings, passing on her way the principal's house, the local Baptist church, and the drugstore on the town square. Two evenings a week she attended classes at the local university where she was almost finished with her master's degree in reading. On Sundays she and her husband sang in the Methodist church choir, where many of her students' families also attended. It was a peaceful life in a town known primarily for the neatness of its surrounding farms, the beauty of its old magnolia trees, and the computer technology developed at the university where her husband taught English. Or, at least, it had been a peaceful life until last year.

It all started during the spring semester a year ago when she took a children's literature course taught by a colleague of her husband's, a woman who, prior to becoming a professor, had been a youth minister in Chicago. One of her assignments had been to select several books written at the upper elementary level that could be used to introduce common themes from several of the world's major religions. From subsequent class discussions on ways in which children's literature could be used for a variety of purposes, Melissa had begun to develop an idea that seemed to solve one of her recurring problems. Because her school was in a university town, her students often represented a greater variety of cultural backgrounds than one would normally expect to find in a small southern town. In the past four years, she had had students from Japan, South Africa, and Ireland as well as a number of students from various parts of this country; all were the children of university faculty. As a result, her own classroom sometimes reflected the same split between local people and newcomers that now and then caused misunderstanding and strife in the community. For the most part, she had been able to help students who were new to the town (and, indeed, the country) adjust to life in Georgia. But there was one element of the cultural differences in her classroom that had stumped her, and that was the difference in religion that had created a number of overt conflicts in the past.

Armed with some new insights about using literature for purposes in addition to reading instruction, Melissa spent the summer developing a series of lessons designed to take advantage of the religious diversity in her class by not only using books and other materials about different religious faiths, but also by planning activities that would lead children to discover more about their own religious backgrounds.

When school began in the fall, she was ready—convinced that it would be a wonderful year. She was doubly excited because students in her class represented a wider variety of religious backgrounds than had been the case the year before. Along with the usual Southern Baptists, Methodists, and Presbyterians were a Catholic student who had come to the United States from Brazil three years ago, three local Jewish students, five African American students who attended the African Methodist Episcopal church in town, two Muslim children from Pakistan whose parents were professors at the university, and two children who had been schooled at home until this year by parents who belonged to a conservative evangelical church. She also had students whose families were part of a small Unitarian congregation made up almost entirely of university faculty and their families.

The year began calmly enough and her initial efforts to weave information about various religions seemed to go well. During the month of September she had made home visits to each of her students' families, some of whom she already knew. In the course of these visits she was able to talk informally with parents and other family members, interact with her students in their home settings, and learn something about the cultural and religious backgrounds of those she did not know well. The father of one of her Pakistani students turned out to be a professor of architecture and promised to come in to her class one day to talk about both the mathematics and the art in Islamic mosque architecture. She was thrilled!

Near the end of October, the school held its annual open house for parents and community members. Her class was eager for everyone to see the exhibit they had been working on since the beginning of school—models of houses of worship from around the world that included a mosque, a Jewish synagogue, a Gothic cathedral, a Greek Revival Congregational church, and a Quaker meeting house. Each model stood against a map of the part of the world where such a building might be found, and each display was surrounded by pictures and books related to that particular place of worship.

About a week after the open house, Melissa's principal asked her to stop in the office after school. After a little small talk, the principal got to the point: "We've had some complaints about the fact that you're dealing with religion in your class."

She was astonished. "Who's complained?" she asked. "And what about?"

"It seems," continued the principal, "that there are two kinds of complaints. Some parents object to their children talking about religion in school at all, and others believe their children are being exposed to ideas that they believe are not Christian. One family wants to come in and look at the books we have in the library to see if there are any offensive materials there."

"Well," said Melissa, "you know what the children and I have been doing; you've seen the models and maps. Did you explain our project to the parents who called? I really didn't intend to upset anyone, you know."

"Yes, I do know," said the principal, "but I'm afraid we've got something of a problem here. At least one of these families has a history of suggesting that the school might not be "purely" Christian. They're part of the small group of parents in this school who objected so strenuously to celebrating Halloween because they felt it encouraged pagan beliefs and devil worship. As you know, several years ago we did away with the Halloween Party in favor of a 'Dress Up As Your Favorite Book Character' day every fall."

"What do you think I should do?" Melissa asked.

"I'm not sure," replied the principal. "Perhaps you should put your models away and let it just die down."

A little shaken, Melissa went home that evening wondering if all her ideas about building on religious diversity would be stalled. She certainly hadn't intended to find herself in the middle of a battle over religion! She also didn't want to stop the discussions and activities in class that had led to such a good project as the models, because her students were learning a great deal and seemed to be loving it. On an impulse, she called her own minister to talk about the problem. She asked if Rev. Southworth could suggest anything.

"Indeed I can," said Maggie Southworth. "The clergy in the area all belong to a regional clergy council that meets next week. Let me bring this up and see what they say. Perhaps you'd like to attend and tell us about what you're doing in class so everyone can hear it at the same time."

Melissa agreed, and the next week she met with the clergy council, where she carefully explained that although she wasn't teaching any particular religious beliefs, she did think that learning about other religions was a good thing for students. She told them that the idea for building the models had come from the students, and that she had been able to bring mathematics and geography as well as both reading and writing into the project, and she told them how proud the students were of their work. At the end of the meeting, each member of the council agreed that what she was doing was a good thing, even if it had never been done before. Several expressed a desire to see the models for themselves, and Melissa promptly issued an open invitation to all. She was pleased that one of those who wanted to see the exhibit was the pastor of the church attended by several of the families who had complained.

"Perhaps," she thought as she drove home, "there is an ecumenical spirit in this town after all." And then she found herself thinking about the coming holidays. "I wonder if we should talk about the way we emphasize Christmas at school?"

Rationale for Attending to Religion in Public Schools

Religion in the American Colonies

Citizens of the United States have, since our national beginnings, been deeply concerned with the role of religion in matters of state. Some of our earliest settlers came to this continent to escape religious prejudice, and all who have come in the years since have brought with them their religious ideas, beliefs, rituals, and habits of mind. Even those who profess to be agnostic or atheist have formed their spiritual values in express rebellion *against* varieties of formalized religion that exist or existed in their particular cultural worlds.

In addition, much of the **cultural capital** of human societies emerges from philosophical, literary, musical, and artistic attempts to answer fundamentally religious questions: Who are we? Where did we come from? What is our purpose on earth? and What happens when we die? Thus, whether individuals see themselves as "religious" or not, religious references and allusions permeate their lives. In most if not all societies, religious references are used in everyday language; families, schools, and other institutions organize time around religious observances; and places of worship exert influence in community affairs. Even money often has religious symbols and language on it.

In part, this connection to religious ideas and symbolism emerges from a seemingly universal human need to be associated with a spiritual dimension. In some societies that connection permeates not only the ways in which the society is organized but also nearly every minute of daily life. When religion plays a large role in society, as it did in our own history in the Massachusetts Bay Colony and as seen recently in such places as Afghanistan, the society is called a **theocracy.** In other societies, the connection is looser, with some degree of separation between secular and religious life. That was the intention of the founders of the United States, who wrote such a separation into the Constitution in the First Amendment, which reads:

> Congress shall make no law respecting an establishment of religion, [**establishment clause**] or prohibiting the free exercise thereof [**prohibition clause**]; or abridging the freedom of speech, of the press; or the right of the people peaceably to assemble, and to petition the Government for a redress of grievances.[1]

U.S. Constitution

Notice that while the writers of the Constitution did not *establish* a religion as a dimension of the state, they also were careful to ensure that religion could be freely practiced by individuals, that religious speech (as well as other forms) was protected by the Constitution, and that peaceable assembly to practice religious beliefs (as well as for other purposes) was guaranteed. It was, however, the passage of the **Fourteenth Amendment** in 1868, which granted to citizens of the states all the rights they had as citizens of the nation, that caused the issue of separation of church and state to have a direct influence on schooling.[2]

Definitions of Religion

Uphoff notes that religion is a concept that seems easily definable until one actually tries to define it.[3] We have available to us definitions of religion that are both universal (those that apply to all religions) and sectarian (those that apply only to a specific denomination or sect). Yinger, for example, defines religion broadly as "a system of beliefs and practices by means of which a group of people struggle with . . . the ultimate problems of human life."[4] The sociologist Durkheim defines it a bit more concretely but still in a universal manner when he says, "A religion is a unified system of beliefs and practices relative to sacred things, that is to say, things set apart and forbidden—beliefs and practices which unite into one single moral community called a church [*sic*], all those who adhere to them."[5] Similarly, Berger and Berger view religion as an overarching view of reality concerned with ultimate meanings which provides a cohesive view of the world, explains evil and prosperity, and offers guidelines for social action in the secular realm."[6] Most broad definitions of religion encompass concepts of a deity, of shared values and an orientation toward the sacred, and of a sense of community.

On the other hand, narrower, sectarian definitions of religion (e.g., Presbyterian, Catholic, Muslim, Jewish, Buddhist, Seventh-Day Adventist) will have relatively different answers to the following questions:

World Religions

1. What theological outlook or point of view does this religion acknowledge?
2. What kinds of religious practice do the people who belong to this religious denomination accept as expressive of proper worship and devotion?
3. What kinds of religious experience—feelings, perceptions, and sensations—ensure that some contact will be made with ultimate reality (i.e., a supernatural agency)?
4. What knowledge about the basic tenets of faith, scriptures, and traditions are necessary to the practice of this particular religion?
5. What are the consequences of this religious belief, practice, experience, and knowledge on an individual's daily life?
6. What are the consequences of falling away from the practice, experience, and knowledge of this particular religion?[7]

Answers to these questions in large measure determine the differences between one religious group and another. Furthermore, it would be a mistake to regard these differences as simply "interesting" variations on a theme. Rather, a person's very identity and relationship with God and other human beings are vested in these beliefs, which are generally regarded by members of a particular faith as true in some ultimate sense. Thus, for example, religious beliefs about the proper kinds of food to eat, the proper way to prepare and eat it, the relative place of males and females in society, and the kinds of rituals required to receive the deity's blessing as well as the number and relative importance of deities themselves, all have a bearing on how an individual conducts his or her daily life. These ideas are so strongly held and so central to a religious person's sense of individual and collective identity that conflicts of belief among different religious groups can—and often have—led to war.

Going to war for religious beliefs is as likely to happen today as it has been throughout history. Indeed, for some contemporary Muslim extremists, terrorist actions are based on and justified by long-remembered people and the battles they fought during the Crusades seven hundred years ago; these extremists sometimes refer to all modern westerners as "Crusaders." Similarly, the torture and horrific murder of thousands of Muslims by Serbian Christians in Kosovo speaks to the potential depth and danger of religious identity.

While the experiences of religious pluralism in the United States are not new, some things have changed over time. First, the degree to which religious belief has been deemed a necessary part of *public* life has changed. In periods of fundamental social change, human beings often turn to the comfort and security of an organized faith and set of absolute values, and many believe that these values should be actively incorporated into the larger society. Second, the advent of technology—especially computer technology—means that it is no longer necessary to actually *attend* a religious service other than your own in order to obtain knowledge of it. Most faiths, and many individual synagogues, mosques, and churches, have numerous web sites on which they can display and promote their religious ideas. Third, the increasing interdependence of the world's social systems means that what happens in one part of the world quickly affects what happens in another part of the world. This connectivity is no less true of religious systems than it is of economic ones.

Religious Pluralism in the United States

Religious pluralism in the United States is so great that a complete accounting is not possible in a short chapter, but it is possible to describe major religious groups that flourish here and to give a brief summary of their histories. Prior to colonization by Europeans in the sixteenth century, the Americas were home to a wide variety of religious practices by native peoples. Although Native American societies differed widely in various aspects of culture, in language, and in appearance, all shared a fundamentally religious outlook that emphasized the centrality of a Creator, a reverence for the natural world, and a belief that human beings were a part of nature and were obligated to preserve and protect it.

Religious Pluralism in the United States

Europeans brought with them another set of religious variations—Christianity and Judaism—as well as a belief that human beings were apart from nature and were intended to conquer and control it. This difference in worldview with respect to the place of human beings in the natural world is perhaps the most significant and profound difference between so-called western religions and most others.

In New England, puritan Protestantism took hold as a dominant theme; in the middle colonies, greater diversity of religious belief, including Catholic, Quaker, and Anabaptist as well as others, meant that no particular denomination prevailed; in the South, the dominant religion stemmed from the Anglican Church of England. Jews also were among the earliest immigrants: first came Sephardic Jews from Spain and Portugal and then German Jewish immigrants, until by the American Revolution, there were about three thousand Jews in the colonies.[8] Religious diversity continued to expand in the late eighteenth century. In the nineteenth century, large numbers of Catholics from Ireland and Italy and Jews from Russia and eastern Europe immigrated to the United States, each group containing within it great diversity of belief and practice. In the twentieth century, particularly since the 1960s, the United States saw increasing Catholic immigration from Cuba, the Caribbean, and Central America.

Activity 7: Proverbs as a Window into One's Culture

In the seventeenth, eighteenth, and nineteenth centuries, large numbers of Africans were brought to the United States as slaves, and they carried with them another large set of their own **nativist religions,** which combined with and enriched the primarily Protestant Christian traditions they found here. Indeed, the creativity with which Africans interpreted and utilized Protestant scriptures and music to make their daily lives more bearable and to further the cause of freedom produced a unique contribution to American religious and political life. Negro spirituals, for example, were very often used as a form of clandestine communication to spread news of slave activities. After slavery was finally abolished in the middle of the nineteenth century, African-American churches continued to have an immense influence on the cultural and educational lives of their members and are today still central to African American culture and African American social and political struggles.

Activity and Reading 8: Cultural Values in American Society

The late nineteenth and twentieth centuries have seen a growth in the Muslim faith in the United States, in part through conversion and in part through immigration. In fact, Islam is presently one of the fastest growing religions in the United States. The converted Muslim population is primarily African American and often identifies itself as the Nation of Islam, a group whose history in the United States that goes back to the 1930s, when it grew out of the works of W. D. Fard and Elijah Muhammad. The Nation of Islam was, and in some respects still is, a separatist group that emphasizes freedom, justice, and equality for African Americans and actively discourages intermarriage with whites. Perhaps its most well-known leader was Malcolm X, the converted son of a Baptist minister who, as a result of his experience during a pilgrimage to Mecca (a hajj) and shortly before his assassination in 1965, began to shift his beliefs away from separatism and toward kinship among all human beings.[9]

Muslim immigrants are from Middle Eastern countries such as Jordan, Lebanon, and Syria, from both North Africa and sub-Saharan Africa, and from such Southeast Asian countries as Malaysia. Like their European counterparts, many Muslims have come to the United States as a result of social and political unrest in their native countries. Al-Ani notes that Muslims have come in three waves. The first, largely poor and uneducated, came from what is known as Bilad ash-Sham, or Greater Syria—an area that after World War I was Jordan, Lebanon, Palestine, and Syria, and also from Turkey, Albania, India, and elsewhere. The second wave immigrated after World War II, particularly from the Middle East and North Africa, and were primarily educated professionals uprooted by political changes including the creation of the states of Israel and Pakistan. The third wave, which continues today, began in the 1960s with the liberalization of American immigration laws. These individuals came not only from the same areas as their earlier counterparts, but also from the former Yugoslavia. In addition, beginning in the 1970s, the oil-producing countries of the Middle East have sent many Muslim students to study in the United States, and these students have played an active role in Muslim communities.[10]

Clearly, while the United States has always been a religiously pluralistic country, today that pluralism is greater than it has ever been. Along with ethnic and racial pluralism, to which it is closely related in a variety of ways, religious pluralism has become a daily experience in classrooms all over the country—a fact that has educational implications in terms of curriculum materials, subject matter, school rules and customs, student services, school calendar decisions, scheduling of student activities, cafeteria offerings, holiday celebrations, teaching methods, and school financing.[11] Rather than looking at these educational implications as problems however, some teachers and schools are finding that such diversity of religion offers unique opportunities for teaching and learning.

Characteristics of a Classroom That Attends to Religious Pluralism

How then, would an educator design a classroom not only to affirm religious pluralism but also to build on it?

Pedagogies: Old and New

Good teaching in a classroom that is sensitive to religious diversity, like teaching in any classroom, is in large measure a matter of getting to know the children with whom you are working, their families, and the communities in which they live. Most teachers quickly learn the individual idiosyncrasies of their students with respect to psychological issues and traits: attention span, motivation, perceived intelligence, and so on. What is often less well known is the sociocultural background of students. Yet, we know very well that the best context for learning is when students are able to build on what they already know. Thus, knowing as much as possible about your students' backgrounds is also central to everything else that happens, because you will be designing your classroom around *your* students and the experiences they bring with them to school.

Because formal religious teachings and values may *or may not* be a part of each of your students' lives, it is important to know something about the religious composition of your class. Chances are good that you will not have an overwhelming number of different religions represented in one room, so you need to know something about only those that are represented at any given time. However, you do need to know something about the worldview of those particular religions as well as the worldview of those students who do not subscribe to any religious tenets, particularly with respect to issues of gender and to the relationship between young people and elders. It is also wise to know whether a particular religious group values such skills as critical thinking and questioning for their children because some do not. In some contexts, a child simply does *not* question authority, age, or religious doctrine.

Knowledge about religious groups does not, of course, mean that you must design a classroom to match each child's unique experience. Indeed, one of the purposes of schooling in a democracy is to help students expand their experience beyond the relatively small world in which they live. However, it is important that you know something about the religious values of your students so that you can know how to approach new learning, where conflicts may develop, and when you can intercede to help students (and often parents) bridge the gap between their own experience and what they are learning in school. At the same time, you must understand and respect the community's primary values so that you do not go too far beyond the readiness level of community members. As Gollnick and Chinn note, schools

are influenced greatly by the predominant values of the community. Whether evolution, sex education, and values clarification are part of instruction in a school is determined in great part by the religious beliefs of a community. Educators must be cognizant of this influence before introducing certain readings and ideas that stray far from what the community is willing to accept within their belief and value structure.[12]

Teachers who want to build on religious diversity must vary the instructional methods used in the classroom. The culture of the traditional American public school stresses certain teaching methods, patterns of instructional interaction, and assessment strategies. For example, teachers talk while students listen, individual students answer teacher-directed questions, individual students give oral reports to their class, students follow detailed, teacher-given instructions in how to carry out a task, and teachers issue paper-and-pencil tests. In the United States, these patterns emerge from a western cultural worldview that emphasizes individualism, middle-class values, and a generally Protestant Christian belief system that stresses the importance of the minister as teacher and the individual's direct relationship with God. These teaching patterns may be relatively or totally unfamiliar to some students. Native American students, for example, whose religious worldview emphasizes communal patterns of interaction and individual choice, may be more interested in the activities of their peers than of the teacher and may feel that the teacher must earn their respect rather than simply get it by virtue of his or her position. That is, these students may believe that they should follow a teacher's directions because they have chosen to rather than because they are compelled to do so.[13] Another example is African American students whose churches use an emotive "call and response" or a choral pattern of interaction; these students may respond to teachers' questions with emotion, with hand gestures, with changes in vocal tonality, or in chorus because those are patterns they have learned.[14] In general, what may be *new* about pedagogy for a classroom that pays attention to religious diversity is the subtle but important ability of the teacher to vary and alter instructional patterns so that all students find both familiar and new ways of learning.

Roles: Old and New

Sensitivity to potential and real areas of conflict among students of different religious backgrounds requires that teachers adopt the role of interpreter and, sometimes, mediator. Once again, teachers must learn as much as they can about the religions represented in the classroom not only so that they can help students find the commonalities among different religious beliefs but also so that they can help students interpret differences. Parents and community members are often helpful in this regard, so long as they understand that their role is to explain rather than to convert. Indeed, perhaps more dissention regarding religious tenets has been caused by the failure of teachers to communicate closely with parents about what they are trying to accomplish in class than by any other single factor. Generally speaking, if parents understand that their children will not be deprived of either respect or affirmation because of their religious beliefs, most will be happy to help teachers in any way they can. Students, too, if they are old enough, can serve as teachers to their peers, as can other school staff and members of the community.

Another set of issues to consider in a religiously sensitive classroom is the role of school rules and customs. Attendance, for example, should be flexible for students involved in religious celebrations and/or duties, and policies such as dress codes should take account of religiously based regulations and customs. Dress codes that stipulate that students cannot wear hats in school must exempt the Orthodox Jewish boy who wears the yarmulke as a token of respect to God or the Amish girl who wears a dimity bonnet and long dress as a gesture of modesty.

Similarly, the fact that the school calendar conveys the importance of religious diversity is significant. For example, vacation times scheduled on traditional school calendars, as well as celebrations usually held in schools, tend to be based on the Christian holidays of Christmas and Easter. Moreover, common practices such as scheduling games on Friday nights (when many Jewish families begin the celebration of the Sabbath) or

Celebrating the Holidays

Allie McNeal was a classmate of Melissa's; the two went through high school and then college together. Allie now teaches third grade at Thomas Edison Elementary School, located in a diverse community in a suburb of Denver. She is a member of the school planning committee for all special events in the school, including the celebration of holidays. Her committee had sent a survey to all the parents, explaining that the school was exploring the possibility of removing "Christmas" from the annual December activities—substituting instead activities having to do with winter—and asking the parents what they thought. The rationale was that because the school has a large number of children from different religious backgrounds, celebrating Christmas spoke to only some of the children, but not all.

Allie has just received an impassioned phone call from one mother, demanding that they not only *keep* Christmas in the holiday schedule, but that they also eliminate Halloween. The mother expressed—in no uncertain terms—the belief that America is a Christian country and that other people had just better get used to it. She went on to say that she was the spokesperson for a large number of other parents who would be asking for an appointment with the principal to discuss the matter. She was especially adamant about Halloween, saying that it was a form of devil worship, and that her group did not want their children to participate in any celebration that included pagan signs and symbols.

Allie was quite taken aback at the intensity of the mother's appeal. She knew she had better speak to the principal about the forthcoming visit, and she also knew she had to make some recommendations to her committee.

- If Allie telephoned you asking for advice, how would you suggest she handle this situation?

homecoming activities early in the autumn (which may fall on the Jewish High Holidays) should also be seriously reconsidered. Later in the school year, teachers need to be sensitive to the demands placed on older Muslim students who observe Ramadan and refrain from eating and drinking during the daylight hours. The customs involved in these special cases must be discussed openly in terms of their religious significance so that other students both learn about different traditions and come to respect the reasons for them. Much of this kind of discussion can take place in the context of learning about religious beliefs and customs as a part of more general curricular study.

Place of Content Knowledge: Old and New

When religion is the cultural focus of your thinking, it is well to remember that religion, unlike some other kinds of difference, has a powerful element of "truth" built into it. That is, it may be more difficult for a student to stand apart from his or her religious worldview in order to look at other religions, because religious "truth" is often linked to fundamental ideas of the relationship between individuals and a supernatural power. Nevertheless, religious history and traditions, architecture, art, music, and ideas can become the basis for an enriched and affirming classroom.

Religion in the Curriculum

Although in recent years educators have been reluctant to consider teaching about religion in public schools, the study of the contributions of various religions to world civilization is worthwhile. Indeed, in 1964 the American Association of School Administrators published a book called *Religion in the Public Schools* in which the authors assert that

> A curriculum which ignored religion would itself have serious implications. It would seem to proclaim that religion has not been as real in men's lives as health, or politics, or economics. By omission it would appear to deny that religion has been and is important in man's history—a denial of the obvious. In day by day practice, the topic cannot be avoided. As an integral part of man's (sic) culture, it must be included.[15]

The study of religion generally can be incorporated into a variety of places in the curriculum; often the best place is the most obvious. Religious dietary regulations might be included in a home economics class, for example, or the intricate, geometrical designs of an Islamic mosque might be part of a math or art class. Because religion is and has been so fundamental to human life and history, locating its study in the context of a variety of subject matters is not difficult. At the same time, separate courses in the study of comparative religion or interdisciplinary courses that study the impact of religion on history, law, and art can be instituted, particularly at the secondary level.

Regular curriculum materials and resources in a religiously sensitive classroom should be carefully screened for bias of various kinds, including omission, not so much in order to exclude those materials as to point out the bias to students and let the bias, itself, become the subject of inquiry, discussion, and debate (see Chapter 13 for an excellent list of forms of bias in curricular materials that can also be applied to religious bias). At the same time, curricular resources—including books, articles, paintings, music, sculpture, maps, and artifacts such as wearing apparel and icons—that represent various religions can be made available for examination by students. Similarly, students who belong to particular religious groups may educate their classmates about their own religious beliefs and values. In all cases, the basis of study and discussion should be inquiry, not evangelism.

Assessment: Old and New

Evolution and Creation Science

When you are teaching or learning about a belief system like religion, you must focus not only on assessing the knowledge that has been acquired but also on the form of that assessment. Uphoff offers a good example of religious sensitivity when he writes about creating exam questions having to do with the concept of evolution. As you may be aware, the teaching of evolution is the subject of much controversy in some communities, with many people calling for balancing the curriculum by including the study of creation science in biology and other classes. The following test questions illustrate the difference between showing respect for those families who accept as fact the story of creation as it is written in the Bible and giving the impression that those families are wrong:

Suggested Reading?

 George Manson, a seventh grade English teacher in the middle school just down the road from Melissa, received a call from the father of one of his students, Rema Assadi, a Muslim girl who had brought home a novel she had selected from George's list of recommended books. The novel, one that had been chosen by librarians in the state as among the best modern fiction for middle schoolers, concerned an American girl going to school in London whose eleven-year-old brother had been killed by a bomb detonated by a Muslim girl attempting to avoid an arranged marriage to a man in his fifties who already had two other wives. The book contained numerous stereotypes of Muslims, portraying them as abusers of women, anti-Semitic, under the control of their religious leaders, and prone to violence. Both Rema and her family were upset and frightened at the thought that other students in the class would be reading this book. After the violent attacks on September 11, 2001, the family feared a major backlash against Muslims.

Mr. Assadi told George that his religious community was mounting a letter-writing and e-mail campaign aimed at the publisher of the book, trying to persuade the company to recall it. In the meantime, he asked, would George please take the book off his recommended reading list? And would he talk to his students about the book, making sure they understood how biased it was?

- If you were George, what would you do?

Poor. It took millions of years for the earth to evolve to its present state. (True/False)

Better. Evolutionists believe that it took millions of years for the earth to evolve to its present state (True/False).[16]

In the first question, the student must agree with a factual statement, while in the second, the student can agree that one group (not necessarily one to which he or she belongs) asserts that something is the case. As Uphoff notes, it is a subtle but powerful difference.[17]

Another issue concerns such assessments as psychological testing and health screening and care. Some families—generally those who profess a fundamentalist Christian faith—believe that psychological assessment by school personnel is an invasion of family rights, a corruption of values based on strict adherence to Biblical teaching, and/or an attempt on the part of school officials to alter or interfere with the religious beliefs of students. These families tend to think that psychological interventions to raise self-esteem or encourage self-expression such as classroom games or the use of puppets as a way to enable children to speak freely are suspect, sometimes in the extreme.

Similarly, health screening and assessment, especially when it involves somewhat invasive procedures such as tine or PPD (purified protein derivative, or Mantoux) tests for tuberculosis, is often the focus of parental objections on a variety of religious grounds. Some parents also may have religious reasons for objecting to their children giving blood in high school blood drives. As schools increasingly become a source of health and social services for children, an increasing number of objections may be raised by families from a variety of religious backgrounds.

Pang and Barba note that culturally affirming instruction should include culturally familiar interaction patterns, culturally familiar strategies, a culturally familiar environment, culturally familiar content, culturally familiar materials, and culturally familiar analogies, themes, and concepts.[18] The next section explores some of the reasons Melissa Morgan's classroom is one in which these guidelines were followed with respect to religious sensitivity and appreciation.

Case Analysis

Educators who have been involved in school disputes about religion might think that this case study has an improbably positive resolution. Certainly many schools have become the center of highly emotional and long-lasting acrimony about issues such as using counseling techniques to build self-esteem in children and have experienced major attempts at censorship of library and other materials.

Yet, Melissa demonstrated several attributes of a good teacher in a religiously sensitive classroom. First, she took advantage of her students' idea to build models as a way to get them to cooperate in a hands-on activity and to encourage individual students from different religious backgrounds to bring their own specialized knowledge to their classmates. Second, she skillfully integrated several aspects of the curriculum into the project so that students could see that knowledge is interrelated. Rather than listening to dry lectures about different religions, the students learned about various religious beliefs by studying the meaning that underlies different parts of the house of worship itself.

When objections came, Melissa did not try to withdraw, nor did she get angry, nor did she dismiss the objections as unreasonable. Rather, she went to her own minister as a way to perhaps create linkages with the religious leaders of the community. That there happened to be a clergy council meeting the next week and that she happened to be a persuasive speaker might be viewed as fortuitous; however, many communities have organizations to which various clergy belong, and the notion of enlisting help from community members is always a good one.

As diversity of all kinds is increasingly prevalent in schools and as teachers like Melissa learn to appreciate and build on those differences, experiences like Melissa's will also increase. Thus, future teachers will want to consider both the opportunities and possible implications of being an educational leader in the classroom and in the community.

Perspectives on Religion and Schooling in the United States

Because a religious or spiritual dimension is so close to the cognitive and emotional lives of human beings and because the founders of the United States believed that religion was so important that it should be addressed in the Constitution, the few words in the First and Fourteenth Amendments have been both the source of religious freedom and the source of educational battles around religion in the schools ever since. In schooling, the fundamental problem has been—and continues to be—how to resolve the tensions created by seemingly opposing principles: (1) the need for schools, as an arm of the state, to support a basic freedom guaranteed by the Constitution, and (2) the need for schools, also as an arm of the state, to uphold the **separation of church and state.** Throughout our history, these tensions have resulted in continually shifting opinions about a number of issues, and because ours is a nation of laws, the courts have been a decisive element in the relationship between religion and schools.

Court Decisions Related to Religion and Public Schooling

Butts has cast these issues into two broad categories. The first is education's role in protecting *private freedoms,* or "those that inhere in the individual, and therefore may not be invaded or denied by the state." He writes,

> In the most general terms, freedom was sought for parents and their children on the grounds that every human being has the right, and should have the opportunity and the ability, to live one's own life in dignity and security. Further he or she is entitled to a chosen cultural or religious group without arbitrary constraint on action or coercion of belief by the state or by other community pressures.

"Most often," he notes, "appeal was made to the free exercise of religion guaranteed by the First Amendment of the Constitution (and as applied by the Fourteenth Amendment to the states) as a protection against coercion of belief or action by school or government authorities."[19]

Butts's second category is education's role in guaranteeing *public freedoms,* "that is, those that inhere in the welfare of the democratic political community and which the . . . state is obligated actively to safeguard, protect, and promote whether threatened by a majority or minority in the community." He describes the ground for public freedoms for teachers and students as the belief that every person in his or her capacity as a teacher, learner, and citizen had the right and should have the opportunity to speak, to read, to teach, to learn, to discuss, and to publish without arbitrary constraint on action or coercion of belief by the state or by other pressures.[20]

The approach to protection of public freedoms has run into opposition by people who see it as a threat to the established order, in other words, a threat to the dominance of Protestantism as the foundation of public schooling. It has also been opposed by people for whom the protection of private freedoms is paramount, that is, who see in the protection of *public* welfare a threat to *private* freedoms of parents to control the education of their children.

Several of the more important concrete issues over which these debates have raged are compulsory attendance, freedom to practice religious beliefs with respect to the Pledge of Allegiance, salutes to the flag, prayer and Bible reading in schools, release time for religious instruction, and the use of public funds for religious schools. Each of these issues has reflected the tension between private and public freedoms.

Private Freedoms: Religion and Compulsory School Attendance

The history of schooling in the United States is characterized by a continually expanding effort to include all children. One way in which inclusion has been accomplished is by requiring all children to go to school until a certain age. This requirement was little regarded in the early years of the country; indeed, for much of our history, schooling was not only not required but also not really necessary to earn a living and develop a good life.

Beginning in the nineteenth century with the advent of industrialization and the major waves of immigration, compulsory schooling gained acceptance largely as a way of protecting young children from exploitation in factories and/or keeping children off the urban streets. In general, however, the move toward compulsory schooling can be seen as part of a larger movement toward the establishment of a social institution (the common school) that would provide the means to ensure a common citizenship and loyalty to the state among diverse individuals. Thus, early on, the issue of compulsory schooling was seen by some Americans as an issue of the rights of parents versus the rights of the state.

In 1922, the state of Oregon narrowly passed an initiative requiring that "all normal children between 6 and 18 must attend a *public* school, or that any who attend a private school must obtain the permission of, and be examined by, the county superintendent of schools."[21] Fearing that such a law would destroy parochial schools, a Roman Catholic teaching order filed suit to have the law declared unconstitutional. In 1925, the Supreme Court did just that in *Pierce* v. *Society of Sisters,* saying,

> The fundamental theory of liberty upon which all governments in this Union repose excluded any general power of the State to standardize its children by forcing them to accept instruction from public teachers only. The child is not the mere creature of the State; those who nurture him and direct his destiny have the right, coupled with the high duty, to recognize and prepare him for additional obligations.[22]

Although affirming the right of parents to send their children to private religious schools, the Court also stipulated that the state had a right to require children to go to *some* school and that the state could also regulate all schools. Thus the precedent was set for the development of a protected parochial school system alongside the public schools.

As is often the case, however, support for compulsory schooling ebbs and flows. By the 1960s and 1970s, many educators had doubts about requiring attendance of all children to the age of sixteen or eighteen. Again, religious beliefs provided the means for the Supreme Court to further the cause of private freedoms and parental rights. In *Wisconsin* v. *Yoder* (decided in May 1972), the Court upheld the decision of the Wisconsin Supreme Court that stipulated that Old Order Amish parents could disobey Wisconsin's compulsory schooling law and remove their children from school at the end of the eighth grade. The Court held that

> a state's interest in universal education, however highly we rank it, is not totally free from a balancing process when it impinges on other fundamental rights and interests, such as those specifically protected by the Free Exercise Clause of the First Amendment and the traditional interest of parents with respect to the religious upbringing of their children so long as they, in the words of *Pierce,* "prepare [them] for additional obligations."[23]

Today the move toward compulsory schooling is once again on the rise, largely because of the perceived interest of the state in a technologically oriented workforce that can compete economically with other nations. Indeed, the second goal of the national education 2000 plan for schooling required that "By the year 2000, the high school graduation rate will increase to at least 90 percent."[24] While that goal has not been entirely met (the 1998 high school graduation rate was about 74 percent) the push is on to graduate as many high school students as possible. Interestingly, at least since the Supreme Court's decisions in 1963 declaring that the *requirement* to begin the school day with prayer and Bible reading was unconstitutional, schools have often dealt with religious issues by ignoring them.

Private Freedoms: The Practice of Religious Beliefs in Classrooms

Public sentiment regarding the role of religion in public schools, like public opinion on other issues, must always be seen in a historical context. In the decisions cited in the previous section, for example, the right of parents to foster religious beliefs in their children versus the right of the state to compel school attendance was part of the larger questions of child labor and the development of schools as the primary socialization agents of citizenship in a democracy.

Similarly, the debates over the practice of religious beliefs in classrooms have often been part of the larger question of loyalty to the United States and the debate about the role of the state to protect a citizen's rights to equality. In the beginning of the common school movement, there was little question that religious practice—and indeed, religious sources of instruction—were a fundamental part of public schooling. Such practices as school prayer and the reading of the Bible on a daily basis were common, if not universal, and curricular materials such as the widely used McGuffy readers taught moral values derived from Christian Protestantism along with vocabulary and grammar. Although the influence of particular religious ideas and values on schooling has always been (and continues to be) partly a matter of the religious composition of the community in which a school is located, the basic structure of public schooling in the United States emerged from an allegiance to a Judeo-Christian heritage as much as it did from the development of an economically capitalist state. Indeed, the Judeo-Christian God has been (and is) a more or less involuntary party to a wide variety of legislative and judicial meetings, deliberations, and decisions at the federal, state, and local levels. Note that while Americans say they separate church and state, it is still common practice that the president of the United States place his hand on the New Testament when taking his oath of office.

The question of loyalty to the government usually arises in times of major political disagreement or war. In 1919, for example, in the wake of World War I and fears of involvement with world affairs, Nebraska passed a law requiring that all instruction in the public schools be given in English and prohibiting the teaching of any foreign language to children younger than the ninth grade. In *Meyer* v. *Nebraska,* however, the Supreme Court ruled that such a law was unconstitutional, stating that the right of parents to guide their children's education is a constitutional right.[25]

Similarly, during World War II, the Minersville, Pennsylvania, board of education set a policy that required all teachers and students in the public schools to incorporate the Pledge of Allegiance and a salute to the flag on a daily basis. One set of parents, who were Jehovah's Witnesses and prohibited by their religion from worshiping images, objected that the requirement set aside their First Amendment rights to free exercise of religion. In *Minersville* v. *Gobitis,* the Supreme Court ruled in favor of the state's right to impose the flag salute rule.[26] The dissent to this ruling was written by Justice Stone, who, on becoming chief justice three years later, reversed the *Gobitis* decision in *West Virginia State Board of Education* v. *Barnett,*[27] saying, in effect, that while the state could require the study and teaching of civic matters, it did *not* have the right to impose an ideological discipline that "invades the sphere of intellect and spirit."[28]

The debate about the role of the state in providing equality of opportunity, on the other hand, has influenced other decisions regarding religion in the public schools. For example, a widely known and still heatedly debated controversy revolves around the issue of prayer and Bible reading in public schools. In a widely referenced case in 1963—*Abington* v. *Schempp*—the Supreme Court ruled that *requiring* student participation in sectarian prayers and reading from the Bible, particularly the New Testament, violated the First Amendment prohibition of separation of church and state.[29] The argument here was that school prayers were fundamentally Christian (and usually Protestant), that all students were not Christian, that so-called nonsectarian prayers satisfied no one, and that therefore the removal of all religious practice from public school classrooms was necessary. More recently, the Supreme Court has ruled that sectarian prayers at high school graduations (*Lee* v. *Weisman,* 1992)[30] and on the football field before a game (*Santa Fe Independent School District* v. *Doe,* 2000)[31] are also unconstitutional. Still, because religious beliefs are so much a part of the identities of many people, the law and the practices of individual schools and people may be somewhat far apart.

Unfortunately, many people, including the national and local media, confused the argument with the actual decision, which did not "ban" prayer in schools but only said that *requiring* students to participate in sectarian prayers and Bible reading was unconstitutional. Indeed, in the majority opinion written by Justice Clark, the Court strongly supported the study of religion in public schools:

> It might well be said that one's education is not complete without a study of comparative religion or the history of religion and its relationship to the advancement of civilization. It certainly may be said that the Bible is worthy of study for its literary and historic qualities. Nothing we have said here indicates that such study of the Bible or of religion, when presented objectively as part of a secular program of education, may not be effected consistent with the First Amendment.[32]

Uphoff suggests that it was the self-censorship of educators and publishers based on both an inadequate reading of the Court decisions and a desire for equal representation for non-Christian religions that is responsible for the relative removal of religion from public schools in recent years. The vacuum created by this removal has enabled a strong challenge from the so-called Religious Right to reinstate religious practices into classrooms. Although this challenge will be discussed in greater detail later in this chapter, for now it is sufficient to say that the pendulum of social opinion on the role of religion in public schools seems to be swinging in the direction of more rather than less influence.

In 1993, for example, Congress passed the Religious Freedom Restoration Act, which laid down several principles about the exercise of religion in schools and elsewhere. In part, the act stated that the government cannot "burden" an individual's exercise of religion unless that exercise conflicted with a compelling government interest and/or if that burden was the least restrictive means of furthering such compelling interest. The constitutionality of this law was challenged in Texas when a Catholic church was denied a permit to build an expansion; the church filed suit under the law, claiming that the denial of a permit infringed on their exercise of religion. A federal court judge ruled the law unconstitutional; that decision was reversed by the fifth U. S. Circuit Court of Appeals; and in *City of Boerne, Texas* v. *P.F. Flores, Archbishop of San Antonio* (1997), the Supreme Court upheld the federal judge's decision, ruling that the law was, in fact, unconstitutional.[33] So, the debate goes on.

Public Freedoms: Public Funding for Religious Schools

Arguments for public funding for religious schools stem from the doctrine contained in the *Pierce* v. *Society of Sisters* decision previously discussed. As Butts notes,

> If parents have a private *right* to send their children to religious and private schools to meet the compulsory attendance requirements of the state, then distributive justice requires that the state provide parents with public funds to enable them to do what they have the private right to do.[34]

Arguments against public funding for religious schools stem, on the other hand, from the establishment clause of the First Amendment on the grounds that the taxpayer has a right to be free of taxation that promotes a religious doctrine.

Until about the middle of the twentieth century, the American public in general was inclined to believe that both national and religious interests were better served if public funds were not used for religious schools.[35] The debate arose again, however, at mid-century, with Americans taking positions about both *direct* and *indirect* aid. Proponents of direct aid argued that since compulsory attendance laws served the state and since parochial schools contributed to the ability of those laws to be enforced, parochial schools should also benefit from public financial support. Further, they argued that since all citizens were required to pay taxes to support public education, those parents who wished—*and had a right*—to send their children to religious schools would have a double financial burden. In addition, they argued that the provision of separation of church and state in the Constitution said nothing about the ability of public and parochial schools to *cooperate* with one another.

A more moderate view favored *indirect aid* to religious schools. As early as 1930, precedent was set for such aid when, in *Cochran* v. *Louisiana Board of Education,* the Supreme Court upheld a Louisiana law that affirmed the purchase of texts for use in private sectarian schools on the grounds that the books benefited the children and thus the state.[36] After World War II, however, a variety of religious groups began to push the limits of *Cochran* by asking for public support for health and medical services and school lunches as well as for books. The greatest demand was for help with transportation of parochial students to their schools.

Perhaps the most cited and argued-over case regarding religion and public education,[37] *Everson* v. *Board of Education,* was the landmark case with respect to busing parochial school children, largely supported by American Catholic Bishops.[38] Emerging from a New Jersey case in which the state allowed public funds to be used to transport Catholic children to parochial schools, the Court ruled that payment for such transportation essentially benefited the children (and thus the state, as it had said in *Cochran*) rather than the school. The vote was five to four, however, with the minority arguing that such support did, indeed, help children and parents to maintain religious instruction at public expense.

A third position, generally taken by Protestant, Jewish, and civil libertarian supporters of the public school, as well as by many professional educators, argues that both direct aid and indirect aid to parochial schools are unconstitutional. Those who take this position base their argument on a strict separation of church and state. In 1950, 1951, and 1952 both the National Education Association and the American Association of School Administrators adopted the following language as policy:

> We believe the American tradition of separation of church and state should be vigorously and zealously safeguarded. We respect the right of groups, including religious denominations, to maintain their own schools so long as such schools meet the educational, health, and safety standards defined by the states in which they are located. We believe that these schools should be financed entirely by their supporters. We therefore oppose all efforts to devote public funds to either the direct or indirect support of these schools.[39]

Over the next three decades, the action regarding federal aid to private schools moved from the courts to the legislature. At the federal level, the School Lunch Act of 1948, the National Defense Education Act of 1958, the Higher Educational Facilities Act of 1963, the Higher Education Act of 1965, and the Elementary and Secondary Education Act of 1965 provided financial support for school lunches in parochial schools; massive funding in a variety of areas for private, often sectarian, colleges; and funds for school libraries, textbooks, and secular instructional materials for private as well as public schools. Courts, however, continued to cut down state statutes supporting direct and indirect services to parochial schools, although it did create some conditions in which such aid was permissible. Thus, in 1977, the Supreme Court ruled that states could use public funds to pay for therapeutic, remedial, and guidance counseling services for parochial school children providing that those services were offered in a "neutral site." That ruling resulted in a great many trailers parked on the tree lawns of parochial schools in which some types of special education, health, and guidance counseling were offered.

Today, the debate about tax support for parochial education continues, made perhaps even more strident because of current efforts to greatly reduce governmental support of social programs. Indeed, this effort is also helping create conditions in which supporters of a greater role for religion in public schools can argue that such a role will either eliminate the need for, or take the place of, governmental support.

Public Freedoms: The Provision of Religious Instruction

Current charges that public schools are too secular and lack the moral tone that will help children grow up to be better citizens are not new. At the end of the nineteenth century, a consensus had developed that religious instruction should not be a responsibility of public schools; but after World War I and II, many citizens thought that the schools were "godless" and that some sort of religious instruction should be returned to public classrooms.

Throughout the 1940s and 1950s, efforts were made to get around Court decisions regarding the separation of church and state, but those efforts were largely unsuccessful. Two arguments were offered.

Some people—mostly Protestants and Catholics—sought a revival of sectarian instruction, usually through the demand for released time in the school day so that students could receive religious instruction from teachers of their own religious faith. Most often, this instruction was to be offered apart from the school building, usually in a nearby church. Others—primarily Protestants—urged that more attention be paid to a nonsectarian religious instruction through daily reading of the Bible and recitation of nonsectarian prayers in school. Both propositions were denounced by many people as an infringement of the separation of church and state.

While a number of states and the U.S. Supreme Court ruled in various ways on the issue of released time for religious instruction, the Supreme Court finally decided in 1952 that a New York case in which students left the school building for religious teaching was permissible under the First Amendment because the schools did not actively promote a sectarian form of instruction and because no public funds were expended for the effort.[40]

The issue of Bible reading has also been decided variously. By the 1970s, a number of states had decided it was *not* religious instruction. At least six state courts, however, ruled that the Bible *was* a sectarian document, at least to Catholics, Jews, and nonbelievers. For Catholics, the King James version of the Bible was thought to be Protestant sectarianism; for Jews, reading the Bible does not hold the same significance that it does for Christians; families of unbelievers objected to any religious practices at all.

Nonsectarian prayers were usually objected to by everyone on the grounds that they watered down any real religious belief in an effort at compromise among belief systems and also on the grounds that such prayers, nevertheless promoted religion against the establishment clause of the First Amendment. In 1963, the Supreme Court did away with most of these arguments in the previously discussed cases that declared *required* prayer and Bible reading to be unconstitutional even while they affirmed the value of teaching *about* religion in public schools.

In the past thirty years, new issues have arisen that bring religious pluralism in the classroom once again into sharper focus. First, immigration from various parts of the world by people whose religious structures and beliefs are very different from the so-called big three—Protestantism, Catholicism, and Judaism—has populated public school classrooms with students from a wide variety of religious backgrounds. Second, changes in the institutions of the family and the economy have weakened the social cohesion that normally helps bind communities together and provide the common socialization processes necessary to raise the next generation. In such circumstances, young people often feel rootless, answerable to no one, and alienated from a system that no longer really exists except in the minds of their elders. One result of these societal conditions is the increase in violence we are now witnessing in all segments of society, but particularly among our youth. Finally, the growth and importance attached to science and technology in our society tends to mask the smaller, more human dramas that contain the very essence of religious questions and meaning. It is small wonder that, in response, the call for religious instruction and moral values in public schools has become a widespread demand.

Perspectives on Religious Identity

Religion as a Form of Personal Identity

Of all the groups to which a person can claim loyalty, religion is perhaps the most common. Indeed, some researchers suggest that Americans are more likely to identify themselves as members of a religious group than as a member of any other group.[41] People who identify themselves as members of a religious group often associate themselves closely with an ethnic group as well. Thus, for example, an Irish Catholic, may consider herself or himself substantively different from an Italian Catholic, and a Russian Jew may feel quite different from a German Jew. We are reminded in this regard of a story related by a colleague who was teaching about diversity at an urban university in a highly ethnic city. After several class sessions on the subject, a student came up after class to tell her that she (the student) could, indeed, relate to the lesson. "You know," the student said, "I went all through Catholic school in my own Irish neighborhood, and it wasn't until I got to college that I met some Italian Catholics. You're right, they sure are different."

This differentiation results in part from differences in ethnic histories and in part from differences in the development of religious practices among members of the same general faith. An individual has only to attend services at churches of three or four different Protestant denominations (e.g., Presbyterian, Southern Baptist, high Episcopalian) to know that there is great diversity *within* the same religious tradition. This diversity is even more true for the world's major religions. The diversity within Christianity, or within Islam, or within Judaism is in many respects far greater than the diversity among them. Moreover, people who identify themselves with a particular religious group have also usually placed themselves in a particular social as well as geographical location. The very term *Southern Baptist* for example, says a great deal about the geographical roots of a person's religious identity, and the term high Episcopalian may indicate something about the social class to which a person belongs.

Religious identity has its strongest roots in the family, and many families not only encourage but demand that their children follow in their religious traditions. Indeed, some families will go so far as to deny the existence of a child who breaks with the faith, and some religious groups, such as the Old Order Amish, will occasionally invoke the practice of "shunning" (never speaking to or acknowledging the presence of the person being shunned) when a community member strays from the fold. The belief that a person's religious identity is an integral part of that person's essential self can be seen in the reaction of parents whose children join a cult of some kind. Such parents believe that their child has been brainwashed and often will hire an expert to deprogram them.[42]

Religious identification also places a person in a particular relationship with the deity (e.g., Catholics as part of a community of believers, Protestants in a one-to-one relationship with God). That relationship may determine a person's view of the possibility of a life after death, that person's set of moral codes for living, and the nature of rewards or punishments for the life that person has, in fact, led. Given the profound nature of these issues, it is not surprising that individuals, families, and communities react strongly to perceived threats to their religious beliefs.

At the same time (and perhaps paradoxically), in a religiously heterogeneous society such as the United States, people often switch from one religion to another. The move from one religious affiliation to another may involve a formal conversion process, or it may be a move from a conservative to a more liberal branch of the same church (or vice versa). It may occur as the result of marriage between people of two faiths, or it may occur in an individual as an outgrowth of intellectual analysis. Gollnick and Chinn note that switching from a conservative to a more liberal church may be the result of upward mobility. They write, "Those shifting to the liberal churches have tended to be older, more educated, holding higher-status occupations, and, as might be expected, more liberal on moral issues. As a group, they tend to be less active in their new churches than the members of the conservative churches they have left."[43]

The switch from conservative to liberal is not, however, the current trend in the United States today. Indeed, the fastest growing churches in the United States tend to be conservative, sometimes evangelical or pentecostal, Protestant denominations, with an accompanying decline in membership of so-called mainline churches. There are probably a variety of reasons for this trend, not least among them the desire of many people for a solid, unquestioning, and dependable religious orientation at a time when change in all institutions means a dissolution of traditional rules for living. Observers might also argue that the trend toward conservatism reflects, in part, the shrinking of the middle class and the increasing economic gap between those who are wealthy and those who are not. If switching to liberal religious affiliations is a function of upward mobility, then the opposite is perhaps also true. For the first time in American history, there is a general perception that children may not "do better" than their parents, and the real or perceived fact of downward mobility can be related to an increasing desire and need to be a part of a community in which an individual can identify with virtue and righteousness.

The Influence of the Religious Right

Although the so-called religious right in this country is composed of a politically oriented and loosely connected set of relatively fundamentalist Christians, it would be a mistake to think that conservatism is the "property" of the Christian faith. Indeed, **fundamentalism** is gaining strength in all the religions of the world as people begin to feel the effects of globalization and institutional change. In the United States, however, the determinedly *political* nature of a coalition of conservative Protestants has had a profound effect on the direction of American government and its legislative and judicial processes. National issues such as the size of the federal government; the need to reduce the incidence of crime; abortion; and violence in and out of schools are the issues of choice of the religious right. Information and exhortations about these issues are carried to millions of people through televangelists, through radio networks sponsored by such organizations as Dr. James Dobson's Focus on the Family, and through national figures such as Pat Robertson and Pat Buchanan as well as through numerous web sites. The influence of the religious right is also observable in the rhetoric of otherwise more moderate politicians, and political campaigns at all levels will in the future undoubtedly be driven in large measure by conservative and even fundamental beliefs.

Fundamentalism and the Religious Right

Nowhere is the influence of the religious right felt more strongly, however, than at the local and grassroots level, and no institution is of more concern than the school. The tension produced by the constitutional separation of church and state has meant a continual debate regarding the part played by schooling in both protecting religious liberty and enabling religious practice.

As it has been in the past, the issue of school prayer is once again at the forefront of public debate, fueled in part by vocal participation of those who believe that the *absence* of regular prayer in schools is one of the elements of what they see as a lack of morality in American society. While the current status of prayer in schools, as determined in part by Supreme Court decisions, is that prayer is individual and voluntary (some wit remarked that as long as there is academic testing, there will be prayer in schools!), conservative groups continue to press for a return of mandated school prayer with the stipulation that individuals can choose not to participate.

Similarly, the issue of funding for private and parochial schools is also the subject of much debate, this time using the language of tuition tax credits. Some proponents argue (again) that because student enrollment in private schools reduces the pressure on public schools and contributes to the overall education of America's children, financial support for private tuition is justified. They argue further that parents should not have to pay twice for the education of their children and that support for private schools encourages pluralism. Interestingly, unlike the Great School Wars in the nineteenth century, in which Protestants opposed parochial schools in general, those proponents of public funding for private schools who are members of the religious right would now like public support for private Christian schools. Opponents, on the other hand, argue that allowing such a use of public funds would weaken the public school system, facilitate the ability of parents to avoid integrated schools, and create a dual system of education that is antithetical to the ideal of a democratically educated citizenry. In a time of social change such as we are experiencing, this debate is likely to continue for some time and promises to be another large part of the conservative political agenda.

Perhaps the most serious challenge by the religious right to public education, however, lies in the area of censorship. Conservative and fundamentalist religious groups are not the only groups to advocate censoring the materials to which school children have access, but they are among the most vocal. Gollnick and Chinn describe the seriousness of this challenge in the following way:

> Censorship, or attempts at censorship, have resulted in violence, where involved parties have been beaten and even shot. It has resulted in the dismissal or resignation of administrators and teachers. It has split communities and in the past thirty years has created nearly as much controversy as the desegregation of schools.[44]

Most people would not doubt that those who urge the censorship of school materials are sincere and fully convinced that they are espousing a cause that is morally right, but the question arises as to whose morality is to be the basis for whatever guidelines are selected. In a religiously pluralistic society, the public schools have an obligation to educate as broadly as possible. Moreover, the issue of academic freedom for teachers to select the materials they deem most suitable is an important one. Of particular concern to many conservative religious groups are those books and materials that deal with alternative family lifestyles and with sex and/or sex education, that contain realistic language, and that are written about ethnic minority groups. Indeed, some people object to any materials that do not portray the ethnocentrically patriotic, small-town, middle-class, family-oriented values of Norman Rockwell.

Among the targets of self-styled censors have been books such as Mark Twain's *Huckleberry Finn* and John Steinbeck's *Of Mice and Men;* curricula such as Man—A Course of Study (a social studies curriculum developed by the National Science Foundation), biology texts that do not give equal space to creation science; dictionaries containing words deemed offensive; the holding of school Halloween parties, which are believed by some people to encourage the worship of devils and witches; and more recently, the immensely popular Harry Potter books. Further, many conservative groups object to any materials and practices that seem to them to represent secular humanism, which they define as thought and action not based on a God-centered universe. Often referred to as a religion by conservative religious groups, secular humanism does not have a church, a set of rituals and practices, or a set of doctrines and dogma. Rather, humanism is a movement begun in the Renaissance that centers its intellectual attention on human beings and their affairs, including the many ways in which they engage in religious endeavors. Nevertheless, some determined religious groups believe that secular humanism exists as a religion and are committed to defeat it.

Attempts to Ban Books

Clearly, those who claim to be part of a religious revival in the United States are currently in a strong position. It is difficult to argue that we as a society should not be concerned about crime, about the high rate of unwed parents, or about raising the next generation to be respectful of the traditions of this country. Indeed, many people who do not profess affiliation with conservative religious groups are deeply concerned about those issues and many others. Furthermore, if the United States is to be a truly religiously pluralistic society, people who profess fundamentalist beliefs have every right to hold them and every right not to be discriminated against because of them. What seems to separate the religious right from more moderate citizens, however, is the belief, based on a strict interpretation of one book—the Bible—that they have the one and only, true, and virtuous answer and that it should be applied to everyone. This very problem, of course, is what led the writers of the Constitution to stipulate that while citizens of a free country should be allowed to practice whatever religious beliefs they espoused, the *government* (and thus, the public schools) should not establish one particular religion as the religion of the state.

This issue is even more urgent today, because we have learned firsthand and tragically to what lengths a rigid fundamentalist belief system may lead its followers. Indeed, perhaps one of the *good* things that may emerge from the devastation of the attacks on the World Trade Center and the Pentagon is a deeper understanding in and support for the tradition of the separation of church and state that is written into the American Constitution.

Ethical Issues

This chapter has emphasized that teachers who address religious issues in their classrooms must understand their communities and not go too far beyond the values that the community holds. This advice may appear to be common sense and carries with it a certain degree of self-preservation, but it also importantly suggests the belief that *all* deeply held religious beliefs are worthy of respect.

Within the classroom, teachers must be on the lookout and intercede for religious prejudice, particularly as it might be expressed in the casual name-calling that children do so easily. Like all other forms of prejudice, religious prejudice is learned—and can be unlearned (though not easily). Respectful behavior toward others, however, can and should be insisted upon.

Another ethical issue concerns the responsibility of teachers to be familiar with federal and state laws with respect to religion and schooling. The classroom teacher often must serve in the role of instructor to parents and community members as well as to students and should be knowledgeable about the development of and debates about religious differences that are a part of the fabric of law and judicial decision in the United States.

With respect to relations with parents and the community, teachers should also be knowledgeable about the bases of different religious beliefs and should be as ready and willing as possible to answer questions and discuss objections calmly. There are times when consensus is not possible to reach and finding effective ways of agreeing to disagree is both useful and wise.

Summary

Because the United States was founded on the principle of religious liberty, the framers of the Constitution built into the First Amendment both a prohibition against a state religion and a prohibition against limiting the free expression of religious beliefs and practices. That ambiguity has led to considerable dispute over the role of religion in American society and particularly in American schools.

The principle of separation of church and state has not prevented many people from believing that schools should be a repository of morality; the question has always been, "Whose morality are we talking about?" Because we are a nation of laws, much of the "action" regarding religion and schooling has been in the courts, which have struggled with this issue over the years, often reversing previous decisions, but always trying to come to a reasonable balance between competing views.

This balance has been impeded by the myth that teachers may not talk about religion in schools; this myth is not true. Indeed, the decision that "banned" school prayer explicitly notes that exposure to the story of the world's great religions is necessary for a complete education. This chapter describes the nature of the debate over religion in public schooling and the importance of attending to the diverse religious backgrounds of American students. In an increasingly interdependent world, it is both necessary and prudent that we understand and respect the religious impulse that influences human identity and guides human behavior.

 # Chapter Review

Go to the Online Learning Center at **www.mhhe.com/Cushner4e** to review important content from the chapter, practice with key terms, take a chapter quiz, and find the web links listed in this chapter.

Key Terms

Cultural capital   251

Establishment clause of First Amendment   251

Fourteenth Amendment   251

Fundamentalism   269

Nativist religions   253

Prohibition clause of First Amendment   251

Separation of church and state   261

Theocracy   251

Reflective Questions

Quite unintentionally, indeed with the very best of intentions, Melissa Morgan found herself in the center of a controversy that could have turned into a major issue both in her classroom and in her community. On reflection, it is likely that Melissa might have asked herself the following questions. Think about how you would answer these questions if you were in Melissa's place.

1. Having grown up in a town very much like the one in which she taught and having taught in her school for five years, how is it that Melissa didn't think about what she knew to be a streak of deep-seated conservatism present in the community?

2. Once her students' project was underway, are there strategies she could have used that might have forestalled the objections voiced by some parents after they saw the exhibit at the open house?

3. As you will see in the case of the new kindergarten teacher in Chapter 10, acting as an agent of change can be a tricky business, particularly when the school in which you teach is a very traditional one. Certainly, it is often easier to go with the flow of traditional school culture than to try to change it. It does not appear, however, that Melissa thought of herself as a change agent; rather, she was attempting only to utilize existing human and intellectual resources in a better way for the sake of her students. What are some of the factors that turn a seemingly innocent curricular activity into a potential source of protest?

4. Melissa attempted to resolve the issue by going to a number of community leaders. Are there dangers in this strategy? What might some of those dangers be?

5. Melissa could have simply dismissed the objections raised to her use of religious information in the classroom as ignorant, unenlightened, or prejudiced behavior. How would that view have undermined her strong belief in religious pluralism?

6. When the episode was over, Melissa began to think about some of the long-standing practices of American schooling, such as the way most schools use Christian holidays—particularly Christmas and Easter—as sources for both curricular and extracurricular activities. Are such traditional practices fitting subjects for review and rethinking?

7. In her meeting with the clergy council, Melissa did not mention that, according to the most recent Supreme Court decisions, she was well within her rights to teach *about* religion in her classroom. Should she have raised that issue? Might there have been some negative results if she had?

References

1. First Amendment to the Constitution of the United States, 1791.

2. James K. Uphoff, "Religious Diversity and Education," in *Multicultural Education: Issues and Perspectives*,

2d ed., ed. James A. Banks and Cherry A. McGee Banks, (Boston: Allyn and Bacon, 1993), p. 95.

3. Ibid., p. 91.

4. J. M. Yinger, *The Scientific Study of Religion* (New York: Macmillan, 1970), p. 7.

5. Emile Durkheim, "The Social Foundations of Religion," in *Sociology of Religion,* ed. R. Robertson (Baltimore: Penguin Books, 1969), p. 46.

6. Peter L. Berger and Brigitte Berger, *Sociology: A Biographical Approach* (New York: Basic Books, 1972), pp. 348–352.

7. Adapted and extended from R. Stark and C. Y. Glock, "Dimensions of Religious Commitment," in Robertson, *Sociology of Religion,* p. 46; cited in Donna M. Gollnick and Philip C. Chinn, *Multicultural Education in a Pluralistic Society,* 3rd ed. (New York: Macmillan, 1990), p. 175.

8. Thomas Sowell, *Ethnic America: A History* (New York: Basic Books, 1980), p. 77.

9. Salman H. Al-Ani, "Muslims in America and Arab Americans," in Christine L. Bennett, *Comprehensive Multicultural Education: Theory and Practice,* 3rd ed. (Boston: Allyn and Bacon, 1995), p. 139.

10. Ibid, pp. 134–136.

11. Uphoff, "Religious Diversity," p. 102–103.

12. Gollnick and Chinn, *Multicultural Education,* p. 196.

13. Ibid., p. 346.

14. Ibid., p. 347.

15. Cited in Uphoff, "Religious Diversity," p. 95.

16. Uphoff, "Religious Diversity," p. 104.

17. Ibid.

18. Valerie Ooka Pang and Roberta H. Barba, "The Power of Culture: Building Culturally Affirming Instruction," in *Educating for Diversity: An Anthology of Multicultural Voices,* ed. Carl A. Grant (Boston: Allyn and Bacon, 1995), pp. 345–356.

19. R. Freeman Butts, *Public Education in the United States: From Revolution to Reform* (New York: Holt, Rinehart, and Winston, 1978), p. 272.

20. Ibid.

21. Ibid., p. 275.

22. *Pierce* v. *Society of Sisters,* 268 U.S. 510 (1925), pp. 534–535. Cited in Butts, *Public Education,* p. 276.

23. *Wisconsin* v. *Yoder,* 406 U.S. 213 (1972).

24. See *Phi Delta Kappan* 72, 4 (December 1990), with articles by L. Cuban, S. L. Kagan, N. L. Gage, L. Darling-Hammond, I. C. Rothberg, L. Mikulecky, and R. A. Hawley, all addressing national goals.

25. *Meyer* v. *Nebraska,* 262 U.S. 390 (1923).

26. *Minersville* v. *Gobitis,* 310 U.S. 586 (1940).

27. *West Virginia State Board of Education* v. *Barnette,* 319 U.S. 624 (1943).

28. Butts, *Public Education,* p. 279.

29. *Abington Township District School* v. *Schempp,* 374 U.S. 203 (1963).

30. *Lee* v. *Weisman,* 112 S. Ct. 2649 (1992).

31. *Santa Fe Independent School District* v. *Doe,* 530 U.S. 290 (2000).

32. Quoted in Uphoff, "Religious Diversity," p. 95.

33. *City of Boerne, Texas* v. *P.F. Flores, Archbishop of San Antonio,* 521 U.S. 507 (1997).

34. Butts, *Public Education,* p. 286.

35. Ibid., p. 287.

36. *Cochran* v. *Louisiana State Board of Education,* 281 U.S. 370 (1930).

37. Butts, *Public Education,* p. 289.

38. *Everson* v. *Board of Education,* 330 U.S. 1 (1947).

39. "School Administrator," *Journal of the American Association of School Administrators* (April 1950): 2; cited in Butts, *Public Education,* p. 291.

40. *Zorach and Gluck* v. *Board of Education,* 343 U.S. 306 (1952).

41. W. Herberg, *Protestant-Catholic-Jew: An Essay in American Religious Sociology* (New York: Anchor Press, 1960), p. 56.

42. Gollnick and Chinn, *Multicultural Education,* p. 193.

43. W. C. Roof and W. McKinney, "Denominational America and the New Religious Pluralism," *Annals of the American Academy of Political and Social Science* 480 (July 1985): 24–38; cited in Gollnick and Chinn, *Multicultural Education,* p. 194.

44. Gollnick and Chinn, *Multicultural Education,* p. 199.

45. Adapted from an incident reported by Manuel Perez-Rivas in the *Washington Post Online* (16 February 2000). Available at http://www.muslimhomeschool. com/mhsnr/index.htm.

Developing a Collaborative Classroom:
Gender and Sexual Orientation

> *Prejudices, it is well known, are most difficult to eradicate from the heart whose soil has never been loosened or fertilized by education; they grow there, firm as weeds among rocks.*
>
> —*Charlotte Brontë*

Chapter Outline

focus questions

1. If you were buying clothes for a newborn, how would you select the color?

2. What do you think about girls who often use vulgar language? How about boys who do?

3. If you were babysitting for a three-year-old boy whose favorite toys were dolls, what might you do?

4. How might you feel if your favorite cousin—or your sister—suddenly declared that she was a lesbian?

5. In school, would you rather work closely with others—in pairs or small groups—or work by yourself?

6. Has anyone (parent, friend, guidance counselor) ever told you that certain subjects were not "suitable" for you because of your gender?

7. What do you think about the increasing number of males who are nurses? What about females who work construction?

case study   Gender and Sexual Orientation in a Collaborative Classroom

It's the beginning of April in Spokane, Washington, and Tom Littleton's combined biological/environmental science class is in full swing.[1] The twenty-seven juniors and seniors in the class are working together in twos, threes, and fours at a variety of tasks—putting together a large display unit, cataloging leaf and bark samples at the two stone-topped lab benches, looking at water samples under a microscope, taking notes from a well-illustrated botany book, and working at a computer in the corner. Three adults who come into the class regularly—Steven's father, a journalism teacher, and a staff member from the local Environmental Protection Agency—are working with some of the students while Tom moves from one group to another watching, listening, answering questions, and giving advice.

Since school started in late August, these students have turned the classroom into what they call a working land lab. Its purpose is to study the ecological characteristics of the land, water, plants, and animals that make up a wooded plot of ground behind the school. They have taken and tested water samples for toxic chemicals, tested the soil for its chemical compounds, identified and cataloged all the trees and plants (including several rare species), and noted the presence of animal and bird life. In short, they have developed a "map" of the ecological system in this area and have come to understand the living relationships existing there. In the process, they have decided to formally request that the school board set aside this land as a nature preserve for use by students and members of the community.

The project began somewhat haphazardly last summer when several of the students noticed that the creek running through the property looked cloudy. When school started, they asked Tom about it and he showed them how to take and test water samples. Since then, the creek area has not only become the catalyst for teaching and learning the subject matter in Tom's class, but has provided an opportunity to accomplish other worthwhile goals. As the school year ends, the class is preparing displays of their findings and writing a report they intend to present to the school board in May. The report contains their recommendations for establishing the nature preserve. On one long wall is a hand-lettered chart that says:

Natural History Perspectives: Goals

- To appreciate the universality of change and the dynamic processes of the physical and biological sciences.
- To obtain a personal standard of scientific literacy that allows for reasonable assessment of the local and global condition in terms of economic, social, legal, and applied science concepts.

- To achieve the ability to distinguish between science, personal opinion, and **pseudoscience** through inquiry, investigation, research, and interpretation of data.

Next to this chart on the same wall is a brightly colored poster of flying geese, with a printed text superimposed on the drawings. It reads:

Lessons from Geese

1. As each bird flaps its wings, it creates an "uplift" for the bird following. By flying in a "V" formation, the whole flock adds 71 percent greater flying range than if the bird flew alone. The lesson to be learned is that people who share a common direction and sense of community can get where they are going quicker because they are traveling on the thrust of one another.

2. Whenever a goose falls out of formation, it suddenly feels the drag of trying to fly alone, and quickly gets back into formation to take advantage of the "lifting" power of the bird immediately in front. The lesson to be learned is that if we have as much sense as a goose, we will stay in formation with those who are headed where we want to go. We should be willing to accept their help and give them ours.

3. When the lead goose gets tired, it rotates back into the formation and another goose flies at the point position. The lesson to be learned is that it pays to take turns doing the hard tasks, and sharing leadership. With people, as with geese, we are interdependent.

4. The geese toward the rear honk to encourage those up front to keep up their speed. The lesson to be learned is that we need to make sure our honking from behind is encouraging, not something else.

5. When a goose gets sick, wounded, or shot down, two geese drop out of formation and follow it down to help and protect it. They stay with it until it is able to fly again or dies. They then launch out on their own, with another formation, or catch up with the flock. The lesson to be learned is that if we have as much sense as geese we, too, will stand by each other in difficult times as well as when we are strong.[2]

Seeing that all the students are occupied and that no one seems to have a question at the moment, Tom moves over to his small, crowded desk, sits down, and takes a spiral-bound notebook out of one drawer. That same drawer also contains portfolios that document the accomplishments of individual students. Tom's notebook is a reflective journal in which he notes observations of students, details of the work they are all doing, and records ideas for future teaching. In a way, the journal is Tom's portfolio, his assessment of himself as a teacher in this class. "One of the great things about this class," he writes, "is that as the year goes by the students need me less and less. They really are learning to work together and to solve their own problems."

When the year began, Tom had two major objectives apart from—although related to—the curriculum. The first was to systematically encourage the girls in this class to actively participate, to willingly put forth their ideas and speculations, and to be outwardly as well as inwardly proud of their accomplishments. For several years he had been encouraging ninth and tenth grade girls to take this class, and this year the class was nearly half female. Tom thought that a science class might be the perfect place for girls to exercise their collaborative skills. After all, discoveries in science are nearly always the result of group effort involving scientists, lab technicians, social scientists, and often students. The process of actually doing science, he thought, should be a particularly fitting one for girls, who were usually socialized to collaborate with others. Unfortunately, he also knew that girls were often guided away from scientific and technical classes by parents and counselors who believed that girls were less suited to such subjects. He knew that girls (and boys) usually thought that science and math were "male" activities.

His second goal was to fully integrate three students from the fairly large Gypsy community that lived in Spokane. These students, Steven, Rebecca, and Ian, had been part of a long-term effort by the Spokane schools to build relations of trust between the schools and Gypsy (or, more accurately, Romani) parents. Because of a long history of persecution by the wider community in both Europe and the United States, these Gypsy parents were hesitant about sending their children to school.

Steven and Rebecca had been in school since they were seven; Ian moved to Spokane when he was ten. All three began school in a program especially designed to accommodate cultural factors within the Gypsy community such as its close family structure, its respect for age, its highly male-dominated society, and its resistance to change. Also, Gypsy children were expected to assume responsibility in the community at an earlier age than were European American middle-class children and were thus somewhat more mature than their-age-mates.

Some aspects of the program were very different from traditional school practice. For instance, because the Gypsy community was a male-dominated society, boys had to be served lunch first and female teachers were expected to wear "female" attire—dresses and skirts. Because Gypsy parents were afraid for their children, phones had to be installed in every classroom so that parents could have direct access to teachers and to their own children regarding after-school activities. Because the community's goal was English literacy but not cultural literacy, the classrooms were explicitly not assimilationist. Because change was feared on a deep level, bus drivers had to keep the same routes and teachers had to stay with the same children. Because respect for elders had to be maintained, illiterate parents could not be taught along with their children but needed separate instruction, younger children could not serve as tutors for older children, and teachers were expected to be over thirty years old. Teachers also needed to be flexible regarding school goals and schedules to allow for participation in community events and rituals.

While Gypsy children had originally been separated from other children in this program, its goal was to eventually build enough trust in the Gypsy community that they would allow their children to be placed in regular classrooms. Steven, Rebecca, and Ian had gone into regular classes when they began the ninth grade. At this point, the three were still inclined to stay together, but Tom had noticed that they all had become deeply involved in the work of the land lab and that even Rebecca seemed willing to venture forth with a suggestion now and then.

As Tom leafed through his notebook and watched the students at work, scenes from the past several months floated through his mind. He remembered the first day of class, when he had introduced the students to the concept of prediction by doing an exercise called Future's Window. In this activity, students divide a piece of paper into quarters and label the top half "Self" and the bottom half "World." The left side of each half is labeled "5 Years" while the right half represents "20 Years" into the future. Students are then asked to make at least five entries in each quadrant, things they expect themselves to have accomplished or to be dealing with in five years and in twenty years, and things they expect the world to be confronting in five and twenty years. Students do this activity at first by themselves and then with two or three others. They have about ten minutes to come up with a compilation of the groups' responses to the activity, after which the whole class discusses what they have generated.

Activity 35: Future's Window

Tom remembers that the list generated by this class was typical:

SELF

5 Years	*20 Years*
In college	Well into my career
Own a car	Have a graduate degree
Married	Married, with children
Have a good job	Traveled overseas
Live on my own	Own a business
Have a good stereo	Own a vacation home
Graduated from college	

WORLD	
5 Years	*20 Years*
More pollution	Still polluted
Increase in AIDS	Cure for AIDS
Many conflicts and war	Human beings on Mars
Decrease in crime	World hunger still a problem
Homelessness still a problem	Still many people without homes and work
Nuclear arms in the hands of terrorists	Nuclear explosions have occurred in
Spread of antibiotic-resistant viruses	a few places on the planet
Another Chernobyl-like disaster	Criminals more sophisticated
Global warming increases	

He also remembers that, like most students this age, this class had a hard time real-izing that there was a connection between their own lives and the life of the larger com-munity and world. He also remembers that not one of the Gypsy students contributed to the discussion and that only one girl said anything at all. How different they are now!

Tom's eyes glance at a page in his journal and he recalls the day, about a month after school started, when he saw Steven's mother standing in the hall watching the class through the partially open door. He had invited her in and she came, somewhat hesitatingly, saying that she only wanted to see that Steven and the other two Gypsy stu-dents were all right. Tom didn't know at the time that she had been one of the first par-ents involved in the Spokane outreach to Gypsy children. In fact, it had been Steven's mother and grandmother who had been primarily responsible for convincing the Gypsy community that "those school people" could be trusted with their children.

Tom also remembered the day that all his careful work to create collaborative working relationships in the class was almost destroyed. For several months, Tom had noticed that many of the students had been avoiding one of their peers, a young man named Kurt. Although he was not overtly excluded from participation in class activities, the boys interacted with him only when necessary and did not include him in the infor-mal conversation and laughter that was often a part of their group work. One rainy Sat-urday morning in November, Tom had taken Kurt with a group of other boys out to the land area behind the school to finish identifying and tagging trees. In dividing the group into pairs, Tom put Kurt with Jimmy, who immediately objected, saying he would rather work with two other boys. Not paying too much attention, Tom told him that since the work would be accomplished much faster if they divided up and since it was raining and they all wanted to get inside, he'd appreciate it if Jimmy would just go along with Kurt and get to work. He was totally unprepared for Jimmy's loud reaction: "I'm not going off alone with that fag, and you can't make me!"

There was a dead silence in the group. All eyes were down except Jimmy's, who stared defiantly at Tom. Tom looked around the group and said, "OK, guys, I guess there is something more important going on here than cataloging trees. Let's go into the school and see if we can sort this out." Somewhat reluctantly the boys followed him into their classroom where they spent the rest of the day talking about what had happened and what they were going to do about it. Tom had told them two things: (1) he was not going to tolerate homophobic (or any other kind of) name-calling; and (2) since it seems likely that homosexuality has a biological basis, hating a person because of sexual orientation was a lot like hating someone because he or she had brown eyes, or was left-handed, or was very tall. Thinking about it now, Tom knew that the discussion didn't change the boys' minds and hearts all at once—homophobia is too emotional and too strong for that. But he did think that the air had been cleared, and in fact, several of the boys were intrigued to learn that sexual orientation was not a simple matter of sexual choice. Afterward, there had been no more name-calling, and Kurt's expertise with the computer earned the admiration of his classmates. He even wrote some programs that enabled the class to classify their data more easily. Although Jimmy was still obviously antagonistic toward Kurt, and Ian and Steven looked at him now and then with some distrust, most of the class seemed to accept him as just another member of the class, and several had become his good friends.

Tom remembered many other incidents during the year: the day the students had finally settled on the three basic goals of the class that were now hanging on the wall; the time Rebecca's father had joined them on one of their field explorations and had told them the name and habits of every bird they saw; the excitement generated by a group of four girls who had been the first to identify the source of the cloudy water; the time Eric had told Penny that she should take the notes in a class meeting because she was a girl; the arguments and the discoveries made by each student in collaboration with others. It had certainly not been a perfect year, but it had been a good one.

And now they were almost ready to present their case to the school board. Tom didn't see how they could fail. In fact, he thought, even if the school board refuses to act on their request, nothing can stop their interest in their project now.

Case Analysis

Tom Littleton's class and its land lab provide numerous examples of a collaborative and **gender-sensitive** classroom in action. It also illustrates the importance of dealing effectively with nonacademic problems that threaten the existence of a learning-community atmosphere. Key elements of a collaborative learning environment that are evident in Tom's classroom include the following.

1. Students have been encouraged to work together on a project that they helped design. During the year, each student had an opportunity to work with others on a variety of tasks that were part of a larger group goal.

2. The use of collaborative teaching and learning has encouraged the girls in the class to think of themselves as equal partners in the group endeavor.

3. Other adults (teachers and parents) have been encouraged to bring their own expertise and experience into the classroom for students' benefit.

4. By combining his own knowledge with that of collaborating teachers, Tom has been able to show how solving real-world problems requires integrating knowledge from a variety of subject areas. His nature study project required measurements and calculations (math); report writing (English); consideration of social, political, and economic issues (social studies); and the preparation of drawings and displays (art).

5. Students have been actively involved in setting their own goals and in planning strategies for accomplishing them.

6. Students have learned how specialized tasks, such as testing water and writing up the results of the tests, are interdependent subgoals that are part of a larger, more holistic goal.

7. Students have learned that their individual successes depend, in part, on the successes of those with whom they are working.

As he reflected on the goals that he had set for this particular class, particularly those related to gender and cultural difference, Tom Littleton realized that he needed more than biological and environmental knowledge: he needed a firm grasp on the basis of collaborative teaching and learning. Furthermore, he realized now how closely related such issues as gender and cultural difference are to both in-school and out-of-school learning. This chapter discusses issues of collaborative learning, gender, sexual orientation, and education from a variety of perspectives, including the differences between collaborative and traditional teaching and learning, the importance of socialization to gender roles, the relation of middle-class values to the creation of gender identity, and the role of the school as a gender socializing agent.

Rationale for Collaborative Teaching and Learning

The rationale for collaborative teaching and learning rests on many of the same ideas as does the rationale for democratic communities of learners and developmentally appropriate and inclusive classrooms. In addition, support for increasing collaboration in schools and classrooms emerges from two other major sources.

First, as it becomes clear that we are members of an interdependent global economic and political community, many theorists suggest that we must learn to live cooperatively with one another rather than continue to engage in the kinds of destructive competition that produce hunger, disease, and war. As the world's population increases, such issues as natural resources, food, and human problem-solving power become critical ones. We must choose between competing for such resources, which has been a major cause of war, and sharing them, which means cooperative efforts at problem solving. Some of the traditional values espoused by the mainstream culture in the United States (e.g., individualism, materialism, an emphasis on technology) may be intensifying rather than ameliorating the major problems that are confronted (e.g., preservation of the environment, increasing poverty, and loss of community). Solutions to such complex social problems demand collaboration and cooperation.

A second and very different source of support for collaborative classrooms emerges from thirty years of research on gender and on the degree to which boys and girls have different experiences in school. Such research suggests two important points: (1) girls and women tend to focus on preserving relationships while boys and men tend to focus on principles of behavior,[3] and (2) girls and women tend to learn more effectively when collaboration rather than competition is central to the teaching-learning process.[4] This research is discussed in more detail later in this chapter. The point to be made here is that gender researchers have developed instructional models based on classroom collaboration and cooperation rather than competition and that these models are currently available for classroom use.

Both of these rationales for collaborative classrooms suggest a shift away from the values of individualism and competition that are so deeply woven into both our political and economic culture and the school curricula that transmit that culture. While teachers and the school curriculum are not the only means of socializing youngsters, they are critical elements in helping students attain the understanding and the skills needed to live cooperatively and comfortably with others.

Characteristics of a Collaborative Classroom

Fortunately, teachers, parents, and supporting school personnel are beginning to recognize both the opportunity and the obligation they have to effect change in this direction.

Collaborative Classrooms

First, while competition is not absent from collaborative classrooms (nor should it be), cooperation and collaboration are woven throughout both instructional and evaluative processes. Similarly, while group activities and group performance are clearly in evidence, individual acquisition of knowledge and skills and individual performance are still stressed. Indeed, one of the primary goals of collaboration is the enhancement of individual learning. In U.S. schools, competition has often been blindly equated with rigor and quality, both of which are regarded as exemplifying American values of hard work and individual achievement. When a competitive environment threatens classroom equity, however, it becomes problematic. Clearly, we need both. As John Goodlad has pointed out, "Equality and quality are the name of the game. These two concepts will frame dialogue, policy, and practice regarding schooling for years to come."[5]

Second, collaborative classrooms involve teachers and other school personnel, parents, and other community members working together to plan and implement instructional goals. In traditional schools, teaching is often a lonely activity that involves little or no interaction with other adults. This isolation is unfortunate on many accounts, not the least of which is that in order to grow professionally, teachers must work in collaboration with others. By observing other teachers in their classrooms, teachers gain new ideas, fresh strategies, and new perspectives on their professional lives.

Third, because teachers in collaborative classrooms work closely with other adults in the school, many of whom have different areas of expertise, lessons and other activities tend to benefit from the integration of different disciplines and skills. Students thus begin to see connections between the subjects they study, and their learning gains relevancy.

Fourth, collaborative classrooms also extend beyond the school, most obviously to the home. Interest in home-school collaboration, often referred to as "parent involvement," initially emerged from concerns about increased student failure and dropout rates among minority groups, particularly immigrant families, many of whom were unfamiliar with the culture and practices of American schools. In truly collaborative classrooms, however, the involvement of parents is perceived as central to effective education, not as a response to difficulties in an otherwise effective schooling system. In short, parents are regarded as the child's first and continuing teachers and, as such, are natural partners in a collaborative relationship with classroom teachers.

Finally, in collaborative classrooms students cooperate with one another in planning their activities. Students may be organized (or organize themselves) in project teams or in dyads and triads, depending on the nature of the work to be done. The assumption here is that students bring to school useful knowledge from a variety of backgrounds and experiences and that they are competent to assist one another in acquiring new knowledge.

Pedagogies: Old and New

Traditionally, schools have always sponsored a variety of collaborative activities. Think, for example, of sports teams, choirs, dramatic productions, and school newspapers and yearbooks, not to mention a wide variety of social and fund-raising activities carried on by students and teachers. Each of these activities requires the skills of teamwork, cooperation, and interdependence. However, each of these activities is also either cocurricular or extracurricular.

In collaborative classrooms the teaching processes and strategies so necessary to cocurricular and extracurricular activities are applied to the very heart of schooling itself, that is, to the formal curriculum. Teachers find themselves working together to plan units and often teach in teams. One excellent example of this collaboration is a middle school in which four teachers have 100 students. During the course of the school day, one teacher may be working with all 100 students while the other three meet to plan future lessons. Or, each teacher may be working with twenty-five students on separate aspects of a unit. The possible combinations of teachers and students, as well as the possible uses of time, are broad.

One of the most widely known pedagogical strategies found in most collaborative classrooms is called *cooperative learning*. Like other instructional strategies, cooperative learning encompasses a variety of instructional techniques. In general, cooperative learning environments are characterized by what is called *positive goal interdependence*. That is, individuals share the same group goals, and members of the group are accountable to one another. In short, the group sinks or swims together as it works in concert in the attainment of a particular instructional goal. Group cohesiveness thus becomes paramount in the attainment of the specific instructional objective or goal.

In discussing his interest in cooperative learning, Kagan relates some findings from his early research on children's play in Mexico.[6] One finding that intrigued him was that children from rural parts of Mexico were more cooperative with one another than were their peers in urban settings. Somewhat bothered by this finding, Kagan extended his work to look at cooperation and competition among children in other parts of the world. What he discovered appears to be nearly universal and has to do with differences between students who live in rural and urban areas. That is, worldwide, regardless of the continent or culture, children in urban environments are more competitive than their rural counterparts. This finding, coupled with the fact that the world is becoming increasingly urban, raised considerable concern in Kagan's mind. Out of fear that the social character of the nation and world would become increasingly competitive, Kagan began exploring ways to help reverse the tendency children had to become more competitive with age. He found that using cooperative teams in the classroom, often referred to as cooperative learning, worked quite well.

Slavin identified two factors that seem to account for the effectiveness of cooperative learning.[7] The first is that cooperative groups must work to achieve a group goal that cannot be mastered unless each member performs his or her assigned task. The second critical factor is that each individual in the group must still be held accountable for learning the required content. That is, members must work together to make certain that all have mastered the assigned content and have earned satisfactory grades or other forms of recognition. The group's success depends on each individual learning the required material. Evidence of group success might be seen in the sum of the individual members' test scores or in the presentation of a group report. In other words, each individual in the group must have differentiated tasks whose successful performance is critical to achieving the group goal. Secondary characteristics of cooperative learning include an emphasis on face-to-face interpersonal interaction, development of social skills, and group reviews that help members analyze how well they are functioning.

Cooperative learning groups may be used to teach specific content (information or skills), to ensure active cognitive processing of information during a lecture, or to provide long-term support and assistance for academic progress.[8] Basically, any assignment in any curriculum area for a student of any age can be accommodated through cooperative learning.

Cooperative learning does not imply either devaluation of individual contributions or lack of individual accountability. Instead, when individuals of diverse cultural backgrounds and differing physical characteristics have the opportunity to work together in pursuit of a common goal, the barriers of stereotype that prevent people from knowing each other as individuals are likely to be broken down. Friendships are more likely to form. Individual accountability is explicitly addressed in cooperative learning strategies in either of two ways: *task specialization,* or determination of *group scores* for team assignments, or both.[9]

Task specialization, or assignment of a specific subtask to each member of a team or group, is particularly effective in ensuring that students with disabilities, for example, contribute significantly to the group effort. In some instances, a student with a disability may be uniquely able to carry out a certain task, because students with physical, academic-cognitive, or emotional-behavioral differences are also people with *abilities.* Thus, not only can the self-image and identity of students with disabilities be enhanced, but all students can, through firsthand experience, realize this fundamental truth.[10]

The corollary to collaborative learning, of course, is collaborative teaching, which refers to interactions among students who are teaching one another, to interactions between teachers and students, and to interactions between teachers engaged in collaborative efforts. In classrooms where collaboration is the norm, teachers do some of the talking but are not necessarily the center of attention even the majority of the time. Students work in teams, discuss issues, engage in group problem solving, and help one another understand the material at hand. Teachers and other adults work with students by encouraging them to inquire, to reflect, and to share and modify ideas.

Roles: Old and New

The traditional roles of teacher as teller and student as listener change in a collaborative classroom. Rather than always being the expert, the teacher often acts as coach, encouraging and assisting students to complete the assigned tasks. Students also serve as coaches for one another and, not infrequently, find themselves acting as experts in particular areas. One of the most obvious examples of this phenomenon is the native Spanish, French, or German speaker in a foreign-language classroom. There are, however, many other ways in which students of all ages can provide expert knowledge and/or skills to their fellow students. For instance, the student who actively uses the computer at home or one who has a well-developed skill in playing a musical instrument can become active as a peer-tutor in these areas.

One of the most important role changes in a collaborative classroom, however, is that of parents. In traditional elementary classrooms, parents ordinarily serve in various "motherly" capacities, such as providing goods for a bake sale, bringing treats on birthdays, and acting as planners for holiday celebrations. Parents also are expected to ensure that homework assignments are completed and to attend open houses and parent-teacher conferences. In traditional middle and high school classrooms, the role of parents is often limited to these latter functions.

In collaborative classrooms, however, parents (and grandparents, and other community members with some interest or expertise) are often central to the instructional program, helping to make and implement curricular and instructional decisions. For example, parents and/or others may take an active role in elementary reading instruction by organizing various small group activities. Or, they may work with small groups of students in math-related activities, thus providing greater opportunity for children to be actively engaged in classroom content.

It is not always easy to encourage such collaboration. Indeed, McCaleb has explored various reasons for the lack of parental involvement particularly among nondominant groups.[11] One reason she offers for a lack of involvement among minority parents centers on the perceived inequality between students from nonstandard-English home environments and students from the dominant culture. She argues that most young children, understandably, identify strongly with their families—their primary teachers. If students happen to come from families with minimal or no schooling or if the educational experience of parents differs significantly from that which is normally experienced by the American middle class, children quickly sense the contradictions between their home and school lives. Seeing many books at school, for example, and few at home, they may begin to question their own potential for educational success. A similarly negative self-attribution may be made by parents if they, in turn, believe that they have little to teach or share with their children. In Hawaii, however, a successful curricular innovation involves grandparents and other community elders regularly coming into elementary classrooms to teach children Hawaiian culture and language from their traditionally oral approach.

Greenspan, Niemeyer, and Seeley conducted a study of how principals perceived parental involvement in school affairs.[12] They cite four reasons for the lack of parental involvement in schools.

1. *A significant transient population.* Many schools have children whose families move frequently, thus forcing their children to attend new schools.
2. *Alienation between the home and school.* Social class differences, for one, tend to separate families from teachers and administrators. Such differences, the researchers suggest, may be accentuated by racial factors. Most of the principals interviewed for the study, however, concurred that poor parents were just as concerned about education and wanted the same things for their children (a good education, good behavior, respect for authority) as other parents. What they did not understand was how to assist their children in attaining these goals.
3. *School-generated problems.* In some instances teachers and other school staff are simply insensitive to the needs and problems of students and their families.
4. *Disintegration of the family.* The researchers inferred this point from the large number of children who seem to be cared for by adults other than their natural parents.

McCaleb, on the other hand, suggests that the perceived "broken family" issue might be a classic case of misunderstanding and misattribution. She suggests that such nonparental caring arrangements do not represent a disintegration of the family but rather a reinterpretation of the concept "family," since many of these families consist of an extended network of caregivers.

To summarize, in collaborative classrooms parents and other community members share with teachers and other school staff the responsibility for educating children. This partnership model views parents as resources and contributors to the education of their children and helps integrate the school and the community. Cummins agrees with these suggestions when he proposes that real changes in schools will take place only when the relationships of power begin to change and when the voices and concerns of parents and the community are heard and acted on.[13]

Place of Content Knowledge: Old and New

In collaborative classrooms where teachers, parents, other school personnel, and students are working together, boundaries between academic disciplines tend to become less defined as cooperative teams pool their knowledge in the pursuit of integrated projects. As teachers learn about what other teachers are doing, they begin to see ways of integrating their efforts. In such classrooms, the language arts and social studies may begin to merge, and the arts may be put to use in the service of scientific and geographical knowledge.

A good example of this "blurring" of disciplinary boundaries is given by Charles Fowler. He writes:

If, for example, students are studying the Grand Canyon, and we want to give them a general idea of it without actually going there, we often resort to a verbal description: "The Grand Canyon, the world's largest gorge, is a spectacle of multicolored layers of rock carved out over the millennia by the Colorado River." If we want to convey its vastness, we use measurements:

"The Grand Canyon is over 1 mile deep, 4 to 18 miles wide, and more than 200 miles long." Each of these symbolic systems—words and numbers—permits us to reveal important aspects, but a picture or a painting can be equally telling.

The arts—creative writing, dance, music, theater/film, and visual arts—serve as ways that we react to, record, and share our impressions of the world. Students can be asked to set forth their own interpretation of the Grand Canyon, using, say, poetry as the communicative vehicle. While mathematics gives us precise quantitative measures of magnitude, poetry explores our disparate personal reactions. Both views are valid. Both contribute to understanding. Together, they prescribe a larger overall conception of, in this case, one of nature's masterpieces.[14]

In a collaborative classroom, content knowledge not only becomes something to be learned, but more important, becomes something meaningful to students who learn to make connections between areas of knowledge that, after all, blend together in the world outside school.

Assessment: Old and New

Methods of evaluating student performance should be compatible with the types of learning activities that characterize a particular classroom. For example, traditional forms of evaluation such as standardized paper-and-pencil tests, answering questions posed by the teacher in a large group format, and student reports all seek to determine what and how much students "know" about a particular subject such as math or English. Each evaluation assumes that subject matter knowledge can be "given" to students who are then able to "give" such knowledge back as a sign that it has been learned. Perhaps the most efficient form of instruction for transmitting subject matter knowledge is that in which teachers talk and students listen, read, and are evaluated on the degree to which they have retained what they have heard and read.

In collaborative classrooms, however, learning is less dependent on teacher talk and more dependent on group activities (projects, problem-solving situations, study groups) that take place over time. In such classrooms compatible evaluation techniques are those that measure performance over time, such as the creation of artifacts and portfolios and demonstrations of individual and group problem-solving ability. Although all these evaluation techniques will be discussed in more detail in Chapter 12, the point to make here is that these forms of assessment are a good match with instructional methods that emphasize collaborative teaching and learning.

With the move toward standardized proficiency testing that is sweeping the country, some of these assessment methods are being called into question by both teachers and parents. However, a report from the National Academy for the Advancement of Science notes that assessment must go beyond standardized tests. They recommend that assessments should (1) include a variety of techniques; (2) encourage students to go beyond simple recall of data or facts; (3) close the gap between the classroom and the real world; and (4) include opportunities for students to perform tasks and solve problems.[15]

In all teaching situations, however, it is well to remember that teachers are not required to choose only one kind of instruction, one kind of role, or one kind of evaluation. Indeed, the more variety teachers have in their repertoire, the more effective they are likely to be and the more exciting the classroom will be for everyone.

Perspectives on Gender Identity

One of Tom Littleton's first goals for his science class was to systematically encourage girls to enroll in and to participate actively in the class. His goal stems from the realization that science is often not considered a "suitable" subject for girls and that girls often do not take higher level science classes in high school for that reason, thus effectively preventing them from pursuing the sciences in college. The reasons for this state of affairs are many and complicated, but central to all of them is the notion of **gender role socialization.**

One of the earliest and most important learning experiences in any society is the development of a sense of self-identity—the knowledge that one is separate from mother, father, and family. This perception begins when an infant is about seven or eight months old and continues throughout an individual's life. It is not unusual for a person's sense of identity to undergo significant changes as new experiences are encountered during the course of that person's life.

Activity 28: Gender Role Socialization

An extremely important part of an individual's identity, and one that begins at least at birth, is gender. It is thought that identification in terms of sex begins at about eighteen months of age and by the age of three is clearly internalized.[16] But sexual identity is more complex than simply "knowing" that you are male or female. More important to your sense of self is your identification as a member of a gender group—"I am a girl"; "I am a boy." Whereas sex is a biological characteristic, gender is a social one. In all cultural groups, gender identity includes knowledge of a large set of rules and expectations for what boys and girls should wear, how they should speak and act, and their "place" in the overall structure of society. Knowledge of these rules is knowledge of our role as a member of a particular gender group and provides us with the ability to deal with many social situations without having to stop each time to figure out what to do. Gender role identity, however, also limits us in terms of our range of choices and, sometimes, the very quality of our lives.

Gender Role Socialization

The rules associated with a person's gender role may vary by race, by ethnicity, by social class, by religion, and even by geographical region. Such socialization takes place in a variety of different ways, many of them small and incremental—simple routines of daily life and language. The process of such learning has been described in three parts:

1. The child learns to *distinguish* between men and women, and between boys and girls, and to know what kinds of behavior are characteristic of each.
2. The child learns to express appropriate gender role *preferences* for himself or herself.
3. The child learns to *behave* in accordance with gender role standards.[17]

Although this process of internalizing knowledge of and identification with gender role is a part of all children's lives, it has been most studied in the lives of middle-class white children, especially girls. This concentration is significant for at least two reasons. First, it reflects the predominant characteristics of the researchers themselves, many of

critical incident

Responsibilities at Home

 Some of the students in Tom Littleton's class were talking about going to the movies on Friday night when two of the Gypsy students, Steven and Rebecca, walked by.
"Hey, Steve," called out one of the boys, "do you want to go to the movies with us on Friday?"

Steven stopped and looked at them. He seemed about to accept their invitation, but then said, "Oh, I can't. My grandmother is coming over that night, and I'm going to help my mother fix dinner."

"Aw, come on!" said one of the students. "You can see your grandmother anytime."

"No," said Steven. "I have a responsibility to be there."

- Why do you think Steven refused an invitation that he might otherwise have wanted to accept?
- Why do you think part of Steven's responsibilities included fixing dinner?

whom have been not only white, middle-class university scholars but also feminists interested in rediscovering the reality of women's lives. Because the focus has been on girls, the consequences of gender role socialization on boys, which are great, often have been minimized.

Second, studies primarily located in the white middle class have reflected the dominant social group in the United States. Because dominance is often equated with universality, norms related to the gender role socialization of middle-class whites are often thought to apply to *all* American girls and boys—indeed, to *all* girls and boys everywhere. Research over the last thirty years, which attempted to look at gender role socialization in terms of racial, ethnic, religious, and national groups, has discovered significant differences in value and orientation between white middle-class socialization practices and those of other groups. This finding is important because the role of the school in teaching gender role attitudes and behavior is second only to the role of the family. Schools normally represent the **dominant culture,** and gender role is no exception. Thus, schools often unconsciously attempt to "mold" boys and girls into the dominant gender role while ignoring the different orientations and behaviors regarding gender that students bring with them to school.

Gender Role Socialization in the Middle Class

For the white middle class, differences in socialization practices for boys and girls are many and obvious. Nearly thirty years ago, Howe describes some of them in the following way. See whether you think things have changed all that much:

We throw boy babies up in the air and roughhouse with them. We coo over girl babies and handle them delicately. We choose sex related colors and toys for our children from their earliest

Should She Go to College?

Anamarie was an extremely bright young Latina in her junior year of high school. Mr. Jordan, her English teacher, thought she should be thinking seriously about going to college. He knew, however, that if she did go, she would be the first in her family to continue school after high school. He also knew that her parents, who owned a very successful restaurant, expected her to help with the business when she finished high school.

One afternoon in April, Mr. Jordan asked Anamarie to come to his office after school. She was a little nervous; what had she done wrong?

When Anamarie sat down, Mr. Jordan came right to the point. "I'd like to talk to you about college," he said. "You have a very good mind, and you're an excellent writer. I'd be very happy to help you look at different college opportunities and to write a good recommendation for you."

Anamarie was astonished. She didn't say anything for a minute; then she said, "Oh, Mr. Jordan, I couldn't do that! My parents want me to help them with the restaurant. They're not getting any younger, you know, and I need to be looking out for them."

She hesitated a moment, and then added, "You know, I think I might really *like* to go to college . . . but I just can't."

- Do you think Mr. Jordan should have considered any ethical issues before talking to Anamarie?
- Would you have handled the situation any differently?

days. We encourage the energy and physical activity of our sons, just as we expect girls to be quieter and more docile. We love both our sons and daughters with equal fervor, we protest, and yet we are disappointed when there is no male child to carry on the family name.[18]

Kramer has suggested a number of socialization agents in early childhood that reflect middle-class values, and these, too, have remained relatively constant.[19] The first, of course, is parents. Studies have demonstrated not only that infant boys are handled more roughly than their sisters and that infant girls receive more verbal attention, but also that young boys are given more freedom to explore than are young girls, who are often kept closer to the supervising parent. In addition, girls receive more help on tasks than do boys, who are encouraged to "figure it out for yourself." Research also shows that parental reaction to the behavior of their children tends to be more favorable when girls and boys are behaving in ways traditionally associated with their gender.[20] Thus parents shape the expectations and abilities of their children not only by overt behavior but also by rewarding them with approval when they behave "appropriately."

In contrast to the usually more traditional socializing influence of the family is another powerful socializing agent—television. Although there is much that is still stereotypical about the images of boys and girls and women and men on television—particularly the sexual images on networks such as MTV—there has been a significant change in the nature of gender role images to be found in commercials. Indeed, males and females of all ages are shown in roles unheard of even fifteen years ago. Thus, young women are competing in sports and young men are taking care of their infants in a variety of commercial messages. Similarly, this kind of change can also be seen in the roles played by older people on television commercials, who are, today, climbing mountains and fording streams in the wild rather than sitting on front porches telling stories to their grandchildren.

A third influence on young children's development of gender role identity is children's books. Although many nonsexist books are being published today, the classics are still being read with enthusiasm. Traditional fairy tales, such as Cinderella, Little Red Riding Hood, Snow White and Rose Red, and Sleeping Beauty present "heroines" who are browbeaten, tricked, chased, put to sleep by wicked witches (another ever-popular female character), and/or eaten. Release from such vicissitudes, when it occurs, is always at the hands of a (handsome) young man who finally shows up at the end of the story to whisk the young girl away on *his* horse, to live out her days in *his* castle.[21]

A fourth important gender socializer of children is toys. If the inclinations of parents and relatives to buy "gender-appropriate" toys is not sufficient to the task, manufacturers provide on their packaging useful clues to the gender of the child expected to use the toy. This influence also extends to the placing of such toys in store aisles. Go to any large toy store and observe the placement of toys (and colors of the signs) for girls and boys. Kramer notes that "with few exceptions, blocks, cars, trains, manipulative games, chemistry sets, doctor's kits, work tools, building games, and of course balls of all kinds show boys on the package. Dolls, kitchen or cleaning toys, needlework or sewing equipment, and nurse's kits show girls on the package."[22] No matter how many Barbie dolls come with briefcases, astronaut helmets, and computers, Barbie is still a *very* well-endowed young lady, and Ken is still lurking in the background.

Boys' toys are relatively more complex, more varied, and more expensive than girls' toys and frequently have no counterpart for girls.[23] Consider, for example, the range of remote-control cars, boats, and airplanes for sale as well as electronic sports and adventure games that are marketed for boys. Take a look at a store that sells computer games for boys and girls in the preteen years: there are a wide variety of action-oriented games (jungle adventures, space travel) for boys and a good many Barbie dress-designing games for girls of the same age. While there is no *law* preventing parents and others from buying cross-gender toys, most people still feel a bit uncomfortable doing so. Even in the twenty-first century, we buy toy lawn mowers for little boys and toy shopping carts for little girls, and seldom do the reverse.

Other socializing influences of young children may be found in a variety of everyday places and activities. From nursery rhymes, we learn that young girls are frightened of spiders while young boys are nimble and quick. In Bible stories, we observe that young boys are brave and able to do away with giants, while women have a tendency toward evil actions such as cutting off a man's hair and robbing him of his strength. From familiar proverbs and sayings, we become aware that sometimes objectionable behavior on the part of boys must be excused on the grounds that "boys will be boys" (did you ever hear "girls will be girls"?), and that "it's a man's world." And from children's songs we learn that John Henry built a railroad while Suzannah was waiting for her young man to return from Louisiana.

Masculine and Feminine Behavior

If middle-class gender roles seem to limit girls more than boys, it may be only that our society favors the active, the adventurous, and the aggressive and that those traits are largely associated with boys. However, there is a high price to be paid by boys for all their "freedom." First of all, boys are socialized much earlier to what is perceived to be "manly." A girl who participates in boys' activities, plays with boys' toys, is impatient with dresses and ribbons and lace, and in general eschews "girlish" things is called a tomboy and is regarded with some tolerance by most adults, at least until adolescence. At that point, according to conventional wisdom, chances are good that she will "grow out of it." At the same time, from the age of three onward, boys who want to play with dolls, spend time with their mothers in the kitchen, cry easily, like to stay clean, and avoid contact sports are called sissies—a much more negative label. Adults viewing such behavior even in very young boys often become enormously uncomfortable and worried that "he is moving in the wrong direction." Adult intervention in these "girlish" activities is usually swift, direct, and unmistakable.

Activity 29: Observing Gender Differences

Second, boys are punished much more harshly for deviation from the norms of "masculine" behavior. Moreover, such punishment occurs at an age when they are too young to really understand the source of their "problem" or the reasons for adult distress. Hartley argues that

> To make matters more difficult, the desired behavior is rarely defined positively as something the child *should* do, but rather, undesirable behavior is indicated negatively as something he should *not* do or be—anything, that is, that the parent or other people regard as "sissy." Thus, very early in life the boy must either stumble on the right path or bear repeated punishment without warning when he accidentally enters into the wrong ones.[24]

One result of this socialization is that boys very early come to regard anything having to do with girls' play and behavior as something to be avoided at all costs, and this attitude increases during the elementary years until most boys would rather "drop dead" than play with girls. This reaction is commonly regarded as a "natural" stage of development rather than the result of careful socialization.[25] Thus little is done to alter practices that lead to separation of the sexes and the masculine disdain for the "feminine," which often lasts a lifetime.

That such lessons are well learned is without doubt, and little has changed in the responses of a representative group of boys (eight and ten years old) asked to describe what boys and girls have to be able to know and do. Boys, they said,

> have to be able to fight in case a bully comes along; they have to be athletic; they have to be able to run fast; they must be able to play rough games; they need to know how to play many games—curb-ball, baseball, basketball, football; they need to be smart; they need to be able to take care of themselves; they should know what girls don't know—how to climb, how to make a fire, how to carry things; they should have more ability than girls . . . they are expected to be noisy; to get dirty; to mess up the house; to be naughty; to be "outside" more than girls are; not to be cry-babies; not to be "softies;" not to be "behind" like girls are; and to get into trouble more than girls do.[26]

Thinking about the roles boys must assume, it is hard not to question, with Hartley, "not why boys have difficulty with this role, but why they try as hard as they do to fulfill it."[27]

Perspectives on Gender and Schooling

One answer to why boys try hard to fulfill their role is that gender roles are **normative**—that is, the ideas about what attitudes, values, and behavior are associated with sex or gender have been coded by the social group into norms or, often, stereotypes. A *norm* is a rule of conduct based on attitudes and values that are usually internalized through socialization until they become "of course" statements.[28]

Schools as Socializing Agents

Schools, of course, have an important function as socializers to societal norms, particularly those associated with the middle class, which is the class most often represented by the school. Because these norms are so much a part of most school folks, they seem "normal" and "right" and are usually taken very much for granted. That sense of "normality" is probably the most powerful force operating to encourage obedience to norms. However, there are other factors involved in encouraging normative thought and behavior. In all societies, there are *sanctions,* or punishments, for deviation from norms.

These sanctions operate in schools on a daily basis, and most of them are particularly *social* santions. Consider again, for example, that girls may avoid taking advanced science or math classes because they don't want boys to think they're "too smart." The assumption of some girls is that the boys will "sanction" them socially for appearing to compete with them academically. Or consider the overt social sanctioning of boys who are gay by those boys who are straight, which is perhaps the most intense sanctioning that occurs. A number of lesser normative rules are broken every day in schools, by both males and females—and it appears that as gender roles change (which they are doing, but slowly), the social sanctions are also becoming less severe. Nevertheless, the power of gender role stereotypes is enormous and frequently costly to both males and females.

Gender Stereotypes in School

**Gender Role
Stereotypes**

In our society, **gender role stereotyping** includes the belief that boys and men are aggressive, independent, strong, logical, direct, adventurous, self-confident, ambitious, and not particularly emotional. Girls and women are passive, weak, illogical, indirect, gentle, and very emotional. Boys, the stereotypes say, are good at math and science, and girls are good at language and writing. Boys are loud and girls are quiet. Girls play with dolls and boys play with balls. Although it is true that not every single boy or girl believes or adheres to these stereotypes, it is generally true that *society,* in part through schooling, attempts to enforce them. Moreover, these stereotypes are reinforced even in the face of contrary evidence, such as the fact that girls and women are now participating in nearly every aspect of life once "owned" by boys and men.

Gender role stereotypes vary not only in their content but also in the value ascribed to the content. In other words, not only are boys and men perceived to be *different* from girls and women, but their learned behavior is generally more highly valued.

Who's Using the Computer?

Joan Thompson was a math education professor at a local university who was working with teachers in a nearby elementary school on incorporating computer technology into their classrooms. In every session of the twelve biweekly meetings she had with these teachers, she stressed the need to include girls in computer work and gave them some background on the need to encourage girls in math, science, and technology.

At the end of the semester, the teachers and students prepared a culminating presentation to demonstrate what they'd learned. In the presentation, students were to be paired in male and female dyads, a fact that the teachers were quick (and proud) to point out. Some students were going to use the computer to find specific information while others were going to write that information on the board. Joan really looked forward to seeing the results of all their work.

When she got there, everyone was excited to show what they'd learned. As the presentation progressed, Dr. Thompson was astounded to observe that, in every dyad, the boys were using the computers and the girls were writing on the board!

- If you were Dr. Thompson, how would you respond to the teachers and students?
- Why do you think the event was planned in just this way?

Thus, gender role stereotypes are the basis for **genderized traits,** traits that any person may be *able* to display but that are assigned value when they are displayed by people of the appropriate sex. Often, these stereotypes are genderized in favor of men, since many of the personality traits valued by society—think of self-reliance, adventurousness, ambition, and directness—are those traits that quite often are socialized into boys and not girls.

Gender role stereotypes are hard on males as well, but in a somewhat different way. As the woman's movement has succeeded in opening up to women public roles that have been traditionally associated with men, women have learned to assume those roles more or less well, and the gender role socialization of young girls has changed somewhat to accommodate their broader life chances. The same is not true of boys and men.

Definitions of masculinity held by boys often are not based on what boys *should* do, but rather on what they *should not* do, and that what they should not do is to be anything like a girl. Two forces that in our society help to enforce male and female stereotypes are misogyny and homophobia. Simply stated, **misogyny** is the hatred of women and **homophobia** is the fear of homosexuality and homosexuals. Thompson argues that while these forces seem to target different kinds of people, they are really different aspects of the same thing. "Homophobia is the hatred of feminine qualities in men, while misogyny is the hatred of feminine qualities in women."[29] In both cases, the assumption is that feminine qualities are less valued, even contemptible.

Carelli has made an effective distinction between sex role stereotyping, sex bias, and sex discrimination. She writes:

Whenever specific behaviors, abilities, interests, and values are attributed to one sex, then sex role stereotyping is taking place. . . . Behavior that results from the underlying belief in sex role stereotypes is referred to as "sex bias." . . . Any action that specifically denies opportunities, privileges, or rewards to a person or a group because of their sex is termed "sex discrimination" if the action is against the law.[30]

Calling another boy a fag because he is exhibiting "female" qualities is an example of gender bias—an action based on gender role stereotypes. If that boy were prevented from, say, taking art classes on the grounds that drawing is a "feminine" activity and that all artists are fags, that would be gender discrimination, since denying access to specific educational activities is against the law.

Clearly, the power of gender role stereotypes is great, and the cost is high for everyone: boys and girls, women and men. Gender role stereotypes serve to prevent girls and boys from having valuable human experiences; they limit growth and development both by denying such experiences and by creating anxiety in children. They also create social and institutional barriers against the development of interests, goals, and talents in young people that may be outside gender role "parameters." The human cost in terms of discouragement, sadness, fear, and alienation is incalculable. Gender role stereotypes also contribute to the organization of schooling and to the subtle and not-so-subtle messages that boys and girls absorb about their identities, their expectations, and their futures.

Productive and Reproductive Processes

Jane Roland Martin has observed that formal education, in content and practice, stresses attitudes and values that are associated primarily with the *productive processes* of society—political and economic activities as well as the creation of art, music, dance, and drama. The *reproductive processes* of society—activities that generally involve caretaking of homes, children, the ill, and the elderly—are not important areas of learning in school, nor are they included in the ordinary criteria used in evaluating the ideal of the educated person.[31]

This emphasis on productive processes has its roots in the Greek tradition, which focused on the *polis,* or political community. Thus, schools were not originally established to meet the needs of the individual, but rather to socialize young people into the adult roles of the larger society. The primary role of the teacher in this regard has been to develop in children loyalties outside the family. This process of encouraging independence from the child's primary social group often begins with transferring loyalty to the teacher.

In accordance with this productive orientation, the typical classroom in our society has maintained a competitive atmosphere. A related value, individualism, characterizes the practice of teaching students as individual units even though large numbers of students are present in any one classroom. Typical evaluation and assessment methods encourage individual competition. The standard bell curve demands that there be both successes and failures in any group. The success of one student, then, lies in the failure of another. This pattern mirrors what we perceive to be the characteristics of the "real" world for which we are preparing students. That real world, moreover, has been until quite recently a world of mostly male competition to achieve individual success.

Gender as an Issue of Legal Equity in Schools

As with laws and court cases involving issues of race, language, and later, of disability, gender became a legal issue in Congress and the courts.

Legislation and Court Cases

Inspired by the civil rights movement during the 1960s and early 1970s, members of the women's movement began to pressure Congress to enact legislation that would guarantee equitable educational experience for girls and women. The result was Title IX of the Education Amendments of 1972. This statute was intended to prohibit discrimination in elementary and secondary schools on the basis of sex; its preamble reads:

> No person in the United States shall, on the basis of sex, be excluded from participation in, be denied the benefits of, or be subjected to discrimination under any education program or activity receiving federal financial assistance.[32]

Not until 1975, however, were the rules and regulations enforcing Title IX published and sent to state departments of education and to school districts. In the interim, there was heated controversy; several bills were introduced in Congress to take the teeth out of the legislation (all of which were defeated); and ten thousand citizens sent in written comments.[33] The initial government agency responsible for enforcing Title IX was the Department of Health and Human Services.

Gender Equity Legislation and Court Cases

In 1980, the U.S. Department of Education was created and the responsibility for Title IX was given to them through the Office of Civil Rights. All was not smooth sailing, however. In the now-famous *Grove City* v. *Bell* case, Grove City College in Pennsylvania attempted to evade compliance with Title IX (and all other civil rights mandates directed toward schools and colleges receiving federal funds) on the grounds that the college took no money from the federal government (although their students did receive college loans from the federal government).[34] In 1984, the Supreme Court agreed with Grove City College and removed the applicability of Title IX in athletics programs by finding that only those programs or activities that receive *direct* federal assistance can be held accountable to Title IX.

The victory was short-lived, however; in 1988, Congress passed the Civil Rights Restoration Act, overriding President Reagan's veto. This act overrode the decision in *Grove City* v. *Bell* by establishing that all educational institutions that receive *any* federal funding—direct or indirect—are bound by Title IX legislation. By 1990, the Office of Civil Rights of the U.S. Department of Education had published an investigation manual to aid in enforcement, and in 1994, Congress passed the Equity in Athletics Disclosure Act, which requires coeducational institutions of higher education to disclose, on an annual basis, information regarding its intercollegiate athletics program.

For the most part, regulation and interpretation of Title IX has affected middle school, high school, and college athletics programs. Lower courts have seen numerous cases involving the participation of girls in athletics, the requirement that expenditures on male and female athletic programs be "substantially" the same, and the canceling of boys' athletics programs in order to better balance expenditures on athletics. In most cases, Title IX has been enforced.

Other cases have been brought in the area of sexual harassment—both adult-and-student cases and student-and-student cases. Court decisions have been mixed in this area. For example, in two cases involving sexual harassment by teachers of students, the decisions were opposite. In *Franklin* v. *Gwinnet County Public Schools* (1992), the Supreme Court ruled that petitioners may claim punitive damages under Title IX when intentional action to prevent Title IX compliance is established.[35] In *Alida Star Gebser and Alida Jean Mccullough* v. *Lago Vista Independent School District* (1997), a California court denied compensatory and punitive damages from both the teacher involved and the school district.[36] However, in the first student-on-student sexual harassment case to be decided successfully under Title IX in federal court—*Doe* v. *Petaluma Unified School District* (1995)—plaintiff was awarded $250,000.[37] Clearly, the whole story of unequal educational opportunity for girls has not been written, but progress has been made, particularly in athletics, under Title IX.

Major Studies on Gender and Schooling in the Last Decade

Studies of Gender and Schooling

In the 1990s, a great deal has been learned about the relationship between gender and schooling. All studies address gender equity issues in schools, but they do so from somewhat different perspectives. A major study published in 1993, for example, done by the Mid-Atlantic Equity Center and The NETWORK under a grant from the Department of Education, found eight areas of concern related to Title IX still to be addressed in order to ensure equal educational opportunity for all students. The eight areas are:

- Girls at risk of dropping out of school
- Gender bias in student-teacher interactions
- The participation and achievement of girls in mathematics and science
- Students enrolling in and completing vocational educational courses historically nontraditional to their sex
- Gender bias in standardized tests
- Gender differences in learning styles
- Teen pregnancy and parenting
- Sexual harassment of students by their peers

Two additional issues not related to Title IX but also of concern were increasing the self-esteem of girls and increasing awareness for both boys and girls of date or acquaintance rape.[38]

In 1997, U.S. Secretary of Education Richard Riley published a report on the increasing achievements of girls in school twenty-five years after Title IX was established. Noting that in 1971, a Connecticut judge asserted that "Athletic competition builds character in our boys. We do not need that kind of character in our girls,"[39] Riley says,

What strikes me the most about the progress that has been achieved since Title IX was passed in 1972 is that there has been a sea change in our expectations of what women can achieve. More important, women have shown skeptics again and again that females are fully capable of being involved as successful and active participants in every realm of American life. Women astronauts from Sally Ride to Shannon Lucid have made their mark in space even as Mia Hamm and Michelle Akers have led the women's national soccer team to Olympic glory and the World Championship. Women have entered the medical and legal professions in record numbers and we have seen a fourfold increase in women's participation in intercollegiate athletics.[40]

Among successes listed in this report are increases for women in college enrollment and completion, earning of graduate and professional degrees, participation in athletics, and success in international comparisons of high school and college graduation rates with women in other industrialized nations.[41]

A bit less sanguine than the government report is a series of studies commissioned by the American Association of University Women (AAUW). Their first study was a national poll in 1991 that assessed self-esteem, educational experiences, and career aspirations of girls and boys ages nine to fifteen. It found lower self-esteem among girls, differentiated educational experiences between boys and girls, and gendered career aspirations among both boys and girls.[42] Following this study, the AAUW funded Susan McGee Bailey at the Wellesley Center for Research on Women to do an in-depth review (more than thirteen hundred studies) of gender and schooling, including the thirty-five major studies of schooling issued by special commissions between 1983 and 1991.[43] What Bailey and her colleagues found was, first, a noticeable lack of attention to gender in national commission reports and, second, a similar lack of interest in assessing the educational experiences of girls and boys across categories of race and class. Thus, what information *was* available on gender was not differentiated by other status categories, thus eliminating the ability of researchers to obtain a full picture of the *diversity* of educational experiences within gender categories.[44]

Following this landmark study, the AAUW funded a series of additional studies on a variety of issues such as the incidence and impact of sexual harassment in American schools, the impact of different educational approaches on girls' school achievement, the influence of school climate on adolescents, and a critical study of single-sex education for girls.[45] These studies and others suggest that in the areas of academic achievement, curriculum materials, learning environments, sexuality education, and college attendance, there remain a number of problematic issues and practices that tend to, if not completely favor boys, at least often fail to take girls' needs into account.[46]

In general, conditions that support the effective education of girls are those that have been recommended in various school reform initiatives and that are recommended in this book for all children. Hansen, Walker and Flom[47] have found that girls are more likely to thrive

> in learning environments that provide mentors and role models; opportunities for leadership and exploration of new ideas; active intellectual engagement with concerned adults and other students; cooperative learning models; and consciousness-raising about gender, race, and class issues.[48]

Where We Are Now

In the past three years or so, the AAUW has published a number of other studies focusing on the fastest growing minority population, Latina girls; on single-sex education for girls; and on educating girls in the technological age.[49] Generally speaking, although these studies show progress, they also show a number of areas in which girls are still "left behind," and they also raise new issues of concern as indicated by research on such newer topics as single-sex education and technology.

Interestingly, as the education of girls has become a matter of interest to the public, so has the education of boys. Some of this interest derives from increasing suggestions that boys, often poor boys, be educated in single-sex classrooms or schools and that girls be educated in single-sex classrooms for mathematics and science classes. Research on such arrangements is, again, mixed at best, and much of it is inconclusive. Another topic relating to the education of boys has to do with the socialization to gender role that this society "imposes" on boys. Of particular interest in this regard seems to be the idea that while we have paid a great deal of attention to altering the socialization of girls, we have spent much less time thinking about altering the socialization of boys. Among concerns in this regard are hyper-masculine media images, increasing violence among boys, decreasing academic achievement among boys, rising numbers of boys on medication for hyperactivity disorders, and confusing messages given to boys that oppose "caring" and "aggression."[50]

The socialization for gender roles among both boys and girls is changing, and these changes are difficult for everyone, particularly for adults. Teachers may have nearly as much responsibility as parents for helping young people understand and adjust to changing roles. In many ways, changing notions of gender role places all of us "in a different country," and we will be following many of the same processes as one who actually finds himself or herself in a foreign place. The good news is that we are surely on our way.

Perspectives on Gender and School Culture

Activity 7:
Proverbs as a
Window into
One's Culture

The cultural values associated with the dominant social group in the United States are also those values that are generally taught in schools. Issues of gender emerge from the question, "Is gender a difference that makes a difference?" From that perspective, an examination of some of these values can illuminate how the culture of the school influences the socialization of girls and boys.

Gender and European American Values in Traditional School Culture

Activity and
Reading 8:
Cultural Values
in American
Society

It has been suggested that European American, middle-class culture rests on six major values.[51] We can explore these values by looking at proverbs and sayings that have become a part of our folk wisdom and also by asking if these values relate differently to males and females.

1. *European Americans have a tendency to view themselves as separate from nature and able to master or control their environment.* As a result, a high value is placed on science and technology as the predominant means of interacting with the world. The study of science is presumed to result in objectivity, rationality, materialism, and a need for concrete evidence. Proverbs and sayings such as "Necessity is the mother of invention" and "We'll cross that bridge when we come to it" reflect this

belief. It is also true, however, that boys are generally encouraged to take courses in math and science while girls are not, usually because boys are thought to "need" these traits, while girls are not.

2. *European Americans are action oriented.* The measurement of progress and change are important concepts here. Our schools expect such an orientation, as evidenced by an emphasis on testing and measurement as well as a nearly religious belief in the efficacy of paperwork assignments. Proverbs such as "Seeing is believing" and "The proof is in the pudding" emphasize this cultural trait. But while girls generally get better grades than boys do, boys are more likely to be challenged to do their work until they get it right whereas girls are often graded on such qualities as neatness.

3. *European Americans have an optimistic, progressive orientation.* Middle-class European Americans believe that change will be in the direction of bigger and better. They are seldom content with the present; they wish not to be considered old-fashioned, and they believe that effort applied in the present will affect their future. Progress is, in many ways, their most important product. Proverbs such as "I think I can, I think I can," and "From little acorns, mighty oaks grow," and even the more recent "No pain, no gain" reflect this tendency. Yet the socialization patterns of schooling are more likely to emphasize this future orientation for boys than for girls. The assumption (often unrealized by teachers) is that girls' futures involve reproductive processes such as caring for families in the private sphere rather than productive processes involving the public sphere. Seldom are girls encouraged to be "mighty oaks."

4. *European Americans are self-motivated and are comfortable setting their own goals and directions.* From an early age, European Americans are encouraged to reach out on their own, to attempt for themselves, to satisfy their own needs. Such proverbs as "Nothing ventured, nothing gained," "If at first you don't succeed, try, try again," and "The early bird catches the worm" reflect this trait. Again, these values are differentially associated with boys and girls. Girls are not often pushed toward the adventurous, aggressiveness traits that seem necessary to "get out ahead." Indeed, aggressiveness is not seen as a "womanly" trait at all.

5. *European Americans have a strong sense of individuality.* They believe that the individual self is separate from the collective self. This belief results in a tendency to emphasize individual initiative, responsibility, independence, action, and an internal locus of control. Individuals are not expected to depend on others for identity but to maintain their individuality even within the larger group. The school expects children to work alone in their seats, rarely coming together with others to share in problem resolution and task assistance. How many of you have heard teachers say, "Keep your eyes on your own paper" or "Don't talk with your neighbors"? A cursory review of most grade school report cards gives evidence of this trait: consider such statements as "Johnny is able to work independently," "Mary works well on her own," or "Shaun is a responsible student." Proverbs such as "Too many cooks spoil the broth," "Don't judge a book by its cover," and "God helps those who help themselves" stress this value. Yet, at the same time, girls are encouraged to help others, and teachers often expect that girls will "know what is going on in the class" and otherwise show evidence of social and caring attitudes.

6. *European Americans believe in the mutability of human nature.* That is, they subscribe to the notion that people's nature is relatively easy to change and that people can be molded by their cultural environment. This belief underlies the assimilationist ideology that has pervaded American public education for so many years. "A stranger is only a friend you haven't met yet" and "Leaders are made, not born" may reflect this notion. Girls, however, are more likely to be protected from strangers and less likely to be encouraged to take "leadership" roles. One of the reasons given for single-sex education, for example, is that in an all-girl class or school, girls have more opportunity to practice leadership roles.

One of the results of such socialization practices is that a middle-class European American boy often attributes success to effort and skill and attributes failure to external factors. A middle-class European American girl is more likely to attribute success to luck and attribute failure to a lack of effort. Both boys and girls from lower socioeconomic groups, who may also be members of ethnic minority groups, more often attribute failure at a task to lack of ability.

Gender and School Rules

Interestingly, the *rules* within school cultures often stress values associated with "feminine" behavior, which are quite different from the values associated with the larger society for which children are theoretically being prepared. LeCompte suggests that there exist baseline conditions that reflect the social and structural demands of schools.[52] Successful students, for example, are expected to:

1. learn the whole range of tasks presented to them rather than selecting those which are of interest
2. learn in particular ways; for example, through the written word rather than orally
3. learn from and be evaluated by adults
4. obey school personnel
5. be task oriented
6. delay gratification of desires in order to win later rewards

In short, children are expected to be relatively passive, obedient, industrious, and malleable, all of which are traits positively associated with girls. In part because of the disjunction between school rules and the overarching societal values of independence and competition, the socialization patterns of schooling are more difficult for boys than for girls because boys tend to receive conflicting messages. Girls (at least middle-class European American girls), on the other hand, tend to fit in to school rules more easily, in part because these rules reflect basic family socialization patterns.

Perspectives on Gender and Sexuality

Although the number of sexually active teenagers is lower than it was ten or fifteen years ago, it is still very high, and the United States has the highest teen pregnancy and birthrates in the industrialized world. The likelihood of sexual activity among teens increases with age: more than half of seventeen-year-olds are sexually active; of these, three-quarters report that their first experience was voluntary, and one-quarter report that it was unwanted.[53]

While we might like to believe that these issues are not part of everyday life in school, we would be wrong. Sexual images are all around us, most with very specific "criteria" for how males and females should look, feel, want, and need. In addition, the increase in AIDS cases among both the homosexual and heterosexual population and the increase in other sexually transmitted diseases means that teenagers are thinking about a great many things besides history, English, math, and science.

Among the most difficult problems facing teachers and students is the relationship between heterosexual and homosexual students. As public awareness of homophobia increases, largely as a result of gay and lesbian activism engendered by the tragedy of AIDS, some professional educators are beginning to consider the need to address issues of homosexuality in schools. Some studies suggest that the more students know about homosexuality, the less homophobic they will be and the more accepting they will be toward homosexual people.[54] However, cognitive knowledge about homosexuality sometimes fails to neutralize deep-seated attitudes of anger and guilt that accompany the issue.[55] Tolerance is also complicated by the gender-related issues that are involved. For example, anger, hostility, and violence are more often directed toward gay men than toward lesbian women, although less physical forms of violence against lesbians, such as losing jobs or being evicted from housing, are common. Furthermore, within the homosexual community, differences in masculine and feminine traits among individuals are wide. The belief that gay men are "feminine" and lesbian women are "masculine" is a stereotype that bears little resemblance to reality, as is reflected by the surprise often expressed by parents, friends, and acquaintances when a person "comes out." Indeed, one of the most difficult aspects of being homosexual in a homophobic society is the separation of sexuality and gender role.

A particularly poignant report was recently published in the newspaper of a small midwestern city. Written by a recent high school graduate who called himself Daniel, this autobiographical statement is telling, both in its genuine pathos and in its demonstration of the power of gender role norms even in today's more liberal society:

I was born in 1979 to a middle-class family that was elated to have a new baby boy brought into the world. My family was very loving and I had a very normal childhood.

At the age of three or four, I began to get little crushes on other boys. I knew that I was different from what society considers to be normal. I never had sexual feelings for these boys because I never knew what sex was. I would instead imagine dancing with them. All around me I saw heterosexual couples kissing and hugging. I began to feel very strange and develop low self-esteem.

As I went through grade school, many of the other kids began to pick on me because they realized that I was different. I would come home and cry because I just wanted to be normal. I tried to befriend everyone I came in contact with. However, because many of my social skills were not in use, others distanced themselves from me. I had a deep loathing for the people of this world. The hate was even greater for myself.

I went into sixth grade and many of the other kids around me started their little boyfriend/girlfriend relationships. I wished I was dead. In art class one day, after being told that I did something wrong, I told the art teacher that I wanted to kill myself. She made me speak with the guidance counselor at the junior high. Through these sessions, we never got anywhere. I wasn't about to tell anyone why I was really hurting.

My summer between sixth and seventh grade was the most traumatic summer up until that point. I would get rushed to the hospital frequently because I was having severe stomach and chest pains. I thought I had AIDS because I knew I was gay.

On to junior high, a child slowly changing into an adult. My body was changing, my voice was getting deeper and I was developing acne. Could life get any worse? I saw all of these kids who thought that they were in love around me holding hands, kissing and sharing what they did over the weekend. I started making up stories about my invisible girlfriends from other schools. I still got teased though. Sometimes people would be very blatant and ask me if I was gay. Of course, I said, "No."

The first time that I actually heard the scientific word "homosexual" was in eighth-grade science. At the time, I made fun of the teacher for teaching it because I didn't want everyone to know that I was one. It was also in eighth grade that a neighbor noticed that I was very depressed. She decided to take me to her church. At the church, I was very happy.

My entire life began to revolve around this church. Although everyone thought that I was a very "good little boy," I had my deep, dark, horrible secret. I thought that if I prayed hard enough, I would be "healed" of this awful affliction. I grew very sad. I didn't get "healed." Each week when it came time to share a prayer request, I mentioned an unspoken request. No one ever knew what it was.

It came time for me to go to high school. I met the first gay person I had ever come into contact with. He was an old, gray-haired, overweight man with a very annoying lisp. I really began to hate myself. I thought that all gay men became like this when they got older. I did not want to be like this. I wanted to lead a normal life.

To gain attention, I began to make up this big whopper of a story about how the doctors found a large tumor on my brain. I finally was found out by my pastor and church. All of the people who knew me were very disappointed in me. No one knew why I lied. I greatly regret it. This was to be the end of lying to myself and to others. I now felt as if I should tell the truth.

I began by telling one of my best friends that I was bisexual. I felt like a weight had been lifted off of my shoulder. She was very accepting. I finally could be understood.

I did not plan on telling anyone else. However, I was "outed" when my friend's boyfriend found a letter and showed it to some of his friends. Now everyone knew my deep, dark secret. People whispered about me and as I walked down the halls, I received horrible remarks and got some very bad looks. At this point, I wanted to kill myself.

As the week progressed, many people approached me and told me that they admired me for the courage to "come out." I felt awful because I never had this "courage" that they spoke of. If it had been my choice, no one would have known.

My pastor's wife approached me one Sunday after I had finally decided to return to church and asked if what she had heard was true. I couldn't bring myself to say "yes," so I lied. She said that she was glad that I wasn't *that* way. She went on to say that the church would not want someone living in such a sin to be there. I was devastated, and since that very moment, I have not and will not ever return to that church again.

I still feel the pain that was inflicted upon my heart, but I am slowly healing. In coming out, I gained many new friends. I also lost many friends. Some people have chosen to hate me even though they have no reason. I sometimes get called names and often have people telling me that my "choice" to be homosexual is wrong. I would never understand why someone would choose this kind of lifestyle. I could not wish this on my worst enemy. The desire to be "normal" will always exist in the back of my mind.

My family is slowly dealing with the whole issue. It must be very hard for them as it was very hard for me to accept myself. I feel much better that I am no longer living a lie. [56]

Another story, told by a teacher, also illustrates the point and supports Daniel's experience:

I was once asked by a teacher in a suburban high school to give a guest presentation on male roles. She hoped that I might help her deal with four boys who exercised extraordinary control over the other boys in the class. Using ridicule and their status as physically imposing athletes, the four wrestlers had succeeded in stifling the participation of the other boys, who were reluctant to comment in class discussions.

As a class, we talked about how boys got status in that school and how they were put down by others. I was told that the most humiliating put-down was being called a "fag." The list of behaviors that could elicit ridicule filled two large chalkboards; the boys in the school were conforming to rigid, narrow standards of masculinity to avoid being called a fag. I, too, felt this pressure and became very conscious of my mannerisms in front of the group. Partly from exasperation, I decided to test the seriousness of these assertions. Since one of the four boys had some streaks of pink in his shirt, and since he had told me that wearing pink was grounds for being called a fag, I told him that I thought *he* was a fag. Instead of laughing, he said, "I'm going to kill you."

He obviously didn't and, in retrospect, I think that what I said was inappropriate. But, in that moment, I understood how frightening it is for a boy to have his masculinity challenged, and I realized that the pressure to be masculine was higher than I ever would have expected. This was, after all, a boy who was a popular and successful athlete, whose masculinity was presumably established in the eyes of his peers; yet because of that single remark from me, he experienced a destruction of his self-image as a male.[57]

It is very clear that the culture of the school is overwhelmingly heterosexist. Butler and Byrne suggest that teachers decrease levels of homophobia by using gender-free terminology such as *partners* and *persons* instead of *husband, wife, boyfriend,* and *girlfriend;* by systematically interrupting homophobic comments, such as Tom Littleton did in the case study; by overtly using homophobic misinformation to encourage students to use critical thinking; and by using educational materials that do not assume that all students are heterosexual.[58] Remember that homophobia is learned behavior; it can be unlearned as well.

Ethical Issues

Clearly, there are many ethical issues involved in the consideration of gender and sexual orientation in the classroom. One important issue has to do with the degree to which all students, regardless of their beliefs and attitudes, are encouraged to be open, reflective, and critical thinkers. Children and adolescents are all in various stages of physical, intellectual, and moral development. It is unwise and unfair for teachers either to impose their own judgments on students or to differentially favor those students whose beliefs and attitudes are most nearly like their own. Rather, students should be enabled and encouraged to discuss all aspects of these issues in a context of thoughtful inquiry.

A second and related issue is the degree to which such inquiry may place students in direct conflict with the values of their families and/or the communities in which they live. A great deal of judgment should be exercised by teachers in this regard, particularly when the family and community context is fairly rigid. It is quite possible for teachers to insist on an equitable set of language and behaviors while still recognizing and affirming contrary beliefs. To do otherwise is to set up a climate of "political correctness" that usually does more harm than good and does not do anything at all to promote self-reflection or inquiry.

While equity as a value is consistent with democracy, so is pluralism. In a society as diverse as the one in the United States, it is not possible—nor is it useful—to insist on a single set of attitudes, beliefs, and values. Rather, the role of the school should be to help students negotiate differences, to understand their origins, and to appreciate what is valuable about them. One of the goals of a collaborative classroom is to nurture *both* similarities and differences among people by enabling them to work together in ways that benefit everyone.

Summary

In this chapter, the importance of gender role socialization to a person's identity is explained through discussion of the ways in which children learn to "become" members of a gender group. The part played by the school and by teachers, administrators, and other adults as socialization agents is also discussed, as is the particular *type* of socialization—generally middle class—exercised by the school and the relation of that socialization to mainstream American values.

It is proposed that traditional gender role stereotypes are both harmful and changing. Indeed, it is the very *change* in the nature of gender roles, as exemplified by Title IX, that is likely to cause some difficulties for students and teachers. In the same way, it is proposed that collaborative classrooms are particularly good vehicles for engendering understanding among both male and female students.

Finally, the issue of sexuality is addressed, in part as a studentwide phenomenon—at least in middle and high schools—and in part in terms of an increasing need to attend to issues raised by students who are gay and lesbian and to issues created by the relations between homosexual and heterosexual students.

Chapter Review

Go to the Online Learning Center at **www.mhhe.com/Cushner4e** to review important content from the chapter, practice with key terms, take a chapter quiz, and find the web links listed in this chapter.

Key Terms

Dominant culture   292
Gender role socialization   291
Gender role stereotyping   296
Gender-sensitive   283

Genderized traits   297
Homophobia   297
Misogyny   297
Normative   296

Pseudoscience   279
Task specialization   287

Reflective Questions

As Tom Littleton reads his journal, he probably asks himself some of the follow
in Tom's place, and think about how you would answer these questions.

1. Both competition and individualism are deeply held values in American society. Have _
   collaboration in a way that omits these values from the students' lives or in a way that weaves them
   together?
2. All people need to feel that they belong, that they have a reliable sense of alliance with others. Has
   this class fostered such feelings?
3. The culture of some students centers on individualism and the culture of others centers on a collective
   spirit. Is there a balance here? For example, are students given enough opportunity to be assessed
   individually as well as in groups?
4. Have I gone too far with Rebecca in stressing equity for girls? Have I put her in a position where she
   feels she has to choose between her community's emphasis on the male and my encouragement of her
   individual talents? How can I help her bridge these two sets of values and still maintain her family's
   trust in me?
5. To what extent has the collaborative structure of this class resulted in individual learning for all students?
   How can I measure that? How can I be sure that real learning is going on for everyone?
6. I can't keep all these students together with me all day or for the rest of their schooling. How are they
   doing, and how will they do, in more traditional classrooms that stress competition and individual
   performance? Is this class just a unique experience that will fade from memory as they get older?

It is obvious that Tom can have few definitive answers for these questions, but the fact that he asks them
is important. He clearly believes that a collaborative classroom is both necessary and valuable. Yet he
knows that this approach to schooling is not shared by everyone, either in the school or outside it. The
decisions he makes as he thinks about these issues are always tempered by what he knows about his
school and his community. Still, he will probably continue to modify and improve his approach, knowing
also that change is incremental and does not come all at once. It is a great challenge.

References

1. Several elements of this case study, in particular the land discovery project, are adapted from the real experience of Bill Elasky and his students at Amesville Elementary School in Amesville, Ohio, and Dan Bisaccio and his students at Thayer Junior/Senior High School in Winchester, New Hampshire. Both are described in George Woods, *Schools That Work* (New York: Penguin Books, 1992). Elements of Gypsy education are taken from *The First S.T.E.P. (Systematic Training and Early Prevention) Program,* prepared by Sam Chandler and Rebecca Boglione, Tacoma Public Schools, 1992.

2. Milton Olson, "Lessons from Geese."

3. See, for example, Carol Gilligan, *In a Different Voice* (Cambridge, MA: Harvard University Press, 1982); and Nel Noddings, *Caring* (Berkeley: University of California Press, 1984).

4. See M. F. Belenky, B. Clinchy, N. Goldberger, and J. Tarule, *Women's Ways of Knowing: The Development of Self, Voice, and Mind* (New York: Basic Books, 1986); and B. M. Clinchy, M. F. Belenky, N. Goldberger, and J. Tarule, "Connected Education for Women," *Journal of Educational Thought* 167, 3 (1985).

5. John I. Goodlad, *A Place Called School: Prospects for the Future* (New York: McGraw-Hill, 1984), p. 45.

...cer Kagan, "The Structural Approach to Coop-...ve Learning," *Educational Leadership* 47, 4 ...989/1990):12–15.

7. R. E. Slavin, *Cooperative Learning: Theory, Research, and Practice* (Englewood Cliffs, NJ: Prentice Hall, 1990).

8. David W. Johnson and Robert T. Johnson, *Learning Together and Alone* (Englewood Cliffs, NJ: Prentice Hall, 1987).

9. Slavin, *Cooperative Learning,* p. 12.

10. Ibid., p. 39.

11. Sudia Paloma McCaleb, *Building Communities of Learners* (New York: St. Martin's Press, 1994).

12. R. Greenspan, J. H. Niemeyer, and D. Seeley, *Principals Speak: Report #2, Parent Involvement* (New York: Research Foundation of City University of New York, 1991).

13. J. Cummins, *Empowering Minority Students* (Sacramento: California Association for Bilingual Education, 1989).

14. Charles Fowler, "Strong Arts, Strong Schools," *Educational Leadership* 52, 3 (November 1994): 4–5.

15. Natalie Nielsen, "Aligning Assessment with Learning Goals,"American Association for the Advancement of Science, Eisenhower National Clearinghouse. Available at http://www.enc.org/topics/assessment/testing/document.shtm?input=FOC-001580-index.

16. L. C. Pogrebin, *Growing Up Free* (New York: Bantam Books, 1980).

17. Lenore J. Weitzman, "Sex-Role Socialization," in *Women: A Feminist Perspective,* ed. Jo Freeman (Palo Alto, CA: Mayfield, 1975), p. 109.

18. Florence Howe, "Sexual Stereotypes Start Early," in *Nonsexist Curriculum Materials for Elementary Schools,* ed. Laurie Olsen Johnson (Old Westbury, NY: Feminist Press, 1974), pp. 25–32.

19. Sylvia Kramer, "Sex Role Stereotyping: How It Happens and How to Avoid It," in *Sex Equity in Education,* ed. Anne O'Brien Carelli (Springfield, IL: Charles C. Thomas, 1988), pp. 5–23.

20. See, for example, B. Fagot, "The Influence of Sex of Child on Parental Reactions to Toddler Children," *Child Development* 49, 2, (1978):459–565; S. Dronsberg, B. Fagot, R. Hagan, and M. D. Lleinback, "Differential Reactions to Assertive and Communicative Acts of Toddler Boys and Girls," *Child Development* 56, 6 (1985):1499–1505.

21. For an insightful analysis of the impact of several fairy tale "heroines" on the socialization of children, see Madonna Kolbenschlag, *Kiss Sleeping Beauty Goodbye: Breaking the Spell of Feminine Myths and Models* (New York: Bantam Books, 1981), p. 7.

22. Kramer, "Sex Role Stereotyping," p. 11.

23. "A Report on Children's Toys," in *And Jill Came Tumbling After: Sexism in American Education,* ed. Judith Stacey, Susan Bereaud, and Joan Daniels (New York: Dell, 1974), pp. 123–125. (If you believe that the age of this citation belies contemporary reality, a short trip down the aisles of any large toy store will rather quickly rid you of the notion that toys—and their packaging—have changed a great deal).

24. Ruth E. Hartley, "Sex Role Pressures and the Socialization of the Male Child," in Stacey, Bereaud, and Daniels, *Jill Came Tumbling After,* pp. 186–187.

25. Kathleen Barry, "View from the Doll Corner," in *Women and Education,* ed. Elizabeth S. Maccia (Springfield, IL: Charles C. Thomas, 1975), p. 121.

26. Hartley, "Sex Role Pressures," p. 90.

27. Ibid., p. 91.

28. Robert S. Lynd and Helen Merrell Lynd, *Middletown in Transition* (New York: Harcourt, Brace, 1937), p. 402.

29. Cooper Thompson, "Education and Masculinity." In Anne O'Brien Carelli, ed. *Sex Equity in Education* (Springfield, IL: Charles C. Thomas, 1988), p. 48.

30. Anne O'Brien Carelli, "Introduction," in Carelli, *Sex Equity in Education,* pp. xiii–xv.

31. Jane Roland Martin, *Reclaiming a Conversation: The Ideal of the Educated Woman* (New Haven: Yale University Press, 1985), p. 6.

32. Title IX of the Education Amendments of 1972.

33. Anne O'Brien Carelli, "What Is Title IX?" in Carelli, *Sex Equity in Education,* p. 85.

34. *Grove City* v. *Bell,* 465 U.S. 555 (1984).

35. *Franklin* v. *Gwinnett County Public Schools,* 503 U.S. 60 (1992).

36. "Information on Sexual Harrassment," Equal Educational Opportunity Commission. Available at http://www.de.psu.edu/harassment/legal/supreme.html.

37. *Doe* v. *Petaluma Unified School District*, 54 F. 3d 1447 (1995, 9th Cir.). Available at http://www.equal-rights.org/about/cases.html.

38. "Beyond Title IX: Gender Equity Issues in Schools" (Chevy Chase, MD: The Mid-Atlantic Equity Center; and Andover, MA: The NETWORK, 1993). Available at http://www.maec.org/beyond.html.

39. "Title IX: A Sea Change in Gender Equity in Education," U.S. Department of Education (1997). Available at http://www.ed.gov/pubs/TitleIX/part3.html.

40. Richard W. Riley, "Introduction," in "Title IX: 25 Years of Progress," U.S. Department of Education (1997). Available at http://www.ed.gov/pubs/TitleIX/ part1.html.

41. "Indicators of Progress toward Equal Educational Opportunity since Title IX," U.S. Department of Education (1997). Availabe at http://www.ed.gov/pubs/TitleIX/part2.html.

42. *Shortchanging Girls, Shortchanging America* (Washington, DC: American Association of University Women Educational Foundation, 1991).

43. *The AAUW Report: How Schools Shortchange Girls* (Washington, DC: American Association of University Women Educational Foundation, 1992).

44. Lynn Phillips, *The Girls Report: What We Know and Need to Know about Growing Up Female* (New York: National Council for Research on Women, 1998), pp. 55–56.

45. *Hostile Hallways: The AAUW Survey on Sexual Harassment in America's Schools* (Washington, DC: American Association of University Women Educational Foundation, 1993); *Growing Smart: What's Working for Girls in Schools* (Washington, DC: American Association of University Women Educational Foundation, 1995); *Girls in the Middle: Working to Succeed in School* (Washington, DC: American Association of University Women Educational Foundation, 1996); and *The Influence of School Climate on Gender Differences in the Achievement and Engagement of Young Adolescents* (Washington, DC: American Association of University Women Educational Foundation, 1996).

46. Phillips, *The Girl Report.*

47. *Growing Smart.*

48. Phillips, *The Girls Report,* p. 70.

49. *¡Si, Se Puede! Yes, We Can: Latinas in School* (Washington, DC: American Association of University Women Educational Foundation, 2000); *Separated by Sex: A Critical Look at Single-Sex Education for Girls* (Washington, DC: American Association of University Women Educational Foundation, 1998); and *Tech-Savvy: Educating Girls in the New Computer Age* (Washington, DC: American Association of University Women Educational Foundation, 2000).

50. See, for example, "Boys to Men: Emotional Miseducation." *American Psychological Association Monitor Online* 30, 7 (July–August 1999). Available at http://www.apa.org/monitor/julaug99/youth.html. See also James Garbarino, *Lost Boys: Why Our Sons Turn Violent and How We Can Save Them* (New York: Free Press, 1999); Daniel J. Kidlon et al., *Raising Cain: Protecting the Emotional Life of Boys* (New York: Ballantine, 1999); and William S. Pollack, *Real Boys: Rescuing Our Sons from the Myths of Boyhood* (New York: Henry Holt, 1998).

51. Larry Samover, Richard Porter, and Nemi Jain, *Understanding Intercultural Communication* (Belmont, CA: Wadsworth, 1981).

52. M. Lecompte, "The Civilizing of Children: How Young Children Learn to Become Students," *Journal of Thought* 15, 3 (1980):105–128.

53. "Statistics on Teens and Sexuality," Planned Parenthood of Chester County. Available at http://www.plan4it.org/education/statisticsonteens.html#sexualactiv.

54. Joel W. Wells and Mary L. Franken, "University Students' Knowledge about and Attitudes toward Homosexuality," *Journal of Humanistic Education and Development* 26, 2 (December1987).

55. Kurt E. Ernulf and Sune M. Innala, "The Relationship between Affective and Cognitive Components of Homophobic Reaction," *Archives of Sexual Behavior* 16, 6 (1987).

56. *The Akron Beacon Journal,* 5 January 1998, p. A6.

57. Cooper Thompson, "Education and Masculinity," in Carelli, *Sex Equity in Education,* p. 47.

58. Karen L. Butler and T. Jean Byrne, "Homophobia among Preservice Elementary Teachers," *Journal of Health Education* 23, 6 (September–October 1992): 357–358.

Creating Developmentally Appropriate Classrooms
The Importance of Age and Developmental Status

The blunt fact is that the American high school was designed for fifteen- to eighteen-year-olds who were children only beginning their journey to adulthood. It is now filled with young adults of the same age. One does not have to subscribe to a Freudian theory of human development to accept the sharp distinction between the years before and after sexual development. And likewise, one does not need to be a professional psychologist to recognize that the way in which one deals with a prepubescent youngster is quite different from the way in which one deals with one in the early states of puberty.

—Leon Botstein

Much of the story of human development must be written in the light of cultural influences in general and of the particular persons, practices, and paraphernalia of one's culture. And chief among these, of course, in any complex culture will be such educational institutions as apprenticeships or formal schools.

—Howard Gardner

C h a p t e r O u t l i n e

1.   How can culture, and schooling, affect students' development?

2.   Are there really stages in children's and adolescents' development? If so, are some of those stages critical?

3.   How do teachers determine what is developmentally appropriate for their students?

4.   How can teachers reconcile demands for educational performance standards and accountability with the goal of education for understanding?

case study   **Age in Developmentally Appropriate Classrooms**

It was a coincidence that Sally Dougherty and Tony Stuart—both recent graduates of the same midwestern university—were hired in the same month at Garfield Elementary School in Asheville, West Virginia.[1] What was not a coincidence was that both Sally and Tony had wanted to come back to the Appalachian Mountains where they had been born.

Settled in waves of people moving westward, Appalachia is ordinarily defined as a set of 397 counties in twelve states, running from southern New York to Mississippi, with a population of some 18 million people. Its population has been comprised predominantly of a mixture of English, German, Welsh, Scots-Irish, and French who, on their arrival, met major civilizations of Iroquois and Shawnee in the north and Creek, Cherokee, Choctaw, and Chickasaw in the south.

Historically, Appalachia has been a hiding place for Native Americans, runaway slaves, and whites escaping from indentured servitude in the early colonies as well as from privation and persecution in Europe. Long cut off from the rest of the world by geography, traditional conservatism, economic hardship, and fear, the people of Appalachia have developed a culture that values kinship, independence, and tradition. They tend to distrust and avoid involvements with major social institutions like church, state, and schooling. Strangers are often regarded as suspect or with disinterest, including all those outsiders who in recent years have descended upon the area in an effort to "fix" it.

Sally and Tony, however, were not outsiders. They knew that out of the pride of independence (some might say the curse of individualism) and the nature of poverty has come a people who are accustomed to making do or doing without, whose experience with the outside world has been largely one of repeated disappointment, who refer to themselves proudly as "highlanders" or "mountain people" and who have produced beautiful folk art in wood carvings, quilts, dulcimer and fiddle music, baskets, and pottery. Indeed, it was because of their sense of loyalty to and admiration for the people and places in which they had grown up that the two young teachers wanted to return to bring the best education they had to offer to a new generation of mountain children.

Garfield Elementary School, with about 350 children in grades K–8, is typical of many elementary schools in the region. Constructed of cement block, it was built in 1968 as part of an effort to "modernize" education. It has twelve classrooms painted in pastel colors, tiled floors, a cafeteria with a kitchen, a library, modern restrooms, dependable heating, and adequate lighting. It serves a number of surrounding communities, has about a 10 percent absentee rate, and has a low budget for books and materials. About 40 percent of its children qualify for free lunches. Most teachers in the school have been there for twenty to twenty-five years, and many are ready to retire. Indeed, that both Sally and Tony were hired at the same time reflected the fact that several teachers had retired the previous June.

Other changes had occurred before they came as well, perhaps the most important one being the conversion two years previously of the sixth, seventh, and eighth grades into a middle school housed in the same building as K–5. While Sally was hired to teach kindergarten, Tony had been hired to teach music to the sixth, seventh, and eighth graders. Although they had known one another slightly in college, neither Sally nor Tony realized that they were going to be teaching in the same school until the week before school began, when they met at the trash bins behind the school. Each was there on the first possible day, getting their rooms ready for the first day of school.

Surprised and excited by their meeting, the two neophyte teachers compared notes.

"I've been planning all summer for this," confided Sally. "I didn't get to see much of the place when I came to be interviewed, but I wanted to get here early so I could arrange my room the way I wanted it. Come and see!"

She practically dragged Tony to her classroom, where she was beginning to organize furniture into activity centers like those she had used in student teaching. Already discernible was a block area, with several kinds of blocks for construction; a part of the room for active games and other large muscle activity; a science center, with a terrarium; an area for counting, sorting, and measuring; a listening center; and also a quiet area, where children could stretch out with picture books. "I had hoped to have a computer and a sand table," she said, "but maybe I can figure out how to get those later. At least I have a sink in my room for cleaning up after painting, washing hands, and getting water for our classroom pets."

Not to be outdone, Tony was also eager to show off his room. One of the first at their university to graduate with licensure in middle childhood, Tony knew that the whole concept of middle school had been devised in part to allow young people more time to explore before committing themselves to futures foreordained by the type of curriculum they chose to pursue. For this reason, there were a lot of things to explore in Tony's room. He had arranged the usual chairs in a semicircle at one end of the room for choral rehearsals and singing, thereby leaving the rest of the rather large room available for bookshelves, tables, and—his pride and joy—a large workbench on which were tools and materials for making and repairing musical instruments.

"I got a lot of these from my grandfather," he explained, pointing to the tools. "He makes both hammered and lap dulcimers and knows just about everything there is to know about mountain music. I'm going to have him come in several times this year and help teach the kids how to play and repair them."

"That's great!" exclaimed Sally. And then, thinking about her own situation, she asked, "Is that part of your curriculum? You know, I didn't get to talk with the principal

about the philosophy of the school, and my *curriculum is certainly laid out without a lot of room for extra stuff!"*

"Well, I'm supposed to do both vocal and instrumental music, and many of these kids are already familiar with the sound of dulcimers, even if they don't know how to play them. And I thought that both dulcimers and flutes could be good introductions to other stringed and woodwind instruments. And the songs of the mountains are also familiar, and I hope they'll get the kids interested in other kinds of singing."

"Sounds good to me," said Sally as she left to go back to her room. But she was thoughtful. I wonder what these folks will think about "developmentally appropriate practice," she said to herself as she thought about the district's goals, which were clearly spelled out for the subjects comprising the kindergarten curriculum, the scope and sequence of which left little to the teacher's, or the children's, imagination.

On the first day of school it was hard to tell who was more excited, Sally and Tony or the new kindergartners. In the kindergarten room, there were a few difficult separations and some tears. Although several of the children had had preschool experience, most had not, and today was their first introduction to "the school." Familiarizing herself with background information that was available, Sally had learned that four of the boys were "late starters" whose kindergarten entry had been delayed based on readiness testing. She wondered fleetingly whether the tests had been accurate assessments. During her student teaching experience, she had witnessed an incident in which a young boy had failed a reading readiness test, although he was fully able to read, because the teacher had never used workbooks or dittos and her students had not had much practice in what she called "the skills test makers want—filling in small dots, sitting for hours, etc." When the teacher had gone to the administrator with samples of the boy's work and the books he was reading in class, the administrator had again referred her to the boy's test scores, which indicated that he wasn't even ready to learn to read. When the teacher pointed out that there was no reading on the "reading readiness" test, the administrator retorted that perhaps she should spend more time getting her students ready to read than in having them read!

Looking across the hall at the other kindergarten classroom, Sally saw that Mrs. Conrad had already passed out worksheets to the quietly waiting children seated around five rectangular tables. She also saw a gaily decorated but otherwise empty bulletin board with the words GOOD WORK *at the top ready to receive the children's efforts. Principal Wilson had told Sally that Mrs. Conrad would be a good mentor for her. "She's an excellent teacher," the principal had said. "She always has things under control and she has a quiet, friendly manner with the children."*

As she invited her charges to look around their room, Sally spent some time observing them as a group. Three other children, two girls and a boy, had "borderline birthdates," but their parents were adamant that they not be held back. Altogether, the group represented more varied ethnicity than Sally had expected, certainly more than she had experienced in her own elementary schooling. This class included four African American and two Asian American pupils; the latter's families had recently immigrated to the United States. Both were just beginning to speak a little English, and one girl spoke scarcely at all. As Sally quickly learned, this girl was by no means the only child in the group that would be difficult to bring out. And that small boy with the sad expression—David; what could be on his mind?

Meanwhile, in Tony's room was a kind of organized chaos. Because Tony was a "special" teacher, his students came to him on a rotating basis. His first group was seventh graders, scheduled for music three times a week, and they were definitely not yet ready to settle into any kind of routine! Remembering his own alarming entry into puberty, Tony grinned at the interplay between boys and girls. Like most young people at this age, the girls were well ahead of the boys in all domains, though most obviously physical development. And like all preteens and early teens, they came in all shapes and sizes and were at diverse points along the road to being grown up, in every sense. He also knew that some had already tried out "adult" behaviors, including sexual and substance-related ones.

Noticing that the students were all clustered around the workbench, Tony went behind it and began to talk with them about what was on the bench. "Might as well begin where they are," he thought to himself. "Here's where my career begins!"

As the year progressed, Sally's room acquired a variety of children's art work, some of it not perfect by any means, some of it unlike anything anyone had ever seen before, but all of it respected and valued because it had been produced by the children's own imaginations. In one corner was the class fairy-tale museum complete with a gingerbread house, and on a low table was a carousel with photographs of each child riding a horse. By January, there was also a list of rules for the classroom hanging on the wall, developed by the children. Rule 1 was "No smoking," and Rule 2 was "No throwing books at the lights." Mrs. Conrad had commented more than once that the list of rules seemed a little silly, but Sally believed that the room was the children's space as well as hers and that the experience of deciding what rules should be followed by everyone was an important step toward building the sense of community she wanted in her class.

Knowing that play is the young child's work and natural mode of expression, Sally had developed a schedule that balanced child-selected activity in especially arranged interest centers with whole-group circle activities. Following opening circle routines—who was here, who would be helpers, today's weather—she introduced a theme through an intriguing "lesson" based on a story or finger play. Afterward, each child was asked to choose from among various centers where that theme could be pursued in different ways, as Sally became a participant-observer, moving from center to center and encouraging children to explore with different media. As new themes were introduced, centers were changed accordingly, but they always enabled children to have experiences with language and other modes of expression, quantities and physical attributes, cause-effect relationships, social interactions, and other curriculum content appropriate for five-year-olds. Noting what each child chose and how each child played, Sally supported mutual helping and other prosocial behavior, intervening as unobtrusively as possible. Then, bringing the children back to the circle, she returned to the theme, urging them to talk about what they had done, often helping them frame this activity in the form of a story in which each child was an important character.

Tony also was learning about his students, and as he was quick to point out to Sally, he had a much wider age range to deal with than she did. Even in a single class, students' interests and needs were far from uniform. Furthermore, while Tony had anticipated needing to establish his own authenticity (and authority), the students at first had seemed to him to be compliant but apathetic. After the first week they had little apparent interest in either the workbench or any of the other activities he planned. Even their singing of familiar songs had a tendency to be dirge-like. Clearly, he thought, he was failing to connect with their concerns and their priorities.

Toward the end of September, a tragic fire in a cabin up in the hills brought the children, at least temporarily, out of their lethargy. Two children had died in the fire, and one was very badly burned. The family had little money, nothing to wear, and no place to live except with cousins down the road who already had cramped quarters. Help came from all the communities in the school district: a hundred families met to fell trees and raise a new cabin, clothes were provided, and money was collected to tide the family over. But the burned child faced months of hospitalization, and her parents were faced with not only medical bills but also the expenses of traveling back and forth to the city in which she was hospitalized, sixty miles away.

As his students continued to talk about the family's plight, Tony got an idea. Perhaps his classes could raise some money for the family themselves by staging a country music fair, performing in a musical review, and selling space for local musicians and crafts-people to sell their wares. Why not?

When presented with the idea, Tony's classes were excited. He formed a grade 6–8 chorus and organized students into groups to write the review, decide on the music, make costumes and build sets, talk with Principal Wilson and other community leaders about finding space for the fair, write an article for the local newspaper to publicize the event, take orders from craftspeople for booth space, and all the other details that had to be worked out. After two weeks, most of the school was involved one way or another: other middle school teachers were using the event to teach English, social studies, and math, and even Sally's kindergartners were drafted to help paint large pieces of scenery. The event itself was scheduled to be held just before Thanksgiving in a local church.

The students decided to write a pageant about the history of the community, which enabled them to choose from a wide variety of music—colonial church hymns, patriotic anthems, and two hundred years' worth of folk music from many countries that had been adopted and adapted over the years until it became true "mountain music."

Tony found himself stretched to provide enough music history—let alone the music itself—for the students' eager needs. He very quickly learned who in the community could be called upon to help (his own grandfather was, of course, one of the first to be asked), and the project became a community effort. Nearly every minute of Tony's time was devoted to advising, guiding, rehearsing, and teaching his students what they needed to know. Everyone had a job (most had several!), and all the students felt that they were participating in something important.

A number of youngsters truly "came out of themselves" during the weeks before the event. Tony's favorite was a boy named Tim, a diminutive, prepubescent loner who strove mightily to affect a grunge persona. Tim, it turned out, had a talent for limericks that could be set to music. Tim's favorite, his signature piece, went as follows:

My name is Tim Bandles.
I eat lighted candles.
I eat them for lunch,
I eat them in a bunch.
Oh, how I wish they had handles!

This little limerick was the source of much teasing and giggling among his peers, but it also gave Tim something to call his own and, in fact, provided a name for the combined chorus—The Lighted Candles. "That's good!" exclaimed Tony when the students suggested it. "'Light a candle where you are is just what we're all doing."

And they were: when the music fair was all over, Tony's students had raised $5,000 to help the stricken family.

By the end of that first year, both Sally and Tony were tired. Sally still did not have a computer or a sand table, the district curriculum was still confining, and Mrs. Conrad was still using xeroxed work sheets. Tony had a hard time coming up with activities in the second half of the year that were as interesting and exciting as the music fair had been in the first half, and his students were still afflicted with adolescent moods and quick mouths. Still, Sally's students had discovered that school was a happy and productive place to be, that they could, in fact, learn to read, and that first grade was something to look forward to. Tony's students had learned a great deal about the history of Appalachian music and instruments and quite a bit about themselves as caring, collaborating, and capable people, which, as the two teachers agreed, is what developmentally appropriate practice is all about.

Rationale for Developmentally Appropriate Educational Practice

Age is one of the two most obvious dimensions of diversity among human beings, and clearly Sally's kindergartners and Tony's "middlescents" are at very different points on the journey to adulthood. In fact, although Tony's specialization of music education is a multi-age field, his middle school licensure identifies him also as an age-specialist, as is Sally (whose licensure in fact qualifies her to teach children from preschool to Grade 3). Both these novice teachers were fortunate in being assigned to children of an age group, and within a cultural context, for which they felt a particular affinity. The teachers also recognized that, those commonalities notwithstanding, each of their students was a unique person making her or his own way along that journey to adulthood.

During the twentieth century, patterns of schooling were radically influenced by increased knowledge of distinctive phases of human development. A striking example was the emergence of junior high schools in the 1920s and 1930s, a trend greatly influenced by G. Stanley Hall's child study movement. Based on questionnaires, interviews, and teacher observations, Hall had argued that early adolescence is a particularly vulnerable and malleable period and that schooling for that age group ought to be quite different from that provided in high schools. The attempt to apply what is known about children's development to school organization is even more sharply reflected in today's middle schools as well as in primary schools and early childhood centers. In brief, **developmentally appropriate practice (DAP)** involves providing learning environments, instructional content, and pedagogical practices that are responsive to the major attributes and salient needs and interests that characterize a given life period in order to facilitate continuing developmental progress.

Developmentally Appropriate Practice

Whatever learners of a given age and stage may have in common, however, the principle of developmentally appropriate practice recognizes both each child's uniqueness and the diversity of the social and cultural contexts that affect children's socialization. This recognition is captured in the following definition:

Developmentally appropriate practices result from the process of professionals making decisions about the education and well-being of children based on at least three important kinds of information or knowledge:

1. *what is known about child development and learning*—knowledge of age-related human characteristics that permits general predictions within an age range about what activities, materials, interactions, or experiences will be safe, healthy, interesting, achievable, and also challenging to children;

2. *what is known about the strengths, interests, and needs of each individual child in the group* to be able to adapt for and be responsive to inevitable individual variation; and

3. *knowledge of the social and cultural contexts in which children live* to ensure that learning experiences are meaningful, relevant, and respectful for the participating children and their families.

Furthermore, each of these dimensions of knowledge—human development and learning, individual characteristics and experiences, and social and cultural contexts—is dynamic and changing, requiring that early childhood teachers remain learners throughout their careers.[2]

Economic Aims for Schooling

Leon Botstein, president of Bard College, offers the "modest proposal" of replacing the American high school and ending secondary education with what is now the tenth grade! If schooling were more *age-appropriate,* he argues, it could be more efficient as well as far more effective. While his argument is essentially for faith in the potential of the American educational system—for "the language of hope"—his critique of what's wrong with the system essentially concerns developmentally inappropriate curriculum and pedagogy. "The challenge," he writes, "is to find ways to engage the early onset of adolescence and its attendant freedoms and habits."[3] Botstein maintains that if we are able to do that and to also capitalize on the learning potential of younger children, what today's eighteen-year-olds have imperfectly learned most students can master by age sixteen, when they can move on to postsecondary academic or technical preparation.

National Education Goals

The currently high profile of early childhood education can be attributed to a combination of factors, not the least of which is mounting evidence of the critical importance of early educational experiences. Recognition of such evidence was reflected in Goal 1 identified by the National Education Goals Panel that, by the year 2000, all American children will enter school "ready to learn."[4] While there is evidence of progress in reducing the glaring discrepancies in participation in quality preschool programs between high- and low-income families, no one would assert that that goal has been achieved, especially for the one child in five who lives in poverty. Moreover, as the Children's Defense Fund 2001 report, *The State of America's Children,* stresses, the discrepancy persists when children enter school, reflected in "the dramatic disparity in resources provided to the poorest children."[5] Kozol depicted this disparity as reflecting *"savage inequalities"* in the educational opportunities provided in American schools.[6]

Some early-twentieth-century Progressive reformers had considered kindergarten "the one thing needful" to redress societal inequities and equalize opportunity; and the growth, since the 1960s, of prekindergarten programs has arguably been directed toward that same goal. Yet, despite the call for all children to have access to developmentally appropriate preschool programs as an important means for achieving the goal of entering school "ready to learn," do educators attempting to meet this goal face a danger of placing developmentally *inappropriate* cognitive, perceptual-motor, and social-emotional demands on young children?

Concerned observers cite two sources of danger. The first is an economic view of educational aims, that is, the view that the major purpose of schooling is to prepare students for the workforce. The second, and related, concern emerges from higher education, which now enrolls many students who might not have gone on to college but have found that a college degree is required for an increasing number of jobs. Such a view begins with the business community and the professorate, and the sequence of attribution goes something like this: employers concerned about workers' literacy skills, and professors concerned about students' "readiness" for college work, blame high school teachers, who attribute responsibility to junior high and middle school teachers for failing to prepare students for the rigors of concentrated academic study. Those teachers in turn think intermediate-level instruction must have been weak, for students lack grounding in the basics (mathematical operations, paragraph construction, reading for meaning, etc.), but those problems, alas, are the fault of primary instruction. The ultimate blame doesn't stop with the kindergarten teacher (who ought to better ensure children's readiness for first grade), it gets passed on to parents. If the ultimate goal is international competitiveness and if American graduates fare poorly when compared to their counterparts in other industrialized nations, one kind of logic argues for "more! earlier! faster!" And that logic inevitably, as advocates for young children maintain, results in inappropriate practices that actually impede children's development in the attempt to accelerate it.

Early Childhood Education and Developmentally Appropriate Practice

Although the principle is relevant to all levels of schooling, *developmental appropriateness* emerged as a particular concern in the rapidly growing field of early childhood education. As New and Mallory summarize, the resulting publication of the National Association for the Education of Young Children (NAEYC), *Developmentally Appropriate Practice,* was—like many other reform ideas—an important political statement:

> The NAEYC effort was motivated primarily by the need to respond to the increasingly pervasive pressure for early childhood programs to conform to an academic model of instruction typical of programs designed for older children. Throughout the document, there is also evidence of the intent to advocate for the field's long-standing core values of respect for and nurturing of young children as among the necessary means to achieve the democratic goals of a just and compassionate society.[7]

Constructivist Thought in Developmentally Appropriate Practice

Cognitive Development Theories

Developmentally appropriate practice, or DAP, is not itself a theory of education (or of child development); it reflects a tradition of child pedagogy that, while centuries old, gained scientific support largely because of Jean Piaget's highly influential theory of cognitive development. Thus, appropriate practice in early childhood education is often described as based on, or at least congruent with, *cognitive developmental theory,* especially Piagetian theory. Also reflecting the *social constructivist* theory of Lev Vygotsky, DAP is clearly congruent as well with the ideas of cross-cultural psychology, which posits that the ways in which individuals construct their worlds are influenced by cultural factors. Williams describes the pedagogical implications of the theoretical orientation intended by the term *constructivism* in this way:

> Children are understood to be active constructors of their own knowledge. Mental activity is enhanced by wide experience with people, materials, and events, through which children form concepts and develop perceptions. Children's skills also are refined through repeated experience. Curriculum is therefore expected to provide multiple opportunities for children's direct and concrete engagement. This view of children's learning places the locus of control of the process within children themselves. Adults are not the pivotal factor in the process. They can provide a conducive setting, but it is the children's inner structures that impel them to learn.[8]

Activity 5: Childhood Experiences

The word *structure* in this context refers to the concepts, ideas, and understandings that children *construct* through their transactions with their social and physical environment. Some scholars call this a *frame,* or a *lens,* or—after Vygotksy—a *scaffold,* but all agree that it is through this construction that individuals filter information and make sense of the worlds in which they live.

Thus, from a **constructivist perspective,** knowledge is "made" by the knower, who (to use Piaget's terms) *assimilates* new experiences within knowledge structures already present and *accommodates* to experiences that do not fit neatly into those structures. Imagine the cognitive manipulation that takes place when a small child who knows the class "dog" as four-legged creatures with bushy tails, and so on, encounters a stub-tailed or pointy-tailed dog . . . or a pony! One five-year-old, his family newly arrived in the United States from the English Midlands, revealed cognitive structures unique among a playground group when he inquired about a small sheltie, of "Is that a *dog?* Then why does it look like a *fox?*"

Motivation to learn emerges from the fact that children's **cognitive structures** are continuously challenged, and the child's inherent need to understand—*epistemic curiosity,* in philosophical terms—provides the impetus for acquiring new knowledge. Note that this need to understand is an *internal* motivating factor and is significantly different from such *external* factors as the praise of adults or the awarding of candy and stickers. Since some conditions are more likely than others to elicit that motivation, the teacher's task is to solve "the problem of the match" between what each child is ready, cognitively and motivationally, to learn and what is made available to the child to learn. (Vygotsky called the range of experiences that are sufficiently challenging yet manageable, "the zone of proximal development.")[9]

While the NAEYC's DAP guidelines constitute a virtual manifesto on the unique-ness of the childhood years from birth through the primary level of schooling, both the concept of developmentally appropriate teaching and its underlying constructivist the-ory of learning and knowing are arguably relevant to the instruction of older children, adolescents, and even adults. Many (most?) college students, experiencing a small epiphany of understanding of some concept or idea, remember that it was introduced in a high school course but they "didn't get it" then. Many also remember lack of interest and boredom with material already too familiar.

The constructivist view differs from the traditional notion of readiness—used as a criterion for determining when a child should enter kindergarten, move on to first grade, and so on—in that constructivists emphasize that cognitive readiness is not determined simply by biological maturation, a kind of natural unfolding. It is rather an interactional—better, a *transactional*—matter. At any point in time, every individual is ready to learn, if learning experiences are at an optimal level of novelty or incongruity. Clearly, what is optimal for one learner is not necessarily optimal for another, even among learners of the same age. Though each of us functions within a particular social-cultural context, everyone undertakes as an individual what Havighurst called the *tasks* of development.[10]

Characteristics of a Developmentally Appropriate Classroom

Pedagogies: Old and New

Though they have historical antecedents, constructivist notions gained scientific support and integrity as a coherent theory through the work of Piaget and other theorists, notably Vygotsky and Bruner, both of whom placed greater emphasis than did Piaget on the social-cultural context of children's development.[11]

Constructivist ideas were actually advanced much earlier by a succession of edu-cational theorists and reformers, including Comenius in the seventeenth century, Condillac and Rousseau in the eighteenth, Pestalozzi and Parker in the nineteenth, and Dewey in the twentieth. Sharply critical of the old methods used to teach reading in the schools—memorization based on recitation from the New England Primer—Mann argued that children could best master reading and writing if instruction were guided by, and built on, the language base a child had. (Does that argument sound like today's "new" whole language approach?) Pestalozzi's object teaching emphasized the child's experience and perceptions as the basis for organizing knowledge and developing powers of reasoning—a faculty the educational psychology of his day considered not available to young children!

In Parker's child-centered approach, school subjects and practical arts were cor-related (integrated) as pupils worked eagerly, without coercion or control by the teacher, at their individual and cooperative jobs. In contrast to the traditional *faculty psychology,* which portrayed the mind as comprised of a number of discrete faculties, and pedagogy

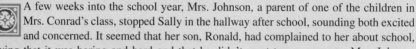

critical incident

The Disgruntled Parent

A few weeks into the school year, Mrs. Johnson, a parent of one of the children in Mrs. Conrad's class, stopped Sally in the hallway after school, sounding both excited and concerned. It seemed that her son, Ronald, had complained to her about school, saying that it was boring and hard and that he didn't want to go anymore. Mrs. Johnson seemed certain that her son's unhappiness in school was related to Mrs. Conrad's reliance on work sheets and excessive seatwork, and the mother was going to ask for a meeting with Principal Wilson to discuss the issue. Mrs. Johnson wondered if Sally might have a talk with the principal with the hope of encouraging Mrs. Conrad to have a greater variety of activities in her teaching.

- If you were Sally, how would you respond to Mrs. Johnson?
- If you were, in fact, called in to speak with the principal, what would you say?

as mental discipline to strengthen them, Parker viewed children's learning as holistic and, like Piaget, inseparable from development. Yet, turn-of-the-century classrooms—with few exceptions, such as Parker's Quincy (Massachusetts) System and Dewey's laboratory school at the University of Chicago, and kindergartens (which were still quite separate from public schools)—were as described by Cuban:

> Generally, teachers taught the entire class at the same time. Teacher talk dominated verbal expression during class time. Classroom activities revolved around teacher questions and explanations, student recitations, and the class's working on textbook assignments. Except for laboratory work in science classrooms, teachers sought uniformity in behavior. The social organization of the turn-of-the-century classroom, then, was formal, with students sitting in rows of bolted-down desks facing the teacher's desk and chalkboard, rising to recite for the teacher, and moving about the room or leaving it only with the teacher's permission. The academic organization of the classroom hinged upon the whole class's moving as one through the course of study, text, recitations, and homework. Those who worked, succeeded; those who didn't, failed.[12]

Does that picture sound familiar to you? Based on his study of American classrooms from 1880 to 1990, Cuban concluded that teacher-centered instruction continued to be the dominant pattern, although at the elementary level, and that in some secondary schools, "a hybrid version of student-centered practices, begun in the early decades of this century, has spread and is maturing."[13] Such practices have included the use of small group organization, activity centers, projects, more provision for student choice, joint teacher-student planning of learning activities, and integration of content.

One fairly mature, and certainly coherent constructivist model that has recently attracted much interest among American educators is the *Reggio Emilia* approach, named for the town in the Emilia Romagna region of northern Italy where it has been developed over about forty years from post–World War II origins.[14] The distinctive qualities of Reggio Emilia include some familiar ideas. Specifically, learning occurs within the context of an emergent curriculum, organized around projects carried out over extended periods of time (determined by children's activity and choice rather than adult-controlled time schedules) that integrate diverse areas of learning and elicit children's expression, in all of their hundred languages,

Reggio Emilia Approaches

> including words, movement, drawing, painting, building, sculpture, shadow play, collage, dramatic play, and music. Leading children to surprising levels of symbolic skills and creativity, the approach takes place not in an elite and sheltered setting of private education, but rather in a municipal system of full-day child care open to all, including children with special needs.[15]

Perhaps the most striking feature of Reggio Emilia may be the most difficult to translate from one cultural setting to another: the view, shared by parents and educators, of the school as an extension of the home. This deeply embedded understanding is a legacy of its origins in a parent cooperative movement that emerged in the region during the years of post–World War II reconstruction. A second distinctive feature perhaps difficult to translate is the valuing, indeed centrality, of artistic expression. Although this approach, like DAP, and the progressive and open education movements, was explicitly designed for preprimary schools (ages three to six) and infant-toddler centers, some of the key concepts would seem valid and applicable with older learners:

- Conscious awareness of the important role of physical space and especially of aesthetic properties of the physical environment in inviting learning
- Not holding students' motivation and accomplishment hostage to the tyranny of the clock, curriculum guide, or textbook
- The importance of true team collaboration, over time, marked by shared ownership of the educational process and continued inquiry on the part of teachers, learners, families, and leaders (principals, supervisors)
- Elimination of artificial compartmentalizations among subjects and between science and the arts, knowledge and creativity, effort and enjoyment
- Trust in and respect for students, expressed through responsibility combined with empowerment, opportunity to work cooperatively as well as independently, and valuing of diverse modes of expression
- A concept of development as a dynamic process rather than static levels

The shift from the traditional junior high to the middle school is another example of DAP being put into practice and uniting an understanding of development of young people with principles of learning. Each age level seems to have a set of characteristics that make it, in a sense, unique from all others, and one of the most marked is that of children who are in the transition between childhood and early adolescence. Whereas administrative organization and grade-level content are often the focus in junior high and secondary schools, in middle schools a focus on broadly defined needs of the learner is fundamental—a focus that encompasses the full range of intellectual as well as social, emotional, and other developmental needs. The challenge of middle school education then is, as the National Middle School Association states, "to develop an educational program that is based on the needs and characteristics of a most diverse and varied population."[16]

Middle Schools

A true middle school, according to the National Middle School Association, will display the following essential elements: (1) educators knowledgeable about and committed to young adolescents; (2) a balanced curriculum based on the needs of young adolescents; (3) a range of organizational arrangements; (4) varied instructional strategies; (5) a full exploratory program; (6) comprehensive advising and counseling; (7) continuous progress for students; (8) evaluation procedures compatible with the nature of young adolescents; (9) cooperative planning; and (10) positive school climate.

Modifying school structures is a continuous process, as communities attempt to respond to perceived local needs. Increasingly, you may find preschool-through-primary age groupings served in early childhood centers, or grades 5 and 6 housed separately from grades 7 and 8, or a return to the junior high model. However, differential organizational structures represent but one way in which schools respond to developmental diversity among students.

Roles: Old and New

Although constructivism (in both its old and new forms) places the student at the center of the learning process and acknowledges that much important learning is done by students entirely on their own or with peers, the teacher's role is of key importance. In the 1997 revision of the NAEYC DAP guidelines, Bredekamp affirms the basic responsibility of teachers as well as the principle that a child's sense of competence and worth is the essential foundation for learning and development:

> The goal is for teachers to support the learning and development of all children. To achieve this goal, teachers need to know children well and use everything they know about each child—including that individual's learning styles, interests and preferences, personality and temperament, skills and talents, challenges and difficulties. Children are more likely to achieve a positive sense of self if they experience more success than failure in the early school years. The teacher must support a positive sense of self-identity in each child.[17]

The one word that best captures the most fundamental change in the teacher's role is *collaboration.* Because the field of early childhood education has been a major influence in bringing about a reexamination of the teacher's role, another look at its history may be instructive.[18]

Soon after Friedrich Froebel's notion of "child-gardening" was brought to America by Margarethe Meyer Schurz in the wake of great German immigration, Elizabeth Peabody described the role of *kindergartner* (the term referred to the kindergarten *teacher*) as a partner and adviser for parents in nurturing young children. Although kindergartens have been around since the mid-nineteenth century, *pre*kindergartens as such have been in existence only about half as long. The common school (not exactly "common," considering that most American children received very little instruction, many none at all) enrolled pupils as young as three years, but they were mixed in with their older brothers and sisters and no provisions were made for early childhood's uniqueness. Nursery schools, like those Margaret MacMillan started for English children of poor families, and kindergartens spread as a facet of the British and American settlement movements, and they had a particular focus on health and nutritional concerns.

History of Kindergarten

Two other important movements fostered the expansion of early childhood education in the United States: child study and mental hygiene. G. Stanley Hall, often called the founder of child psychology, was a key influence in both. He influenced the latter by introducing to American intellectuals and professionals psychoanalytic theories of the formative significance of early childhood experiences (and to Freud himself at the historic conference at Clark University in 1909!). Arnold Gesell, Hall's student, had by 1930 led the growth of nursery education, in his words, "from a no man's land to an every man's land," although of course nursery teachers, like "kindergartners," were invariably women.[19] What Gesell meant was that a broad range of professionals—psychologists, physicians, social workers, public health workers—had become involved. Universities had established laboratory programs, like Gesell's own Guidance Nursery at Yale, as centers for child development research and teacher training. He and other professionals viewed programs for young children as important both in identifying problems early in life so that timely ameliorative measures could be provided and in promoting the healthy development of mind and body.

The Great Depression halted the spread of nursery education, but when the Second World War called multitudes of women to defense industry work, the Lanham Act created another role for such programs—day care. The years since World War II and especially since the 1960s have witnessed an enormous increase in the need for outside-the-home child care in the United States and other nations, and a crisis has developed, certainly for families but also for providers and policy makers. Parents and child advocates insist that child care must be more than custodial, but is it "education"? In the United States, the NAEYC joined forces with other major child advocacy groups such as the Children's Defense Fund in working for policies to ensure that day care is accessible and affordable yet also adheres to high-quality standards of professional nurture and guidance that are in the interests of children and, consequently, of society itself. That is, whether provided in a center or in someone's home, child care must be *developmentally appropriate.*

Children's Defense Fund

Growth in families' need for child care led to new discoveries about young children and, consequently, to a redefinition of adult roles. Conventional wisdom in the burgeoning field of child psychology had held that group experiences were of no value for children until at least age three. But as necessity truly became the mother of invention, caregivers (and psychologists) discovered that toddlers were quite interested in each other, and even babies were, in their fashion, social creatures. Such discoveries implied a *teacher* role (developmentally appropriate) for adults caring for infants and toddlers, and a number of roles (model, partner in parallel play, friend, leader) for very small children themselves. These new roles became ever more influential in the course of children's development through and beyond the early childhood years. Educators who observed the ways young children learn from and with each other sought to reapply Parker's and Dewey's less-teacher-centered concepts through such strategies as *cooperative learning* and small-group activity. From birth through all the years of schooling, *learners* have a central role in their own learning and an instrumental role in the learning of their peers.

Head Start Programs

Early childhood programs, especially Project Head Start and Early Start, emphasize collaborative relationships with families to promote optimal development during the most formative years. The teacher's role has increasingly become a collaborative one in other respects. Rather than being expected to function on their own, teachers can anticipate the support of peers through building-level planning and problem-solving teams and actual team teaching. And, of course, working collaboratively with others—fellow professionals, parents and other family members, and community resource persons—requires a unique set of sensitivities and skills.

Place of Content Knowledge: Old and New

DAP means a change in the place of content knowledge in early childhood education that involves rediscovery of some old wisdom undergirded by new knowledge about human development. What is often called the "cognitive revolution" in American psychology that began in the 1950s and 1960s brought new respect for young children's intellectual resources and for the potential of early childhood programs to influence the course of development. But it also contributed to an unduly narrow emphasis and raised what Piaget called the "American question": How much can we accelerate the pace of cognitive learning in order to create smarter adults?

The discourse concerning DAP is more concerned with *process* than with content, which Spodek attributes to the fact that "early childhood educators are more concerned with the effects of early childhood education on a child's development than with what a child comes to know as a result of that education."[20] What Piaget called "social knowledge" (information)—imparted by parents, teachers, Sesame Street, siblings, and peers—is important, but cognitive development is an active, transactional process, not a passive one. The deductive reasoning basic to mathematical understanding and the inductive questioning that is the hallmark of scientific inquiry are inherent capabilities of young children as they strive to reconcile incongruities and impose structure on their constantly expanding experiential world. In related fashion, literacy learning begins in early childhood—in fact, in earliest infancy—and is fostered to the degree that the child's active and creative use of language, and pleasure in its use, are encouraged.[21] However, to put basal readers or phonics worksheets in the hands of all three-year-olds would be developmentally inappropriate. In the constructivist perspective, learners *generate* content knowledge, not just *receive* it. As Howard Gardner emphasizes, the goal of effective education is not merely transmitting information, but ensuring understanding.[22] Moreover, Gardner emphasizes that since understanding is itself a developmental process—proceeding from sensorimotor, to intuitive, to application of logical reasoning—school instruction must support this progression if learners are ultimately to gain discipline mastery.

Assessment: Old and New

When we consider assessment in the context of learners' developmental status, we need to distinguish different purposes of assessment. Statewide proficiency tests and international comparisons of educational achievement indeed reflect urgent American concerns for accountability and a national effort to identify and maintain educational standards as essential for educational reform. "Setting the bar" higher, some educators argue, will only widen the gap between the more and the less advantaged children and schools. Yet conversely, two decades of research have demonstrated the strong link between expectations and student (and school) performance: *expectancy* becomes a self-fulfilling prophecy.[23] Whatever standards are agreed upon for progression through the educational system and ultimate graduation, there must be some means of assessing the status of individual students in terms of those standards. While it may be imperfectly implemented, assessment is certainly essential to educational accountability.

But assessment of student progress vis-à-vis performance standards should not be confused with sorting, a questionable and potentially invidious use of assessment. In the past, assessment was often used to validate beliefs about limited learning potential of children of poor and low-income families and immigrants, children of color, and children with disabilities. Although inappropriate assessment procedures have also been used to identify which children are ready for school and which ones are not, the DAP guidelines are quite explicit about the responsibility of schools to be ready for all children. As Meisels has said, screening and assessment should never be used to close educational doors for a child, but to open them.[24]

A new view of assessment goes beyond reliance on narrow and fallible tests in linking knowledge about individual learners with instructional planning and decision making. This view is frequently identified by the term *authentic assessment*. Noting the limited value of traditional, norm-referenced assessment procedures with young children, DAP guidelines emphasize the importance of observation of children in natural activity contexts, collections of children's work, and ongoing communication with parents "for the purpose of improving teaching and learning."[25]

To Gardner, with students of any age, understanding can only be meaningfully assessed through opportunities to apply learning to new situations:

> Whereas short-answer tests and oral responses in classes can provide clues to student understanding, it is generally necessary to look more deeply if one desires firm evidence that understandings of significance have been obtained. For these purposes, new and unfamiliar problems, followed by open-ended clinical interviews or careful observations, provide the best way of establishing the degree of understanding that students have obtained.[26]

Perspectives on Age and Development

School experiences both profoundly influence and are influenced by peoples' development as human beings. That statement may seem on the surface so obvious that it scarcely deserves mention. But consider more closely. What is "development," and precisely what implications does it have for learning and teaching in schools? As Shaffer summarizes, "Simply stated, *development* refers to systematic changes in the individual that occur between the moment of conception . . . and the moment the individual dies."[27] You are probably familiar with important concepts involving patterns of change that humans experience over time, such as nature versus nurture, sensitive or critical periods, individual differences, and developmental stages and domains. What implications do such concepts have for schooling?

Sensitive Periods and Developmental Crises

Since critically important systematic changes occur before schooling begins (indeed, from the moment of conception) as well as afterward, it may appear that development proceeds relatively independently of formal education. While the so-called **nature versus nurture debate** has revolved more around what young children experience at home than what older children and youth experience in school, major social programs such as Project Head Start have reflected the belief that education, especially in the early years of life, can indeed alter the course of children's development. And probably most people believe their own lives have been affected in crucial ways by school experiences that occurred at some point in their lives when they were particularly receptive or particularly vulnerable.

While those points of receptivity and vulnerability are to a great extent an individual matter—associated with a major change in an individual's family situation like parental divorce, separation, or death; a person's own or a family member's illness; a move to a new community and a new school; a new friendship; even a certain teacher or coach—some are fairly universal. In Erik Erikson's familiar formulation, the development of *ego identity* is a lifetime enterprise, involving eight stages of psychosocial development, each marked by a conflict to be resolved.[28] The adolescent identity crisis is preceded by successive childhood crises, or turning points, emerging from conflicting influences or needs: basic trust versus mistrust; autonomy versus shame and doubt; initiative versus guilt; industry versus inferiority. Everyone remembers—happily, painfully, or ruefully—their own adolescent years and the changes they brought. For centuries, in fact, adolescence, though not identified as such, was assumed to be the critical period for learning, and schooling often didn't begin until then. Infancy, traditionally the first seven years of life, was accorded little importance.

Clearly, the kinds of experience that are critical will change in the course of development. Yet, as Gardner notes in *The Unschooled Mind,* formal instruction often fails to challenge students to move beyond the *intuitive* modes of knowing that served them well as young children. Matching instruction to the developmental level of learners requires, he reminds us, challenging students to demonstrate understanding by applying knowledge to new situations.[29]

Individual Differences and Developmental Domains

Developmentally appropriate practice is based not only on age and stage differences, but also on another key concept in the psychology of human development: individual differences. Many such differences are culture related, while others are situational, influenced by circumstances in a person's life and quite idiosyncratic. Wide variations, even within cultures, are to some degree attributable to built-in factors, certainly to biological heredity. Gesell, well-known for his detailed descriptions of nearly universal characteristics of infants, children, and youth that are virtually programmed in humans as in other species, asserted, "No two infants were ever born alike."[30] While the nature side of the nature versus nurture debate involves both common (i.e., maturational) and highly idiosyncratic (i.e., hereditary) influences, development involves the subtle interaction of these influences with a host of environmental influences, many cultural and many specific to the individual. All the characteristics or traits that distinguish everyone's unique personality reflect some interactive mix of biological and environmental influences. This impact is true of even some physical attributes, such as skeletal structure, although others (e.g., eye color) are entirely biologically influenced.

Human development proceeds on many fronts, often referred to as developmental domains (e.g., motor, cognitive, language/communication, social/emotional). The notion of domains in some ways involves arbitrary distinctions, for babies, children, youth, and adults are whole beings, not just composites of discrete parts. Language development, for example, is virtually inseparable from cognitive and social development. During the critical period for language acquisition—the first three years of life— language is also mightily influenced by sensory and motor development. But language can be analyzed on the basis of domain-specific concepts (phonology, morphology, syntax, semantics, and pragmatics). Appropriate educational practice requires knowledge of such concepts and patterns of change associated with major domains. It is not developmentally appropriate to expect three-year-olds to cut expertly with scissors or know (in the adult sense) what clouds are; five-year-olds to be physically inactive for extended periods or argue the merits of a bicameral legislature; or ten-year-olds to do grueling labor or solve algebraic equations. Nor is it developmentally appropriate, Gardner reminds us, to fail to challenge learners to apply their developing powers of understanding.

Because milestones, such as first words and independent walking, as well as transitions from one stage to another are reached by different children at different times, it is necessary to be aware of normal ranges of variation in the timing and sequencing of developmental changes. Such variations are attributable to many factors, including gender, geography (e.g., climate), genetics, specific environmental influences, and differential cultural values and expectations. And for some children, such as a child who is blind or one who has cerebral palsy, developmental processes may differ *qualitatively,* rather than quantitatively, from their typical peers. It makes no sense to say, for example, that a child who cannot see has delayed visual development or that a child with cerebral palsy who cannot walk independently has delayed motor development. The first child learns to complement functional vision with other sensory information more than do most children; the second child may accomplish mobility with the aid of adaptive equipment, such as a wheelchair.

The Importance of Developmental Knowledge

What should teachers know about children and adolescents in order for their instruction to be developmentally appropriate? Until the latter half of the nineteenth century, most American and European teachers and school officials knew very little, because not much attention was paid to the unique features of successive stages. In some common schools, children as young as three or four were instructed along with older students, even adolescents, seated on hard benches inappropriate for all, awaiting their turn to recite. Age-grading supplanted such arrangements, however, and though instruction could be more age-appropriate, it rarely took into account individual variations. Pupils who deviated considerably from the norm—who didn't "fit"—presented problems that were addressed through grade repetition or ungraded classes and classes for "unrulies" (forerunners of special education classes, which are discussed in Chapter 11).

The child study movement, while promoting more positive awareness of differential rates of development among children, mainly inspired more age-appropriate practices, such as the introduction of the junior high school. From the child study tradition, through the work of Gesell and his associates, a generation of aspiring teachers who were trained in the 1940s and 1950s also learned about the terrible twos, trusting threes, and general attributes characteristic of successive ages and stages. What they didn't learn about development was the extent to which, and the ways in which, it is influenced by *experience* and the wide variability among children that can be expected within each of the successive stages. Nor did they learn about variability associated with diverse cultural norms, expectations, and values.

Stage theories of human development emphasize the universality of developmental milestones and the manifestations of specific attributes of successive stages. In addition to Gesell's normative descriptions, some well-known theorists have focused on personality development (Sigmund Freud, Anna Freud, Erik Erikson), on cognitive development (Jean Piaget), on language (Noam Chomsky), and on moral development (Lawrence Kohlberg). While many of these aspects of development may emerge in much the same way among the world's children, it is also the case that they may be differentially valued and expressed in different cultural settings.

One instance of culturally different values placed on developmental skills involves the notion of *independence,* or autonomy, and developmental domains labeled on assessment scales as *self-help, adaptive,* or *social-emotional.* Noting aspects of the Reggio Emilia early childhood approach that may be culture-specific, Rebecca New comments on a standard routine that children in American day care centers quickly learn: how to put on one's jacket, when it's time to go home or for outdoor play, by flipping it, arms in sleeves, over one's head. This maneuver may require concentration and involves occasional mistakes, but the pleasure in accomplishment and sense of mastery youngsters experience is apparent in their expression. "Few Italian 2-year-olds have been taught how to put their coats on unassisted," she notes, for "adults . . . enjoy the opportunity to assist children, even as they encourage children to also help one another."[31] This example illustrates a difference in culturally valued independence versus cooperation that is expressed in various ways. What implications do such differences have for developmentally appropriate expectations concerning children?

The concept of Developmentally Appropriate Practice emerged in a political context, with a certain agenda, of establishing consensus concerning the uniqueness of early childhood, defined as the first eight years of life. But developmental appropriateness, at least as defined in DAP, cannot be the sole determinant of *educational* appropriateness, in the early childhood years or beyond. The guidelines as they were originally formulated and generally understood may have been insufficiently responsive to diverse cultural values, a concern addressed in the revised version of DAP. For example, Williams contrasts widely shared Native American traditions of interconnectedness, interdependence, and respectful listening with DAP's original strong emphasis on individualism, independence, and overt expression of language.[32] The constructivism underlying DAP's guidelines has thus been criticized as being ethnocentrically narrow and inadvertently legitimizing social and educational inequities by expressing a preconceived and prescribed version of what is developmentally appropriate.

Responding to a Disgruntled Board Member

Things seemed to take a positive turn for Tony once he and his students began planning for the music program; many of the students seemed to be actively engaged and interested in the program planning and in the variety of preparatory activities that needed to occur. Then one morning, about three weeks before the scheduled program, Tony was called into Principal Wilson's office. One of the members of the school board, a rather influential individual who was quite supportive of the existing school band, had complained that Tony might be setting a bad example for other teachers—especially ones new to the school. While this board member acknowledged that it was of benefit to raise money to assist the family with their expenses, it was pretty clear to him that this activity was outside the standard music curriculum and that it was setting a bad example. And besides, he reasoned, there was a pretty good music curriculum in place that was approved by the state. The Principal wanted to let Tony know of the concern because the board member was coming in to discuss the issue in two days, and he had asked to speak with Tony. The principal asked Tony to think about how he might best present his argument and rationale for the activities in which he and the students were presently engaged.

- If you were Tony, how would you best structure your meeting with the board member?

A broader *social constructivism*, on the other hand, implies a more inclusive and collaborative perspective of educational practices that not only considers family and culture but recognizes their primacy in the lives of children and respects children in both their uniqueness and interconnectedness. In the Reggio Emilia educational approach, for example,

> the child is understood as having not only needs but competencies and rights as well. . . . Implicit in this view is the recognition of the child's embeddedness in a family, a community, a culture, and a society. It is thus the responsibility of the teachers, in active collaboration with parents and other members of the community, to acknowledge and respect those rights, to identify and understand those competencies, and respond collectively to those needs. In order to fulfill this role, teachers in Reggio Emilia become researchers in their own classrooms, regularly making and sharing hypotheses about learning and development rather than reifying existing conceptions.[33]

There are in fact different constructions of what constructivism entails, ranging from those that encompass applied behavior analysis and direct instruction to those that consider *teaching* a dirty word (in the sense that it connotes adult direction and management of children's learning).[34] Exclusive commitment to any doctrinaire approach in teaching risks blinding a teacher to the differences among students at any particular stage of development or level of schooling. In its essence, constructivist teaching recognizes that learning, though it occurs in and is supported by social contexts, is an individual affair. Developmentally appropriate practices are those that respond to each student's uniqueness.

Summary

The concept of developmentally appropriate practice, or structuring an educational program that is sensitive to factors of age and experience, is introduced in this chapter. In particular, the concept of constructivist learning is introduced as a pedagogical approach that integrates both development of the learner and practice of the teacher.

 # Chapter Review

Go to the Online Learning Center at **www.mhhe.com/Cushner4e** to review important content from the chapter, practice with key terms, take a chapter quiz, and find the web links listed in this chapter.

Key Terms

Cognitive structures   322

Constructivist
    perspective   322

Developmentally appropriate
    practice (DAP)   319

Nature versus nurture
    debate   330

Reflective Questions

1. Consider for a moment what it might mean to integrate developmentally appropriate practice into a variety of content-area disciplines. Give an example of developmentally appropriate practice when considering: (a) a physical education class on basketball for students in grades 3, 7 and 10; (b) a social studies class discussion related to the topic of slavery in the United States for children in grades 6 versus grade 10; and (c) basic literacy and reading readiness activities for a class of nonreading six-year-olds compared to a class of nonreading adults in a basic literacy evening class.

2. How does the more recent development of middle schools address developmentally appropriate practice differently than the more traditional junior high schools, even though they both are designed to serve children of similar ages?

References

1. The setting for Garfield Elementary School as well as elements of Sally Dougherty's classroom have been incorporated from a true story related by George Wood about a first grade classroom in southern Ohio in *Schools That Work: America's Most Innovative Public Education Programs* (New York: Penguin Books, 1992), pp. 9–12.

2. Sue Bredekamp and Carol Copple, eds., *Developmentally Appropriate Practice in Early Childhood Programs,* rev. ed. (Washington, DC: National Association for the Education of Young Children, 1997), p. 9.

3. Leon Botstein, *Jefferson's Children: Education and the Promise of American Culture* (New York: Doubleday, 1997), p. 85.

4. National Education Goals Panel, *Profile of 1994–95: State Assessment Systems and Reported Results* (Washington, DC: National Education Goals Panel, 1996).

5. *The State of America's Children: A Report from the Children's Defense Fund, Yearbook 2001.* (Boston, MA: Beacon Press, 2001), p. 62.

6. Jonathan Kozol, *Savage Inequalities: Children in America's Schools* (New York: Crown Publishers, 1991).

7. Rebecca S. New and Bruce L. Mallory, "Introduction: The Ethic of Inclusion," in *Diversity and Developmentally Appropriate Practice: Challenges for Early Childhood Education,* ed. Bruce L. Mallory and Rebecca S. New (New York: Teachers College Press, 1994), p. 1.

8. Leslie R. Williams, "Developmentally Appropriate Practice and Cultural Values: A Case in Point," in Mallory and New, *Diversity and Developmentally Appropriate Practice,* p. 158.

9. L. Vygotsky *Mind in Society: The Development of Higher Psychological Processes* (Cambridge, MA: Harvard University Press, 1978).

10. Robert J. Havighurst, *Developmental Tasks and Education*, 3rd ed. (New York: David McKay, 1972).

11. Unless otherwise noted, the source consulted for historical background information discussed in this chapter is Philip L. Safford and Elizabeth J. Safford, *A History of Childhood and Disability* (New York: Teachers College Press, 1995).

12. Larry Cuban, *How Teachers Taught: Constancy and Change in American Classrooms, 1890–1990,* 2nd ed. (New York: Teachers College Press, 1993), p. 37.

13. Ibid., p. 272.

14. Carolyn Edwards, Lella Gandini, and George Foreman, eds., *The Hundred Languages of Children: The Reggio Emilia Approach to Early Childhood Education* (Norwood, NJ: Ablex Publishing, 1993).

15. Ibid., pp. 3–4.

16. National Middle School Association, *This We Believe* (Columbus, OH: National Middle School Association, 1992), p. 4.

17. Sue Bredekamp, "Developmentally Appropriate Practice: The Early Childhood Teacher as Decision-maker," in Bredekamp and Copple, *Early Childhood Programs,* p. 40.

18. See Lillian Weber, *The Kindergarten: Its Encounter with Educational Thought* (New York: Teachers College Press, 1969) for an excellent analysis of the impact of the progressive movement on the philosophy and goals of the American kindergarten.

19. Arnold Gesell, "A Decade of Progress in the Mental Hygiene of the Preschool Child," *The Annals of the American Academy of Political and Social Sciences* 151 (1930):143.

20. Bernard Spodek, "Early Childhood Curriculum and Cultural Definitions of Knowledge," in *Issues in Early Childhood Curriculum, vol. 2 of Yearbook in Early Childhood Education,* ed. Bernard Spodek and Olivia N. Saracho (New York: Teachers College Press, 1991), p. 1.

21. See recommended guidelines of the Early Childhood and Literacy Development Committee, International Reading Association, in Richard Vacca, Jo Anne Vacca, and Margaret Gove, *Reading and Learning to Read* (Boston: Little, Brown, 1987), p. 65.

22. Howard Gardner, *The Unschooled Mind: How Children Think and How Schools Should Teach* (New York: Basic Books, 1991).

23. Botstein, *Jefferson's Children.*

24. Samuel J. Meisels, "Testing Four- and Five-Year Olds: Response to Salzer and to Sheppard and Smith," *Educational Leadership* 44, 3 (1981): 90–92.

25. Bredekamp and Copple, *Early Childhood Programs,* p. 17.

26. Gardner, *Unschooled Mind,* p. 145.

27. David R. Shaffer, *Developmental Psychology: Childhood and Adolescence,* 3rd ed. (Pacific Grove, CA: Brooks/Cole, 1993), p. 4.

28. Erik H. Erikson, *Childhood and Society,* 2nd ed. (New York: Norton, 1963).

29. Gardner, *Unschooled Mind.*

30. Arnold Gesell, "Human Infancy and the Ontogenesis of Behavior," *American Scientist* 37 (1949): 529–553, 548.

31. Rebecca S. New, "Culture, Child Development, and Developmentally Appropriate Practice: Teachers as Collaborative Researchers," in Mallory and New, *Diversity and Developmentally Appropriate Practice,* p. 72.

32. Williams, "Cultural Values."

33. Ibid., p. 158.

34. Karen R. Harris and Steve Graham, "Constructivism: Principles, Paradigms, and Integration," *Journal of Special Education* 28, 3 (1994): 233–247.

Creating Inclusive Classrooms:

The Ability/Disability Continuum and the Health Dimension

> *Wow! I would love to be able to show yesterday to others and say,*
> *THIS is inclusion! . . . I really enjoyed visiting Tim's class . . .*
> *It's good to see him in the classroom environment, so mature and confident.*

—A parent

C h a p t e r   O u t l i n e

focus   questions

1.   What determines which students are "exceptional"?

2.   What is meant by the term *inclusion* of exceptional students?

3.   What is the philosophical basis of inclusion? its legal basis?

4.   What is its educational basis?

case study   **Schools That Include All Students**

Located in an affluent suburb of a large midwestern city, Burlington Elementary School serves the children of middle- and upper-middle-class families.[1] The community is a relatively conservative one, but it wants what is best for its children and is willing to pay for it. Inspired by a state initiative encouraging schools to develop alternative models to include students with disabilities in the regular school program, Burlington's faculty, with the administration's blessing, developed a proposal designed to enhance the educational opportunities of all students.

In its first year, the program focused on including primary-age children with specific learning disabilities in regular classrooms. Planning for this step was accomplished through regular meetings of the participating teachers with a special educator, who was present in each inclusion classroom during the seventy-five minutes scheduled daily for the language arts block, the area of greatest difficulty for most of the identified students.

*By the fourth year of the project, all Burlington students with disabilities, including children with significant delays and multiple impairments as well as disabilities requiring less intensive intervention, were served in nine inclusion classes. These classes comprised typical pupils experiencing no particular difficulties, pupils considered at risk for learning or behavior problems, and pupils with identified disabilities ranging from mild to severe. For each student eligible for special education, the specific goals and related services identified in the student's **IEP,** or **Individual Education Program,** would be implemented within the context of regular classroom activity. While joint planning is continuous, each Inclusion Team meets once a month to review progress and consider needs to modify the strategies. In addition, all teams come together for periodic Building Inclusion Meetings, joined by the school psychologist, counselor, speech-language pathologist, art and physical education teachers, and librarian.*

While all nine classes reflect a common philosophy and employ the same basic strategy of collaboration and individualized adaptation, each is a unique community in many respects, including the specific needs presented by its members with disabilities. One variable is the amount of time each day that a special educator is physically present and is sharing in ongoing instruction that is determined by the varying degrees of support and by curricular and instructional adaptation individual students need. These factors also determine class size, ratio of typical students to those with special needs, and whether an instructional aide is assigned to the teacher, or to individual students, throughout the day. Related services are integrated within ongoing class routines (e.g., physical therapy in the context of physical education, occupational therapy in art and other activities), except where certain objectives (e.g., self-care for a child with cerebral palsy) suggests the need for brief, unobtrusive pullout by a therapist.

Carol is enrolled in a first grade classroom on a full-time basis. Although Carol's IEP indicates a label of "multihandicapped," she is an accepted and integral part of Mr. Beeman's classroom. The supports and services she needs have also become an integral part of the classroom routine; that is, as Carol needs assistance, everyone knows that the support is needed and will be provided, sometimes by the classroom aide assigned to that role, sometimes by Mr. Beeman or by another student.

On this particular day, the class is learning about units of measurement. Working in small, cooperative learning groups, the children are engaged in a variety of tasks, including determining how many "hands" it takes to measure the length of a doorway, or how many "knuckles" it takes to measure the length of a table. Today's lesson also involves walking heel-to-toe across the room to determine its length and width in "feet." As Mr. Beeman is providing directions for this part of the lesson, he notes that Carol will be unable to participate as the other children will because she requires a wheelchair to move across the room. Without missing a beat, he interests the class in another unit of measurement. He instructs the students in the group with Carol to place a piece of tape on the wheel of her chair and determine the number of rotations required as she moves from one side of the room to the other.

The students view this instruction simply as another part of their lesson on units of measurement, while Carol is happy to have yet another opportunity to participate in the ongoing activities of her classroom. Despite the apparent inspired brilliance of Mr. Beeman's response, he gives it little thought and moves on to engage students in other explorations. In his view, he provides the assistance that Carol needs not because of her label or goals on her IEP, but simply so Carol can participate along with her learning group. "Isn't that what being included should be?" he reflects. "It's no big deal."

Carol's parents have been gratified by her teachers' willingness to regard her as just another one of the students. Prominent in her file is the letter they wrote last year to the principal:

Watching our daughter go off to kindergarten was the beginning of a new adventure. The anticipation of riding the "big yellow school bus" and entering a world of all new learning was thrilling! She was filled with excitement and energy. As the school year progressed, each day brought much joy. She loved making new friends and learning new skills. Carol's confidence and willingness to learn is only enhanced by the surrounding of real life with real children of all walks of life. It has been fulfilling to watch her grow in a classroom where the teacher reaches out to all the children's potential. All children deserve to discover their abilities and develop their talents regardless of their circumstances. It has been a positive experience for Carol to be given the opportunity to expand her mind in an exceptional classroom . . . where all children are invited and encouraged to pursue their academic and social challenges . . . [and] where the teachers know the importance of developing the whole child and including all children.

Since teachers' participation has been voluntary, some negotiation has been involved. Elizabeth Sims, a first grade teacher with nineteen years of experience, recalls being "very apprehensive" when Sheila Marks, a special education colleague, approached her. "She assured me it would be fun and listed the benefits: a full-time aide's help with running off papers and monitoring recess, a hand-selected class with fewer children, specials such as art and gym at the time we would choose, and the largest classroom in the building. After listening to her litany, being one who does not say no easily, I agreed."

Mrs. Sims continues, "It was a wonderful decision . . . I have truly enjoyed being in this total inclusion classroom. I am a teacher who has done a 360-degree turn-around! I always felt 'those children' needed to be in a class by themselves with teachers who were trained to meet their needs. I saw no benefit to including them in regular classes, and I felt a disservice was being done to the typical child. Now, I see that the advantages far outweigh the disadvantages for everyone involved. The children are accepting of differences and very helpful to each other, whether they are typically developing or have special needs. I also feel that the children with special needs try more challenging things when seeing what their peers can do."

"The fact that there are two teachers is great (two heads are better than one!). We have come up with some fantastic projects and ideas while putting our heads together. I find I really need to be organized because we plan on Wednesday for the following week. I must have everything planned and available so Sheila is able to adapt the material for the children with special needs. Flexibility is also a must! There are times when the best-laid plans must be changed because something is not working correctly. Although flexibility is a necessity in an inclusion classroom, I've always felt it must be present in a typical classroom as well. I really have not had to change the program I have always used, except with Sheila's help to adapt it to make sure the children with special needs are being reached."

Margaret Burns, a kindergarten teacher, also stresses the importance of flexibility in combination with collaboration. As her reflections on the matter of balance make clear, her concern is for all the children in her class. "My elementary education background, with one overview class in special education," she says, "gave me little specific knowledge of the population that this program might serve. As it has turned out, my preparation as a regular teacher, combined with the expertise of the specialist I'm privileged to work with, has allowed me to create an effective and positive learning environment for all the children."

"Our class is composed of twenty typical children and four with disabilities identified as **low-incidence.** *The teaching team includes the special education specialist, a kindergarten aide, two student teachers, and myself for part of this year. There are several critical factors to the success of this type of program. Perhaps the most basic is having a team of teachers with the same philosophy and vision for all the children being served. Hands-on time with the children is fundamental, especially at the kindergarten level, where every child has very immediate needs; therefore, a workable teacher-pupil balance is essential. The specifics of this number would vary, as do the profiles of the children from year to year. Having a special educator with broad-based knowledge and experience on the team has been instrumental in making this program successful. Perhaps our greatest strength as a team is the flexibility that is visible every single day in*

our classroom. Knowing that our bottom line is meeting the emotional and educational needs of each of our students gives us the freedom to exchange roles, modify plans, and adapt as situations warrant."

"Three necessities are a small enough enrollment to accommodate all the typical and special children being served, the extra adults that are routinely present in the classroom and the eventuality of special equipment that children may need. For example, this year one of our students went progressively from braces, to a total lower body cast and wheelchair, then to crawling on his stomach, and finally to an unassisted walking gate. Particularly during the time he was using the wheelchair our space was taxed to the limit. Also, it is important to keep the number of children slightly low, so that flexibility is maintained to accommodate additional children as the year progresses if the need arises. It is unfair to assume, because an 'extra teacher—the specialist'—is present to specifically meet and modify for special needs, that the dynamics of an inclusion classroom are just the same as any regular classroom . . . we feel that they are not, but they can be positive if they have been planned for appropriately."

"It is critical to the success of inclusion, in my opinion, that the class be truly a representative sample of a normal population distribution. Placing many identified children in one room and calling it 'inclusion' would defeat its most important purpose—to be a model for the world we live in outside the school walls. Indeed, we've had wonderful feedback from parents of children without disabilities. Listen to this letter from the parents of two boys, both of whom have been in inclusion classrooms."

Our fourth grade son was in a homeroom with several multiple-handicapped children last year. This school year our first grade son has been in an inclusion room. Both boys have had wonderful learning experiences as a result of this. They have been able to be involved directly on a day-to-day basis with special children. We as adults have not been exposed to this! Imagine how great it has been for their learning environment to know that not all people are alike. Everyone has special gifts, and at such a young age my children have been able to realize this! I think it has brought out in them responsibility, increased sensitivity to others and a sense of pride in being involved with these special children. As parents we have been very pleased with the inclusion environment for all these reasons. Our children are receiving an excellent education . . . both scholastically and socially.

"And here's another," Ms. Burns says, waving a second letter:

We thought being in an inclusion class would be a great experience for Shana but we didn't realize to what extent. Her acceptance of the disabled children in the class, we feel, is far beyond her years and extends to the typical children as well. Being a part of this class has given her more self-confidence and a chance to make friendships she may not have had the opportunity to do. Being in this inclusion atmosphere has greatly added to her education. We only wish our other children had this opportunity.

Elementary children are not the only ones to benefit from inclusive classrooms in the Burlington schools. As the district's inclusion program progressed, such classrooms have been developed at both the middle and high schools.

Marty, for example, is in the seventh grade. For anyone who has spent any time in a middle school, the definition of "normal" may be difficult. In Marty's school, eight hundred students between the ages of twelve and fifteen are grappling with the everyday developmental tasks of adolescence.

*Because he had entered school before the inclusion program was implemented, Marty spent most of his elementary school years in a self-contained class with other similarly labeled children. It had often been believed "necessary" to implement **behavior management plans** in response to his displays of inappropriate social behaviors, especially his incessant drooling and frequent bathroom accidents. A significant amount of professional time was invested in ensuring that Marty made it to the bathroom according to a prescribed schedule. When Marty entered middle school, his educational program underwent significant changes, because he was included in regular classes for most of the school day. Interestingly, within a short time Marty's drooling practically disappeared, and he also began to show a much greater interest in monitoring his own bathroom schedule—with very positive results.*

One of the intended by-products of being included in regular education settings is involvement in the ongoing social milieu of the school and the community. This outcome was truly realized for Marty the day he was hanging out with other students in the school lobby after lunch. It seems that he and several of his "regular" friends were taken to the office when an exchange of taunting and teasing with members of the opposite sex escalated. The assistant principal determined that every member of the group involved would be subject to a sentence in the in-school suspension program, but neither Marty's resource teacher nor his parents viewed this event negatively. In fact, they were excited that he was an integral member of the group of students being disciplined. Welcome to adolescence, Marty!

Similarly, students in the high school also participate in inclusive classrooms. James, now seventeen, spent much of his childhood in segregated residential facilities and special schools, but within the last three years his life has undergone a dramatic change: James came to live in a foster home and was given the opportunity to attend a regular high school, enrolled in regular classes.

One of the first assignments in his Public Speaking class required recitation of a poem, which presented a challenge for James because he does not read. He also has difficulty maintaining conversation because of a tendency to repeat phrases or sentences spoken by the individual with whom he is conversing, which a clever teacher turned into a teaching strategy. The poem selected for James was recorded on tape by another student, who left a lengthy pause on the tape between each line and stanza. When the time came to recite, he was given the tape recorder and a set of headphones. When the voice on the tape recited a line into James's ears, he repeated it flawlessly. This continued until he had recited the entire poem. As he finished reciting, the entire classroom erupted into applause and cheers, his classmates relishing the success James had achieved and sharing in the joy of his accomplishment.

Rationale for Inclusive Classrooms

From its inception, a fundamental characteristic of American schooling has been its intended inclusiveness across social boundaries of gender, class, and—belatedly—race. Today, the term **inclusion** refers to the practice of including another group of students in regular classrooms, those with chronic health problems and those with physical, cognitive developmental, or social-emotional disabilities.

The argument for inclusion has both a philosophical and legal basis. Philosophically, proponents of inclusive classrooms believe that communities of learners are, by definition, inclusive communities—cohesive groups with common goals, each member of which is a unique individual, different from every other member but sharing with every other member the characteristics that distinguish the age (e.g., middle school), affinity (e.g., computer club), or other basis for forming that particular community. All members have their individual contributions to make, and each will derive his or her own benefits from membership.

The philosophical basis of inclusive education does not rest on the manifestly wrong notion that everyone is the same as everyone else. It rests, instead, on the principles that heterogeneity within a group is both unavoidable and desirable, and that differences in ability—to read printed material or use Braille, to speak or use sign, to walk or use a wheelchair, to acquire and master skills rapidly or slowly, to express thoughts with pen and paper or with a keyboard—are not marks of greater or lesser worth.

Another key philosophical basis for inclusive education is the concept of **normalization,** an idea that emerged in work with persons with mental retardation in the Scandinavian countries in the 1970s. It was originally defined as "making available to all mentally retarded people patterns of life and conditions of everyday living which are as close as possible to the regular circumstances and way of life of society."[2] Subsequently extended to all areas of disability, normalization means that the lives of exceptional individuals of any age should be characterized as much as possible by the same kinds of experiences, daily routines, and rhythms as those of persons who do not have disabilities.

For a person living in an institution rather than with a family in the community, normalization implied radical changes in practice—a shift from institutional care to community-based services, such as group homes and supported employment. This principle also has had important implications for exceptional children and youth in school, not in suggesting they do not need supportive services, but concerning *how* assistance is provided. The idea is to provide whatever adaptations are needed as unobtrusively as possible, ensuring that the student can participate in all classroom experiences and, as much as possible, in the same manner as everyone else.

While philosophical principles transcend the letter of the law, civil rights legislation represents their expression in public policy. In the legal sense, an inclusive classroom is one from which no "otherwise qualified" student who would ordinarily be a member has been excluded because of a disability, if the student's needs can be addressed through "reasonable accommodations."

Those key phrases—"otherwise qualified" and "reasonable accommodations"— were contained in two pieces of civil rights legislation. First, Section 504 of the Vocational Rehabilitation Act of 1973 prohibited discrimination based on disability on the part of agencies receiving federal funds (including public schools) and was extended to the private sector by the Americans with Disabilities Act (ADA) of 1990.[3] As a practical matter for schools, that means no a priori policies can be adopted consigning pupils who have, have had, or have been thought to have a certain "type" of disability to a certain "type" of program. It means that pupils with impairments affecting major life functions cannot be deprived of access to learning opportunities by architectural or attitudinal barriers and that all pedagogical decisions, including placement, must be based on individual rather than categorical considerations. This legal protection from discrimination affects pupils who are not eligible for special education (including many with special health-care needs, but no difficulties in learning) as well as those who are.

Least Restrictive Environment

The other legal cornerstone of inclusive education is the principle of **least restrictive environment** (LRE), expressed in Public Law 94-142, which was federal legislation that was reauthorized in 1990 as the Individuals with Disabilities Education Act (IDEA).[4] While recognizing a continuum of potential placements, this principle states that, to the maximum extent appropriate, students with disabilities must be educated in a regular classroom with nondisabled peers and must be removed from such settings only if the student's needs cannot be met there, even with supportive aids and services. Moreover, each student's Individual Education Program (IEP) must include a statement of the extent to which the student will participate in regular education and an explanation of why any needed services cannot be provided in a regular class. While this law, like Section 504 and the ADA, was most compellingly based on the need to prohibit exclusion, in this instance of children from public schooling, its intent was also to promote inclusion of exceptional children in the learning experiences shared by other children. Congress clearly meant to ensure that each student found eligible actually receive specialized instruction and related services (e.g., speech, physical, occupational therapy; adapted physical education; counseling; **adaptive equipment** or technology; etc.) appropriate to their individual needs in the most normal setting considered feasible for that student.

Although the legal basis for inclusion has not changed—nondiscrimination and LRE—changes in language used by educators, advocates, and exceptional individuals themselves reflect philosophical changes. *Mainstreaming,* a word often used in the 1970s, implied movement out of a special placement, most often for limited periods of time, and into regular school experiences—the "mainstream." In the 1980s, reflecting the legacy of the civil rights movement, the word on the lips of many educators and parents was *integration,* sometimes merely physical, preferably social, but rarely instructional.

Like societal inclusion, inclusive education implies fully shared participation of diverse individuals in common experiences. As you might expect, this concept is interpreted somewhat differently by different people and, therefore, is implemented with varying degrees of inclusiveness. The most straightforward interpretation of *full inclusion,* which many educators endorse as the standard, is that a pupil should attend the school she would attend if she did not have a disability, with her neighbors and siblings, and is enrolled with whatever group or groups of learners she would be part of if she did not have a disability. A key proviso is that any needed supportive aids or services are provided, including those requiring the direct service or consultative expertise of specialists, so that special education is defined as a *service,* not a *place.*

What is Exceptionality?

Ability/disability and health are distinct dimensions of human exceptionality. They do not necessarily overlap except in conditions such as **muscular dystrophy** that entail high risk for health problems. People who are in any way "exceptional" with respect to ability/disability—such as those with cerebral palsy, a hearing loss, or impaired vision or who are intellectually gifted or intellectually impaired—are not necessarily "exceptional" with respect to health. Like everyone else, these people may experience health problems. The inclusive classroom is one in which class members *include* students who are considered exceptional on either of these two dimensions; they have not been *excluded* because of their exceptionality.

The Ability/Disability Continuum

Defining childhood exceptionality is a circular affair; exceptional children and youth are those eligible for special education services, which in turn are services provided for exceptional pupils. However, this definition restricts the scope of human differences, which may include:

**Activity 32:
The Student
with Special
Needs**

• sensory differences (vision and hearing)
• other physical differences (e.g., those affecting mobility or other voluntary control of motor activity, vitality, and such basic life functions as eating)
• communication differences (speech and language)
• cognitive, or intellectual, and information processing differences
• emotional and behavioral differences

Federal guidelines under IDEA delineate thirteen disability categories based on these dimensions (e.g., *deaf* is distinguished from *hard of hearing;* some children are both deaf and blind or are otherwise multiply impaired; **autism** and **traumatic brain injury** are now distinct categories, etc.) Explicit definitions of each category are important because allocation of financial resources is involved, and schools must ensure that eligible pupils receive services to which they are entitled. But because many such differences occur along a continuum (e.g., cognitive, social-emotional, communicative, etc., as discussed in chapter 10), differentiating exceptionality from normality in the course of children's development is often a matter of judgment and somewhat arbitrary. While some disabilities, and some special health care needs, involve qualitative differences that must be considered and addressed, most exceptional children have the same needs, interests, and concerns that their "typical" peers have, and they have the same right to public education.

Historical Perspectives on Special Education

Horace Mann believed that the goal of education as preparation for citizenship in a democracy applied to all children.[5] Accordingly, Massachusetts' compulsory attendance law of 1851 explicitly encompassed "crippled" children, and Boston's Horace Mann School was named in recognition of Mann's efforts to provide day classes so that deaf children could live at home and interact with hearing children. His staunch ally, Samuel Gridley Howe, was nineteenth-century America's most influential special educator. Though he founded the world-renowned Perkins Institute and was an important figure in the spread of day classes for deaf children, he saw institutions for persons with disabilities only as a last resort. "The practice of training . . . blind and [deaf] children in the common schools," he wrote, " . . . will hardly come in my day; but I see it plainly with the eye of faith and rejoice in the prospect of its fulfillment."[6]

**Samuel Gridley
Howe**

Pioneers in Research and Treatment of Disabilities

Special education's history is studded with tales of pioneers like Howe, the first to teach a pupil who was both deaf and blind; like Jean-Marc Gaspard Itard, the physician who taught Victor, the "wild boy of Aveyron"; and Edouard Seguin, who defied received wisdom by undertaking to instruct pupils who were thought unable to learn, fated to be beggars, dependents, or even a threat to society. The historical record also reveals that many of the key breakthroughs were made by persons who themselves had disabilities. Arguing that in blindness lay a key to understanding human reason, the Enlightenment philosopher Diderot advised that to understand blindness, one must consult blind persons themselves.

Special education emerged in the context of social reform, inspired by belief in natural rights and individual worth and in the conviction that, through education, every person can contribute to society. Valentin Hauy, who founded the world's first school for blind students in Paris in 1784, heeded Diderot's counsel and learned from his first pupil how reading could be accomplished through touch. Since then, the pantheon of "greats" in this field has included blind individuals like J. W. Klein, Louis Braille, Helen Keller, Thomas Cutsworth, and Robert Irwin. Deaf persons have had a critical role in gaining recognition of Deaf culture and the legitimacy of signed languages. While deaf education has had hearing pioneers, their own "teachers" were their deaf pupils, some of whom, such as Laurent Clerc, became influential leaders.

In important respects, special education began as a rescue mission, for in 1860 nearly two-thirds of the countless "unfortunates" who languished, untaught and uncared for, in American almshouses were children with sensory or other physical impairments or mental retardation. By the 1870s, state boards of charities, supporting the work of local charity groups and benevolent societies, had undertaken a major child-saving effort, organized nationally as the National Conference of Charities and Corrections. In some families of more privileged circumstance, parents advocated for schooling for their children, a tradition that since has been pivotal in bringing about major policy reforms.

History of Disability and Special Education

Although the most urgent concern of nineteenth-century reformers was to provide proper care and some form of instruction, the goal then, as now, is to achieve maximum independence and integration in society. However, as attitudes toward deviance became less accepting, that goal was for a time abandoned for many children with mental or physical abnormalities, such as epilepsy. While nineteenth-century facilities were often called asylums, they were intended as schools, in the United States as extensions of the common schools. But they were "training schools," employing a highly utilitarian pedagogy to enable pupils to become, as much as possible, able to support themselves through certain prescribed trades, such as boot making.

The Settlement House Movement

Specialized instruction began its gradual move into the common schools by the beginning of the last century. At the same time, school officials, pressed by Settlement leaders like Lillian Wald and Jane Addams, were struggling to meet the challenge of pupil diversity compounded by massive immigration from southern and eastern Europe. Special classes were a facet of a more general diversification effort: steamer classes to expose immigrant youngsters to the English language (which led to programs for children with actual speech impairments); classes for unrulies; fresh air schools for pupils with tuberculosis or who were physically weak (which led to classes for children with other health impairments); and ungraded classes for those who "just didn't fit" (from which classes for pupils with mild retardation evolved). Except in cases of deafness and blindness and in speech training for "young stammerers," special pedagogy was secondary to the perceived need to separate pupils who were different as a way of making schooling more manageable.

Although the early programs were centralized residential facilities, they represented an important step in enabling children with disabilities "to share in the blessings of education" (as Howe eloquently persuaded the Massachusetts legislature in 1848).[7] By the first decades of the twentieth century, day classes were increasingly a component of the common school. The first public school program for blind children, in Chicago, involved them in many ways with seeing peers, a model emulated in other cities. In rural areas, because blindness is a low-incidence impairment (compared, for example, to specific learning disabilities), many children, even those using Braille, have been enrolled in regular classrooms and have received periodic assistance from itinerant specialists. Many schools made "reasonable accommodations" for pupils with other physical impairments long before such action was legally mandated. But as American attitudes toward differentness became less accepting, special education increasingly took the form of a "system-within-a-system," separately administered and often separated physically from other classes. It seemed as though schools sought to manage pupil diversity by trying to make it go away, that is, by segregating or excluding altogether students who "didn't fit" in special classes.

By the 1930s, as schools adopted IQ testing, the basis for separation of students who had difficulty learning presumably became more scientific, but such students' instruction was distinguished from regular instruction mainly because it was provided in somewhat smaller groups, comprising pupils of various ages: urban versions (in most instances) of the one-room schoolhouse. However, curricula emphasizing life skills necessary for adult living emerged in these programs. For children with physical impairments, chronic health problems, and (by the 1960s) emotional and behavioral problems, special pedagogy was truly an afterthought, decidedly secondary to the medically oriented treatment focus. Until the parent-led learning disability movement gathered force in the 1960s, special education was more likely to mean special place than special pedagogy. And with implementation of systematic exclusionary policies, the special place was often likely to be somewhere other than public school—home, or an expensive private facility if parents could afford it, or an institution.

Yet, even as special education expanded, the majority of children and youth with special needs who were not excluded from schooling altogether were included in the mainstream because their problems had not been identified or services were not available. For students who had difficulty learning, and also students who were exceptionally capable, there was a downside. A pupil who needed more time, or much less time, than others, or one who could succeed only with some adaptation in the way material was presented or assignments could be completed, often paid a considerable price for being treated like everyone else. In 1975, a watershed year from the standpoint of social policy, the Education of All Handicapped Children Act (P.L. 94-142, re-authorized in 1990 as P.L. 101-476, the Individuals with Disabilities Education Act) required schools to identify all students whose disabilities adversely affected their educational functioning and provide them—excluding none—with a free appropriate public education. But

**Special
Education
Law**

even earlier, some special educators (and parents) questioned whether special education must mean special placement, while many regular educators (and parents) were concerned about students who were experiencing difficulties but were not eligible for special education.

In the 1920s, a few leaders, like Leta Hollingworth, were concerned also that gifted children were not being challenged to realize their potential.[8] It was at this time that some large urban school districts, such as Cleveland, initiated programs for students identifed as academically gifted, using the special class model. Support for separate programs for gifted students has waxed and waned since then, with advocates concerned that the brightest students are insufficiently challenged in inclusive classrooms and with opponents arguing that what is presented as appropriate for gifted students would be appropriate for *all* students. Two other major concerns involve (1) the inclusiveness of schools' definition of giftedness, and (2) gifted students who are hard to identify, including ethnic and linguistic minority students and students with disabilities who are also gifted.

What constitutes an appropriate education for a student who is identified as academically gifted? For students with disabilities, IDEA defines *appropriate* on the basis of the IEP developed for each student, stipulating that the student's educational placement must be in the LRE. In some states, such as Pennsylvania, identification and education requirements for children and youth who are gifted are the same as for those with disabilities, though federal legislation addresses only the latter.

Subsequent amendments to the original federal legislation (P.L. 94-142) extended these provisions to children as young as age three; added a family-focused early intervention component for infants and toddlers; stipulated a required **transition plan** (by age sixteen) in anticipation of a student's leaving school and entering the adult world; clarified definitions; and distinguished two forms of disability (autism and traumatic brain injury) from other forms. No doubt the legislation will continue to be amended as it is revisited by the Congress for periodic reauthorization. Many advocates for gifted and talented children and youth hope that eventually an *individually appropriate education* will be mandated on a national basis for these children, as well.

The Health Dimension

Although certain forms of disability may involve greater vulnerability to health problems (for example, many people with **Down syndrome** tend to experience cardiac difficulties and middle ear and upper respiratory infections), health is a dimension encompassing everyone. Some disabilities, such as **spina bifida,** may involve health services such as **clean intermittent catheterization (CIC).** A child with cerebral palsy may have significant motor, sensory, communication, and possibly cognitive impairment, yet experience no health problems, while a child with no such involvement may experience chronic asthma. Most of us enjoy reasonably robust good health most of the time, but all of us will, at some times in our lives, experience debilitating illness. Some of us, were it not for anticonvulsant or other forms of medication, special diet, or other adaptations, would experience continuous, significant disruption in our daily lives or impairment of critical life functions such as self-care, working, and going to school. And for some of us, supplemental oxygen, kidney dialysis, or other adaptations make it possible to take in nourishment or eliminate waste, which are essential life functions. Children with leukemia or other forms of cancer may experience times of great fatigue; those with **sickle cell disease** may experience times of excruciating pain.

While they represent a very small proportion of students eligible for special services, children with significant health-care needs are often a matter of concern in discussions of inclusion. Actually, a great many American children, estimated at more than one in ten, experience some form of chronic illness, although the number with relatively severe conditions is much less. However, that number has risen in the last two decades, because of a number of factors: interventions that sustain life in utero and facilitate the survival of newborns at very low birth weight and with other biological risk factors, such as respiratory distress; medical advances in bringing certain childhood diseases into remission during the vulnerable first year of life; marked increases in drug-affected pregnancies; and HIV transmission to newborns. Given these factors, the 1987 Surgeon General's Report estimated that 1 to 2 percent of all surviving American newborns are likely to have conditions implying special health care needs.[9]

Some conditions involve *established risk* (that is, the condition is known to involve lasting impairment), but much more often the future of a newborn at *biological risk* (e.g., very young gestational age at birth, very low birth weight) cannot be reliably predicted, for much depends on the quality of nurture the child will have. Although many of the great numbers of children born each year prenatally exposed to alcohol, crack or powder cocaine, or other drugs continue to have special needs, biology is not destiny. These and other biological factors interact in subtle ways with environmental ones, most crucially the quality of attachment and caregiving.

After a brief period of time in the neonatal intensive care unit, a still-tiny infant is likely to come home dependent on life support equipment that parents will need to manage as they attempt to normalize the baby's life and their own. Many young children soon cease to be technology-dependent, but some will continue to need a respirator, perhaps, or require nasogastric or gastrostomy tube feeding. While the term *medically fragile* is really inappropriate considering the struggle a child may need to put forth, some children who may require no special adaptations to support life functions may be particularly susceptible to infection, experience debilitating allergies, or have other special health care needs throughout their school careers, perhaps throughout their lives.

The notion that children with special health care needs require special educational arrangements had its origins in efforts to contain the spread of tuberculosis. Fresh air classes were first established in the United States in Providence, Rhode Island, in 1908. Like the adult sanitoriums, open air schools in Europe were often located in the mountains or forests. However, many of the fresh air schools in the United States were in the large cities, where the disease was epidemic; classes were sometimes held on tenement roofs. (Tragically, little effective intervention was done on the reservations and in the boarding schools established for Native Americans, where tuberculosis decimated tribal populations.) In the eastern states, siblings of infected children were often removed to "preventoriums." Where children were thus gathered, hospital schools were provided, and school districts collaborated with charity groups and health agencies to provide instruction, mild exercise, and rest. Generally, as public health measures worldwide were brought to bear, segregation strategies to halt the spread of tuberculosis became less necessary. However, the special class or special school model established in response to tuberculosis was adopted for children with other health care needs, such as heart defects.

Also, for children experiencing lengthy hospital stays for any reason, the convention of establishing a hospital school, introduced in Europe, was adopted in the growing number of pediatric hospitals and pediatric units in general hospitals. Increasingly, operation of such schools was also assumed by public education, especially in large metropolitan communities. For many children believed unable to manage the physical demands of school attendance, whether hospitalized or at home, public education established tutoring for "homebound and hospitalized children."

Health needs of children and youth have, as we know, changed with the presumed conquest of tuberculosis, poliomyelitis, and a number of diseases, such as smallpox, scarlet fever, and diphtheria, to which children had been particularly vulnerable. And philosophies of medical care have changed also. Extended periods of hospitalization are now rare for children (as for adults), and while that practice has been influenced by crass realities of cost and insurance coverage limits, it also reflects awareness of the importance for children to experience conditions of growing up that are as normal as possible. Most children who in times past would have been excluded, either by formal policy or assumed dependency, weakness, or vulnerability, now go to school with their siblings, neighbors, and friends.

Children with Multiple Health Problems

What are the implications for inclusive education? First, remember three basic, and obvious, principles: (1) we can all expect to experience serious health problems at some time in our lives, for they are part of the universal human condition; (2) serious health impairment in children is certainly not a new phenomenon, historically speaking, as can be evidenced in epidemics and pandemics of the past to which children were especially vulnerable; and (3) a health problem is, for a child or an adult, certainly not a person's only identifying characteristic or need.

Our own vulnerability helps to explain an element of fear, particularly of contagion, that in antiquity focused on leprosy, a century ago on tuberculosis, then on poliomyelitis, and today on AIDS, although other conditions (e.g., hepatitis B) are much more readily transmitted than the HIV virus is. Today, all school personnel are strongly advised to adopt universal health precautions to lessen the risk, to themselves or to pupils, of any form of infection, especially if there is possible exposure to blood or any body fluids. The need for such precautions is not affected by whether a school adopts an inclusive education philosophy. While contagious disease is understandably feared, it is conquered not by avoidance, ignorance, or blaming the victim. This point is certainly the message of AIDS awareness.

Another source of fear has to do with a different type of vulnerability, implied by inappropriate terms such as *medically fragile*. Teachers neither want a child to be endangered nor want themselves to be vulnerable to self-imposed guilt feelings or even to a lawsuit should a pupil in their charge incur injury or even die. As with many human fears, these feelings are best allayed by information, availability of appropriate resources and supports, and most importantly, personal experience. Teachers can feel vulnerable whether they are dealing with a child who has a condition that is actually life threatening or with a child who has no chronic special health care needs per se but does have significant physical impairment. A fourth grade teacher participating in an inclusion project in Virginia spoke of "fear of the unknown . . . You're afraid they might hurt you or you might hurt them." Janney and her coauthors, reporting on the success of that project, summarized:

teachers who initially had been hesitant to get involved (22 of the 26) judged that their original fears and expectations were based on inaccurate perceptions about the integrated student's needs and abilities. By getting to know the students with disabilities on an individual basis, they had gained knowledge of the student's unique abilities and a new perspective on disabilities in general. "I guess we just really had never thought about them being 'normal.' They really are," explained the junior high math teacher in District C. These general education teachers' attitudes toward integration also had been changed by finding that it was personally and professionally rewarding to work with the integrated students, a sentiment expressed in these words by the high school physical education teacher in District A: "These kids seem to appreciate you a lot more . . . and that's a little pat on the back for the teacher."[10]

Characteristics of an Inclusive Classroom

The discussion in the preceding section, although it gives a sense of what inclusion in this specific sense means, is likely to raise questions in a teacher's, or prospective teacher's, mind about how, or even whether, inclusion works. Inclusive schools and classrooms do not just happen, nor do they require each individual teacher to be "all things to all students." Some of the major ideas reflected in this chapter's case study are based on legal requirements, but most derive from or are congruent with emerging principles and practices in general pedagogy and in the way Third Wave schools operate.

Inclusion and Human Diversity

One fundamental idea is an old one, and it is that a major purpose of schooling is to prepare the young for citizenship in a democracy, which is also a heterogeneous society. Another idea is relatively new: that the young must be prepared for successful participation in a global economy. The adult world that children will enter is not one in which everyone is like themselves; this fact has important implications for the necessary learning experiences of any child, with a disability or health impairment, or without. The former will not live in a society comprised only of other people with cerebral palsy, mental retardation, autism, dyslexia, diabetes, and so forth; the latter will not live in a society comprised only of people who do not have these conditions or characteristics. Related to that societal reality is another that can be seen in any school and in any classroom: even if it were desirable to eliminate heterogeneity in a group of learners by putting anyone who is "different" in another group, it is impossible, for every group is necessarily heterogeneous; *all* children are "different."

Another major idea emerging in general pedagogy, *collaboration,* involves new kinds of teacher-specialist relationships and team models, more mutually supportive school-family relationships, and new awareness of the important role of interactions

**Activity 27:
What Does
It Feel Like to
Be Excluded?**

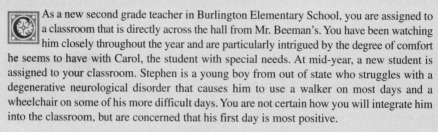

critical incident

Integrating the New Student with a Disability

As a new second grade teacher in Burlington Elementary School, you are assigned to a classroom that is directly across the hall from Mr. Beeman's. You have been watching him closely throughout the year and are particularly intrigued by the degree of comfort he seems to have with Carol, the student with special needs. At mid-year, a new student is assigned to your classroom. Stephen is a young boy from out of state who struggles with a degenerative neurological disorder that causes him to use a walker on most days and a wheelchair on some of his more difficult days. You are not certain how you will integrate him into the classroom, but are concerned that his first day is most positive.

- How will you go about introducing Stephen to the other students in your class?
- What will you do to familiarize your students with disabilities in general and with Stephen's in particular?

among learners. Each of these sets of relationships is multifaceted. For example, Pugach and Johnson have described four different roles—*supportive, facilitative, informative,* and *prescriptive*—underlying collaborative relationships of adults within schools.[11] The IDEA legislation implies such relationships with respect to the education of students with disabilities, but the concept of collaboration goes beyond the legal requirements:

1.   The law requires only multidiscipline participation in assessing a student's current functioning and in planning and monitoring the student's IEP, but collaboration suggests continuing interdisciplinary teamwork on the part of regular and special educators and other specialists in implementing the student's program.

2.   The law requires parents' informed consent prior to multifactored evaluation, participation in developing the IEP, and right to procedural due process in the event of disagreement; collaboration suggests going beyond these bare legal requirements to ensure that a student's IEP reflects the family's concerns and priorities, that a student's home and school expectations and experiences are mutually supportive, and that professionals respect the primacy and continuing influence of families on children's development.

3.   The law requires that students with disabilities be educated as much as is appropriate with peers who do not have disabilities; collaboration implies optimizing the potential benefits for both by fostering positive classroom interactions and creating opportunities for students to respect and learn from each other and to develop feelings of group identification.

Policy requirements have a critical role in determining how students with disabilities are educated, but as in all aspects of schooling, other factors such as research findings influence pedagogical practices. The next sections summarize some contrasts between old and new characteristics, keep in mind that, in one sense, everything before the IDEA legislation was enacted is "old," yet what is "new" continues to emerge.

Pegagogies: Old and New

While traditional methods of teaching are incorporated in pedagogies for inclusion, a major influence on inclusive pedagogy is *constructivism,* a way of understanding students' learning as a process of cognitive development influenced, but not controlled, by adult instruction. Constructivist perspectives are fundamental to current conceptions of developmentally appropriate practices for young children,[12] but they are also reflected in current discussions of elementary, middle school, and even high school curriculum and instruction, especially in the areas of literacy, mathematics, social studies, and science. Is all genuine and meaningful learning—though externally influenced by family and peers as well as teachers and textbooks—internally motivated and internally organized? And if so, is it true of all learners? Beliefs about *how* children learn are key determinants of *what* is taught.

This issue is critical with respect to the pedagogy of inclusion because special education, strongly influenced both by a *medical model* of treatment and a *behavioral model* of learning, has traditionally placed great emphasis on skill acquisition through training strategies employed by teachers and therapists. The assumption has been that most children "naturally" learn important skills, such as language skills, and generalize what they have learned to new situations, but that children with delayed development, or disabilities for which they must learn to compensate, require more direct adult intervention. This issue is far from simple, considering the wide variation among children with disabilities, and such distinctions have certainly been unduly emphasized; generally speaking, children with disabilities, and certainly children with health impairments, are more *like* other children in the way they learn, and in what they need to learn, than they are *different* from their peers.

Moreover, some constructivist practices were actually introduced or readily adopted by special education pioneers like Howe, Seguin, and early educators of deaf children. Seguin, Maria Montessori, and Ovide DeCroly were convinced that the experiential methods they developed in working with children with mental retardation, which were based on faith in every child's ability and motivation to learn, should be extended to instruction of all children. Some learners do require more adult direction and adult-imposed structure than other learners, but the same can be said of many students who do not have disabilities. Arguably, the diverse needs present in any group of learners can more effectively be accommodated with constructivist approaches to teaching than with approaches that assume all pupils learn the same things at the same pace. This individualized approach represents an important legacy of special education that is applicable for all students.

Roles: Old and New

The most dramatic difference between old and new affecting the education of children with disabilities is that today most children live at home with their families and attend public schools. That fact implies fundamental changes in the roles of both families and educators and critically important changes in their relationships. Moreover, the increasing number of students with disabilities who participate to some degree in regular education suggests fundamental changes in the roles of both special and regular educators and in *their* relationships. To appreciate the significance of these changes, consider other contrasts between old and new roles of regular and special educators.

The special educator of the past was indeed a specialist, not only as a special educator but as a teacher of a specific category of students. As children were segregated, so too were their teachers. Early special educators were trained in residential schools and followed a medically oriented, preceptor model, which was quite unlike the preparation their counterparts were provided in normal schools. Even as preparation for both types of teachers moved to degree-granting colleges and universities, special and general educators were most often prepared separately; they were taught different content by different instructors. Those barriers like the separate structures in schools, have been gradually receding.

Except in schools for deaf students, which had a strong pedagogic tradition, the special educator was a clinician, albeit a junior one, and was increasingly likely to be a woman who was, as Seguin insisted, "supervised by a competent physician."[13] In school and in clinical settings, special education teachers were (and are today) members of teams, collaborating with (or carrying out the recommendations of) psychologists; sometimes physicians and/or social workers; and physical, occupational, and speech/language therapists. In medical settings—hospitals, rehabilitation centers, and residential treatment facilities—the team was often led by a physician; in schools, by a school psychologist or special education supervisor. Because team members were expected to work together, each applying her or his own expertise, the model was referred to as *multidisciplinary*. To the extent that diverse perspectives on the child as patient or client were integrated within a unified plan (difficult, since members had been trained in their respective disciplines in relative isolation from each other), teams increasingly evolved an *interdisciplinary* approach. In clinical settings a social worker often provided the only link teachers had with parents, but in schools home-school cooperation and consistency were often seen as critical. A more integrated *transdisciplinary* team model has recently emerged, most notably with young children, and it is characterized by *role exchange* and *role release,* whereby professionals share and synthesize perspectives on an ongoing basis.[14]

Like their fellow team members, then, and quite unlike regular education teachers, special educators were imbued with a clinical orientation influenced more by a medical than an educational model. Just as their preparation was relatively distinct from that of elementary and secondary teachers, their work environment was often in relative isolation from other teachers. Their classrooms were located "next to the boiler room" (as many veteran special educators recall), and their pupils were often transported separately, used the playground at separate times, and ate lunch in their classroom, with their teacher, rather than in the cafeteria. Like their students, many special educators perceived themselves as outsiders, and in fact they were more likely to be accountable to a central office supervisor, or "inspector," than to the building principal.

Regular educators, for their part, were often the first line of identification of children experiencing difficulty in school as well as those who might be gifted. Their principal role vis-à-vis an exceptional student, then, was identification of suspected problems and, as the law stipulates, an attempt to address such problems within the regular classroom. Only if their attempt was unsuccessful did educators refer a student for a **multifactored evaluation** with parents' **informed consent.** However, the **placement continuum** of possible school arrangements, mandated since 1975, implied that most exceptional pupils would have varying degrees of involvement in regular education; either they were pulled out for special help, or they were provided supportive aids and services in the mainstream.

Place of Content Knowledge: Old and New

As suggested in the previous section, *what* was to be learned has long been a key issue in special education, and it is a key issue in discussions of inclusion. Generally, content issues have involved the same fundamental question, posed by Herbert Spencer, that has been raised for all learners: what knowledge is of most worth?[15] In the case of blindness, deafness, and other physical impairment, the answer to that question was: knowledge that can enable an individual to be maximally independent and self-supporting as an adult. In the past, such knowledge generally implied training in a trade. Although their societal role shifted from instruction to containment, facilities for persons with mental retardation and epilepsy were also intended originally to be training schools, a designation that was maintained even though residents were "trained" based on the expectation of lifelong institutionalization. As the European day class model was introduced in the United States, at first in the form of ungraded classes for relatively undifferentiated low achievers, the goal of economic self-sufficiency shifted to imply that pupils with mild retardation needed to develop habits that would make them reliable workers as well as good citizens. Consequently, the distinctive curricular tradition that emerged in special classes focused on relatively generic and social *employability skills.* With extension of schooling under the **zero exclusion mandate** of P.L. 94-142, a "criterion of ultimate functioning" was advanced as the basis for curriculum for students with severe disabilities, including severe cognitive disability. This criterion means that what is taught must be age appropriate, future oriented, functional, and community referenced.[16]

The advent of the concept of specific learning disabilities (SLD), which today comprises more than half the special education enrollment (encompassing many pupils who previously would have been designated as having mild mental retardation), brought a greater focus on differential instructional strategy than on curricular content. Based on an educational diagnostic profile showing specific areas of strength and difficulty, or intraindividual differences—in other words, differences *within* an individual student—a plan of remediation or compensatory instruction could be devised for each pupil, usually within the context of the standard curriculum. This distinctive feature, individually tailored instruction, was subsequently mandated for all eligible students with disabilities through the IEP, which specifies individual annual goals and short-term objectives for each area in which a student is to receive special education. Though not required by federal law, in some states an IEP and other provisions are required for students identified as gifted.

Assessment: Old and New

With respect to children with disabilities, assessment has both a general and a specific meaning. While emerging trends in educational assessment (general) are relevant for all learners, two assessment concerns (specific) have unique importance: the determination, as a result of assessment, of eligibility for special education services and the determination of how accountability for those services is demonstrated. The former concern also pertains to possibly gifted and talented students, but for those with "suspected handicaps" the IDEA requires that, to be eligible for special education services, a pupil must have a disability (as defined in the law) that adversely affects educational functioning. Such determination cannot be based on only one measure, or one criterion, but is based instead on a multifactored evaluation, conducted with informed parental consent by appropriately qualified, multidisciplinary professionals using appropriate and nondiscriminatory procedures.

While the IDEA broadly defines criteria for each disability category, individual state standards may specify what types of assessment must be carried out, such as medical or psychological evaluations. In the case of gifted and talented programs, mandated in some states but not in others, state or local district policies stipulate certain criteria and identification processes. In both cases, norm-referenced, standardized tests (e.g., IQ or ability tests) play an important role, but must be used in combination with other appropriate procedures (e.g., criterion-referenced tests of academic skills, teacher reports and ratings).

Individual Educational Plan (IEP)

With respect to outcome as well as process, the IEP is an accountability document. It states what services the pupil will be provided, and for each goal that is listed, it states the evaluation procedure that will be used and who is responsible. These two key functions reflect the legacy of a medical model and a behavioral model, the former in such concepts as *screening* (to identify indications of need for thorough diagnostic evaluation) and *diagnosis,* the latter in stipulating that objectives must be stated in the form of observable, measurable behavior. While medically oriented diagnostic evaluation may be essential in determining eligibility, it has limited value as a guide to the individualized instruction that is the hallmark of special education.

Although the term *diagnostic/prescriptive teaching,* a legacy of the medical model tradition, has been closely associated with special education, more instructionally relevant types of assessment have been developed. Moreover, whether special learning difficulties are believed to reflect underlying process differences (e.g., in information processing, perception, or visual-motor coordination) or viewed as specific skill deficiencies to be identified and remediated, the most useful types of assessment are criterion-referenced rather than norm-referenced. The purpose of such assessment is to ascertain a pupil's current status and progress on the basis of age or stage expectations (developmental assessment); the school's or state's curricular expectations (curriculum-based assessment); through systemic observation, a pupil's ability to function in the classroom (behavioral assessment); a pupil's skill acquisition (task-analytic assessment); or a pupil's ability to accomplish skills required to function in present and/or future environments (ecological assessment).

With young children, diagnostic profiles are often based on *developmental domains,* which are described in Chapter 10. For older students and those with severe or multiple impairments, diagnostic profiles often are based on *functional domains,* that is, important life functioning areas such as work and leisure skills. For children with visual impairments, critical assessment concerns are assessing how the child uses his or her vision, orients in space, and progresses in achieving independent mobility. For children with hearing impairments, critical concerns are use of residual hearing or of compensatory communication modes (hearing aid augmentation, lipreading) or alternative communication modes (sign language). In both instances, progress in communication and literacy as well as in general curricular areas are continuously assessed. For children with impaired mobility or communication, specific assessment concerns involve possible needs for adaptive equipment or procedures.

While every student is unique, some indeed have differences that require adaptations or certain support services in order to receive an appropriate education as required under federal law. Can these services be provided within normalized classroom settings in which they learn side by side with typical peers? That is the challenge of inclusive education.

Successful Inclusive Teaching

The Importance of Collaboration

Students with and without disabilities are intended to benefit from participation in inclusive classrooms. Perhaps the greatest benefits are the positive self-esteem of all the students and the fact that more students have their needs met than in a conventional classroom. The special education student doesn't experience the stigma and confusion associated with the daily journey to a "special" room for "special" instruction. The day is less fragmented, and the student doesn't feel different or left out. Also, special education teachers have hands-on experience with their interventions—applying them to real, daily learning situations—and can make more precise changes in those interventions as they are needed. With a coteaching situation, there is always a teacher available to help a student. Also, coteaching provides two perspectives on any situation and increases creativity in teaching.

Mutual understanding and mutual respect are essential elements in any true collaboration. The Burlington teachers in the case study agreed that the special educator and the regular educator should acknowledge that both have specialized knowledge and skills but that their perspectives and knowledge bases may differ. For example, it is important for the special educator to recognize that regular educators' instructional and behavior management techniques can be effective in working with students with special needs. They must also understand that teachers in regular classrooms must respond to the needs of many students in rapid fashion and that having a student with disabilities does not relieve the teacher of responsibilities to the other students. Thus, the teacher cannot devote disproportionate time and attention to any one student, and some techniques that may be successful in a separate special education class may not be appropriate for the regular classroom environment.

At the same time, the regular educator should strive to understand that the special education consultant may be responsible for supporting many students in a variety of settings and therefore have a limited amount of time to devote to each student. Further,

The Reluctant Parents

 Not long after Stephen moves into your classroom, a number of parents approach you concerned that their children will now be missing out on valuable time with you as the primary teacher and may not themselves develop as fully as the parents expect. You, of course, are both knowledgeable as well as concerned that all students receive the education to which they are entitled.

- How will you go about addressing the parent's concerns?
- What issues would you want to be certain they understood?
- What kinds of activities might you engage them in so they become better informed and more positive about the opportunities that are forthcoming?

the regular education teacher must realize that a new intervention strategy is unlikely to have an immediate effect and that a fair trial is needed before judging it ineffective. Acknowledging that students differ in the extent of instructional adaptations they need, regular classroom teachers should understand that many of the adaptations that the consulting teacher recommends will be extensions of regular education techniques. They should also maintain familiarity with each exceptional student's IEP, sharing responsibilities with the consultant for determining how goals and objectives can be reinforced during the course of classroom activities.

The Burlington teachers developed the following set of principles to guide their communication and collaborative team functioning: establish a communication system; discuss each placement together; assist each other in individualizing instruction; work together to adapt subject matter; share materials; assist each other in adapting evaluative procedures; exhibit characteristics of flexibility, dedication, reliability, organization, imagination, energy, initiative, and enthusiasm; involve others by sharing plans and ideas; seek support and suggestions from others; set realistic goals; work to improve interpersonal relations; be happy and proud about working with students with special needs; and remember that presenting a positive attitude will change attitudes about inclusion both inside and outside the school.

The Importance of Flexibility

The Burlington teachers often use the word *flexibility* in describing their inclusion program. While flexibility is important in any teaching situation, as they note, it is critical to the success of inclusion of students whose learning characteristics and needs may require adaptations, both planned and spontaneous, in the instructional program. Classroom adaptations to accommodate differential individual needs among *all* students can be delineated in terms of four basic parameters: curriculum materials, instructional strategies, classroom organization, and behavior management.

Curriculum Materials

Within the context of the regular curriculum, instructional materials and experiences can be adapted in a wide variety of ways. The Burlington teachers offered the following suggestions: when working with fractions, provide recipes that include measurements and have students identify all the fractions on the recipe; when instructing about time on the hour and the half-hour, help students develop a personal schedule showing daily activities matched to a clock face showing the time of the activity; when working with adding two columns of numbers and regrouping, help students practice balancing a checkbook or compile a shopping list with prices, using a calculator to add; when administering a spelling test, have students practice identifying functional words; when identifying U.S. presidents, have students practice keyboarding skills by locating letters of presidents' names.

Instructional Strategies

Adaptations may include the following: the way instruction is delivered (e.g., use of visual aids, learning centers, cooperatively structured activities, cooperative learning, small group instruction, auditory aids); the way the learner can demonstrate knowledge (e.g., oral versus written response, pictures that can be pointed to, computer, augmentative communication devices such as picture boards, tape recorder, language master, calculators); or the number of items the learner is expected to complete (e.g., spelling words, math problems).

Classroom Organization

Adaptations can be made in such aspects as: the skill level, problem type, or rules on how the learner may approach the work (e.g., using calculators or computer, simplifying task directions, changing rules to allow for participation, breaking task down to sequential steps, providing more planned opportunities to achieve success); the amount of individual instruction with a specific learner (e.g., peer partner, use of teaching assistant); or the time allowed for learning, task completion, or testing (e.g., extra time to practice new skills, individualized timelines for work completion, flexible class schedules).

Behavior Management

Adaptations can be used to anticipate and prevent inappropriate or disruptive behavior. For instance, a student's participation may involve assisting with visual aid equipment while some other students are being instructed; students can take on a teacher's role by sharing a favorite activity or interest; or goals or outcome expectations can be individualized while using the same materials (e.g., a language arts activity of diagramming a sentence can be, for some students, a verbal language activity of hearing and speaking in full sentences).

As a way of conceptualizing variations in individual students' needs for instructional adaptation and/or curricular modification, the Burlington teachers devised a continuum of levels, each defined by a question for the team to resolve through discussion.

- *Level I.* What can the student learn in the regular program of instruction with the same performance standards as nondisabled peers?
- *Level II.* What can the student learn with nondisabled peers, but with adjustments in performance standards according to the student's needs as identified through curriculum-based assessment?
- *Level III.* What can the student learn with adjustments in pacing, method of instruction, and/or special materials or techniques provided with consultant support to the teacher?
- *Level IV.* What can the student learn with adjustments in pacing, method of instruction, and/or special materials or techniques provided jointly with regular and support or ancillary staff?
- *Level V.* What can the student learn with adjustments in the content of the classroom curriculum to be taught jointly by regular and special support or ancillary staff?
- *Level VI.* What classroom curriculum content must be modified significantly and taught by special staff?
- *Level VII.* In what situation is some or all of the content of the classroom curriculum inappropriate for this student? What alternative curriculum program will be used to provide for this student's educational needs?

Ethical Issues in Inclusive Education

Federal legislation does not mandate inclusion, as defined earlier in the chapter, although it does forbid exclusion. The legal basis for inclusion continues to be least restrictive environment (LRE), the requirement that education occur "as much as appropriate" in a regular classroom setting, with supportive aids and services as may be needed. Some professionals, organizations, and also parents have reservations about any concept that could be interpreted to mean "one size fits all," especially if legislators and school officials construe inclusion to mean less costly services. (While individual needs differ widely, the cost per year of educating a student with disabilities is, on average, about twice the cost of educating other pupils, only a part of which is provided through IDEA.)

The American Federation of Teachers, in fact, called for a moratorium on inclusion until all schools were ensured of being provided the kinds of supports (resource specialists and classroom aides) and other provisions (such as manageable class size) that they needed. But advocates compare such proposals to similar situations in the civil rights movement, in which a moratorium on school integration was suggested until all European Americans fully accepted their African American fellow citizens. The question in both situations is, should the crucial years of childhood be allowed to pass irretrievably while their elders await optimal conditions?

What percentage of children with disabilities are currently included in regular classrooms? Based on data compiled for the U.S. Department of Education's annual report to Congress, about three-fourths of the students identified as having mental retardation still receive their instruction in separate classes or even separate schools. Although more than 70 percent of all students with disabilities receive at least some instruction in regular classes, less than one-third of those students are fully included. Resource room arrangements represent the most frequent type of placement—especially for pupils with learning disabilities, by far the largest group—whereby the pupil is either pulled out for certain purposes or mainstreamed in for selected subjects or activities.[17]

Resource room arrangements may seem to offer the best of both worlds—normalizing experiences supplemented by more intensively individualized instruction by specialists. But Joanne Yatvin, a superintendent, found that many students dislike "being sent 'down the hallway' to learn." Moreover,

> When students return to their classrooms, their regular teachers, believing that they have had their daily dose of "special education," feel little need to modify other instruction during the rest of the school day. Under such a system, students get far less instruction than they would if they were grouped with their peers, by age and interest, in regular classrooms with teachers who knew that they had to modify instruction for everyone."[18]

Many educators, parents, and persons with disabilities themselves maintain that if the society of the twenty-first century is to be an inclusive one in which human differences are recognized and celebrated, it must begin with inclusive schools and inclusive classrooms. They point out, correctly, that it is not inclusion that needs to be justified but rather separation, even for part of the school day. That is precisely what the IDEA legislation requires: a child with a disability may not be removed from the regular classroom unless it has been demonstrated that that child's needs cannot be met within the regular classroom, even with supportive aids and services. Policies and practices that segregate children on the basis of a categorical label, whether the label refers to ability/disability, health, or race, are in violation of the U.S. Constitution.

Can every individual child with special needs receive an individually appropriate education without having to be segregated in a special place? Can these students still get the services they need? And what about the typical students? As such questions are debated in local schools like those in the Burlington case study, many teachers in collaboration with parents are making inclusive education a reality. From such examples, the Advocacy Board for the Center on Human Policy at Syracuse University has developed the following statement:[19]

INCLUSION MEANS

1. Educating all children with disabilities in regular classrooms regardless of the nature of their disabling condition(s).
2. Providing all students enhanced opportunities to learn from each other's contributions.
3. Providing necessary services within the regular schools.
4. Supporting regular teachers and administrators (e.g., by providing time, training, teamwork, resources, and strategies).
5. Having students with disabilities follow the same schedules as non-disabled students.
6. Involving students with disabilities in age-appropriate academic classes and extracurricular activities, including art, music, gym, field trips, assemblies, and graduation exercises.
7. Students with disabilities using school cafeteria, library, playground, and other facilities along with non-disabled students.
8. Encouraging friendships between non-disabled and disabled students.

9. Students with disabilities receiving their education and job training in regular community environments when appropriate.
10. Teaching all children to understand and accept human differences.
11. Placing children with disabilities in the same schools they would attend if they did not have disabilities.
12. Taking parents' concerns seriously.
13. Providing an appropriate individualized educational program.

INCLUSION DOES NOT MEAN

1. "Dumping" students with disabilities into regular programs without preparation or support.
2. Providing special education services in separate or isolated places.
3. Ignoring children's individual needs.
4. Jeopardizing students' safety or well-being.
5. Placing unreasonable demands on teachers and administrators.
6. Ignoring parents' concerns.
7. Isolating students with disabilities in regular schools.
8. Placing students with disabilities in schools or classes that are not age-appropriate.
9. Requiring that students be "ready" and "earn" their way into regular classrooms based on cognitive or social skills.

Perhaps the most important ethical issues involved in inclusion, however, are the degree to which it can have a positive effect on an individual student and the degree to which educators are committed to seeing that positive effect occur. Consider, if you will, the case of Stevie as it is described by his parents:

Stevie ends each day by asking if it's a school day tomorrow. When it is, he picks out his clothes promptly for the next day so that he won't be late. . . . We believe that his eagerness reflects his joy in being included in a kindergarten classroom just like every other child in his neighborhood. In so many ways, Stevie is just like all of the other children. But he does face extra challenges due to his diagnosis of Down syndrome. We recognize that Stevie's learning style and ability does differ when compared to his typically developing peers. What we have found critical, though, is not the differences in style and ability, but the desire to do what his peers are doing. We believe that this desire is shared by all children. And for Stevie, this desire becomes his greatest source of motivation and thereby his success.

In an inclusive classroom, Stevie's classmates become his positive role models. In the last six months, Stevie has made considerable progress in his academic and fine motor skills. He is now able to write his name with minimal prompting, count to five with meaning and begin to identify the beginning letters of words by their sounds. His speech, self-help and social skills continue to improve because he wants and expects to interact with the other children. . . . Probably one of the most important benefits of an inclusive classroom is that our life is just *more normal*. As parents, we volunteer in the classroom and participate in school-sponsored events just like every other parent. Thus, we are constantly talking to other parents about mutual parenting concerns. For Stevie's younger brother, it gives him the opportunity to follow the footsteps of his big brother just like other siblings do. And, for Stevie, he has *friends*. Stevie's friends include classmates who are both typically developing and others who have special needs. This too we believe will become the norm for all children because of inclusion. Thus, inclusion leads us to focus our attention on the *child* first and his disability second. Stevie needs that focus. We will always strive to maintain it.

Summary

This chapter has drawn attention to both the historical foundations of the field of special education and current practice of inclusion for children with special needs. In addition, it addresses issues related to the health of children and the responsibility of teachers and schools to consider the means by which children with a variety of health concerns can be integrated into the classroom. Of most importance is the critical role the teacher can play in ensuring that all children are fully integrated into the life and activities of today's classroom while they develop the skills necessary to function effectively in the society at large.

 # Chapter Review

Go to the Online Learning Center at **www.mhhe.com/Cushner4e** to review important content from the chapter, practice with key terms, take a chapter quiz, and find the web links listed in this chapter.

Reflective Questions

A number of questions were posed toward the end of the chapter. Here they are again for your consideration:

1. Can every individual child with special needs receive an individually appropriate education without having to be segregated in a special place? How might this education best be accomplished?
2. How can teachers make certain that all students still get the services they need?
3. What about the typical students? How will they benefit or otherwise be impacted by the concept of inclusion?

Key Terms

Adaptive equipment   344

Autism   345

Behavior management plans   342

Clean intermittent catheterization (CIC)   348

Down syndrome   348

Inclusion   342

Individual Education Program (IEP)   338

Informed consent   355

Least restrictive environment   344

Low-incidence   340

Multifactored evaluation   354

Muscular dystrophy   344

Normalization   343

Placement continuum   355

Sickle cell disease   349

Spina bifida   348

Transition plan   348

Traumatic brain injury   345

Zero exclusion mandate   355

References

1. The case study in this chapter is a composite that reflects the experiences of children, parents, and educators in two communities. Appreciation to the educators who, with parents' consent, provided material for this case study is repeated here. The names of all children and adults are pseudonyms.

2. Bengst Nirje, "The Normalization Principle," in *Changing Patterns in Residential Services for the Mentally Retarded,* rev. ed., ed. R. B. Kirgel and A. Shearer (Washington, DC: President's Commission on Mental Retardation, 1976), p. 231. Also see Wolf Wolfensberger, *The Principle of Normalization in Human Services* (Toronto: National Institute of Mental Retardation, 1972).

3. Vocational Rehabilitation Act of 1973 § 504, P.L. 93-112, 29 U.S.C. § 794 (1983); Americans with Disabilities Act of 1990, 42 U.S.C. § 12101 (1990).

4. Individuals with Disabilities Education Act of 1990, P.L. 101-476, 20 U.S.C. §§ 1400–1485 (1990, reauthorized in 1995).

5. The source for this and subsequent historical information in this chapter is Philip Safford and Elizabeth Safford, *A History of Childhood and Disability* (New York: Teachers College Press, 1995).

6. Laura E. Richards, *Letters and Journals of Samuel Gridley Howe, the Servant of Humanity,* vol. 2 (Boston: Dana Estes, 1909), p. 516; p. 25.

7. Samuel Gridley Howe, *Report of Commission to Inquire into the Conditions of Idiots of the Commonwealth of Massachusetts* (Boston, MA: Senate Document No. 51, 1848).

8. Leta S. Hollingworth, "Provisions for Intellectually Superior Children," in *The Child: His Nature and His Needs,* ed. Michael V. O'Shea (New York: Children's Foundation, 1924), pp. 277–299.

9. Surgeon General's Report, U.S. Department of Health and Human Services, *Children with Special Health Care Needs: Campaign '87* (Washington, DC: U.S. Government Printing Office, 1987).

10. Rachel E. Janney, Martha E. Snell, Mary K. Beers, and Maria Raynes, "Integrating Students with Moderate and Severe Disabilities into General Education Classes," *Exceptional Children* 61, 5 ():425–439.

11. Lawrence Johnson and Marlene Pugach, *Collaborative Practitioners, Collaborative Schools* (Denver, CO: Love Publishing, 1995).

12. See Chapter 10 for a comprehensive discussion of constructivism as reflected in developmentally appropriate practice.

13. Edouard O. Seguin, *Report on Education: U.S. Commissioner on Education at the Vienna Universal Exhibition* (Washington, DC: Government Printing Office, 1880).

14. For a detailed explanation and discussion of collaborative team strategies, see Beverly Rainforth, Jennifer York, and Cathy Macdonald, *Collaborative Teams for Students with Severe Disabilities: Integrating Therapy and Educational Services,* 2nd ed. (Baltimore, MD: Paul H. Brookes Publishing, 1997).

15. Herbert Spencer, "What Knowledge Is of the Most Worth?" *Education: Intellectual, Moral, and Physical* [Essays, 1854-1859] (Patterson, NJ: Littlefield, Adams, 1963), pp. 21–96.

16. See Martha Snell, ed., *Instruction of Students with Severe Disabilities,* 4th ed. (New York: Macmillan, 1993).

17. U.S. Department of Education, *Annual Report to Congress on the Implementation of the Education of All Handicapped Children Act* (Washington, DC: Government Printing Office, 1991).

18. Joanne Yatvin, "Flawed Assumptions," *Phi Delta Kappan* 76, 6 (1994): 482–484.

19. Center on Human Policy, "Inclusion (Inclusion in Education: A Choice for Your Child)," *Newsletter, TASH: The Association for Persons with Severe Handicaps* 20, 9 (1994): 27.

ARTS

Enjoys and participates in art
activities
Recognizes eight basic colors
Cuts on line
Uses glue sparingly

PHYSICAL SKILLS

Hops on one foot
Walks a balance beam
Catches and throws a ball
Kicks a rolling ball
Skips
Jumps rope
Climbs stairs using alternating feet

First Report Period

TEACHER'S COMMENTS

Teacher's Comments:

Your student is possessing
nicely. He has a positive
attitude and is a pleasure
to have in my class.

Assessing Progress:

The Importance of Social Class and Social Status

> *Alice: Would you tell me, please, which*
> *way I ought to go from here?*
> *The Cat: That depends a good deal*
> *on where you want to get to.*
>
> —*Lewis Carroll*

Chapter   Outline

1.   What do you think about the emphasis on state-mandated educational standards for learning?

2.   What has been your experience in taking state competency or proficiency tests?

3.   Do you think that all children can learn?

4.   Do you believe that all children should be educated to the same level?

5.   Do you prefer paper-and-pencil tests over demonstrating your knowledge in other ways?

6.   Do you believe that social class influences the ability of students to succeed in school?

case study   **Redesigning the Jefferson Schools' Math Assessment Program**

It had been a busy semester, and Beth Bradley, chair of the Jefferson City School District Mathematics Committee in Jefferson, Texas, was relaxing with some of her fellow teachers in the conference room at the district office one particularly hectic Tuesday afternoon in mid-January.[1] The day was gray and chilly outside, but students and staff throughout the district were busy preparing for the first mid-year evaluation to be held the next week. This evaluation was to be like no other they had ever experienced in this school system. No longer were grades at the middle and high school so heavily dependent on examinations, as had so often been the case at this time of the year. This was the first year the new evaluation plan was to be put into effect. Parents, teachers, and students would come together over three afternoons and evenings to review student work that was now in the process of being displayed throughout the three elementary schools and the newly combined middle and high school. It had not been an easy transition, and there were still quite a few uncertainties as the evaluation days approached. While most teachers were enthusiastic and optimistic that the transition would be made smoothly, not all the teachers shared that enthusiasm. Even after the two years of discussion and planning that had preceded this year, some teachers still resisted the changes that had been decided on. Beth thought that they would come around after they saw the success of this year's activity. At least, she sure hoped the evaluation would be a success!

Beth, a veteran junior high and then middle school math teacher who had been with the school district for fifteen years before taking over responsibility as chair of the math committee, was talking with John Pinto, a new student teacher in math who was just beginning his student teaching experience at the high school. John was finishing a program at a nearby state university where he would graduate with a master of arts in teaching. Prior to his schooling, John had spent five years as a computer consultant, and he felt fortunate to have been so warmly welcomed at the high school. He was especially excited about being with the math faculty as they were in the process of redesigning the entire math curriculum—including their practices in evaluation.

With them in the district office were two other math teachers, Paul Goodwell, who was responsible for the math program at the elementary level, and Kate van Ryan, the math teacher at the high school who was to be John's cooperating teacher. Because all the mathematics teachers in the district were to have started using multiple means of assessment this year, Beth was telling John how some of the changes had taken place, at least for her.

"Our decision to redesign the way we did math assessments was based on the National Council of Teachers of Mathematics Curriculum and Evaluation Standards," began Beth. "When I first read them, I was impressed and excited about the depth and breadth of the changes they recommended. Before I started to think about making any changes in my classes, I took the time to do a thorough self-evaluation of my own assessment practices. And was I surprised at what I discovered! First, I realized that one of the main reasons I gave most tests was to produce a score that could be entered into my grade book. But while I may have had a score in my book, I really didn't know much about my students' learning or their abilities with respect to the content of the exams. Another thing that really stood out for me was that as I thought about the way I constructed exams, I knew that I could accurately predict which of the students could answer which questions. And, I also had to admit that my predictions were often based on—or at least consistent with—my knowledge of the students' socioeconomic status. Finally, it occurred to me that unless I designed tests that provided opportunities for students who worked at different paces to demonstrate their abilities, I was not really testing learning, but speed instead."

Beth recalled her first attempts to introduce multiple forms of assessment in her eighth grade general math class. "My goal was not to give separate, stand-alone tests, but to assess student growth and understanding through the use of performance assessments, observations of students, interviews with students, and oral as well as written student reports. Nevertheless, old habits die hard. After administering and grading one early test, I realized that I still had no new information from the results. You see, we really should use tests primarily as diagnostic tools, and I had no 'diagnosis' to offer. I somewhat hesitantly abandoned the testing approach in favor of having students assigned to groups or pairs, each having certain tasks to perform. Then, through coaching, observing, and interviewing students as they worked on these tasks, I began to be more aware of each student's work and more able to assess each student's knowledge and growth. This information was much more comprehensive and complete, and I was able to give students grades that more accurately reflected their progress. The students, too, seemed much more relaxed with this approach. Now that I have more experience with these methods, I find that tests do not have to be the primary, or sometimes even a necessary, means of assessment. Furthermore, I suspect that tests may sometimes be an impediment to effective instruction because they tend to reinforce what I already 'know' about my students—that is, who is likely to do well and who is not."

"How did you get started?" asked John. "I mean, textbooks don't seem to offer much more than they did years ago. Just what does it mean to provide students with performance-based assessment?"

"That's a good question, and it did take quite a bit of rethinking and reformulating at first," replied Beth. "I found that the first step in using performance tasks was to find or create some intrinsically useful and interesting activities and problems. A good initial source of these activities is, in fact, the textbook itself. Using these activities, you then have to consider how students might demonstrate their understanding of a given concept. They might use manipulatives, for instance. Class presentations, constructing mathematical models, keeping journals, or producing bulletin boards are other ways students can demonstrate their understanding. You can also change the wording of textbook word problems so that they elicit further explanation. For example, instead of asking, 'How many are left?' you can change the directions to read, 'Explain how you would find out how many are left.' What's important is that students learn how to organize data, set up their own problem-solving strategies, identify their own mistakes, and demonstrate their own thinking as much as possible. This approach will require students to do things that many of them have not been asked to do before. It may be difficult at first, but you will be amazed at how fast they come around."

"There are many ways students can be asked to demonstrate their understanding of mathematical concepts," added Paul, entering the conversation. "For instance, by using manipulatives, young children who are studying fractions can show how they would divide different items, such as five candy bars, ten pencils, or eleven comic books among four students. Instead of being given a traditional division test with twenty items, groups of students can be given different problems to solve. Groups can then be responsible for making posters that explain to others the methods they tried in solving their problem. Older students can be asked to find and demonstrate the value of pi by measuring diameters and circumferences, expressing the ratio, and finding decimal equivalents on the calculator. Students can be free to choose the way they explain and display their findings. When studying sampling techniques, students might be asked to estimate how many bicycles, or any other item, are within two miles of the school. A group can be asked to make a plan for investigating the question and to prepare an oral report, complete with graphs or other displays. They might also keep a log of their activities. Our major goal, you must remember, is to design ways that make it possible for students to demonstrate what they know and the ways in which they went about solving their problem. Students should be the active workers and decision makers. It is ultimately what we do in the real world on a daily basis anyway. We balance our checkbooks, we decide which price is a better buy. We must learn to estimate expenses and live within a budget. Life doesn't test us with rows or columns of problems to solve. And more often than not, the problems in real life are open-ended and might have more than one correct answer. We should strive in our work with young people to integrate the understanding that there might be more than one solution to many problems. This approach not only provides the teacher with insight into the student's thinking, but it encourages the student to verbalize and share her or his strategies."

"That's right," said Beth as she eagerly rejoined the conversation. "Teachers really must decide what is important for students to know and what skills are really

essential. Part of this decision making must take account of state requirements at each grade level and of state proficiency tests. But there are other factors, too. Many of our students do not go on to college, but the jobs they will find are increasingly skilled and technical and require rather sophisticated leadership and problem-solving capacities. We also have to get away from thinking that every bit of student work or activity must be evaluated or observed. You might start by assessing a single simple but important idea. For instance, over a period of several days we might want to find out if students can paraphrase the problem they are working on, while we continue to teach in our usual way the rest of the time. We might then observe whether students can formulate a plan. And always, we keep notes or other records of our observations."

Kate chimed in. "I had an interesting experience with my secondary classes. At the start of last year I persuaded our principal to replace my standard desks with tables that could seat four students. I was then forced to change my entire approach to teaching mathematics. Since last year I've taught my students in a cooperative manner. I'm really thrilled with the results. I have never known students to be so involved with mathematics. I am convinced that their learning was more effective when they were allowed to work in groups, to discuss concepts, and to solve problems with their peers. Even the noise is productive—students actually talk about mathematics!"

"Of course," Kate continued, "my assessment strategies had to change as well. I couldn't justify assessing group work only with written quizzes and unit tests as I had always done, so I added three additional techniques of assessment: by pairs, by observation, and by individual presentation to the whole group. Assessment by pairs of students was very effective. Students are randomly paired. I give each pair two copies of the quiz— one for a rough draft and one to turn in to me. Both students are awarded the same mark. They particularly like this approach because it allows for collaboration and adds another dimension to the thought process—students feel responsible for each other's success."

"Assessing students by observation is also quite natural when teaching in a small group format. I assess students on their contribution to the group, their observed understanding of the concepts, and their ability to clarify and explain questions as they arise. I move freely among the groups and can also easily identify students who are in need of extra help. And because students are accustomed to talking with one another about math problems, they are not as shy about asking for help from me."

"Assessment by presentation allows students to demonstrate the solution to a problem that I present on the overhead projector or chalkboard that comes from the work they are currently studying. Each group is responsible to make certain that all members understand and can explain the solution. I then randomly choose individual students to present their solution to the entire class in a clear and concise manner. The same mark, based on quality of presentation, clarity, creativity, and correctness of solution, is then awarded to each member of the presenter's group."

John was pretty surprised at what he was hearing and glad he had the opportunity to listen to others from the department. "What about the use of portfolios in math?" he asked. "I've heard quite a bit about them, but I've not had the opportunity to see them in use. Has anyone here been using portfolios?"

"We all have," replied Paul. "I began with my fifth grade math class's unit on ratio, proportion, and percents just this year. I told my students that the basic reason for the

change was to encourage quality work. I was really challenged each day to think of different ways to present topics so that the portfolio would show variety. The textbook by itself certainly wouldn't, nor would any of my supplemental work sheets. Most of the activities and applications had to come from me. Quality was the criterion. Growth in thinking and understanding needed to be seen in assignments that involved applications in activity-based projects. Such assignments were not readily available and required considerable time and thought at first. It's gotten quite a bit easier as time has gone by and I become more experienced. Needless to say, I found my teaching style had to change and found new excitement within my classroom. I looked forward to seeing how the various assignments would be received and to discovering what value they had in promoting understanding. We became more like partners in learning—my students and I."

"I did not abandon testing altogether, but I felt better about having something to back up my test scores," said Kate. "The criteria for evaluating the portfolios was listed—usually in the form of a rubric. A cover sheet was required that had a list of all the assignments given. Students had to indicate how many activities they had done out of the total assigned. They were to select four samples of their best work and include them with two assignments I required. The work had to show variety and evidence of thought. They had to explain why they chose what they did. Students quickly went to work. They were allowed to make revisions and attach them to the original work. At first, students balked at having to tell why they chose a particular piece of work, but in time, this hitch seemed to smooth out. We took two days with this final activity, but the end result was quite rewarding and definitely worth the time. Parents will see the results when they come in for conferences."

"When it comes to grading, I use a holistic method. I sort portfolios into three main piles and then subdivide within those piles. I find myself basing my decisions on the kinds of assignments selected, and I tend to value those with writing rather than those with strict calculations. I also look at the quality of the assignments and value those that show more mathematical understanding over others. I feel very good about the whole process. And the students seem to like the portfolio process as well. They think it allows them to 'mess up' a bit and not be penalized. They like being able to choose the quality of the work. A test is only one grade, and it may not always be the student's best effort. They think that a combination of the two, tests and portfolio, is a good measure of what they have learned. The portfolio really is a culmination of everything I've been trying to do. It reflects a wide variety of assessments and assignments. It also forced me to use and acknowledge some of the principles of learning that are currently being uncovered by researchers. Students like being a part of something new and exciting as well."

"You know, we've studied quite a lot about diversity and education across cultures and socioeconomic groups in college," said John, "and there seems to be considerable diversity here in the Jefferson schools. Has this approach been beneficial to all the individuals from various backgrounds who are in this school?"

"It sure has, at least from my perspective," replied Beth. "We are a school with tremendous diversity, and we haven't always been good about addressing particular needs or reaching some of our students, particularly those whose families are poor. Exciting some of these students about school seemed to be difficult if not impossible at times. Now that we've begun to alter our assessment strategies, and our instructional

approaches as well, a much greater percentage of students seem to be more actively involved in their learning more of the time. The more verbal student, for instance, is now encouraged to discuss and reflect more with open-ended questioning, and she or he has more opportunity to dialogue with others. Because we use more interviews and individual conferences, there is a greater opportunity for both teacher and student to get to know one another, to develop trust, and to increase that essential sense of belonging among students. This method, incidentally, also helps build confidence and self-esteem in students."

"With portfolios, students become an integral part of the system," Paul added. "Students are co-creators of what they are to be responsible for. No longer is it only the teacher who tells students what it is they are to know. Students help determine the direction of their learning, the means by which it is assessed, and the level of acceptability. It is also easier for students to see how their progress has evolved. They are no longer merely collecting a series of marks on papers and exams. They become part of the process of documenting growth over time."

"We also find that there is greater opportunity to communicate with parents," interjected Kate. "First, our method of reporting student progress had to change. We are now piloting a variety of checklists and descriptive reports to determine the most beneficial way to communicate student progress. It is also much easier to sit down at conferences and be specific with parents about their child's strengths and weaknesses when you have a collection of their actual work in front of you. It becomes much more meaningful than merely looking at numbers in a gradebook, which, I'm now embarrassed to say, I've done in the past. It's easier to take a more individualized approach to my teaching and working with students now that we all are much more focused on their actual products. This approach also helps build the necessary bridges within the community between parents and the schools. We've started asking students to assess themselves and to become critical of their own progress as well as of our work. This step is somewhat difficult for many of the students to do well, but I'm pretty sure they will become better self-evaluators as time goes on."

"Are other teachers using multiple forms of assessment?" asked John. "Can they be used outside the traditional classroom?"

"Of course," replied Beth, "this effort is district wide. The same principles that we have applied in math are used across the curriculum. We are constantly seeking out ways that our students can demonstrate the skills they are learning. Why don't you spend some time during the evaluation period observing what others are doing? I think you'll find it quite interesting."

"And," Paul added, "our emphasis on performance assessment has forced us to ask the bigger questions: those dealing with our narrow approach and perspective that we have always found so comfortable and easy to adopt. We're all learning a tremendous amount about how our own culture, for instance, has conditioned us to see the world from one particular perspective and to therefore judge others according to our own culture's standards. This new method means that we have had to develop more elaborative, comprehensive, and inclusive means to evaluate students across the board. We're beginning to rethink our whole policy on participation in many of the so-called extracurricular activities. Our goal really is full inclusion. We do want as many students to participate in as many activities as possible. We think we can create a structure that

will allow students who wish to participate in an activity to do so while they are at the same time striving toward quality and excellence. Maybe we won't build school spirit by having the region's best sports teams, but we'll build it by having more students who are active and involved in their school community. By looking at multiple forms of assessment, we have been forced to concentrate on actual student behavior—and in the process, encourage greater participation in all areas of school life."

At that moment, Dr. Gerard, the district superintendent, was passing by the office. "Hope you're looking forward to our upcoming evaluation activities," she said as she put her head in the office. "I've never seen faculty so busy and excited. I think we're on the long-overdue road to uniting the schools. Hope it all goes well." As she left the group, she added, "And I hope that these new forms of evaluation will pay off when the students take the state proficiency tests in April!"

Rationale for Broadened Definitions of Assessment

The task of assessing student progress has always been of central importance to educators, but in the last decade or so schools, teachers, and students have felt increasing pressure to demonstrate competence in their teaching and learning. Indeed, since the publication of *A Nation at Risk* in 1983, the debate about how well our children are learning has become both ubiquitous and emotional.[2]

Accountability and the Educational Standards Movement

In the mid to late 1980s, after the publication of numerous state-of-the-schools reports funded and/or sponsored by groups with widely divergent interests, concern grew that America's schools were not functioning very well and that students were not learning much—certainly not as much as their counterparts in other industrialized nations.

History of the Standards and Accountability Movement

In 1989, President George H. W. Bush convened the nation's governors for an education summit, out of which came a set of national education goals—**Goals 2000**—designed to improve America's schools in eight specific areas, including improvement in reading and math and graduating 90 percent of America's high school students by the year 2000. In 1992, Congress convened a thirty-two-member panel of educators, business leaders, and public officials, called the National Council on Education Standards and Testing. That panel concluded that creating national standards and assessments was both highly desirable and feasible.[3]

In 1994, President Clinton signed the Goal 2000: **Educate America Act,** which awarded states additional money for education and granted them considerable flexibility as to how that money would be spent. The Educate America Act was based on five principles: (1) all students can learn; (2) lasting improvements depend on school-based leadership; (3) simultaneous top-down and bottom-up reform is necessary; (4) strategies must be locally developed, comprehensive, and coordinated; and (5) the whole community must be involved in developing strategies for systemwide improvement. Central to the whole idea was the belief that states and local districts should set high standards for achievement, should test to see how well students were achieving, and should hold schools, teachers, and students accountable for the results. Thus was the **accountability movement** born.

As part of the act, Congress created a National Standards and Improvement Council, with nominations for membership to be made by congressional leaders, the Secretary of Education, and the National Education Goals Panel. Nominations were slow in coming in, and by 1996, amendments to the Educate America Act eliminated the council altogether. One central aspect of the problem of setting national standards for education is that it implies a national curriculum, something that states have resisted mightily over a long period of time. Questions that arose across the nation with respect to national standards included not only how to decide on specific definitions of standards in major academic subjects, but also how the standards would be tied to some reasonable assessment of what students really needed to know to be good citizens and productive workers, how student learning would be measured, and how the standards would affect poor and minority children, children with special needs, and children for whom English was not their primary language.[4]

When the battle to set national standards failed, states began to come up with subject-area standards of their own. The federal role in the accountability and standards movement diminished somewhat, and the states came to the forefront. Although the Educate America Act defined three kinds of standards—**content standards**, **performance standards**, and **delivery standards**—the states concentrated on content and performance standards, and especially on testing. As of today, academic standards in at least some subjects are in place in forty-nine states, fifty states test student learning, and twenty-seven states hold schools accountable for results, some by issuing state report cards, some by tying graduation to test results, and all by rating school performance.[5]

By the year 2001, the Educate America Act was eliminated in favor of a new Elementary and Secondary Education (ESEA) Act, called the **"No Child Left Behind" Act of 2001,** signed into law by President George W. Bush in January of 2002. This law increases the pressure on failing schools through a series of consequences and continues the emphasis on testing by mandating that all children be tested in reading and math each year in grades 3 through 8. The new law also increases federal spending for education reform, seeking to target resources for high-poverty schools.

The "No Child Left Behind" Act of 2001

According to an American Federation of Teachers study, there is still no coordinated effort to align standards, curriculum, tests, and accountability measures.[6] Further, an increasing number of teachers, parents, administrators, and policy makers are questioning the nature and outcomes of traditional evaluation practices as well as the uses to which these are put. Particularly called into question is the primary use of standardized objective tests—called high stakes tests—to make decisions about students with respect to placement and graduation.

The Case for Standardized Testing

Throughout the 1970s and early 1980s, the use of standardized tests increased across the United States in response to the minimum competency testing movement that swept the nation. Proponents of this movement argued that U.S. students, in comparison with students in other industrialized nations, were lacking basic skills, particularly in literacy and mathematics. Such insufficiency, they argued, was due to two factors. First, American education suffered from too much child-centered educational practice and the wide latitude of curriculum in U.S. schools that was comonplace. Second children from racial minority groups, poor children, and those for whom English was a second language routinely scored lower than white upper- and middle-class children on tests of basic skills. Proponents argued that these combined factors only proved that U.S. schools were not doing their job with respect to basic knowledge.

The Case for Standardized Testing

Today the loudest calls for educational reform from business and government include insistence on standardized testing as a way of measuring how well American schools are doing. So popular is the appeal of an objective and standardized test as a way of measuring student achievement and so strong is the belief that such tests actually do measure the knowledge that students have acquired, that standardized testing has come to be accepted as a principle measure by which many legislators assess academic achievement of students. Moreover, the reports on results of testing are becoming more complex: the new ESEA reauthorization requires not only that individual student scores be reported, but also that they be reported by race and income and that the reports show "gaps between, and the progress of, various subgroups."[7]

The Case against Standardized Testing

Over the years, many concerned educators as well as some well-informed politicians have been raising questions and concerns over such issues as poor validity between the stated purpose of a given test and what it might actually measure; the reliability and comparability of test scores; cultural bias in the design and use of tests; the often unethical or questionable use of test results; and the narrow approach and application of tests that, although they provide easy quantitative analysis, tend to measure out-of-context learning while downplaying actual student performance. Most standardized tests, for instance, don't truly tell us if a student can write a coherent sentence but rather indicate only if she or he can identify one. Further, there is little correlation between a student's ability to identify which word in a series of words is misspelled (which is easy to measure on a standardized test) and the individual's subsequent ability to spell correctly (which is really the preferred goal).[8] Performance-based assessment, on the other hand, requires that students demonstrate their ability to perform the actual skill.

While the goal of most responsible policy makers was to improve the outcomes of schooling by ensuring that most students mastered some basic skills, the effect was often quite different. For example, on multiple-choice standardized tests, complex academic and intellectual skills often must be broken down into discrete elements that, while easy to measure, often tend to neglect both the context in which knowledge and skills can be used and the ability to connect one idea or skill with another. Teachers, on the other hand, often teach within a context that is familiar to their students but unknown to test makers. Thus, two results are common: (1) students don't recognize out-of-context questions, and (2) students' thinking skills and ability to synthesize information or to solve problems is not ordinarily tested very well. In addition, because areas of knowledge such as art, drama, and music are difficult to assess in this

How Is My Child Really Doing?

Stan Morrison is worried. His son, Dave, is a student at Jefferson High School and has shown a good deal of aptitude in math all during his school years. Stan thinks that Dave's aptitude is a good thing because the boy wants to be an engineer, just like his dad. But lately, Dave has been talking about the "new" kinds of math instruction that his trigonometry teacher is using. The students work in small groups; they try to find answers to problems with little guidance from the teacher; they write *papers* in math class, for heaven's sake.

Tomorrow, Stan and his wife are going to the school for a presentation and demonstration of the new math evaluation procedures. What Stan wants is to hear that his son is getting an A in trig. He knows what that means—that Dave is doing well. But Stan has a suspicion that he is going to hear a lot more than that, and he wonders if he will understand all the educational jargon he thinks he'll probably hear. All this new "assessment" stuff sounds pretty weird to him!

- If you were Dave's trig teacher, how would you deal with Mr. and Mrs. Morrison?
- What might you say to alleviate their worries?

manner, many schools have deemphasized these aspects of the curriculum. Educators, feeling pressure to "teach to the test," have often overemphasized the discrete low-level elements while ignoring the more complex cognitive, affective, and behavioral skills and processes needed by individuals in a highly interrelated and rapidly changing society.

The Case for Multiple Forms of Assessment

In recent years a number of national organizations have made policy statements asserting that so-called **high stakes testing** should be abandoned or at least modified in their impact on students. These organizations also call for a wide range of assessment practices. The American Educational Research Association's position statement says:

The Case for Multiple Forms of Assessment

> Decisions that affect individual students' life chances or educational opportunities should not be made on the basis of test scores alone. Other relevant information should be taken into account to enhance the overall validity of such decisions. As a minimum assurance of fairness, when tests are used as part of making high-stakes decisions for individual students such as promotion to the next grade or high school graduation, students must be afforded multiple opportunities to pass the test. More importantly, when there is credible evidence that a test score may not adequately reflect a student's true proficiency, alternative acceptable means should be provided by which to demonstrate attainment of the tested standards.[9]

Similarly, the National Education Association's position "supports ongoing, comprehensive, aligned assessments of student growth that are directly linked to lessons and materials used by teachers. NEA believes that standardized tests should only be used to improve the quality of education and instruction for students."[10]

Three ideas are central to the argument underlying multiple assessments. First, students must leave school with more than low-level basic skills. Indeed, they should have the ability to solve complex problems and be able to integrate knowledge across disciplines as well as have an appreciation for and knowledge of the arts. Multiple forms of assessment enable teachers to more accurately determine if, in fact, a student can actually perform the skills or behavior that are expected of them.

Second, because the world in which students will live is becoming increasingly interdependent, young people must learn the skills of cooperation and collaboration. Thus, instruction and evaluation must become somewhat less individualistic, and students should be able to work with others in groups, both as leaders and as followers.

Third, greater accuracy in assessment across cultural groups must be achieved in order to understand more clearly just what students do know and can do and to assist all students in developing their own potential to the highest level possible. Since the use of standardized tests has become so widespread, educational researchers have been investigating reasons why some groups tend to perform less well than others. Theories to explain discrepancies between groups have tended to look for deficiencies in the people and not in the tests themselves. Thus, explanations for poor performance have included sociocultural and genetic deficiencies among particular groups of people. Critics of these theories point out that differences in test results do not represent deficiencies in upbringing or in genetic differences of certain groups of children. Rather, research suggests that many tests are inherently unreliable because of such factors as cultural bias or the fact that tests may not measure features of intelligence that are deemed essential among particular groups. Thus, children may lack exposure to certain knowledge and experiences that become the basis of the tests or the test administration as well as the basis of the inconclusiveness of basic assumptions about intelligence and its inheritability.[11]

Various forms of performance assessment are quite congruent with the practice of many groups. Prior to European contact in the Americas, for instance, nearly all native people used performance-based assessments to determine how each individual could best contribute to the survival of the group. As children grew up, adults observed their level of knowledge and skill in such tasks as hunting, running, building consensus, healing, and spiritual leadership. Children who demonstrated superior skills were the ones who later led hunting parties, provided spiritual guidance, and performed other necessary tasks. Today, various forms of performance assessment are gaining wide acceptance as legitimate ways to evaluate learner success.

At the same time, proponents of multiple forms of assessment argue that teachers are most often the best judges of student performance, because they are aware of both the context in which students have learned and the individual variations in students' learning styles. Furthermore, proponents assert that since standardized means of assessment, particularly multiple-choice tests, do not lend themselves well to analysis of these more complex behaviors and skills, teachers should develop the skills necessary to make informed and accurate judgments in a variety of contexts and across a variety of groups. These goals have prompted educators to look more closely at multiple forms of assessment and to develop more comprehensive approaches in the area of performance assessment.

Characteristics of Classrooms That Use Multiple Forms of Assessment

It is important at the outset to distinguish between the process of assessment and the process of testing. **Assessment** looks carefully at the whole individual within the educational process and context; it implies a comprehensive, individualized evaluation of the person's strengths as well as areas that are in need. Assessment is formative; that is, it is an in-process act in which the information derived is used as feedback to both teachers and students as to how and where they might begin to look if change is desired.

Testing, on the other hand, implies standardization in which the individual is compared against some norm-referenced set of scores or to a known group of individuals. Testing tends to be a summative activity. That is, the resultant scores represent a final statement of how an individual compares to others who have taken the same test. Too often teachers neglect the ongoing nature of assessment and rely on some form of summative test to obtain a picture of how well a student has performed. Once this result is obtained it is usually too late, at least in the standard classroom, to take corrective action.

Pedagogies: Old and New

Classrooms that actively use performance-based, multiple forms of assessment are typically classrooms where students are engaged in meaningful projects, multiple activities, and discussion with teachers about self-evaluation as well as teacher evaluation. Rather than completing workbook page after workbook page or endlessly doing repetitive exercises from a textbook, students may be seen working on open-ended projects that begin with focused problems and move into larger, more complex problems that demand a variety of skills. Such classrooms are characterized by a lack of standardized, objective-type tests. Rather than an accumulation of test papers, a certain number of projects may be required each grading period—a certain percentage of which must be passed better than satisfactory. And there is a certain understanding that the entire community may also wish to have knowledge and access to student work. As a result, performance tasks and portfolios of student work often become the means by which students demonstrate mastery of particular content.

Roles: Old and New

In multiple-assessment classrooms, a variety of forms of performance assessments, such as **portfolio assessments,** or exhibits, or experiments, allow students to become active contributors and responsible partners in documenting their learning. For a portfolio assessment, each student puts together a folder that may contain classwork, journals, and projects. At the end of a grading period, teachers and students work together to select the pieces that provide an honest picture of the work the student can accomplish and has accomplished. Portfolios developed early in the year enable students and teacher to see growth and changes that occur over time. Together they choose what is worth documenting—because the ideas are important, because the work is something the student is especially proud of, or because progress and growth over time is easily visible. Based on the contents of the portfolio, students are given narrative reports that detail strengths, areas for improvement, development, special interests, and so forth. Parents may also become active in such an evaluation process by being encouraged to review the contents with their child and to call or write a response to the teacher. All the while, students reflect on what they have learned and what they desire to know in the future.

Place of Content Knowledge: Old and New

Like in many, if not all, of the classroom case studies presented in previous chapters, content knowledge in classrooms that use a variety of assessments has a somewhat different place. First, much of the time in such classrooms, content is presented and acquired in the service of other activities. Thus, language arts content is necessary for the production of a newspaper or a report or a story. Similarly, math content is necessary for building models, measuring water samples, or mapmaking. This attitude toward content information closely mirrors the way we acquire knowledge and skills outside of school; in general, we learn something because we need to know it in order to do something else.

It may be argued that if the only information and skills we acquire are directly linked to what we need to know, we will miss much that is both useful and beautiful. Schooling is, in part, an invitation to escape the boundaries of our current lives by discovering that which lies outside our experience. Such was the case, for example, in Chapter 8, when students were encouraged to build models of various types of places of worship and, in the process, discovered much about comparative religion that was "unnecessary" in their daily lives. It is up to teachers to provide the context and the environment in which students do learn to go beyond their present experience. Indeed, it is the very nature of a liberal education to provide students with new experiences of all kinds (including exposure to literature, music, and art) that will enrich their lives. The major difference here is that such knowledge is not taught only as an end in itself, but rather as a means toward other ends.

Assessment: Old and New

Multiple Forms of Assessment: Examples

As teachers have become more sophisticated in their understanding of the manner in which students learn and as they have paid particular attention to the variety of learning styles, they have recognized the relative inadequacy of a single approach to assessment. Some children who perform tasks quite well in real life demonstrate poor performance on paper-and-pencil tests, the result not of an inability to demonstrate the requisite skill but of an incongruency between their knowledge and the manner in which it is assessed.

Often, in classrooms that employ multiple means of assessment, students and teachers together arrive at acceptable standards for good work. Assessment of such projects is not based on terms such as *neat* or *correct*. Rather, students are evaluated on their ability to solve problems, to clearly demonstrate how thinking was done, or to collaborate well with others.

Time limits and criteria of acceptability are also generally broader. It is understood that some students may take more time than others to complete various projects; the standards, however, remain the same for all students. It becomes more important that students ultimately achieve the objectives—not that they achieve them by a certain deadline. In such classrooms, students might also keep working and submitting their work for suggestions and critique, not only from the teacher but from other students as well. Rather than considering a project or particular learning task completed at a particular date, as with a final test, students are encouraged to return to earlier work time and time again as they gain new knowledge.

Student work may also be used to teach others. Classroom folders may contain student work from previous years. Students can see others' thinking and realize that projects may have multiple solutions. Students may also be encouraged to, and in fact evaluated on, their ability to find good help—in the form of primary source material or outside people. Parents and other community volunteers may take an active role in student work and in such activities as after-school homework halls where cross-age tutoring may be encouraged.

At the end of each semester there may be a portfolio week, much like the old finals week, where student work is displayed, like the Jefferson schools faculty were preparing for in this chapter's case study. The portfolio, in such circumstances, becomes the basis for a conference with the teacher or advisor. The subject of the conference focuses not only on the content of the portfolio but also on the student's future plans, major learning tasks still to be addressed, and any changes in direction that might have occurred since the previous conference. Students ultimately take their work home and share it with another adult.

Perspectives on Means for Assessing Student Learning

Among all the issues involved in assessment, several stand out as truly basic. Chief among these are the importance of criteria in any kind of assessment and the issue of the reasons for grading.

The Importance of Criteria

Determining the specific criteria for satisfactory performance may be the most difficult aspect of assessment.[12] Educators must step back and ask what it means to master a specific ability or skill. Just what would a student who has mastered certain skills be able to do?

For instance, a long-term goal of an American history class might be for students to demonstrate empathy for people in different periods in history. To demonstrate this goal using the Civil War as a context, students might be given assignments such as these: (1) Write a diary as though you are the parent of two sons during the Civil War, one fighting for the South and one fighting for the North. Attach a statement about what you think was hardest for the parent. (2) Create a play about a family in the Civil War, and make the action revolve around a family member's decision to join the army. Attach a commentary about how the members of this family are like or unlike families you know. (3) Create a chart of aspects of the Civil War that affected families. Compare these aspects to the experiences of Afghan families during the recent war in Afghanistan.

What About the State Assessment Tests?

John Pinto, the student teacher at Jefferson High School, is worried about how the new forms of assessment are going to help in ensuring that his math students do well on the state tests. He thinks the assessments are a good idea—indeed, he looks forward to trying some of them out. But will they translate into improved math scores on the Texas Assessment of Academic Skills (TAAS)? President George W. Bush is very high on the TAAS tests and often uses them as a model for what the whole nation could (and should) do.

John isn't completely sure that the evaluation system developed by the Jefferson city schools can, in fact, "match" the TAAS.

- If you were Beth Bradley, how might you answer John's concerns?

Making judgments as to the appropriateness of student responses is another issue. Some criteria that might be used in the analysis of student responses to the Civil War assignments might include: (1) The student accurately uses information from the historical period. (2) The student uses sufficient detail to create a sense of what it was like for people who lived at the time under study. (3) The student draws out relationships between that period of history and the present. (4) The student uses affective language in dealing with the experiences of people—in history as well as today.

Finally, communicating achievement to students and parents becomes a critical issue. Teachers have always been faced with the difficulty of integrating a number of sources of student information into a single grade. But especially today, with the emphasis on broadening the range and types of assessments, boiling all the information down into a single grade can be overwhelming, if not impossible, to do. Seeking alternative methods of reporting grades has also been a focus in recent years.

The Issue of Grading

Although issues of assessment (how well students are doing) have long been a part of the educational landscape, grading (how well students are doing in relation to others) seems to be a relatively recent phenomenon. As far back as ancient Greece, assessment was used in a formative manner. Teachers questioned students orally so they could demonstrate what they knew, which thus provided insight into what areas or topics required more work or instruction. Grading and reporting were virtually unknown until the mid-1800s. Prior to this time, few students went beyond an elementary education. It wasn't until later, as school populations grew and the new ideas of scientific measurement gained popularity, that the perceived need to grade children emerged. A brief history of grading can be seen in Table 12.1.

In any discussion of grading, especially if traditional methods of grading are being called into question, it is well to consider the basis on which grades are assigned in the first place. Kohn suggests three levels of inquiry into questions regarding the

t a b l e   1 2 . 1   History of American Grading

Mid to late 1800s
Progress evaluations begin to be issued by schools. Teachers simply record the skills students have mastered. Once students have completed the requirements of one level, they move onto the next.

Early 1900s
As the number of high school students increases, teachers begin introducing percentages as a way to certify students' accomplishments in specific subject areas. While written descriptions continue to be used in elementary schools, few educators question the gradual shift in emphasis at the high school level.

1912
Starch and Elliott publish a study that questions the use of percentages as a reliable measure of student achievement.[13] Their study asked 142 teachers to grade two papers written for a first-year high school English class. Grading on a scale from 0 to 100, 15 percent gave one paper a failing mark while 12 percent gave the same paper a score of 90 or more. The other paper received scores ranging from 50 to 97. Neatness, spelling, and punctuation influenced the scoring of some of the teachers, while others simply considered how well the paper communicated its message.

1913
In light of criticism that good writing is, by its very nature, subjective, Starch and Elliott repeat their investigation, this time using geometry papers.[14] Greater variation occurs during this assessment, with scores on one paper ranging from 28 to 95. Some teachers deducted points only for wrong answers, while others took neatness, form, and spelling into account.

1918
Teachers begin using grading scales with fewer and larger categories. One three-point scale uses categories of Excellent, Average, and Poor. Another scale has five categories: Excellent, Good, Average, Poor, and Failing, with some corresponding letters of A, B, C, D, and F.

1930s
Grading on a curve increases as an attempt to minimize the subjectivity of grading. This method begins to group students according to some arbitrary scale, with top percentages receiving As, the next percentage receiving Bs, and so forth. Some educators even go as far as suggesting that the proportion of grades be assigned as 6-22-44-22-6. Grading on a curve seems fair and equitable, especially in light of research at the time that innate intelligence approximates a normal probability curve.

(Continued)

table 12.1   (*Concluded*)

1930s (*continued*)

The debate over grading and reporting intensifies. Many schools abolish formal grades altogether and return to using verbal descriptions of student achievement. Some schools introduce pass-fail systems, distinguishing only between acceptable and failing work. Still other schools emphasize a mastery approach; once students demonstrate mastery of a skill or content they are allowed to move on to other areas of study.

1958

Ellis Page investigates how student learning is affected by grades and teacher's comments.[15] In his classic study, seventy-four secondary teachers administer a test and assign a letter grade of A, B, C, D, or F to each paper. Scored papers are then randomly assigned to one of three groups. Papers in one group receive only the numerical score and a letter grade. The second group, in addition to the score and letter grade, receive the following comments: A—Excellent! B—Good Work. Keep at it. C—Perhaps try to do better. D—Let's bring this up. F—Let's raise this grade! For the third group, in addition to the score and letter grade, teachers write individualized comments.

Page looks closely at students' scores on the next test as a measure of the effect of the comments and grades. Results demonstrate that students in the second group achieved significantly higher scores than did those who received only a score and grade. The students who received individualized comments did even better. Page concludes that grades can have a beneficial effect on student learning but only when accompanied by specific or individualized comments from the teacher.

Source: H. Kirschenbaum, S. B. Simon, and R. W. Napier, *Wha-ja-get? The Grading Game in American Education* (New York: Hart, 1971); and T. R. Guskey, "Making the Grade: What Benefits Students?" *Educational Leadership* 52, 2 (October 1994):14–20.

assignment of grades that distinguish educators' depth of analysis and their willingness to question the basic assumptions about why grading is undertaken.[16]

> *Level 1* considers the most superficial elements, primarily, how to grade students' work. The assumption at this level is that everything that students do must receive some grade and that, as a result, students should be concerned about the grades they ultimately will receive.

> *Level 2* begins to question whether, in fact, traditional grading is really necessary or even useful for assessing student performance. Multiple forms of assessment, when used for more than merely determining a letter grade, fall into this category. The basic idea here is to provide a deeper description of students' achievement.

> *Level 3* moves beyond the discussion of how to grade and begins to question why students are to be evaluated. Regardless of how we go about evaluating students, if our reasons for doing so are not valid, our results will not be constructive.

Grading to Sort

One reason we evaluate students is to sort or categorize them into groups based, generally, on their performance. Questions at Level 1 ask whether we are placing individuals in the "correct" group. A major problem here, it is said, is that at the secondary and university levels, too many students are placed in the "excellent" category. Most studies, interestingly enough, suggest that there is no subsequent increase in student performance when teachers grade more stringently. And conversely, students do not do inferior work when it is relatively easy to get a good grade.

At Level 2, discussion centers around whether grades are reliable indicators with which to sort students. The subjectivity as well as the variability of grading suggests the rather questionable nature of much of our "objective" assessment.

Concerns at Level 3 question not whether we are sorting students poorly, but why we are sorting them at all. What are our reasons for sorting students? Is it to segregate students and to teach them separately? Are we acting as inexpensive personnel screening services for business? Are we attempting to maintain a power structure built on an outdated foundation? Whatever the ultimate reasons, it is suggested that sorting is often incompatible with the goal of helping all students learn.[17]

Grading to Motivate

A second often-stated reason behind the giving of grades is to motivate students to work harder so they will, in turn, receive favorable evaluations. This use rests on the assumption that there exists a single entity, called motivation, that students have to a lesser or greater degree. What is often overlooked or not well understood, however, is the distinction between extrinsic and intrinsic motivation. That is, some motivation comes from outside the student (extrinsic), as in an attempt to avoid punishment or receive greater rewards; other motivation comes from within the student (intrinsic), as when learning occurs for its own sake. These two sources of motivation, unfortunately, often conflict with one another. That is, when people work for external rewards, they tend to lose interest in whatever they have to do to earn those rewards. The principle motivator becomes either obtaining the reward or, in some instances avoiding a punishment. Many studies, across age as well as culture, have found that the more students are induced to think about their evaluation on an assignment, the less they desire to learn and the less they will do, especially in areas where creativity is the focus.[18] As Butler and Nissan suggest, grades may actually encourage an emphasis on quantitative aspects of learning, depress creativity, foster fear of failure, and result in a loss of interest on the part of the student.[19]

Grading as Feedback

Some educators state that their purpose in evaluating students is to provide feedback so that students can learn more effectively. From a Level 2 perspective, this goal is legitimate. Unfortunately, grades, as reported in the previous section, are not good means to provide feedback. In most instances, students experience grades as rewards and punishment, not as information. Reducing something to a B+ or D– provides the student with little information about how a paper might be improved. A good Level 3 question asks, Why do we want the student to improve?

Increasingly across the United States, such questions are being asked—and answered in surprising and interesting ways. When teachers and administrators begin to seriously question the form and function of traditional grades, the answers they come up with frequently alter traditional views.

Case Analysis

Performance assessment and authentic evaluation have been the buzzwords of the past few years when it comes to looking closely at the manner in which teachers gain knowledge about student achievement. Such efforts force educators like those in the case study's Jefferson School District to look well beyond simply testing students. When teachers look at the broader issue of assessment, they are encouraged to examine such aspects as the purposes of education, stating clearly the specific skills they wish students to master and, at the same time, empowering themselves to take greater charge of their curriculum.[20] This process also brings into question the manner in which individual teachers tend to make judgments about students as well as attempts to broaden that approach. Indeed, testing of individuals in and of itself seems to be solely a western concept associated with western models of schooling.[21]

In addition, the desire to compete with others may also be a rather foreign concept for some cultures or groups. In other words, the whole concept of testing, in the formal sense that we use the word, may be relatively uncommon to some groups of people. Educators are also forced to look closely at the manner in which schools communicate achievement to both students and parents.

In the traditional sense, testing as we have known it draws our attention to whether students get the right answers. How students arrive at their answers, while perhaps important in the development of such tests, are typically not evident or even asked about at this stage. When students take a multiple-choice test, in math for instance, there is no way a teacher can differentiate students who select the correct answer because they truly understand the problem, those who understand the problem but made a simple careless mistake, or those who do not know where to begin but simply guessed correctly. A key feature of performance assessment is that students demonstrate their knowledge or skill. The process by which they go about solving problems therefore becomes as critical as the final solution. Whereas a traditional test might ask students the steps involved in preparing a biological specimen to be viewed under a microscope, a more authentic assessment might ask students to demonstrate how to prepare a slide for use on a microscope. Instead of testing students' knowledge about the rules of grammar, students might be asked to edit a poorly written passage. Whereas a traditional technology test might ask students to identify the steps involved in programming a computer, a performance assessment would have students produce a program that runs well.

Another key element of all performance assessments is that students become active participants. Instead of choosing from preselected options, as is typical of multiple choice or most other simple objective measures (e.g., true-false, matching), students become active learners, responsible for creating or constructing their responses. A wide range of assessment techniques are possible, some of which are summarized in Table 12.2.

table 12.2   Some Examples of Performance Assessment Techniques

Projects

Projects are comprehensive demonstrations of skills or knowledge. They are often inter-disciplinary in focus, require a broad range of competencies, and require student initiative and creativity. Teachers or trained judges score each project against standards that are known to all participants ahead of time.

Projects can take the form of competitions between individual students or groups, or they may be collaborative projects that students work on over time. Students may be required to conduct a demonstration or give a live performance before a class. Science fair projects are a form of this type of assessment. Group projects enable a number of students to work together on a complex problem that requires planning, research, discussion, and group presentation. Such an approach helps develop and integrate skills of cooperative learning.

Interviews and oral presentations

Such approaches allow individuals to verbalize their knowledge. This approach is especially useful with young children, with students with learning disabilities, or with students relatively new to a second language. In such an approach, the interview is likely to elicit more information than open-ended written questions will.

Examples occur rather frequently in foreign language education, where fluency can be determined only by hearing an individual speak. Use of audio and video technology allows these approaches to be used more frequently.

Constructed-response questions

Such questions require students to produce their own responses rather than select from an array of predetermined responses (such as multiple choice). Constructed-response items may have just one correct response or may be more open-ended, allowing for a range of possible answers. Examples include fill-in-the-blank, writing a short answer, producing a graph or diagram, or writing out a proof for geometry.

Essays

This approach has long been used to assess a student's understanding of a subject through written description, analysis, explanation, or summary. Essays can demonstrate how well a student uses facts in context. Answering well-constructed essay questions may also allow a teacher to assess a student's ability to use higher-level cognitive processes, such as critical thinking, analysis, and synthesis. Essays may also be used to assess students' composition skills such as spelling, grammar, and sentence structure.

(Continued)

t a b l e   1 2 . 2   (*Concluded*)

Experiments

Experiments allow teachers to assess how well students understand various scientific concepts and can carry out scientific processes. Students are encouraged to "do" science by posing hypotheses, designing experiments to test their hypotheses, writing up their findings, and applying various scientific skills, facts, and concepts.

Demonstrations

Demonstrations allow students the opportunity to show their mastery of subject-area content and procedures. Students in biology class might demonstrate the production of a microscope slide. Students in a first-aid class might demonstrate skill in bandaging by working with a partner.

Portfolios

Portfolios are usually files or folders that contain collections of a student's work. They provide a broad portrait of an individual's performance over time. Students, if allowed to put together their own portfolio, gain skill in evaluating their own work. Portfolios are increasingly common in English and language arts where drafts, revisions, works in progress, and final papers demonstrate student development.

Source: Lawrence M. Rudner, "Assessing Civics Education," *ERIC Digest Series* (1991), and *Testing in American Schools: Asking the Right Questions* (Office of Technology Assessment, Congress of the United States), cited in Lawrence M. Rudner and Carol Boston, "Performance Assessment," *The ERIC Review*, vol. 3, no. 1 (Winter 1994), p. 3.

Another issue that is central to multiple forms of assessment is the assumption that some students will take longer than others to arrive at mastery. The concern, however, is not that some students will take longer or need extra help to achieve the goals and objectives that have been set. The standards will remain the same for all students. What differs is how they are achieved. We must ask if it is more important for a student to "get the concept" by a certain date or that they "get it" at all. Underlying multiple forms of assessment is the notion that learning is developmental and that assessment is not final or summative, but rather provides insight into where on the path a student is at a particular time. Assessment thus plays a more important role as a formative tool that enables all parties—teacher, student, and parents—to derive a sense of where a student is at a particular time so that subsequent learning experiences can be developed that aid in student growth.

We must ask some important questions before we even begin to determine the most appropriate form of test questions to use. In most cases in the past, teachers and schools have focused solely on the content they were teaching. The goals of a biology course, for instance, were often stated in terms of phyla of plants and animals that students were expected to study. Emphasizing what it is we want students to know and to be able to do forces us to look at the curriculum in much broader terms. We begin to ask what personal abilities and sensitivities we want students to develop? What behaviors and orientations should students exhibit toward the environment around them? What will they be able to do that demonstrates these abilities?

In many ways, an individual's cultural experiences (defined rather broadly) determine the kinds of abilities that are important and are therefore learned as well as the context and strategies in which they are expressed. Gardner's theory of multiple intelligences is useful to consider here in that it challenges our more traditional concepts of intelligence and suggests that there are multiple contexts in which individuals develop and demonstrate their skills.[22] Gardner hypothesizes that there are at least seven areas in which people can express competence—musical, linguistic, logical-mathematical, spatial, body-kinesthetic, interpersonal (social or streetsmart), and intrapersonal (showing great insight into self). Note that only three of these—linguistic, logical-mathematical, and spatial—are presently assessed by standard intelligence tests. All seven of these dimensions, it is proposed, are of importance in today's world. When applied to school, the main emphasis of Gardner's theory suggests that children may demonstrate the different kinds of intelligence in ways not necessarily associated with traditional subjects in school and certainly not associated with traditional methods of assessment.

Perspectives on Social Class and Social Status

Previous chapters have suggested that differences in school achievement may be attributed to a variety of cultural influences. Two of those influences that have not yet been addressed are the cultural aspects of social class and social status.

Most Americans believe they live in a classless, egalitarian society. At the least, American ideology promotes the idea that, through proper attention, diligent effort (and some luck, which Americans also believe in), an individual may "rise above" his or her social class. Part of what has been called an "American religion,"[23] this faith in the reality of upward mobility may account for the relative lack of attention given to the concept of social class in much of the educational and psychological literature in the United States.[24] Certainly it accounts for the difficulty encountered by sociology professors in helping young people understand the bases of class differences in this society. Nevertheless, as we all know, there are significant variations in economic standard of living, status of occupation, and extent of expectations for upward mobility among American citizens.

Definitions of Social Class

Social class has been defined in a number of ways, all of which refer in some sense to a hierarchical stratification or "layering" of people in social groups, communities, and societies. Assignment to social class categories is one of several stratification systems that can be used to distinguish one individual or group from another in such a way as to assign "worth." The urge to organize people in layers almost appears to be a human characteristic; indeed, it has been said that whenever there are more than three people in a group there will be stratification; someone will be more respected, more powerful, or more "worthy" than the rest. While many Americans would identify class membership in terms of income,[25] it is important to understand that money alone does not determine a person's social class. Rather, social class standing depends on a combination of prestige, power, influence, and income.[26]

Traditional class markers in the United States include family income, prestige of one's father's occupation, prestige of one's neighborhood, the power one has to achieve one's ends in times of conflict, and the level of schooling achieved by the family head. Among other nations and cultures, markers of one's social class may include such determiners as bloodline and status of the family name, the caste into which one was born, the degree to which one engages in physical labor, and the amount of time that one might devote to scholarly or leisurely activities of one's choosing.[27]

One reason that social class is so difficult to talk about and truly understand is that while class distinctions are real and observable in concrete daily experience, they are also highly abstract. It is no accident that social class categories are often "assigned" by others (often sociologists), for social class in the real world is often in the eyes of the beholder. Nevertheless, for purposes of analysis, American society can be divided into five social classes.[28] At the top is a very small upper class, or social elite, consisting of people who have generally inherited social privilege from others. Second is a larger upper middle class whose members often are professionals, corporate managers, and leading scientists. This group usually has benefited from extensive higher education, and while family history is not so important, manners, tastes, and patterns of behavior are.

The third (or middle) social class has been called the lower middle class.[29] Most members of this group are people employed in white-collar occupations earning middle incomes—small business owners, teachers, social workers, nurses, sales and clerical workers, bank tellers, and so forth. This class is the largest of the social classes in the United States and encompasses a wide range of occupations and incomes. Central to the values of the lower middle class are a "desire to belong and be respectable . . . friendliness and openness are valued and attention is paid to 'keeping up appearances.' "[30]

Fourth in the hierarchy of social class is the working class, whose members are largely blue-collar workers (industrial wage earners) or employees in low-paid service occupations. Working-class families often have to struggle with poor job security, limited fringe benefits, longer hours of work, and more dangerous or "dirtier" work than people in the classes above them. It is not surprising, then, that members of the working class often feel more alienation from the social mainstream.

Finally, fifth in the hierarchy is the lower class, which includes both the so-called working poor and those who belong to what has been termed the "underclass"—a designation that refers to people who have been in poverty for so long that they seem unable to take any advantage at all of mobility options and thus lie nearly outside the class system. Clearly, poverty is both the chief characteristic and the chief problem of this group. Webb and Sherman point out that this simple fact needs to be underscored:

> Being poor means, above all else, lacking money. This statement would be too obvious to mention were it not for the fact that most Americans see poverty in other terms. Middle-class conversations about the poor often depict them as lazy, promiscuous, and criminal. Misconceptions about the poor are so widespread that it is difficult to appreciate fully what life is like at the lowest stratum of society.[31]

Social Class and Minority Group Membership

Complicating the issues of social class is the fact that in the United States there is a large overlap between lower-middle-class, working-class, and lower-class membership and membership in minority groups. African Americans, Hispanics, and Native Americans (including American Indians, Eskimos, and Hawaiians) are the most economically oppressed and depressed of all groups in the United States. The highest school dropout rates also occur among these groups. To the extent that social class status depends on income and occupation (and therefore, usually, prestige and power), women and children across racial, ethnic, and religious groups constitute a large proportion of the lower classes. This fact is in part a consequence of the descent into poverty that characterizes the lives of divorced women and their children. In the year 2000, one in six American children lived in poverty, and 77 percent of those live in families in which a family member worked at least part of the year.[32]

The Working Poor

Members of the **working poor**—those people who do work but in jobs that are minimum wage or slightly above, with no benefits and hardly any job security—must also struggle to make it in today's society. With changes in welfare laws and the economic uncertainty of today's world, not only are more working people confronting poverty, but because of massive layoffs in a number of economic sectors, those who never expected to encounter poverty are now doing so.

In a recent (2001) survey of twenty-seven U.S. cities, the U.S. Conference of Mayors found that (1) in the past year requests for emergency food assistance increased 23 percent; (2) an average of 14 percent of those requests went unmet; (3) 54 percent of those people requesting assistance were members of families; (4) in 100 percent of the cities, food assistance was relied on by families for both emergencies and as a routine source of food; and (5) low-paying jobs, unemployment, high housing costs, changes in the food stamp program, economic downturn, utility costs, welfare reform, medical or health costs, and mental health problems were the major contributors to hunger in the United States.[33]

Social Class and Child-Rearing Practices

Those people who share similar socioeconomic status, whatever its level may be, also share similar cultural knowledge, attitudes, and values. These similarities can be seen in various patterns of child rearing; various attitudes toward and expectations about dress, food, and shelter; and various beliefs about the necessity and value of schooling. Gordon suggests that the socioeconomic level to which a family belongs may be the strongest factor in determining differences among groups.[34] Of prime interest to educators is the influence social class has on educational opportunity, behavior, and achievement in schools.

Brislin has reviewed a number of sources in this area that are useful.[35] Kohn, for example, argues that parents from different class backgrounds emphasize different values when raising their children.[36] Parents in the middle classes tend to emphasize intellectual curiosity, self-control, and consideration of others. This emphasis leads to adult characteristics of empathetic understanding and self-direction. Working-class parents, on the other hand, stress neatness, good manners (often involving quietness and invisibility when adults are present), and obedience.[37] These emphases lead to a concern with external standards, such as obedience to authority, acceptance of what other people think of as good manners, and difficulty in articulating one's wishes to authority figures. The middle-class emphasis leads to adolescents and adults who are relatively comfortable with self-initiated behaviors and at ease when interacting with others outside their immediate family or friendship networks. Kohn suggests that the skills learned by children of the middle classes prepare them to assume professional and managerial positions that demand intellectual curiosity and good social skills.[38] In addition, Argyle suggests that social skills, such as those learned by children of the middle classes, may be central to success in the professions because they may take precedence over purely intellectual skills in many promotion and hiring decisions.[39]

In contrast, the skills learned by working-class children lead them to take wage labor jobs that are closely supervised and demand physical effort. The implication is that these jobs are taken partly as a result of less emphasis on intellectual curiosity and partly as a result of parental concern for external standards and obedience to the expectations and demands of a visible supervisor. However, jobs involving strictly physical labor have all but disappeared, a fact that makes life for lower-class individuals only that much more frustrating.

Lindgren and Suter suggest many reasons why students from middle-class backgrounds may do better in school than their working-class peers.[40] One difference can be attributed to perceived parental expectation. Students from working-class backgrounds think their parents expect less of them with regard to future school achievement, even when those parents don't really have lower expectations. Children of parents who have attended college or participated in other forms of postsecondary education are more likely to encourage their children to attend college than are parents who have not.

Family income may be a factor that discourages college attendance among the lower classes, but the cultural context of schooling may also discourage many lower-income and inner-city children.[41] Success in school, for example, demands linguistic competence. Children from working-class backgrounds tend to have less exposure, less expertise, and less confidence with language skills. Working-class children may not understand the teacher's questions as well as middle-class children do. Gullo found that three- to five-year-old working-class children had more difficulty answering various "wh" questions (who, when, where, and why, but not what) than did middle-class children.[42] Since a considerable amount of teacher-student interaction consists of questioning, it is conceivable that lower-class children may benefit less from lessons that employ questioning.

Another view, however, is taken by Knapp and Shields, who seriously question the efficacy of emphasizing the so-called deficits of "disadvantaged children."[43] To do so, they assert, is to

> risk making inaccurate assessments of children's strengths and weaknesses. . . . [to] have low expectations . . . and set standards that are not high enough to form the foundation for future academic success . . . [and, in] focusing on the deficits of students from disadvantaged backgrounds . . . [to risk] overlooking their true capabilities. Finally, a focus on the poor preparation of disadvantaged children often distracts attention from how poorly prepared the school may be to serve these youngsters.[44]

While statistically there are significant differences in school performance of students from different class backgrounds, there are some students from working- and lower-class backgrounds who do quite well in school. Social class, by itself, may not be the best predictor of school success. Rather, the relation of school success to social class appears to be mediated by a number of other factors, not the least of which is the teacher's perception of what social class means.

Social Status

As discussed in Chapter 3, the term **social status** refers to a hierarchical position determined not so much by one's wealth (or lack of it) but by the prestige, social esteem, and/or honor accorded one within one's own social milieu. It is quite possible, in fact, to have high social status without having commensurate money. Members of the clergy are good examples of this condition, as are, quite often, teachers. Conversely, it is also possible to have a great deal of money but occupy a low-status position, at least in terms of general community norms, for example, drug lords and leaders of gangs.

In the social hierarchy of schools, individual students usually achieve high status because of roles they assume, such as star athlete, academic achiever, cheerleading captain, and so forth. Interestingly, the social status of a particular student often differs from the point of view of students and of teachers. Thus, students may often accord athletes with high status, whereas teachers generally accord high status to students who achieve well academically. In neither case are economic considerations necessarily predominant.

All of which, of course, is not to say that social class and social status don't sometimes go hand in hand. To the extent, for example, that teachers believe that middle- and upper-middle-class students will achieve more than working- and lower-class students, such expectations are often reflected in reality.

The Importance of Teacher Expectations

Teacher expectations regarding the possibilities and potential of academic success for individual students are a critical factor in student achievement. **Teacher expectation** refers to the attributions that teachers make about the future behavior or academic achievement of their students, based on what they presently know about them. Teacher expectation effects refers to student outcomes that occur because of the actions taken by teachers in response to their own expectations.[45]

Teacher Expectations

An important type of teacher expectation is the self-fulfilling prophesy. In this effect, a false or untrue belief leads to specific behavior that causes that expectation to become true. For instance, if false rumors begin to spread that the stock market is going to crash and if millions of people then rush to sell off their stock holdings, the market may in fact crash. The outcome, however, is not due to any event that was predicted accurately but because people responded to the false information that was rumored.

In the classroom setting, teachers may tell themselves about the potential for success or failure of the students in their charge. For instance, assume that a teacher looks at her roster for the upcoming year and sees that she will have in her classroom a particular student, named Sandra, whose sister, Sally, was in the same classroom two years earlier.

Assume further that Sally had a difficult year. Not only did she struggle academically, but (perhaps as a result of academic failure) also had behavior problems. This teacher, vividly remembering her problems with Sally, may expect that Sandra will repeat the pattern. When Sandra walks into the classroom at the start of the year, the teacher may greet her in a cool manner, may be hesitant to approach her, and may even avoid personal contact with her as much as possible. Such behavior on the part of the teacher may alienate Sandra, may make her feel as if she doesn't belong, and may generate many feelings of anxiety and uncertainty. These feelings may, in turn, result in certain acting-out behaviors on Sandra's part. The teacher may then have set the stage for a self-fulfilling prophesy.

Just the opposite can also be true. A teacher may, for whatever reason, believe a certain child will be a good student when in fact he or she may be just about average. This belief may translate into particular actions on the part of the teacher that demonstrate care and concern and an expectation of success to the student. The teacher may call on this particular student to read more than other students, may trust this student with particular responsibilities, and may afford greater attention and privilege to this student, which may, in turn, result in increased gains in achievement. This outcome may not have happened if the teacher did not have high expectations for this student.

A tremendous amount of research has been undertaken over the past twenty-five years that looks at the effect of teacher expectations on student achievement.[46] Many teachers expect students of color as well as those from lower socioeconomic groups to perform less well on school-related tasks than their middle-class peers do. When these expectations are upheld, the teacher's beliefs are reinforced, thus perpetuating an erroneous cycle.

It is a part of our folk wisdom that children tend to live up (or down) to the expectations that significant adults have for them. For some children, their teachers will be the only adults who may ever have high expectations for them. Clearly, to automatically disregard the possibility of achievement because of the color of a child's skin or the evidence of a child's economic situation is discrimination of the most insidious kind because it is unspoken and largely invisible. The greatest gift that a teacher can offer a child is not knowledge, not skill development, not evaluation, but rather a fundamental faith that the child can acquire knowledge, develop skills, and demonstrate ability.

Perspectives on Multiple Forms of Assessment: Demand versus Support

The belief that all children can and should learn is, in essence, at the heart of multiple forms of assessment, and a number of scholars have looked at ways in which this philosophical position can be translated into classroom practice.

Kohn suggests that certain classroom orientations distinguish between what we as educators expect that students ought to be able to do and how we as educators can support students' development, thereby helping them to learn.[47] He calls these opposing approaches "demand" versus "support."

In the demand model, students are perceived as workers who are obligated to do a better job. Students who do not succeed are said to have chosen not to study or not to have earned a given grade. Under such an approach, responsibility is removed from the teacher and attention is deflected away from the curriculum and the context under which learning is meant to occur. In reporting to parents, teachers state whether students did what they were supposed to do. Even programs that reportedly emphasize performance objectives often adopt such an approach under the guise of the common buzzword—outcomes. Unfortunately, in the context of the demand model, many working- and lower-class students appear to choose not to study and thus earn lower grades.

The support model, on the other hand, assumes that students are active contributors to the learning process, or as Kohn puts it, the "adventure of ideas."[48] Under such an approach the teacher has a major responsibility to guide and stimulate all students' natural curiosity and desire to learn and explore the unfamiliar, to construct meaning in their world, and to develop the competence for using words, numbers, and ideas. Teaching and learning become child-centered or student-centered, and the goal becomes helping students build on their desire to make sense of, and to become competent in, their world. Student evaluation becomes, in part, a way to determine how effective we have been as educators. We seek to measure improvement in students because it indicates that we have been successful in engaging students and in creating a context in which they become motivated. Assessment, then, becomes supportive.

Kohn offers five principles of assessment that follow a supportive model.[49]

1. Assessment should not be overdone. The United States seems to be a test-happy nation, and American young people are the most tested in all the world. When students become preoccupied with how they are doing, they begin to lose interest in what they are doing. An excessive concern with performance can erode curiosity and thus reduce the quality of performance. Students excessively concerned with their performance may tend to avoid difficult tasks so they can avoid any negative evaluation.

Alfie Kohn

2. The best evidence we have of whether we are succeeding as educators is to observe the behavior of children. Test scores only tell us if students perform well on that specific test. Most tests are not true indicators of a student's subsequent ability to perform a specific task. When we observe children actively engaged in dialogue or conversation about a given topic, seeking out answers to their own questions, or reading on their own, we know that we have sparked their interest and that skills are often subsequently acquired.

3. Schools must be transformed into caring, safe communities. Such characteristics are critical for helping students become good learners willing to take risks and seek guidance and support. Only when there is no fear of humiliation or punitive judgment will children be free to acknowledge their mistakes and take the guidance of others. When the environment stresses grades and standardized testing or when teachers feel that a certain amount of curriculum must be covered, pressures increase, and subsequently, learning diminishes.

4. Any responsible discussion about assessment must attend to the quality of the curriculum. The easy question to answer is whether the student has learned anything. The more difficult question to answer is whether the student has been given something worth learning. Research has supported the notion that good teachers

already know. That is, when students have interesting things to do, artificial inducements to boost their achievement are not necessary. If the need to evaluate students has directed the design of the curriculum, students will not be actively engaged in their learning.

5. Students must become part of the discussion in determining the criteria by which their work will be judged and then play a role in that judgment. Such participation gives students greater control over their own education, makes evaluation feel less punitive, and provides an important learning experience in and of itself.

If you as an educator must give letter grades, consider the following suggestions. Refrain from giving a letter or number grade for individual assignments, even if you must give one at the end of the term. Numerous research studies support the use of comments instead of grades as more effective assessment devices. Also, never grade students while they are in the process of learning something. Never grade on a curve, which limits the number of good grades available. If students master the work, let them know by giving them the appropriate grade. Do not artificially limit the number of students who are said to do well.

Ethical Issues

Regardless of the specific means of communicating performance to others, assessment is inherently a subjective process. Ornstein has suggested that the more detailed the reporting method and the more analytic the process, the more likely it is that subjectivity will influence the results.[50] Subjectivity, however, is not always a negative factor. After all, teachers who truly know their students understand their progress in far greater detail than any test might uncover.

It is when subjectivity turns into bias that educators get into trouble. Teacher's perceptions and subsequent expectations can significantly influence their judgments of scholastic performance. Students with behavior problems, for instance, often face the obstacle that their infractions will overshadow their performance. These effects are especially evident with boys. Such aspects as a student's handwriting, dress, family background, and so forth can all influence a teacher's judgment.

The official labeling of children and identification of cognitive difficulties happens chiefly in the elementary years. Public schools typically label children as mentally retarded when their measured IQ is below seventy-nine. Children with African American and Spanish surnames are more likely to score below seventy-nine than are European American counterparts and subsequently are more likely to be placed in special education classes. Of the students placed in special education classes, only 19 percent ever get out—23 percent drop out of school, 46 percent are ultimately placed in other institutions or other programs, and 11 percent age out of the system. Children with African American and Spanish surnames are overlabeled as mentally retarded by public agencies; European Americans are underlabeled when compared to the general population. Such a situation suggests that educators are using tools of analysis that favor some students over others and/or actively discriminate against some groups. The special education literature is replete with evidence of individuals wrongfully identified as in need of special education services when all that was really at issue was their inability to communicate as expected in the English language at the time the exam was administered. How many children have been cheated or wrongfully labeled as failures because of an inadequate means of assessment?

Standardized testing in its many forms often results in the use of labels that may not be accurate and comprehensive. Such labels may be quite limiting on the individual as well as quite difficult to shed. The unofficial labeling of students, usually in the form of teacher expectations with respect to social class attributes, can occur at any age. All that is required is a teacher who does not really know the child. Do we really want to use our power as teachers to prematurely limit a student's growth and development or to make judgments that will be perceived by others as final statements of a student's skills and abilities? What about the late bloomer? What about the individual who is penalized because his or her first language is not English? What about the child who has not had all the early advantages that other students may have had? Are we willing to say that these children cannot and will not succeed as well? As a teacher you can provide the structure and opportunity for all children to develop to their full potential—whenever they are ready.

Imagine, for a moment, that you are viewing the files of the following two students.[51] What kinds of judgments would you make about these children? What kind of academic program would you recommend? Would you expect them to fit in with your regular class program? Would you suggest any special intervention, such as special classes for gifted or handicapped students? Would you recommend any extracurricular activities that would help develop special skills in these children?

Sam Edder did not begin speaking until he was three years old. He has always had trouble with school, often remaining withdrawn and unsociable. He was even removed from school at one time because of his emotional instability. Sam's test scores are well below average except for his performance on creativity measures. In this area he shows some potential. Other than reading intently and playing a musical instrument, Sam seems to have few interests and expresses little in the way of personal or vocational goals. Sam's parents are of European descent, with high school educations.

Bill Ridell has never spent much time in school. He started late because of an illness and was withdrawn several times because of continued sickness. Bill has been labeled "backward" by school officials. He has suffered from a variety of ailments and is going deaf. Although his creative performance shows some promise, Bill's IQ score is low (81), as are his scores on other achievement indices. However, Bill enjoys building things and mechanical pursuits, has good manual dexterity, and would like someday to be a scientist or railroad mechanic. Although Bill's mother is well educated, his father has no formal schooling and is unemployed.

What do you think? What judgments are you able to make about these two children, given this descriptive information? As a teacher, what other information would you like to have? How might you go about working with these children?

This little exercise can be used to check the accuracy of your attributions as well as the assumptions you are making. The descriptions of Sam Edder and Bill Ridell are actually case studies of real people. Sam Edder's file is that of Albert Einstein and Bill

Ridell's is that of Thomas Edison. How quickly did you make faulty attributions about the potential for success of these students? How many other potential geniuses have been overlooked or have slipped through the cracks because of our narrow approaches to assessing and judging students?

Increasingly, teachers are searching for more effective ways to communicate performance to both students and parents. Many issues converge as we consider what it is, exactly, that we wish to communicate to others. For one, as already discussed in Chapter 10, children develop at different rates. Educators face the difficult task of determining specific outcomes that all students could be expected to learn by the end of a given school year. In addition, educators must identify which outcomes are the most critical to assess.

Summary

Assessment is a critical part of both the debate and the substance of school reform issues today. This chapter presents some history of the standards and accountability movements, as well as the arguments for and against standardized testing and the arguments for the use of multiple forms of assessment. Further, the role played by social class and social status in student learning and assessment is discussed, and suggestions are made for a model of supportive assessment.

 # Chapter Review

Go to the Online Learning center at **www.mhhe.com/Cushner4e** to review important content from the chapter, practice with key terms, take a chapter quiz, and find the web links listed in this chapter.

Key Terms

Accountability
   movement   375

Assessment   379

Content standards   375

Delivery standards   375

Educate America Act   374

Goals 2000   374

High stakes testing   377

"No Child Left Behind"
   Act of 2001   375

Performance standards   375

Portfolio assessments   379

Social class   389

Social status   393

Teacher expectations   393

Testing   379

Working poor   391

Reflective Questions

1. Beth Bradley and her colleagues in the Jefferson schools undertook a major change in the way they assessed students in mathematics, based on guidelines set by the National Council of Teachers of Mathematics. These guidelines, like those set by other subject area teacher associations, are often adopted by individual states as requirements for all teaching of that subject in the state. As a teacher, how might you become involved in the organizations that set these standards?

2. Two years of planning went into the new assessment program discussed in the case study. Why do you think it took so long? What happens to teachers who continue to disagree with a proposed change?

3. One of the first things that Beth and her colleagues discovered was that using multiple forms of assessment required them to alter their instruction in significant ways. What does that finding imply about the relation between instruction and evaluation?

4. Beth recalls in the case study that even though she believed in the assessment changes that were to be adopted, she continued to test in the old way because "old habits die hard." What do you think might help teachers develop new habits? What characteristics of the school environment would facilitate change in teachers' behavior?

5. How might tests be an impediment to effective instruction (that is, instruction that results in student learning)?

6. A common criticism of multiple forms of assessment is that two teachers using the same assessment procedures may arrive at different evaluations of students' achievement. Assuming that this criticism has some validity, how might conditions be set so that variation in teachers' evaluation might be minimized?

7. Multiple forms of assessment raise critical issues about the relation between project-based collaborative work in classrooms and standardized testing. Given the political climate of the United States at the present time, it is unlikely that standardized testing, at least on the state level, is going to be abandoned any time soon. Many teachers believe that knowledge and skills acquired through new types of instruction and assessment will transfer easily to demonstration through standardized tests. Others are not so sure. What are the arguments on each side?

References

1. This case study has been adapted from material found in J. K. Stenmark, *Mathematics Assessment: Myths, Models, Good Questions, and Practical Solutions* (Reston, VA: National Council of Teachers of Mathematics, 1991).

2. *A Nation at Risk: The Imperative for Educational Reform* (Washington, DC: National Commission on Excellence in Education, 1983).

3. Robert Rothman, "Council Calls for a New System of Standards, Tests." *Education Week on the Web* (29 January 1992). Available at http://www.edweek.org/ew/ewstory.cfm?slug=19ncest.h11.

4 Asa Hilliard, "The Standards Movement: Quality Control or Decoy?" *Rethinking Schools Online* 12, 4 (summer 1998). Available at http://www.rethinkingschools.org/Archives/12_04/hill.htm.

5. "Seeking Stability for Standards-Based Education," a report of *Education Week Quality Counts 2001, A Better Balance: Standards, Tests, and the Tools to Succeed.* Available at http://www.edweek.org/sreports/qc01/articles/qc01story.cfm?slug=17exec_sum.h20.

6. Kathleen Kennedy Manzo, "No State Has Coordinated Standards Effort," *Education Week on the Web* (7 November 2001). Available at http://www.edweek.org/ew/newstory.cfm?slug=10stand.h21.

7. "An ESEA Primer," *Education Week on the Web* (9 January 2002). Available at http://www.edweek.org/ew/newstory.cfm?slug=16eseabox.h21.

8. Ron Brandt, "A Fresh Focus for Curriculum," *Educational Leadership* 49, 8 (May 1992):7.

9. "AERA Position Statement Concerning High Stakes Testing in PreK–12 Education." Available at the American Educational Research Association web site: http://www.aera.net/about/policy/stakes.htm.

10. "NEA's Position on High Stakes Testing." Available at the National Education Association web site: http://www.nea.org/issues/high-stakes/neaposition.html.

11. A. M. Villegas, *Culturally Responsive Pedagogy for the 1990s and Beyond,* Trends and Issues Paper, no. 6 (Washington, DC: ERIC Clearinghouse on Teacher Education, 1996), ED 339 698.

12. M. E. Diez and C. J. Moon, "What Do We Want Students to Know? . . . and Other Important Questions," *Educational Leadership* 49, 8 (May 1992):38–41.

13. D. Starch and E. C. Elliott, "Reliability of the Grading of High School Work in English," *School Review*, 20 (1912):442–457.

14. D. Starch and E. C. Elliott, "Reliability of the Grading of High School Work in Mathematics," *School Review* 21 (1913):254–259.

15. E. B. Page, "Teacher Comments and Student Performance: A Seventy-Four Classroom Experiment in School Motivation," *Journal of Educational Psychology* 49 (1958):173–181.

16. Alfie Kohn, "Grading: The Issue Is Not How But Why," *Educational Leadership* 52, 2 (October 1994):38.

17. Ibid. For additional views of grading and the standards and testing movement, see Alfie Kohn, *The Schools Our Children Deserve: Moving beyond Traditional Classrooms and "Tougher Standards"* (Boston: Houghton Mifflin, 1999).

18. Ibid.; see also R. Butler, "Task-Involving and Ego-Involving Properties of Evaluation," *Journal of Educational Psychology* 79 (1987):474–482; W. S. Grolnick and R. M. Ryan, "Autonomy in Children's Learning: An Experimental and Individual Difference Investigation," *Journal of Personality and Social Psychology* 52 (1987:890–898; and M. Kage, "The Effects of Evaluation on Intrinsic Motivation" (paper presented at the meeting of the Association of Educational Psychology, 1991, Joetsu, Japan).

19. R. Butler and M. Nissan, "Effects of No Feedback, Task-Related Comments, and Grades on Intrinsic Motivation and Performance," *Journal of Educational Psychology* 78 (1986):210–216.

20. M. Smith and M. Cohen, "A National Curriculum in the United States?" *Educational Leadership* 49, 1 (September 1991):74:81.

21. B. Nurcombe, *Children of the Dispossessed* (Honolulu: University Press of Hawaii, 1976).

22. Howard Gardner, *Frames of Mind: The Theory of Multiple Intelligences* (New York: Basic Books, 1983).

23. Robert N. Bellah, "Civil Religion in America," in *American Society: Problems and Dilemmas,* ed. Alan Wells (Pacific Palisades, CA: Goodyear Publishing, 1976), pp. 351–368.

24. R. Brislin, "Increasing Awareness of Class, Ethnicity, Culture, and Race," in *The G. Stanley Hall Lecture Series,* vol. 8, ed. I. Cohen (Washington, DC: American Psychological Association, 1988), pp. 137–180.

25. Gilbert and Kall, for example, suggest that in the United States individual or family income is the central variable from which other opportunities follow. For instance, income reflects the neighborhood in which one lives. Neighborhood determines, to a great degree, the educational experience one has, in school and outside it. The education one has then influences one's profession or occupation, which determines the prestige one obtains, and so forth. D. Gilbert and J. Kahl, *The American Class Structure: A New Synthesis* (Homewood, IL: Dorsey, 1982).

26. Rodman B. Webb and Robert R. Sherman, *Schooling and Society*, 2nd ed. (New York: Macmillan, 1989), pp. 397–398.

27. Brislin, "Increasing Awareness," p. 144.

28. Webb and Sherman, *Schooling and Society,* pp. 399-417.

29. Ibid., p. 405.

30. Ibid., p. 407.

31. Ibid., p. 412.

32. "Frequently Asked Questions About Child Poverty," Children's Defense Fund (14 January 2002). Available at http://www.childrensdefense.org/fairstart-faqs.htm.

33. "Hunger and Homelessness Up Sharply in Major U.S. Cities," Report of the U.S. Conference of Mayors (12 December 2001). Available at http://www.usmayors.org/uscm/news/press_releases/documents/hunger_121101.asp.

34. J. Gordon, *Assimilation in American Life* (New York: Oxford University Press, 1964).

35. Brislin, "Inceasing Awareness."

36. M. L. Kohn, *Class and Conformity*, 2nd ed. (Chicago: University of Chicago Press, 1977).

37. Gilbert and Kahl, *American Class Structure.*

38. M. L. Kohn, *Class and Conformity.*

39. M. Argyle, "Interaction Skills and Social Competence," in *Psychological Problems: The Social Context* ed. M. P. Feldman and J. Orford (New York: John Wiley & Sons, 1980).

40 H. C. Lindgren and W. N. Suter, *Educational Psychology in the Classroom*, 7th ed. (Monterey, CA: Brooks/Cole, 1985).

41. A. W. Boykin, "The Triple Quandary and the Schooling of African-American Children," in *The School Achievement of Minority Children: New Perspectives,* ed. V. Neisser (Hillsdale, NJ: Lawrence Erlbaum, 1986).

42 D. Gullo, "Social Class Differences in Preschool Children's Comprehension of Wh—Questions," *Child Development* 52, 2 (June 1981):736–740.

43. Michael S. Knapp and Patrick M. Shields, "Reconceiving Academic Instruction for the Children of Poverty," *Phi Delta Kappan* 71, 10 (June 1990):753–758.

44. Ibid., p. 754.

45. Thomas Good and Jere Brophy, *Looking in Classrooms*, 4th ed. (New York: Harper and Row, 1987).

46. Ibid.

47. A. Kohn, *School's Our Children Deserve,* pp. 39–40.

48. Ibid., p. 40, citing J. G. Nichols and S. P. Hazzard, *Education as Adventure: Lessons from the Second Grade* (New York: Teachers College Press, 1993).

49. A. Kohn, *School's Our Children Deserve.*

50. A. C. Ornstein, "Grading Practices and Policies: An Overview and Some Suggestion," *NASSP Bulletin* 78 (1994):55–64.

51. From a simulation developed by John Rader.

Tomorrow's Classrooms Today

It is change, continuing change, inevitable change, that is the dominant factor in society today. No sensible decision can be made any longer without taking into account not only the world as it is, but the world as it will be. . . . This, in turn, means that our statesmen, our businessmen, our everyman must take on a science fictional way of thinking.

—Isaac Asimov

Chapter Outline

1.   What are the factors in individuals that inhibit change? How might these be overcome?

2.   What are the factors of organizations that inhibit change? How might these be overcome?

3.   What is the relationship between communities and schools as they undergo change to address the needs of a more diverse society?

In many ways, this book is about boundaries—boundaries that we impose on ourselves, that we impose on others, and that are imposed on all of us by factors often beyond our conscious or direct control. It is a book about physical boundaries of geography; about social boundaries of language, gender, race, ethnicity, and religion; and about political and economic boundaries of many kinds. However, and more important, it is also a book about breaking boundaries, building bridges, and finding commonality across differences.

In today's world, many old boundaries are fading away and new ones are emerging. In Germany, the Berlin Wall has disappeared. In the former Yugoslavia, in Eastern Europe, and in Russia, newly revived ethnic boundaries are reappearing. In the Middle East, political and religious boundaries shift and harden as all people struggle to ensure an identity for their grandchildren and great-grandchildren. Around the globe, the old antagonisms of political ideology that pitted East against West during the Cold War have given way to new global antagonisms based on economics in which the countries in the South struggle to survive in the face of an inequitable distribution of resources weighted toward those in the North. And at home, even within our schools, boundaries seem to be hardening between ingroups and outgroups to such an extent that atrocities such as school shootings in Littleton, Colorado, and in other communities result.

Social categories of various kinds do not arise arbitrarily—they help us understand the world we live in; they offer the comfort of familiarity; and they allow us to proceed through our days without having to identify and reidentify everything and everybody. Social categories help to give meaning to our lives. They are also often responsible for sustaining hatreds among people, for enabling human beings to turn away from human suffering, and for the occurrence of war.

In the age we live in, old boundaries created by traditional definitions are becoming increasingly dysfunctional. We are well on the way to shedding many of our Second Wave characteristics as we evolve into a Third Wave society. It is necessary, in the face of new circumstances, to continuously rethink some of our old ideas and to find ways to cross the boundaries that separate people. Many people may not like this expectation. Indeed, many today are reacting to change by pulling back, by hardening their resolve to "keep things as they were." Note the resistance to talk of a new world order, the rise in membership of various hate groups, and the recent terrorist attacks within the United States, including the Oklahoma City bombings and the rash of anthrax attacks that originated within our own nation. It is quite likely that we will see much more of this kind of response in the years ahead; but in the end, change will have its effect. Whether that effect is positive or negative is up to us. And, in large measure, teachers may play a very important part in the process, because it is teachers who can exercise the power to engender new ideas and new ways of doing things in the children with whom they come in contact.

This book has presented a number of ideas that will be helpful in leading us to remove, redefine, or bridge old definitions or theories that may stand in our way as we attempt to create educational environments that are more inclusive in terms of culture, gender, race, exceptionality, and the many other aspects of culture from which we derive our own sense of cultural identity and loyalty. Recall that this book's goals are: (1) to recognize social and cultural change; (2) to understand culture and the culture-learning process; (3) to improve intergroup and intragroup interactions; and (4) to transmit cross-cultural understandings and skills to students. But what does it mean to change? How might we go about making the significant personal and organizational changes necessary to realize these goals? What factors might facilitate change? What might a changed educational environment look like?

The Process of Change

It is in schools, perhaps more than in any other social setting, that opportunities exist to have close and regular interactions with a wide variety of people. But even though teachers, administrators, and even the community might sanction such efforts, it will be no easy feat to change schools and institutions in such a manner that they are attentive to issues of diversity and inclusive of all people in society. This book contains much of the theory and ideology that supports certain changes in the educational context. Unfortunately, to date there has been little evidence that teachers and administrators actually apply much of what is known or that their efforts have had the intended impact. Facilitating change in schools is, in many ways, dependent on the combined motivation and skill level of individuals and the organizational climate that is maintained in the school districts and in the schools. The path to support such change efforts, while paved with good intentions, is often barred by numerous roadblocks, detours, and areas that are still under construction. And, we must continually remind ourselves that, contrary to what some people may desire, there will be no quick fixes. Efforts to change schools must be seen as an evolutionary—not a revolutionary—process.

In his early work, Lewin proposed a model of change suggesting that the status quo is maintained when opposing forces, that is, those supportive of change and those resistant to change, are relatively equal in strength.[1] He argued that the most effective way to institute change was to reduce the resistance rather than add to the forces favoring change. Resistance to change, and especially resistance to efforts designed to improve intercultural relations, exists at both the individual and organizational level.[2] It is important that we consider individual as well as institutional characteristics when considering factors that facilitate or hinder change efforts. The greatest opportunities for real change arise when the individuals and the organization work in concert with one another.

Barriers to Change at the Individual Level

At the individual level, several factors hinder changes that might lead to improvements in our schools. Chapter 1 pointed out the considerable concern about the relative lack of diversity among the teaching population itself as well as a lack of intergroup experience that most teachers bring with them to the field. Chapter 4 introduced Bennett's developmental model of intercultural sensitivity (DMIS).[3] This model helps us better understand individual resistance to intercultural change. Recall that the DMIS provides a framework for understanding individual development and awareness with respect to group differences along a continuum from a highly ethnocentric to a highly ethnorelative perspective. Knowledge of where along the continuum an individual lies can provide a basis for intervention strategies that can facilitate that person's understanding of intergroup relations. The model can also be used to obtain a picture of where on the continuum an organization is, thereby providing important information on factors that might hinder change. Reluctance to change is likely to be higher among teachers, administrators, and students who are on the ethnocentric side of the continuum, whereas support for change should be evident among those on the ethnorelative side of the divide. One challenge to improving intergroup relations is to move people from an ethnocentric to an ethnorelative perspective.

Change cannot occur on a large scale until the individual or individuals involved are able to alter their perceptions and see themselves as active participants in the process. Change is also facilitated when it is a welcomed and sought-after process. Individuals pass through predictable stages as they internalize any new situation. People must also perceive themselves from a new perspective in order to fully internalize and actualize their new situation. Only then can they become role models for change. Change does not come about simply as a result of new information—active participation in efforts designed to bring about significant change are required if the individual is to be an active part of the process.

Combs stressed the importance of recognizing and involving the individual's beliefs and patterns of behavior when considering the change process:

> [Changing] must concern itself with the inner life. Simple exposure to subject matter (or new information or ways of doing things) is not enough. The maturation of an effective professional worker requires changes . . . in perceptions—his feelings, attitudes, and beliefs and his understanding of himself and his world. This is no easy matter, for what lies inside the individual is not open to direct manipulation and control. It is unlikely to change except with the active involvement of the . . . [person] in the process.[4]

Barriers to Change at the Organizational Level

The institutional barriers to bringing about change can be even more complex and difficult to surmount. Institutions, by virtue of their adherence to tradition, have a tendency to maintain the status quo. This tendency may be especially true of educational institutions. Studies undertaken by the National Council for the Accreditation of Teacher Education suggest that although a growing number of educational institutions profess to address issues of cultural diversity, very few actually do so.[5]

The effective management of change, thus, must take into consideration the nature of the educational institution. There is evidence to suggest that those institutions that tend to be internally focused are less likely to espouse change. Conversely, those institutions that are externally oriented, that is, those with greater links to the community, are generally better able to respond to social and political factors and are more responsive to change efforts.[6] If change is not perceived to be part of the organizational culture, efforts to bring it about are likely to fail. Fullan argues that "You cannot have an educational environment in which change is continuously expected alongside a conservative system and expect anything but constant aggravation."[7]

Resistance to organizational change may also have historical roots that are often related to the failure of past change efforts within a school.[8] Most changes involve some sense of loss, anxiety, or conflict, and resistance may arise because of the anticipation of the turbulence, chaos, and stress that change will cause. Think back to the culture-general themes introduced in Chapter 3 and the importance of understanding such emotional concerns as anxiety, ambiguity, and disconfirmed expectations of intercultural interactions. If the uncertainty and disruption caused by the threat of change are ignored, resistance can become even more deeply entrenched and can drive conflict underground to such an extent that it may be difficult to overcome.[9]

A range of concerns and issues have been identified in studies of teachers involved in organizational change efforts related to improving intergroup relations and intercultural understanding.[10] Teachers report that it takes a significant amount of money to initiate change, and most schools are currently struggling to meet basic expenses. Teachers feel that an appreciation and understanding of the time and effort that is required to change students, especially younger ones, is lacking. Also, teachers feel that there is often insufficient collaboration with families and guardians, poor connections with minority communities, a lack of understanding of minorities' unique needs, and oftentimes a lack of minority faculty and staff involved in the change effort from the very beginning. And all too frequently, there is a lack of follow-up and support services available once a program or experience has been provided. These findings pinpoint a wide range of organizational barriers to change that must be overcome if intergroup relations are to be improved in schools.

Chapter 6 made reference to Gordon Allport's contact hypothesis, which was originally developed to address prejudice in settings outside schools, but later provide much of the groundwork for efforts to improve intergroup relations in schools.[11] The elements that Allport first identified as being critical to improving intergroup relations remain as solid today as they were when they were originally proposed. It is clear that merely putting students from differing backgrounds together in the same environment, such as a school, does not guarantee that positive relations will result. Recall that relations between students from different racial, ethnic, religious, and cultural groups are most likely to improve when the following conditions are met: individuals are on equal status with one another in the contact situation, implying that they have equal access to the rewards available in a given setting; students interact with one another on a repeated basis while in pursuit of some common goals; students have the opportunity to get to know one another as individuals in a rather intimate manner, thus interacting with a wide range of people and disproving the prevailing stereotypes of the group; and their interactions are sanctioned by administrators and others in authority.

Applying the contact hypothesis directly to school settings, however, has always been problematic for a variety of reasons. For example, many schools are relatively monocultural and thus provide little opportunity for intergroup contact to occur. In many schools, patterns of racial and ethnic segregation remain, often as a result of segregated housing patterns, which reduces the possibility of intergroup contact.[12] If contact is to serve as a route to intergroup understanding, then segregation constitutes a major obstacle that must be addressed.

Even when cultural, ethnic, racial, and socioeconomic diversity is evident in the school, other factors often mitigate against regular, meaningful intergroup interaction. One problematic issue, when applying the contact hypothesis in schools, centers on the criterion of equal status contact. Although equal status contact provides much of the foundational structure that underlies many group activities in the classroom, including cooperative learning strategies, it may be undermined by the inequality that exists among groups outside the school.[13] Students do not leave their social status at home when they come to school. Unless efforts are made to counteract these inequalities, contact in the schools may lead to increased stereotyping.[14]

Generalizing changed attitudes beyond the immediate context in which an intervention occurs also presents a problem when applying the equal status concept. That is, while intergroup relations may appear to improve between individuals who come into contact in the school setting, such attitude change may not transfer to other contexts outside the classroom or the school. Also, equal status between two specific groups in school may not generalize to other outgroups or to situations in which status is not equal, as in so many community contexts.

Another organizational problem that is relatively common is that many integrated schools end up resegregating themselves through the practice of ability tracking. Grouping students by academic ability continues to be practiced in many schools and may result in the unintended segregation of students by ethnicity or race.[15] Tracking often relegates a disproportionate number of low-income students and students of color to lower-tracked classes, which has the result of limiting the intergroup interaction that can occur. Segregation, however, can also occur for other reasons. In some instances, students segregate themselves into like-groups on the playground, in the lunchroom, or as a result of participation in extracurricular activities. For whatever reason it occurs, within-school resegregation limits intergroup interactions, and teachers should look for ways to reduce its occurrence.

The Change Process: From Self to Others

Restructuring schools in such a manner that they become more inclusive and that individuals become empowered toward equity and excellence on all fronts does, however, require individual teachers to become mavericks, so to speak. This idea may go against the typical image people have of teachers. Teaching tends to be a rather conservative activity, with most teachers acting in such a manner that the status quo is maintained. In fact, some innovative teachers may rightly perceive themselves to be punished by the system in which they work when it comes to taking a stand and encouraging change. Yet change must occur if schools and society are to become more equitable and inclusive.

Schooling in the United States has two principal functions: to preserve the society and, at the same time, to change it. Historically, these two functions have been viewed as at odds with one another: either schooling acts to preserve or to alter the society, but it doesn't do both at the same time. In a society characterized by pluralism, it frequently appears that the primary role of schooling is to bind us together. Indeed, one of the fundamental notions at the heart of the common school movement was the provision of a common educational experience that would provide a kind of "glue" to hold the society together. This belief is a powerful factor in resisting attempts to alter schooling; there is a sense in which such alteration can be perceived to go against the preservation of our democratic experiment.

Apart from the degree to which the transformation of schooling is perceived to be a disservice to the nation, there are other difficulties inherent in the nature of the school as a social organization. Seymour Sarason is one of a few people who has attempted to look at the problems inherent in changing organizations, including the school.[16] In his work, Sarason has developed several propositions about changing organizations that are worth considering.

First, "real" or fundamental change, as opposed to cosmetic or surface change, requires a different way of thinking. New thought processes are extraordinarily difficult for people to do, particularly when they are caught up in day-to-day activities embedded in traditional ways of thinking and acting. Some evidence for this proposition can be found in the knowledge that schools seem always to be "changing"—curriculum content changes; new activities take place; the things people talk about in terms of the school change. But life in schools goes on pretty much as it did before.

Second, altering thinking about schools requires the questioning of what Sarason calls "existing regularities," or structures that have become unquestioned givens in schools. This proposition requires that some alternative perspectives exist, for purposes of contrast if for no other reason. In other words, people must be aware of other possibilities in order to seriously question what exists. The "regularities" of schooling are so much a part of our way of thinking about schools that it is often hard to distance ourselves from them long enough to imagine them in different ways. Ask yourself, for example, the question that Sarason asked a number of school personnel: why is it that math is taught every day? Sarason writes:

> The naive person might ask several questions: Would academic and intellectual development be adversely affected if the exposure was for four days a week instead of five? Or three instead of five? What would happen if the exposure began in the second or third grade? What if the exposure was in alternative years? Obviously, one can generate many more questions, each of which suggests an alternative to the existing programmatic regularity. From this universe of alternatives how does one justify the existing regularity?[17]

The responses—many of them emotional—that Sarason received to this question reveal a good deal about the difficulty inherent in thinking differently about that which already exists. The first response, he relates, was usually one of humor: the listener assumed he was making a joke and laughed. In order to keep the discussion going, he often set forth the view that no one, with the exception of those whose work entailed the use of mathematical concepts, used any but the simplest computation skills in life after school, and thus the legitimacy of twelve years of mathematics every day was at least open to question. He then continues:

> And now the fur begins to fly. Among the more charitable accusations is the one that I am anti-intellectual. Among the least charitable reactions (for me) is simply an unwillingness to pursue the matter further. (On one occasion some individuals left the meeting in obvious disgust.) One can always count on some individuals asserting that mathematics "trains or disciplines the mind" and the more the better, much like Latin used to be justified as essential to the curriculum.[18]

Clearly, the consideration of alternatives to existing regularities is a profoundly difficult matter. Moreover, asking questions about existing structure often connotes on the part of the listener a feeling of threat to the establishment, and on the part of the questioner a feeling of being alone and somehow different. Neither of these feelings is conducive to an environment in which asking fundamental questions is encouraged.

A third problem, too often ignored by those who wish to see significant change undertaken, is that not all people in the school can be counted on to share that wish. As Sarason notes,

> There are those among the "change agents" whose ways of thinking are uncluttered by the possibility that others see the world differently than they do. In my experience, the number of these individuals is far exceeded by those, in and out of school systems, who know that their plans and intended changes will not be viewed with glee but who seem to assume that either by prayer, magic, sheer display of authority, or benevolence, the letter and the spirit of the changes will not be isolated from each other. Far more often than not, of course, letter and spirit are unrelated in practice if for no other reason than that in the thinking of planners the relation between means and ends was glossed over, if it was considered at all.[19]

These discussions about the difficulties of instituting change, of course, do not in any way mean that attempts to fundamentally alter schooling should not be made. Yes, the processes of fundamental change are difficult, are fraught with distractions and unconsidered problems, and probably will not occur in the lifetime of one set of transformers. In practical terms, we have to realize that success will not be immediate nor even, perhaps, in the foreseeable future; nevertheless, we must act as if it were just around the corner. Change will be evolutionary, not revolutionary.

A final difficulty to be considered here (and there are, of course, more difficulties that are not even being discussed), is that people who wish to undertake new ways of thinking about and doing things in schools often are ignorant of the history of education and thus are simply unaware of possible alternatives that have already been conceived and attempted. This situation is one reason for the common belief that there is nothing new under the sun. This problem is not, of course, unique to educators who do a poor job of educating teachers in the history of their own profession. Most professions and skilled crafts today exist in a kind of modern time warp in which past and future are lost to one another. What this problem leads to, in part, is a double bind: because we don't know much about our own history, we are inclined to think that what is, has always been. At the same time, we are deprived of examples of potentially useful alternatives for thought and action. Thus, educators have been criticized either for moving too slowly or, worse, for retaining models and strategies deemed effective in the past that fail to recognize the times in which we now live. The words of June Edwards echo the concerns of many before her:

> Today's secondary schools are designed as though students will face the same kind of life as their grandparents did. In previous generations, children were trained for industrial work. They learned to be punctual, obedient to authority, and tolerant of repetition, boredom, and discomfort, for such was the lot of factory workers. Judgment, decision-making ability, creativity, and independence were neither taught nor desired.
>
> Industries have changed in recent years, but schools have not. Students, herded by bells, are still for the most part expected to be obedient, dependent, and accepting of discomfort and boredom. Though some outstanding instructors encourage creativity and critical thinking, the majority of secondary classrooms are teacher-centered, focused on isolated facts, and constrained by standardized curricula and tests.[20]

Edwards follows this statement with a review of an educational model designed by Helen Parkhurst known as the Dalton Plan, a model she suggests would serve our needs well today.[21] In examining this plan, think about the ways in which it required a way of thinking about schools that is significantly different than the way we currently approach schooling. Under the Dalton Plan, the entire school day was restructured into subject labs whereby students determined their own individual schedules. Traditional classrooms were dismantled, bells were eliminated, schedules were dropped, and students were entrusted to have considerable say in the manner in which they carried out their day. Basically, the Dalton Plan was student centered, self-paced, and individualized by means of monthly contracts. Teacher-designed contracts stressed academic learning as well as independent thinking and creativity. Homework was not assigned; however, students could complete work at home if desired. Movement from one grade to another was carried out when students completed their contracts for a year's work; and like college today, students graduated when they completed the requisite number of courses. Edwards suggests that this model is quite appropriate today given the postindustrial or Third Wave society in which we are living—even though it was proposed in 1921!

> As we move into the postindustrial age—with corporations splintering into minicenters, with work being done on home computers at all hours of the day and night, and with diversity rather than standardization fast becoming the norm—the single-skilled employees who are punctual and can follow orders are no longer in great demand. Instead, the need is for employees who are self-disciplined, creative, capable of carrying out a variety of tasks, and able to work well alone or with others.[22]

The Dalton Plan could benefit students in many ways. Students might learn responsibility and self-discipline. They might work slowly and learn more thoroughly, or they might work quickly and advance rapidly if they so desired. Students might feel freer to take risks and fail without penalty, and they might be actively involved at all times. Students might work in a nonthreatening, noncompetitive environment and be able to request individual help as needed. They might develop and enjoy long-term relationships with peers and teachers, or they might be able to miss school for days if needed without falling behind. And students and teachers might have the freedom to vary the hours that they spend in school. Teachers might benefit by spending all their time on educational matters, having the opportunity to be friend and counselor as well as teacher to students. They might be able to work in a room free from disruptions, working with students who are interested, motivated, and self-reliant, and they might be able to specialize as well as work cooperatively with colleagues as needed. School districts, too, might benefit by reducing complex scheduling and by being able to accommodate midyear and other transient students more readily. Such flexibility might enable limited-English-proficient students to join English immersion groups as needed. And students and first-year teachers might be more easily integrated into the culture of the school by having the flexibility to reassess the organization of the school day to include early morning, evening, and holiday hours.

Notice that this discussion indicates that students, teachers, and school organizations *might* benefit from this plan. The point is not that the Dalton Plan is a model for imitation; the point is that it is an actual plan that was carried out at one time and that seems to have some potential for today's school life. Serious consideration of the Dalton Plan requires questioning, discussion, and thought on the part of educators. Would such a plan really resolve some of the issues we face? How? What constraints would there be to adopting such a plan? Are there any portions of the plan that seem more applicable than others? Why? And so on.

Significant change must occur with the individual teacher in the classroom, but a teacher's responsibilities, especially the new teacher's, are such that it will be extremely difficult to attend to behavioral and curriculum modification in the task of day-to-day teaching. Such change takes time. It also takes an awareness of the processes by which change occurs on an individual basis, and at the same time, it takes a vision of what is desired and possible.

Building Community through the School

This book has also been about building community, and perhaps a few words about this concept are necessary at this time. The term *community* is used in the context of the school to mean "spirit" or "sense of community." In this sense, all individuals need to be "in community" with one another. In such a context, diversity becomes central to our way of perceiving and acting—it is not seen as an obstacle that must be overcome. In a true democratic community, all members' contributions are actively sought out and viewed as equally worthy of consideration. But creating a classroom community, as in creating any viable community, is not an easy task. Community growth and identification is an evolutionary process that, with concerted effort and constant guidance, emerges over time.

Peck described the qualities of a community, which are particularly relevant to multiculturalism, in the following manner:

Community is integrative. It includes people of different sexes, ages, religions, cultures, viewpoints, life styles, and stages of development by integrating them into a whole that is greater—better—than the sum of its parts. Integration is not a melting process; it does not result in a bland average. Rather, it has been compared to the creation of a salad in which the identity of the individual ingredients is preserved yet simultaneously transcended. Community does not solve the problem of pluralism by obliterating diversity. Instead it seeks out diversity, welcomes other points of view, embraces opposites, desires to see the other side of every issue. It is "wholistic." It integrates us human beings into a functioning mystical body.[23]

Not too long ago children, parents, and teachers lived, worked, and interacted in relatively close proximity to one another. It was, thus, relatively easy and common to feel a true sense of community—parents could expect to run into teachers while doing their shopping, many parents and teachers shared common places of worship, and teachers had extended interaction and involvement with children as they grew and developed. Such a situation allowed for numerous models of good parent-teacher inter-action and resulted in the community being a central, supportive component in a child's development. Today, in most instances, the situation is quite different. Many teachers, especially those who teach in urban areas, tend to live in neighboring suburbs, a good distance from the school, and they leave the school neighborhood soon after the school bell rings. The result is that the so-needed sense of community knowledge and experi-ence is more difficult to achieve. Teachers have a difficult time understanding the world in which their students live and are socialized, they struggle to build relationships with parents, and thus, they cannot be as effective at reaching students as they might be.

Woodruff suggests that the mostly untapped bridge between urban teachers and more desirable levels of student knowledge is the local community itself.[24] And Banks reminds us that the most effective schools are those in which the curriculum is rooted in the needs and experiences of the children served.[25] The emphasis within the school as such should be as much about the child's life as it is about the curriculum and academ-ics. Life in the school should reflect to a large extent life in the home and community, and classrooms should be organized in such a manner that children feel central and cared for. Teachers and staff should strive to reflect and value the child's community, belief systems, and culture if school is to be seen as relevant in the eyes of the child.

Parents are often the key element in linking successful schools to students and community. Yet, one of the most difficult and unresolved issues for many schools has been the problem of how to involve minority and low-income parents in the education of their children. Irvine found that parents who consistently participate in school activities and have frequent interactions with their child's teachers and principal are a key element in a school's success.[26] Unfortunately, in some urban schools these good parent-teacher interactions do not exist.[27]

A significant gap often exists between the culture of the school and that of the community and family. Many researchers have recognized that a key obstacle to estab-lishing fruitful home-school relationships and academic focus among students is the misunderstanding that exists between these cultures.[28] In many situations, the interper-sonal dimension in the community is often at odds with that of the school, thus creating ongoing problems that are rooted in cultural dissonance. When there is agreement, this harmony, which extends between the school and the wider community, is critical for stimulating parental involvement and teacher effectiveness. Comer, when discussing the evolution of a school-community development program, identified this dissonance:

We quickly discovered an extremely high degree of distrust, anger, and alienation between home and school—the two most important institutions in the developmental life of a child—that were only vaguely apparent and routinely misunderstood. School people viewed parents' poor participation . . . as indicative of a lack of concern . . . Parents often viewed the staff as distant, rejecting, and sometimes even hostile toward them and their children.[29]

Maximizing parent and community involvement in the school has been the subject of much debate and considerable effort. The concept of culturally relevant pedagogy for teachers' use of students' lived experiences and backgrounds has been suggested as one way to link the students to the broader world of learning.[30] In this approach, academic development is viewed as inextricably linked with psychosocial and emotional growth and development, and it is the teacher's responsibility to understand these dimensions and how they intersect. Culturally responsive pedagogy links the classroom curriculum to the learning styles and experiences of the students in a manner similar to Bell's description of holistic learning.[31] In Bell's description, sociopolitical, historic, and economic factors outside the school are recognized as having impact in the classroom; the students' background, not that of the teacher, is the determinant of culturally responsive teaching; school language and communication patterns reflect the students' home and community language and communication structures; teacher effectiveness is dependent on both personal warmth and academic rigor; and the curriculum reflects students' lived experiences.

There are well-founded reasons related to academic success and cognitive development that support community or culturally relevant teaching, particularly in terms of language, communication, and the development of curriculum materials. A variety of cognitive processes that are important for school success, such as memory, comprehension, task focus, and attention to cues, have been enhanced in many students by teachers who use culturally appropriate pedagogy.[32] Such research suggests that the cognitive demands required in problem-solving tasks are reduced when the tasks are introduced in ways that are familiar to the students' existing knowledge background. Linking instruction with contextual relevance enables teachers to add a personal dimension to their school and classroom and thus link more closely with students.

The sense of community, however, is not static. It is a process that we must constantly work at. Peck contends that community can happen on national and international levels.[33] In fact, if we are ultimately to survive as a species, we all must strive toward these levels. It is incumbent on educators, then, to continue to work at the classroom and school level to build community.

Creating an Inclusive Environment

In Chapter 11 the term *inclusive* was used to refer to the field of special education, but in this section the term is used in a more global sense to refer to the process of creating a classroom and school environment that welcomes the contributions of *all* its members. The raw material to achieve full inclusion, at least in terms of ideology, has existed in our nation since its inception, and in some ways, as we come to the end of this book, we go back to our beginnings as a nation. The United States is a democracy and is truly one of the first experiments in such a process of government. The Declaration of Independence, signed on July 4, 1776, contains these words:

> We hold these truths to be self-evident, that all men are created equal, that they are endowed by their Creator with certain unalienable Rights, that among these are Life, Liberty, and the pursuit of Happiness.—That to secure these rights, Governments are instituted among Men, deriving their just powers from the consent of the governed.

On September 17, 1787, eleven years after the Declaration of Independence laid the foundation for our nation, the Constitution was signed. This document outlines the structure of the American government and captures the basic principles on which the nation is to operate. The first ten amendments of the Constitution, known as the Bill of Rights, establish the basic rights to life, liberty, and property that are to be available to all the citizens of the republic. Included are freedom of speech, the press and religious practice; freedom to assemble and petition the government; freedom from unwarranted search and seizure; and freedom to a speedy and public trial by jury.

Our nation embodies these principles today more than ever and is constantly faced with the awesome task of preparing a populace that not only is knowledgeable about them but is able to put them into everyday practice. The American common school originated as a way of enabling young people to learn to participate in a democratic polity. Today, not only does that polity have global implications, but it also seems that the common school must be revised so that it works for all its members. In a sense, we must learn to establish an effective, dynamic, multicultural community.

Knowledge alone is rarely sufficient to bring about significant change in behavior. The educational philosopher John Dewey reflected this idea when he insisted that children learn through experience as well as through instruction. Jean Piaget has been known to utter the simple phrase, "Teaching is not telling." Transmission of the democratic ideals of our nation, then, cannot be relegated to the mere giving of information. Students *must* have concrete experiences that enable them to develop the necessary skills and outlooks needed to fulfill the goals of our nation's charter.

The school and classroom provide a perfect environment in which to put into practice the very ideals and behavior we hope our students will one day express and exhibit as adults—those of participatory, reflective, and informed decision makers who act within their multicultural community, nation, and world. Educators must create an environment that enables individuals to act in such a manner that the ideals sought by our founding fathers become second nature. The school, then, can be envisioned as a minisociety in which appropriate classroom structure ultimately creates a climate conducive to democratic and inclusive practice. Establishing a democratic, learning community classroom and school content ensures that all students participate, are recognized, and have a say in building a structure that considers the needs of all its members.

Building an inclusive Third Wave environment, whether it be the learning community within the classroom or a sense of community from within as well as outside the school, requires a comprehensive approach. Educators must remove barriers of access to knowledge, to the mainstream society and culture, and to each person's own identity.

In general schools that are successfully addressing this challenge are concerned with at least four distinct areas: sociocultural inclusion, curriculum expansion, modification of pedagogy, and modification of assessment strategies.

Sociocultural Inclusion

The classroom that accepts and integrates various cultures, languages, abilities, and experiences helps its students learn to negotiate life in a society characterized by multiple layers of identity and affiliation. This lesson can be realized in many different ways and at numerous levels. In successful schools, the physical surroundings might be transformed in an attempt to make the school look less "institutional" and to reflect the various groups that are present. Hallway walls may include photographs of children, of families, of the local community. The school, like the wheat-growing society described in Chapter 1, integrates the ideas, perspectives, and contributions of everyone and begins to look like a place where real people live and work together—people who can be identified, recognized, and admired as participants and role models. The family is woven into the fabric of the child's experience in school. Parents may become tutors, classroom aides, and/or decision makers in the school community. Such efforts go far in helping children see the ethnic (or other) makeup of adults as more congruent with that of their local community. Remember that until a greater diversity of people enter the teaching force, most people who become teachers will be members of the dominant culture. Children will come into contact with few role models similar to themselves. Educators thus have a responsibility to establish greater opportunity for children to interact with people in a variety of roles and from a variety of backgrounds.

Equally important here is a dialogue that can develop within a community and its schools, particularly with regard to negotiating between the purposes of the school and community expectations. Culturally appropriate means to introduce the community to the school are critical. The frequent complaints of Vietnamese immigrants, for instance, that the school does not value respect for age or authority or that children waste time in school without significant teacher-directed instruction suggest that distinctly different values exist. A variety of approaches are possible in this situation; however, one approach may be better than another when care is taken in advance to think about the approach from the point of view of the immigrants. Prudence as well as good sense and a simple interest in justice, for example, may suggest that specific learning styles inherent in the socialization of particular populations be accommodated at the outset. Later on, as has been demonstrated by various culture-specific programs in different parts of the country, individuals can be taught other styles that then allow for successful entry into a greater society.

In addition, a sense of community can be developed within the ranks of teachers and administrators as well as within the student population and between teachers and students. In successful schools teachers share ideas, materials, and feedback. They perceive themselves as helpers to their colleagues. Parents are often included in school activities and learn ways of keeping their child's learning alive outside the school day and during the summer months when many gains made during the school year are lost. And, teachers work to establish a sense of order in the school. For many children, life at home and in the neighborhood is chaotic and hazardous. In such circumstances, a relatively high degree of anxiety, ambiguity, and uncertainty may exist. In order for children to feel safe, secure, and loved, the school must strive to be an orderly, predictable environment.

Children, too, can work to create a sense of community within a school environment. Pairing younger and older children within a school, between schools, or even across district lines can go a long way toward helping individuals reach out and participate in the lives of those around them. Successful "reading buddy" programs that bring early readers and older students together over a continuous period of time help to develop bonds such that children begin to look out for one another. All these efforts act to include individuals at various levels in the activities of the school, recognize and encourage various contributions, and enable diverse individuals to find their niche. Thus a sense of belonging and personal identity develops, and a reduction in anxiety and ambiguity occurs.

Curriculum Inclusion and Expansion

Until recently, little attention was given to the more subtle messages conveyed by school curricula and classroom materials. Sensitivity to gender, ethnicity, and disability, among many other sources of diversity, were seldom thought to impact the learner. In reality, exclusion of such factors harms all, the individual or group that has been excluded as well as the majority group, which may develop an unrealistic perception of the world around them. We now know that to build positive self-esteem for all children as well as a sense of inclusion or belonging, the educational materials presented to children must reflect the diversity of groups found in the society at large.

Materials also must be free of bias or extreme ethnocentrism in which the tendency is to view or express an event from one firmly held point of view. Biases and stereotypes are especially powerful when people deny that they exist, ignore them or accept them when they occur, deny that they affect their own as well as others' lives, and support them, knowingly or not, through their own behaviors. While subtle and often implicit, these behaviors may have significant impact on the values and attitudes of teacher behavior and intentions and may be evident as exclusion or tokenism, stereotyping, use of language, inequality or imbalance, unrealistic perception (or ethnocentrism), and isolation or segregation.

Exclusion suggests elimination or invisibility in curriculum materials. Many groups in society, including women and people of many ethnic groups, have historically been absent from most educational material; and if they have been present, it is often in such a token manner as to be trivialized or perceived as a second-class status. The discoveries, inventions, and contributions of people of color or women are often absent from history books. Exclusion and tokenism are also apparent when persons with disabilities rarely appear in curriculum materials or when the origins of ideas, concepts, or technology are not credited with its founders but are merely assumed to be associated with the mainstream, for example, the fact that the concept of zero was first used extensively by the Mayans. Consider the fact that the number of children's books portraying people of color even in the mid-1980s was only 1 percent.[34] This figure has only recently begun to change.

Inequality or imbalance refers to the practice of representing only one side of an issue or event. When we learn of Martin Luther King Jr. and not Rosa Parks in a study of the civil rights movement, or when children learn about colonization of the Americas without learning that the people who were already present had well-developed cultures and societies, we are not providing a balanced perspective on the issue. Too, when the origins of our democratic principles do not credit the Iroquois nation, we are not providing adequate balance and perspective.

Often, events are glamorized or sanitized and, as a result, present an unrealistic image. When children study the atrocities of the Holocaust but do not learn of the internment of Japanese Americans during World War II; or when students do not learn that Thomas Jefferson, one of the authors of the Declaration of Independence, was himself a slave owner and fathered at least one child with a slave, they are being presented not with the reality of the times but rather with an image that can go far to create a false impression.

Isolation or segregation occurs when the history or concerns of a particular group are relegated to special sections in the textbook or special times of the year. If February is the only time of the year when African American contributions are discussed, or if women's contributions to the development of the nation are presented only as a special chapter at the end of the book, this content is often overlooked, viewed as extra credit, or simply passed over because of lack of time.

Attention to issues of diversity through curriculum transformation requires the teacher and/or school to look at issues of process as well as content. Educators must determine what knowledge, skills, and attitudes already exist as well as those that must be developed. Teachers should strive to achieve multiple perspectives by emphasizing many different groups in many different ways, not just the experiences of one group. Certainly in a pluralistic nation like the United States, more than one kind of cultural content is valid and worth knowing. Beyond providing an expanded knowledge base, multicultural content also helps reduce the tendency people have to form and use stereotypes in their thinking. As much as possible, a curriculum that addresses diversity should be interdisciplinary. That is, efforts to address issues of diversity should not be restricted to the social studies, language arts, or performing arts. Attention to diversity in all areas, including mathematics, the sciences, and physical education, for example, is necessary. Equally important is that if the curriculum is to help students make broad connections, it must develop cognitive, affective, and behavioral skills. Especially in the areas of culture learning and in developing students' skills in making change, significant active participation on the part of the student is necessary. As has been repeatedly stressed throughout this book, these goals are not achieved using only a cognitive approach. Finally, in efforts to bring people from different backgrounds into closer contact and thus to improve understanding while broadening people's experience base, local populations should be emphasized and enlisted whenever possible. Educators should utilize individuals from the community who are able to share their lives and their special knowledge and talents and who can thus help bring community members closer together.

Modification of Pedagogy

Successful teaching reflects both the living hand of cultural tradition, including culturally specific learning styles, and the particular social, linguistic, and cognitive requirements of the future in a rapidly changing industrial society. This combination suggests that it becomes necessary for teachers and other school personnel to meet the student wherever he or she is, to accommodate and adapt learning activities to the needs and abilities that the student presents, and to work from that point toward assisting the student to become better able to function effectively in diverse settings. Teaching from this perspective does not mean throwing out knowledge and understanding necessary for success in the dominant society. Indeed, quite the reverse is true. So long as we live in a society where individuals are punished, economically, socially, and sometimes physically, for their inability to participate in a dominant society, it is the responsibility of the teacher to see that children acquire that knowledge and those skills. However—and this is a big "however"—it is not at all necessary to do so by negating, ignoring, and not taking advantage of the knowledge and skills children bring with them to school. Indeed, it could be argued with little effort that the dominant society in the United States has not done well in terms of its relations with its fellow citizens and with its international co-citizenry. Clearly, members of the dominant society have a great deal to learn from those who live "other" lives. Viewed from this perspective, teaching and learning among diverse individuals becomes a transactional experience. Just as it is possible for people to function quite effectively in bilingual settings, so too can all individuals become increasingly bicultural, multicultural, or pluralistic. Such functioning is not in any sense a process of loss but rather a process of gain.

Assessment Strategies

Methods of student assessment that consider the complex interrelationships of race, class, ethnicity, religion, gender, and disability in students are also found to vary in effective schools. Assessment is used in determining student achievement vis-à-vis particular instructional objectives, in decisions on advancement from one grade level to another, in diagnosing individual student needs, and also as a means to gain insight into the appropriateness of a given curriculum or instructional intervention. Test reliability studies have repeatedly indicated that considerable bias (cultural, gender, linguistic, experiential, etc.) may exist such that a given test administered to an individual may produce results that are significantly determined by factors other than actual achievement or ability. Based on such testing, students are often limited a priori from the variety of curricular and instructional choices available in a school. For example, students with inferior skills in the majority language who perform poorly on a given test early in their educational careers may have restricted subsequent educational experiences and thus be prevented from access to knowledge that is potentially available.

Students and parents need accurate assessment of their work. Behavior described in terms of individual performance and development, often taking advantage of parent participation in the process, frequently provides a more accurate and sensitive measure of achievement than do paper-and-pencil tests. Assessment strategies that consider cultural and other differences provide students and parents with better indicators of actual student performance. Assessment strategies that measure individuals in terms of their achievement relative to a particular starting point provide a clearer picture of an individual's growth in a given area.

Summary

This book strives to better prepare today's teachers to achieve their goals of delivering an effective education to diverse students who are living in a complex, interdependent world. The approach used in this book begins by recognizing the kinds of experiences many, but not all, individuals who become teachers bring with them. It is with the classroom teachers in concert with their peers and community that effective education can occur. For the most part, today's teacher education students are from the majority culture and have limited experience with people of different backgrounds. For that reason this book attends to such issues as people's emotional responses and other kinds of experiences people have when they encounter difference or diversity. Understanding the socialization process in terms of cultural development and the obstacles to culture learning helps educators gain insight into the reasons for typical responses and facilitates the processes necessary to transcend, or move beyond, one's conditioning. Understanding how many of the various processes, such as communication and learning style, impact on interaction and learning is also critical to effective teaching. This book looks at how society and education has responded to cultural diversity in a variety of contexts. Each of the various diversities addressed in this book mediate one another and do not act in isolation, which further complicates an educator's task but is nonetheless critical to an understanding of classroom interaction.

Only recently has our nation been addressing issues related to diversity in any real sense. In a few short decades, development in related fields has tended to move from that of totally ignoring diversity in the hopes of complete assimilation to that of encouraging and recognizing the value of pluralism in a diverse democratic society. Schools—as well as individuals who have been successful at addressing such issues— *have been working on these issues for a long time.* Innovations in individual perspective and behavior as well as in curriculum and instructional modification do not come quickly and cannot show immediate results. Such efforts require a long-term commitment on the part of many actors—teachers, administrators, students, parents, community, and material developers—before any of the hoped for changes can be realized. Removing the various barriers and modifying conditioned behavior takes time. We must be willing to act and work accordingly over the long haul; that is, we must take whatever time is needed to realize such changes and not be discouraged in the short run. Successes must be measured in inches rather than miles and must be perceived by all actors as being developmental, or evolutionary, in nature, not revolutionary. As such, efforts must begin in the early stages of education, both for children and adults, and must continue throughout. Such efforts are not ones that can be effectively addressed in one short course or class or for a short period of time. Continuous efforts must be made at many different levels in the educational process. It is hoped that, for you, this book is just one step on a personal and professional path of continual growth, development, and interaction.

References

1. Karl Lewin, *Field Theory in Social Science* (New York: Harper and Row, 1951).

2. See N. P. Greenman and E. B. Kimmel, "The Road to Multicultural Education: Potholes of Resistance," *Journal of Teacher Education* 46, 5 (November/ December 1995): 360–368; and Kenneth Cushner, "Organizational Environment Factors That Support Positive Intergroup Relations," in *Educational Programs to Improve Intergroup Relations,* ed. Stephan and Vogt (in press).

3. Milton Bennett, "A Developmental Approach to Training for Intercultural Sensitivity," *International Journal of Intercultural Relations* 10 (1986): 179–196.

4. A. W. Combs, *The Professional Education of Teachers* (Boston: Allyn and Bacon, 1965), p. 14.

5. Donna Gollnick, "Multicultural Education: Policies and Practices in Teacher Education," in *Research and Multicultural Education*, ed. C. A. Grant (London: Falmer, 1992), pp. 218–239.

6. J. W. Schofield, "Promoting Positive Intergroup Relations: A Review of the Literature," *Review in Education* 17 (1995): 335–409.

7. Michael Fullan, *Change Forces: Probing the Depths of Educational Reform* (New York: Falmer Press, 1993), p. 3.

8. A. I. Morey, "Organizational Change and Implementation Strategies for Multicultural Infusion," In *Multicultural Course Transformation in Higher Education: A Broader Truth,* ed A. Morey and M. Kitano (Boston: Allyn and Bacon, 1997).

9. L. G. Bolman and T. E. Deal, *Reframing Organizations: Artistry, Choice, and Leadership* (San Francisco: Jossey-Bass, 1991).

10. K. A. Myers, R. Caruso, and N. A. Birk, "The Diversity Continuum: Enhancing Student Interest and Access, Creating a Staying Environment, and Preparing Students for Transition," in *Cultural Diversity: Curriculum, Classroom, and Climate*, ed. J. Q. Adams and J. R. Welsch (Illinois Staff and Curriculum Developers Association, 1999), pp. 429–442.

11. Gordon Allport, *The Nature of Prejudice* (Reading, MA: Addison-Wesley, 1954).

12. C. Bagley, Y. Mizuno, and G. Collins, "Schools and Opportunities for Multicultural Contact," in Grant, *Research and Multicultural Education,* pp. 203–217.

13. Paul Vogt, *Tolerance and Education: Learning to Live with Diversity and Difference* (Thousand Oaks, CA: Sage, 1997).

14. E. Henderson-King and R. E. Nisbett, "Anti-Black Prejudice as a Function of Exposure to the Negative Behavior of a Single Black Person," *Journal of Personality and Social Psychology* 71 (1996): 654–664. See also E. G. Cohen, "The Desegregated School: Problems in Status, Power, and Interethnic Climate," in *Groups in Contact: The Psychology of Desegregation,* ed. N. Miller and M. B. Brewer (New York: Academic Press, 1984), pp. 77–96

15. Walter Stephan, *Reducing Prejudice and Stereotyping in Schools* (New York: Teachers College Press, 1999).

16. Seymour B. Sarason, *The Culture of the School and the Problem of Change* (Boston: Allyn and Bacon, 1971).

17. Ibid., p. 69.

18. Ibid., p. 70.

19. Ibid., pp. 8–9.

20. J. Edwards, "To Teach Responsibility, Bring Back the Dalton Plan," *Phi Delta Kappan* 72, 5 (January 1991): 399.

21. Ibid.

22. Ibid., p. 400.

23. M. S. Peck, *The Different Drum: Community Making and Peace* (New York: Simon and Schuster, 1987).

24. D. W. Woodruff, "Keeping It Real: The Importance of Community in Multicultural Education and School Success," *Theory into Practice* 35, 4 (1996): 234–235.

25. James Banks, *An Introduction to Multicultural Education* (Needham Heights, MA: Allyn and Bacon, 1994).

26. J. J. Irvine, *Black Students and School Failure* (New York: Praeger, 1991).

27. Woodruff, "Keeping It Real."

28. B. A. Allen and A. W. Boykin, "African American Children and the Educational Process: Alleviating Cultural Discontinuity through Prescriptive Pedagogy," *School Psychology Review* 21, 4 (1992): 586–596. See also C. Ascher, "Improving the School-Home Connection for Poor Minority Urban Students," *The Urban Review* 20, 2 (1988): 109–123; and S. Forham and J. Ogbu, "Black Students' School Success: Coping with the Burdens of 'Acting White,' " *The Urban Review* 18 (1986): 176–206.

29. J. Comer, "Parent Participation: Fad or Function," *Educational Horizons* 69, 4 (1991): 185.

30. G. Ladson-Billings, "Culturally-Relevant Teaching: Effective Instruction for Black Students," *The College Board Review* 155 (1990): 20–25.

31. Y. R. Bell, "A Culturally-Sensitive Analysis of Black Learning Style," *Journal of Black Psychology* 20, 1 (1994): 47–61.

32. C. L. Lopez and H. J. Sullivan, "Effect of Personalization of Instructional Context on the Achievement and Attitudes of Hispanic Teachers," *Education, Technology, and Research* 40, 4 (1992): 5–13.

33. Peck, *Different Drum.*

34. K. M. Reimer, "Multiethnic Literature: Holding Fast to the Dream," *Language Arts* 69 (1992): 14–21.

Glossary

A

Accent Pronunciation habits of the standard language acquired by people from a particular geographic region.

Accountability movement The national interest in and reform of schooling that began in the 1980s, continues to the present time, and rests on the idea that schools, teachers, and students are responsible for meeting standards of learning in all major subjects.

Acculturation The changes that take place as a result of continuous firsthand contact between individuals of different cultures; usually refers to the experiences of adults.

Adaptive equipment Appliances, materials, and supplies that are used to assist people with disabilities to write, read, move, speak, hear, and otherwise conduct normal activities.

American Sign Language The only signed system of communication that is recognized as a distinct language.

Anglo-conformity The belief that all immigrant children must be socialized into the culture and worldview of the dominant Anglo society in the United States.

Assessment A comprehensive, individualized evaluation of the student's strengths as well as areas that are in need.

Assimilation The process whereby an individual or group is absorbed into the social structures and cultural life of another person, group, or society.

Assimilationist model The practices by which children were socialized into the culture and worldview of the dominant Anglo society in the United States.

Attribution The judgments people make about others based on the behavior they observe.

Autism A brain disorder that typically affects a person's ability to communicate, form relationships with others, and respond appropriately to the environment.

B

Behavior management plan A formal plan for classroom organization and instruction designed to elicit good behavior on the part of all students as well as to plan for adaptations required for children with disabilities.

Bidialectalism The ability to speak and understand two (and sometimes more) dialects and to switch back and forth between or among them.

Black English A dialect of English spoken primarily by urban African Americans also called Ebonics.

C

Categorization The process of dividing stimuli into classes or groups according to a particular system. In the cultural context, categorization refers to the manner by which people's culture teaches them to view the world around them.

Clean intermittent catheterization (CIC) A process by which a hollow plastic tube (catheter) is inserted into the bladder to drain it; CIC is normally done on a regular schedule during the day and night and is used to assist children and adults who, for one reason or another, cannot control bladder function.

Cognitive structures The ways in which individuals organize or scaffold knowledge so as to learn, remember, think, and otherwise use it.

Collaborative classroom A classroom in which cooperation and group (small or large) activity is in evidence; in which students, teachers, administrators, parents, and members of the community work together; and in which all take part in at least some decision making.

Collaborative teaching A style of pedagogy in which teachers collaborate with one another in planning instruction, may team-teach with one another, and often collaborate with students in setting instructional goals and designing instructional activities.

Communication style A set of culturally learned characteristics associated with both language and learning style, involving such aspects of communication as formal versus informal, emotional versus subdued, direct versus indirect, objective versus subjective, and responses to guilt and accusations.

Cooperative learning A pedagogical strategy or method in which students work in groups to maximize the learning of all individuals in the group.

Constructivist perspective The belief that all knowledge is built, or "constructed," by individual learners; it is thus important when teaching and learning *new* knowledge to connect it to knowledge already known.

Content standards One of three kinds of standards (the others are performance standards and delivery standards) for learning; refers to standards for subject-area knowledge.

Cultural capital The accumulation of both subjective and objective cultural knowledge that one uses to advance or be a leader in one's society.

Cultural pluralism A system of social and/or political organization that stresses and promotes mutual understanding and respect among disparate ethnic, religious, and racial groups existing in a society.

Culture The totality of socially transmitted behavior patterns, arts, beliefs, institutions, and all other products of human work and thought characteristic of a community or a population.

Culture-general approaches Cross-cultural training approaches that prepare people for the kinds of interactions and experiences they are likely to encounter, regardless of the groups that are interacting.

Culture-specific approaches Cross-cultural training approaches designed to prepare people to live and/or work with people of a particular culture or group.

D

Delivery standards One of three kinds of standards (the others are performance standards and content standards) for learning; refers to standards for the context of the classroom such as class size, materials available, instructional time, and so on.

Demographics Vital statistics that characterize human populations, including age, gender, ethnicity, and so forth. Demographics, often generated from population census data, can be used to project future trends and needs of relevance to educators.

Developmentally appropriate practice (DAP) Instructional practices that are organized and designed on the basis of the age and development of the student.

Dialect A variation of some standard language form that includes differences in pronunciation, word usage, and syntax; such differences may be based on ethnicity, religion, geographical region, social class, or age.

Differentiation The process of distinguishing the finer points among elements of a given category, such as a wine connoisseur is able to do; in the cross-cultural context, differentiation refers to distinctions made between aspects of a category that are important to a given group of people.

Dominant culture Culture of the social or political group that holds the most power and influence in a society.

Down syndrome A genetically inherited condition caused by extra genetic material (genes) from the twenty-first chromosome and resulting in a combination of features including some degree of mental retardation or cognitive disability and other developmental delays.

E

Educate America Act Legislation signed into law in 1994 stemming from the Governors' Conference in 1989 that set eight goals for education and their implementing requirements to be met by the year 2000; the law expired in 1991, and its requirements were incorporated into the reauthorization of the Elementary and Secondary Education Act of 1992, called the "Leave No Child Behind" Act.

Empathy A psychological sense of understanding and "feeling for" another person's situation.

Enculturate The process of raising a child to be a member of a particular culture or culture group.

English as a second language An approach to teaching linguistically diverse students in which the student's background and cultural experiences become the focal point for learning English; in ESL programs, children are kept in the regular classroom for most of the day but are pulled out at various times for English instruction.

Establishment clause of First Amendment The clause in the First Amendment that prohibits the government from establishing a state religion.

Ethnic group Groups who share a common heritage and reflect identification with some collective or reference group, oftentimes in a common homeland. Identification with an ethnic group is reflected in a sense of peoplehood, or the feeling that a person's own destiny is somehow linked with others who share this same knowledge.

Ethnic identity A sense of belonging and identification with one's ancestral ethnic group.

Ethnocentrism The tendency that people have to evaluate others from their own cultural reference.

F

Field dependent A learning style proposed by H. A. Witkin; students who are field dependent learn best when given a larger context, or "field," in which to embed new learning.

Field independent A learning style proposed by H. A. Witkin; students who are field independent can learn material that is separated from its context. For example, a student learns the table of elements without an explanation of its history or purpose or how it fits into the larger scientific enterprise.

Fourteenth Amendment The Constitutional amendment that prohibits states from abridging rights granted to all U.S. citizens, born or naturalized; the amendment also guarantees that no person shall be deprived of life, liberty, or property without due process of law and that all persons shall be guaranteed equal protection under the law.

Free exercise clause of First Amendment Clause of the First Amendment that prohibits the government from preventing the free exercise of religious belief among its citizens.

Fundamentalism A movement or attitude stressing strict and literal adherence to a set of basic principles, usually religious ones.

G

Gender A socially defined category in which the biological specialization of *male* and *female* are transformed by associating specific personality, role, and status traits to each sex.

Gender bias Behavior that results from the underlying belief in sex role stereotypes.

Gender discrimination Any action that specifically denies opportunities, privileges, or rewards to a person or a group because of their sex.

Gender role identity The sense of identity that one acquires as a result of internalizing specific social requirements of behavior based on one's sex.

Gender role socialization The process by which young children acquire the knowledge and internalize the values of socially determined sex roles.

Gender role stereotyping The process of attributing specific behaviors, abilities, interests, and values to one sex.

Gender-sensitive Instructional and other practices that take differences in gender into account.

Genderized traits Traits such as aggression or empathy that are differentially valued by a society when displayed by males and females.

Generalization The tendency of a majority of people in a cultural group to hold certain values and beliefs and to engage in certain patterns of behavior. This information can be supported by research and can be applied to a large percentage of a population or group.

Genotype The whole complex of genes inherited from both parents; the genotype determines the hereditary potentials and limitations of an individual from embryonic formation through adulthood.

Global perspective A worldview that takes into account the fact that individuals and societies are a part of a larger, worldwide system.

Globalization The process by which nations of the world become connected and interdependent through ties created by electronic communication, rapid means of travel, and interlocking economies.

Goals 2000 A set of goals for education created by the national Governors' Conference in 1989, to be achieved by the year 2000; goals included the following: (1) all children will be ready to learn when they enter school; (2) 90 percent of high school students will graduate from high school; (3) all students will be proficient in major content-area subjects; (4) all teachers will have access to effective preprofessional and professional development; (5) U.S. students will be the first in the world in mathematics and science; (6) every adult American will be literate; (7) all U.S. schools will be free of drugs, violence, and unauthorized firearms and alcohol; and (8) all schools will promote partnerships to increase parental involvement and participation in the education of their children.

H

High stakes testing A system of statewide or national testing on the basis of which important decisions—such as promotion in grade or graduation—are made that profoundly affect students' lives.

Homophobia The irrational fear of homosexuality and of those whose sexual orientation is homosexual.

Hypodescent A type of categorizing racial membership in which any amount of biological inheritance from a group considered to be a socially lower or minority group automatically places one in that group.

I

Immigrants People who voluntarily move to a country of which they are not natives with the purpose of taking up permanent residence.

In-context learning Learning that takes place through direct participation in real-world events.

Inclusion The belief in and practice of creating heterogeneous classrooms; more particularly, the practice of teaching students with disabilities in regular classrooms.

Indigenous people People living in an area generally since prehistoric (or pre-European contact) times; related terms include *aboriginal people* (particularly in Australia), *first nation people* (particularly in Canada).

Individual Education Program (IEP) A formal plan for instruction mandated by laws governing special education that sets forth the educational needs of a student, the goals and objectives that direct his or her program, the educational programming and placement, and the evaluation and measurement criteria that were developed during the IEP creation process.

Informed consent The legal requirement that parents must approve their child's multifactored evaluation, that parents participate in developing the child's IEP, and that parents know they have a right to procedural due process in the event of disagreement.

Integration The coming together of ideas, things, people, or objects in such a manner as to form a common unit that cannot be distinguished from the original parts. In the educational context, integration refers to the positive interaction of all people along equal lines of power, authority, status, and involvement in the school process.

K

Kinesics The study of nonverbal communication in the form of body movements, often called body language; kinesics includes gestures, posture, facial expressions, and eye contact.

L

Learning community An approach to classroom organization and instruction, based on democratic ideals, which is characterized by active teaching and learning, collaboration, belonging, shared decision making, and a strong sense of democratic participation.

Learning style A consistent pattern of behavior and performance by which an individual approaches educational experiences; learning style is derived from cultural socialization and individual personality as well as from the broader influence of human development.

Least restrictive environment The aspect of laws regarding special education that requires that children with disabilities be educated in the most unrestrictive context possible.

Low-incidence A type of disability that does not occur very often, for example, blindness.

M

Marginalization The practice of excluding a social group from the mainstream of the society, placing that group—legally or socially—on the "margins" of the society.

Microculture A social group that shares distinctive traits, values, and behaviors that set it apart from the parent macroculture of which it is a part. Microculture seems to imply a greater linkage with the parent culture and often mediate the ideas, values, and institutions of the larger political community.

Minority group A social group that occupies a subordinate position in a society, that often experiences discrimination, and that may be separated by physical or cultural traits disapproved of by the dominant group.

Misogyny An irrational hatred and fear of women.

Mountain English A dialect of English that is spoken primarily in the nineteen states of the Appalachian region of the United States.

Multifactored evaluation An evaluation that looks at many possible aspects of the learning problems of children with disabilities; may include cognitive, physical, social, and psychological factors.

Muscular dystrophy An inherited disease that causes increasing weakness in muscle tissue; the muscles affected are the skeletal muscles and, occasionally, the muscles of the heart.

N

Nativist religions Religions practiced by native peoples, often based on a sense of oneness with the earth.

Nature versus nurture debate A long-standing argument about which is more important in the outcome of an individual's development: a set of inborn and immutable characteristics, or education, that is to say, learning.

"No Child Left Behind" Act of 2001 The name given to the reauthorization of the Elementary and Secondary Education Act of 1992.

Normalization A philosophical view that the lives of exceptional individuals of any age should be characterized as much as possible by the same kinds of experiences, daily routines, and rhythms as those of persons who do not have disabilities.

Normative The fact that the norms of a society influence and regulate an individual's beliefs and behavior.

Norms Accepted ways of agreed-upon behavior that enable similar groups of people to function in a similar manner.

O

Objective culture The tangible, visible aspects of a culture, including such aspects as the artifacts produced, the foods eaten, the clothing worn.

Out-of-context learning Learning that typically occurs in the abstract as opposed to with concrete objects and references.

P

Paralanguage Forms of nonverbal communication involving vocalizations that are not words.

People of color Nonwhite minority group members, but reflects recent demographic realities of the United States. The phrase *people of color* refers to groups such as African Americans, Mexican Americans, Puerto Ricans, and Native Americans and is often preferred over the phrase *ethnic minority* because these groups are, in many schools and communities, the majority rather than the minority.

Perception The process by which people are aware of stimuli in the world around them.

Performance standards One of three kinds of standards (the others are content standards and delivery standards) for learning; refers to standards for achievement in subject-matter knowledge.

Phenotype All the observable characteristics of an organism, such as shape, size, color, and behavior, that result from the interaction of its genotype (total genetic inheritance) with the environment. The common type of a group of physically similar organisms is sometimes also known as the phenotype; the phenotype may change constantly throughout the life of an individual.

Placement continuum The degree to which students with disabilities are involved in regular education.

Portfolio assessments Comprehensive evaluations of student work, usually selected by students themselves and contained in a notebook or other venue, that demonstrate knowledge and skills acquired by the student.

Prejudice Nonreflective judgments about others that are harsh, are discriminatory, or involve rejection.

Proxemics The normal physical distance between speakers when they are communicating with one another and is normally acquired as part of one's culture; sometimes referred to as social space.

Pseudoscience A set or system of beliefs claiming to be "scientific" without the benefit of the scientific method used to make further inquiries that might suggest that the belief system is wrong in any particular way.

R

Race In a biological sense, the clustering of inherited physical characteristics that favor adaptation to a particular ecological area. Race is culturally defined in the sense that different societies emphasize different sets of physical characteristics when referring to the concept of race. Thus, race is an important social characteristic not because of its biology but because of its cultural meaning in any given social group or society.

Racial identity One's sense of belonging and identification with a racial group; may also refer to the categorization of an individual in terms of a racial group by society or other social groups.

Racial profiling The practice of constructing a set of characteristics or behaviors based on race and using that set of characteristics to decide whether an individual might be guilty of some crime and therefore worthy of investigation or arrest.

Refugee A person who flees for safety to another country.

Rural English A dialect of English, sometimes called mountain English, spoken primarily in Appalachia and derived from the language of early English settlers in the area.

S

Segregation The act of separating or setting apart from others. In the educational context, segregation may refer to the establishment of separate schools for students of different races or abilities/disabilities.

Separation Situations in which two or more social groups voluntarily decide that it is of value for each to maintain its own cultural identity but not of value to maintain relationships with the other groups.

Separation of church and state The philosophical belief that religion and government should not be cojoined; in the United States, this belief is codified in the First Amendment to the Constitution.

Sickle cell disease An inherited condition in which an abnormality of the red blood cells causes a variety of serious medical and physical problems.

Social class A term used to categorize individuals in a stratified social system; social class characteristics are often related to (but may not be limited to) child-rearing practices, beliefs, values, economic status, prestige and influence, and general life chances.

Social institution A formal, recognized, established, and stabilized way of pursuing some activity in society.

Social reconstructionist One who believes that education can, and should, be devoted at least in part to the rebuilding or reform of a society.

Social status The degree to which an individual has power, influence, or leadership in his or her social group.

Socialization The process whereby individuals learn the appropriate behavior that allows them to be functioning members of a particular group, such as a family, work, or social group.

Sojourner A person who stays in a place for a relatively brief period of time; often used in reference to tourists or short-term visitors or strangers to a country.

Spina bifida A condition in which there is a congenital cleft or opening in the vertebral column.

Standard English A dialect of the English language, usually taken to mean that version of the English language most acceptable or most "correct," used by educated middle and upper classes and thus the dialect taught in public schools; standard English may vary by geographical location, but in general it is the dialect used in formal writing and in the broadcast and print media.

Stereotypes Beliefs about the personal attributes of a group based on the inaccurate generalizations that are used to describe all members of the group and that thus ignore individual differences.

Structured immersion programs Educational programs for students for whom English is a second language in which students are taught by teachers who are fluent in the native language of the child; while students are allowed to speak in their first language, the teacher usually responds in English.

Subculture A social group with shared characteristics that distinguish it in some way from the larger cultural group or society in which it is embedded. Generally, a subculture is distinguished either by a unifying set of ideas and/or practices (such as the corporate culture or the drug culture) or by some demographic characteristic (such as the adolescent culture or the culture of poverty).

Subjective culture The invisible, intangible aspects of a group, including such aspects as attitudes, values, norms of behavior—the things typically kept in people's minds.

Submersion programs Educational programs for children for whom English is a second language in which language minority children are placed in the regular classroom with native speakers of English; may be referred to as a "sink-or-swim" approach; found to be unlawful by the Supreme Court.

T

Task specialization The practice of assigning a specific subtask to each member of a collaborative learning team or group.

Teacher expectations A construct used to refer to the phenomena associated with the relation between what a teacher believes a student can do and what the student can actually do; generally, the more a teacher believes a student can do, the higher the achievement of the student, without respect to such factors as measured intelligence, social class, or family background.

Testing A process of evaluation that implies standardization in which the individual is compared against some norm-referenced set of scores or to a known group of individuals.

Theocracy A system of government in which a particular set of religious beliefs, or an organized religion, is completely intertwined with the processes of government.

Transition plan A formal education plan that elaborates the steps to be taken to move a student with disabilities into adult and working life.

Transitional bilingual education Educational programs for children for whom English is a second language in which efforts are made to phase out the student's native language while developing the student's facility in English as quickly as possible.

Traumatic brain injury An injury to the brain that causes subsequent cognitive or psychomotor disability; usually the result of an accident, but sometimes can be sustained at birth.

W

Working poor A categorization that refers to individuals who are employed (often underemployed) but still fall within the category of poverty because their income does not enable them to participate fully and effectively in everyday life.

Z

Zero exclusion mandate Section of P.L. 94-142 that requires that all children with disabilities must be provided a free, appropriate, public education; local school systems do not have the option to decide whether to provide needed services.

Author index

Subject Index

Photo Credits